Oxford University Press
Digital Course Materials for

In Mixed Company
Communicating in Small Groups and Teams

ELEVENTH EDITION

J. Dan Rothwell

Carefully scratch off the silver coating to see your personal redemption code.

This code can be redeemed only once.

Once the code has been revealed, this access card cannot be returned to the publisher.

Access can also be purchased online during the registration process.

The code on this card is valid for two years from the date of first purchase. Complete terms and conditions are available at learninglink.oup.com

Access Length: 6 months from redemption of the code.

OXFORD
UNIVERSITY PRESS

Directions for accessing
Oxford University Press

MW00851934

Your OUP digital course materials can be delivered several different ways, depending on how your instructor has elected to incorporate them into his or her course.

BEFORE REGISTERING FOR ACCESS, be sure to check with your instructor to ensure that you register using the proper method.

VIA YOUR SCHOOL'S LEARNING MANAGEMENT SYSTEM

Use this method if your instructor has integrated these resources into your school's Learning Management System (LMS)—Blackboard, Canvas, Brightspace, Moodle, or other

> Log in to your instructor's course within your school's LMS.

> When you click a link to a resource that is access-protected, you will be prompted to register for access.

> Follow the on-screen instructions.

> Enter your personal redemption code (or purchase access) when prompted.

VIA OXFORD learning link

Use this method if you are using the resources for self-study only. **NOTE:** *Scores for any quizzes you take on the OUP site will not report to your instructor's gradebook.*

> Visit oup.com/he/ rothwell-mixedcompany11e

> Select the edition you are using, then select student resources for that edition.

> Click the link to upgrade your access to the student resources.

> Follow the on-screen instructions.

> Enter your personal redemption code (or purchase access) when prompted.

VIA OXFORD learning cloud

Use this method only if your instructor has specifically instructed you to enroll in an Oxford Learning Cloud course. **NOTE:** *If your instructor is using these resources within your school's LMS, use the Learning Management System instructions.*

> Visit the course invitation URL provided by your instructor.

> If you already have an oup.instructure.com account you will be added to the course automatically; if not, create an account by providing your name and email.

> When you click a link to a resource in the course that is access-protected, you will be prompted to register.

> Follow the on-screen instructions, entering your personal redemption code where prompted.

For assistance with code redemption, Oxford Learning Cloud registration, or if you redeemed your code using the wrong method for your course, please contact our customer support team at **learninglinkdirect.support@ oup.com** or 855-281-8749.

In Mixed Company

In Mixed Company

Communicating in Small Groups and Teams

Eleventh Edition

J. Dan Rothwell

New York   Oxford
OXFORD UNIVERSITY PRESS

Oxford University Press is a department of the University of Oxford.
It furthers the University's objective of excellence in research, scholarship,
and education by publishing worldwide. Oxford is a registered trade mark of
Oxford University Press in the UK and certain other countries.

Published in the United States of America by Oxford University Press
198 Madison Avenue, New York, NY 10016, United States of America.

Library of Congress Cataloging-in-Publication Data

Names: Rothwell, J. Dan, author.
Title: In mixed company : communicating in small groups and teams / J. Dan
    Rothwell.
Description: Eleventh edition. | New York, NY : Oxford University Press,
    [2022] | Includes bibliographical references and index.
Identifiers: LCCN 2021015032 (print) | LCCN 2021015033 (ebook) | ISBN
    9780197602812 (paperback) | ISBN 9780197602843 (epub)
Subjects: LCSH: Communication in small groups.
Classification: LCC HM736 .R678 2022 (print) | LCC HM736 (ebook) | DDC
    302.34—dc23
LC record available at https://lccn.loc.gov/2021015032
LC ebook record available at https://lccn.loc.gov/2021015033

9 8 7 6 5 4 3 2 1
Printed by LSC Communications, Inc., United States of America

To my family: Marcy, Hilary, Geoff, Barrett, and Clare

Brief Contents

Table of Contents

Preface

▶ With each new edition, I find it ever more challenging to make significant changes that improve *In Mixed Company*. With the Covid-19 crisis, however, and the abrupt transition to online learning and pervasive virtual group communication, significant revisions naturally emerged and are comprehensively addressed in this eleventh edition.

Even with the abundant changes made for this edition, listed later, *I have preserved the essence of previous versions*. The *communication competence model* continues to guide discussions of key small group concepts and processes. *Systems theory* also remains as a key theoretical component of the text, providing a conceptual framework for analysis and insights. A comprehensive, atypical *chapter on roles* continues to inform on the dynamic, complex nature of group communication. Finally, *the unique focus on power* in groups remains. Power is a central underlying element in small group conflict, teamwork, decision making, problem solving, normative behavior, roles, and leadership. No other small group communication text provides the breadth and depth of coverage on this significant topic.

In addition, I continue to place great emphasis on *readability*. Textbooks are not meant to read like spy thrillers, but neither should they induce a coma by reading like instructions for filling out your income tax forms. I have searched in obvious and not-so-obvious places for the precise example, the poignant instance, and the dramatic case to enhance reader enjoyment. I have employed a more *narrative or storytelling style* than is usual in textbook writing. Chapter 7, for example, lists several perspectives on effective leadership, but I try to connect these perspectives to the story of how each evolved one from the other. The several case studies, vivid examples, and personal experiences are also narrative in nature, included to illustrate ideas and concepts and trigger reader interest. Research confirms that the narrative style not only adds interest but also increases comprehension and recall of information (Dahlstrom, 2014).

I also have attempted to *enliven and personalize the writing style* by incorporating colorful language and lively metaphors that bring interesting images to mind, and to depart from standard academic practice by employing the "perpendicular pronoun" I. Occasional use of first-person singular speaks more directly and personably to readers than the more impersonal style of writing commonly used in textbooks (such as "in this author's view"). Although it has been suggested that I employ the "editorial we" instead of the first-person singular, I tend to agree with Mark Twain, who said that "people with tapeworms have the right to use the editorial 'we,'" but others should avoid it.

Finally, I am a great believer in the potential of *humor* to gain and maintain the attention of my readers. Humor can often cross generational divides and spark interest in scholarly subjects that can seem distant and abstract until a humorous example, quip, or story enlivens the reading and ignites interest, even promotes understanding. There is humor to be found throughout *In Mixed Company*. I have attempted to infuse some amusement whenever possible.

Significant Substantive Changes

There is often the suspicion, not always without merit, that a new edition of a textbook offers mostly cosmetic changes (a few new photos or an occasional new example or reference). This is emphatically not the case for *In Mixed Company*. *This eleventh edition incorporates the most comprehensive revision I've ever undertaken*. Major changes include:

1. A completely **new chapter on meetings**, both standard and virtual, *co-authored with my colleague and friend Michelle Waters*, a past instructor at Cabrillo College in the Communication Studies Department and a longtime, highly successful international business consultant, has been added. This chapter reflects the radically changing environment triggered by the Covid-19 pandemic and the changing landscape of international business. Both standard and virtual meetings are discussed with detailed analysis and specific advice offered far beyond the relatively short treatment of this subject that appeared in earlier editions. This has become the new Chapter 3, which recognizes the more immediate needs of students to receive credible advice on how to navigate the often tricky virtual environment now that teaching and learning have become increasingly an online small group experience.

2. Virtual groups and teams receive significant additional treatment throughout the text. **Chapter 12, on technology and social media in previous editions, has been dismantled and that material has been disseminated to various relevant chapters**. Virtual groups and teams, once more of a fledgling enterprise, are now a centerpiece of small group activity in countless venues and contexts, especially since the inception of the Covid-19 pandemic. Thus, leaving a direct discussion

of virtuality in small groups mostly until a final chapter seems too much like an afterthought when an infusion of new research and insights should be incorporated much earlier and more comprehensively. **I am reasonably confident that no more thorough treatment of virtual groups is available in a foundational small group communication text.**

3. Research and theory, as always, have been thoroughly updated in every chapter. Almost **400 new references**, *a third of the total number of citations*, incorporate the most current research and theory on small group communication. **More than half of all references are dated from 2015 to 2021.**

4. A **vastly improved visual package of photos, custom cartoons, and graphics** has been included. In some cases, new photos make a point not noted in text material. In other cases, new photos illustrate important concepts. Custom cartoons, created by Marcy Wieland, who has skillfully rendered cartoons for other textbooks that I have authored, add a unique quality to the text.

5. **New, sharper examples** have replaced shopworn illustrations. I have also included numerous recent events, especially incorporating the Covid-19 challenges, to illustrate key points and to give the text a contemporary feel.

6. Expanded and extensive treatment of **culture** is blended throughout this edition. The breadth and depth of this coverage can be easily ascertained by simply glancing at the Table of Contents and the index under "culture." Blending the discussion of culture throughout *In Mixed Company* underlines the inseparable nature of this subject from an abundance of topics.

7. Expanded coverage of **diversity** is apparent. Diversity issues are incorporated throughout the text, not as mere sidebars or afterthoughts, but in carefully developed embedded segments.

8. Expanded coverage of **"truth decay,"** an increasingly important topic in this age of polarized politics, has been included.

9. **Listening** has received additional treatment, with special emphasis given to active, empathic, and competitive listening, including discussions on impediments to competent listening. Check the index for a delineation of extensive discussion of this important subject.

10. **Considerable new material** has been added. For example, emotional contagion and the ripple effect, creating a psychologically secure group environment, the fallacy of 93% of message meaning being communicated nonverbally, conducting Zoom meetings, virtuous

cycles of respect and servant leadership, steps for choosing a mentor, and much more have been included.

11. Some **new case studies** have been added, and others have been deleted.

12. Additional coverage of **nonverbal communication** has been highlighted. **Trust** has also received expanded treatment.

Continued and Expanded Pedagogical Features

Several acclaimed features of previous editions have been maintained and expanded. A few new features have been introduced.

1. Oxford University Press offers **extensive tutorials on teaching online**, available at https://oupeltglobalblog.com/2020/03/12/online-teaching-getting-started/ for the more technical aspects, and https://oupeltglobalblog.com/2020/03/13/online-teaching-practical-tips/ for practical teaching tips, and https://oupeltglobalblog.com/2020/03/17/online-teaching-engage-motivate/ for tips to engage students online.

2. Enhanced e-book version. The e-book version of *In Mixed Company* will incorporate **easily accessible links to short video clips in every chapter** that illustrate points and can provide opportunities for thoughtful analysis.

3. Tables, each called **Second Look**, act as succinct summaries of complicated or detailed material. These can be useful when studying for exams.

4. **Self-Assessment Instruments** in previous editions were well received. Some of these instruments have been slightly revised.

5. The very popular **Video Case Studies** segment appearing at the end of every chapter has been expanded and includes many recent examples. Some reviewers have requested a DVD with all of the video case studies provided as a free ancillary. As advantageous as this would obviously be, the cost of gaining permission to use copyright-protected videos for such a DVD would require a major donation from Bill Gates or would send the price of the text into the stratosphere. Given my commitment to drastically lowering the price of *In Mixed Company*, such an option is unfortunately not feasible.

6. *A new feature has been added*—**TED Talks and YouTube videos** for illustration and analysis. These appear at the end of each chapter, and students can easily access them on the *Learning Link*.

7. A **glossary** of key terms for quick reference appears at the end of the text. Terms that are boldfaced in each chapter are included in the glossary. Many new terms have been added for this edition.

8. **Practice exams**, called **"Quizzes Without Consequences,"** appear at the end of each chapter in the enhanced e-book. These quizzes help prepare students for graded exams. Students frequently mention to me how helpful these practice quizzes have been to them.

9. **PowerPoint slides** have been prepared for classroom presentation of material. Most instructors prepare their own slides, but a potpourri of slides is available for those who may want to supplement their file.

10. The comprehensive **Instructor's Resource Manual** has been revised. Extensively classroom tested activities, simulations, exercises, and suggested video clips provide an abundance of options for enriching the learning experience for students. The **Test Bank** of exam questions for each chapter has been expanded with more than one version of each question (single answer or multiple answers) available. Both the extensive activities and the test bank included in the manual have been extremely well received.

Text Organization

Although there is no ideal organizational pattern, my schema for the sequence of chapters is quite simple. A theoretical foundation is discussed first (**Chapters 1 and 2**). Given the recent necessary embrace of virtual group meetings, a new detailed chapter has been composed addressing not just standard meetings but especially virtual group meetings (**Chapter 3**). This is then followed by how groups are formed and developed (**Chapter 4**). Then a discussion of how to establish the proper climate for the group to work effectively is presented (**Chapter 5**). An explanation and analysis of what roles group members are likely to play comes next (**Chapter 6**), followed by a discussion of group leadership (**Chapter 7**). Then, how to build teams and instill effective teamwork in groups is addressed (**Chapter 8**). A discussion of decision making/problem solving—the primary work to be performed by most groups—with special focus on critical thinking is next (**Chapters 9 and 10**). The close connection between power and conflict is then explored (**Chapters 11 and 12**). I can see other ways of organizing this same material, and instructors are obviously free to shift the order as they please, but the order I have chosen works well for me, students seem satisfied with the sequence of topics, and reviewers have praised the organization.

◣ Acknowledgments

My sincere thanks are extended to all those who reviewed this edition of *In Mixed Company*. They include: Marlene Adzema, *Red Rocks Community College*; Michelle R. Bahr, *Bellevue University;* Evan Billingsley, *Arizona State University;* Samantha L. Gonzalez, *Manchester Community College;* Richard Groner, *Ivy Tech Community College;* Kyle Hanners, *Arizona State University;* Jami Blaauw-Hara, *North Central Michigan College;* Richard A. Knight, *Shippensburg University;* Marla Lowenthal, *University of San Francisco*; Christine J. Moore, *Texas State University;* and Nancy Stillwell, *Madison College.*

I also wish to extend a sincere thanks to Steve Helba, acquisitions editor, and Alyssa Quinones, associate editor.

Finally, to my amazing and immensely talented wife, Marcy, who lovingly endured my persistent requests for her to create new custom cartoons, which she did with great imagination and skill, I offer a special thanks. Artist, singer, writer, musician, computer program analyst—her talents seem boundless. Our three decades as partners have been a joy that words cannot adequately reflect.

◣ About the Author

J. Dan Rothwell is the former chair of the Communication Studies Department at Cabrillo College after 30 years heading the department. He has a B.A. in American History from the University of Portland (Oregon), an M.A. in Rhetoric and Public Address, and a Ph.D. in Communication Theory and Social Influence. His M.A. and Ph.D. are both from the University of Oregon. He is the author of four other books: *In the Company of Others: An Introduction to Communication*, *Telling It Like It Isn't: Language Misuse and Malpractice*, *Interpersonal Communication: Influences and Alternatives* (with James Costigan), and *Practically Speaking*. He is also working on a sixth textbook, with his colleague and friend Michelle Waters, on business communication, to be published by Oxford University Press.

During his extensive teaching career, Dr. Rothwell received more than two dozen teaching awards, including the *Ernest L. Boyer International Award for Excellence in Teaching, Learning, and Technology* conferred by the Center for the Advancement of Teaching and Learning, Florida State College, and the National Council of Instructional Administrators; the *Cabrillo College "Innovative Teacher of the Year"* award; the National

Communication Association *"Community College Educator of the Year"* award; an official resolution by the California State Senate acknowledging Dr. Rothwell's excellence in teaching; and the *"Master Teacher"* award from the Western States Communication Association.

Finally, Dr. Rothwell's public speaking book, *Practically Speaking*, received the national Textbook Excellence Award from the Textbook and Academic Authors Association. Having never achieved one of his early goals in life—to be a Hall of Fame major league baseball pitcher—this, and his teaching awards, will have to partially compensate for his lifelong disappointment.

Professor Rothwell encourages feedback and correspondence from both students and instructors regarding *In Mixed Company*. Anyone so inclined may communicate with him by email at jdanrothwell@gmail.com.

Communication Competence in Groups

If you want to find out what people think about participating in groups, ask them. I have on numerous occasions. Comments include: "If God had ordered a committee to create the world, it would still be discussing proposals." "Working in groups is like eating tofu. I'm told it's good for me, but it makes me gag." Then there is this caustic gem: "I've had the flu and I've had to work in groups. I prefer the flu." Another student offered this biting assessment: "I hate groups. I hate group assignments. I hate teachers who require group assignments. Take the hint." Finally, there is this tongue-in-cheek suggestion: "Group work can be improved only if we threaten actual duels-to-the-death between slackers and perfectionists." This hyperbolic and negative view of working in groups is a common student reaction (Isaac, 2012; Muir, 2019). Surveys of full-time workers in the United States find similar results. One survey found that 95% of more than a thousand respondents agree that working in teams serves an important function in the workplace, but only 24% preferred to do so ("University of Phoenix Survey," 2013). Another survey found that fewer than 10% of employees prefer to work exclusively in teams, while 43% prefer to work alone ("Organizational Dynamics Survey," 2016).

Why is there such widespread antipathy for working in groups? A survey of almost 19,000 workers found that the top "pet peeves" that spark actual hatred for group work include: unfair workload, having to depend on others, and lack of full control over a project (Jerabek & Muoio, 2017). Having to depend on others who may not have the same motivation or commitment to produce excellent results can be annoying, even nightmarish. Groups can be time consuming, sometimes indecisive, conflict provoking, and slow to react to urgent needs. Personality clashes, irritating communication behaviors, and having to deal with difficult group members all encourage reticence to work in groups. Sorensen (1981) coined the term **grouphate** to describe how troublesome the group experience is for many people.

Despite these negative views of groups, almost everyone can point to positive group experiences, including some that are profoundly rewarding. The rewards include a feeling of belonging and affection gained from **primary groups** (family and friends), social connection from **social media networks** (Facebook, Instagram, LinkedIn, Reddit, Snapchat, Twitter, and numerous developing sites—see "101+ Social Media Sites," 2021), and social support in difficult times from **support groups**

objectives

The purpose of this chapter is to begin the exploration of how to improve the small group and team experience. Toward this end, there are three chapter objectives:

1. To correct common misconceptions regarding the human communication process.

2. To explain what communication is and is not.

3. To establish the theoretical groundwork for a communication competence approach to small groups and teams.

(Alcoholics Anonymous, cancer survivors groups). Also, you gain satisfaction from solving challenging problems by working in **project groups** (task forces, self-managing work teams), you enhance your knowledge from participating in **learning groups** (class study groups, Bible study groups, mock trial teams), you experience thrills and entertainment from participating in **activities groups** (chess club, sports teams), and you gain a sense of community from joining **neighborhood groups** (homeowners associations). Finally, you can acquire an identity and achieve pleasure from helping others through **social** and **service groups** (fraternities, sororities, Rotary, Lions, Habitat for Humanity), and you may find a creative outlet in **music** and **artistic groups** (bands, choirs, quilting circles). This is an impressive list of potential rewards from participating in small groups.

Not surprisingly, the most successful groups are composed of members who enjoy working in groups and who experience the rewards. The least successful groups are composed of members who dislike working in groups and primarily experience the disadvantages (Karau & Elsaid, 2009). Communication plays a central role in achieving group success and producing rewarding experiences. Thus, competent communication is a principal means of counteracting grouphate.

Whatever the degree of your satisfaction or dissatisfaction with groups, there is no escaping them, unless you plan to live your life alone in a cave as an out-of-touch survivalist. Reliance on groups will increase, not diminish, in the future. The American Association for the Advancement of Science, the National Council of Teachers of English, and the National Communication Association, among other organizations, all recommend frequent group activity in the college classroom. Four-fifths of both Fortune 1000 companies and manufacturing organizations use **self-managing work teams**—teams that regulate their own performance free from outside interference while completing an entire task (MacDonald, 2019). Organizations are increasingly becoming "team-centric" (Singh, 2019). A broad study by Microsoft found that the prevalence of working in teams has doubled in the workplace and will continue to increase (Wright, 2018). A survey of 1,372 respondents from 80 countries concluded that **virtual groups**—groups whose members rarely, if ever, meet face to face, and are connected by electronic technology—are an integral part of conducting business globally (Solomon, 2016). With the emergence of the Covid-19 pandemic, virtual group work has become even more prevalent. For example, a broad study showed that 64% of organizations expected virtual group work to be a permanent change even after the Covid-19 pandemic (Meluso et al., 2020). Maximizing the benefits of your unavoidable group experiences is obviously a worthy goal.

The central purpose of this textbook, then, is to teach you how to be a competent communicator in small groups and teams. Because we all have participated in many groups, it may be tempting to conclude that these experiences already prepared you for group success. Experience, however, sometimes teaches us bad habits and misinformation (note the myths discussed in the next section). I will not presume to tell you what you do and don't know about small group communication. That is for you to assess, perhaps with the help of your instructor.

When making this initial self-assessment, however, please consider this: Most Americans have a common tendency to overestimate their communication proficiency in groups. A long-term study of 600 teams and 6,000 team members in a wide variety of organizations found that assessments of leaders by team members were a whopping *50% lower* than the leaders' self-assessments (LaFasto & Larson, 2001). A more recent study parallels these findings. An exceedingly generous 96% of self-identified leaders of corporate virtual teams rated themselves as "effective" or "very effective." Only 19% of team members, however, agreed that most team leaders were adequately prepared to lead virtual teams effectively, and 58% rated their own team leaders as underprepared (Solomon, 2016). Ironically, it is the poorest communicators who inflate their self-assessments the most (Dunning, 2003). It is called the Dunning-Kruger effect.

Blulz60/Shutterstock.com

Hero Images/Getty Images

Iakov Filimonov/Shutterstock

fizkes/Shutterstock

We participate in a wide variety of small groups that serve many purposes and provide numerous rewards. Identify the potential purposes and rewards illustrated in these images.

Myths about Communication

Before tackling the question "What is communication?" and then "What is competent communication?" let's sweep out some of the musty misconceptions many people have stored in their intellectual attics regarding the communication process. As American humorist Will Rogers reputedly remarked, "It isn't what we don't know that gives us trouble; it's what we know that ain't so." Foolishness springs from holding firmly to indefensible **myths**—beliefs contradicted by fact. Consider five prominent ones.

Myth 1: Communication Is a Cure-All

Improving communication is not the magical answer to all your group woes. Research reveals that some problems between individuals are not solvable (Fulwiler, 2018). A group member may never develop a sunny disposition and a less cynical view of the world. Your group leader may never be more than an imperious, narcissistic, inconsiderate tyrant. Competent communication can help us cope with our recurring disagreements and challenges, but it may not change some people for the better.

Ysbrand Cosijn/Shutterstock

Some problems, such as an arrogant, imperious, bullying boss, may not be improved even if you communicate competently. Does this person even look approachable much less interested in possibly improving his communication competence? Looks can be deceiving, but they also can either invite or repel others from confronting communication difficulties. Communication is a significant tool, but not a panacea for all problems that arise in small groups.

In addition, a dysfunctional organizational system characterized by unclear roles and responsibilities and poorly designed decision-making processes may be the root cause of poor communication (see Chapter 2). Training to improve communication in such circumstances is likely to prove futile without systemic changes (Baker, 2015). Sometimes groups dismantle, not because the communication is poor but because members simply don't like each other or because they have contradictory visions for the group.

Communication is a tool that, in the possession of someone knowledgeable and skillful, can be used to help solve most problems that arise in groups. Communication, however, is not an end in itself, but merely a means to an end. You will not solve every conceivable problem in groups by learning to communicate more effectively, because not all group problems are communication based.

Myth 2: Communication Can Break Down

Communication does not break down. Machines break down; they quit, and if they belong to me, they do so with amazing regularity. Human beings continue to communicate even when they may wish not to do so. For example, not showing up for a group meeting, remaining silent during group discussions, or walking out in the middle of a group discussion without saying a word does not bring communication to a halt. Group members infer messages from these nonverbal acts—perhaps incorrect messages, but potentially important ones nonetheless.

The view that communication can break down comes partly from the recognition that we do not always achieve our goals through communication; the group may disband in failure. But failure to achieve group goals may occur even when communication between the parties in conflict is exemplary. So, where's the breakdown?

Myth 3: Effective Communication Is Merely Skill Building

The skills orientation to communication assumes that if you learn a few key communication skills, you will become a much better communicator. Without understanding the complexities of the communication process, no amount of skills training will be meaningful, and it may be harmful. Merely teaching the skill of assertiveness to a battered woman, for example, without addressing the volatile and often unpredictable circumstances of abusive relationships in families, could prove fatal for the abused woman and her children (Dombeck, 2010). Assertiveness with your boss or team leader may get you fired or demoted to a position equivalent to cleaning up after parading elephants. Effective communication is not a one-size-fits-all skill set.

Teaching communication skills in isolation is like constructing a house without a carefully developed set of blueprints. The blueprint offered later in this chapter that provides the foundation to help you succeed in small groups and teams, to learn when and how to employ acquired communication skills, is the communication competence model.

Myth 4: 93% of Meaning Is Communicated Nonverbally

Some communication texts and numerous Internet sites misinterpret research by Albert Mehrabian and assert that 93% of all meaning in messages is communicated nonverbally (see Konstantinova & Astakhova, 2018; Lapakko, 2007, for detailed critiques). Mehrabian (1971) never drew such a broad conclusion from his research. In fact, he repudiated it directly. In 2009, BBC reporter Tim Harford asked Mehrabian if 93% of communication meaning is nonverbal. He responded: "Absolutely not, and whenever I hear that misquote or misrepresentation of my findings I cringe" (quoted by Lovett, 2016). Mehrabian's research consisted of a speaker uttering a single word in an inconsistent voice, with no context provided, and a judgment required from a very small sample of subjects regarding the feelings of the speaker. That's it!

Why bother learning a language, a difficult undertaking, if only a minuscule 7% of meaning is derived from verbal communication while the remaining 93% is from nonverbal cues? Consider how many English proficiency classes are required throughout your education, even if you are a native speaker of the language. Turn off the sound when watching a movie scene of two characters quarreling and see if you can ascertain 93% of the meaning of their argument. Yes, you can know they are quarreling, ascertain emotional expression (anger), and even gauge the intensity of that emotion, but can you discern the informational content? What are they fighting about? Who has the stronger arguments? Travel to China without understanding the language and observe people in casual conversation. Can you understand more than a hint of the meaning in their transaction? Why do movies whose dialogue is in a language other than English come with translation captioning as an option if verbal communication is so insignificant? As I will explore later, nonverbal communication can be highly significant, especially in certain contexts, but don't fall for this oft-repeated massive exaggeration of its importance to the communication process.

Myth 5: Effective Communication Is Just Common Sense

Consider **hindsight bias**—the "I-knew-it-already" tendency (Cherry, 2020). We are inclined to overestimate our prior knowledge once we have been told the correct answers. Anything can seem like mere common sense when you've been given the correct answers, or as psychologist David Myers (2002) observes, "How easy it is to seem wise when drawing the bull's-eye after the arrow has struck." Everybody knows that opposites attract, right? When told this by Myers, most students find this conclusion unsurprising. But wait! When college students are told the *opposite* ("Birds of a feather flock together"), most also find this result unsurprising and merely common sense.

The hindsight bias may influence us to view competent communication as mere common sense once we have received communication training. **If, however, competent communication is just common sense, why does miscommunication occur so often?** For example, a survey of a thousand U.S. employees conducted by Dynamic Signal warned businesses: "Repair the way we communicate with employees at work or risk crippling financial consequences" (Hannah, 2019). Another study found that 86% of corporate executives, employees, and educators say that poor communication is a key reason for widespread workplace failures (Sanders, 2020). As one expert concludes: "That communication problems are omnipresent in companies or organizations is simply an understatement" (Odine, 2015).

Although a huge majority of recent college graduates believe they have the necessary communication skills to be successful in their careers, employers mostly disagree (Bauer-Wolf, 2018). Principal deficiencies are in verbal communication and working in teams, sometimes referred to as "soft skills" (Gould, 2016). As Michael Hansen, chief executive officer of Cengage Publishing, notes, "There is a need for more soft skills training, both in college and on the job, and today's learners and graduates must continue to hone their skills to stay ahead" (quoted by Bauer-Wolf, 2019). **This is not a one-and-done process. It is a lifelong enterprise that requires constant updating as our world changes.** Just contemplate the enormous, unexpected communication challenges and often clumsy attempts to adapt initially that have emerged as a result of the Covid-19 pandemic!

The simple way to test whether competent communication in groups is merely common sense and you knew it all along is to be quizzed before training is received. For years, I tested my students at the beginning of a term on general knowledge of small group communication. I did not ask technical questions or definitions of concepts (making this the least challenging test of the term). Consistently, students did very poorly on this quiz (most flunked). Such results are not surprising or cause for ridicule. It is foolish to expect students to do well on this exam before they've taken the class.

Learning requires a degree of humility, a willingness to recognize and address our shortcomings. To paraphrase Alfred Korzybski, no one knows everything about anything. Communication is not mere common sense. It is arguably the most complicated, pervasive activity we humans do, and **learning how to do it**

better should never end. Everyone has more to learn. You are invited to approach this text, not with an attitude of contentment with your knowledge and skills (whatever their level), but with a strong desire to learn more and to improve your communication in small groups.

Communication Defined

Thus far, I have indicated what communication is not, but not what it is. The definition of communication involves several fundamental attributes discussed in this section.

focus questions

1. How do the content and the relationship dimensions of messages differ?
2. "Communication is a process." What does this mean?

Communication as Transactional: Mutually Influential

Human communication is **transactional**. This means that all parties engaged in communicating mutually influence one another. Each person is both a sender and a receiver simultaneously, not merely a sender or a receiver. Thus, as you speak, you receive *feedback* (responses), mostly nonverbal, from listeners. This, in turn, influences the messages that you continue to send. Skillful communicators read feedback accurately and adjust their ensuing message appropriately.

You can see this mutual-influence process clearly by examining the two dimensions of a message—content and relationship (Watzlawick et al., 1967). The **content dimension** refers to the information transmitted. The **relationship dimension** refers to how messages define or redefine the relationship among group members. Consider the following transactional dialogue:

Anne: We should meet to prepare our group presentation.
Benny: I can't meet until Wednesday night after 6:30. I work.
Charise: Wednesday, say about 7:00, works fine for me. How about the rest of you?
David: No can do! I'm busy.
Eduardo: Well, get unbusy because our project is due in a week, and we're way behind.
David: Hey, Satan's spawn, come up with another time.

Benny: Come on, everybody. No need to get ugly.

Anne: Exactly how busy are you on Wednesday night, David? Can't you change plans?

David: I'm busy. Let's leave it at that.

Eduardo: Why don't you come up with a time that works with your "busy" schedule.

Charise: How about next Monday evening?

Anne: Now I've got a schedule conflict.

The content of this group transaction is the need to schedule a group meeting and the schedule conflicts that exist. The relationship dimension, however, is far more complex. Group members are not merely identifying scheduling difficulties; they're maneuvering for power positions in the group. Who gets to tell whom what to do is a subtext. How messages are spoken (as a demand or a request) influences group members' responses. Whether group members are being cooperative or competitive with each other affects the discussion.

When you are in a group, every utterance, choice, and action continually defines and redefines who you are in relation to other group members and who they are in relation to you. This is ongoing and unavoidable. Individuals affect the group, and the group influences the individual. Communication in groups is a continuous series of transactions.

Communication as a Process: The Continuous Flow

Identifying communication as a process recognizes that nothing stands still, or as the bumper sticker proclaims, "Change is inevitable—except from a vending machine." Communication reveals the dynamic nature of relationships and events.

Communication is a process because changes in events and relationships are part of a continuous flow. You can't understand the ocean by freezing a single wave on film. The ocean is understood only in its dynamism—its tides, currents, waves in motion, plant and animal life interacting symbiotically, and so forth. Similarly, communication makes sense not by isolating a word, sentence, gesture, facial expression, or exclamation, but by looking at currents of thought and feelings expressed verbally and nonverbally as a whole.

As a student, for instance, you affect the quality of instruction by your attitude and degree of interest in the subject matter. Show indifference by exhibiting inattention and you will suck the life out of a teacher's enthusiasm and invite a negative reaction. Relationships between teachers and students may change in the short span of a single class period or in the flash of an ill-chosen phrase, especially when controversial material is presented.

We cannot freeze relationships in time. Every conversation is a point of departure for an ensuing conversation. Every communication experience is the result of the accumulation of experiences preceding the present one. Each new experience affects future transactions. Human communication is a process.

Communication as Sharing Meaning: Making Sense

The term *communication* is derived from the Latin word *communicare*, which denotes "to share." Sharing from this perspective does not mean merely exchanging information like one would exchange gifts. Communication is not just transferring "stuff" from one person to another. This isn't just the postal service delivering packages or Door Dash delivering takeout. You attempt, and often achieve, something deeper when you communicate with other humans. You attempt to share meaning, which is "the conscious pattern humans create out of their interpretation of experience" (Anderson & Ross, 2002). You construct meaning by making connections and patterns in your mind that "make sense" of your world. You then attempt to share this constructed meaning with others, who in turn reconstruct your message to try to understand your meaning. For example, when you view a relationship with a team member as a friendship and the other person sees it likewise, there is an overlap, and meaning is shared, approximately. The depth of that friendship, or even what constitutes friendship, however, is not identical between two people. There are always subtle differences. Those subtle differences can be quite meaningful, as when one party views the friendship as potentially romantic but the other party does not. Welcome to the world of the awkward! You share this meaning both verbally and nonverbally.

Verbal Communication: Telling It Like It Isn't We share meaning verbally with language. **Language** is a structured system of **symbols** for sharing meaning. Symbols are representations of *referents*—whatever the symbol refers to. Because symbols represent referents but are not the objects, ideas, events, or relationships represented, symbols have no meaning apart from us. Meaning is in the mind of the beholder. Words are symbols, so meaning is not contained in words. We aren't "telling it like it is" (identifying objective reality); we're telling others what our subjective perception of the world is.

The meaning and usage of words depend on common agreement. As a speech community, English speakers tacitly agree to certain meanings and appropriate usages for words, even if this sometimes seems odd. For example, comedian Steven Wright asks, "Why is it that when you transport something by car it's called a shipment but when you transport something by ship it's called cargo?" Why does *slow down* and *slow up* mean the same thing? Why does *fat chance* and *slim chance* also mean the same thing? The simple answer is that when decoding words, we give them agreed-upon meanings.

Common agreement among language users determines the meaning of words, even though at times literal meaning would seem odd at best. For example, our feet can smell but our noses can run. Misunderstandings, especially cross-culturally, can easily occur because common agreement also has to be understood for language to function effectively. Those group members who speak English as a second language may struggle with deciphering common understanding of word choices.

This common agreement, however, doesn't always avoid misunderstandings because words can be ambiguous; they can have double or multiple common meanings, as Groucho Marx famously illustrated with the quip: "Time flies like an arrow; fruit flies like a banana." A *booty call* could be an invitation to a treasure hunt or a search for something quite different. Consider actual newspaper headlines reported by the *Columbia Journalism Review*: "Prostitutes Appeal to Pope"; "Kids Make Nutritious Snacks"; and "City Manager Tapes Head to District Attorney." Imagine a nonnative speaker of English trying to decode this sentence: "The woman was present to present the present to her friend, presently." A study of "problematic communication" among crew members and in pilot–air traffic controller interactions concludes that "it is almost certain that communication has played a central role in a significant proportion of aviation accidents" (Howard, 2008, p. 371). "Multiple meanings of words and phrases" was listed as one of the principal problems. A survey of 2,070 airline pilots likewise found that "words, phrases, and sentences with more than one meaning" was "the biggest communication issue" with ground control (Wilson, 2016).

Culture further complicates verbal misunderstandings. Electrolux, a Scandinavian vacuum cleaner manufacturer, once used the sales slogan in the United States, "Nothing sucks like an Electrolux." In preparation for the 2008 Summer Olympics in Beijing, China, a retired army colonel named David Tool, who resided in the capital city, was hired to correct notoriously poor translations featured on English signs. "Beijing Anus Hospital" was changed to "Beijing Proctology Hospital," and "Deformed Man Toilet" thankfully was changed to "Disabled Person Toilet" (Boudreau, 2007).

Ambiguous verbal communication between cockpit crews and ground control has caused near disasters and actual catastrophes. Seemingly simple messages can produce potentially deadly incidents when multiple meanings for words create misunderstandings.

Tatiana Popova/Shutterstock

The increasing globalization of business makes even the choice of language to communicate within and among multicultural groups and organizations an important consideration (Weedmark, 2019). "Those who share a mother tongue have a linguistic bond that differs from those who speak the same language as a second language" (Victor, 2007, p. 3). If English is chosen as the preferred language of business, this can create an in-group/out-group dynamic between those who speak it easily and those who do not. The choice of language to conduct business can directly affect teamwork and long-term business relationships for good or ill (Tenzer et al., 2017). When a group speaks a language not well understood by all its members, as can occur in our increasingly multicultural workplaces, those left out of the conversation because of difficulties fully understanding the language spoken may feel socially ostracized and angry (Morrison-Smith & Ruiz, 2020). This *linguistic divide* can reduce group productivity (Dotan-Eliaz et al., 2009).

The emergence of global virtual teams has also created an international linguistic challenge. Increasingly, virtual teams in the realm of international business are composed of members from diverse cultures, many of whom speak English as a second language. English is the dominant language of the Internet ("Internet World Users by Language," 2021). Inevitably, the nuances and complexities of mastering a language such as English lead to problems of interpretation and translation. One study of virtual groups showed that 75% of respondents found language difficulties challenging (Solomon, 2016).

Seemingly straightforward messages can also produce difficulties sharing exact meaning. Consider, for example, whether the email from your team leader saying that the team project "is fine" should be interpreted as damning with faint praise or as giving a genuine thumbs up for a job well done. In addition, "maybe" to an American means possibly yes, but to a Japanese, "maybe" typically means a polite no (Kameda, 2014).

Finally, we indicate linguistically our identification with a group (Van Swol & Kane, 2019). A study of language used by group members on Reddit, for example, found that their language styles and word choices converged. Redditors revealed their group identification by adopting the linguistic norms of their social media group (McEwan, 2016). In other words, Redditors share a common language to indicate group affiliation.

Nonverbal Communication: Wordless Meaning We share meaning nonverbally as well as verbally. **Nonverbal communication** is sharing meaning with others without using words. Our facial expressions, eye contact, personal appearance, tone of voice, gestures, posture, touch, and use of space and time all have the potential to communicate messages to group members. For example, the strength of your handshake can communicate degree of confidence. The intensity of your anger is exhibited mostly nonverbally (e.g., tone of voice, facial expressions, gestures, and posture). Anxiety is chiefly communicated nonverbally. Touch can be a source of comfort and compassion or a key indicator of sexual harassment in the workplace. Direct eye contact can be critical to presentational effectiveness. The top nonverbal mistake candidates make when interviewing is failure to make eye contact (Hayes, 2018). A smile can communicate a host of differing messages (e.g., approval, affection, sarcasm, contempt, discomfort). As noted previously, however, the significance of nonverbal communication has often been wildly exaggerated. Nevertheless, if it were merely incidental to verbal messages few would pay it notice or experience difficulties sharing messages accurately.

One of the difficulties with communicating in virtual groups can be the absence of nonverbal cues, in whole or in part, that accompany verbal, face-to-face messages (Yang et al., 2018). One study of virtual teams revealed that "lack of face-to-face contact" was identified by 89% of respondents as a significant problem (Solomon, 2016). The emotional tone of an online written message can easily be misinterpreted as hostile, impersonal, or disagreeable because vocal tone, facial expressions, posture, gestures, and the normal array of nonverbal cues are missing (Myers, 2017). One study found that the tone of our emails is misinterpreted 50% of the time (Kruger et al., 2005). Internationally recognized consultant Erica Dhawan (2021) notes that we are often "tone-deaf not tone-deft" when writing our emails. This can be a generational issue. A study conducted by Grammarly "found workers under 35 were 50% more likely than older workers to be told their tone was too informal, even though more younger workers said they spent time agonizing over meaning, tone and grammar in their emails" (Carino, 2019). Even assuming that friends are more likely to interpret accurately emotions conveyed in emails better than strangers is not supported by research (Riordan & Trichtinger, 2017).

Emojis help with tone but are still limited. Individuals may also be hesitant to use them in business communication for fear of appearing too informal and unprofessional, but the increasing prevalence of virtual group work has encouraged some researchers to advocate their wider use in employment environments (Meluso et al., 2020). One study, however, found that smiley emojis, "contrary to actual smiles . . . do not increase perceptions of warmth and actually decrease perceptions of competence" (Glikson et al., 2017).

Skyping or Zooming can add a nonverbal element to business meetings, but it has its own limitations (Morrison-Smith & Ruiz, 2020). For example, "a frozen screen or a weird echo makes it hard for attendees to feel that their contributions are being heard and valued" (Dhawan, 2021). Staring at your own image on screen during a video meeting amongst an assemblage of additional participants' images isn't the same as communicating while physically present with others. We're not accustomed to seeing ourselves as we converse. Myriad additional challenges of engaging in videoconferences are discussed later.

Nonverbal communication, like verbal communication, is often ambiguous. When group members look down for several minutes while you are speaking, does it mean they are bored, uncomfortable with your message, not listening, carefully considering your message, or devising a plan to exit the meeting early? When a group member frowns, is he or she showing confusion, taking offense at something said, disagreeing, or suddenly remembering the dog was left alone in the house with no exit for using the outdoors as a toilet? Rich Matthews, a jury consultant with Decision Analysis in San Francisco, states that it is "practically impossible and it's just dangerous to interpret facial expressions and gestures and reactions" during a trial (quoted in Sulek, 2004, p. 9A; see also Hoffer et al., 2013). Research from Decision Quest, a U.S. legal support company, concludes that jurors "overestimate what you can know about a person based on his or her nonverbal behavior. Jurors assume that a person whose lips are pursed is rigid or arrogant, that someone who cocks his head back is condescending, that a person who fidgets is lying." As this report notes, however, such interpretations fail to consider "that the witness is trying to concentrate, is likely nervous about being in a new situation, and is trying to make a good impression" ("Jurors' Body Language," 2017).

Sharing meaning nonverbally between cultures can be equally problematic (Cotton, 2013; Manolaki, 2016). For example, the "A-OK" gesture that forms a circle with the index finger and the thumb is obscene in Brazil, and it means "worthless" in France, "money" in Japan, and recently has become a white power sign in the United States. Raising the index finger to signify "one," as Americans often do to signify "We're number one," means "two" in Italy, so the gesture becomes "We're number two," a less satisfying source of celebratory pride. In Japan, however, the upright thumb means "five" (counting begins with the index finger, and the thumb is the last digit). Nodding the head up and down means "yes" in the United States, and shaking it side to side means "no." In Bulgaria, Turkey, Iran, and Bengal, however, it is the reverse. In Greece, tipping the head back abruptly means "no," but the same gesture in India means "yes." (Nod your head if you understand all of this.) You can imagine the potential for misunderstandings and even international incidences when gestures are misinterpreted during intercultural team negotiations.

Even though nonverbal communication can be ambiguous and difficult to read accurately, it can nevertheless have a big impact on our impressions of others (Knapp et al., 2014). In 2004, Scott Peterson was found guilty of murdering his pregnant wife and unborn child. Jurors revealed after the trial that they chose the death penalty as his punishment partly due to Peterson's nonverbal communication. Juror Richelle Nice said, "For me, a big part of it was at the end—the verdict—no emotion. No anything. That spoke a thousand words—loud and clear. Today—the giggle at the table. Loud and clear." Jury foreman Steve Cardosi echoed this reaction: "He lost his wife and his child, and it didn't seem to faze him" (quoted in Sulek, 2004). Similarly, one study of jurors' reactions to nonverbal communication by judges during mock trials showed a negative reaction to

fizkes/Shutterstock

Gestures, such as the thumbs-up, do not necessarily have universal meaning. In some cultures, thumbs-up is obscene, even when done with a big smile. In a very simple way, this highlights the challenges you face when groups are composed of members from very diverse cultures.

a judge's perceived lack of involvement (e.g., pen tapping, paper shuffling) and apparent bias (e.g., scornful facial expressions) during trial proceedings (Burnett & Badzinski, 2005).

Mixed messages also show the impact of nonverbal cues. A **mixed message** occurs when there is positive verbal and negative nonverbal communication, or vice versa. A group member may verbally endorse the group's decision but nonverbally exhibit disagreement, even contempt. It is easier to hide our real feelings verbally than it is nonverbally. Attempting to wipe an opinion off your face is challenging.

I have thus far discussed what communication is not and, conversely, what communication is. To summarize by way of definition, **communication** is a transactional process of sharing meaning with others. The intricacies of sharing meaning with others in group situations will become more apparent when I discuss what constitutes competent communication, the next topic for consideration.

Communication Competence

Defining communication does not tell you how to communicate competently. To accomplish this goal, let's begin with a definition. **Communication competence** is engaging in communication behavior with others that is both effective and appropriate in a given context (Spitzberg, 2015). This definition requires brief elaboration.

focus questions
1. How do you determine communication competence?
2. Does appropriate communication require strict conformity to group rules?

Effectiveness: Achieving Goals

Communication competence is partially predicated on results. Consequently, **effectiveness** is defined as how well we have progressed toward the achievement of goals. Someone who knows the changes in communication behavior that need to be made, and who wants to make these changes but never does, can hardly be deemed a competent communicator.

A Matter of Degree: From Deficiency to Proficiency   Communication effectiveness is a relative concept—a matter of degree. We speak of communicators along a continuum, from highly proficient in achieving goals to woefully deficient, with designations in between such as ordinary and average. All of us have our communication strengths and weaknesses in certain situations and circumstances. Some individuals are at ease in social situations such as parties or gatherings of strangers, but they would rather be dipped in molasses and strapped to an anthill than confront conflict in their own group. We can be highly proficient in one circumstance but minimally skillful or depressingly ineffective in another situation. Therefore, the label "competent communicator" is a judgment of an individual's degree of proficiency in achieving goals in a specific context, not an inherent characteristic of any individual.

We (Not Me) Oriented: Primacy of Groups A We-orientation means that your primary attention is on the group (we), not the individual (me). Zander (1982) long ago claimed, "A body of people is not a group if the members are primarily interested in individual accomplishment" (p. 2). This, however, doesn't mean that group interests should always supersede individual interests. Nevertheless, trying to achieve your individual goals at the expense of the group's goals usually produces unsatisfactory outcomes for both you and the group (Platow et al., 2015). Research by the Gallup organization found that 60% of government workers are miserable because of "horrible bosses" who exhibit less interest in the welfare of employees than in nailing a good tee time on the golf links (Bradberry, 2020).

There are potential dividends when group members assume a We-orientation. Teams win championships, businesses innovate, and students earn better grades. A We-orientation requires concern for others, not merely concern for self. Consequently, communication competence in groups necessitates behavior that is both effective and appropriate.

Appropriateness: Following the Rules

The appropriateness of a person's communication is determined by examining the context. Every communication transaction has a context, or an environment in which meaning emerges. Context consists of *who* (sender) communicates *what* (message) to *whom* (receiver), *why* (purpose) the communicator does it, and *where* (setting), *when* (time), and *how* (way) it is done. Every communication context has rules that create expectations regarding appropriate behavior. A **rule** is a prescription that indicates what you should or shouldn't do in specific contexts. (Shimanoff, 2009). Thus, **appropriateness** means complying with contextual rules and their accompanying expectations.

Rule Violations: Consequential Effects Groups expect rules to be followed, but when rules are violated the consequences can be significant. Consider some examples. A study of student-to-teacher email and text messaging showed that students often send overly casual messages to teachers. Messages such as "R U Able to Meat Me" incline an instructor "to like the student less, view them as less credible, have a lesser opinion of the message quality, and make them less willing to comply with students' simple email requests" (Stephens et al., 2009, p. 318). Text abbreviations ("R U" instead of "are you") are particularly disliked by teachers, and misspellings and apparent lack of proofreading ("meat" instead of "meet") clearly diminish the sender's credibility. Standard implicit rules for teacher–student communication dictate that students communicate thoughtfully and respectfully with teachers. If your study group or project team needs to email or text message your instructor, show care and respect by avoiding overly casual, inappropriate messaging.

This study also underlines the importance of proofreading all emails and text messages before sending them, especially to all members of teams in work and professional settings. It isn't that misspelled messages cannot be deciphered. For example, read this edited version found on the Internet:

> Aoccdrnig to stdees at an Amrcan uinervtisy, ltteer oredr in a wrod is uniprmeotnt. Olny the frist and lsat lttr msut be in the crrocet pclae. The rset of the wrod can be a cmolpete mses. Tihs is bcuseae we raed words as a wolhe, not by idndvidaul ltters.

Were you able to decipher the message without much difficulty despite the disastrous spelling? Have you ever received an email or text message that resembled this jumbled mess? Imagine the impression you leave if you send such an error-filled message to your boss, instructor, or team leader.

Beware the risks of autocorrect! It is notorious for changes to text messages that make you seem moronic or weird if you do not catch the ludicrous "corrections." True story: A friend of mine texted a colleague at work about a delicious "nut taco" recipe. Autocorrect had changed it to "butt taco"—not so delicious.

Finally, a survey of more than 2,600 hiring and human resource managers conducted by Harris Interactive for Career Builder, a web-based employment organization, listed answering a cellphone or text message during the interview, appearing arrogant or entitled, dressing inappropriately, and failing to make eye contact as the most common mistakes made by job applicants (Grasz, 2017). An interviewing panel expects appropriate behavior from applicants. Interrupting an interview to answer a cellphone or to send a text message communicates less interest in the job and more interest in immediate communication with others. Dressing too casually for a formal interview sends the message, "I don't take this interview seriously." Displays of arrogance and entitlement can instantly kill an interview.

Then there are the "most unusual" things job interviewees have done according to hiring employers and managers: candidate asked for a cocktail; candidate broke out in song during the interview; candidate came to the interview wearing slippers; and candidate asked to taste the interviewer's coffee (Hayes, 2018). Know the rules and meet expectations accordingly to be effective and appropriate.

Rule Changes: Context Specific The appropriateness of your communication cannot be determined by merely examining a message that is isolated from the rich complexity of **context**—an environment in which meaning emerges, consisting of who communicates to whom, why the communicator does it, and where, when, and how it is done. For instance, you may self-disclose intimate information to members of some groups but not others. If you attend a therapy group on marriage, self-disclosing will be expected and encouraged because it is compatible with the group's purpose. If, however, you are talking in a meeting of the Student Senate or the Dormitory Advisory Committee, intimate self-disclosure will likely make members squirm in their chairs and wish for an earthquake as a distraction. The purpose of these groups is not therapeutic, so the rules that dictate appropriate communication in these contexts are different from rules found at meetings of Alcoholics Anonymous or Marriage Encounter.

Halfpoint/Shutterstock

Some rules may need to be modified. No rule is sacrosanct. With the advent of the Covid-19 pandemic, rules regarding social contact had to be changed. Such rule changes were not always greeted with alacrity.

Achieving Communication Competence

Defining communication competence identifies what it is, but not how to achieve it. There are five general ways, each explored throughout this text in much greater detail, to improve your effectiveness and appropriateness in groups: You can acquire knowledge, hone communication skills, improve your sensitivity, redouble your commitment, and apply ethical standards to your communication choices (see Figure 1.1).

Figure 1.1 Communication Competence Model

Knowledge: Learning the Rules

Knowledge in any communication situation is critical. We cannot determine what is appropriate and effective without knowing the rules operating in a given situation, and rules can change. When first hired, for example, there is a period of adjustment where you learn to navigate in your new job based on the rules that become apparent. What authority do you have to influence decision making in your project group? How should you address your team leader—formally or casually? What information technologies are you permitted to access at work to advance your team proposal?

Then there are rules, often misunderstood or volatile, regarding how to relate to LGBTQ group members. Canela Lopez and Marguerite Ward (2020) identify thirteen things to avoid saying to LGBTQ coworkers. Among these are: (1) Never offer a "compliment" by saying "You don't strike me as gay"; (2) do not keep mentioning your one gay family member; and (3) avoid saying, "I would never have guessed you were transgender." Rules are changing as gender fluidity has become a more transparent issue, so remaining current in your knowledge is important if you hope to avoid appearing insensitive and offensive.

Skills: Showing, Not Just Knowing

Communication competence encompasses the ability to apply your knowledge in actual situations. To be effective, you must combine knowledge with skill. Despite the increasing popularity of teams in organizations, researchers have discovered that such groups are often unsuccessful because members lack teamwork knowledge *and* skill (Hollenbeck et al., 2004). They may know what to do but not how to do it skillfully.

A **communication skill** is the ability to perform a communication behavior effectively and repeatedly. Clearly, fluently, concisely, eloquently, and confidently communicating a message is an example. Practice, of course, is essential to the mastery of any communication skill. Group members who are trained and practice together acquire skills and improve group performance (Ellis et al., 2005). Business consultant Greg Satell (2015) claims that "communication is today's most important skill." A LinkedIn study found that communication and teamwork were ranked #1 and #3 as the most "essential business skills for success in the workplace" (Beqiri, 2017; see also Bean-Mellinger, 2019).

Sensitivity: Receptive Accuracy

Having the knowledge to determine what constitutes appropriate communication in a specific context and having the skills to be effective are great, but what if you aren't attentive to signals from group members that indicate hostility, tension, anger, irritation, disgust, or uneasiness? Sensitivity is also important. **Sensitivity** is receptive accuracy whereby you can detect, decode, and comprehend signals and emotional cues sent within groups (Bernieri, 2001).

Failure to attend to and comprehend signals can severely affect group performance (Hall & Bernieri, 2001). Sensitivity is even more important than the general intelligence of group members. Google conducted a huge study called Project Aristotle and found that members of effective teams had high scores on sensitivity; members of ineffective teams had low scores (Duhigg, 2016). Women exhibit a greater facility for sensitivity, so including women in task-oriented groups is highly advisable (Woolley et al., 2010).

Fortunately, sensitivity can be learned, especially if we give social media a rest. A major aspect of sensitivity is being mindful, not mindless, about your communication with others. We exhibit **mindfulness** when "we think about our communication and continually work at changing what we do in order to become more effective" (Griffin, 2006). Put down the electronic gadgets, view your surroundings, engage others face to face in your classes or workplaces, and be mindful. We exhibit **mindlessness** when we pay little attention to our communication with others and put little or no effort into improving it. One of the functions of this text is to assist you in developing greater sensitivity by identifying patterns of communication that pose problems in group transactions and by providing solutions.

Commitment: A Passion for Excellence

Effectiveness requires commitment. **Commitment** is persistent effort to achieve goals and produce excellence. Little that is worthwhile comes without commitment. The predominant motivation of the competent communicator is the desire to avoid previous mistakes and to find better ways of communicating with group members. Someone who makes the same mistakes repeatedly and shows little interest in altering his or her behavior is a nuisance or, worse, a deadweight who can sink a group.

Commitment to improving your communication effectiveness requires self-monitoring. When you interact in groups, be a **participant-observer**. Assume a detached view of yourself. Analyze your communication behavior; look for areas to improve while noting successes. Ultimately, the competent communicator

Rawpixel.com/Shutterstock

Dr. Louisa Parks of the Brain Health Center at California Pacific Medical Center notes that people are spending so much time on social networking devices instead of face-to-face interactions that "the ability to recognize things like sarcasm, humor, or even the emotions on a human face" are on the wane (quoted in Brown, 2013, p. A16). This poses problems for exhibiting sensitivity—that ability to accurately decode subtle emotional cues.

considers it a personal responsibility to make the necessary effort to interact with group members as effectively and productively as possible.

Ethics: The Right and Wrong of Communication

Competent communicators concern themselves with more than what works for them personally. Lying, cheating, and abusing others to gain group leadership, for example, is self-oriented and reprehensible. This violates standards of ethics related directly to appropriateness.

Ethics is a system for judging the moral correctness of human behavior by weighing that behavior against an agreed-upon set of standards of what constitutes right and wrong. Five essential values, based on the Credo for Ethical Communication adopted by the National Communication Association (www.natcom. org), constitute the set of standards for judging the moral correctness of our communication behavior. They are as follows:

1. *Honesty.* "There is no more fundamental ethical value than honesty" (Josephson, 2002). Unfortunately, the demand for honesty often exceeds the supply. "Indeed, lying is so commonplace in corporations that it often passes without comment" (Jenkins & Delbridge, 2016).
2. *Respect.* Relationships in groups fall apart, and groups can't function effectively when members show disrespect for each other. One survey by the

Ethics is a critical element of communication competence. As humans, we care about right and wrong behavior (appropriateness). It is one of the characteristics that separates humans from the beasts-as-feasts daily killing field that occurs on the African Serengeti. The We-orientation of communication effectiveness and rules of appropriateness make ethics a significant element of the competence model.

Josephson Institute of Ethics reported that 99% of respondents rated receiving respect as "very important" or "essential" to them, and treating others with respect received a similar rating (Jarc, 2012).

3. *Fairness.* Students recognize immediately how unfair it would be if an instructor gave a better grade to some project groups in class and penalized others based on their sex, ethnicity, age, or lifestyle. Everyone should play by the same rules. One study of community college students reported that fairness was perceived to be "very important" or "extremely important" by most respondents (Kidder et al., 2002). Millennials (born between 1982 and 1997) consider fairness in the workplace as more important than even recognition or opportunity (Knights, 2017). Research of Generation Z members (born between 1997 and 2013) reveals that perceived fairness is significant and affects their performance, satisfaction, commitment, trust, and self-esteem (Schroth, 2019).

4. *Choice.* Freedom to choose for oneself without threat of force or intimidation is a basic ethical value (Jaksa & Pritchard, 1994). **Coercion**—forced choice—prevents free choice. There is no real option presented. Choice goes hand in hand with honesty. If you fear reprisals for telling the truth, then your freedom to choose truthfulness instead of deceit is compromised.

5. *Responsibility.* Every group member has a responsibility, a duty, to be concerned about more than merely what works to achieve personal or even group goals. How goals are achieved is also a vital consideration. The study of community college students previously cited reported the highest score among a list of choices was for the importance of responsibility as a "moral value."

These general ethical values serve as guidelines for appropriate communication behavior. Group communication is so complex, however, that any list of standards used to judge members' communication ethics, applied absolutely, would immediately create problems. Ethical communication is a matter of context. A lie that accuses a member of your study group of cheating on a test is different from a lie that covers up an embarrassing event that is private and none of the group's business. Exceptions also will inevitably surface. Students don't have complete freedom of choice. Few would freely take a public speaking course even to improve important group presentations unless mandated by general education requirements because most people fear giving speeches. Honesty, respect, fairness, choice, and responsibility, however, are strong values in most cultures, and they should act as basic standards for evaluating our communication.

Culture and Communication Competence

Multicultural small groups are becoming the norm, not the exception. Consequently, membership diversity poses challenges when applying the communication competence model. So, what is culture? Lord Raglan asserted that "culture is roughly anything we do and the monkeys don't." To be more specific and accurate than Raglan, **culture** is a learned set of enduring values, beliefs, and practices that are shared by an identifiable, large group of people with a common history. To explain this definition, a **value** is the most deeply felt, generally shared view of what is deemed good, right, or worthwhile thinking or behavior. Values constitute a shared conception, not of what is, but of what ought to be. A **belief** is what a person thinks is true or probable. Two individuals may *value* human life, for example, but one may *believe* that capital punishment preserves life by deterring homicides, while the other may believe the contrary. Finally, a **co-culture** is any group that is part of a dominant culture yet often has a common history and shares some differences in values, beliefs, and practices from the dominant culture. African Americans, Asian Americans, Native Americans, and Mexican Americans are some obvious examples of co-cultures within the United States. The LGBTQ community is also a co-culture, as is the deaf community and a variety of other groups.

Rules of appropriateness vary widely among cultures and co-cultures, sometimes surprisingly so. Knowing cultural rules can be critical. Consider, for example, the common practice of tipping after a meal at a restaurant. In cultures such as China, Japan, South Korean, New Zealand, and Costa Rica, there is no tipping, and Americans who do are perceived to be disrespectful. Even if you are intending a magnanimous gesture by picking up the lunch check for your sports team while traveling abroad and you add a healthy tip, you are communicating the insulting message that the waitperson must be bribed to provide decent service. Tipping in Egypt is permitted but tricky. Attendants staff most public restrooms, and some dole out toilet paper based on the size of the tip ("Tipping," 2020). The awkwardness of such events will be left to your imagination.

Individualism–Collectivism Dimension: The Prime Directive

All cultures vary in the degree of emphasis they place on individuals exploring their uniqueness and independence versus maintaining their conformity and interdependence. This **individualism–collectivism dimension** is thought by many scholars to be the most important, deep-seated value that distinguishes one culture from another (Santos et al., 2017). "It is widely considered as the quintessential marker of a society's prevalent mentality and culture" (Beugelsdijk & Wetzel, 2018). The individualism–collectivism dimension is at the center of the communication competence model's We-orientation perspective and the importance of rules that determine appropriate communication in varying cultural contexts.

Individualist cultures have an "I" consciousness. The autonomy of the individual is of paramount importance in individualist cultures. Words such as *independence*, *self*, *privacy*, and *rights* imbue cultural conversations. Competition, but less so cooperation, is encouraged. Decision making is predicated on what benefits the individual, even if this jeopardizes the group welfare. Individual achievement and initiative are stressed. Self-promotion is expected, even encouraged (Hofstede & Hofstede, 2010).

In collectivist cultures, by contrast, commitment to the group is paramount. Words such as *loyalty, responsibility* (to the group welfare), and *community* imbue collectivist cultural conversations. Collectivist cultures have a "We" consciousness. Cooperation within valued groups (family, friends, coworkers, teams) is strongly emphasized, although transactions with groups perceived as outsiders (foreigners, strangers) can become competitive (a threat to a valued group) (Yu, 1998). Individuals often downplay personal goals in favor of advancing the goals of a valued group. Self-promotion is discouraged, and harmony is encouraged (Hofstede & Hofstede, 2010).

All cultures have both individualist and collectivist influences, but one tends to predominate over the other. A worldwide study of 50 countries and three geographic areas ranks the United States as the number one individualistic country, followed by other Western countries such as Australia, Great Britain, and Canada (Hofstede & Hofstede, 2010). Evidence shows that the United States is slowly

In the United States, self-promotion is encouraged, even expected when interviewing for a job. Such self-enhancement, however, is not typically viewed as appropriate in the context of many collectivist cultures that prefer self-effacement, which downplays one's performance and exhibits modest talk and self-deprecating messages (Ting-Toomey & Dorjee, 2018).

Gutesa/Shutterstock

becoming even more individualistic than when this global study was first conducted (Twenge et al., 2017). Latin American, Asian, West and East African countries, such as Guatemala, Ecuador, Indonesia, Taiwan, and Singapore, rank high on collectivism (see Figure 1.2). Most people live in collectivist cultures (Hofstede & Hofstede, 2010), but one study of 78 countries utilizing 51 years of data found a 12% increase worldwide in individualism. Despite this increase in most cultures studied, "cultural differences remain sizable" (Santos et al., 2017) and "relative country rankings tend to be rather stable" (Beugelsdijk & Wetzel, 2018). Very little has changed in the rankings on the individualism–collectivism dimension since Hofstede's original research (Beugelsdijk et al., 2015).

Differences on the individualism–collectivism dimension can lead to inappropriate and ineffective communication. For example, when brainstorming ideas in diverse face-to-face small groups or global virtual teams, group members from more individualist cultures such as the United States and Australia tend to voice unfiltered ideas and opinions during brainstorming sessions. Members from more collectivist cultures such as China, Korea, and Taiwan, however, are far more reluctant to contribute, fearful that they will appear superficial or foolish and, consequently, lose face (Toegel & Barsoux, 2016). From the perspective of these Asian cultures, this lopsided difference in brainstorming participation rates can lead to misperceptions that Americans are domineering, rude, and arrogant bullies instead of eager participants. They violate accepted cultural rules with impunity. Conversely, Americans can misperceive these Asian participants as docile, timid, and uncreative. They don't meet American expectations of appropriate behavior.

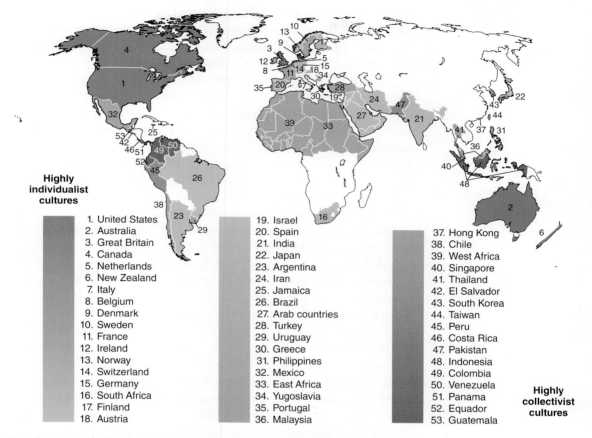

Figure 1.2   Map of individualist and collectivist cultures (Hofstede & Hofstede, 2010).

Highly individualist cultures

1. United States
2. Australia
3. Great Britain
4. Canada
5. Netherlands
6. New Zealand
7. Italy
8. Belgium
9. Denmark
10. Sweden
11. France
12. Ireland
13. Norway
14. Switzerland
15. Germany
16. South Africa
17. Finland
18. Austria

19. Israel
20. Spain
21. India
22. Japan
23. Argentina
24. Iran
25. Jamaica
26. Brazil
27. Arab countries
28. Turkey
29. Uruguay
30. Greece
31. Philippines
32. Mexico
33. East Africa
34. Yugoslavia
35. Portugal
36. Malaysia

37. Hong Kong
38. Chile
39. West Africa
40. Singapore
41. Thailand
42. El Salvador
43. South Korea
44. Taiwan
45. Peru
46. Costa Rica
47. Pakistan
48. Indonesia
49. Colombia
50. Venezuela
51. Panama
52. Equador
53. Guatemala

Highly collectivist cultures

Applying the Communication Competence Model: Several Steps

Working in increasingly diverse small groups is a challenge that requires direct application of the communication competence model. There are several steps that you can take to adapt appropriately and effectively to the challenge of cultural diversity in groups:

1. *Embrace diversity.* As Henry David Thoreau once said, "It's never too late to give up your prejudices." **Ethnocentrism**—exalting one's own culture while disparaging other cultures (Samovar et al., 2021)—is prejudice on a culturally grand scale. All cultures are ethnocentric to some degree (Triandis, 2009), but you can recognize it and vow to rise above it. Diversity is part of the colorful tapestry of humankind. Move beyond personal preferences. Be open to new experiences and views of others.

2. *Reduce uncertainty.* **Uncertainty reduction theory** posits that when strangers first meet (the getting-to-know-you initial phase of group development), the principal goal is to reduce uncertainty and increase predictability (Rahmani, 2017). Uncertainty often produces anxiety. This is especially true in highly diverse small groups, or when you might be the lone member from an individualist culture in an otherwise collectivist-oriented group. We fear embarrassing ourselves or causing offense if we say or do the wrong thing in unfamiliar intercultural situations. Uncertainty reduction can improve the effectiveness of your communication in diverse groups (Neuliep, 2014). Engaging others in conversation is an important way to reduce uncertainty by getting to know others. Ask questions. Explore group members' cultural stories. Be accessible. Demonstrate true interest in another person's culture.

3. *Listen and learn.* "Listen" is an anagram for "silent" (same letters, different words). Too often we are more interested in hearing ourselves talk than in remaining silent, the first step in the listening process. No one ever insulted individuals from another culture by actively listening to them. Think about that! It's when we open our mouths or act in inappropriate ways that trouble can emerge. Encourage contributions from group members, and resist interrupting them when they do contribute. Doing a quick "whip-around" in which each team member is given an opportunity to speak in turn before opening a more free-for-all brainstorming session markedly improves brainstorming participation rates among members of collectivist cultures (Aritz & Walker, 2014).

4. *Don't stereotype.* Allow for individual differences. Describing cultures as primarily individualist or collectivist is a generalization that does not accurately reflect every member of a specific culture. The individualist-collectivist dimension is a cultural tendency, not an immutable law.

5. *Employ the Platinum Rule.* The Golden Rule is treat others as you want to be treated. This is a nice sentiment, and it works well in homogeneous (similar membership) groups and cultures. Not everyone, however, wants to be treated the same, especially when cultures clash. "That doesn't bother me; why should it bother you?" and "That wouldn't offend me" are comments that reveal the problem with this rule applied interculturally. The **Platinum Rule** is more useful in multicultural groups: Treat others as they want to be treated (Alessandra, 2020). In many collectivist cultures, direct eye contact can be perceived as disrespectful, but in individualist cultures shifting your gaze is often perceived as disrespectful, a show of disinterest (Crowley, 2016). You can vary your eye contact depending on the cultural composition of your group and individual interactions.

6. *Learn to style shift.* There are two main communication styles that differentiate individualist and collectivist cultures: low-context and high-context communication (Hall & Hall, 1987). **Low-context communication** is verbally

precise, direct, literal, and explicit. A legal contract is an example of low-context communication. Every legal detail is clearly specified, often in dozens, even hundreds of pages. **High-context communication** is indirect, imprecise, and implicit. For example, an indirect verbal expression, such as "I'll think about it," may be a face-saving means of saying no in Japan, or it may be assumed that no verbal expression is required to state what should be obvious from the nonverbal context. You are expected to "read between the lines" by recognizing hints and knowing the cultural context and unspoken rules. If group members are mostly or entirely from individualist cultures, a low-context communication style is appropriate. If group members are mostly or entirely from collectivist cultures, a more high-context communication style is appropriate. Don't insist on everyone else adapting to your accustomed way of communicating, particularly if you are the lone individualist member in a collectivist group. Be flexible, as persons from collectivist backgrounds must be to adapt to typical American groups with individualist cultural values.

SELF-ASSESSMENT

Be Ye Individualist or Collectivist?

How closely do you personally reflect individualist or collectivist values of your culture or co-culture? Consider the following statements and, using a scale from 1 (*strongly disagree*) to 9 (*strongly agree*), indicate in the blanks your degree of agreement or disagreement with each statement.*

1. I prefer to be direct and forthright when I talk with people. _____

2. I would do what would please my family, even if I detested that activity. _____

3. I enjoy being unique and different from others in many ways. _____

4. I usually sacrifice my self-interest for the benefit of my group. _____

5. I like my privacy. _____

6. Children should be taught to place duty before pleasure. _____

7. I like to demonstrate my abilities to others. _____

8. I hate to disagree with others in my group. _____

9. When I succeed, it is usually because of my abilities. _____

10. Before taking a major trip, I consult with most members of my family and many friends. _____

Total your score for all odd-numbered statements (1, 3, etc.), then total your score for even-numbered statements (2, 4, etc.). All odd-numbered statements reflect individualism and all even-numbered statements reflect collectivism. Which are you?

For the entire 63-statement measuring instrument, see Triandis (1995).

Definition of a Group

Both communication and communication competence have been defined and discussed in detail. In this section, for clarification, the definition of a group is offered and distinguished from interpersonal communication and public speaking.

Groups: More than People Standing at a Bus Stop

A **group** is a human communication system composed of three or more individuals, interacting in a quest to achieve some common goal(s), who influence and are influenced by each other. The group process can be adversarial or collaborative, but in either case members interact and influence each other attempting to achieve a desired goal.

SECOND LOOK

Groups versus Aggregations

Groups	Aggregations
Crowd doing "the wave"	Crowd in a shopping mall
Cheerleading squad performing	Individuals waiting for cheerleading tryouts
Crossing guard leading children	Children waiting at stop signal to cross street
Jury deliberating	Individuals waiting for jury duty assignment

A group is different from a mere collection of individuals, called an **aggregation** (Goldhaber, 1990). Twenty-five people standing in line to buy tickets for a movie are not a group, but simply an aggregation. Because they do not interact with and influence each other to achieve a common goal (strangers standing in line are not there expressly to help each other secure tickets), they do not qualify as a group. The same holds for a crowd shopping in a mall or waiting for a plane departure delayed by fog, or people sitting on benches in a public park. In such cases, the presence of other people is irrelevant to the achievement of the specific goal (buying clothes, traveling from point A to point B, or enjoying the outdoors). Crowds, of course, can become groups if they satisfy the definition provided (e.g., flash mob).

This text will focus on *small* groups. Trying to draw a clear line between small and large groups, however, can prove to be difficult. When does the addition of one more member transform a small group into a large one? When you attend a group meeting and you can't remember afterward whether some members were even present, you've probably reached large-group status. When groups grow to the point where problems of coordination emerge and formal rules for discussion and debate (parliamentary procedure) during meetings become necessary, the group can reasonably be designated as large.

Rawpixel.com/Shutterstock

A mere collection of people is not a group. They can be in proximity to each other but unless they are interacting to achieve a common goal, then they are called an aggregation.

Interpersonal Communication and Public Speaking: Ungroups

Communication between only two individuals is usually referred to as **interpersonal**, or **dyadic communication.** Distinguishing interpersonal communication and group communication, however, is more than numerical. There is an important qualitative dimension as well (Moreland, 2010). As most couples experience, interpersonal communication between spouses is massively changed with the addition of a child. In such cases, three individuals seem like many more than two. Communication between two individuals is far less complex than the complicated network of transactions found in groups of three or more. Thus, the unit of analysis is structurally different when focusing on three or more individuals, not just two (see Chapter 2 for more detailed discussion). Coalition formation and majority–minority influence occur in groups, not dyads. A group dynamic seems to begin with no fewer than three individuals. For example, one study showed that two individuals working together to solve a complex problem performed no better than two individuals working apart. Three individuals working together, however, proved to be the point at which superior problem-solving begins (Laughlin et al., 2006). I doubt that you would deem it unusual to refer to a family as a group, but you might think it odd to label a married or dating couple as a group. We typically say, "They're such a cute couple" but not "They're such a cute group." The dynamics between two people are qualitatively different from the dynamics experienced among three or more people.

Group communication is also distinct from public speaking. **Public speaking** involves a clearly indicated speaker and an audience, and the speaking situation is far more formal than what is usually found in group discussions. Verbal feedback is often delayed in public speaking events, but during group discussions verbal feedback often is almost immediate. Public speakers usually prepare remarks in advance and speak from notes or even a manuscript. Group members usually don't make formal preparations to speak during group discussions but may do so when participating on group panels, symposiums, or public forums (see Appendix A for details).

In summary, human communication is a transactional process of sharing meaning with others. Communication competence, a recurring theme throughout this book, is communicating effectively and appropriately in a given context. It is achieved generally through knowledge, skills, sensitivity, commitment, and ethics. Learning to communicate competently in groups is of vital importance to all of us. With this as a backdrop, let's explore in the next chapter how groups function as systems.

QUESTIONS FOR CRITICAL THINKERS

1. Are there any circumstances in which a Me-orientation becomes necessary when participating in a small group?
2. Does competent communication ever necessitate dishonesty? Explain.
3. Should you always exhibit commitment to the group, or are there exceptions? Explain.

TED TALKS AND YOUTUBE VIDEOS

This ancillary activity, added to each chapter, provides video presentations and segments that both illustrate key communication concepts and provide opportunities for specific analysis, discussion, disagreement, and application of text material. These TED Talks and YouTube videos can be accessed by going to the Oxford Learning Link for *In Mixed Company* or by typing the title of the video into a Google search window.

"Communication in the 21st Century: Is It What You Say, Not How You Say It?"

"It's How You Say It—The Science of Emotions"

"The Power of Nonverbal Communication" | Joe Navarro

"Why Language Is Humanity's Greatest Invention"

VIDEO CASE STUDIES

This activity presents video case studies from a variety of films for you to analyze. A movie rating (PG-13, R, etc.) and category (drama, romantic comedy, etc.) are included to help you decide which movies are suitable for your viewing. You are asked to analyze each video case study, applying key material presented in each chapter.

American Factory (2019). *Documentary; TV-14*

A Chinese billionaire opens a factory in an abandoned General Motors plant, employing 2,000 American workers. Cultural clashes ensue. Examine the clashes from the perspective of individualism and collectivism in this Oscar-winning documentary.

Brooklyn (2015). *Drama/Romance; PG-13*

Outstanding tale of an Irish immigrant trying to make her way in 1950s Brooklyn. Identify and analyze the rules that operate both interpersonally and in groups. What impact do these rules have on communication behavior? What are the consequences of rules violations?

Crazy Rich Asians (2018). *Drama/Romance/Comedy; PG-13*

Native New Yorker Rachel Chu follows her boyfriend to Singapore to meet his family. Identify differences in cultural rules and inappropriate behavior that results.

The Hunger Games: Catching Fire (2013). *Action-Adventure; PG-13*

Katnis (Jennifer Lawrence) and Peeta (Josh Hutcherson) become enemies of the Capitol and must participate in a second Hunger Games event pitting previous winners against each other. Examine the ethics of the Hunger Games participants, applying the five standards of ethical group communication. Identify instances in which communication is interpersonal and when it is small group. Are participants ever just an aggregation?

Return to Paradise (1998). *Drama; R*

Underrated film about a harrowing ethical dilemma involving three friends who vacationed in Malaysia. Yes, this film is "old," but the issues that it raises are not. Analyze this film from a communication ethics perspective. Is Anne Heche's character justified in lying to the Vince Vaughn character? Does Vince Vaughn's character have a choice, or is he being coerced unethically? Does he have a responsibility to return to save his friend?

Groups as Systems

2

In one of my small group communication courses, six women formed a project group. During their first meeting in class, communication was warm, friendly, and task oriented. They accomplished a great deal in a short period of time: deciding which of the five project options they would pursue, dividing labor to develop the project, and setting deadlines for accomplishment of specified tasks. They said they all were very pleased with their new group.

During the next week, the six women met one more time for a lengthy session, and again they were pleased by their progress on the project and increasingly comfortable with their harmonious interactions. Then a male student who had missed a week of class and had no project group approached me and asked which of the four class groups he should join. I told him to join the all-women group for two reasons: I typically encourage mixed-sex, not same-sex, groups (there were far more women than men in the class), and the other groups had seven members already. From the moment he joined the six women, he transformed this harmonious, task-effective group into a frustrating experience for every group member. His opening introductory remark upon joining the group of women was, "I hope PMS won't be a problem for us." He guffawed at his supposed humor, but all six women seemed stunned. During the group meeting he made sexist remarks, offered derogatory comments about the choice of project already decided by the women, and made a complete nuisance of himself. As he left class, he loudly proclaimed to everyone that he was "leader of a chicks group."

All six women bolted to the front of the class and asked me to assign this disruptive individual to another group. I explained that moving him would make the other groups too large and would merely pass the problem to another group, not solve it. I noted that this was an opportunity to experiment with communication strategies for dealing with difficult members, but I gave them a choice: I could "rescue" them by intervening, or I could let them handle their bad apple without my interference. To their credit, they chose the latter.

This example illustrates that every group is a complex system (Ramos-Villagrasa et al., 2018). A **system** is a set of interconnected parts working together to form a whole in the context of a changing environment (Littlejohn et al., 2021). A group is composed of individual members interrelating with each other—not as individual parts operating in isolation from each other, but as a unit. The behavior of one member affects the entire group because of the interconnectedness of

objectives

This chapter's principal purpose is to explain and discuss systems theory and how it can be applied to groups. There are three chapter objectives:

1. To explain interconnectedness of parts in a system.

2. To discuss how groups must adapt to a changing environment.

3. To explore the influence of size on a group's ability to function effectively.

system parts (all group members), especially if the behavior is disruptive. In this opening case, the six women had to adapt to the jarring change introduced by their disruptor. He changed the group environment, and the communication dynamics also changed from warm and friendly to defensive and strained. Research shows that system failure can be the result of even a single "weak link" group member who is unmotivated to help the group achieve its goals or learn to become a productive member (Valcea et al., 2019).

In general, a system is composed of input, throughput (processes), and output (Katz & Kahn, 1978). **Input** consists of resources that come from outside the system, such as energy (sunlight, electricity), information (Internet, books), people (a new group member), and environmental influences (organizations, society, culture). If input ceases, a system deceases. A system inevitably wears down without continuous input. This wearing-down process is called **entropy**—a measure of a system's movement toward disorganization and eventual termination. All living systems combat entropy with input. No group, for example, can survive without new members. The group will dismantle because current members will lose interest and leave to join different groups or the members themselves will eventually die.

Consider the religious sect called the Shakers (members shook to rid themselves of evil). Now near extinction, two Shaker decisions foreordained their inevitable demise: a belief in celibacy and a group decision in 1965 to admit no new members. From a peak membership of 6,000 in the 1830s, there were only two remaining members at the Sabbath Day Lake, New Gloucester, Maine, community in 2020 ("Shakers," 2020). Contrary to the Shakers' aversion to new members, interjecting "new blood" into a group can bring new information, ideas, experiences, energy, and even different values and perspectives. New members can thwart entropy, and energize and revitalize a group. New members, however, can also shake up the system by disrupting traditions and stable patterns of behavior—undesirable eventualities from the Shaker point of view.

Throughput is the *process* of transforming input into output to keep the system functioning. Input is transformed in a group by its members engaging in communication activities, such as presenting information during group discussion and then taking that information and engaging in creative problem solving. According to **structuration theory**, a system, such as a small group, establishes structures for such discussion and problem solving. **Structure** gives form and shape to a group with the establishment of rules, roles, norms, and power distribution (all subjects for later discussion) (Poole et al., 1996). These structures are used to permit the system (the small group) to function effectively and to sustain itself, but they can also constrain the process (West & Turner, 2020). For example, establishing both procedural and ground rules for group meetings, as explained in Chapter 3 (e.g., "Meetings will follow a prepared agenda"; "The chairperson will lead the group discussion"; "Interruptions will be kept to a minimum") permits an orderly dialogue to occur among group members—it gives it a clear form. At the same time, however, it constrains unfettered discussion from occurring. Rules permit certain communication behaviors (polite discussion) while restricting others (raucous debate). Through the discussion process, the rules, roles, norms, and distribution of power may be reinforced and even institutionalized within an organization, or they may change over time.

Output comprises the continual results of the group's throughput (transformation of input). Group outputs include decisions made, solutions to problems created and implemented, projects completed, group procedures modified, team member cohesiveness enhanced, member relationships improved, and so forth. This chapter discusses input, throughput, output, and more.

Given this brief overview of what constitutes a system, this chapter's principal purpose is to explain and discuss systems theory and how it can be applied to groups. Understanding at least the basics of systems theory provides useful insights into why some small groups succeed and others fail.

Interconnectedness of Parts

Interconnectedness of parts is a major element of systems theory. The effects of interconnectedness can be seen in two ways: the ripple effect and synergy.

Nejron Photo/Shutterstock

Groups are systems composed of interconnected parts that form a whole. These are not four individuals playing independently. That would produce a cacophony—a meaningless, irritating mixture of sounds. These band members must blend as a unit.

focus questions

1. What is the ripple effect and how does it affect groups?
2. What is synergy? What is negative synergy? How is each produced?

Ripple Effect: A Chain Reaction

In a system, one part can have a significant impact on the whole. This **ripple effect**, or chain reaction, spreads across the entire system, much the way a pebble tossed into a pond disturbs the water and forces adjustments. On a global scale, this ripple effect can be plainly seen from the example of the Covid-19 pandemic. What began as a report by a physician in Wuhan, China, in early December 2019 about a group of patients who exhibited signs of a severe respiratory syndrome quickly became an international phenomenon. On January 30, 2020, the World Health Organization (WHO) declared a Public Health Emergency of International Concern (PHEIC). The first case reported in the United States was confirmed in mid-February 2020. On March 11, WHO declared Covid-19 a pandemic. The number of confirmed Covid deaths in the United States by August 2021 approached 650,000, according to the Worldometer tracking site ("COVID-19 Coronavirus Pandemic," 2021). Medical facilities struggled mightily to keep up with the influx of Covid cases as the virus spread rapidly. Restaurants, bars, consumer services, and entertainment events of almost every kind were closed or severely restricted. Shelter-in-place orders were issued in most states, sequestering people in their homes and prompting a 734% increase in sales of toilet paper, dubbed the Great Toilet Paper Panic (Krieger, 2021). Online purchases skyrocketed. Schools at all levels were closed, necessitating an abrupt and often difficult transition to online learning formats. An already apparent **digital divide**, benefiting wealthier students with greater access to technology and disadvantaging poorer students whose families have more limited options to access necessary technology, was exacerbated by the pandemic. Educational delivery was uneven and often clumsy. Many students, especially those from low-income families, struggled as a result (Wu, 2020). Psychological distress and feelings of social isolation from friends and classmates also emerged (de Marcellis-Warin et al., 2020). Travel restrictions became the norm. Citizens began wearing protective masks and social distancing as a matter of course, although this became a fiercely argued controversy in the United States. The most devastating recession since the Great Depression of the 1930s crippled the American economy (Nicola et al., 2020). Even the rollout of the vaccination campaign to beat back the virus was initially fraught with difficulties. Welcome to the ripple effect that severely impacted the United States and the rest of the globe as Covid continued its devastation with frustrating persistence.

Even a small part of a huge system can generate an enormous ripple effect. The Writers Guild of America went on strike in late 2007 and didn't settle its strike until mid-February 2008. If you look at the screen credits for movies and television programs, screenwriters are but a blip among the vast network of individuals and groups that compose the system required to complete a single film or an episode of a TV series. Yet this strike shut down film and television production, cost an estimated $3.5 billion in lost revenue, forced a starkly abbreviated Golden Globes award ceremony, threatened the cancellation of the Academy Awards, and required viewers to watch endless reruns and banal "reality shows." Entire production crews, caterers, gardeners, agents, and actors were out of work during the strike ("What Did the Writers' Strike Cost?" 2008). A strike by the Writers Guild was barely averted in 2017, which would have produced similar effects.

Marina Poushkina/Shutterstock

Drazen Zigic/Shutterstock

Group emotional contagion illustrates the ripple effect inherent in systems. The contagion can be highly positive or it can also be negative, markedly affecting group output. Your mood, alone, can have a profound effect on the entire group. Have you ever noticed what impact your personal mood has had on a group?

The ripple effect, of course, does not have to be a negative experience. When a parent gets a job promotion or a significant raise in pay, all members of the family stand to gain from the good fortune. If a child wins a scholarship to a major university, the entire family potentially benefits from the news. Accomplishments of individual family members may motivate others in the group to seek similar goals. When group members view their leader with the same affection as a skunk in their clothes closet, and the leader is replaced with a competent, well-liked leader, then optimism and enthusiasm can spread throughout a group. Research on **group emotional contagion**—"the transfer of moods among people in a group and its influence on work group dynamics"—has shown that positive group emotional contagion, such as spreading joy, happiness, and compassion, "improved cooperation, decreased conflict, and increased perceived task performance" (Barsade, 2002). Emotional contagion can be a force for positive results for groups, but it can also go the other direction when the emotions are potentially negative, such as spreading anger, fear, depression, and hatred (Barsade, 2020; Barsade et al., 2018).

Recognizing the significance of the ripple effect means paying close attention to your own impact on groups. Your level of communication proficiency or deficiency can mean success or failure of the entire group. "The power of one" should not be underestimated, as the chapter opening case study so glaringly illustrates.

Synergy: One Plus One Equals a Ton

United Airlines Flight 232 left Denver and headed to Chicago on a perfectly lovely sunny day. Without warning, well into the flight, a loud explosion from the tail of the plane was heard. The plane's tail engine, one of three engines, was gone. Even worse, shrapnel severed the main and backup hydraulic control lines. In short, there was a catastrophic failure. The pilots had no ability to control the plane. "The plane was now wobbling through the Iowa sky like a poorly made paper airplane, porpoising up and down thousands of feet each minute" (Coyle, 2018). One of the passengers happened to be Denny Fitch, a pilot trainer who worked for United. He offered to help the crew frantically trying to wrestle the plane into some semblance of controlled flight. Fitch, along with Captain Al Haynes and first officer Bill Records, "began to do something that no pilots had ever done: fly a DC-10 without any controls." The makeshift crew communicated in short bursts called notifications. Working together, despite a fiery landing when a wingtip dug into the runway, 185 passengers, including the entire crew, survived. Afterward, the National Transportation Safety Board tested experienced crews in flight simulators and recreated the conditions faced by Flight 232. In 28 simulations, the plane never reached the runway and crashed catastrophically with no chance of survivors. "The crew of Flight

232 succeeded not because of their individual skills but because they were able to combine those skills into a greater intelligence. They demonstrated that a series of small, humble exchanges—*Anybody have any ideas? Tell me what you want, and I'll help you*—can unlock a group's ability to perform" (Coyle, 2018).

This group genius, or "wisdom of the crowd," is called synergy. **Synergy** occurs when group performance from joint action of members exceeds expectations based on perceived abilities and skills of individual members (Salazar, 1995). Thus, the whole is not necessarily equal to the sum of its parts. It may be greater than the sum of its individual parts. NASA did not reach the moon through the combined efforts of individuals working alone, and the Apollo 13 near-disaster "stands today as an example of . . . NASA's innovative minds working together to save lives on the fly" (Howell & Hickok, 2020).

The synergistic quality of group decision making is analogous to mixing drugs or chemicals. Some combinations of drugs, such as those used in chemotherapy, can significantly boost effectiveness (Mokhtari et al., 2017).

Synergy is produced in primarily three ways. First, when group members are highly motivated to achieve a common goal, such as when grades, jobs, helping others, or lives are at stake, synergy may occur (Forsyth, 2019; "Teams Work Better," 2020). Habitat for Humanity "has helped more than 29 million people achieve strength, stability and independence through safe, decent and affordable shelter" ("Habitat's History," 2020). Habitat work crews, composed of both skilled and unskilled volunteers who are highly motivated to help poor

Nathan Denette/The Canadian Press via AP

After barely avoiding elimination in the preliminary rounds, the U.S. curling team pulled off stunning upset after stunning upset and won the 2018 Olympic gold medal in a synergistic miracle.

people, divide into small subgroups and erect portions of modest houses a section at a time.

Second, synergy is produced from relatively equal participation, not individual, independent effort (Carey & Laughlin, 2012). If group members work independently by completing individual assignments on their own and the group merely compiles the results, no synergy will occur. For instance, if your group took an essay test and each member was assigned one question to answer, no synergistic benefit would occur if group members did not discuss rough draft answers with the whole group and make improvements prior to a final draft. Google's Project Aristotle found that "if only one person or a small group [within a larger team] spoke all the time, the collective intelligence declined" (quoted in Duhigg, 2016). Relatively equal time speaking *and active listening* among team members were key to effectiveness.

Third, groups whose members have deep diversity have greater potential to produce synergy than groups with little such diversity (Pentland, 2016). **Deep diversity** is substantial variation among members in task-relevant skills, knowledge, abilities, beliefs, values, perspectives, and problem-solving strategies (Harrison et al., 2002). Basketball teams, for example, thrive when players have a diverse set of skills. A team of great shooters but limited defensive abilities is unlikely to be successful. In a simulation study comparing small groups with deep diversity and those without, the groups with deep diversity were synergistic and outperformed even their best individual member. Groups without deep diversity performed much more poorly (Larson, 2007). Groups with diverse cognitive abilities—"differences in perspective or information processing styles"—and "intuitive and analytical" skills are especially synergistic (Keck & Tang, 2020; Reynolds & Lewis, 2017).

Finally, groups are much more likely to be synergistic when group members are competent communicators (Rogelberg et al., 2012). There is simply no substitute for competent communication, an essential component of any successful group experience. The quick, decisive, collaborative communication exhibited by the crew of Flight 232 was critical to the ultimate outcome.

Negative Synergy: Results Beyond Bad

Systems don't always produce synergy. If you're sharing ignorance (misinformation based on lack of knowledge), no group genius is likely to emerge (Krause et al., 2011). The National Geographic–Roper Public Affairs Geographic Literacy Study (2006) revealed some major gaps in geographic knowledge of young Americans ages 18 to 24. The 510 randomly selected respondents answered only slightly more than half of the geography questions correctly. Half of the respondents could not find Japan on a map, and 65% did not know where our "mother country" Great Britain is located. More locally, half did not know where New

York is, and *6% were unable to locate the United States.* (When asked the trivia question on a roll sheet I circulated in my classes, "What is the tallest mountain in the world?" one student wrote Mountain Dew. I laughed, then remembered the results of this geography study. I wasn't completely sure this answer was meant as a joke.) A more recent survey of 1,203 college students by the Council on Foreign Relations and the National Geographic Society asked geography-related questions about global issues "critical to the United States." The average score was 55%, and only 1% achieved 91% correct or better (Haass & Knell, 2016).

Groups with limited knowledge on a subject of interest aren't likely to perform magic. If you can't locate a country on a map, and you know next to nothing about a country's culture, government, policies, values, and practices, no good would likely come from decision making based on such ignorance.

Shared ignorance among group members can produce **negative synergy**—when group members working together produce a worse result than expected based on perceived individual skills and abilities of members (Salazar, 1995).

Group synergy can be fostered when members exhibit knowledge, skills, sensitivity, commitment, and ethics while working in concert with each other. Groups can produce negative synergy, however, when they share ignorance and exhibit incompetent communication.

The whole is worse than the sum of its parts. Negative synergy is like mixing alcohol and tranquilizers, risking death. When group members know little about a subject, compete against each other (Me-orientation), resist change, or share a collective bias or mindset, the result of mixing their individual contributions can produce decisions beyond bad. As David Lykken (1997) observes, "A gang is more dangerous than the sum of its individual parts." Even groups uniquely talented and trained for a specific task may fail disastrously at a distinctly different task that requires other specialized knowledge and skills. For example, military groups may be quite effective in warfare but inept as a peacekeeping police force that requires cooperation, diplomacy, and creative problem solving (Weiss, 2011).

Adaptability to a Changing Environment

Systems are never in a static state. They are in a constant state of becoming until they terminate. They must adapt to their changing environment, not always an easy task (Malhotra et al., 2020). The **environment** is the context within which a system operates, such as a team within an organization or a student project group within a college class. You do not have a choice between change and no change. The relevant question is, can a system (group) adapt to the inevitable changes that are certain to occur?

Every system reacts to change in its own way. Groups with a similar or identical final goal (e.g., financial security) may reach that end in highly diverse ways. One family may invest in the stock market; another family may rely on retirement plans or real estate investments. This process is called **equifinality**, in the somewhat ponderous systems lingo. In this section, the process of adapting to change in a system in search of goal achievement is discussed.

focus questions

1. What relationship do stability and change have in groups?
2. Why do groups establish boundaries? How do they control boundaries?
3. In what circumstances can groups become too open? Too closed?
4. Is it better for a group to be more open than closed? Explain.

Dynamic Equilibrium: Regulating Stability and Change

There is always a dynamic tension between stability and change in any system (Dovidio et al., 2009). All systems attempt to maintain stability and to achieve a state of equilibrium (*homeostasis*) by resisting change, but no system can avoid it.

Too much stability can produce stagnation and tedium. Too much change can produce chaos and group disintegration. There is no perfect balance point between stability and change in any system, but there is a range in which systems can manage change effectively to promote growth and success without destroying the system with too much instability. This range is called **dynamic equilibrium** (Forsyth, 2019). A system sustains dynamic equilibrium when it regulates the *degree*, *rate*, and *desirability of change*, allowing stability and change to coexist.

Consider what happens when the three variables of change are not sufficiently regulated. As the owner of a small business, a friend of mine decided to go high-tech and computerize his office with the very latest, most sophisticated equipment. At the same time, he embarked on an office renovation project. To add to the disruption, he moved in a new partner. His small office staff went berserk. Staff members hadn't been trained to run the sophisticated computer programs and equipment. They resented the renovation, which displaced them from their normal work areas and created a huge mess that interfered with their efficiency. The new partner turned out to be a very demanding individual who expected instant results from the beleaguered staff. His favorite saying, posted on the wall of his office, was "Impossible is a word found only in a fool's dictionary." The final disastrous change, however, was my friend's insistence that his staff work half-days on weekends until the office was returned to a more normal state. Three of the four members of his staff quit, and they were spitting fire as they stomped out of the office, never to return. They left a gift for my friend's partner—a thesaurus renamed with black marker pen *Fool's Dictionary* with words such as *idiot*, *pompous*, *twit*, *jerk*, and *moron* highlighted. The business had to be shut down for two weeks, resulting in a substantial loss of revenue.

Mongkolchon Akesin/Shutterstock

The Covid-19 pandemic stressed group systems to the maximum. The *degree* of change required for protection from the virus was huge, the *rate* of change instituted was almost overnight because the virus didn't wait for preparations, and the *desirability* of protective changes such as social distancing and wearing masks and plastic face guards was hotly debated, especially in the United States.

Too much change (degree) was required in too concentrated a period (rate) without a concerted effort to persuade the staff of the value (desirability) of the changes demanded. Groups can often adapt even to large changes if given sufficient time to absorb them and if members are convinced the changes have merit. A key element of the latter is "mobilizing people around a common purpose" that is inspiring, clear, and perceived as achievable (Walker, 2017)—more on this in later chapters. In some instances, of course, the dismantling of an ineffective system may be necessary to replace it with a better system—one that institutes wholesale change and radical departure from the way things were. Sports teams, for example, may fire entire coaching staffs and dump numerous weak performing players, rebuilding a losing team from the ground up.

Dealing with Difficult Group Members: Disruptive Change

This chapter opened with a narrative about a difficult group member who dramatically changed the dynamics of a harmonious group of women and required adaptation to new environmental circumstances. Research by Will Felps and his colleagues (2006) on "**bad apples**"—disruptive members who poison the group ("One bad apple spoils the barrel")—demonstrates just how disturbing such a group member can be. A skilled student actor portrayed three versions of disruptive, or bad apple, behavior in several small groups. He played a *jerk* who made insulting remarks to other group members, such as "Do you know anything?" and "That's a stupid idea." He played a *slacker* who wouldn't contribute during a 45-minute challenging group task, text messaged a friend, and responded with "Whatever" or "I really don't care" to other group members' ideas. Finally, he played a *depressive pessimist* who put his head on the table, complained about the task being boring, and predicted group failure. (For more bad apple behavior, see "disruptive roles" discussed in Chapter 6.)

The results were startling. No matter how talented team members were, those groups that had to deal with the one bad apple scored 30% to 40% lower on a challenging task than teams with no bad apple. Disruptive behavior was also contagious. When the actor played the jerk, group members would respond to insults from the bad apple with insults of their own; when the actor pretended to be the slacker, group members would assume slacker behavior and say, "Let's just get this over with. Put down anything"; and when they played the depressive pessimist, other group members became cynical and disengaged.

There are several fundamental steps that should be taken by a group when dealing with a difficult member who interjects unwanted change, even chaos, into the group. First, make certain the group climate is cooperative. If your group creates a ruthlessly competitive, politicized climate where decision making is influenced by rumor-mongering, backstabbing, dealmaking, and sabotaging the efforts of other members, then difficult group members will appear like flies at a summer picnic. The group of six women had established a very cooperative group climate, so this was not what precipitated their troublemaker's offensive behavior. (Chapter 5 discusses group climate in depth.)

Second, the group should establish a clear code of conduct for all group members (Sverdrup et al., 2017). This code should spell out specific unacceptable behaviors (insults, rudeness, threats, bigoted statements, and any other disrespectful communication). The Joint Commission on Accreditation of Healthcare Organizations required just such a code of conduct for its 15,000 healthcare organizations because of disruptive behavior between doctors and nurses. The code is viewed as "an essential element" in addressing such disruptive behavior (Grenny, 2009). A code of conduct takes a systems approach by viewing disruption as every member's concern.

Third, change your communication in relation to a difficult person's behavior. In the Felps bad apple study, there was one group that performed well despite the concerted effort of the actor playing the part of a difficult group member. Coyle (2018) examined the taped encounters and concludes that there was one group member who consistently avoided being sucked into the bad apple's disruption. This individual responded to the jerk behavior with warmth, "deflecting the negativity and making a potentially unstable situation feel solid and safe." He encouraged participation from other group members, even from the "jerk." His communication behavior actually thwarted the bad behavior and contributed to the success of the group.

In the case study of six women faced with a bad apple, initially all six women laughed nervously at their troublemaker's sexist "jokes" and comments, and they let him dominate conversations. Soon, however, at my prompting, they stopped laughing, and, collectively, they wouldn't let him interrupt, as he was prone to do. They began saying to him, "Please wait; let her finish." Disrupters thrive on provoking retaliation. Don't counter abusive remarks with abusive remarks of your own. Fighting fire with fire ignites a firestorm. To their great credit, none of the six women reciprocated the inappropriate behavior of their tormenter. It required a group effort (a systems approach) because had even one member taken the bait, the disrupter would have been encouraged to continue his sophomoric behavior.

Fourth, confront the difficult person. If the entire group is upset by the behavior of the difficult person, then the group should confront the disrupter. The group's code of conduct should be enforced systemwide. Even truly abrasive individuals will find it tough to ignore pressure from an entire group. Be descriptive. State what behavior is offensive and encourage more constructive behavior. For example: "Your comments about women offend me. Please stop." I strongly encouraged the six women to confront their troublemaker. Although they did indicate their discontent, their efforts were more indirect than clear-cut.

Fifth, separate yourself from the difficult person if all else fails. Some individuals leave no other option except removal from the group, and this may be very positive. One clothing retailer, for example, fired his top-selling employee who otherwise was a bad apple. The sales at the store skyrocketed nearly 30% once the bad apple was jettisoned from the small sales group (Sutton, 2011). One rather amazing study bolsters the results of this example. Analyzing data from 50,000 employees at 11 businesses, two researchers found that the average benefit derived from firing a toxic employee is about four times greater than adding a good employee. Even adding a superstar employee, someone in the top 1% of job performance, doesn't negate a toxic group member. Dumping the toxic employee is twice as beneficial financially as hiring the superstar (Housman & Minor, 2015).

If the difficult person is powerful, expulsion may not be an option. In this case, try putting physical distance between you and the problem person. Keep interactions to a minimum. Because of the unusual experience the women had with their male disrupter, I subsequently gave groups the option to expel a troublemaker as a last resort, provided that other strategies were attempted.

SELF-ASSESSMENT

Are You a Difficult Group Member?

Instructions: Rate honestly your likely behavior in each of the scenarios below. Use a 5-point scale varying by degrees from 1 (*rarely*) to 5 (*frequently*). Mark the appropriate number (1, 2, 3, 4, or 5) in the blank after each scenario. This should reveal whether you are a difficult group member. *Optional alternative*: After answering this questionnaire, ask fellow class or team members to complete this same assessment about you, but only if you feel comfortable making such a request. If team members are hesitant, encourage them to complete the assessment without identifying themselves on the questionnaire. Compare the results by following the scoring system at the end of this assessment.

1. When a topic of great interest to me is discussed in my group, I tend to talk much longer and more forcefully than I know I should. _____

2. During group discussions, I typically remain silent, exhibiting lack of interest in the proceedings. _____

3. When my group attempts to work on a task, especially one in which I have little interest, I prefer to joke around and be comical instead of focusing on the task. _____

4. When I oppose what my group decides, I am inclined to reintroduce the issue already decided even though I know there is little chance the group will change its decision. _____

5. I quarrel openly with group members by raising my voice, interrupting other members to forcefully interject my own opinion and criticizing those who disagree with me. _____

6. I have strong opinions that color my participation during group discussions, and I attempt to convert group members to my way of thinking even if they are unresponsive. _____

7. I predict failure of the group, especially if a risk is involved, and I focus on what will go wrong, not on what will go right with my group's decisions. _____

Total your responses for all seven of your answers (maximum score = 35; minimum score = 7). Determine your average score (total score divided by 7). If your average score is 3.0 or higher, you tend toward being a difficult group member. Any single answer that is 3, 4, or 5 indicates trouble for your group on that particular behavior. These seven scenarios correspond to the seven disruptive informal roles discussed in Chapter 6.

So how did the six women do on their project? They all performed wonderfully, giving an excellent presentation to the class. Their troublemaker, however, missed several group meetings outside of class, and he embarrassed himself by performing poorly during his presentation. His presentation on a second project with a different group, however, was much improved primarily because this group enforced their code of conduct without hesitation, and his disruptive behavior was instantly confronted and squelched.

I have presented a rational model for handling troublemakers. Nevertheless, we are not strictly rational beings. Difficult people can provoke intense anger and deep frustration. In my own experience, even if I lost my temper and let my emotions get the better of me, this response seemed less problematic than ignoring or enduring the disruptive behavior. At the very least, you have served notice on the troublesome group member that his or her pattern of behavior is unacceptable and will not be suffered in silence.

Boundary Control: Communication Methods for Regulating Input

Openness and change go hand in hand in a system. **Openness** refers to the degree of continuous interchange with the outside environment. As systems open to the outside, new input enters the system, inevitably disturbing it. Admit women into a previously all-male club, boardroom, or law firm, and change is inevitable. Add a single member to your small group and, as powerfully illustrated in the chapter opening case study, massive disturbance can occur. A group must adapt to change or suffer strife, even possible demise. **Adaptability to change** is the adjustment of group boundaries in response to changing environmental conditions.

Boundaries regulate input and consequent exposure to change in a system. When groups establish boundaries, they regulate the degree, rate, and even the desirability of change. This **boundary control** determines the amount of access to input a group has. Boundary control is a critical group function. As you'll see, too much or too little input can dramatically impact a group's effectiveness, even its existence.

Boundaries, however, are permeable (Lifshitz-Assaf, 2017). They leak. No group can close off so completely to its environment that no change is possible. There is always some interchange with the environment that oozes through the boundaries. Group boundaries are also permeable because they are not static; they can change (Wimmer et al., 2019). Groups establish boundaries by using a variety of communication methods. They can erect physical, psychological, and linguistic barriers, and they can establish rules, roles, and networks.

Physical Barriers: Protecting Group Space There are many possible physical barriers that can communicate "stay out" to those outside a group. These physical barriers include locking group meeting rooms or choosing an inconvenient location in a building to discourage people from just dropping by and disturbing a group meeting. A board of supervisors' public meeting might place the board on a raised stage or rope off audience members from direct access to board members. One study found that simply putting up curtains around selected teams at an open manufacturing plant increased productivity 10% to 15% (Bernstein, 2014).

Psychological Barriers: Member in Name Only Groups can communicate to an individual that they do not belong in the group (Nezlek et al., 2012). When this occurs, the group is erecting a psychological barrier. Such barriers occur when a member's contribution during group discussion is ignored or the member is treated as an outcast. The group may even tell the member directly to leave the group. Women and ethnic minorities historically have been made to feel like outsiders and tokens when first joining mostly white, male groups.

Being treated as an outcast creates a psychological barrier. You become a group member in name only.

fizkes/Shutterstock

Linguistic Barriers: Having to Speak the Language Groups erect linguistic barriers when members use a private vocabulary or slang meant to camouflage meaning outside of the group. Cyberbanging, the high-tech tagging, taunts, and threats on thousands of gang-related websites, creates virtual turf warfare (Patton, 2017). Rival gang members exchange threats and "throw up" gang numbers and names on sites operated by other gangs. Police seeking to address gang warfare effectively must attempt to decipher street lingo found on various social media used by gangs. This street talk can vary widely among gangs and their geographic locations (Cohen, 2014). Those who understand the lingo are presumed to be group members. Those who don't are clearly outsiders.

Even when "sharing" a common language across cultures, linguistic barriers can arise. For example, there are a number of British business phrases that Americans would likely find confusing when negotiating in a diverse group ("12 UK Phrases," 2017). For example:

> "We have to set prices on a *wash its face* basis." (an action that pays for itself)
> "I'm going to *look under the bonnet on that*." (look under the hood of a car = analyze a situation)
> "I think I'll modify the *strategic staircase*." (business plan)

When you know the lingo, you are an insider; when don't, you are an outsider. George Bernard Shaw once remarked that England and America are two countries separated by the same language.

Rules: Permission Not Granted Membership rules establish who can join a group and who is barred. They also define appropriate behaviors in specified social situations. Rules can establish what constitutes disruptive and inappropriate behavior, thus drawing boundaries regarding what will and will not be tolerated by the group. Rules may also specify who can talk to whom, thus controlling input from outside. For example, the Federal Judicial Center's publication *Benchbook for U.S. District Court Judges* offers this suggested jury instruction: "You may not communicate with anyone about the case on your cellphone, through email, Blackberry, iPhone, text messaging, or on Twitter, through any blog or website, including Facebook, Google+, LinkedIn, or YouTube" (Yurkiw, 2013). These judicial rules are meant to prevent juror misconduct and consequent mistrials and reversals. A fair, unbiased trial is at stake. Twitter tweets, Internet searches, and text messaging all have become sources of concern in court cases (Thanawala, 2016). In a murder case in Syracuse, New York, one juror sent and received more than 7,000 texts during the trial, including one from her father urging a guilty verdict (Prudenti, 2020). California passed a law permitting judges to exact a $1,500 fine on any juror caught using social media (Temme, 2019). Unfortunately, evidence shows that jurors just hide their social media use during trials (Turgeon, 2017). Eric Robinson, co-director of the Press Law and Democracy Project at Louisiana State University, used to track cases of juror Internet or social media misconduct, but he stopped because such instances were so numerous that "it got to be more trouble than it was worth" (quoted by Thanawala, 2016).

Roles: Staying in Bounds A **role** is a pattern of expected behavior associated with parts we play in groups. The expectations attached to group roles specify appropriate behavior, thereby fostering predictability and controlling variability. Once the pattern of behavior is associated with a group member, a boundary is set. Role constraints are discussed in Chapter 6. Leaders of groups can dictate tasks for members to complete, but they don't have the prerogative to dictate behavior in a group member's private life. That would be stepping out of bounds. For example, commenting on a female's lack of a husband and informing her that she will be attending a luncheon to meet an eligible male would be clearly overstepping the boundaries separating supervisor from employee.

Networks: Controlling Information and Interaction Flow Groups set boundaries by establishing networks. A **network** is a structured pattern of information flow and personal contact. Networks control the access and flow of information within the group, and they may also isolate the group from outside influences (Lifshitz-Assaf, 2017). Facebook, for example, was originally limited to Harvard students only. Outsiders could not get access. It was a relatively closed network. Quickly, Facebook broadened to include almost three billion monthly users and counting (McLachlan, 2021), but each participant can control who has access to his or her home page by either accepting or rejecting a request for access to become a Facebook "friend." The more open the network, the more accessible information is to a broad range of individuals. Open networks encourage change and potential disruption; closed networks emphasize stability, privacy, and permanence. Finding a moderate level of network flow of information and interaction appears to be optimal for group effectiveness (Troster et al., 2014).

Open and Closed Systems: Setting Effective Boundaries

Although all groups set boundaries, there is a strong bias in American culture that encourages openness, or loose boundaries, and discourages closedness, or rigid boundaries (Afifi et al., 2017). We preach the value of fostering an open society and maintaining an open mind, and in groups risk-free questions, constructive feedback, fluid roles and responsibilities, information sharing, and collaboration should be encouraged as a general perspective. Having a closed mind is linked to an authoritarian personality and dogmatism. A closed society is likened to North Korea.

The unqualified belief that openness is good and closedness is bad, however, is a faulty one (Klapp, 1978). **No group can long endure unless it closes off to some outside influences and restricts access to some information.** This is why boundary control is an essential group function. For example, the Golden State Warriors professional basketball team hired Kevin Sullivan, a communications strategist, to instruct team members about managing social media—when and how to set boundaries. Warriors coach Steve Kerr noted, "We're all human beings, so we all have a desire to know what people are saying about us, and we all have a desire to be liked. So imagine that times 100 on your phone, access to it nonstop all day, every day, including at halftime of games" (quoted by Rohlin, 2018).

A group must close off when both the quantity and type of input place undue stress on the group and/or prevent it from accomplishing its task. There are times, for instance, when a family seeks advice and counsel from friends and relatives (input), but there are also times when a family should close itself off to intrusion from outsiders. In-laws who are overly free with advice and criticism impose stress on the family. Permitting even well-intentioned relatives and friends to hammer immediate family members with unsolicited counsel can easily lead to bickering, increased tension, conflict, and even family disintegration.

Group members should watch for signs of excessive openness or closedness, such as when groups experience debilitating stress and tension, divisive conflicts, boredom and malaise, and poor productivity (Lifshitz-Assaf, 2017). Loosening or tightening boundaries may be in order. Whether to relax or tighten boundaries depends on whether the group is already very closed or very open.

SECOND LOOK

Group Boundary Control

Types of Group Boundaries Regulating Change

Physical barriers	Psychological barriers
Linguistic barriers	Rules
Roles	Network

Boundary Control and Group Effectiveness

Signs of Excessive Openness or Closedness:

Debilitating stress	Divisive conflicts
Boredom	Malaise
Poor productivity	

Adjust boundaries when signs of excessive openness/closedness occur.

Influence of Size

Size is a central element in any human system. Fluctuations in size have enormous influence on the structure and function of a group (Laughlin et al., 2006).

focus questions

1. What is the most appropriate size for a decision-making group?

2. What distinguishes a small group from a large one?

3. How are groups and organizations different?

Group Size and Complexity

As groups increase in numerical size, complexity increases. Try scheduling a meeting for a group of 15 or 20 members. Consider how difficult it would be to find a time that doesn't conflict with at least one or more members' personal schedules and preferences. There are numerous complications that increased complexity produces. This section discusses these complications.

Quantitative Complexity: Exponentially Complicated As the size of a group increases, the possible number of interactions between group members increases exponentially (Bostrom, 1970). The calculations are as follows:

Group Size	Possible Relationships
3	9
4	28
5	75
6	186
7	441
8	1,056

In a dyad, only two relationships are possible, namely, person A to person B, and vice versa. A and B may not have the same perception of their relationship. Person A may perceive the relationship with B as a close friendship, whereas B sees the relationship with A as merely acquaintanceship. In a triad, or three-member group, there are nine possibilities:

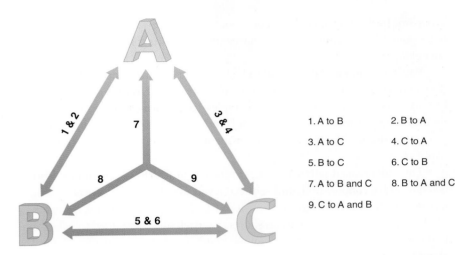

1. A to B   2. B to A

3. A to C   4. C to A

5. B to C   6. C to B

7. A to B and C   8. B to A and C

9. C to A and B

Adding even a single member to a group enormously complicates the group dynamics.

Complexity and Group Transactions: Size Matters Variations in size affect group transactions in several specific ways. First, larger groups typically have more nonparticipants than smaller groups ("Is Your Team Too Big?" 2006). This occurs partly because in larger groups there is more intense competition to seize the floor. More reticent members are apt to sit quietly rather than fight to be heard.

Second, smaller groups inhibit overt disagreement and signs of dissatisfaction more than larger groups. Smaller groups can apply more intense pressure to conform to majority opinion than can be applied in larger groups. Splinter groups and factions are more likely to emerge in larger groups. In a 6-person group, there may be only a single deviant who must stand alone against the group. In a 12-person group, however, two or more deviants may more easily emerge, forming a supportive faction ("Are Six Heads as Good as Twelve?" 2004).

Third, group size affects levels of cooperation (Artinger & Vulkan, 2016). When groups of 12 to 30 members were compared, the smallest groups were found to be the most cooperative, meaning they worked together on tasks more interdependently, engaged in collaborative effort, and exhibited consensus leadership. As groups increased in size, cooperation decreased. This resulted in diminished task effectiveness, unmet goals, and increased conflicts (Benenson et al., 2000). One reason for diminished cooperation is that as groups increase in size, more members tend to claim greater than their fair share of credit for group output. Research shows that even members who have contributed nothing to the group's output sometimes claim equal contributions. Such brazen **overclaiming of responsibility** invites furious disagreement and antagonistic feelings (Schroeder et al., 2016).

Fourth, group members tend to be less satisfied with groups of 10 or more (Carter & West, 1998). The overall group climate often deteriorates when groups become large. Tasks become more complex to perform, tension mounts, and dominant group members can trigger interpersonal disharmony by becoming too aggressive and forceful with other members while trying to impose order (Aube et al., 2011).

Thus, decreased participation, inhibition of overt disagreement, diminished levels of cooperation, and reduced levels of satisfaction characteristic of larger groups all lead to significantly diminished group productivity. Research by Marcia Blenko and her colleagues shows that each member added to a decision-making group that starts with seven members reduces decision effectiveness by about 10% (Blenko et al., 2010). If this **rule of seven** is taken to its logical conclusion, they explain, a group of 7 members or more "rarely makes any decisions" (p. 88). Too many group members can create decision paralysis, not cooperative decision making. Another study of 2,623 members in 329 work groups shows that groups composed of 3 to 8 members are significantly more productive than groups composed of 9 or more members. Groups of 3 to 6 members are the most productive (Wheelan, 2009). One final study showed that group productivity peaked at 7 members (Molavi, 2015).

So, what is the ideal size for a group? Is it 3 to 6, or maybe 7 or 8? There is no perfect number. Amazon's CEO Jeff Bezos follows the "two pizza rule." A group is too large if two pizzas are insufficient to feed all members (Yang, 2006). Obviously, this rule is an imprecise standard for determining ideal group size (small, medium, or large pizzas? Thin crust or deep-dish? Big eaters or nibblers?). The best size for a group is the smallest size capable of performing the task effectively. This admittedly is also somewhat imprecise advice, but there is a trade-off between *quality* and *speed* when trying to determine ideal group size. If the primary group goal is the quality of the decision, then a group of 7 or 8 members is advisable. These smaller groups are especially effective if the group has deep diversity and the group task requires such (Larson, 2007). If the primary goal of the group is speed, however, then very small groups of 3 or 4 members are advisable. Larger groups, especially those with a dozen or more members, potentially provide a diversity of resources but typically slow decision making and problem solving. Contextual factors (politics, legal requirements, institutional norms, availability of members, task complexity, etc.) may necessitate groups larger in size than what works for greatest efficiency.

sirtravelalot/Shutterstock

There is a trade-off between *speed* and decision *quality* as groups increase in size. In a jury trial, for example, the large size of the group (12 members) purposely constrains a speedy decision. The quality of the decision, not the speed, should be the prime focus. If your freedom depended on a jury verdict, you would certainly want the primary group goal to be the quality and not the speed of the decision.

An Organization: A Group of Groups

When groups grow, they reach a point where they may become organizations with bureaucracies. For instance, suppose you and two friends decide to open a small business together. Let's say you call it Computer Repair Use and Distribution (CRUD for short—easy to remember but not genius marketing). In its initial stages, the structure of your group is informal, and the division of labor is most likely equal. Since the three of you work together as friends (Crud Buds), communication is not hampered by cumbersome chains of command, middle managers, and the bureaucratic complexities of a large, formal organization. Standards of operation and procedures for decision making are informally negotiated among the three of you as situations occur.

If your little enterprise booms, employees will have to be hired, thus expanding the business and increasing the complexity of the entire operation. Work schedules will have to be coordinated. Perhaps a fleet of vans (Crudmobiles) will have to be purchased to form a computer repair "strike team." Standardized codes of dress (Crud Duds) and conduct on the job (Crudiquette) may be required. Constant training (Cruducation) in ever-changing computer technology will be necessary. Formal grievance procedures may also be required to settle disputes among employees and management. You may decide to open additional CRUD outlets (Crudlets), and even become a chain, selling franchises around the country. Now you must hire managers, accountants, and lawyers; establish a board of directors;

maybe sell stock in the company; and become business executives. What began as a small group enterprise can grow into a large, complex organization.

In typical organizations, research shows that complexity increases, on average, 6.7% per year (Morieux, 2017). Consider Facebook. It began as a small enterprise in 2004 at Harvard University. Mark Zuckerberg, along with roommates Eduardo Saverin, Dustin Moskowitz, and Chris Hughes, developed Facebook as an online Harvard student directory that quickly mushroomed into a global social networking behemoth. Despite disputes regarding whether Zuckerberg stole the original idea for Facebook, no one can dispute its meteoric rise from a small group of four into a large organization of more than 6,300 employees worldwide in just its first decade (Martin, 2014).

When small groups grow into larger groups, finally graduating into complex organizations, the structure and function of these human systems change. With increasing group size comes greater formality. Traditional large organizations become hierarchical (members of the organization are rank ordered from top to bottom), with clearly demarcated power structures, lines of authority, and top-down communication networks. In traditional organizations, the company is more important than any single individual. Employees can be replaced with relative ease, whereas in a small intimate group, loss of a single member may bring about the demise of the group. Although recently there has been a trend toward *flattening the hierarchy* by placing greater emphasis on teamwork, some formality remains. The flow of information is one of the most important differences between small groups and complex organizations. Normally, little negative information from below reaches the top of the corporate hierarchy, or, if it does, it is delayed (Reitzig & Maciejovsky, 2015). Who wants to be the bearer of bad tidings? Bad decision making, however, cannot be hidden easily when the group is small. Almost any blunder will become incandescent when the black hole of bureaucracy is not present to shroud it. If you have three people running a small business and one of the three does something boneheaded, your choices immediately narrow to two possibilities (unless, of course, you are guilty but playing dumb). One of your partners must be the culprit.

Information distortion usually is a bigger problem in organizations than in smaller groups. Managers act as gatekeepers, screening messages and selecting which ones will be brought to the attention of higher-ups. By the time a message from below reaches top executives in an organization, it can easily become unrecognizable nonsense. Similarly, information from the top can be distorted by the time it filters down to the bottom of the organization (Adler et al., 2013). In smaller groups, the communication is usually more direct, with fewer opportunities for distortion from messages being transmitted serially through several people. If the message is communicated to the entire group at the same time—a comparatively easy task if the gathering is small—then the problems of message distortion are reduced.

SECOND LOOK

Effects of Increasing Group Size

Increases

Complexity

Factionalism/cliques

Formality—more hierarchical

Information distortion

Quality decision making (unless group becomes too large and unwieldy)

Difficulty achieving consensus/majority vote often substituted

Decreases

Participation in group discussion

Cooperation (in very large groups)

Pressure to conform—coalitions likely to form in opposition to group norms

Member satisfaction with group experience (10 or more)

Access to information

Flow of negative information to top of hierarchy

Speed of decision making

Although organizations are not emphasized in this text, I include examples from organizational settings because many of you can relate meaningfully to such an environment, and small groups and teams often function within large organizations. Virtually all of what is discussed is immediately relevant to enhancing communication competence in organizations.

In summary, groups are systems. The three main elements of a system are interconnectedness of parts, adaptability to change, and the influence of size. There is no precise dividing line between small and large groups, and the ideal size for most decision-making and problem-solving groups is the smallest group capable of performing the task effectively. Having now laid the theoretical foundation for analyzing small groups, I discuss the process of group development in the next chapter.

QUESTIONS FOR CRITICAL THINKERS

1. In groups you belong to, what boundaries are erected?
2. Have you experienced group boundaries that are too rigid in any groups to which you belong? How can you tell that the boundaries are too rigid?
3. What's the largest group you've ever belonged to that didn't experience serious problems because of its size? Why did it work?

TED TALKS AND YOUTUBE VIDEOS

"The Pandemic Is Forcing Everyone to Face the Digital Divide"
"How to Deal with Difficult People" | Jay Johnson
"3 Ways to Deal with Difficult People"

VIDEO CASE STUDIES

City Island (2010). *Comedy/Drama; PG-13*

Vince Rizzo, played by Andy Garcia, is a corrections officer who secretly wants to be an actor. He hides this fact and his secret acting lessons from his wife Joyce, played by Julianna Margulies, so she thinks he is having an affair. Secrets abound throughout the family. Analyze boundary control issues and openness versus closedness concerns from a systems perspective.

Contagion (2011). *Drama; R*

Fairly graphic presentation of a pandemic virus and its consequences. You have to have a strong stomach to watch this movie. Analyze this film for the ripple effect and systems theory dynamics.

The Host (2013). *Adventure/Sci-Fi/Romance; PG-13*

Average but intriguing story about the human race being infected with small parasitic aliens called "souls." Analyze from a systems perspective the isolated cave-dwelling humans who have created a protective enclave from the aliens. What are the interconnected parts, adaptability to change, boundary control, and influence of size elements? How does environment influence the group?

The Post (2017). *Drama/History; PG-13*

This is a Steven Spielberg dramatization of the famous Pentagon Papers case that pitted the *Washington Post* and the *New York Times* against the government's attempt to prevent release of damaging documents revealing awareness that the Vietnam War was unwinnable. Analyze boundary control issues at the center of this controversy, the ripple effect, and adaptability to changing circumstances as the events unfold.

Wonder (2017). *Drama; PG*

This is a heartwarming depiction of a boy with facial differences who enters fifth grade in a mainstream school for the first time. Analyze the family dynamics from a systems perspective. How does August Pullman's entry into the school produce change and boundary issues?

Meetings: Standard and Virtual

3

Do you ever remember anyone saying, "I sure wish we had more meetings"? Columnist George Will once remarked, "Football combines the two worst things about America: it is violence punctuated by committee meetings." You may disagree with Will's opinion about football, but most seem to agree with his assessment of meetings. A Harris poll found that almost half of the 2,066 respondents would suffer "any unpleasant activity" instead of attending a meeting, with 18% of this group preferring a trip to the DMV, 17% preferring to watch paint dry, and 8% opting for a root canal ("Meetings," 2015). In a more recent survey of almost 7,000 business professionals from the United States, Germany, Switzerland, and the United Kingdom, 100% of these respondents said disorganized meetings were a waste of time and money (Doodle, 2019). How much money? According to the same study, the United States wasted $399 billion in unproductive meetings in 2019 when the study was conducted.

Group meetings don't have to be a common source of grouphate, but they often are viewed with the same distaste one might have for the return of disco. Common complaints associated with group meetings include the following: There is an unclear purpose for the meeting, participants are unprepared, meetings begin and end late, they are poorly organized, attendees fiddle with their social media, key individuals are absent or late, discussion drifts into conversation on unrelated topics, some participants dominate the conversation and stifle discussion, and decisions made at meetings are not implemented (Doodle, 2019; Levitt, 2013).

Then there was the unique disgruntlement that emerged in 2020 with the pervasive spread of virtual meetings necessitated by the Covid-19 pandemic. Campus quarantines moved college classes mostly online for entire semesters. Virtual meeting attendees reported feelings of exhaustion and dread when classrooms and boardrooms took solely to the virtual platform during the pandemic (Supiano, 2020). Group projects to fulfill class assignments became more challenging. "Zoom fatigue" quickly set in.

objectives

The purpose of this chapter is to explain how to conduct effective standard and virtual meetings. Toward this end, there are three chapter objectives:

1. To determine what to do before, during, and after a meeting when you are in charge.

2. To explore how to use communication competence to participate fully in any meeting, regardless of your role.

3. To learn how to navigate virtual meetings with ease.

The fatigue from virtual meetings is intensified as our brains are required to process more information in lieu of the missing or diminished nonverbal elements present in face-to-face meetings. We are working harder to decipher message cues such as tone, facial expression, and pitch—elements essential to the processing of messages. Even pauses are cause for distress. "Silence creates a natural rhythm in a real-life conversation. However, when it happens in a video call, you become anxious about the technology" (quoted by Jiang, 2020). As anyone who has experienced the frustrating stop-start dance of interruption when trying to contribute at the same time as others on conference calls can attest, our latest way of communicating disrupts conversational cadence. The merest millisecond delay of accessing the mute/unmute button takes more than twice as long as what we experience in-person (Yorke, 2020). No wonder we are so tired.

Despite this dismal perception of group meetings, "Meetings-R-Us." One study found that business executives spend an average of almost 23 hours a week in meetings, not including unscheduled "drive-by" confabs (Perlow et al., 2017). Meetings are an unavoidable and potentially significant part of successful group decision making and problem solving when conducted competently (Atlassian, 2019). "Meetings are critical venues for groups and teams. Group decision making, problem solving, sense making, and communication come to life in meetings" (Rogelberg et al., 2012, p. 236). They are an essential vehicle for collaboration and communication. Great minds come together, enabling the possibility of synergy, decision making, and camaraderie. Meetings provide a place to share information, create strategies, and make agreements.

Cecilia Sharpe, who was managing an audit team, decided to calculate the effects of eliminating the team's weekly meeting with the understanding that group members would maintain direct communication to coordinate their efforts (see Shaffner, 1999). When a proposal to revise work schedules for her team emerged, she discovered that this one decision in the absence of group meetings resulted in a net loss of 18 person-hours in productivity. There were 102 disruptions to discuss the proposal by phone but only 7 disruptions of any kind during team meetings. The decision was two days late and uniformly disliked. Clearly, group meetings have many potential benefits, but poorly designed meetings will not be productive. Consequently, the purpose of this chapter is to explain how to conduct effective standard and virtual meetings.

Ensuing chapters explore more complex elements of the small group process. For now, I prefer to get you up and running quickly on the basics of meeting effectively in small groups before doing a deep dive into the intricacies of competent communication in small groups. Whether a student or an employee, engaging in a small group meeting is likely to be one of your most frequent activities.

Standard Meeting Preparation

You can neutralize negative attitudes group members have about formal meetings by conducting them efficiently and effectively. Adequate preparation is critical. As the facilitator, there are several ways that you can accomplish this.

focus questions

1. What are reasons not to hold a group meeting?

2. Which meeting preparations are essential for success?

Clarify the Purpose: Avoid Aimlessness

Don't call a meeting unless there is no good alternative. Disseminating information, holding a meeting because you are scheduled to do so every Tuesday afternoon even though an email or phone call would suffice, or hoping to try out new ideas on colleagues or classmates all are lousy reasons to call a meeting. One of life's little pleasures is the surprise notification, "Meeting has been canceled." Hold a meeting if an immediate response is required, group participation is essential, participants are prepared to discuss and act on relevant issues, and key players can be present.

Once you have decided that a meeting is required, determining a meeting's purpose cascades into every decision you make about the meeting including whom to invite, what to discuss, and how to discuss it. The *purpose* is the rational outcome—that is, the tangible, measurable result that needs to be achieved by meeting. Much like the thesis of a research paper, the purpose of your meeting should be clear, specific, and meaningful, and all meeting content should align with that purpose. As important as it is for you to clarify the meeting's purpose, it is equally important to communicate it to those coming to the meeting so they can best prepare.

To determine the purpose, begin with broad strokes: What is the overarching objective of the meeting? Most meetings are called to generate ideas, solve a problem, or make decisions (Goff-Dupont, 2018). Which best suits your meeting? Once you have determined the general objective, it is time to refine it by creating your **purpose/impact (P/I) statement**. Follow this template:

The Purpose of this meeting is to _____ in order to _____(Impact).

This is the question on everyone's mind: Is this meeting really necessary? Be clear on your meeting purpose before calling one, and reiterate it to all in the agenda and again when the meeting begins.

For example, instead of routinely calling the team together for the Monday staff meeting, drill down to the importance of *why* you are calling a meeting and *what* the most desirable result will be after its conclusion. Steer clear of vague descriptions. Aim for P/I statements that capture the detail needed to gain clarity and momentum around the required gathering. For example:

> The purpose of Monday's meeting is to check in with everyone in order to be updated.

This statement fails to signify the importance of the meeting, and the stated impact is weak at best. Conversely, here is a better P/I statement:

> The purpose of Monday's meeting is to review project group members' weekly progress on specified tasks in order to ascertain any problem areas to explore.

Here is a more compelling sample of a P/I statement for a brainstorming meeting:

> The purpose of our brainstorming session is to generate a minimum of five strong, feasible ideas to pursue in order to choose one of these ideas for our class project.

Do not get lazy with your P/I statements or ignore the process altogether to save time. Doing this correctly will ultimately save you time.

Create an Effective Meeting Agenda: Simple Steps

Once you have formulated your P/I statement, consider *what* you need to do in the meeting, *how* you will do it, and with *whom*. Absence of an agenda is a primary cause of failed meetings. Research found that almost two-thirds of group meetings had no planned agenda. Consequently, about a quarter of typical meeting time is spent discussing irrelevant issues, and 9 out of 10 individuals attending meetings lapse into daydreaming ("The Trouble with Meetings," 2017). The agenda serves to keep the meeting on track and on topic, communicates participation expectations, specifies the processes used throughout the meeting, and highlights what pre-meeting preparation is needed. Constructing an agenda takes time, but it can pay big dividends.

Creating a well-structured agenda may not be necessary for every small group meeting, especially when the purpose of the meeting is more casual and social than decision making or problem solving. When groups meet to discuss and debate important issues and make impactful decisions or solve significant problems, however, a carefully constructed agenda can be critical to success. Here is how to put together an effective agenda:

1. **Print your P/I statement at the top of your agenda.** Consider displaying it on a whiteboard, flip chart, or poster board for all to see at the actual meeting.
2. **Draft agenda items from the P/I statement.** What must be done? In what order? By whom? What can be saved for an email, a one-on-one, or a different meeting?
3. **List your agenda items as questions** to encourage participation and drive clarity (see Table 3.1).
4. **Identify the item leader.** Next to every agenda item question, label who will take the lead on each topic. This not only saves you from being the only voice in the room, but it increases contributions and thwarts surprises during the meeting.
5. **Manage your guest list.** Consider key decision makers, subject matter experts, stakeholders, influencers, and even perhaps those with dissenting opinions. Keep the meeting size as small as possible to promote productive engagement. Curating your guest list clarifies meeting logistics such as the timeline, required meeting space, and activities.
6. **Seek input.** Email your tentative list of agenda items to meeting attendees and get their feedback. What would they like added to the agenda if anything and why (Schwarz, 2017)? If their request fits the purpose of the meeting, add it to the agenda. If not, respond in an email or a one-on-one conversation.
7. **Estimate time needed.** Designate the anticipated time needed for each agenda item, considering the time needed to solicit information, have discussions,

Attachments (pre-reads) can easily become unmanageable and stressful. No group member is likely to pre-read lengthy attachments, so they usually become useless appendages to emailed agendas. Brevity should be the watchword for attachments whenever possible.

and make decisions if needed (see Table 3.1). Check your time allotment and estimates with the meeting contributors. Is it too much? Too little? About right? **Pre-reads**—essential materials you assign for review before the meeting begins—can save time on the agenda and prepares participants for productive conversation (Dhawan, 2021). Pre-reads should be concise and essential to the discussion. Avoid encyclopedic-sized pre-read attachments to the announcement of a meeting unless you like being ignored or teased.

8. **Create your final agenda.** Two versions are provided in Table 3.1. Send out your completed agenda so participants know what to expect, when to attend, and what materials, if any, each participant should bring to the meeting. Schedule meetings clearly by notifying participants by email or other means, so everyone is well informed.

Get There First: Expect Problems

Whether you are the meeting facilitator or meeting attendant, arrive early to the meeting whenever possible. There is no need to make a grand entrance. This is

Table 3.1 Sample Agenda A

Agenda for Group Project Team Meeting, Monday, 8:00 am–9:00 am

Location: Library Study Room (reserved)

Purpose/Impact: *The purpose of our brainstorming session is to gather a minimum of three strong focus areas to consider in order to make progress on our final group project.*

Time	Topic/Question	Leader
8:00–8:05 (5 minutes)	Welcome: What is the purpose of this meeting?	Anne
8:05–8:10 (5 minutes)	Assignment review: What are the criteria for the final group project?	Anne
8:10–8:20 (10 minutes)	Brainstorm in pairs: What topics could we present and why?	All
8:20–8:35 (15 minutes)	Group brainstorm: Report best ideas.	All
8:35–8:45 (10 minutes)	Which ideas merit further exploration? Vote for top three.	Arun
8:45–8:55 (10 minutes)	Determine next steps: Who will do what by when (**WWDWBW**)? When will we meet again?	Anne and Arun
8:55–9:00 (5 minutes)	Revisit parking lot: Issue? Action item? Agenda? Rate the meeting.	Anne

Alternate Sample Agenda B: Business Meeting (*e.g., Meeting of the Student Senate*)

Date:

Location: Boardroom

Time: 2:00–4:00 pm

Purpose/Impact: *Biweekly meeting to report committee progress on items of interest and to address new issues of significance to students and the campus at large.*

I.   Call meeting to order; introduce any new members (Margaret) [5 minutes]

II. Discussion/approval of minutes of last meeting (Margaret) [5 minutes]

III. Additions to the agenda (Margaret) [2 minutes]

IV. Committee reports

    A. Student fee committee (Adolpho) [5 minutes]

    B. Student activity committee (Brandon) [5 minutes]

    C. Student union committee (Mariana) [5 minutes]

   V. Officer's reports

      A. Treasurer's report (Roberto substituting for Annabeth) [5 minutes]

      B. President's report (Margaret) [10 minutes]

   VI. Old business

      A. Textbook prices: Any solutions? (JoBeth Donello, bookstore director) [10 minutes]

      B. Campus parking problems: What's been done? (Sgt. Phillipe Rodriguez) [10 minutes]

   VII. New business

      A. Safety on campus: Progress? (Sgt. Rodriguez) [10 minutes]

      B. Computer access on campus: What changes need to occur? (Open discussion) [10 minutes]

      C. Pub on campus: Pros and cons? (Breakout groups—samples not included) [15 minutes for discussion; 10 minutes for reporting to full group]

   VIII. (**WWDWBW**)? [5 minutes]

   IX. Parking lot issues? [3 minutes]

   X. Building agenda for next business meeting [2 minutes]

   XI. Assess the meeting and decide when will we meet again? [3 minutes]

   Adjournment

not a coronation. Anticipate problems. Arriving early will give you an opportunity to double-check the room and equipment for problems. Notice the room's layout—are there enough chairs, adequately spaced apart, and is a table required and available? Test the equipment and your Internet connection (if using) before the meeting starts. Check the temperature of the room: If it is too hot or too cold, adjust the room's temperature control. If not possible, consider sending a quick text or email to attendees suggesting they dress accordingly. While they might sound trivial, these little considerations such as seating, climate, and technology can greatly influence the conditions necessary for a participative group.

Conducting a Meeting

Benjamin Franklin said, "If you fail to plan, you are planning to fail." Though that typically holds true, simply having a plan (P/I statement and carefully conceived meeting agenda) and preparing the meeting room does not guarantee success.

focus questions

1. Is parliamentary procedure necessary to conduct effective meetings?
2. How can you keep a meeting on track instead of going off the rails?

Type of Meeting: Formal or Informal

There are additional steps required when actually facilitating a meeting. Using parliamentary procedure, however, isn't necessarily one of them. **Parliamentary procedure** is a set of hundreds of rules for conducting meetings (see Robert's Rules of Order at *www.robertsrules.com*). Parliamentary procedure is appropriate for large, formal groups (e.g., the U.S. Senate) and even a few smaller groups with formal responsibilities (e.g., boards of directors), but for most small groups the rules are too rigid and artificial (Sunwolf & Frey, 2005). They can stifle productive discussion and squash the creative process. Saying "I rise to a point of privilege" or "I move to table the motion" during your study group's discussion would also sound ridiculous.

Using a relaxed version of parliamentary procedure, however, is a viable option in some circumstances. Relatively informal small group meetings can abbreviate the procedural rules as follows (Jennings, 2020): Skip formal motions and a required second from another group member; speak freely without formal recognition by the chair of the meeting when opportunities occur without competitive interruptions that fight to seize the floor; avoid motions to limit debate because time limits listed on an agenda can be extended; allow minutes for the meeting to be skipped, although the chair of the meeting might make brief notes for later reference; and avoid technical terminology. A detailed agenda may also be deemed unnecessary when the issues are very limited and the group is very small, but a P/I statement is still useful.

Some small group meetings such as standing committees that meet regularly may find it appropriate to combine some formality with informality. For example, require clearly stated and concise motions, formal votes, and recognition from the chair before speaking when the issues discussed are controversial, but follow the remaining suggestions for abbreviating parliamentary procedure. The group can decide how formal or informal they prefer the rules for discussion and debate to be.

The degree of structure (i.e., rules, roles, and norms prescribed) determines the difference between formal and informal small groups. A study group, for example, is normally an informal group of students who gather to prepare for an exam. As such, you may forgo an agenda, a P/I statement is likely unnecessary since the purpose and impact are obvious (i.e., to ace the exam), and you can simply rely on a list of study guide questions if your instructor provides such a list. A somewhat relaxed structure might also include a pre-read of the study questions, an opportunity to review subject matter to answer the questions individually before meeting as a group, writing down preliminary answers, definitely coming prepared and not expecting other group members to supply answers, usually agreeing as a group regarding who might act as a facilitator of the study discussion, encouraging participation from all group members, and if possible, achieving a consensus (unanimity) on the correct answers for each question (Lange et al., 2016). As groups become more formal, additional guidelines detailed in the ensuing sections are useful, and some also apply even to casual groups, such as this next step.

Begin on Time; End on Time: Punctuality Is a Virtue

Begin your meetings, whether formal or informal, at their stated time and end them accordingly. Do not wait for the terminally tardy to arrive. Yes, cultures vary widely in their view of punctuality. In Spain, Italy, and Argentina, being 30 minutes late for a meeting is not unusual. Many Arab and African cultures do not highly value punctuality. Nevertheless, when meetings occur, especially formal ones, there is a strong cultural expectation in the United States that punctuality will be highly regarded so as not to appear rude and insensitive to members' busy lives (Samovar et al., 2021). Research also shows that, especially in Western cultures such as the United States, punctuality is not only highly prized but arriving late to meetings (especially 15 minutes or longer) negatively affects other group members. These negative responses include feeling disrespected, frustrated, and upset, and judging the late member or members as rude. Also, late members can disrupt the flow of group discussion and negatively impact decision making (Rogelberg et al., 2013; see also Allen et al., 2018). Clearly, these negative outcomes are not universal among group members. Some members are quite tolerant of even substantial lateness, but the negative consequences of meeting tardiness can be quite disruptive especially if it becomes widespread among group members.

Delaying the start of a meeting because some members have not arrived communicates the message to those who are present that being on time does not really matter, but it usually does in American culture. If you will just wait around for people to join, why should anyone bother to be punctual for your next meeting? As for meetings that run late, consider that others may have back-to-back meetings scheduled, and while it is a big deal to you, yours may not be the most important one of the day to others. Punctuality, of course, is a matter of perception, but perception matters.

Communicate Ground Rules: Avoid Chaos

While many might assume professionalism and competent communication are unspoken yet understood guidelines for how to behave during group meetings, it is not so often the case. There are two types of ground rules: **procedural ground rules** that help the meeting process and **behavioral ground rules** that assist in managing contributions and communication (Schwarz & Heinecke, 2016). Common procedural ground rules include: "Turn off phones," "Start every meeting on time," and "No multitasking." Previous discussion of whether and to what extent parliamentary procedure and structure might be imposed is also procedural. Impactful behavioral ground rules focus on the way people are expected to participate at the meeting. "Stay curious and ask tough questions" encourages participants to challenge ideas and information. "Stay on topic and monitor time" asks participants to be mindful when contributing. Research warns about a group meeting **babble effect** in which participants seem to believe that filling the airwaves with aimless and seemingly endless discussion improves decision making. It clearly does not (Yoerger et al, 2018). Participants must stay focused on agenda items and keep contributions terse and on point. Finally, "discuss the undiscussables" urges addressing tough topics.

Ground rules not only help the flow of the meeting, but they also make communication expectations known to all. Well-established ground rules can also eliminate the counterproductive but all too common "meeting after the meeting"—the informal conversations where employees discuss what they *really thought* about the meeting.

Use the Best Process: No One-Size-Fits-All

Change the monotonous meeting script of going around the conference table and seeking input from each attendee by trying different methods of involvement and inclusion that match agenda items. Better techniques might include: creating small break-out groups that debate a question for 10 minutes and then coming

wavebreakmedia/Shutterstock

The standard "I talk/ you listen" process is tedium times tedium equals tedium squared. Try periodically breaking free from this traditional meeting equation.

back and discussing with the larger group; or having meeting participants "vote" for their favorite three ideas on a prepared flip chart, using a colored sticky dot (found in office supply stores). Many virtual meeting platforms offer similar capabilities such as breakout rooms, shared whiteboards, and poll voting. Carefully planned processes can dramatically affect the quality of participation.

Stay on Track: Parking Lots, Jellyfish, and Perception Checks

Choosing the right participants, starting on time, and sharing the well-designed, detailed agenda will help keep your meeting on track, but good meetings require competent communication. An efficient meeting should be necessary, focused, organized, and as short as feasible. This requires steady leadership from the chair of the meeting.

You may want to assign a timekeeper. When the time on a discussion item has elapsed (see the agenda), the group may decide to extend the time allotment or move to the next item. Time limits establish a crisp pace for the meeting.

Discourage stage hogs. This may require purposeful interruption. Divert the talkaholics with a comment like "Let's hear from others," "George, what are your ideas about X?" or "Let's keep our comments targeted so everyone can join the conversation."

Establish a visual **parking lot** for questions and topics that are worthy of discussion but not on the agenda. Put the words "Parking Lot" on a white board or on a piece of flip-chart paper that is easily accessed by all. When an item comes up that is important though not necessarily relevant to this meeting, encourage participants to capture it on the parking lot. This ensures the importance of participant contributions and concerns, while keeping the meeting on track. At the conclusion of your meeting, take two to three minutes to revisit the parking lot. Determine whether or not each item has been resolved, needs action, or requires further exploration, perhaps in the form of a follow-up conversation or meeting. Take a picture of the parking lot with your phone so you can refer to it later if needed.

A light and humorous method that empowers all meeting attendees to monitor time, contributions, and communication is by saying "jellyfish" (or some other agreed upon, neutral term) when conversations veer off-track (Frisch and Greene, 2017). Gelatinous jellyfish are the drifters of the sea. Invoking their name reminds people not to drift. Saying "jellyfish" or "I'm feeling the sting of a jellyfish" suggests getting back to the originally stated goals (remember the P/I statements?) of the meeting. The jellyfish tactic works best in small groups composed of members who get along and can appreciate a bit of whimsy to lighten the atmosphere of long or dense meetings. To be most effective, it needs to be understood, agreed upon, and used correctly (Schwarz & Heinecke, 2016). Caution participants to use the tactic judiciously, infrequently, not carelessly.

Of course, you are not limited to jellyfish. Australian start-up Atlassian swears by squeezing a squeaky rubber chicken named Helmut (Castles, 2017). I've used a Kermit the Frog puppet with everyone trying to impersonate his Muppet voice ("It's not easy to intervene"). **Almost any word or object will work, as long as all meeting attendees know what it is and how to use it.** Introduce the tactic at the beginning of a meeting. Let participants know that anyone can use it, regardless of stature, for the purpose of maintaining meeting focus. This helps participants monitor their own contributions, and it is a safe way for all to interrupt constructively if conversations get hijacked or derailed. It also diminishes status differences that can stifle productive discussion. The first attempt by the most powerful member of a group to imitate Kermit never fails to trigger laughter and loosen the conversational atmosphere.

If jellyfish, rubber chickens, or Kermit imitations are not preferred, another option is the use of a quick perception check. Perception checking has three parts: (1) neutral description of an observable fact, (2) two possible interpretations of the aforementioned fact; and (3) a request for clarification. For example, "You're talking about the budget (neutral description), and I am unclear how that relates to the research we're reviewing for changes on this project, or maybe I missed something in your explanation (two possible interpretations). Will you help me make the connection, or, if we have veered off track, should we put this on the parking lot so it can be addressed at a different time (request for clarification)?" **Even the most perfectly crafted perception check can come across as rude or dismissive if paired with contradicting nonverbals.** Keep your voice tone, eye contact, and posture in alignment with the intention of your communication: respectful, direct inquiry intended to keep the topic, and thus, the meeting, on track.

Concluding the Meeting: Don't End with a Whimper

With so much planning around the facilitation of a meeting, it would be a shame to end it with a shoulder shrug while saying "That's it." Great meetings close with purpose. Every participant should leave knowing who does what by when (WDWBW). Allow a few minutes for these useful questions (Axtell, 2015):

> Is there anything left that needs to be said before we adjourn? (check for completion)
> How do you feel about where we ended up? (check alignment with decisions)
> Who is doing what by when to ensure progress before our next meeting? (ensure agreement on next steps)

After the Meeting: Clean-Up Time

The meeting is over, but you are still not finished. Jot down any must-dos or reminders as soon as you can while they are fresh in your mind. This might include your list of *who does what by when*. Check to see if anyone outside of the meeting needs an update. Next, revisit the parking lot—what requires follow-up from you? Should you schedule a one-on-one, or will an email or phone call suffice? Finally, start planning your next meeting. If further work and discussion are deemed necessary, schedule discussion of unfinished business for the next meeting. If the group has made decisions, implementation of those decisions must be monitored (see the PERT method detailed in Chapter 10).

Distribute the minutes of the meeting as soon as possible. Someone attending the meeting should be delegated the responsibility for taking notes and turning them into meeting minutes. The minutes should indicate what was discussed, who said what, what action was taken, if any, and what remained to be deliberated and decided. Minutes record the gist of a meeting, not an exact transcript. Also, do not include confidential information, and keep language neutral ("Fred freaked," "Jamie had a meltdown," or "Stephanie begged" lacks neutrality).

Participating in Meetings

As important as participation of group members is to group synergy, no one wants to encourage participation from bad apple members. The quality of member participation is more important than the mere quantity (Dowell et al., 2017). Low quantity of participation from group members, however, especially from those who are merely shy or reticent to contribute, can impact group effectiveness. In this section, ways to engage low participators in group discussion and addressing the challenge of cultural diversity and rates of participation are explored.

focus questions

1. What are your responsibilities as a meeting participant?
2. Should nonminority Americans value silence as much as some cultures do?
3. Should you expect some group members to become more assertive and outspoken participators in small groups, even though this is not highly valued in their culture?

Be Prepared: Don't Act Like a Potted Plant

Elevate your pre-meeting knowledge by requesting the meeting agenda and asking the person who coordinated the meeting how they would like you to contribute. Are you there to observe? Participate? Take notes? Critique? Specific clarification of your role will help you prepare and show up the best way possible. If you are truly needed at the session, complete any necessary pre-reads or research. Write down any questions you hope to get answered. If you have a suggestion for an agenda item, send it to the coordinator in advance so they are not caught off guard and can work it into the agenda.

Preparation includes punctuality, regardless of your meeting role. Make the meeting a priority, not an afterthought. If you are on time, you are late. Aim to arrive five minutes early. Secure parking (if traveling for the meeting), find the room, set up your seat, say hello, and center yourself.

Preparation also means coming ready to listen, not half-listen while you discreetly text status updates on all of your social media accounts. Research shows that when it comes to cellphones, simply silencing them during the meeting isn't enough. In fact, people who leave their phones in a different room when they attend a meeting significantly increase their ability to process relevant information, reason, and solve problems. It turns out it is the mere *presence* of a phone that is distracting, not just the alerts (Ward et al, 2017).

WAIT: Avoid Stage Hogging

Embrace consultant Laura Schloff's acronym **WAIT**: "Why Am I Talking?" (Lublin, 2017). Before talking, determine your intention (to contribute, to challenge, to add, to encourage, etc.) and ask yourself if your comment will add or subtract from the conversation. In an effort to be clear and to the point, think before you speak. Do not ramble. Look for a balance of contributions. Do not always be the first one to comment on a presentation or proposal, particularly if you're not an expert. If nobody raises what you were going to say, then continue but be mindful of the impact of how you make your contribution. Model excellent participation—others might follow your lead.

Be Attentive: Monitor Your Nonverbal Communication

You are sending messages even when you're not speaking. Watch your posture and facial expressions. Posture should be attentive (standing or sitting up straight, facing the leader or screen, arms uncrossed). Facial expressions should convey interest, not boredom or disbelief. Tone of voice should be congruent with the level of respect you are trying to convey. Stay curious, listen well, and ask relevant questions.

Recognize Cultural Diversity: Is Silence Golden?

The year 2009 marked the beginning of Japan's first jury system since World War II. The idea of participating in jury deliberations and deciding court cases does not immediately appeal to Japanese citizens (Johnson, 2016). There is a deep cultural reticence to expressing opinions in public discourse, to arguing different points of view, to judging others publicly, and to questioning authority (Ryall, 2019; Vanoverbeke, 2015). In keeping with the respect for authority, the new system combines three trained judges and six citizens picked by lottery to make decisions (Tabuchi & McDonald, 2009; Watanabe, 2012). Hundreds of mock trials were held prior to the official start of jury trials in Japan, but jurors remained mostly silent, failing to participate in deliberations despite prodding from judges. After a decade of experience with lay juries, an ever-increasing number, almost 70% of Japanese citizens called for jury duty, refused to serve (Ryall, 2019).

The value of verbal participation in decision making is perceived differently across cultures. Speaking is highly valued in the United States. Talking in an individualist culture is a way of showing one's uniqueness and importance (Samovar et al., 2021). In collectivist cultures and co-cultures, by contrast, speaking is not highly prized. Among Cambodians, Chinese, Japanese, Thais, and Vietnamese, among others, emphasis is given to minimal vocal participation. A Chinese proverb by Lao Tzu states, "Those who know do not speak; those who speak do not know." A Thai proverb says, "A wise man talks little; an ignorant one talks much." A Japanese proverb states, "It is the duck that squawks that gets shot" (Samovar et al., 2021).

Cultural value differences concerning verbal participation in small groups pose a challenge. Finding ways to boost the verbal participation rates of cultural

Japanese do not view participation in jury deliberations with particular relish. Americans don't especially look forward to jury duty either, but when placed on a jury, Americans are much more likely to embrace active group discussion about the court case. This image is one of the many mock trials conducted to prepare Japanese citizens to be jurors in real trials. Small group participation is not universally valued.

jeremy sutton-hibbert/Alamy Stock Photo

minorities in an American culture that values speech is a worthy undertaking. The methods outlined in the next section for encouraging constructive participation from low contributors in general apply well.

Increase Participation: Constructive Engagement

There are several steps that can be taken to promote constructive participation, especially from members of multicultural groups. First, encourage contributions from low participators. Solicit input from reticent members by asking open-ended questions (e.g., "What does everyone think?"). When low participators offer contributions, indicate that their participation is valued by actively listening to what they say and perhaps thanking them for their contribution.

Second, make issues and problems for discussion relevant to the interests of low participators. When groups work on interesting, involving, or challenging tasks, member contributions increase (Forsyth, 2019).

Third, give low participators responsibility for certain tasks. If low participators believe that their efforts have an impact on the group's final decision or product, they are less likely to remain uninvolved.

Fourth, establish a cooperative group climate. This is particularly important for members from collectivist cultures who highly value cooperation. See Chapter 5 for a detailed, complex exploration on developing a positive group climate.

Virtual Meetings

In-person meetings are what most of us are accustomed to, favored by 92% of the Solomon (2016) survey respondents and 72% of respondents who attend professional conferences ("The Surprising Truth," 2020). Electronic alternatives to the standard in-person meetings have emerged, however, from necessity. College instruction had become increasingly virtual but exploded when the pandemic hit, and business has become more global in its reach. Virtual meetings have become commonplace, even among families and friends.

Types of Virtual Meetings: Audio and Visual

Virtual meetings take the form of teleconferences (audio only) and videoconferences (video and audio). The audioconference is commonly referred to more simply as the **conference call**. The Solomon survey found that 93% of respondents deemed conference calls as beneficial. This version of a virtual group allows several individuals to conduct a joint meeting over the telephone or in some instances by a computer-based voice link. Once the exclusive province of corporations, a conference call can now be easily set up by almost anyone. Student

sirtravelalot/Shutterstock

Remember that an audioconference is not merely a phone conversation. You're conducting an efficient meeting. *The conference call should be necessary, focused, organized, and as short as feasible.* This meeting is utilizing a classic Polycom Soundstation to conduct the meeting. More sophisticated equipment is available, but this version works well (Hanson & Turner, 2020). Simple cellphone conference calls are also easily available when student groups need to connect as a team. The easy availability of options such as Zoom has made audioconferences instead of videoconferences less common.

groups working on a project can easily establish a conference call with little effort. Both Android and iPhones have conference call capabilities with easy instructions readily available online. Its primary purpose for virtual groups is to conduct meetings. **Most of the guidelines for conducting efficient and effective meetings already discussed apply.**

Videoconferences **have become commonplace in the workplace**, and 84% of survey respondents view them as beneficial (Solomon, 2016). The videoconference, like the teleconference, is a useful option when participants cannot meet easily in person. Videoconferences provide nonverbal cues, such as facial expressions, gestures, posture, and eye contact, unavailable in teleconferencing. Body language cues help participants assess messages more accurately, and they are instrumental in defining relationships between participants. The meeting environment is much more engaging than audioconferencing can provide.

There are numerous software options available for videoconferencing. Highly rated options include: Zoom, GoToMeeting, ClickMeeting, Google Meet, RingCentral Video, Microsoft Teams, BlueJeans, and Skype. These are just some highly rated choices, each offering slightly different tools and benefits (Drake & Turner, 2021; McLaughlin & Brame, 2020). Undoubtedly, new software options will be added in the future. Zoom, for example, had only 10 million users in December 2019, but by March 2020 daily users ballooned to 200 million with the advent of Covid-19 and shelter-in-place requirements (Patnaik, 2020). Videoconferences in any form, as with any meeting, should be necessary, focused, organized, and as short as feasible.

Pros and Cons: A Mixed Bag

Virtual meetings present a mixed batch of advantages and disadvantages (Yang et al., 2018). They save time and money. Meeting others online axes travel costs such as flights, food, gas, and lodging, and it eliminates venue charges should the meeting be held off campus or away from the office. Virtual meetings also allow remote or global employees instant access and connection with the rest of the team. Experts typically unavailable for in-person meetings because of distance can be blended rather seamlessly into virtual meetings (Morrison-Smith & Ruiz, 2020). Group members can communicate with each other at the speed of light over vast distances, even continents. Finding one central meeting place available at a specific time is not an issue for virtual groups. **Work-from-anywhere** has become increasingly popular in the world of business, especially with the arrival of the pandemic (Choudhury, 2020). Members can connect at home, at their office, even in airport terminals or restroom stalls—one survey showed that 75% of respondents use a cellphone while answering nature's call (Heaney, 2013). Another survey found that 45% of employees working remotely do so from their beds for 11 hours per week (Anthony, 2020). There are few limitations on where and when a group member can join virtual discussions and meetings. Pragmatically, virtual meetings can be recorded so people who missed the meeting can catch up.

Limitations, however, include distractions disguised as multitasking, a lack of nonverbals from the meeting facilitator and participants in audioconferences that can lead to misinterpreted communication, and the absence of interpersonal interactions that build trust and connection with a team, such as small talk, handshakes, and getting coffee together before or after the meeting (Speagle, 2017). Being able to communicate over vast distances removes group members from physical proximity to each other and can seem more impersonal than in-person meetings. Also, differences in time zones was considered the single most difficult issue by 85% of global virtual team members in the Solomon (2016) study. If a virtual meeting is scheduled at 6:00 PM San Francisco time, for example, members living in London would have to meet at 2:00 AM. That tends to make people crabby.

A study of 20,000 employees from the United Kingdom and United States noted that **people have a love-loathe relationship with virtual meetings.** More than half (56%) said they would like to spend less time on video calls. In the same study, participants ranked technology issues, such as slow Internet connections and trouble accessing a meeting along with the communication frustration of people talking over one another, as their top videoconference frustrations (Mendoza, 2020). **Groups that are 100% virtual may have more difficulty remaining effective than virtual groups that mix in at least some face-to-face contact** (Trees, 2017).

With these limitations in mind, it is no surprise that **one of the biggest challenges that leaders of virtual meetings encounter is keeping participants engaged and connected.** Virtual meetings follow several of the same guidelines established for successful face-to-face meetings. For the best participation and meeting outcome, however, some important challenges need to be addressed.

Facilitating a Virtual Meeting: New Challenges

To avoid surprising anyone, the meeting invitation should specify that cameras are expected to be on if this is not already obvious (i.e., Zoom meeting). When cameras are required, people are more engaged. They cannot hide or multitask without others noticing (I have heard of people who work from home and do all of their housecleaning while muted on audio-only conference calls), and expressions are easier to read (Edinger, 2018). Attach an agenda to the meeting invitation if the meeting is formal.

Make certain each group member is well versed in the technology used to conduct the meeting. Remind members that sensitive microphones may pick up whispers between members during videoconferences. This could cause embarrassment or create crosstalk that interferes with the fidelity of message transmission. Virtual meetings, at first, may seem stilted and difficult to manage, but with practice the technology can almost seem to disappear. Nevertheless, **check all technological equipment before each meeting to be sure that everything is in top working order.** Technological glitches can disrupt the flow of a meeting, even destroy it. "Easy to use" and "usually works great" were the two top requirements when respondents were asked about virtual group meeting technology (Courville, 2017). Have someone available at short notice, if feasible, who can correct technological problems during a virtual meeting.

Conclusions from Forbes Insights, the strategic research practice of *Forbes* media, in a July 2017 global survey of executives supports the **preference of videoconferences to audioconferences.** From the more than 300 executives surveyed, 62% agreed that when compared to teleconferences, videoconferences significantly improve the quality of communication, while 50% said that video-conferencing improves comprehension (Forbes Insights Team, 2017).

As the facilitator, you are in charge of moving the meeting toward stated objectives. **Consider rotating helpful roles** such as timekeeper, whose sole job is to remind others of time constraints, and notetaker, who captures meeting highlights and commitments, summarizing them quickly at the meeting's close (Tsao, 2017). Bestselling author and business consultant Keith Ferrazzi suggests recruiting several volunteers to act as "Yodas" in each meeting. Wise peacekeepers, the Yodas keep a pulse of what's not being said, call out difficult to discuss topics, and help others follow agreed-upon ground rules (Ferrazzi, 2017). Further discussion of group roles applicable to both in-person and virtual groups are addressed extensively in Chapter 6.

Finally, **call on people directly** to increase participant involvement. In the spirit of transparency and fair warning, let attendees know early on that you'll be calling on people directly to solicit their input and collaboration. (Axtell, 2015).

Girts Ragelis/Shutterstock

Nonverbal communication challenges escalate in two-dimensional meetings as we struggle to interpret meaning beyond words. Gestures can appear forced or awkward, even hidden from view if the camera angle becomes just a headshot. When everyone but the speaker is muted to screen out barking dogs, rustling papers, and other background noise, applause that might normally erupt naturally during in-person meetings cannot be heard. Some virtual groups have taken to doing a jazz hands version of silent applause. It is a different world we occupy online.

Virtual Meeting Participation: A Few Unique Considerations

Several considerations will influence the impression that you make and the impact you have when attending virtual meetings. Log on to the website or set up your call early—at least five minutes before the meeting begins. Forget about sneaking in unnoticed. Once you've successfully logged on to the meeting, test your camera, your Internet connection, and volume. Next, make sure you know how to mute yourself. Though the mute button slows the flow of communication, it is imperative for people in busy, noisy environments that would distract from the meeting (Ferrazzi, 2014). While you might not even notice your barking dog or the blaring background music of the coffee shop you are in, your fellow meeting attendees surely will. "Look around" the virtual room. Just as we familiarize ourselves with a physical meeting room, choosing the best seat and noting the exit, for example, we can do something similar in the virtual meeting room: Locate the chat and exit buttons so you can access them with ease.

When preparing for a videoconference, dress as you would dress in the office or classroom to convey respect, unless the meeting is casual by design (study groups preparing for an exam would likely appear odd if everyone or even some members dressed formally). Check out your background, too. Stacks of dirty dishes or piles of papers send messages you might not want to convey. Even bookshelves can be distracting as viewers try to read book titles in the background and discern interests and even political viewpoints.

Videoconferencing can be a challenge. Preparation and following "A Participant's Guide to Successful Video Conferences" provided in Table 3.2 are critical. As international consultant Erica Dhawan (2021) notes, "Digital meetings demand more preparation than in-person meetings."

Review Table 3.2 for a comprehensive list of tips for getting the most out of virtual meetings.

In conclusion, though many people would like to eliminate the preponderance of meetings, they are still a prominent vehicle of communication in small groups. When leading a meeting, especially if it is a formal one, it's imperative to consider the meeting process carefully, from beginning to end. Before the meeting, identify the meeting purpose, carefully craft the guest list, and create a worthy agenda. During the meeting, keep participants engaged and keep the meeting on track. After the meeting, tend to unanswered questions and action items. As a meeting participant, aim to arrive at the meeting early and prepared, and monitor your contributions—find the delicate balance between too little or too much communication. Whether virtual or face to face, implementing these guidelines will help immunize yourself and others from the delirium of meeting madness.

TABLE 3.2 A Participant's Guide to Successful Video Conferences

Before the meeting	
Make some time: Check the meeting platform, the invite, and your Internet connection	**Try a test run.** If using the meeting platform for the first time, Microsoft Teams, Zoom, Google Hangouts, and WebEx all have test links you can try before your meeting.
	Download any required meeting software. If joining the meeting by cellphone, **check to be sure you have a strong signal**. If joining by computer, use a wired connection over Wi-Fi, and check your camera, speakers, and microphone.
	When working from home, **be aware of any Wi-Fi dead zones** before your meeting begins. Move your router to a central location and in an unobstructed but hidden area.
	Wipe off those fingerprints: **Make sure your camera lens is clean.**
	Sign into the meeting a few minutes early to make sure the meeting invite is valid. Contact the meeting organizer if you cannot join through the provided link.
	Once in the virtual meeting room, look around.
	Find your communication options and know how to use them: Locate chat, mute, screen share, and video icons so you can participate without hesitation once the meeting begins.
	Keep the meeting password handy, especially if you need to log in again anytime during the meeting. Things happen.
	Pro-tip: If you have back-to-back virtual meetings and a less-than-stable connection, **restart your computer** or, at the very least, log out of and back into the meeting application between meetings.
	Close all unneeded applications as well. **Improve connection** even more by reducing movement: Keep your computer in the same spot (don't move it around during the call) and turn off the ceiling fan, TV, or any other source of movement in your visual background in order to improve video streaming.

Get ready for your close-up: Appearance, camera, and lighting

Position your webcam at eye level or a bit higher, but no higher than your hairline. Sit far enough away from your camera so that your shoulders are showing.

Don't be a webcam zombie: washed out and weary. **Ensure that you are clearly visible and illuminated.** Appearance matters as much as, if not even more than, in a face-to-face meeting.

Sit facing your light source. Lighting from above or below casts unflattering shadows. Natural lighting is great. Three-point lighting—creating dimension and eliminating shadows by using a key light, fill light, and backlight—is even better. Face your key light, the main light source. Place a fill light on either side, at about face level, and use a backlight to separate yourself from your background.

If you wear glasses, beware the glare. Let others see your eyes by paying closer attention to the angle, height, and distance of your light source. A large, soft light, above eye level and off to the left or right can greatly decrease glare.

Dress appropriately, as you would if you were meeting in an office or classroom, unless your meeting is extremely casual by design.

Look behind you: Backgrounds

Everything speaks: Keep your background clean and free of anything that will give meeting participants' eyes reason to roam. Let the focus be on you, not the piles of paper (or dishes!) behind you. Even decorations such as family photos can be a visual distraction.

Clear the clutter, but don't make your background so sterile that you're one screenshot away from a mugshot. If you must choose between sterility or clutter, pick the former. If using a virtual background, test it before the meeting to make sure your system supports it. Choose a virtual background that contrasts with your hair, skin, and clothing. Be sure your background doesn't compete for your attention (visual noise), particularly when uploading your own background image.

Get ready to roll!

Keep a pen and paper nearby for notes.

Grab a beverage (but consider that the container will be seen on the call—not a good time for your "I hate meetings" mug or any alcoholic beverage in a formal meeting).

When working from home, put pets away and hang a "Do not disturb" Post-it on your door.

During the Meeting

Monitor your nonverbals

Your goal is to appear attentive, yet natural. Keep these in check:

Posture: Sit up straight or stand up tall. Whether sitting or standing, limit unnecessary movement.

Eye contact: When talking, look into your camera often, not just the images on the screen. This makes it appear as if you are looking your audience members in the eye. When listening, look at the people on the screen so you can capture their nonverbal messages.

Vocal qualities: Use your indoor voice. Keep volume loud enough for all to hear but avoid shouting.

Facial expressions: *Show* others you are listening. Follow along with the conversation and reflect your reactions accordingly. You can show you're paying attention by nodding in agreement, smiling for encouragement, or raising your brow in surprise. Whatever the case, be authentic.

Gestures: Make them purposeful and relevant. As with a public presentation, know what your hands are doing.

Eliminate the desire to multitask	**Commit to the meeting.** Though tempting, this is not the time to get up and use the bathroom, scroll your Amazon cart, or tidy up around you while others are watching. Remember: Your audience can see you!
Participate	**Mute and unmute with ease.** Since you logged in early, you already know where the mute button is—now is the time to use it! For meetings with many participants, commit to the sequence: Mute when you're not talking, unmute when you have something to say, mute yourself when finished speaking, repeat. To paraphrase a tweet: "Not muting is the new reply all." Finally, anticipate when to unmute yourself. Sitting in virtual meetings in which participants fumble around trying to unmute themselves while everyone waits for their comments can be annoying if it occurs repeatedly. Talking while muted can also be tedious as the facilitator and/or other members remark, "You're muted; we can't hear you."
	Narrate yourself. To avoid looking like you're not paying attention, let meeting participants know what you're doing when you are looking away for prolonged periods of time or silence. For example, say, "I am looking up the details of that right now . . ." or "Let me pull up the latest version of that report." You can also let the meeting host know why you need to go off camera or leave the meeting by sending them a private chat.
	Get comfortable with silence. Whether it be from lagging Internet or fumbling for the unmute button, expect delays from others who ask and answer questions. "Even a delay of five-tenths of a second is more than double what we're used to during in-person conversations" (Yorke, 2020).
	Know how to interrupt. The rules of interrupting vary with meeting size. Smaller group meetings of, say, three to five familiar attendees can more easily mimic the cadence of a normal conversation, with people exchanging ideas quickly, though at times clumsily. As the participant list grows, however, so does the complexity and formality of interrupting. If prescribed, follow the leader's protocol on participation by using the hand-raise symbol or raising your real hand for all to see when you have something to say. (Likewise, understand that simply because you are raising your hand on camera doesn't mean it's being seen by all—it depends on how others are viewing the meeting.) You can also type questions in the chat (if this feature is used) or save comments to the end of a meeting. To ensure comprehension and etiquette, use transitions liberally. Say some iteration of, "Before we move to the next agenda item, I have something to add." And if your contribution isn't on the agenda or would derail the timing of the meeting, indicate such by saying something like, "I just thought of something that could support that. Can I say it now or should I wait until the end of (or after) the meeting?" Be patient. Be polite.
After the meeting	
Exit with ease	In most video calls there are those few people who don't know how to exit the meeting and stare awkwardly at the screen, mumbling apologies, while trying to figure it out. Remember all that meeting orientation prework you did? It pays off when you can smoothly say goodbye and exit the meeting with the press of a button at a meeting's end.

Source: Michelle Waters

QUESTIONS FOR CRITICAL THINKERS

1. Is there ever a time when an agenda might actually interfere with the smooth, effective functioning of a group meeting?

2. Would you ever use an agenda during a group study session for an exam?

3. Can you have too many procedural and ground rules for effective group meetings?

4. Clearly, you can have too many meetings, but can you ever have too few? If so, what determines this?

TED TALKS AND YOUTUBE VIDEOS

"**Authenticity in Meetings**"

"**Every Meeting Ever**"

"**9 Brilliant Virtual Meeting Tips in Under 9 Minutes**" | **Will Wise and Chad Littlefield**

VIDEO CASE STUDIES

The Hobbit: An Unexpected Journey (2012). *Adventure/Fantasy; PG-13*

Examine the ability to shift the mood and participation of a chaotic meeting in the first portion of this film.

Moneyball (2011). *Biography/Drama; PG-13*

Oakland A's general manager Billy Beane is depicted attempting to assemble a winning baseball team. Analyze his meetings with scouts and assistants.

Group Development

4

On April 24, 1997, the board of directors for Delta Air Lines announced the unanimous decision not to renew the contract of Delta's chairman, Ronald Allen. He was forced out because, as one board member put it, there was "an accumulation of abrasions over time" (Brannigan, 1997, p. A8). So, what were these "abrasions" that led the board to replace him? Allen had a caustic management style that concentrated on the financial "bottom line" at the expense of relationships with workers. He developed a reputation for berating employees in front of other workers. He was known as autocratic, intolerant, and harsh (Brannigan, 1997). Employees were extremely upset with his cost-cutting measures and the heavy-handed way in which they were done. Allen acknowledged that workers were upset, but his glib response was "So be it." Soon, buttons reading "So Be It" began appearing on the chests of pilots, flight attendants, and mechanics. Worker morale plunged. An exodus of senior managers began. Many experienced workers were laid off or quit. Delta service, once the envy of the industry, rapidly deteriorated. Dirty planes and frustrated flight attendants became the norm. On-time flights sank from the top to the bottom of the industry. Passengers began joking that Delta stood for "**D**oesn't **E**ver **L**eave **T**he **A**irport." Tough measures were necessary to save Delta financially when Allen took over, but, as Wayne Horvitz, a Washington, D.C., labor relations consultant notes, "You don't have to be an SOB to be tough" (Brannigan, 1997, p. A1). Under Allen's direction, "What the airline embarked on was nothing less than a suicidal mission" ("PlaneBusiness Ron Allen," 2008).

Delta filed for bankruptcy protection and reorganization in 2005. Richard Anderson became CEO of Delta. "After the bankruptcy, Delta spent millions to rebuild morale, flying in many of its 47,000 employees for a series of events that were equal parts team-building and tent revival. Delta also convinced creditors to cede 15% ownership to employees" (Foust, 2009). Anderson established the practice of flying in a Delta cockpit jump seat once a month to garner suggestions for improving the company from pilots and crew teams, and he spent a two-day stretch soliciting suggestions from 2,000 employees. Delta posted its first profit

objectives

The primary purpose of this chapter is to explore the interconnectedness of task and social dimensions through phases of group development. There are two related chapter objectives:

1. To explain the connection between task and social dimensions of a group.

2. To discuss task and social dimensions within the periodic phases of group development.

since bankruptcy, $500 million, in 2007. The company made an aggregate profit of $3.2 billion between 2010 and 2013 with Anderson at the helm, surviving the "Great Recession" that hit hard in 2008 (Caulderwood, 2013). In 2015, $1.5 billion was disseminated to employees under its profit-sharing plan. Delta returned as an industry leader in on-time performance. In 2014, Anderson was named one of the World's Best CEOs by *Barron's* magazine. Delta was named Airline of the Year by *Air Transport World* magazine in the same year. Anderson retired in 2016 (Mouawad, 2016).

This case study provides a long view that spans initial calamity to eventual resurrection, and highlights the strong connection between the task and social dimensions of groups. Put simply, how group members are treated and the quality of their relationships within a group can markedly affect task accomplishment (Tran et al., 2018). Try getting your housemates to keep your joint apartment clean and tidy (task) when relationships among housemates are strained. Relational friction can produce inane squabbles about division of labor and result in juvenile boycotts by housemates of work entirely while the apartment becomes a health hazard. As groups move through phases of development, as discussed in this chapter, the relationship between task and social dimensions of every group can become a critical factor in achieving success or experiencing failure.

Primary Dimensions of Groups

The Ronald Allen/Richard Anderson case study illustrates diametrically opposite effects when the importance of social relations to group performance and effectiveness receive either indifference or optimal focus. In this section, the systemic interconnection between the two primary dimensions of groups, task and social, is explored.

focus questions

1. How do the task and social dimensions of groups interconnect?
2. How are the task and social dimensions integral to both the formation and development of decision-making groups?
3. How does a group build cohesiveness?

Task and Social Dimensions: Working and Relating

All decision-making groups have both task and social dimensions. The **task dimension** is the work performed by the group. The **social dimension** encompasses the relationships that form between members in the group and their impact on the group as a whole. Because groups are systems, the task and social dimensions are interconnected and affect each other.

The output from a group's task dimension is **productivity**—the result of the efficient and effective accomplishment of a group task. The output from the social dimension is **cohesiveness**—the degree to which members feel a part of the group, wish to stay in the group, and are committed to each other and to the group's work. Cohesiveness is produced primarily by attention to social relationships.

TASK DIMENSION	→	**Productivity**
SOCIAL DIMENSION	→	**Cohesiveness**

Neither the task nor the social dimension can be ignored for a decision-making group to be successful. Finding the optimum balance between productivity and cohesiveness is an important goal for all groups (Wise, 2014). Too much attention to productivity can diminish cohesiveness by producing stress and conflict. Ronald Allen's single-minded focus on the task of returning Delta Air Lines to profitability disrupted the interpersonal harmony within the company. This disruption ultimately led to poor service, diminished worker morale, loss of valuable employees, and a negative image within the industry and among passengers. Conversely, too much emphasis on cohesiveness can produce a group of socializers ("It's party time!") who like each other a great deal but accomplish nothing in particular (Eys & Kim, 2017). This is a problem unless, of course, the purpose of the group is merely to have a good time and no task needs to be accomplished, in which case, knock yourself out.

Chaay_Tee/Shutterstock

The task dimension (productive achievement of a goal) and the social dimension (cohesiveness) influence each other in groups. Ignore either and you won't be doing high fives (or medium fives in this case) celebrating group success.

In general, cohesiveness enhances group productivity, unless it is overemphasized (Evans & Dion, 2012). The reverse is also true, namely, that high productivity can enhance group cohesiveness while low productivity typically lowers cohesiveness (Braun et al., 2020). The more interconnected group members must be to accomplish a task (e.g., flying a passenger jet, performing surgery, playing team basketball) the stronger is the cohesiveness–productivity relationship (Gully et al., 2012).

Building Cohesiveness: Bringing Us Together

Because cohesiveness can improve group productivity, enhancing it is worthwhile. So, how do groups build cohesiveness? There are several main strategies ("Group Cohesiveness," 2017).

Encourage Compatible Membership When group members enjoy each other's company and share an attraction for one another, cohesiveness can be easily built (Muceldili & Erdil, 2015). When difficult, disruptive individuals join the group, cohesiveness can suffer. Of course, a group doesn't always have the luxury of choosing who can join. Sometimes, membership is mandated by the system within which the small group operates (e.g., an institution or corporation).

Develop Shared Goals One aspect of cohesiveness is sharing a common vision. When all group members are pulling together to achieve a common goal valued by all, cohesiveness is likely to increase. When goals are unclear, both cohesiveness and productivity can suffer. One study found that only 40% of employees thought they were well informed about their company's goals, strategies, and tactics. This lack of a clear mission produced chronic stress and damaged workers' ability to interact cohesively as a team (Zak, 2017).

Accomplish Tasks Productive groups usually become more cohesive from task accomplishment and less cohesive when productivity lags (Anwar, 2016). If group members feel good about work accomplished, this often pulls the group together and promotes team spirit. This is true unless some members suspect that they are doing the lion's share of the work and others are slackers. As a rule, successful teams exhibit harmony. Unsuccessful teams, however, frequently manifest frustration and disappointment by sniping, sniveling, and pointing the finger of blame. Poor productivity can lead to group disintegration, as losing sports teams can often attest.

Develop a Positive History of Cooperation If group members work together cooperatively rather than competitively, cohesiveness can flourish (Anwar, 2016). Groups and workplace environments that encourage individual competition instead of cooperation, however, typically diminish motivation of members to share skills and information to enhance productivity (Morrison-Smith & Ruiz, 2020). Constructing cooperation in small groups is a complicated process, discussed extensively in the next chapter.

Increase Proximity It may be surprising to you at first, but physical proximity increases the likelihood of group cohesion (Coyle, 2018). Research shows that distance makes a big difference. It boils down to the old adage "Out of sight, out of mind." In fact, as MIT professor Thomas Allen puts it, "If you're on a different floor in some organization, you may as well be in a different country" (quoted by Coyle, 2018). What Allen calls "clusters of high communication" are essential to the development of group cohesiveness, and these clusters occur when members are within eye-contact distance. Increase the distance to 50 meters and communication just stops, and so does cohesiveness. Decrease the distance to 6 meters and communication explodes and a sense of belonging increases. It's called the **Allen Curve**. In one study, workers who shared a proximate location emailed each other four times as often as workers who were distant from each other. They completed their projects 32% faster as a result (Coyle, 2018).

Nurture Virtual Group Social Relations Virtual groups pose unique challenges in regard to the development of group cohesiveness. Proximity, as just discussed, is an important cohesiveness builder, but how do you identify with team members who aren't merely 50 meters away or on a different floor but perhaps in a different time zone or a continent away? How do you nurture cohesiveness when you have never met group members personally or ever seen them in some cases (i.e., audioconferences)? Some virtual groups, however, attempt to address these difficulties by directing participants to Facebook or LinkedIn personal sites for profiles of group members. Those who have not created such a profile are encouraged to develop one. Connecting with members by social media can also speed up the "getting to know you" phase of virtual group development (Yang et al., 2018). Texting photos of family gatherings, amusing animated GIFs—yes, even cat (and dog) videos—and the like can create a sense of familiarity and identity. The key point here, however, is to avoid images that might make virtual group members uncomfortable or offended. Also, don't inundate group members with a flood of images. This shouldn't be an opportunity to show your family photo album.

 Virtual groups seem to require more time than face-to-face groups to develop positive social relationships and cohesiveness (Johnson et al., 2009). Trust, a key element of group cohesiveness, is especially difficult to build virtually. "Swift trust in virtual teams is particularly fragile due to the unexpected disruptions and differences across time, distance, organization, and culture in virtual teams. Teams that interact virtually are considerably less likely to develop trust" (Morrison-Smith & Ruiz, 2020). One study found that developing trust matters more in virtual groups than in face-to-face groups (Breuer et al., 2016).

The difficulty virtuality poses in building trust can be overcome. **Research found that use of social media was rated as significant for communicating with team members to enhance trust** (Gupta, 2015). Regular and timely feedback and sharing information freely is critical to building trust and cohesiveness among virtual group members (Ebrahim et al., 2009). Competence (demonstrating expertise and skills), integrity (keeping promises, respecting deadlines, and complying with team norms), and benevolence (demonstrating commitment by effort) are other key ways to bolster virtual group trust and ultimately cohesiveness among members (Sciacovelli, 2017).

So, developing cohesiveness as just detailed can be accomplished, even in virtual groups. That is an important step in building productive small groups, but just where the task and social dimensions operate within the lifespan of a group can be ascertained by exploring the periodic phases of group development.

Periodic Phases of Group Development

Tuckman (1965) describes the four phases of group development as forming, storming, norming, and performing (see also Bonebright, 2010; Wheelan et al., 2003). **Groups do not, however, necessarily pass through these phases of development sequentially,** like a person does when growing older (i.e., youth, middle age, old age). Groups tend to be far messier than this, sometimes cycling back around to a previous phase that was seemingly completed. (Unhappily, such cycling back is not possible with aging.)

Admittedly, group development can be classified in terms of an initial phase where individuals join for some reason (forming), a tension phase (storming), a standards and rules of conduct for members phase (norming), and a phase where effort is targeted toward goal achievement (performing). **These phases can be periodic, meaning that they are apt to appear, disappear, reappear, and even overlap** (Chang et al., 2006). Complicating this process are new realities of group membership fluidity and simultaneous multiple group memberships. Group membership is simply less stable and more complicated than in previous eras before "job hopping," virtual groups, and online learning became widespread (Benishek & Lazzara, 2019).

Forming, storming, norming, and performing are also *global phases* of group development relevant to groups in general, large or small. **Specific phases of decision emergence in small groups, such as the multiple sequence model's three phases, are discussed in Chapter 10.**

focus questions

1. Does why we join a group make any difference to the group?
2. How does group composition affect group efficacy?
3. Is tension in a group always undesirable?
4. Where do group norms come from? Why do we conform to group norms?
5. Under what conditions do groups outperform individuals?

Forming: Gathering Members

A group begins with its own formation. In this section, two issues are addressed: (1) why we join groups, and (2) how diverse membership affects groups.

Reasons We Join Groups: Motivation   The reasons we join groups act as catalysts for group formation. There are six main reasons we join groups:

1. *Need to Belong: No One's an Island.* Humans are communal beings. We have a powerful need to belong, one that is as much an imperative as the need for food (Aronson & Aronson, 2018). Our brains "are wired to be social" (Lieberman, 2013). Such wiring has survival value for humans. Forming social bonds with group members can provide protection from outside threats to one's person and possessions and ward off loneliness. As one study of group dynamics during the Covid-19 crisis notes, "The need to belong as well as the importance of reducing loneliness during uncertain times often encourages people to connect, despite recommendations to remain socially distant" (Marmarosh et al., 2020). In addition, we find mates by joining groups (e.g., Parents Without Partners), and we satisfy our desire for affection from family and groups of friends.

2. *Interpersonal Attraction: The Drawing Power of Others.* We join a group because we seem drawn to others who are similar in personality, attitudes and beliefs, ethnic origin, gender orientation, and economic status (Youyou et al., 2017). Many campus clubs and support groups are attractive because of member similarity. Physical attractiveness may also draw us to join a group. We may have no other reason to join a group than that we'd like to get to know an attractive group member.

3. *Attraction to Group Activities: Joining for Fun and Frolic.* Sometimes we join groups to participate in the group's activities. This is a primary motivation for joining most college athletic teams, fraternities, and sororities.

4. *Attraction to Group Goals: A Purpose-Driven Membership.* We join most volunteer groups (e.g., Habitat for Humanity, Food Not Bombs) because we are attracted to the groups' goals. Political groups gain members because individuals are drawn to the cause or the candidate. When you join a group for a worthy cause, however, you don't have the luxury of interacting only with members that you'd enjoy inviting to dinner. You adapt to the various personalities and quirks of fellow members because the task supersedes the social dimension.

5. *Establishment of Meaning and Identity: Groups-R-Us.* **Social identity theory** explains that groups provide us with a meaningful identity (Hogg, 2018). We feel socially connected to cultural, ethnic, political, gender, and other groups (Croucher et al., 2015). You may join a choir, a marching band, or an athletic team because it gives you an identity that enhances your pride and self-esteem. As this social identity increases, individuals see their membership as personally significant and their group attachment as strong. Even members of antisocial groups, such as gangs, find meaning and identity from their membership (Hennigan & Spanovic, 2012).

6. *Fulfillment of Unrelated Needs: Our Miscellaneous Reasons.* Finally, we join groups to satisfy needs that are unrelated to the group's task, goals, members, or even our desire to belong. We may become group members to enhance our résumé or establish business contacts. Sometimes we join a group because other members familiar to us have joined, removing some of the uncertainty associated with group formation. Occasionally, we are told by persons in authority to join a group. You may be summoned for jury duty. It is wise to comply. The instructor of your class may put you into a group of people who interest you very little. If you are pragmatic, you will make the best of a less than satisfactory situation because your grade may depend on it.

The reasons individuals join groups have noticeable effects on the productivity and cohesiveness of those groups (Wax et al., 2017). If they join because they are attracted to the other members, the likelihood of cohesiveness in the group is certainly more probable than if they join to meet self-oriented needs. If they join because they are attracted to the group's goals, productivity is likely to be enhanced. If they join groups for personal gain only, they'll likely end up as deadweight and drag down the entire group.

Member Diversity: The Benefits and Challenges of Difference   By 2044, minorities composed largely of Hispanic/Latino[1] Americans, African Americans, and Asian Americans are projected to constitute the majority of the U.S.

---

[1]The term *Latinx* is preferred by only 3% of this group in a recent Pew poll (Noe-Bustamante et al., 2020). A majority (61%) prefer the term *Hispanic* and another 29% prefer the term *Latino*.

Rawpixel.com/Shutterstock

We join groups for many reasons. What might be the reasons depicted in this photo?

population (Poston & Saenz, 2019). In addition, with the advent of virtual groups whose members may vary widely in age, ethnicity, and culture, the likelihood that you will join groups whose membership mirrors yourself is becoming ever more remote. This offers opportunities and challenges.

Groups usually benefit significantly from diverse membership (Eswaran, 2019). "Decades of research by organizational scientists, psychologists, sociologists, economists and demographers show that socially diverse groups (that is, those with a diversity of race, ethnicity, gender and sexual orientation) are more innovative than homogeneous groups" (Phillips, 2014). Diverse groups are more likely to have members with **deep diversity**—varied skills, perspectives, backgrounds, information, and experiences (briefly discussed in Chapter 2).

This deep diversity can provide a wider array of problem-solving and decision-making resources than are likely to be found in homogeneous (nondiverse membership) groups. For example, research shows that, overall, gender diversity enhances team performance (Kelemen et al., 2020). One study found that both ethnic and cultural diversity improved "profitability and value creation" for businesses (Hunt et al., 2018). Groups whose membership includes a rich mixture of Asian, African, Hispanic/Latino, and Anglo Americans have superior performance to groups that include only Anglos (Phillips, 2014). Professor Samuel

R. Sommers (2006) of Tufts University summarizes his findings in one study of 200 participants on 29 racially diverse mock juries: "Such diverse juries deliberated longer, raised more facts about the case, and conducted broader and more wide-ranging deliberations." More important, "they also made fewer factual errors in discussing evidence and when errors did occur, those errors were more likely to be corrected during the discussion." Even generational diversity can benefit groups. College professors appreciate having older students in classes. They provide a rich mixture of life experience and historical perspective that younger group members do not have. As 70-year-old undergraduate at UC Berkeley, Delores Orr, notes, she has a repository of historical knowledge learned firsthand. "They [younger students] call me the living archive. I love it!" (quoted in DeRuy, 2018).

Diversity in group membership, however, poses significant challenges (Fernandes & Polzer, 2015). Diversity may result in increased difficulty achieving agreement because of strong cultural value differences (Hong & Cheon, 2017). Cohesiveness and group satisfaction may also be more challenging to develop and maintain. A competition for power and resources between majority and minority

oneinchpunch/Shutterstock

Despite significant benefits, diverse composition of groups can pose serious challenges. For example, five generations work together in the world of business for the first time in history. Although older workers often have a wealth of experience, a variety of differences in work-life balance, flexibility, technological proficiency, and values arise among diverse generations. Michelle Raymond, founder of the People's Partner consultancy, also notes, "The disparity arises when young, often highly ambitious people are accelerated into senior positions and then are supervising and leading older workers. This can cause resentment and hostility" (quoted in "Managing Age Diversity," 2020).

members may emerge and result in hostile communication and discrimination. With group diversity comes the potential for conflict and misunderstanding (Phillips, 2014).

Finally, **diversity in age can be challenging**. A study by Pew Research Center reported the largest generational differences in the United States in decades ("Generation Gap," 2018). Those 65 years and older differ significantly from those 18 to 29 on issues of politics, religion, social relationships, use of technology, and other topics. Generalizations based on generation gaps should be embraced cautiously, but generational differences do pose significant challenges for groups. Older members in college groups composed mostly of teens and 20-somethings may have a tough time identifying with younger members, and vice versa (DeRuy, 2018). Older members may feel isolated and become nonparticipants, or they may "take charge" as in a parental role without the willing acceptance of younger members. Individuals fresh out of college who join the business and professional world may find it intimidating working with more mature, experienced team members. Issues associated with following rules, respect for authority, and attention to task and details may trigger clashes. Even choices associated with a "digital divide" regarding preferences for communication technologies in virtual teams pose generational challenges (Ferrara et al., 2016). **Despite these challenges, diverse membership in groups is generally a positive influence.**

There is no magic, however, from merely adding traditionally excluded members when forming groups. **An atmosphere of inclusion, of openness and acceptance, must be established to reap the benefits of diversity** (Adesina, 2017). Sexism, sexual harassment, and stereotyping continue to plague mixed-sex groups ("Sexual Harassment," 2019). Adding a single ethnic minority, woman, or person of a markedly different age or gender identification to a group can easily appear to be **tokenism**—giving the appearance of diversity inclusion without exhibiting such in actual practice (Sherrer, 2018).

Potential negative side effects of group diversity can be addressed by recognizing that initially team members will need some time to address any friction that emerges because of broad category differences (race, age, etc.). Also, these category differences, instead of being highlighted (e.g., "People of my generation believe . . ."), can be minimized during group discussion and problem solving, making conflict less likely (Homan et al., 2010).

In conclusion, **the competent communicator can show sensitivity to the needs of the group during the forming phase in the following ways** (Mannix & Neale, 2005):

1. *Encourage a "getting-to-know-you" conversation.* A common, productive strategy when a group meets for the first time is to eschew immediately addressing the agenda and instead having all members introduce

themselves one at a time, even encouraging simple opening conversation. Small group research found that this simple initial communication process created a collaborative environment in which women more easily emerged as group leaders (Lindzon, 2016).

2. *Find areas of commonality and cooperation.* Problems mostly arise when group members concentrate on differences, not similarities, among members. Try finding commonalities in values and perspectives and explore ways to cooperate.

3. *Avoid aberrant behavior.* This phase is the getting-acquainted stage of group development. Avoid oddball behavior (e.g., displaying embarrassing lapses in social etiquette, making abrasive remarks or provocative statements, wearing outrageous dress). Don't put your foot in your mouth. Put your best foot forward.

4. *Establish clear group goals.* Groups function better when clear goals are established early in the formation phase (Crown, 2007).

Storming: Feeling the Tension

All groups experience some social tension because change in any system can be an ordeal. Tension can be a positive force. Athletes perform best when they find the proper balance between complete relaxation and crippling anxiety. Excessive tension, however, can produce damaging conflict that may split the group apart. The relative absence of tension in a group can result in lethargy, haphazard attention to the task, and weak productivity. Finding both the level of tension that galvanizes the group and effectively managing group tension are important factors in successful group development.

There are two types of social tension: primary and secondary (Bormann, 1990). All long-term groups experience both types.

Primary Tension: Initial Uneasiness When you first gather in a group, you normally feel some jitters and uneasiness, called **primary tension**. When you initially meet roommates, classmates, or teammates, primary tension occurs. Even groups that have a lengthy history can experience primary tension at the outset of every meeting. This is especially true if groups such as the PTA, homeowners associations, or student senate meet infrequently. Also, when contact with a virtual group is infrequent, primary tension can emerge.

There are many signs of primary tension. Group members may become cautious and hesitant in their communication. Long periods of uncomfortable silence and tentative statements are all indicators of primary tension. Group members are often overly polite and careful to avoid controversy. Interruptions normally invoke immediate apologies.

Primary tension is a natural dynamic of group life. In most instances, it tends to be short-lived and cause for little concern. With time, you become comfortable with the group and your primary tension diminishes. Joking, laughing, and chatting about your interests, experiences, and beliefs on noncontroversial subjects all serve to reduce primary tension. You're not trying to "support gay marriage," "promote conservative causes," or "raise an alarm about climate change." An introduction such as "Hi! My name is Malcolm; what's your position on abortion?" would likely induce one to flee. Controversial subjects can increase tension among members. Your purpose is to become acquainted with other group members, not change their worldview. As you get to know each other better, there is less perceived threat and, consequently, less primary tension.

If a group is too anxious to get down to business and forgoes the small talk, primary tension is likely to create an atmosphere of formality, stiffness, and insecurity. Communication will be stilted and hesitant. The ability of the group to work on a task will be hindered by excessive and persistent primary tension.

Engaging in small talk to relieve primary tension has cultural variations. In the United States, we tend to view small talk as wasting time, especially if our primary focus is on a task (e.g., starting a meeting), not social interaction. Many Asian (e.g., Japanese, Chinese, and Korean), Middle Eastern (e.g., Saudi Arabian), and Latin American (e.g., Mexican, Brazilian, Chilean) cultures view small talk as a necessary ritual engaged in for several hours or several meetings, during which the group's task may not even be mentioned. Ethiopians view tasks that require a great deal of time to complete as important (Samovar et al., 2021).

Secondary Tension: Later Stress and Strain The stress and strain that occur within the group later in its development is called **secondary tension**. Having to make decisions produces secondary tension. Disagreements and conflicts—*storming*—inevitably emerge when group members struggle to define their status and roles in the group. Tight deadlines for task completion can induce tension. Intense time pressure also can produce poor small group performance on tasks (Bowman & Wittenbaum, 2012). Whatever the causes, you should expect some secondary tension in a long-term group. Low levels of secondary tension may mean that the group is highly harmonious. It may also mean that group members are unmotivated, apathetic, and bored.

Signs of secondary tension include a sharp outburst, emotional exhibitions, a sarcastic barb, hostile and antagonistic exchanges between members, or shouting matches. Extreme secondary tension is unpleasant for the group. If it is left uncontrolled, the group's existence may be threatened.

Secondary tension has become an issue in jury deliberations (Weingart & Todorova, 2010). Court officers have broken up fistfights, jurors have flung chairs through windows, and some jurors have screamed so loudly that they could be

Photo by United Artists/Getty Images

The classic jury movie *12 Angry Men* graphically depicts both primary tension and especially secondary tension. The influence on the group's decision-making ability is palpable. Tension in groups can be smooth sailing for some groups but white-water rafting for others.

heard on other floors of the courthouse (Marzulli, 2014). Jurors have been caught wandering away from the jury room, and in one case a juror tried to escape the deliberations permanently by leaping off the jury bus. Courts all around the United States have begun providing booklets to jurors detailing how to deliberate while remaining courteous and even-tempered.

The goal is not to eliminate secondary tension in groups. Most decision-making groups experience secondary tension. Within tolerable limits, it can be a positive force. Tension can energize a group, challenge the members to think creatively, and bring the group together. Trying to avoid or to camouflage secondary tension merely tricks us into believing that the group is functioning well. Beneath the surface, the group may be disintegrating or the decisions coming from the group may be ill conceived, even disastrous.

There is no mathematical formula for determining an ideal degree of secondary tension. Some groups can tolerate a great deal of disagreement and conflict. Other groups are more vulnerable to disintegration because members are more thin-skinned or insecure and view even minor disagreements as personal repudiations and character assassination. Generally, a group's inability to accomplish tasks and to maintain a satisfying social climate is a rule of thumb for determining excessive tension in a group. In the 2016 so-called Bridgegate trial, which concerned a lane closure on the George Washington Bridge used as political payback by members of New Jersey Governor Chris Christi's administration, jurors on the second day of deliberations experienced intense secondary tension. Tears and emotional arguments erupted. Deliberations became so heated that the judge elected to send the jury home at 2 PM. As one juror reported, the early break gave fellow jurors time to reflect. "Once we could put the emotional stuff behind us, things started to come together" (Berger, 2016). Sometimes you just need a break to find balance.

There are four steps that you can take to find that balance:

1. *Tolerate, even encourage, disagreement.* Suppressing differences of opinion will likely increase tension and exacerbate conflict. Focus disagreements on the task, not social relationships (unless, of course, the conflict is social in nature). Resist the temptation to drift into irrelevant side issues, especially contentious ones.

2. *Keep a civil tongue.* Disagree without being disagreeable. You want to foster a cooperative, not a competitive, atmosphere for discussion. You can express opinions with conviction and exuberance without raging against those who do not agree with you.

3. *Be an active listener.* Clarify significant points that are confusing. Resist the temptation to interrupt. Make an honest effort to understand the point of view that is in opposition to your own.

4. *Use humor* (Romero & Pescosolido, 2008). In a study of the 414-page transcript of a real death penalty trial, 51 instances of laughter, not all involving humor (some revealed embarrassment), were identified. Tension release was the most common reason for the laughter (Keyton & Beck, 2010). Humor, of course, can increase tension if it is used as a weapon to put down other group members. Self-deprecating humor works well to avoid the negative uses of humor. In the death penalty trial, one juror misstated another juror's position on sentencing, stating "30 days" as the preferred penalty instead of "30 years." Laughter ensued, but you could imagine self-deprecating humor here lightening the tension of a serious discussion: "Sorry, 30 years. I stand corrected. Wow, 30 days for a homicide. That's almost as serious as a stack of unpaid parking tickets. How could anyone think I'm soft on crime!"

There are numerous sources of conflict within a group that raise the level of tension. Reasons for stormy transactions in groups and strategies for effectively managing them are discussed in greater detail in Chapters 11 and 12. For now, recognize that conflict and tension are a normal part of the group experience.

Norming: Regulating the Group

In groups, rules that establish standards of appropriate behavior are called **norms**. In this section, types of norms, their development, and conformity and nonconformity to norms are discussed.

Types of Norms: Explicit and Implicit There are two types of norms: explicit and implicit. **Explicit norms** are rules that expressly identify acceptable and unacceptable behavior. Such rules are codified in constitutions and bylaws of student senates, fraternities and sororities, campus clubs, and the like. All laws in our society act as explicit norms. The Motley Fool, a stock advising company, has a corporate dress code that is certainly on the casual side, but the stated norm is to "not wear anything that would embarrass your parents" (O'Malley, 2019). Most norms in small groups, however, are not so obvious. **Implicit norms** are rules that are indirectly indicated by patterns of behavior and uniformities of members' attitudes. Examples might include the following: All members dress neatly, humor is never sarcastic or offensive, and no one gossips about other group members. These norms are learned by how others react. Violate an implicit norm, and reactions from group members will undoubtedly set you straight. Make fun of your boss, for example, in a business meeting expecting good-natured laughter, but seeing terrified facial expressions from participants instead, sends a message that you simply do not tease your boss. That is an unwritten rule determined from likely hard-earned experience.

Is providing comfort to a group member who is experiencing an emotional moment an implicit norm, explicit norm, or no norm at all? Explain.

topperspix/Shutterstock

A college seminar to discuss advanced academic research and debate controversial ideas illustrates the difference between explicit and implicit norms. If participating in a seminar qualifies as a new experience for you, group norms could be determined in several ways. Usually, the professor teaching the seminar will provide a syllabus that delineates explicit norms, such as "avoid absences," "all assignments must be turned in on time," and "turn off all cellphones during class." The implicit rules for the seminar class might be such things as "don't interrupt the professor," "sit in chairs at the table," "be polite when disagreeing with classmates," and "don't hide the professor's notes, even in jest" (it happens). You can ascertain these norms by observing the behavior of classmates and your professor.

Degree of Conformity: Strength of Group Pressure Solomon Asch (1955) found that when a group composed of confederates of the experimenter unanimously judged the length of a line incorrectly, participants unaware of the setup chose the obviously erroneous group judgment 35% of the time. Most of these same participants (75%) conformed to the group error at least once during the study. Social psychologist Anthony Pratkanis of the University of California, Santa Cruz, replicated this study for *Dateline NBC* in August 1997. In his study, 9 of 16 college students studied fell in line with the unanimous choice made by six other group members, even though the choice was clearly incorrect. **Conformity** is the adherence to group norms by group members, in this case "following the crowd" by choosing the wrong answer. Group pressure can change behavior, but research shows that it can also alter attitudes, either strengthening or changing them with long-term effects (Levitan & Verhulst, 2016).

Conformity can have serious negative consequences. Consider binge drinking by college students. The National Institute on Alcohol Abuse and Alcoholism defines binge drinking as "4 drinks for women and 5 drinks for men—in about 2 hours" with a standard drink amounting to a 12-ounce beer, 5 ounces of wine, or 1.5 ounces of distilled spirits with 40% alcohol content. Based on this definition, about one out of three college students ages 18–22 engaged in binge drinking in the month before the survey ("College Drinking," 2020). One study reported that 14% of college students consumed 10 or more drinks in a row at least once in the two weeks prior to the survey and 5% consumed 15 or more drinks in a row ("Binge Drinking Statistics," 2013). Binge drinking is especially pervasive among students living in fraternities and sororities (Juergens & Hampton, 2020). Among students ages 18–24, an estimated 1,800 or more college students die each year from heavy drinking, about 600,000 are injured, about 700,000 college students are physically assaulted by an intoxicated student, and almost 100,000 college students are sexually assaulted or raped because of binge drinking ("College Drinking," 2020). Excessive consumption of alcohol among college students is encouraged by group norms, especially among socially desirable small groups ("Drinking and Drug Abuse in Greek Life," 2018; Fitzpatrick et al., 2015).

Image Source/iStockphoto

Group pressure is a key cause of binge drinking among college students. Despite the seemingly cheerful peer pressure, the consequences of binge drinking can be catastrophic.

Conforming to group norms, even when risky behavior is encouraged, increases the likelihood of acceptance by the group (Sleek, 2016).

Conformity, however, isn't always a negative experience (Sleek, 2016). Without some conformity, a society would disintegrate into anarchy. Conformity creates a sense of belonging, helps groups accomplish important goals, and can be a positive force. Groups could not exist without some conformity. Group discussion would be tumultuous if there were no rules governing such interactions (e.g., taking turns speaking).

Group pressure to conform can be applied for prosocial reasons. At Shaker Heights High School in Ohio, the Minority Achievement Committee (MAC), a small group of high-achieving African American male students, is working to establish the norm that being smart and doing well in school is cool, not "acting white." Students must earn at least a 2.8 GPA to gain membership into the MAC program. Weekly MAC meetings begin with a firm handshake and the MAC credo, "I am an African American and I pledge to uphold the name and image of the African-American man. I will do so by striving for academic excellence, conducting myself with dignity, and respecting others as if they were my brothers and sisters." The MAC program success has been expanded and widely emulated by schools across the United States (Kuhel, 2020).

Why We Conform: Fitting In So why do we conform to norms, especially in a society as individualistic as the United States? We conform for two principal reasons (Aronson et al., 2016). First, we want to be *liked*. Conformity brings social acceptance, support, companionship, and recognition. We must "go along to get along." Our natural desire to belong and to be liked makes conformity attractive. Individual goals, such as making friends or increasing social activities, can be satisfied by conforming to group norms.

Second, we conform to norms because we want to be *right*. Acting incorrectly can be embarrassing and humiliating. Group norms identify correct behavior. In this case, we may not want to be liked by group members as much as we want to avoid social disapproval. We seek emotional support not group ridicule and rejection (Yu & Sun, 2013).

Conditions for Conformity: When We Bow to Group Pressure There is greater conformity to group norms when certain conditions exist (Burn, 2019). First, the stronger the cohesiveness in the group and the social identity with the group, the greater the conformity to group norms (Eys & Kim, 2017). If there is minimal attraction to the group and nebulous desire to be a member, then there is scant reason to adhere to the rules of behavior. A group has little leverage against apathetic or scornful members. Conversely, individuals who are strongly attracted to the group and wish to remain members in good standing are much more likely to conform and bow to peer pressure. Second, conformity is greater when individuals expect to be group members for a long time. After all, you must live with this group. Why make your life unpleasant by not conforming? Third, conformity is greater when individuals perceive that they have somewhat lower status in the group than other members or that the group does not completely accept them. Higher status members have earned the right to dissent, but lower status members must still earn that right to occasional nonconformity. Lower status members also feel a greater need to prove themselves to the group, to show fealty.

Addressing Nonconformity: When Groups Get Tough Because behavior in groups is governed by rules, a violation of a norm can be quite unsettling for group members. Nonconformity disturbs the system. Groups usually do not appreciate such violations, called **nonconformity**, except within limited boundaries.

There are four communication strategies groups typically use to command conformity from nonconforming members (Leavitt, 1964; Lipman-Blumen & Leavitt, 1999). These strategies tend to follow a sequential order, although there may be some variation. First, group members attempt to **reason** with the deviant. The quantity of talk aimed at the nonconformist initially increases substantially.

Although often awkward for Americans, the Japanese cultural norms regarding bowing as a greeting between businesspeople are important. When greeting a person of superior status, the rule is that you bow lower and longer and your eyes should be respectfully cast downward (Axtell, 1998). Nonconformity in such instances would communicate disrespect.

Rawpixel.com/Shutterstock

Groups show an intense interest in convincing nonconforming members of their folly. Second, a group will often try **seduction**. Telling the nonconformist that his or her efforts are fruitless is one form of the seduction strategy. "You won't get anywhere anyway, so why cause such turmoil?" is the seduction strategy at work. Offers of promotions, perquisites, and monetary incentives to tempt conformity are other examples. The third line of defense against nonconformists is **coercion**. Groups attempt to force conformity by using nasty and unpleasant tactics. Members may harass or intimidate nonconformists. Threats of group expulsion or actual ouster are other examples (Levin, 2010). The final strategy of group pressure to induce conformity is **isolation**. Often referred to as *ostracism*, this strategy ignores or excludes a member by giving the silent treatment or isolating the member from social interaction with the group. It is a kind of social death that produces significant psychological pain (Yaakobi, 2017). When an opportunity arises to get back into the good graces of the group, ostracized members will often seize that opportunity by conforming to group norms (Williams, 2007).

Studies show that even **cyberostracism**, a remote form of ostracizing virtual group members, can be quite potent (Abrams et al., 2010; Smith et al., 2017). Acts of cyberostracism occur when a group of online team members deliberately ignores a member who violates the group's norms (e.g., for incorrect use of technology, using profanity, flaming). Even when the ostracism isn't clearly deliberate (e.g., using English when a member speaks primarily Spanish or vice versa), the negative effects occur (Dotan-Eliaz et al., 2009; Hitlan et al., 2006).

Considering the power of group norms to pressure conformity and the disruption caused by nonconformity, responding appropriately and effectively to the norming periodic phase of group development is important. Here are three suggestions:

1. *Adapt communication to the norms of the group.* Communication becomes inappropriate when violation of norms could be averted by more prudent action. Don't violate norms without a strong justification.

2. *Encourage change when norms are excessively rigid.* Some norms can be suffocatingly rigid—too closed to permit adaptation to change in the system (e.g., cults). Norm rigidity fosters nonconformity and disruption. Violating the norm is one avenue of change if rational argument proves unsuccessful, but expect backlash from the group. Leaving the group is certainly an option. Failure to loosen norms from within may require intervention from without, such as court suits and protests.

SECOND LOOK
The Norming Process

Types of Norms

Explicit—Preferences and prohibitions specifically stated in some form

Implicit—Preferences and prohibitions determined from observation

Degree of Conformity

Negative consequences

Positive consequences

Why Group Members Conform to Norms

Desire to be liked

Desire to be right

Conditions for Conformity to Norms

The stronger the cohesiveness, the greater the conformity

Greater conformity when individuals expect to be group members for a long time

Greater conformity when individuals perceive they have lower status in groups

Typical Group Responses to Nonconformity

Reason

Seduction

Coercion

Isolation/Ostracism

3. *Encourage change when norms are too elastic.* Excessive openness in a system can be counterproductive. Apply the same guidelines for changing overly rigid norms.

Performing: Group Output

If I had a dollar for every time I have been told that a camel is a horse designed by a committee, I'd be downing dark beers on a white sand beach, enjoying a blissful life of leisure. Winston Churchill, always armed with his sardonic wit, fired this salvo: "A committee is the organized result of a group of the incompetent who have been appointed by the uninformed to accomplish the unnecessary." Then there is this anonymous offering: "Trying to solve a problem through group discussion is like trying to clear up a traffic jam by honking your horn."

In terms of performance, groups as decision-making units need better public relations. Too many people are inclined to believe that groups are assembled to stymie progress and to serve as roadblocks to decision making, not to produce better alternatives. Previous discussion of group synergy and conducting group meetings effectively bely such cynical views. Nevertheless, groups do not always perform better than individuals. This section compares group to individual decision making and performance.

Motivation to Perform: Social Loafing and Social Compensation Why are some group members strongly motivated to work hard on a task, but other members are not? The **collective effort model** (**CEM**) suggests that group members are strongly motivated to perform well in a group if they are convinced that their individual effort will likely help in attaining valued results (Hoffman, 2020). If members view the task as unimportant or meaningless (mere busy work) or if a member's effort is expected to have little effect on the group outcome even when the outcome is highly valued (a person of low ability working with high-ability members), then social loafing will likely occur.

Social loafing is the tendency of a group member to exert less effort on a task when working in a group than when working individually (Synnott, 2016). Social loafing is more than lackluster participation during group meetings, already explored in Chapter 3. It also is exhibited by failing to start or complete individual tasks requested by the group or exerting minimal effort to perform as a trustworthy and effective group member. Please note here that reluctance to participate during group discussions because of shyness does not constitute social loafing. Loafers put out little effort because of poor motivation, disinterest, or a bad attitude.

Not surprisingly, social loafing can significantly diminish group performance, especially in virtual groups (Robert, 2020). Confronting a loafer is problematic in text-only virtual group formats. If the loafer refuses to read the messages, deletes them, or does not respond when confronted, group members

The Ringelmann effect is named after a French agricultural engineer who did an experiment in which individuals pulled on a rope attached to a pressure gauge. He found that as the number of individuals pulling on the rope increased, the further they dropped below their collective potential. For example, eight individuals pulling together reached only half of their individual sum total (Hoffman, 2020). This became known as social loafing. Additional research found that social loafing tends to be a bigger problem in individualist cultures than in collectivist cultures (Early, 1989). These Thai children, for instance, learn early to pull for the group and avoid social loafing.

have few options. Members can try working around the loafer by ignoring lackluster participation, but this merely increases the workload of more motivated members. Online classes that require team projects are especially subject to this problem. **Preventing social loafing at the outset, discussed next, is the most effective option available to virtual groups, as it is for in-person groups as well.**

There are several ways to address the annoying, even infuriating, problem of social loafing (Forsyth, 2019; Robert, 2020; Synnott, 2016). The first few steps may be all that are necessary in some instances, but a complete list is offered just in case loafers are intransigent.

1. *Choose meaningful tasks.* Groups can't always choose their tasks, and sometimes they are given dull tasks to perform by those with higher authority. If required to choose a project from a list of several options, choose the option most interesting to the entire group, not the option interesting to only one or two relatively dominant members. Meaningful tasks can motivate most even all group members whether the groups are in-person or virtual.

2. *Establish a group responsibility norm.* Emphasize individual responsibility to the team and the importance of every member contributing a fair share to the

videoTD/Shutterstock.com

Social loafing is typically not a group problem when the task is meaningful and each member's effort is perceived to be critical to success. Read *The Boys in the Boat* by Daniel James Brown (2013), the epic story of the University of Washington rowing team that stunned the world by rising from obscurity to win the 1936 Olympic gold medal with Adolf Hitler watching his highly touted German team just barely lose. It's a terrific and very relevant book. Social loafing was never a problem for the Washington crew. Quite the opposite, because they pursued an exceedingly meaningful goal and each member of the crew was committed to giving maximum, often extraordinary effort.

successful completion of a task. Fairness and responsibility are important ethical concerns. Virtual group members immediately reveal that they embrace responsibility as a norm by how responsive they are when group tasks begin.

3. *Note the critical importance of each member's effort.* Impress upon all members that their individual effort is essential to the group's success. When members believe that their contribution is indispensable to group success, they often exert greater effort.

4. *Enhance group cohesiveness.* Members of weakly cohesive groups are more prone to social loafing than members of highly cohesive groups. Highly cohesive groups, however, with a *mediocrity norm* that sets low expectations for performance, could produce an entire group of social loafers. (See the steps for enhancing cohesiveness discussed earlier in this chapter.)

5. *Hold members accountable.* **Behavioral-output control theory** posits that social loafing, especially in virtual groups, can be addressed effectively by comparing group members' performance with predetermined behavioral expectations and holding members accountable to meeting those expectations. Control strategies include directing expected behavior (i.e. defining and assigning specific tasks), monitoring members' progress (i.e., communicating

with members to check progress and offering assistance), and assessing members' behavior. Either the leader of the group, a designated member, or the group should approach the loafer either in-person if possible or via a Zoom meeting, and ask why the lethargic attitude exists. Encourage stronger participation, reaffirm the importance of the loafer's contribution to the team effort, and solicit suggestions regarding how the group might help the person become a contributor. Do not name-call or personally attack the loafer.

6. *Consult a higher power* (not to be confused with divine intervention, although that would be impressive). If the previous steps fail, consult a supervisor, teacher, or someone with greater authority than the group members and ask for advice. The authority may need to intervene.

7. *Boot out the loafer.* This is a last resort. Do not begin with this step, as many groups prefer to do. You may not have this option available, however.

8. *Sidestep the loafer.* If expulsion isn't an option, reconfigure individual responsibilities and tasks so even if the loafer contributes nothing to the group effort, the group can still maneuver around the loafer and produce a high-quality result.

Some group members don't attempt to change the loafer's behavior. They engage in **social compensation**—an increased motivation to work harder on a group

---

SELF-ASSESSMENT

Social Loafing

Make honest assessments of your participation in small group decision making and problem solving by using the scale 1 (*rarely*) to 5 (*almost always*). Mark the appropriate degree of frequency (1, 2, 3, 4, or 5) in the blank for each situation.

1. _____ I am on time for small group meetings.

2. _____ I leave small group meetings early.

3. _____ I am quiet during small group discussions.

4. _____ My attention during small group discussions is focused on the task.

5. _____ I am strongly motivated to perform well in small groups.

6. _____ When other group members show little interest in accomplishing a task successfully, I lose interest in achieving success.

7. _____ When other group members seem uninvolved in participating on the group task, I also reduce my participation.

Your scores on statements 1, 4, and 5 should be high (4–5), and your scores on statements 2, 3, 6, and 7 ideally should be quite low (1–2)—little social loafing.

task to counterbalance the anemic performance of others (Hoffman, 2020). Social compensation is especially likely when a high-ability group member senses that his or her maximum effort is required for the group to be successful on a meaningful task. Compensation is less likely when the group is largely composed of high-ability members who are disengaged. Few wish to play the sucker and cover for the very capable but unwilling sluggards in a group (Hoigaard & Ommundsen, 2007).

When Groups Outperform Individuals: Three Heads Are Better than One Despite the common complaint about social loafing, groups often outperform individuals (Hsieh et al., 2020). Groups usually outperform individuals when certain conditions exist.

First, when the task requires a wide range and variety of information and skills, groups tend to be superior to any individual (Xie et al., 2018). It does this by *pooling knowledge*. Humorist Will Rogers once said, "Everybody is ignorant, just on different subjects." A key to successful group performance is putting together a team composed of members with *deep diversity* who can share non-overlapping knowledge.

Second, groups generally outperform individuals when both the group and any individual compared are without expertise on the task (Laughlin et al., 2006). Here, *synergy* is at work. There is a Japanese proverb that says, "None of us is as smart as all of us."

Third, groups will usually outperform an individual when both the group and the individual have expertise (Wolf et al., 2015). *Diversity of knowledge* and *error correction* both contribute to the superiority of groups. The ability of a group to divide labor, to *share the load*, will normally result in a better decision than any overburdened expert individual could manage. Shaffner (1999) provides the arithmetic logic for sharing the load. If one person had all the knowledge and skills to single-handedly build a Boeing 777, it would take about *250 years* to deliver one plane. The logic of working in groups is indisputable when the task is large and complex.

A group of experts is especially effective when members are highly motivated and trained to work as a team. A group of experts is not an expert team without appropriate training in teamwork (Reyes & Salas, 2019). *Teamwork* allows a group to coordinate efforts and to work at optimum effectiveness.

Fourth, even when comparing a group of reasonably bright and informed nonexperts to an individual with special expertise, group decisions are sometimes superior. One of the reasons for this superiority is that when groups are functioning effectively, members perform an *error correction* function for the group. Assumptions are challenged, and alternatives are offered that an individual might overlook. In addition, the collective energy and chemistry of the group may produce a *synergistic result*.

When Individuals Outperform Groups: No Group Magic Although groups frequently outperform individuals, this is not always the case. There are five conditions supported by research in which individuals outperform groups.

First, groups composed of uninformed laypersons will not usually outperform someone with special expertise, such as a doctor or lawyer, on issues of medicine and law, despite the "Google University Effect" in which Internet searches and YouTube videos, usually from obscure self-proclaimed "experts" spreading misinformation, may substitute for real expert advice. There is certainly no advantage to be gained from *pooling ignorance* from lack of knowledge or simply being misinformed. This can result in *negative synergy*.

Second, individuals outperform groups when groups establish a norm of mediocrity. Some groups are composed of members who are satisfied with relatively low productivity. If a norm of mediocrity prevails in a group, performance will be sluggish, or worse (Grenny, 2017). Even individual members who may wish to perform at a higher level will become discouraged because of *insufficient motivation* to excel. Since the group rewards middling performance, why bother trying harder than the rest?

Third, when groups become too large, individuals outperform groups. Again, the rule of thumb is to select the smallest group capable of performing the task effectively. Quality performance is usually enhanced in smaller or moderately sized groups of seven to eight members (Kao & Couzin, 2014). Much larger

SECOND LOOK

Group versus Individual Performance

Group Superior to Individual

Conditions	Reason(s)
Broad-range task	Pooling knowledge, deep diversity
Neither have expertise	Synergy
Experts	Sharing the load, teamwork, diversity, error correction
Individual expert, informed group	Error correction, synergy

Individual Superior to Group

Conditions	Reason(s)
Individual expert, uninformed group	Pooling ignorance, negative synergy
Groups establish mediocrity norms	Insufficient motivation to excel
Group becomes too large	Difficulty coordinating, social loafing
Simple task	Minimal resources required
Time is a critical factor	Groups are too slow

than this and *problems of coordination and efficiency* increase. *Social loafing* also becomes a bigger problem in large groups where one can hide in the crowd (Chidambaram & Tung, 2005). Loafers can hide their anemic effort more easily in large groups.

Fourth, when the task is a simple one, groups are not superior to individuals. There is no special advantage in having a group work on a remedial task. *Minimal resources* are required. If any individual can likely do the task, why involve a group?

Finally, when time is a critical factor, groups usually perform less effectively than individuals. In emergency situations or in circumstances where speed and efficiency are paramount, individuals can often perform better than groups, especially large groups. The reason is simple. *Groups tend to be abominably slow*, and larger groups usually take longer to make decisions than smaller groups. There are exceptions, such as disaster teams and emergency surgical teams trained to perform under pressure and time constraints. Most groups, though, are not trained to operate swiftly and efficiently under pressure.

SECOND LOOK

Competent Communication and Group Development

Forming Periodic Phase

Express positive attitudes and feelings

Appear friendly, open, and interested

Encourage a "getting-to-know-you" conversation

Find areas of commonality and cooperation

Establish clear group goals

Storming Periodic Phase

Tolerate, even encourage, disagreement and deviance

Keep a civil tongue

Be an active listener

Use humor, especially self-deprecation

Norming Periodic Phase

Adapt communication to the norms of the group

Encourage change when norms are excessively rigid

Encourage change when norms are too elastic

Performing Periodic Phase

Focus on the task

Encourage participation from group members (in most instances)

In conclusion, the performance phase of group development is a complex process. I have merely laid the groundwork for more detailed discussion of group performance in later chapters. Nevertheless, some general advice can be offered.

1. *Focus on the task.* Because task and social dimensions of groups are interconnected, focusing on the task to the detriment of social relationships among members obviously makes little sense. Nevertheless, when there is work to be done, the primary focus is on the accomplishment of the task. Cohesiveness can be built when the pressure to perform has lessened. Task accomplishment also increases cohesiveness.

2. *Encourage participation from group members.* The group needs to utilize its resources fully, which means that even social loafers may have much to contribute. As noted in Chapter 3 on participating during meetings, however, encouraging member participation should not be a blanket rule. Some group members should not be encouraged to participate because they disrupt the group's decision-making process.

In summary, all groups have a task dimension and a social dimension. The output of the task dimension is productivity. The output of the social dimension is cohesiveness. Productivity can affect cohesiveness and vice versa. Group development encompasses four periodic phases: forming, storming, norming, and performing. These periodic phases do not occur in rigid sequence. They frequently overlap, and groups may jump around between phases depending on the circumstances and situations groups face. Some groups never progress beyond the forming and initial storming phases. These are groups that dissolve because they do not work.

QUESTIONS FOR CRITICAL THINKERS

1. When is it appropriate to be a nonconformist in a small group?
2. Are there ever times when the task is so important that concern for the social dimension of the group must be ignored?

TED TALKS AND YOUTUBE VIDEOS

"Dangerous Conformity"

"Conformity: Are We Afraid to Stand Out?" | **Mina Whorms**

"Resisting Conformity: Juggling Expectations & Cultural Foundations" | Maya Cheaib

"My Identity Is a Superpower, Not an Obstacle" | America Ferrera

VIDEO CASE STUDIES

Easy A (2010). *Comedy; PG-13*

Hilarious take on high school in the land of Twitter, texting, and YouTube. Emma Stone, in a stunningly sharp depiction, plays a high schooler who begins to "act out" the *Scarlet Letter*, the famous novel that is assigned in her favorite class. Her lies about having sex get her noticed and then eventually ostracized. Analyze the stages of reactions to her nonconformity and how she addresses the group's reactions.

Hacksaw Ridge (2016). *Drama, Biography; R*

This is the story of Desmond T. Doss, World War II American Army medic, who refused to kill enemy soldiers at the Battle of Okinawa but received the Medal of Honor for heroic life-saving action under fire. This film is essentially about nonconformity. Analyze the consequences of his nonconformity. Which of the typical communication strategies used to command conformity—reason, seduction, coercion, and isolation—are employed?

Lord of the Flies (1963). *Drama; NR*

There is a 1990 remake of William Golding's grim allegory of schoolboys stranded on a deserted island, but it is a pale, lifeless effort compared to the splendid original film. Analyze in detail all four phases of group development.

Lord of the Rings: *The Fellowship of the Ring (2001). Drama; PG-13*

Movies don't get much better than this fantasy epic. Analyze this first-rate thriller in terms of the four *global phases* of group development (forming, storming, norming, and performing). This film is rich with applications to group development.

The Croods (2013). *Animated comedy; PG*

Animated story of early cave-dwelling family abruptly forced to journey through an unfamiliar fantasy world with the help of an inventive boy. Hilarious group dynamic that offers plentiful examples of conformity and nonconformity to norms. Also, examine cohesiveness of the group, group diversity, and task and social dimensions of the family.

Developing the Group Climate

5

IDEO is Silicon Valley's most influential design firm (Budds, 2016). Begun in Palo Alto, California, in 1991, the company's 700 designers in nine cities around the world work on hundreds of projects each year. From an early concentration on individual products (e.g., AT&T answering machines, virtual reality headgear, the animatronic whale in the movie *Free Willy*), IDEO has expanded to providing design expertise for some of the largest and most respected companies and institutions in the world. More recently, IDEO has embarked on trying to solve intractable social and political issues, such as gun violence, preparing New Yorkers for inevitable floods and streamlining access to resources once such disasters hit the city, and designing citizen-centered websites and social learning environments. IDEO has won more design awards than any competing design firm ("About IDEO," 2021).

What IDEO has accomplished, however, is not nearly as impressive as how the firm has accomplished it. David Kelley, the founder and driving force behind IDEO, is a unique corporate executive. Kelley wanted three things when he established IDEO in 1991: to work with friends, to have no bosses in charge of employees' lives, and to eliminate jerks from the workplace (O'Brien, 1995).

The company is designed to encourage "creative disruption." Clarke Sheffy, speaking as managing director at IDEO/San Francisco explains, "I believe in intentionally creating moments—spaces, walls to draw on, the piano, culture-building events—to [help employees] bring their whole selves to the workplace" (quoted in Lamb, 2015). IDEO encourages "culture-building events" such as personal storytelling group sessions by the staff. IDEO teams go to baseball games and movies, and they take field trips to recharge team members' creative energy. Teams engage in poetry slams and "IDEO-centric parties." The atmosphere is laid-back and fun-loving. At IDEO, developing and maintaining a positive group climate of fun, excitement, and support that is free of negative infighting is essential ("About IDEO," 2021).

A positive group climate, such as that created at IDEO, is imperative to group and team success. For example, a large LinkedIn study of full-time professional workers found that 70% would avoid working even at a leading company if they had to endure a negative workplace environment. These same employees would also

objectives

The purpose of this chapter is to identify and explain what communication patterns encourage both positive and negative group climates. There are four related chapter objectives:

1. To distinguish positivity from negativity in the development of group climate.

2. To explore competition and cooperation as underlying forces for group climate development.

3. To discuss communication patterns that create positive and negative group climates.

4. To address difficulties often experienced by virtual group members regarding the establishment and maintenance of a positive communication climate.

choose to accept lower pay and forgo a fancy title instead of tolerating a bad workplace climate (McQueen, 2018). At work, at school, at home, or wherever small groups gather, just about everyone prefers a positive, constructive communication climate instead of a Lord of the Flies environment.

Positive versus Negative Climates

A **group climate** is the emotional atmosphere, the enveloping tone that is created by the way we communicate in groups. A communication climate permeates all groups and affects every aspect of a group's social and task dimensions. A **positive climate** exists when individuals perceive that they are valued, supported, trusted, and treated well by the group. A **negative climate** exists when group members do not feel valued, supported, trusted, and respected. Abundant incivility, for example, can turn off individuals' desire to expose themselves to persistent negative communication from others, resulting in a backlash avoidance reaction (Muddiman et al., 2020). This section explores the significance of diminishing negative communication in small groups and establishing and maintaining a positive group climate.

focus questions

1. How does the negativity bias impact small group climate?
2. Why is negative information more impactful than positive as a general rule?

Negativity Bias: Short-Circuiting a Positive Climate

If someone described a potential group member to you as "outgoing, intelligent, fun-loving, and deceitful," what would be your impression of this person? Would the single negative quality cause you to pause despite the three very positive qualities? Conversely, if someone described another potential group member to you as "abrasive, unethical, domineering, and smart," would the one positive quality even make a dent in the negative initial impression created by the first three qualities? This perceptual process is called the **negativity bias**—our strong tendency to be influenced more heavily by negative than positive information (Jaworski, 2021). One negative quality can neutralize a bunch of positive qualities, but one positive quality is unlikely to override several negative qualities. This negativity bias is built into the human brain (Moore, 2019). As comedian Stephen Colbert once observed, "Mother Nature is on your side, keeping fear alive." Your amygdala, "the alarm bell of your brain," uses about two-thirds of its neurons to search for bad news. Why? Because recognizing negative information promotes human survival. Identifying risks quickly can save lives. Your brain "is like Velcro for negative experiences but Teflon for positive ones" (Hanson, 2016). Even though most negative information ("deceitful") isn't usually an immediate threat to a person's survival, your brain doesn't make that nuanced assessment. Hesitation when faced with a real threat could prove fatal. It's best to be constantly on guard.

The negativity bias can be particularly strong during job interviews (Tierney & Baumeister, 2020). In fact, negative information, especially if it is received early in the interview, is likely to lead to a candidate's rejection by a hiring committee selecting finalists even when the total quantity of information about the candidate is overwhelmingly positive. In a hypercompetitive job market where differences in quality between candidates can be hard to discern, one poorly chosen phrase or inappropriate remark during an interview can negate a dozen very positive letters of recommendation.

aiyoshi597/Shutterstock

Most people won't sit on a rock watching crashing waves because their brains alert them to potential danger (being swept into the sea). This is the negativity bias at work. The negativity bias is built into your brain as a survival mechanism, as an alarm to warn against potential disaster, even though at times it may go unheeded. Nevertheless, the bias is difficult to overcome in groups where risk is minimal or no threat to personal well-being exists, but your brain wants to insist that you be ever vigilant.

Sometimes the negative information, of course, should outweigh the positive. Movie mogul Harvey Weinstein was instrumental in advancing the careers of many actors and producing numerous highly regarded and successful films for several decades, and he gave millions of dollars to social causes, but he was a predatory lecher who sexually preyed on young women in the industry. Here, the one clearly outweighs the many.

Positive Emphasis: The "Magic Ratio"

Presenting an abundance of positive information that contradicts a single bad act can overcome negativity bias, unless the bad act is egregious (Tierney & Baumeister, 2020). In an analysis of almost 300 scientific studies that incorporated more than 275,000 subjects, the power of positivity was strongly supported (Lybormirsky et al., 2005). What this research showed was that frequent positive communication both verbally ("We're making progress"; "I hadn't thought of that") and nonverbally (giving a card on a group member's birthday; sharing lunch with coworkers) can create a climate for success manifested by greater satisfaction at work, higher salaries, and greater productivity, among other life-affirming benefits. More specifically, a study conducted by the University of Michigan found that the best-performing teams made about six times as many positive comments ("I agree"; "Terrific idea") as negative ones ("I disagree"; "Don't consider doing that"). The worst performing teams, on average, made three negative comments for every positive one (Ko, 2013). Additionally, research by the Corporate Leadership Council found that employee performance declined 27% when managers focused mostly on workers' weaknesses, but improved by 36% when managers mostly focused on employees' strengths (McQuaid, 2015).

POSITIVE COMMUNICATION	NEGATIVE COMMUNICATION
"Clear, concise writing style"	"Too many grammatical errors"
"Thanks for meeting our deadline"	"Late reports are unacceptable"
"Let's organize an office party to recognize how hard everyone has been working lately"	"Too much socializing at work has reduced productivity"
"This is a great team"	"We're under-achieving as a team"
"Your time off is well deserved"	"We're way behind schedule, so expect to work longer hours until project completion"

Must you be positive all the time to reap these benefits? That would be unrealistic and probably somewhat irritating. Psychologist Barbara Fredrickson (2009) notes, "To experience 100-percent positivity defies and denies the humanness of life" (p. 32). Studying several sets of data, however, she has concluded that there is a clear ratio of positive to negative behavior that leads to important benefits. This "tipping point" occurs when there is at least a **3-to-1** positive-to-negative ratio in how you act toward other group members. An even higher ratio of **5-to-1** for optimum results, sometimes referred to as the "magic ratio," has research support (Benson, 2017). Notice that the ratio is not 5-to-0. Even if your life is a bed of roses, there are thorns that can sometimes prick personal positivity. Working with classmates on a group project may not always be a smooth, harmonious process, but a key to success is to make the more negative moments the exception and the positive communication experiences the rule.

Competition and Cooperation

The evidence supporting the importance of establishing a positive group climate is abundant. When discussing how to build a positive group climate, addressing competition and cooperation cannot be ignored. They both impact group climate enormously but in different ways. In this section, the relationship between increasing competitiveness and negative group climate is explored. Conversely, the relationship between increasing cooperativeness and positive group climate is also addressed.

focus questions
1. In what circumstances might competition be constructive in small groups?
2. Why is cooperation more likely to foster a positive group climate than competition?

Definitions: Conceptual Clarity

Although seemingly straightforward, the terms *competition*, *cooperation*, and *individual achievement* aren't always used in a conceptually clear manner. To avoid any confusion, these three terms are defined, and the term *hypercompetitiveness* is introduced.

Alfie Kohn (1992) defines **competition** as a mutually exclusive goal attainment (MEGA) process. When transactions in groups are competitive, individual success is achieved at the expense of other group members. Competition, by definition, necessitates the failure of the many for the success of the few. When the city of San Francisco solicited applications for 50 new firefighters, more than 10,000 individuals applied. That's 50 winners and more than 9,950 losers. Pick any contest and the disproportionate number of losers compared to winners is usually substantial.

Cooperation is a mutually inclusive goal attainment (MIGA) process. A common goal is achieved by group members working together, not against each other. Cooperation is a process, not an outcome (King et al., 2009). For example, two groups can both negotiate cooperatively by striving to satisfy the goals of all

PHOTOCREO Michal Bednarek/Shutterstock

For conceptual clarity, it is important to understand the difference between competition and individual achievement. Often, individual achievement is likened to "competing with yourself." If you "compete with yourself," however, you will be both the victor and the vanquished—a conceptual absurdity. It is like saying that you arm wrestle with yourself. All competition is an interactive phenomenon necessitating at least one adversary. Here this climber appears to have no adversary but seeks individual achievement. For him, the goal is not a race to the top, but simply reaching the top as a personal accomplishment.

parties, listening respectfully to everyone, offering encouragement to find mutually satisfactory solutions to joint problems, avoiding the temptation to blame others and "win" a debate, and more, but still end up at an impasse because of fundamental disagreements that cannot be easily resolved.

Individual achievement is the attainment of a personal goal without having to defeat another person. Independently accomplishing a goal, such as performing your best dance routines or earning a higher grade on a calculus exam than at any other time are examples.

Finally, **hypercompetitiveness** is the excessive emphasis on defeating others to achieve one's goals. In a study of 198 of the world's top athletes, more than half of the participants said that they would take a drug that would improve their chances of winning every competition for a five-year period. Here's the stunner: These same top athletes would take the performance-enhancing drug even if they knew that it would kill them at the end of the five years ("Superhuman Heroes," 1998). Americans "manifest a staggering cultural obsession with victory" (Aronson & Aronson, 2018). Our education, sports, economic, judicial, and political systems are all based on intense competition.

Constructive Competition: Tempering Hypercompetitiveness

It is hypercompetitiveness, not competitiveness itself, that poses the greatest challenge to establishing a positive group climate of trust, openness, directness, supportiveness, and accomplishment. Hypercompetitiveness can create a toxic group environment (Schur, 2019). Research shows that hypercompetitiveness often results in unethical behavior (Mudrack et al., 2012). It can inhibit sharing knowledge (task-relevant information, ideas, and suggestions) and encourage hoarding of that knowledge for personal gain. Also, it can stifle a team's ability to adapt to changing situations and challenges. Finally, hypercompetitiveness can produce hostility and trigger anxiety, stress, and even depression among group members (Gilbert et al., 2008). All of these effects inevitably diminish group cohesion and productivity (He et al., 2014).

Arguing that all competition is bad, however, and that our goal should be to replace every instance of competition in small groups with cooperation is unrealistic and pointless. There will be numerous times in groups where, despite Herculean efforts to cooperate, competition prevails. In some cases, a cooperative alternative may not exist. How does a hiring committee, for example, transform the competition among hundreds of candidates into a cooperative endeavor when there is only a single position? In such cases, the competent communicator must have the flexibility of skills to adapt to an adversarial, competitive situation, and the hiring committee will have to make the competitive choice concerning which candidate "wins." Also, as discussed in Chapter 12, sometimes a competitive communication style is required to manage a group conflict.

Despite the inevitability of competition in some circumstances, competition does not have to become hypercompetitive. Competition can be constructive. **Constructive competition** occurs when rivalry produces a positive, enjoyable experience, and generates increased efforts to achieve goals without jeopardizing positive interpersonal relationships and personal well-being (Tjosvold et al., 2003, 2006). Establishing a positive, but competitive group climate, however, is no small challenge. What may start as a friendly rivalry among group members can devolve into a nasty conflict if certain conditions are not strictly observed.

There are three conditions that can thwart hypercompetitiveness (Fulop & Orosz, 2015; Sheridan & Williams, 2011).

1. *When winning is deemphasized.* The less group members emphasize winning as the primary goal of competition and instead focus more on having fun and developing skills while competing, the more positive will be the group climate (Tjosvold et al., 2006).
2. *When opponents are equally matched, allowing all participants a reasonable chance to win.* Clearly, competition is often rewarding for those with

skills who have a reasonable shot at winning. The prospect of being a persistent "loser," however, can be demoralizing.

3. *When there are clear, specific rules that ensure fairness.* When there are clear rules enforced without bias, group competition can produce a positive climate.

These three conditions must be viewed as a wholly trinity. Remove one condition and constructive competition erodes. Apply rules unfairly, for example, and watch mildly competitive teams enjoying the experience transform into hypercompetitive, wild-eyed crazies. Also, the less these three conditions for constructive competition are met, the more likely that competition will turn negative. Being "a little bit fair" or a little less intensely competitive might reduce the negative effects, but it won't likely eliminate them.

Cooperative Group Climates: Cultivating Positivity

Competition can produce both positive and negative group climates. Developing a positive group climate, however, is far more likely when cooperation is cultivated. More than 1,200 research studies have been conducted on the relative merits and demerits of competition and cooperation (Johnson & Johnson, 2009, 2015). Reviews of these studies clearly show that cooperation is more likely to produce higher levels of group achievement and performance on a wide variety of tasks (Johnson et al., 2014). Groups that perform at a high level typically enjoy a positive group climate. Groups that perform more poorly often flounder in dissension and blame (Guenter et al., 2016). Also, a review of more than 180 studies concluded that cooperative communication promoted significantly greater liking, support, acceptance of group members, and cohesiveness—all elements of a positive group climate—than did competitive communication (Johnson, 2003). Social relationships thrive in a cooperative environment.

The principal difficulty with competing in groups while maintaining a positive climate is that attempting to achieve excellence and trying to beat others are different goals. A series of studies conducted at a business school at Cambridge University makes the point. Teams composed of members with high IQ scores performed worse on a challenging task than teams whose members had more ordinary IQ scores. (The groups did not compete against each other but were merely compared based on results.) High-IQ members spent a great deal of time in hypercompetitive debate, attempting to outshine each other. They became immersed in a negative group climate of adversarial egocentrism. Moderate-IQ members, however, worked as a team, uninterested in competing for intellectual star status. They enjoyed the challenge and worked cooperatively (Belbin, 1996). Trying to beat other group members can diminish teamwork and divert attention from achieving group excellence.

Communication and Group Climate

Urgent pleas and pious pronouncements ("Let's all just get along") rarely produce cooperation in groups, even if our intentions are noble. Learning cooperative communication skills, however, is critical to the establishment of a positive group climate (Johnson, 2003).

focus questions

1. Why are praise and recognition important to the creation of a positive group climate?
2. When is controlling communication appropriate and when is it inappropriate?
3. What's the difference between a shift response and a support response?

Praise and Recognition: Basic Building Blocks

A key element of establishing a positive, cooperative communication climate is offering recognition and praise, especially in work groups and teams ("The Power of Praise and Recognition," 2014). Praise and recognition are highly desired but often absent (Weisser, 2013). Surveys consistently reveal that scant praise and limited recognition for quality performance produce job dissatisfaction and a desire to leave (Lipman, 2013). A Gallup study of more than 80,000 managers concluded: "Praise and recognition are essential building blocks of a great workplace" (Buckingham & Coffman, 2002b). Even a simple recognition that the facilitator of your Zoom class project team meeting did a "good job" navigating the technological challenges can be meaningful and appreciated.

Understand, however, that praising or offering recognition inauthentically or indiscriminately produces no benefits, and it may poison the group climate. You do not want to be perceived as a phony or a manipulator (e.g., offering praise to gain favor from a more powerful group member). This shouldn't be engaging in a daily checklist: "Positive comment made to my team leader—check!"

Nevertheless, following a few clear steps for praising others and offering recognition can produce meaningful small group benefits. First, praise specific behavior not general personal qualities. "You handled that complaint about Melanie very adroitly by keeping calm and on task" is preferable to "You are a good team member." Vague praise does not identify particular behavior that can be repeated. Second, praise improvement. Do not wait until excellence has necessarily been achieved. Use praise to motivate positive steps toward ultimate excellence. Third, praise and offer recognition occasionally. Abundant praise and recognition for mediocre achievement can diminish the impact. Praise effort that leads to meaningful accomplishments and recognize overtly those accomplishments either by

Reactions to Defensive and Supportive Communication

Project yourself into each situation below and imagine how you would react. Choose a number for each situation that reflects how much you would like or dislike the statements presented.

1. You live with two roommates in an apartment. You forgot to clean your dishes twice this week. One of your roommates says to you, "Do your dishes. I'm tired of cleaning up your mess."
    STRONGLY DISLIKE   STRONGLY LIKE
    5   4   3   2   1

2. You're working with your team on a group project. One member says to the group, "I'm feeling very concerned that we will not finish our project in time. We're about halfway and we only have two days before our presentation. What do the rest of you think?"
    STRONGLY DISLIKE   STRONGLY LIKE
    5   4   3   2   1

3. You are a member of a softball team. Your coach says to you in front of the team, "You blew the game last week. Are you prepared to do better this game?"
    STRONGLY DISLIKE   STRONGLY LIKE
    5   4   3   2   1

4. At work, you tripped and badly bruised your shoulder. Your boss says to you, "I heard that you injured yourself yesterday. Do you need time off? That must really hurt. Can I do anything to make you more comfortable while you work in your office?"
    STRONGLY DISLIKE   STRONGLY LIKE
    5   4   3   2   1

5. Your support group meets once a week to share experiences and solve personal problems. The group facilitator announces to the group, "We haven't got time to hear from [your name]. We have more important things to consider."
    STRONGLY DISLIKE   STRONGLY LIKE
    5   4   3   2   1

6. During a group problem-solving session, one member says to the group, "I have a suggestion that might solve our problem. Perhaps this will move us forward."
    STRONGLY DISLIKE   STRONGLY LIKE
    5   4   3   2   1

7. You are a member of the student senate. During discussion on a controversial campus problem, the senate president says to the group, "We're obviously divided on this issue. Because I'm the president of this body, I'll have to make the final decision."
    STRONGLY DISLIKE   STRONGLY LIKE
    5   4   3   2   1

8. During a dorm council meeting, one member says to the council, "I know we all have strong feelings on this issue, but let's put our heads together and see if we can find a solution everyone can support. Does anyone have ideas they wish to share with the group?"

STRONGLY DISLIKE   STRONGLY LIKE
5   4   3   2   1

9. During a heated group discussion with fellow classmates, one group member says, "I know I'm right and there's no way any of you will convince me that I'm wrong."

STRONGLY DISLIKE   STRONGLY LIKE
5   4   3   2   1

10. Your class project group approaches your teacher and proposes an idea that your teacher initially dislikes. She says to your group, "I can see that you really like this idea, but it doesn't satisfy the requirements of the project. I suggest that you keep brainstorming."

STRONGLY DISLIKE   STRONGLY LIKE
5   4   3   2   1

11. You're a member of a hiring panel. During a break from an interviewing session, one member of the panel takes you aside and says, "Look, I want you to support my candidate. We've been friends a long time. This is important to me. Whadd-aya say? Can I count on you to back me up?"

STRONGLY DISLIKE   STRONGLY LIKE
5   4   3   2   1

12. You've been asked to work on a committee to solve the parking problem on campus. The chair addresses the committee: "It is my hope that this committee can come to a consensus on solutions to this parking problem. I'll conduct our meetings, but I only have one vote, the same as everyone else."

STRONGLY DISLIKE   STRONGLY LIKE
5   4   3   2   1

13. An individual addresses his work team: "I'm sick of you losers constantly pushing your political stupid agenda. You're all pathetic."

STRONGLY DISLIKE   STRONGLY LIKE
5   4   3   2   1

14. "Please, let's all disagree without being disagreeable, OK?"

STRONGLY DISLIKE   STRONGLY LIKE
5   4   3   2   1

Answers 1, 3, 5, 7, 9, 11 and 13 = **defensive communication** (control, evaluation, indifference, superiority, certainty, manipulation, and incivility—in that order); 2, 4, 6, 8, 10, 12 and 14 = **supportive communication** (description, empathy, provisionalism, problem orientatin, assertiveness, equality, and civility—in that order). Find your average score for each set (divide by 7 both the sum of the odd-numbered items and the sum of the even-numbered items). Which do you like best (lower average score)—defensive or supportive communication?

group members or a team as a whole. Finally, **praise and recognition do not have to be a top-down process** coming only from group leaders. Any group member should be prepared to offer deserved praise.

Defensive and Supportive Communication: Shaping Climates

Jack Gibb (1961), in a classic eight-year study of groups, identified specific communication patterns that both increase and lessen **defensiveness**—a reaction to a perceived attack on our self-concept and self-esteem. Typical responses to feeling attacked include *denying* the truth of the attack, *counterattacking* or striking back at those who diminish us, and *withdrawing* from defensive situations (Ellison, 2009). These responses occur because **defensive communication patterns heighten negativity. Conversely, supportive communication patterns, as discussed in this section, heighten positivity.** As each of these communication patterns (with some modification from Gibb's list) is discussed, see if you recognize any of them in your own experience with small groups and teams.

Criticism versus Description A friend of mine was in his townhouse when the 6.9 magnitude Loma Prieta earthquake hit Santa Cruz, California, in October 1989. Objects flew across the rooms, kitchen cabinets emptied onto the counters and floor, and glass shattered throughout his home. When the 15 seconds of rocking and rolling to Mother Nature's syncopation subsided, a momentary quiet ensued. Then, from the back room came the timid, frightened little voice of his five-year-old daughter: "Daddy, it wasn't my fault." We are quick to criticize each other in American society, and we are ready to defend ourselves with **self-justification**—providing excuses that absolve us of blame—even when no evaluation occurs (Tavris & Aronson, 2016).

Sometimes aggressive, hurtful remarks about a group member are excused as merely "constructive criticism." Although criticism is not always avoidable, it can be demoralizing or trigger anger. Describing behaviors instead of alleged character flaws is less likely to ignite defensiveness. Also, remember the 5:1 "magic ratio" of positive to negative communication.

Pixelvario/Shutterstock

Criticism can have very negative effects on group members and ignite counterproductive defensiveness, as more than 40 years of research at the Gottman Institute has shown (Ryan, 2020). Criticism can be traumatic, especially when it is harsh and you feel blindsided, but one study found that even rather mild criticism ("Make your emails less flowery or soft") still packs a punch felt long after the delivery (Grenny, 2019). Criticism immediately puts people on the defensive for two reasons: (1) it requires submission—copping to mistakes, and (2) it devalues a person (Stosny, 2014).

A disturbing study regarding who gets criticized most often in the workplace found an astounding gender difference. Negative personal criticism, such as "Watch your tone," "Stop being so judgmental," and "You come across as abrasive," appeared twice in 83 performance reviews (2.4%) received by men but in 71 of 94 reviews (75.5%) received by women. There was no gender difference, however, in who wrote these performance reviews, men or women (Snyder, 2014).

Despite the negative effects of criticism, a criticism-free group environment is a fairy tale. When individuals are not pulling their weight in groups at work, at school, or socially, performing in ways that may even be dangerous or creating dissension among group members, criticism is warranted and necessary. Criticism, however, does not have to be delivered with a sledgehammer, pounding people into submission. How you deliver the message is critical.

Description is necessary feedback delivered in ways that can minimize defensiveness. Description is composed of the following steps (Stosny, 2014):

1. *Make suggestions as "I-statements."* Here's an example of an I-statement: "I feel good about this report, but I have just a couple of suggestions." This statement avoids pointing the finger of blame and offers to help, not tear down a person (Ryan, 2020). Focus on improvement, not on what's wrong.

   A *You-statement* of negative evaluation, on the other hand, places the focus on someone who is an object of attack. "You haven't helped your class project team finish on time" is a statement that blames. Assigning blame may be necessary eventually if improvements do not materialize, but avoid it when possible. Expect denial when a person is blamed for inadequate results ("No I haven't") or a counterattack ("I've worked a lot harder than the rest of these simpletons"). Any statement that begins with "You didn't . . ." or "You shouldn't . . ." or "You haven't . . ." can seem like an accusation will follow (Shonk, 2020a).

2. *Describe specific behaviors, not perceived character flaws.* "You're lazy" or "You're irresponsible" identifies perceived character flaws. Constructive feedback describes what specific behavioral change is desired. For example, "Let's be on time. Do we need to discuss our starting time for meetings?"

3. *Eliminate editorial comments from descriptive statements.* Some I-statements are undisguised personal assaults. "I feel uncomfortable when you act like an idiot" uses the I-statement form without the supportive intent or phrasing. Even an I-statement that may appear to be a specific description devoid of judgment sometimes inadvertently travels into evaluative territory.

"I get irritated when you waste the time of this committee by commenting on trivial side issues" loads the statement with provocative phrasing. "Waste time" and "trivial" retain the evaluative and attack elements likely to induce defensive responses. Simply jettison the provocative, loaded language.

There is a debate regarding whether the positive power of praise, already documented, might also cushion the negative effects of criticism. Some have advocated using a **criticism sandwich**: praise–criticize–praise. Psychologist Clifford Nass (2010), however, argues that the human brain forgets the praise when the more impactful negative criticism follows (remember the negativity bias). While praise occurs initially, people tend to wait for the "but," expecting criticism to follow the praise. Nass suggests beginning with the negative, then following that with plentiful praise.

I have mixed feelings about both approaches. Although praise can sometimes soften attending criticism and is useful, my preference is that meaningful praise should be offered as often as feasible separate from the anticipated "but" of criticism that follows. The more often praise can be offered without the "but," the less likely receivers will associate praise packaged with inevitable criticism.

So, what if your teammates do not exhibit competent communication skills and instead clumsily engage in hurling hurtful criticism your way? How should you respond? Here are several suggestions:

1. *Ask for clarification*. Your first reaction likely will be to defend yourself by denying the correctness of the criticism, or counterattacking. Instead, request elaboration if the criticism is too vague. Insist that the conversation be laser-focused on behaviors, not personal qualities.
2. *Listen carefully*. Even if you disagree with the criticism, it is best that you at least understand what exactly bothers those who criticize you. If the criticizer becomes verbally disagreeable, note that you can listen and understand more effectively when both parties remain calm and respectful.
3. *Agree if the criticism is factual*. If you have been late or absent from class or team meetings, for example, cop to it without offering lame excuses. Just say, "You're right. I'll take steps to correct this immediately," and then enjoy the stunned looks.
4. *Disagree without becoming disagreeable*. You do not have to accept the criticism if it is not factual. Nevertheless, stay calm and provide credible information dispassionately to counter factually incorrect criticism.
5. *Seek a solution*. You may be able to find a compromise or a mutually acceptable solution if you pursue one. "Perhaps a more flexible schedule would meet your expectations and help me avoid tardiness and absences. What do you think?"

Control versus Problem Orientation English poet Samuel Butler once said, "He who agrees against his will, is of the same opinion still." Issuing orders and demanding obedience, especially when no input was sought from group members who were told what to do, is controlling communication. Dictatorial, demanding behaviors exhibited by teachers are poorly received by students (Schrodt et al., 2008).

Jack Brehm (1972) developed a theory of psychological reactance to explain our resistance to efforts aimed at controlling our behavior. **Psychological reactance** means the more someone tries to control us by telling us what to do, the more we are inclined to resist such efforts or even to do the opposite. Even supportive, comforting messages can take on an appearance of dominance (unsolicited advice) and trigger psychological reactance (Tian et al., 2020). Controlling strategies challenge our sense of personal freedom to choose (Moore, 2019). The Covid-19 mask-wearing debate illustrates this in a stark way. The following bit of popular wisdom captures the essence of psychological reactance: "There are three ways to make sure something gets done—do it yourself; hire someone to do it; *forbid* your kids to do it" (Landers, 1995).

Tell someone they can't do something and, typically, it is what they want to do most. Consider a common scenario. Imagine while returning to your car in the congested college parking lot, another car follows you and then waits for your space. Are you inclined to leave faster or slower? What if your parking stalker

When communication seems to be an order, not a request, psychological reactance can easily emerge, even when individuals might be inclined to act like lemmings. Both individualist and collectivist cultures typically experience reactance, but in individualist cultures such as the United States, not restricting one's personal freedom is highly significant, whereas in collectivist cultures "it is more important that their group's freedom is not restricted" (Sittenthaler et al., 2015).

honks at you to encourage a faster exit? One study found that most people slow their exit, especially if honked at (Ruback & Jweng, 2006). When I've posed this exact scenario to dozens of classes, there usually is a split result when the car is just waiting. When the driver honks, however, I usually hear uniformly negative responses, such as "I'd get out of my car and walk away" (accompanied by an obscene gesture) or "I'd sit there and browse my smartphone until the jerk left." Such is the typical reaction to perceived controlling strategies.

You help prevent psychological reactance from emerging when the orientation is on the problem and how best to solve it, not on how best to control group members' behavior. A study of decision making at 356 U.S. companies discovered that 58% of strategic plans were rejected when executives overseeing the plans attempted to impose their ideas on teams. When executives asked instead for problem-solving ideas from team members and worked cooperatively, 96% of the plans were approved (McNutt, 1997). Ownership of a solution to a problem comes not from mandating it ("This is what I've decided, so do it") but from collaborating as a group and brainstorming possible solutions. All controlling communication can't be eliminated, as every parent knows, but it can be kept to a minimum. Employ controlling communication as a last resort not a first choice.

Manipulation versus Assertiveness Most people resist being manipulated. If you are like most people, simply knowing that someone is attempting to influence you for his or her own benefit is repellent. A study of 6,000 team members in 600 organizations found that playing politics, an especially cutthroat hypercompetitive version of manipulative communication, destroys social relationships and team effectiveness (LaFasto & Larson, 2001). **Hidden agendas**—personal goals of group members that are not revealed openly and that can interfere with group accomplishment—can create a defensive atmosphere. When you suspect that a team member is complimenting your performance merely to gain an ally against other members in a dispute, this hidden agenda will likely ignite defensiveness.

Assertiveness is the alternative to manipulation. Assertiveness is honest, open, direct, and nonaggressive communication (discussed in detail in Chapter 11). It is the opposite of game-playing and strategic manipulation. "I feel manipulated, and it is making me uncomfortable. Please stop asking me to become a member of this sales group" is an example of assertiveness.

Indifference versus Empathy We like being acknowledged when we are present in a group. We dislike being treated like a piece of furniture. Indifference from group members makes us defensive. Making little or no effort to listen to what a coworker or member of your project team wants to say exhibits indifference. When online team members don't respond to phone calls, emails, text messages, or postings on social media, this apparent indifference can be a frustrating experience and a huge impediment to team success. **Research shows that responding indifferently to others damages an interpersonal relationship as much or more than outright rejection** (Brittle, 2015).

You counter indifference with empathy. **Empathy** is the capacity to share what someone else is thinking and feeling (Denworth, 2017). Empathy is built on concern for others and striving to make a connection. **It requires that we try to see from the perspective of the other person**, perceiving the needs, desires, and feelings of a group member because that is what we would want others to do for us (Fisher & Shapiro, 2005). One way is to engage in **empathic listening**. Dr. Carl Marci, a neurologist at Harvard who has studied this skill, explains it this way: "It's very hard to be empathic when you're talking. Talking is really complicated, because you're thinking and planning what you're going to say . . . When you're really listening, you lose time. There's no sense of yourself because it's not about you. It's about this task—to connect completely to that person" (quoted by Coyle, 2018). One study shows that "active-empathic listening" by supervisors at work has a positive effect on employees' perceptions of their working conditions and quality of life. Supervisors who have lower levels of such empathy produce an opposite effect (Kristinsson et al., 2019). Microsoft's CEO Satya Nadella, who led the company to a $250 billion turnaround in less than four years, preaches the critical importance of empathy. He believes that humans are wired for empathy and that it is essential not only for establishing workplace harmony but also for creating products that will resonate with consumers. "Our growth mindset culture requires us to truly understand and share the feelings of another person" (quoted in McCracken, 2017, p. 99).

A study by Businessolver found that 96% of employees view empathy as important for their employers to demonstrate, but 92% do not believe employers value its importance enough (Higginbottom, 2018). A cross-cultural study of almost 7,000 managers in 38 countries found a positive correlation between empathy and job performance (Gentry et al., 2016). The expression of true empathy by a CEO or group spokesperson in a time of crisis was found to be especially important (De Waele et al., 2020).

Superiority versus Equality   Communicating superiority sends the message that one is Me-deep in self-importance. It is often called arrogance or egocentrism. Group leaders who exhibit superiority to group members undermine their credibility and influence (Silverman et al., 2012). As consultant Peter Barron Stark (2017) notes, "Arrogance is leadership kryptonite." Whatever the differences in our abilities, talents, intellect, and the like, treating people with respect and politeness—as equals on a personal level—encourages harmony and productivity.

Texting during a group meeting can communicate indifference, as in "I find a personal message more important than this meeting." It exhibits a focus on self, not on others.

Monkey Business Images/Shutterstock

Treating people like they are IRS agents at the award ceremony for the state lottery winner will invite enmity and retaliation.

Equality does not mean we all have the same abilities. Equality from the standpoint of group climate means that we give everyone an equal opportunity to succeed and display whatever potential they possess. We recognize that everyone has faults and limitations. One way of demonstrating equality to minimize defensiveness is to share your own shortcomings with group members, perhaps by using self-deprecating humor (Greengross & Miller, 2008). Former major league baseball catcher Bob Uecker frequently made sport of his career .200 batting average. "Look, people have differing opinions on many issues. Take my career. Half the people thought I was the worst player they've ever seen, and the other half thought I was a disgrace to the uniform." Poking fun at yourself just makes you seem more human and likable if it's done occasionally. It is the antithesis of ego.

One study compared a leader's self-deprecating humor to "aggressive" humor. At the end of a leader's introduction of a new employee named Pat, the leader says, "I am so glad that Pat took this job despite knowing all about me" (self-deprecating humor) in one condition, and in another condition says, "I am so glad Pat took this job despite knowing all about you [other employees]" (aggressive humor). Admittedly, neither is thigh-slapping funny, but perhaps mildly amusing to those familiar with the leader. More importantly, despite no differences in ratings of how funny each statement was, the self-deprecating leader received significantly higher positive ratings on trustworthiness and leadership ability than the leader who used aggressive humor (Hoption et al., 2013).

If using self-deprecating humor is done too frequently, however, it could diminish your credibility. During a job interview in which you are attempting to enhance your status and credibility in the minds of the interviewing panelists, self-deprecating humor is inadvisable unless your interviewing panel is composed of colleagues who already know you well and might appreciate some light humor.

Certainty versus Provisionalism There are very few things in this world that are certain—death, taxes, your clothes dryer will eat your socks, your toast will fall buttered-side down, and your technological devices will fail at the most inopportune times are a few that do come to mind. Certainty is reflected in terms such as *never, always, impossible, can't,* and *won't.* "We'll never finish this project on time" and "We always procrastinate" are two examples of using terms of certainty. They can ignite a defensive argument regarding who is right or wrong.

Provisionalism counters certainty. **Provisionalism** means you qualify statements, avoiding absolutes. Provisionalism is reflected in the use of qualifying terms such as *possibly, probably, perhaps, occasionally, may, might,* and *sometimes.* "We may have difficulty finishing this project on time unless we organize our effort" is a provisional statement. This is the language of precision, not fence-straddling. Problems are approached as issues to be investigated and discussed, not ego-protecting verbal contests. When others use the language of certainty, note it out loud and rephrase the issue in provisional terms: "I know that it seems that the team is always late and disorganized, but to be fair, that occurs only occasionally, but let's all try to improve."

Incivility versus Civility Christine Porath (2016), author of *Mastering Civility: A Manifesto for the Workplace,* found in a poll she conducted that 78% of respondents were less committed to their employer and half reduced their effort because of on-the-job incivility. One study concludes, "Incivility in America has risen to crisis levels" (Shandwick & Tate., 2017). A stunning 84% of survey respondents report having "personally experienced incivility" which made them feel intimidated, threatened, and harassed. A worldwide survey found that 47% of millennials and 44% of Gen Z respondents believe that incivility is growing ("The Deloitte Global Millennial Survey," 2020). Social media was considered a major cause (Shandwick & Tate., 2017).

Incivility is the commonplace acts of rudeness and disrespect that most groups and organizations recognize exist, but few act to discourage it (Ross, 2017). Research shows that name-calling and vulgarity are perceived to be the most egregious forms of incivility, and that there tend to be different norms for women and men. Women "have heightened sensitivity to uncivil comments" and they are "less willing themselves to engage in such discourse" than men (Kenski et al., 2020).

Conversely, **civility** is treating people with respect both verbally and nonverbally. As Porath notes, "Civility is smart, it's savvy, it's human. By being civil, you get to be a nice person, and you get ahead. People are more likely to support you and work harder for you" (quoted in Ross, 2017, p. D1). One study of social media interactions found that even brief exposure to civil discourse created a positive communication environment (Antoci et al., 2018). Creating a civil group environment is everyone's responsibility, but group leaders must set the tone by example. Incivility is contagious but so is civility.

SECOND LOOK

Defensive versus Supportive Communication

Defensive	Supportive
Criticism	Description
Control	Problem orientation
Manipulation	Assertiveness
Indifference	Empathy
Superiority	Equality
Certainty	Provisionalism
Incivility	Civility

Once a group climate develops from these seven defensive or supportive patterns of communication, it can set in motion a **reciprocal pattern**—tit for tat. One famous tit-for-tat exchange occurred between Lady Astor, the first female member of the British Parliament, and Winston Churchill. Exasperated by Churchill's opposition to several of the causes she espoused, Lady Astor acerbically remarked, "Winston, if I were married to you, I'd put poison in your coffee." Churchill replied, "And if you were my wife, I'd drink it" (Fadiman, 1985). Verbal attack begets verbal attack. Remember the "bad apple" research by Felps and his colleagues (2006) discussed in Chapter 2? Insults (criticism) from the bad apple begat insults from other group members, slacker behavior (indifference) begat slacker behavior, and cynicism (indifference and certainty) begat cynicism. Remember, however, in that same study one group with a harmonious leader found positivity contagious and was successful.

The challenge in any group is to maintain the positive reciprocal pattern of support and to break the cycle of the negative reciprocal pattern of defensiveness. A positive reciprocal pattern of support and cooperation should emerge from the communication transactions among group members. Group leaders may play an important role in this process by setting a cooperative tone for the group. The responsibility for establishing a positive group climate, however, rests on all group members.

Listening: Enhancing Positivity

Listening effectively is one of the most critical communication skills group members can exhibit (Cole, 2016; Yavuk & Celik, 2017). Research confirms that people spend more time listening than in any other communication activity (Janusik & Rouillard, 2020). One study of almost 2,200 hiring managers, human resource professionals, and college students found that competent listening is the most sought-after business "soft skill" (Bauer-Wolf, 2019). Competent listening interjects positivity into group discussion. Poor listening interjects negativity.

Unfortunately, despite the obvious importance of listening well in groups, evidence shows that for the most part we don't listen effectively. A study of more than 3,000 professionals from 30 countries at all levels of organizational hierarchies concluded that those who self-report their excellent listening skills are the same ones who also confess to frequent multitasking and difficulties maintaining attention on others (Cole, 2015). Another study of college students found that a quarter of in-person class time is wasted from non-course-related digital activities (Rabi et al. 2019).

The emergence of the Covid-19 pandemic only exacerbated the problem of digital distractions. One of the first studies to incorporate Covid into the distraction equation found "high levels of distraction" among online college students (Gillis & Krull, 2020). The distractions aren't always digital. Working at home can produce myriad distractions from family members, environmental noises, attempts to multitask (e.g., washing dishes while Zooming), and others. Listening to class lectures or virtual group discussions becomes compromised. As opportunities to connect and actually practice our listening skills diminish in our digital age, conversation and connection with group members are often replaced with brief texts or emojis (Murphy, 2020). Amazon's Siri may be the only one left listening if we aren't careful. Clearly, despite its importance, most people are not good listeners.

Active listening is focused listening. We make a conscious effort to focus our attention on the speaker and his or her message. Unlike empathic listening previously discussed, however, active listening attempts to understand messages from others, not necessarily connect with others on a personal or emotional level. Too often when sitting in groups, whether in-person or online, we do not make the effort to listen actively. We allow our minds to wander and our attention to be distracted. Competent listening, however, goes far beyond actively listening to other group members. Listening can become a competitive event.

The typical college student plays with a digital device (smartphone, laptop, tablet) an average of 11.43 times a day during in-person classes for purposes unrelated to class, according to one survey. Such digital distraction is virtually universal, with few students resisting the temptation (McCoy, 2016, 2020).

Gorodenkoff/Shutterstock

Shift Response versus Support Response: Focusing on Me or Thee   When we vie for attention during a group discussion, our listening becomes competitive. Conversation becomes a contest. An attention-*getting* initiative by a listener, called the **shift response**, is a key competitive listening strategy. Here the listener attempts to shift the focus of attention from others to oneself by changing the topic of discussion. The shift response is Me-oriented and inserts negativity into group discussions. The **support response**, in contrast, is an attention-*giving*, cooperative effort by the listener to focus attention on the other person, not on oneself (Derber, 1979; Vangelisti et al., 1990). The support response fosters positivity into group discussions. We like being shown respect by others listening to us.

Consider examples that highlight differences between shift and support responses:

> **Maria:** I'm feeling frustrated by our group's lack of progress on our project.
> **Michael:** I was more frustrated by Jerry's snotty attitude during yesterday's meeting. (*shift response*)

Notice that Michael does not respond to Maria's frustration. Instead, he shifts the focus to his own frustration about another issue. Compare the shift response with this support response:

> **Maria:** I'm feeling very frustrated by our group's lack of progress on our project.
> **Michael:** I hear you. What do you think we should do about it? (*support response*)

Here, the response from the listener keeps the focus on the speaker and encourages Maria to explore the topic she initiated.

A shift response can easily provoke shift responses from other group members in a hypercompetitive battle for attention, such as in the following example:

Beth: I don't think our project fulfills the requirements for the class assignment. I'm worried that we will get a bad grade.

Lucius: The assignment is confusing. I don't understand what we are supposed to do. (*Shift response*)

Aniyah: The assignment is clear. It's the speech that concerns me. (*Shift response*)

Beth: But what about our written report on this project? I still don't think we've fulfilled the assignment. (*Shift response* to refocus attention on the initial topic)

Lucius: I need help on my speech. What's the main point I need to make first? (*Shift response*)

Although the shift response may be appropriate in some instances where individuals drift from the main topic of conversation and need to be refocused, competent communicators emphasize support responses and use shift responses infrequently. *Background acknowledgment* ("really," "uh-huh"), a *supportive assertion* ("That's super," "Nicely done"), and a *supportive question* ("How do you think we should proceed?") are the types of supportive responses that encourage cooperative discussion, not competitive struggles for attention.

Competitive Interrupting: Seizing the Floor   Nathan Miller bitingly asserted that "conversation in the United States is a competitive exercise in which the first person to draw a breath is declared the listener" (quoted in Bolton, 1979). Competitive interrupting is closely related to the shift response. It differs, however, in one key way. Listeners who use the shift response usually observe the "one speaker at a time" rule of conversation. Competitive interrupters do not. Interrupting becomes competitive when the listener attempts to seize the floor from the speaker and dominate the conversation. Not all interrupting, of course, is competitive. Sometimes group members interrupt to express support ("I agree with Joe") or enthusiasm ("Great idea"), seek clarification ("I'm confused. Could you explain that again before we move on?"), warn of danger ("Look out. You're falling over backward"), or cut short a nonstop monologue that stymies group participation (James & Clarke, 1993).

Competitive interrupting is Me-oriented. The focus is on individual needs, not group needs. Competitive interrupting creates antagonism, rivalry, hostility, and in some cases withdrawal from group discussion by frustrated members. Group members often mirror the interrupting patterns of others. If one member interrupts to seize the floor, another member will likely interrupt to seize it back. If members rarely interrupt and, when they do, primarily offer support, others will likely follow suit and keep the conversation supportive and cooperative.

Ambushing: Preparing Rebuttals When a group member is ready to pounce on a point made by a speaker, this is called **ambushing**. That member is listening with a bias. The bias is to attack the speaker verbally, not try to understand the speaker's point of view. Ambushing is clearly competitive listening. Ambushers aim to defeat a speaker in a verbal jousting match. Preparing a rebuttal while a speaker is still explaining his or her point shows little interest in comprehending a message except to find flaws. In competitive debates, message distortion is a common problem. The focus is on winning the argument, not discerning a message accurately.

Debating ideas is a useful and important process in a democratic society. Ambushing, however, interjects negativity into group discussion. Defeating an opponent becomes the driving force for ambushers. During group discussion, try to understand messages clearly and accurately *before* evaluating them.

Probing and paraphrasing can short-circuit ambushing. **Probing** means seeking additional information from a speaker by asking questions. Probing includes clarifying questions ("Can you give me an example of an important goal for the group?"), exploratory questions ("Can you think of any other approach to this problem?"), and encouraging questions ("Who can blame us for making a good effort to try a new approach?").

Paraphrasing "is a concise response to the speaker which states the essence of the other's content in the listener's words" (Bolton, 1979). Paraphrasing should be concise and precise. For example:

> **Gabriela:** I'm sick and tired of slaving on this report and we have so little to show for it. If we'd started earlier, we would be done by now.
> **Frank:** You seem frustrated and unhappy with the group's effort.
> **Gabriela:** Frustrated? Yes! Unhappy with the group effort? No! We all just have impossible schedules to coordinate.

Paraphrasing can reveal misunderstanding. Ambushing merely assumes a message is understood without checking. Noncompetitive listening is a useful communication skill that nurtures a positive group climate.

◤ Virtual Group Climate

Lindred Greer, professor of organizational behavior at Stanford Graduate School of Business, explains, "People are more likely to be less inhibited [in virtual groups], they are likely to be aggressive, and they are more likely to say opinions that could spark very negative reactions in other people" (quoted by Petersen, 2014).

The absence of normal constraints on incivility and insults found in face-to-face transactions, such as implicit norms discouraging nasty public displays of emotion, coupled with the ease and swiftness of text-only, impulsive communication, encourages more negative interactions. This is called the **disinhibition effect**—the tendency to say online what you wouldn't normally say in person (Voggeser et al., 2018). "Men are tone-deaf in general but are worse online. They become more aggressive, more rude. Women pick up social cues online," says Professor Lionel Robert. He continues by noting "that the online environment historically has been a hostile one for women, and it can be even more so in the decision-making process, causing them to be less inclined to participate" (quoted by Thomas, 2018).

Sensitivity, the accurate decoding of messages discussed in Chapter 1, is a significant challenge in the virtual group arena. Text and email messages can seem to be outright criticism when no such message is intended. Zoom crosstalk can seem like competitive interrupting when inherent technological difficulties emerge and transform conversation into a garbled mess. Zoom fatigue can make active listening challenging.

Enriching the virtual group environment is especially important during the initial stages of group development to instill a positive group climate (Yang et al., 2018). Professor Greer suggests a "face-to-face kickoff when you start working together in virtual teams. It is really critical to give team members a few days together to get to know one another so they have a context and an understanding of the relationship and the person" (quoted by Petersen, 2014). If that is not possible, using a variety of social media to connect with virtual group members to share stories and information that permit connections is important.

In summary, there is perhaps no greater challenge or more important task in a group than establishing a positive, cooperative climate. A negative, hypercompetitive climate will bode ill for your group. Defensive climates promote conflict and disharmony. Supportive climates do not free groups entirely from conflict, but such an atmosphere enhances the likelihood of constructive solutions to conflict in groups. Active listening, not competitive listening, helps establish a positive, cooperative group climate. Although virtual groups pose unique challenges, a positive climate can be created with a few direct steps.

QUESTIONS FOR CRITICAL THINKERS

1. Are there instances when you should act as a model of cooperative behavior even though other group members will take advantage of you?

2. Is hypercompetitive communication ever ethical? Explain.

3. In what ways might positive evaluation of others produce defensiveness?

4. When is interrupting appropriate?

TED TALKS AND YOUTUBE VIDEOS

"Cultivating Collaboration: Don't Be So Defensive" | Jim Tamm
"How Not to Take Things Personally?" | Frederik Imbo
"Let's Try Emotional Correctness" | Sally Kohn

VIDEO CASE STUDIES

August: Osage County (2013). *Drama; R*

A Meryl Streep and Julia Roberts vehicle depicting family dysfunction. Focus on the abundance of defensive versus supportive communication patterns and competitive and noncompetitive listening examples.

Authors Anonymous (2014). *Comedy; PG-13*

A dysfunctional group of hopeful, unpublished writers attempts to remain unconditionally positive and supportive in their communication in the face of constant rejection. Not for everyone, but this movie has many amusing moments. Analyze the effects of unconditionally supportive communication and what occurs when praise turns to criticism and envy.

Girls Trip (2017). *Comedy; R*

Four lifelong friends rekindle their sisterhood when they travel to New Orleans for the annual Essence Festival. Identify both supportive and defensive communication during this admittedly raunchy, but often hilarious comedy.

Paddington 2 (2018). *Animated Comedy/Adventure; PG*

Yes, this film is about a chipper little bear happily settled with the Brown family in London, but it is an adorable, sweet movie, and a welcome respite from the cornucopia of explosive comic book sequels. Examine defensive and supportive communication patterns, especially the role of empathy in Paddington's creation of a positive group climate.

Who's Afraid of Virginia Woolf? (1966). *Drama; R*

Engrossing but lengthy film depicting George and Martha, a troubled couple, "entertaining" another couple in the wee hours of the morning. This film is loaded with examples of defensive communication. Identify as many examples as you can find.

Roles in Groups

6

It happened one Sunday morning. Police officers, with vehicle sirens screeching, swept through the college town and arrested 10 male college students. Charged with a felony, the students were searched, handcuffed, and taken to police headquarters for booking. They were blindfolded and transported to the "Stanford County Prison," located in the basement of the Stanford University psychology department building. Upon arrival they were stripped naked, issued a smock-type uniform with an ID number across the front and back, and forced to wear a nylon cap to simulate a shaved head. Jail cells were sparsely furnished—cots and bucket toilets. Personal belongings were prohibited.

The 10 inmates were guarded by 11 other college students. This group of guards carried nightsticks, handcuffs, and whistles. They dressed in khaki uniforms and wore reflecting sunglasses to make eye contact difficult. They remained nameless. Guards' communication to prisoners consisted mostly of commands, insults, verbal and physical abuse, degrading references, and threats. Guards, working together, established a set of rules that the prisoners were to follow without hesitation or resistance. The rules were rigid: no talking during meals, rest periods, or after lights were out. Punishment for disobedience included cleaning toilets with bare hands, doing push-ups, and spending time in solitary confinement (a closet). Head counts during sleeping hours were used as a means of harassment.

The inmates initially discussed and developed a plan to revolt against the repressive conditions. Some barricaded the doors of their cells with cots. Some engaged in hunger strikes. The guards became increasingly abusive and authoritarian in response to the revolt. They used a fire extinguisher to quash the rebellion. Within a short time, some of the prisoners began to act depressed, dependent, and disturbed by their incarceration. One prisoner wept uncontrollably. He flew into fits of rage and experienced disorganized thinking and bouts of severe depression. Three other inmates developed similar symptoms.

Stanford psychologist Philip Zimbardo (2007; see also Gilmour, 2016), who conducted this mock prison study, terminated the experiment after only six days. The study was originally planned for a two-week period, but he decided that the roles had become real. "In guard roles, college students who had been pacifists and 'nice guys' behaved aggressively—sometimes even sadistically. . . . As prisoners, psychologically stable students soon behaved pathologically, passively resigning

objectives

The principal purpose of this chapter is to discuss roles and how they function within groups. There are five chapter objectives relevant to this purpose:

1. To explain the significance of roles in groups.

2. To identify types of group roles and their corresponding communication patterns.

3. To explore the role emergence process.

4. To discuss role adaptability in the group system.

5. To explain the newcomer role and the socialization process in groups.

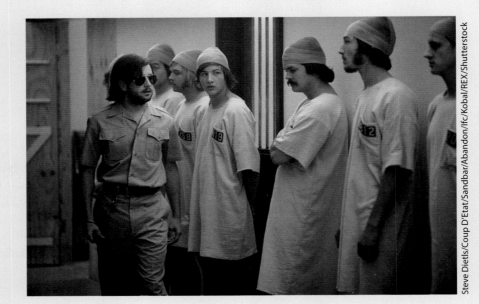

Steve Dietls/Coup D'Etat/Sandbar/Abandon/Ifc/Kobal/REX/Shutterstock

The Stanford Prison Study showed the awesome power of group roles.

themselves to their unexpected fate" (Gerrig, 2013). The guard and prisoner roles were randomly assigned by the flip of a coin, so pathological behavior cannot be explained by looking for character flaws in the men acting as guards. Clearly, the young men in this controversial study became the product of their designated roles. As one guard in the prison study explained afterward,

> Once you put a uniform on, and are given a role . . . then you're certainly not the same person if you're in street clothes and in a different role. You really become that person once you put on the khaki uniform, you put on the glasses, you take the nightstick, and you act the part. (quoted in Zimbardo, 2007)

The parallels of the Stanford study to the shocking abuse by American soldiers of Iraqi inmates at Abu Ghraib prison near Baghdad in 2004 are alarming (Gilmour, 2016; Zimbardo, 2007). In both the real and the experimental prison, guards stripped prisoners naked, forced them to wear bags over their heads, chained prisoners together, and finally forced prisoners to endure sadistic sexual degradation and humiliation. Guards said to a group of prisoners, "Now you two, you're male camels. Stand behind the female camels and *hump* them." This was just one of the many examples of abuse heaped upon prisoners, not by guards at Abu Ghraib but by college students playing the role of guards in the Stanford prison study.

In the drama of life, we play many roles often with telling consequences. A group **role** is the pattern of expected behavior associated with parts that we play in groups. Individuals act out their roles in transactions with group members. What might have begun as a casual or unnoticed pattern of behavior may quickly develop into an expectation. For example, when you tell a few jokes during the initial meeting of your group, you may be assuming the role of tension reliever without even noticing. Other group members may come to expect you to interject humor into tense situations.

Norms and roles form the basic structure of a group. Norms are *broad* rules that designate appropriate behavior for *all* group members, while roles create expected *specific* behaviors for *individual* group members. A norm for a group might be that every member works hard to achieve the group's goal. Group roles, however, differ regarding each member's expected behavior while working hard toward that end. This chapter explores the power of group roles.

Influence of Roles

The expectations attached to roles can have a marked influence on group members' perceptions. This influence is discussed in this section.

focus questions
1. Are some roles more prestigious than others?
2. When two roles conflict, which role is likely to prevail?
3. How is role reversal influential?

Role Status: Playing by Hierarchical Rules

Not all roles are valued equally. **Role status** is the relative importance, prestige, or power accorded each group role. Middle managers have higher status than staff members. College professors usually are accorded greater status than elementary school teachers. Teachers typically have greater status than students, although research shows that status differences are not always respected. One in five educators in the United States report being verbally and/or physically threatened, and 6% were actually physically assaulted ("Protecting Teachers," 2020). Higher

A younger teacher commands the respect and attention of a much older audience because of role status. Early in my teaching career, I once had a student who was 91 years old and had several graduate degrees, but because of my position, offering him knowledge that he valued, and role status, he accorded me respect.

vm/iStockphoto

role status doesn't always translate into respect from all those in lower status roles who are expected to comply with the wishes and directions of higher status individuals.

Referring to the Stanford Prison Study, Zimbardo (2007) notes that, although students are unlikely ever to play the roles of prisoner or guard in real life, this study is analogous to more commonplace role status differences. Whenever the power accorded certain roles establishes unequal power distribution, the potential for abuse is real. Teacher–student, doctor–patient, supervisor–employee, and parent–child relationships are just a few examples of role status differences that can potentially lead to verbal, even physical mistreatment.

Role status differences can be a source of great discontent in groups. For example, surgical teams, by necessity, have clearly defined roles of uneven power. This role status disparity can lead to abusive behavior by the more powerful doctors leading the team (Robbins, 2015). Results from a survey of more than 2,100 physicians and nurses conducted by the American College of Physician Executives show that the clash of roles between doctors and nurses and the abusive behavior it produces is stunningly frequent. Almost 98% of those surveyed reported witnessing bad behavior between physicians and nurses. A surprising 40% said that these clashes occurred at least weekly or daily. Typical incompetent communication included cursing, yelling, and demeaning behavior, and doctors initiated most of it. In one case, a doctor told a nurse, "You don't look dumber than my dog. Why can't you at least fetch what I need?" In another instance, a surgeon shouted for all to hear, "Monkeys could be trained to do what scrub nurses do" (Johnson, 2009; see also Brewer et al., 2013). A New York critical care nurse noted, "Every single nurse I know has been verbally berated by a doctor. Every single one" (quoted by Robbins, 2015). In addition, a third of nurses report sexual harassment perpetrated by physicians and in 74% of these cases, no action was taken (Knowles, 2018).

Abuse by doctors has serious consequences. The more that abuse is heaped on nurses, the more likely they are to quit their jobs ("Why Do Hospital Nurses Leave," 2018). Aside from the deleterious effects on nurses, patient care is also at risk from the bad behavior of "superior" doctors (Robbins, 2015). Role status differences are inevitable in many small groups, especially within organizations, but these differences do not have to be opportunities for mistreatment of those with lesser status roles.

Role Conflict: Torn Between Two Roles

The influence of roles can be seen in another way. When we find ourselves playing roles in different groups that contradict each other, we experience **role conflict**. Usually, we are forced to make a choice between the two roles, and this can produce serious turbulence in family relationships, for example (Worley & Shelton, 2020). Women with careers and families are increasingly concerned with perceived role conflict (Herley, 2015). When a woman is in an important business meeting in which colleagues depend on her input and she receives a phone call from her child's school, what does she do? Please note that the same role conflict could also exist for a man, but women are still typically cast as the primary caregiver except in single-parent situations. The perception that family demands will intrude upon a woman's work world more than on a man's can impede women's advancement in organizations (Padavic et al., 2019).

Students increasingly find work–family and student–work role conflicts emerging (Waheed & Malik, 2013). Students who have children are often faced with conflict between their student role and their parent role. Do you participate in your group's presentation, or do you stay home with your sick child? Faced with such a dilemma, do you ask your instructor whether you can present your speech virtually using Zoom or Skype, risking the perception of asking for favoritism? As the cost of a college education skyrockets, students must work full- or part-time to cover the costs of higher education and living expenses. Work obligations can interfere with students' need to meet with their group to work on projects for class. This is a common source of tension within small student groups, whose members' grades may depend on responsible and enthusiastic participation from everyone involved.

When individuals feel role conflict at work (e.g., family role vs. professional role), they often exhibit job burnout and an increased tendency to leave (Celik,

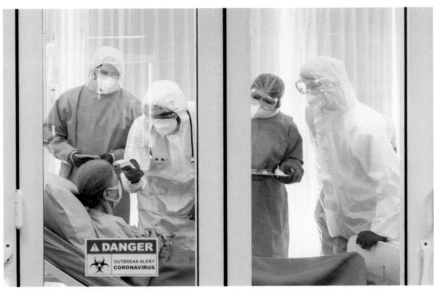

Emergency hospital teams during the Covid-19 crisis often worked double, even triple shifts to save victims' lives. Such commitment to their roles surely conflicted with their roles as partners, parents, and family members. Often quarantined from their family for long periods of time to protect them from exposure to the disease, they experienced profound role conflict between their jobs and family obligations and desires.

Gukzilla/Shutterstock

2013; Gauche et al., 2017). Emotional demands caused by role conflict can distress workers, risk their health, and lower their productivity on the job (Johannessen et al., 2013).

Some roles have a greater impact on us than others. The role that has the greatest importance and most potent effect on us is usually the one we choose when we must decide between conflicting roles. The expectations associated with group roles and the perception of the value, prestige, influence, status, or stigma attached to each role by both the group and the individual can strongly affect us. Finding a balance between conflicting roles and adjusting to inevitable changes in the small group system are keys to addressing role conflict (Lenaghan & Sengupta, 2007).

Role Reversal: When Students Become Teachers

The effects of roles on perceptions can be seen in a dramatic way by doing a **role reversal**, which is stepping into a role distinctly different from or opposite of a role we're accustomed to playing (from child to parent, student to teacher, and employee to employer, or vice versa). Role reversal can be quite powerful (Bagchi et al., 2016). The CBS show *Undercover Boss* uses role reversal to dramatize how different it is for CEOs of companies to experience the day-to-day trials of ordinary workers. The boss, unbeknownst to employees, becomes an ordinary worker

Photo by Quantrell Colbert/CBS via Getty Images

CEOs from the TV program *Undercover Boss* underscore the power of role reversal. Bosses said that they learned empathy and even changed some policies as a result of their experience acting as an employee instead of the boss (Cumberland & Alagaraja, 2016).

at his or her company. An admittedly contrived gimmick made for "reality" television, nevertheless the presented insight gained from reversing roles from CEO to worker is often profound.

As a student, I complained on more than one occasion about the quality of instruction I was receiving from my college professors. When I became a college professor, however, similar complaints from students seemed unjustified, and I initially made excuses for some ineffectual teaching practices. As a teacher, I began to appreciate the many challenges instructors face when attempting to stimulate student interest. Reversing roles can promote an appreciation for the constraints of roles on your behavior (e.g., you're required to grade students even if you dislike the practice because of its potential for triggering defensiveness). Role reversal can also promote changes in behavior, as it thankfully did early on in my teaching career.

Types of Roles

It is not possible to enumerate here all the roles a person can play in groups. In the broadest sense, there are two types of roles: formal and informal. A **formal role** is a *position* assigned by an organization, group, or specifically designated by the group leader or the result of a formal election. Titles usually accompany formal roles. A college student group, for example, might have a designated president, vice-president, secretary, treasurer, director of communications, event officer, and membership officer. Especially within larger organizations, a set of expected behaviors to fulfill the role is explicitly designated. A job description used to hire an individual to fill a specific position is an example. Formal roles exist within the structure of the group, team, or organization. These roles do not emerge naturally from communication transactions. Formal roles are often independent from any person filling the role.

In most small groups, however, the roles are usually informal. An **informal role** emerges from the group transactions, and it emphasizes *functions*, not a position. A group member may fulfill leadership functions, that is, perform as a leader, without any formal designation. Actual duties and specific behaviors expected from a group member playing an informal role are implicitly defined by communication transactions among members. The group does designate how to play a specific role, but members do indicate degrees of approval or disapproval when an individual assumes the role. Informal role playing is improvisational, not scripted.

Informal roles, the principal focus of this discussion, are typically classified into three types: task, maintenance, and self-centered (Benne & Sheats, 1948; Mudrack & Farrell, 1995). This next section explores each type.

Is the speaker at this meeting playing a formal or informal role? How can you tell? How about the other group members? Are they exhibiting formal or informal role playing? What nonverbal cues suggest which type of role is exhibited?

Monkey Business Images/Shutterstock

focus questions

1. Are there some group roles that the competent communicator should avoid?

2. How do communication patterns differ among the three types of roles?

Task Roles: Focusing on Maximum Productivity

Task roles move the group toward the attainment of its goals. The central communicative function of task roles is to extract the maximum productivity from the group. Consider a sample of the most common task roles.

1. *Initiator-contributor.* This person starts the ball rolling by offering lots of ideas and suggestions. Trying to come up with an idea for a group project in class requires an initiator. Imagine the uncomfortable silence that occurs without an initiator in the group. The group becomes mired in a state of dysfunctional inertia. When a group has one or more initiators, fruitful discussion can ensue. Groups typically function more effectively when the initiator-contributor role is shared and rotates depending on the context. At some point, however, contributions need to stop, and decisions need to be made (e.g., choose a project topic).

2. *Information seeker.* When a group begins a task, the information seeker takes an inventory of the knowledge base of group members, such as "So, does anyone know why textbooks are so expensive?" The information seeker solicits research, experiences of group members, and any supporting materials to bolster ideas once they have been initiated. Informational deficits quickly become apparent once information seekers probe the level of knowledge of group members.

3. *Information giver.* The information seeker and the information giver roles have a symbiotic relationship. They feed off each other in an interdependent relationship. If no member can provide credible information, the role of information giver becomes one of researching the topic for the group. In a group devoid of expertise, lack of at least one information giver results in sharing ignorance or group impotence.

4. *Opinion seeker.* Without an opinion seeker, a group can assume agreement where none exists. Dominant members may squelch or discourage the viewpoints from others. The opinion seeker helps the group determine where agreement or perhaps disagreement exists: for example, "Does everyone agree, or does anyone have a differing opinion on the subject?" The false assumption that agreement is universal within the group can lead to disastrous groupthink, a topic discussed at length in Chapter 9.

5. *Clarifier-elaborator.* A group member playing this role explains, expands, and extends the ideas of others and provides examples and alternatives that piggyback on the ideas of group members. During heated disagreements, group discussion can deteriorate into murky confusion. The clarifier can step in and provide refreshing clarity, such as "I actually don't believe we are as far apart as everyone seems to believe. Consider how similar we are on the following issues...."

6. *Coordinator.* This role requires organizational skills. Scheduling issues need to be resolved and the coordinator organizes where, when, and how a meeting will take place.

7. *Secretary-recorder.* This role serves a group memory function. The secretary-recorder takes minutes of meetings, prepares reports for further discussion and decision making, and reminds members of past actions that may have been forgotten as time passes: for example, "That was only an information item in our last meeting. No action was taken."

8. *Facilitator.* A group member acting as a facilitator keeps participants on track, guides discussion, reminds the group of the primary goal that informs the discussion, and regulates group activities: for example, "I think we've drifted from our main focus. Let's bring back the discussion to what we can actually accomplish in the next two weeks."

9. *Devil's advocate.* This is a critical role for any group and one that is often absent from group decision making. A devil's advocate gently challenges a prevailing point of view for the sake of argument to test and critically evaluate the strength of ideas, solutions, or decisions. You raise questions and potential objections, not because you necessarily disagree with other group members but because you don't want the group to rush headlong into making a rash decision that has not been carefully considered. "So, what happens if our plan doesn't work the way we think it will?" and "Do we have a backup strategy?" are the kind of questions a devil's advocate asks. Chapter 9 discusses this role in more detail.

Maintenance Roles: Focusing on Cohesiveness

Maintenance roles focus on the social dimension of the group. The central communicative function of maintenance roles is to gain and maintain the cohesiveness of the group. Maintaining a positive group climate is essential to group success, so these roles are quite significant. Consider a sample of common maintenance roles:

1. *Supporter-encourager.* A group member playing this role bolsters the spirits and goodwill of the group; provides warmth, praise, and acceptance

of others; and invites reticent members into the discussion: for example, "Good job everyone. Great group!"

2. *Harmonizer-tension reliever.* This role aims to maintain the peace and reduce secondary tension by using humor and by reconciling differences among members. This isn't just a "can't we all just get along" approach. When tempers flare and communication turns defensive, a harmonizer-tension reliever can call for a brief break to calm anger ("Let's try not to get personal, and let's take a break. I think we are getting weary").

3. *Gatekeeper-expediter.* Someone playing this role controls channels of communication and flow of information, regulating the degree of openness within the group system so all group members are given an opportunity to participate. Rules may be suggested to expedite efficient meetings, such as "Perhaps we should set a time limit for discussing this item."

Disruptive Roles: Focusing on Self

Self-centered or disruptive roles serve individual needs or goals (Me-oriented) while impeding attainment of group goals. Individuals who play these roles often warrant the tag "difficult group member" or "bad apple." The central communicative function of self-centered, disruptive roles is to focus attention on the individual. This focus on the individual can diminish group productivity and cohesiveness. Competent communicators avoid these roles (*see* Chapter 2 for ways to deal effectively with disruptive group members).

1. *Stage hog.* An individual playing this role seeks recognition and attention by monopolizing the conversation and preventing others from expressing their opinions fully. The stage hog seeks the spotlight like a moth to a flame. "Listen to me! I'm not done yet."

2. *Isolate.* An isolate deserts the group and withdraws from participation. Isolates act indifferent and resist efforts to be included in group decision making. A person playing this role is a group member in name only. Isolates can be dead weight on a group. They are particularly prevalent and troublesome in virtual groups. They can easily disappear.

3. *Clown.* This role is not merely one of offering humor to lighten the tension in the group. The clown engages in horseplay, thrives on practical jokes and comic routines, diverts members' attention away from serious discussion of ideas and issues, and steps beyond the boundaries of mere tension reliever. Humor taken to extremes says, "Look at me. I'm so funny." This is self-centered, not group centered.

4. *Blocker.* This role is obstructionist in nature. The purpose is to prevent the group from taking action, especially action the blocker finds objectionable.

A person who plays the blocker thwarts progress of the group by refusing to cooperate and by opposing much of what the group attempts to accomplish.

5. *Fighter-controller.* Some group members love to fight and control group discussions. A fighter-controller tries to dominate group discussion, competes with members, picks quarrels, interrupts to interject his or her own opinions into discussion, and makes negative remarks to members ("You're really kind of slow on the uptake, aren't you? Try keeping up."). The fighter-controller is a bully.

6. *Zealot.* When a group member plays this role, he or she tries to convert members to a pet cause or idea, delivers sermons to the group on the state of the world, and often becomes obsessively political in remarks ("Once again, politics reigns supreme. I've been telling you this all along, haven't I?"). It is one thing to be enthusiastic when expressing a point of view, but it is quite another when one's zeal becomes that of a fanatic. As Winston Churchill once remarked, a fanatic is "one who can't change his mind and won't change the subject." Zealots incessantly reintroduce dead issues, maximizing group members' frustration. "I know I keep saying this and you don't like it, but if you would just listen to me . . ."

7. *Cynic.* This role is a climate killer. A cynic displays a sour outlook, engages in fault-finding, focuses on negatives, and predicts group failure ("We're never going to agree on a decent topic"). H. L. Mencken described a cynic as someone who "smells flowers [and] looks around for a coffin." When the group may need a cheerleader, the cynic becomes a jeerleader by providing a disheartening message ("I told you we wouldn't succeed. This was a stupid idea").

SECOND LOOK
Sample of Informal Roles in Groups

Task Roles

1. *Initiator-contributor:* Offers lots of ideas and suggestions; proposes solutions.
2. *Information seeker:* Requests clarification; solicits evidence; asks for suggestion.
3. *Information giver:* Provides information based on research, expertise, or experience.
4. *Opinion seeker:* Requests viewpoints from others, both pro and con.
5. *Clarifier-elaborator:* Explains, expands, and extends the ideas of others.
6. *Coordinator:* Organizes and schedules meetings.
7. *Secretary-recorder:* Takes minutes of meetings; keeps group's records and history.
8. *Facilitator:* Keeps group on track; guides discussion; regulates group activities.
9. *Devil's advocate:* Gently challenges prevailing point of view for the sake of argument to test and critically evaluate the strength of ideas, solutions, or decisions.

Maintenance Roles

1. *Supporter-encourager:* Bolsters the spirits and goodwill of the group; provides warmth, praise, and acceptance of others; includes reticent members in discussion.
2. *Harmonizer-tension reliever:* Reduces tension through humor and by reconciling differences.
3. *Gatekeeper-expediter:* Controls channels of communication and flow of information.

Self-Centered/Disruptive Roles

1. *Stage hog:* Monopolizes conversation; prevents others from expressing their opinions.
2. *Isolate:* Withdraws from participation; acts indifferent, aloof, uninvolved.
3. *Clown:* Engages in horseplay; diverts members' attention; distracts by acting goofy.
4. *Blocker:* Opposes group direction; incessantly reintroduces dead issues.
5. *Fighter-controller:* Domineering; pugilistic; abusive.
6. *Zealot:* Tries to convert members to a pet cause or idea; exhibits fanaticism.
7. *Cynic:* Displays sour outlook; engages in fault-finding; predicts failure.

This is a static list and description of task, maintenance, and disruptive roles. Roles, however, unfold dynamically in the context of group discussion, debate, and disagreement. One minute you may be an information-giver and the next you may switch to harmonizer-tension reliever depending on the flow of the group's interactions. During the course of a single group meeting you may play many roles. Consider the following brief group transaction as a sample illustrating this process of dynamic role-playing:

> **Jeremy:** Maybe we should do our project on campus safety. (Initiator)
> **Maria:** Do any of you know anything about campus safety? (Information seeker)
> **Charlise:** I did a survey last semester in another class and discovered some interesting results. (Information giver)
> **Peter:** That just sounds boring, just like this project. (Cynic)
> **Darnell:** I don't see you offering anything constructive, so stifle yourself. (Fighter-controller)
> **Peter:** And I suppose you love this project? And who uses words like *stifle*? (Fighter-controller)
> **Maria:** Come on guys, this isn't getting us anywhere. (Harmonizer-tension reliever) We can do better. (Supporter-encourager) So, can we get back to discussing Jeremy's idea for a topic? (Facilitator) What do you all think? (Opinion seeker; Facilitator)

In this brief sample discussion, you see some group members assuming roles in response to other members. There are task, maintenance, and disruptive roles

Individuals may play many roles during the life of the group, even during a single event. Some bands have more than one singer, as does this band (woman on the left), and sometimes singers meld into the group while playing an instrument.

LightField Studios/Shutterstock

represented, and some members play more than one role in rapid-fire succession, while other members play a single role. Role-playing in small groups is a dynamic, transactional process.

Assuming appropriate task and maintenance roles during group discussion is a matter of timing. For example, a *devil's advocate* is not needed during initial discussion. You do not want to kill potentially creative ideas by immediately challenging them. A *harmonizer-tension reliever* is needed when conflict emerges and threatens to derail the group discussion. This role is irrelevant if there is no tension or disharmony. Which roles to play at which time is an important aspect of leadership, discussed at length in the next chapter.

Role Emergence

In large groups and organizations, roles are largely determined by their formal structure. Even within this formal structure, however, role emergence occurs. Functional roles operate in smaller group meetings within the organization or in factional subunits of large groups.

Role emergence, however, is a relevant concern primarily to small, informal, leaderless groups without a history. These groups could be ad hoc project groups set up within formal organizations (e.g., self-managed work teams), classroom discussion groups formed to complete a class project, or a jury in a criminal trial.

Playing by the Roles

Fill out this self-assessment for an important group: family, study group, project group, and so on. This should reveal which roles you play most often in your group. Use the 5-point scale from 1 (*low*) to 5 (*high*), by writing in the blanks the appropriate number (1, 2, 3, 4, or 5) indicating frequency. *Optional alternative:* After answering this questionnaire, ask fellow class or team members to complete this same assessment about you, but only if you feel comfortable making such a request. If team members are hesitant, encourage them to complete the assessment without identifying themselves in the questionnaire (ideally, all team members should complete the assessment to preserve anonymity). Compare the results.

_____ **1.** Your degree of participation in group activities was

_____ **2.** How task-oriented (showed interest in meeting group goals) were you?

_____ **3.** How socially oriented (concerned about the relationships among group members) were you?

_____ **4.** How much influence did you have on the group's decisions?

Using the same 5-point scale, indicate the degree to which you played the following roles (see Second Look: Sample of Informal Roles in Groups) by writing the appropriate number (1, 2, 3, 4, or 5) in the blanks:

Task

_____ Information giver   _____ Opinion seeker   _____ Initiator-contributor

_____ Clarifier-elaborator   _____ Coordinator   _____ Information seeker

_____ Devil's advocate   _____ Facilitator   _____ Secretary-recorder

Maintenance

_____ Supporter-encourager

_____ Gatekeeper-expediter

_____ Harmonizer-tension reliever

Disruptive

_____ Stage hog   _____ Isolate   _____ Cynic

_____ Fighter-controller   _____ Blocker

_____ Zealot   _____ Clown

The roles each member will play have not been designated in advance but emerge from the transactions conducted among group members. How roles emerge in zero-history groups has been studied extensively at the University of Minnesota (Bormann, 1990).

focus questions

1. How do roles emerge in small groups?

2. What is role specialization and why is it important?

Group Endorsement: Accepting a Bid

Individuals initially make a bid to play a role. They may bid for a role because they have special skills that suit the role, or they may succumb to gender role stereotyping. Group endorsement of the bid to play a specific role must occur before a person gets to play that role. In a competitive culture, high-status roles are generally perceived to be those that are task oriented. Accomplishing tasks brings victories, tangible accomplishments, and recognition. The roles of facilitator, initiator-contributor, information giver, and devil's advocate are high-status roles because individuals are perceived as doers—they accomplish important tasks that advance the group's success.

Despite their critical importance to group success, maintenance roles are often viewed as lower status in a competitive culture such as the United States. Those who play maintenance roles are viewed as the helpers, not the doers, yet they are critical to maintaining a positive group climate. Women have been socialized to play primarily the lower status maintenance roles (Wood, 2019). Thus, group roles such as supporter-encourager, harmonizer-tension reliever are roles traditionally played more by women than men. When women are underrepresented in groups, it is particularly difficult to receive the endorsement of the group to play nonstereotypical, higher status roles or to enhance the perceived status of maintenance roles.

The endorsement process proceeds by trial and error. A group member tries out a role, perhaps initiator-contributor, for example. If the group does not reinforce the effort (members ignore the contributions), then the member will try another role, hoping to get an endorsement. An individual who insists on playing a specific role in the face of group resistance may be characterized as inflexible and uncooperative.

Role Specialization: Settling into One's Primary Role

Once a role for a member has been endorsed by the group, **role specialization**—when an individual member settles into his or her primary role—occurs. If the group wants you to be an information giver, then that will be your principal function. This specialization doesn't preclude assuming other roles, however. Role specialization does not grant a monopoly to a single member. There may be more than one harmonizer in the group, although there is likely to be only one member with the primary responsibility. Attempting to "poach" another member's primary role can invite negative feedback from the group.

Role Adaptability

Playing roles is a fluid, dynamic process. Individuals in a system are so interconnected that what one group member does can significantly influence the roles other group members play. Clashes regarding who gets to play a particular task role, for example, may ignite disruptive role behavior from the "losing" group member.

focus questions
1. Why should group members exhibit role flexibility?
2. What are the disadvantages of role fixation?

Role Flexibility: Adapting to Context

Roles are not static entities. When the composition of your group changes, when phases of development change, when the group climate shifts either toward or away from a cooperative/supportive one, or when you move from one group to another, you have to adapt to these changes in the system. The required behaviors for your role may change as a consequence, or the roles members play may change.

The most competent small group members are the ones who exhibit **role flexibility**—"the capacity to recognize the current requirements of the group and then enact the role-specific behaviors most appropriate in the given context" (Forsyth, 2019). For example, if group discussion becomes confusing, an alert member recognizes the need to play the clarifier role. If members' discussion veers off topic, a competent member recognizes the need to play the facilitator role and refocus the discussion. Playing devil's advocate by challenging a group idea in its formative stage may squash creativity and the generation of further innovative ideas. Having your ideas challenged immediately by a devil's advocate will likely discourage further contributions to idea generation during brainstorming sessions for fear of evaluation.

Role Fixation: Failure to Adapt

Sometimes, the necessary flexibility of small group roles escapes individual members and they become so enamored with a single role that they exhibit **role**

fixation—the acting out of a specific role and that role alone no matter what the situation might require. Professional comedians sometimes don't know when to be serious in social gatherings. They are always "on." Lawyers who cross-examine their spouses and children as they do hostile witnesses on the stand at a criminal trial may find their role fixation is a ticket to a court of a decidedly civil sort. Competent communication requires the ability and the willingness to adapt communication behavior to changing situations. Some individuals, however, get locked into the mindset that they must play a certain role. Facilitator, information giver, feeling expresser, and tension reliever are among the most likely candidates for role fixation.

Role fixation in decision-making groups can occur when an individual moves from one group to another, or it can happen within a single group. If you were a gatekeeper in your last group, you may insist on performing the same role in your new group. There may be another member, however, who can play the role better. If you insist on competing for the role instead of adapting to the new group by assuming another role, you will be a source of conflict and disruption.

Sometimes the group insists on role fixation to its own detriment. The reluctance of men to accept women in high-status roles, for instance, can lead to role fixation against a woman's wishes. Women should have the opportunity to play roles that require more than nurturing (e.g., supporter-encourager) or low involvement (e.g., secretary-recorder).

In a larger sense, you don't want to become fixated on even a category of roles. Those members who become fixated on task roles to the virtual exclusion of

Role ambiguity, being unclear what role you are expected to play in a group and how you should behave, can provide too much role flexibility. You don't want firefighters struggling over who should operate the hoses while your house burns down, nor do you want them looking around for other team members to run into the burning house to rescue family members. Teams typically require role specialization to avoid role ambiguity.

Dmitry Pistrov/Shutterstock

maintenance roles, or vice versa, exhibit a counterproductive imbalance between productivity and cohesiveness. Having noted the importance of role flexibility and avoiding role fixation, research cautions that too much role flexibility can lead to poor group performance. This can create problems of coordination and role ambiguity among group members, especially for crisis-management teams (Jobidon et al., 2016).

Newcomers and System Disturbance

Group members learn their roles over time as they emerge from group transactions. Once established, members' roles can become solidified and resistant to change. Consequently, the interconnectedness of all components of a system makes the entry of even a single new member into an established group a highly significant event (Delton & Cimino, 2010). As groups develop, relationships among members stabilize, and the roles and norms in the group become more complex. "The entry of a newcomer into the group can threaten this development by forcing members to alter their relationships with one another" (Moreland & Levine, 1987). Acceptance of newcomers into an established group is especially challenging.

focus questions

1. What aspects contribute to or thwart acceptance of a newcomer into the group?
2. What responsibilities should newcomers and long-standing group members have to make the socialization process work?

Nature of the Group: The Challenge of Acceptance

Several characteristics of a group directly affect the acceptance of a newcomer. First, the level of group development has a direct bearing on newcomer acceptance (Hare, 2013). A newcomer in a recently formed group is less disruptive because he or she enters early in the group development process. Entering a long-standing group, where development has progressed far beyond the initial stages, can be a much greater shock to the system and requires greater adaptation by the members. The newcomer seems more like an outsider in long-standing groups than in recently formed ones.

Second, the level of group performance affects the acceptance of newcomers. When the system is functioning well, group members may not want to take a chance on altering a successful formula. Accepting a newcomer may pose a big risk. When a group is performing poorly, however, there is a strong impetus for change. The arrival of a newcomer may be perceived as a fresh resource that might improve the group (Phillips et al., 2009).

Third, the number of members affects acceptance of a newcomer into a group. Groups that have too few members to perform necessary tasks well are usually eager to accept newcomers. Newcomers mean less work for each member and potentially greater success for the group. Groups that have too many members to function efficiently, however, will probably view a newcomer as an additional burden.

Fourth, the degree of turnover in a group also affects acceptance of newcomers. Groups accustomed to frequent entry and exit of members will accept newcomers more readily than groups unaccustomed to turnover.

Finally, and probably most important, groups are more accepting of a newcomer when members believe the newcomer embraces and will conform to the norms, values, and practices of the group. This can be more difficult for women entering a group than for men, especially in the workplace. "Given that workplace cultures tend to be masculine, it's a lot easier for men to assimilate. Women, on the other hand, must negotiate around masculine norms, which often exclude them" (King, 2020).

One all-too-common method for determining such willingness to conform in advance of actual membership is using hazing or initiation rituals. **Hazing** is defined as "any activity expected of someone joining or participating in a group that humiliates, degrades, abuses, or endangers them regardless of a person's willingness to participate" (Allan & Madden, 2008). Hazing rituals are widespread with 55% of college students who are involved in clubs, teams, and campus organizations (e.g., fraternities and sororities) experiencing hazing. At least 40 college students have died from hazing rituals since 2007 (Freeman, 2019). The lack of physical proximity on college campuses because of the Covid pandemic did not stop hazing. It continued on virtual platforms (Apgar, 2020).

The list of silly, stupid, dangerous, and illegal activities required by some groups as a rite of passage into groups is long and sometimes lethal. Hazing rituals have included forcing students to swallow quarter-pound hunks of raw liver slathered with oil; abandoning students in remote areas in bitter cold conditions without suitable clothing; repeatedly punching the stomach and kidneys of students who forget parts of ritual incantations; incarcerating initiates in a locked storage closet for two days with only salty foods, no liquids, and only a small plastic cup to catch urine; and forcing initiates to abuse alcohol or illegal drugs (Allan & Madden, 2008; Forsyth, 2013).

There are two main reasons newcomers submit to hazing. First, humans tend to place greater value on that which is difficult to achieve. The more severe the hazing ritual, the more desirable a group appears to be. Second, hazing creates group cohesiveness and conformity (Lodewijkx et al., 2005). If you had to swallow a slimy, oil-soaked slab of raw liver, freeze off the south side of your

Photo by Luis Sinco/Los Angeles Times via Getty Images

Hazing rituals as a rite of passage into full-fledged group membership can seem harmless, even fun, but they also can be lethal when they become excessive. This is a protest at California State University at Northridge following the death of Armando Villa that resulted from hazing.

anatomy, or risk your life to gain membership, chances are you would slavishly conform to the norms of the group once you were admitted. Nevertheless, hazing is outlawed in most states.

Group Socialization: Mutual Adaptation to Change

In any system, interconnected parts must adapt to changing conditions. Newcomers require adaptation in a group because they inherently produce change by their mere presence. The communication process in which new and established group members adjust to one another is called **group socialization** (King, 2020). This process is one of mutual adaptation. Newcomers must acquire the necessary knowledge and skills to blend successfully into the group (Moring, 2017). They must play the role of newcomer, not act initially like an established group member. Established members must also adjust to the newcomers. This may include changing roles that require learning new skills when replaced by a newcomer (Forsyth, 2019).

For their part, newcomers can employ several strategies to improve their chances of gaining acceptance from a group (Dean, 2009b; Moring, 2017).

1. *Conduct a thorough reconnaissance of the group.* Most newcomers do a poor job of scouting a group to determine whether they and the group are a good match. Newcomers should exploit all available sources of information about the group to form a reasonably accurate assessment of the group they contemplate joining.

2. *Play the role of newcomer.* "The temptation when joining a new group is to try and make a splash, to impress others. . . . Groups are hostile to criticism from newcomers and are likely to resist, dismiss, or ignore it" (Dean, 2009b). Seek information and advice from longtime members and coworkers or team partners who "know the ropes" (Moring, 2017). Try to fit in by conforming to the norms and values of the group. Again, this can be more difficult for women, especially women of color, entering a group in predominantly white male workplaces (King, 2020). Avoid disagreements with old-timers and talk less than they do. Listen to show respect and to learn valuable information. Emphasize similarities to other members in the group (Burke et al., 2010). As you become more accepted by the group, your communication can move away from the newcomer role pattern.

3. *Embrace your new group; distance yourself from previous groups.* "This is the way we successfully met this challenge where I used to work" is unlikely to be a welcomed comment from a newcomer. It suggests superiority of your previous group that likely evokes defensiveness from your new group members. Embracing your new group and distancing yourself from a previous group ("This group is much better prepared to handle this challenge than my previous group") inclines group members to listen, even accept suggestions or criticism more readily (Hornsey et al., 2007).

4. *Seek mentors within the group.* Mentors are old-timers who develop a close personal relationship with the newcomer and assist the newcomer's entry into the group. Unfortunately, even though both men and women are equally mentored in organizations upon entry (Artz et al., 2018), men are "more likely to be sponsored by senior executives who would use their influence to help advance their mentees' careers" (King, 2020). Nevertheless, the mentoring process can increase the newcomer's understanding of the group and enhance both women and men's level of group satisfaction and advancement (Oglensky, 2008).

5. *Collaborate with other newcomers.* When more than one newcomer enters a group, they stand to gain from banding together. Newcomers can lend emotional support and encouragement to each other, provide useful information about the group, and act as a friendly face, making the group climate more inviting.

Established group members also have a responsibility to engage in the socialization process. Old-timers may have expectations regarding how newcomers should act that may not be shared by new members. A period of adjustment occurs as new and older members adapt to one another. There are several strategies that established members of groups can employ to make the role of newcomer less challenging and intimidating (Anderson et al., 1999).

1. *Welcome new members into the group.* An initial meet-and-greet gathering of group members in which newcomers introduce themselves and old-timers provide brief narratives about themselves works well. Providing opportunities for socializing outside of group task responsibilities also helps.

2. *Orient new members.* Provide a tour of the facilities, offer a brief history of the group, and discuss expectations the group has for newcomers. Inform newcomers of any politics or environmental influences from outsiders that may be challenging.

3. *Mentor newcomers.* Have a structured mentoring process for newcomers if this is a long-standing group; brief ad hoc groups typically do not require mentoring programs.

Competent communicators learn about the nature of the group to which they seek membership, and they learn the strategies that will assist their acceptance into the group. Women and ethnic minorities, who are often in the newcomer role, add diversity to a group, which presents challenges but usually benefits group decisions (Phillips et al., 2009). Newcomers can revitalize stagnant groups and provide creativity and innovation (Perretti & Negro, 2007). It should be the goal, however, of both newcomers and long-standing members of a group to work together to make the socialization process successful for all.

In summary, there are many roles to play in small groups. Competent communicators learn to play a variety of roles. A formal role is a position assigned by an organization or specifically designated by the group leader. An informal role emerges from group transactions and emphasizes functions. There are three general types of informal roles: task, maintenance, and disruptive roles. I've explained the roles we play during the life of a group and how to function effectively in those roles. In the next chapter, the leader role, often the most coveted of all the roles in groups, is discussed.

QUESTIONS FOR CRITICAL THINKERS

1. Is hazing ever an acceptable initiation process for newcomers?
2. Are self-centered disruptive roles ever appropriate?
3. Have you ever experienced role reversal effects?

TED TALKS AND YOUTUBE VIDEOS

"Disrupting the Cycle of Hazing" | Will Clarke

VIDEO CASE STUDIES

One Night in Miami (2020). *Drama; R*

Fictional meeting on night of February 25, 1964, in Miami motel room in which Cassius Clay joins Jim Brown, Sam Cooke, and Malcolm X in a powerful discussion of each mans role in the civil rights movement. Examine the dynamic informal roles of each character as the discussion develops.

The Experiment (2010). *Drama; R*

Mostly faithful dramatic recreation of the Stanford Prison Study. Analyze formal and informal roles played by all of the characters. Explore the impact of each role on their behavior. Would you have preferred to be a prisoner or a guard? Why?

The Saffires (2013). *Biography/Drama; PG-13*

Based on a true story, in 1968, four young, talented Australian Aboriginal girls become a singing group called the Saffires, who entertained U.S. troops during the Vietnam War. Analyze role emergence and informal roles played by each of the women. Does role status emerge as an issue? How does the group respond to the newcomer played by Chris O'Dowd?

Wind River (2017). *Murder Mystery, Drama; R*

Graphic, sometimes chilling depiction of the story of a rookie FBI agent teaming up with a local game tracker and the tribal police chief to solve the murder of an 18-year-old native American girl who froze to death in the wilds of Wind River Indian Reservation in the remote Wyoming wilderness. What formal roles exist? What informal roles emerge? Are there any disruptive roles that impede the investigation? How do roles influence the investigation? How does the newcomer (rookie FBI agent) adapt to the group? How do others adapt to the newcomer?

Group Leadership

7

Scholars, philosophers, social scientists, and even novelists have exhibited an intense interest in leadership. In politics, leadership is a buzzword and a subject of intense, although not always informed or fruitful debate. Conduct a Google search of articles, books, and viewpoints on leadership, and you'll get millions of hits. Enter "leadership" in the Amazon search window and almost 60,000 titles are referenced, and the list continues to grow. Business executives and management consultants regularly author books on leadership, mostly consisting of anecdotes that purport to prove allegedly sage advice garnered from years of corporate experience or management training. Matthew Stewart (2009), a former management consultant turned disapproving critic, comments: "Upon putting the gurus' books down, however, I find that I get the same feeling I get after reaching the bottom of a supersized bag of tortilla chips. They taste great while they last, but in the end, what am I left with?" (p. 8). He later answers: "platitudes," "bundles of nonfalsifiable truisms," and "transparently unsubstantiated pseudotheories."

Echoing Stewart's criticism, what I see most of these business executives and management consultants too frequently offering is ego gratification for the authors who endlessly tout their self-proclaimed mastery of leadership based on experience only as CEOs, and sometimes not even that. Untroubled by the lack of social scientific research to support this supposed mastery of leadership, they provide advice that may have worked for them, but it doesn't readily translate to others who must adapt to markedly different situations and circumstances than a corporate CEO might face (Vroom & Jago, 2007). As a college student, trying to follow advice offered by a billionaire CEO should strike you as mostly irrelevant to your current circumstances, unless of course you are a billionaire and have a start-up company.

Insightful academic research on leadership effectiveness too often is ignored, while the press and the popular culture lionize these flashy, quick-fix books. With few exceptions (some referenced in this chapter), they have minimal merit. Fortunately, you don't have to depend on the self-promotional and self-congratulatory peppy platitudes of these personal testimonials on leadership. One highly acclaimed reference book takes more than 1,500 pages to review the vast research and theory on leadership (Bass & Bass, 2008), and much additional research has been conducted since this monumental work was released (see DuBrin, 2019).

objectives

This chapter's principal purpose is to explore leadership effectiveness in groups. Five chapter objectives are addressed:

1. To define leadership.

2. To discuss how to gain leadership.

3. To explore which perspectives on effective group leadership have the most merit.

4. To address cultural applications of leadership theory.

5. To provide insight regarding virtual group leadership effectiveness.

167

This reservoir of research serves as the foundation for this chapter's principal purpose, namely, to explore leadership effectiveness in groups, in far fewer than 1,500 pages, much to your relief, I'm sure.

lentamart/Shutterstock.com

Stanford business professor Jeffrey Pfeffer (2015) observes critically: "There are no 'barriers to entry' into the leadership industry; no credentials, rigorous research, knowledge of relevant scientific evidence, or anything else required to pass oneself off as a leadership expert." He notes that "anyone and everyone can write a book" on leadership, and "it seems that virtually everyone does" (p. 24).

Definition of Leadership

There is an evolving consensus among academics that leadership is a social influence process (Northouse, 2019). "Exercising influence is the essence of leadership" (Hackman & Johnson, 2019). This influence can come from status, authority, personality, credibility, interpersonal and group communication skills, and a host of other factors.

Too often, however, the **romance of leadership**—the tendency to give too much credit to leaders for group outcomes, both good and bad—makes it appear that one can lead successfully without willing and capable followers (Ladkin, 2020). This next section discusses this fallacy.

focus questions

1. What is meant by "leadership is a process, not a person"?
2. What are the key differences between managing and leading a small group?
3. What role does communication play in leadership of small groups?

Leadership and Followership: Let's Dance

Former House Speaker John Boehner once remarked, referring to his many challenges trying to corral his rebellious Republican caucus, "You learn that a leader without followers is simply a man taking a walk" (quoted in Grove, 2014). Acclaimed business professor Warren Bennis (2007) notes, "The only person who practices leadership alone in a room is the psychotic" (p. 3). Leaders influence followers, but followers also influence leaders by making demands on them, requiring them to meet members' expectations, and evaluating their performance based on expectations. A Deloitte survey of 1,531 Gen Z respondents (born after 1995) draws this conclusion: "Gen Z has the opportunity to shift the 'balance of power' between the employer and the employee to a model where instead of workers trying to fit into a box called a 'job,' organizations will need to tailor work around the curated skillset of a worker." The report continues: "We think Gen Z will have the ability to demand greater personalization in how they move along their career journey" (Gomez et al., 2019). Followers can also influence leaders dramatically by mounting responses to leaders' decisions on social media platforms (Gilani et al., 2019). Thus, a definition of leadership must reflect the interconnected relationship between leaders and followers (DuBrin, 2019).

Negative connotations, however, have been associated with the term *follower*, such as passive, pliable, sheeplike, and even unintelligent (Gilani et al., 2019). Henry Ford, who pioneered the mass-production assembly line, articulated an apparent contempt for his workers who he expected to follow directions from their supervisors like robots: "The average worker," Ford (2003) asserted, "wants a job . . . in which he does not have to think" (p. 124). Ford further claimed that of the 7,882 operations necessary to construct a Model T automobile, "670 could be filled by legless men, 2,637 by one-legged men, 2 by armless men, 715 by one-armed men, and 10 by blind men" (p. 130). Continuing in this vein of supposedly amusing contempt for the worker/follower, he asked, "Why is it that when I ask for a pair of hands, a brain comes attached?" This vision of followers parking their brains at the door and mindlessly obeying whatever orders are issued by those in powerful positions has been relegated to the trash can of archaic thinking.

Modern researchers and scholars see leadership as a partnership (Yung & Tsai, 2013). Leaders and followers act like ballroom dancers. One leads and the other follows, but they influence each other, and they must work in tandem, or they will look like stumbling drunks on a binge. Thus, leadership is primarily a process, not a person (Platow et al., 2015). When you look at leadership from this angle, there can be no doubt that focusing only on leaders without analyzing the complex communication transactions that take place between leaders and followers misses the mark.

It should become apparent as this chapter unfolds that opportunities for you to exercise leadership regardless of your age, experience, job résumé, or a host of additional factors are plentiful. You do not have to be accorded an official title or position within a group to exhibit competent leadership. Learning early how to become a competent leader can boost your career choice and hasten your progress toward achieving personal life goals.

Although some authors and scholars offer special advice on how to be a good follower, that seems unnecessary and redundant. There are no special guidelines for being an effective follower that diverge from what makes an effective team member (see Chapter 8) and a competent communicator in groups. Leaders and followers are interconnected parts of a system, not separate entities.

Leader and Manager: Different Types of Influence

Have you ever, perhaps while working at a juice bar, grocery store, sporting goods store, or some other service-oriented job, worked for a manager who seemed less capable to lead than a disoriented person lost in a maze? Ask employees how they respond to "being managed." On my campus, even referring to "managing" employees—whether they be faculty, staff, or students—is a surefire way to trigger a Krakatoa-like eruption of verbal rebellion. "Being managed" has negative connotations. As one report puts it, "Newsflash: No one WANTS to be managed. Even the term 'manage' evokes feelings of control and manipulation" ("People Hate Being Managed," 2018). Most people do not equate managing with leadership, and for good reason. They are not the same. There are important differences between a leader and a manager (Hackman & Johnson, 2019).

Difference #1: Positional versus Interpersonal Influence A leader does not ordinarily operate from positional authority; a manager does. Anyone in a group can exhibit leadership even without being designated the leader. Only a manager is permitted to manage the group. Thus, managers are formally assigned the position of authority. A leader exercises interpersonal influence persuasively (leader–follower relationship), but a manager exercises positional influence, sometimes coercively (supervisor–subordinate relationship). One global report on leadership, involving more than 7,000 business executives from 130 countries, concluded, "The whole notion of 'positional leadership'—that people become leaders by virtue of their power and position—is being challenged. Leaders are instead being asked to inspire team loyalty through their expertise, vision, and judgment" (Wakefield et al., 2016). This means that as a student you won't exercise managerial authority, but you can become a leader on your project team, during discussion sessions, or in study groups through your communication with group members.

Difference #2: Maintaining versus Changing Leaders work to change the status quo; managers typically maintain it. Managers do this by working with budgets, organizing tasks, solving problems as they arise, and keeping things running smoothly by carrying out policies, plans, and visions devised by leaders. Managers enforce rules when they are broken, but they don't create the rules (Bryant & Higgins, 2010). Their primary goal is efficiency, not transformation. As Muriel Wilkins, C-suite advisor and cofounder of leadership development firm Paravis Partners, explains, a manager is "the individual who aims to keep things within the lines and the leader is the one who creates new lines" (quoted by Hoch, 2021).

Leadership implies change, not merely implementing or enforcing policies and rules. "Leadership deals with change, inspiration, motivation, and influence" (DuBrin, 2019). Some have called this **transformational leadership**, and they have distinguished it from transactional leadership (Bass & Bass, 2008). **Transactional leadership**, however, is essentially the same as management,

Photo by: Jeffrey Greenberg/Education Images/ Universal Images Group via Getty Images

Unlike leaders, for example, if you act as a designated manager of a fast-food restaurant, you do not set the rules of operation. You may even believe that some of the rules and regulations are silly, but nonetheless you enforce them because that is your job as the manager. The goal is efficiency, not transformation. Does this preclude managers exercising real leadership in some circumstances?

not leadership (Ebert & Griffin, 2011). I agree with Rost (1991) and his postindustrial model of leadership, when he claims, "Leadership, properly defined, is about transformation, all kinds of transformations" (p. 126). The social influence process (persuasion) that is the essence of leadership inherently implies transformations, small and large—changes in attitudes, beliefs, or behavior (Haslam et al., 2011). **All leadership, therefore, is transformational to a greater or lesser degree.** Leaders perceived to be *highly* transformational are sometimes referred to as **charismatic leaders** (Judge & Piccolo, 2004). Charismatic leaders have a significant impact on group members' lives and they provoke fierce loyalty, commitment, and devotion from followers. Believing that you have to be charismatic to be an effective leader, however, is called "the charisma myth" by Professor of Business Psychology Tomas Chamorro-Premuzic (2019). He concludes from extensive research that "the most effective business leaders in the world are not exactly known for their charisma."

Charisma—a constellation of personal attributes that people find highly attractive in an individual and strongly influential—is subjective, of course, and is determined by followers, not by some inherent list of objective qualities (Cohen & Yoon, 2021). Given the right person in the right set of circumstances, however, charismatic individuals can sometimes be highly transformational leaders in good ways. In one of my small group communication classes, I assigned a difficult group project due by midterm. The class was divided into four groups of 6–7 members. A member of one of these groups, an assemblage of individuals who on an initial assignment performed at a mediocre level, had an appealing personality and a gentle, articulate way of communicating that resonated immediately and strongly with fellow team members. He was a terrific, empathic listener, always showing an interest in what other group members could bring to the task. It was clear that he exuded charisma, but he also demonstrated competent communication. It was that combination that worked. He inspired members' commitment to excellence and generated an energetic work ethic, and ultimately his team was an outstanding success. When he moved to another group as required for the final class project, his initial group members were visibly glum when they ended up in a group that didn't include him.

Differences Not Categorically Exclusive: Matter of Emphasis So, the terms *leader* and *manager* are not synonymous. Distinguishing the two, however, does not exclude one person from being both (Blom, 2015; DuBrin, 2019). The point is not to denigrate managers to exalt leaders. Leaders are most effective when they can inspire followers and manage a budget, problem solve, and organize a plan of action. Conversely, a manager may be interested in more than merely maintaining the status quo, thus exercising leadership by lobbying for meaningful changes. These distinctions between leaders and managers are matters of emphasis. They are overlapping not completely separate categories. Thus, if you have the capacity to inspire and motivate group members to make changes, then you have the capacity to lead.

Having distinguished leaders from managers, a more complete definition of leadership emerges. **Leadership** is a leader–follower social influence process, directed toward positive change that reflects mutual purposes of group members and is largely accomplished through competent communication (Hackman & Johnson, 2019).

Leadership Emergence

Defining leadership sets the parameters of this discussion, but gaining and retaining leadership in small groups is complex and requires complex communication processes. A first relevant issue is whether a leader is designated or emergent. **Designated leaders** are appointed by a higher authority or elected by the group membership. They typically have the positional title of chair, facilitator, or coordinator when conducting small group business. Designated as "leaders," they may be expected to fill that role, but remember that a position does not automatically make one a true leader. **Emergent leaders**, the focus of this section, earn the admiration of group members and significantly influence them even though they have no formal authority.

Emergent leaders can rise quite unexpectedly during challenges small and large. When Covid-19 struck, requiring everyone to bunker in a Zoom room, those more technologically savvy but lacking formal authority could exercise greater influence over their group than the person with the formal title of chair, facilitator, or the like with limited technological skills to keep group transactions up and running smoothly. In one case that I observed, the chair of a board of trustees kept appearing on screen during a Zoom meeting, then quickly disappearing into a blank screen, only to soon reappear with hair askew and clothes disheveled, having obviously crawled under his desk trying desperately to find the cause of connection problems that clearly were beyond his technical knowledge. The meeting continued without him, interrupted occasionally as the chair came up for air to display his rather comical exasperation, as other group members, including the student trustee board member, swooped in to assume influential task roles (e.g., information giver, coordinator-director) despite lack of designated authority.

Leader emergence is not necessarily a one-time, permanent affair. In long-standing groups, several leaders may emerge at different times, rotating through the life cycle of the team, especially when circumstances change and team tasks differ markedly requiring alternative sets of knowledge and skills (Horila & Siitonen, 2020). Again, leadership is primarily a process, not just a person. Thus, the leader emergence process in small groups is a significant topic for exploration.

focus questions

1. What should you avoid if you want to emerge as a leader of a group?

2. What are the most likely ways to emerge as a group leader?

How Not to Become a Leader: Communication Blunders

A survey of millennials reported that 91% aspire to be leaders (Haynie, 2016). Another survey found that 81% of Gen Z respondents aspire to be leaders (Miller, 2018). Why do people want to become leaders? There are numerous reasons, but the most obvious ones are *status* that comes from running the show, *respect* for doing a good job of guiding the group, and *power* accorded leaders that allows them to influence others and produce change. Students who campaign to be representatives on the student senate may be motivated by all three of these reasons, but wanting to produce meaningful change is likely to be a more driving force than either status or respect.

It is often easier to determine what you shouldn't do more than what you should do if you wish to emerge as leader of a small group for any of the reasons just cited. As a college student, you undoubtedly have numerous opportunities to emerge as a group leader. For example, the local university in my geographic location is the University of California Santa Cruz. There are more than 150 registered student groups at this college "based on academic, athletic, ethnic, religious, political, and cultural interests" ("Student-Led Clubs & Organizations," 2021). At larger colleges, there are even far greater numbers of groups to join. Ohio State University, for example, has more than 1,400 such groups and 70% of the vast student body participates in at least one group ("Student Activities," 2021). So, heed the following dictums that likely will prove quite relevant to you now or at some near future time:

1. *Thou shalt not exhibit Me-orientation.* Groups typically do not endorse would-be leaders who seem more interested in advancing self-oriented goals than group goals (Grace & Platow, 2015). It is preferable to exhibit a We-not-Me orientation. Relationship building is strongly associated with perceived leadership (Horila & Siitonen, 2020).

2. *Thou shalt not be uninformed about a problem commanding the group's attention* (Riggio et al., 2003). Leaders are expected to be relevantly knowledgeable. A previously cited Career Builder survey that identified the "most unusual" mistakes made by job interviewees seeking professional employment included one candidate who proudly offered "Fake it until you make" as his personal philosophy (Hayes, 2018). You can imagine how his tacit know-nothing confession was received by the hiring panel.

3. *Thou shalt not manifest sluggish participation in group discussions.* Group members are not impressed by "vigor mortis." Participation is a sign of commitment to the group, and commitment to the group and its goals is part of the leadership process.

4. *Thou shalt not attempt to dominate conversation during discussion.* Leadership is not "loudership" (Kluger, 2009). Although those who talk the most are perceived initially as potential leader material (Jones & Kelly, 2007), quality of participation, not mere quantity, is what groups typically desire (Jiang et al., 2015). Loudmouths who try to dominate discussions and won't dial down the volume and the intensity of their speech patterns can be repellent. An armor-piercing voice demanding unyielding attention is infantile. Women, unfortunately, must be especially careful to not come across as shrill, while men typically are permitted wider latitude to be overbearing, at least up to a point (McClean et al., 2017).

5. *Thou shalt not listen poorly.* As the sign says sarcastically, "Oh, I'm sorry. Did the middle of my sentence interrupt the beginning of yours?" Interrupting will not endear you to the group. Leadership is not a monologue; it's a dialogue. Dialogue means leaders and followers listen carefully to each other without constant interruption. Groups prefer leaders who listen effectively (Daimler, 2016). Avoid being an annoying "know-it-all," and become more of a "learn-it-all" by listening actively to others (McCracken, 2017).

6. *Thou shalt not be rigid and inflexible when expressing viewpoints.* Group members prefer open, not closed, minds. The attitude of certitude (see Chapter 5) provokes defensiveness, not a willingness to be influenced.

7. *Thou shalt not display "emotional incontinence."* Emotional outbursts, or what Birgitta Wistrand, CEO of a Swedish company, called "emotional incontinence," will likely brand you as unstable and unfit to lead a group of any size (Goleman, 2013).

General Emergence Pattern: Process of Elimination

In general, small group leaders emerge by a process of elimination (Bormann, 1990). Potential candidates are systematically removed from consideration.

Pressmaster/Shutterstock

If crying at work is perceived to be a serious workplace taboo (Wilding, 2018), it is nevertheless a common occurrence. One survey found that of 3,078 respondents, 5.2% admitted to crying at work daily, 8.3% did it weekly, and an additional 50% reported doing it occasionally (Bolden-Barrett, 2019). "Rightly or wrongly, workplace tears do not communicate leadership potential—especially if you're a man. While 59% of executives say crying makes a woman look bad, 63% believe it's a top mistake for men" (Goudreau, 2012). Emotional incontinence can be a leadership deal-breaker. Better to cry in private if the need arises. Established leaders should also take note concerning the group climate that may be the stressor that triggers tears.

HBRH/Shutterstock

We may be quite clear on what we don't want in a leader, but we may not be as sure about what we do want. Also, there can be variability in leader emergence over time, and that can be productive for a group as it responds to changing circumstances (Guastello et al. 2018).

Two Phases of Emergence There are two phases to the process-of-elimination explanation of leader emergence. During the first phase, roughly half of the members are eliminated from consideration. The criteria for elimination are crude and impressionistic. Negative communication patterns—the "thou shalt nots"—weigh heavily.

In the second phase, groups look for task-competent individuals who are committed to the group's goals, not personal advancement, to emerge as leaders. Leaders are expected to be *doers*, persons ready to act to help the group achieve its goals (Platow et al., 2015). If the group feels threatened by some external or internal crisis (e.g., the inability to choose a topic for a symposium presentation or the loss of members with expertise relevant to successful completion of a class group assignment due to illness or attrition), the group often turns to the member who provides a solution to the crisis, and he or she becomes at least the temporary leader. Also, those individuals who exhibit high levels of **emotional intelligence**—"the ability to perceive, glean information from, and manage one's own and others' emotions"—emerge as group leaders more readily than those who don't (Cote et al., 2010). In fact, based on two studies, "the ability to understand emotions was the most consistently related to leadership emergence" (DuBrin, 2019). This affirms the importance of sensitivity and skills in the communication competence model discussed in Chapter 1.

Finally, during the phase two process, members who acquire an advocate who promotes them—their ideas, positions, and abilities—find their chances of becoming a group leader boosted (e.g., "Rodney has the most knowledge and experience dealing with fundraising. I think he should steer us in the right direction"). A person can acquire an advocate in a variety of ways: through friendship, charisma, common interests and goals, competence, or self-interest and pursuit of power. If more than one member gains an advocate, then the process can become contentious, or it may end in shared leadership.

Virtual Group Leader Emergence Research on leader emergence in virtual groups mostly parallels findings of leader emergence in standard, face-to-face groups. Degree and quality of participation is an important consideration, as it is in standard groups. Virtual group participants have a negative view of those positioning themselves to emerge as leaders when they are perceived to be "dominant, opinionated, outspoken, uncompromising, and pursuant of their own agenda." Virtual group participants have a positive view of those who are "inclusive, collaborative, concerned about others, good listeners, and in search of consensus" (Shollen, 2010). More importantly, as a very large study of 220 student groups found, doers are even more likely to lead virtual groups than they are in-person groups (Purvanova et al., 2020). As lead author of the study, Radostina

Purvanova explains, "Virtually, we are less swayed by someone's personality . . . But those chosen as remote leaders were doers, who tended towards planning, connecting teammates with help and resources, keeping an eye on upcoming tasks and, most importantly, getting things done" (quoted by A. Cohen, 2020). Displaying emotional intelligence is more challenging in virtual groups, and charisma seems to have less influence on virtual group members.

Additional Factors: Implicit Theories of Leadership

When group members first meet, **implicit theories of leadership**—individuals' expectations, beliefs, and assumptions about what traits and abilities constitute an effective leader—influence the dynamics that favor emergence of certain individuals as group leaders. When survey respondents are asked to picture a "leader," for example, they typically picture "male" (Koenig et al., 2011; Murphy, 2018). Data from Equilar's Gender Diversity Index of the 3,000 largest public U.S. companies show that fewer than a quarter of corporate board members are women, no boards are entirely comprised of women, 180 companies have no women on their boards, and only 71 companies (2.4%) have boards that are at least half female (Boorstin, 2021). This sorry record is especially ironic because several studies reveal that women score markedly higher on measures of leadership effectiveness than men even when both men and women make the assessments (Young, 2016). In fact, Tomas Chamorro-Premuzic (2019), previously cited, has written a bestselling book titled *Why Do So Many Incompetent Men Become Leaders*? He concludes from voluminous research that "most leaders are bad and that most leaders are male." Studies also show that when asked to "think leader," respondents "think White" (Gundemir et al., 2014). The situation for African Americans, both male and female, in regard to executive positions at large companies is especially bleak (Guynn & Schrotenboer, 2021). Gaining advocates (e.g., men supporting women as group leaders) and being assertive are especially important in overcoming gender and ethnic bias in leadership emergence, in addition to more detailed advice and discussion provided in Chapter 11 on the effects of power imbalance in small groups.

We develop prototypes in our minds that picture what a leader should be. Unfortunately, "people tend to equate leadership with the very behavior—overconfidence, for example—that often signals bad leadership" (Chamorro-Premuzic, 2019). These implicit theories of leadership can produce some odd choices. One disturbing study (Babiak & Hare, 2006) found that nearly 4% of 200 business executives qualified as **psychopaths**—"someone who has no conscience and feels no remorse or empathy" (Perman, 2011). More recent research by forensic psychologist Nathan Brooks, however, bumps the prevalence of psychopathic business executives to an astounding 21%, about the same percentage as found "in a prison population" (cited by Agerholm, 2016). Whatever the actual prevalence, these are "horrible bosses," not cold-blooded killers.

So why do psychopaths ever emerge as leaders? They project an image of a leader that dovetails with common implicit theories of leadership (Dutton, 2016). Initially, they are typically charming, confident, decisive, fearless, risk-takers, and mentally tough. Nevertheless, they are ruthless and manipulative (i.e., ethically challenged). They make toxic leaders who create negative group climates. The negative qualities, however, may not become apparent until after the psychopath has emerged and subsequently solidified his or her image as group leader.

Similarly, **narcissists**—those who exhibit "a grandiose sense of self-importance; arrogant behavior or attitudes; a lack of empathy for others; a preoccupation with fantasies of unlimited success or power; . . . [and] a desire for excessive admiration from others" (Pfeffer, 2015)—frequently emerge as leaders in groups. This occurs because they "possess many characteristics that people associate with a prototypical leader (e.g., confidence, extraversion, dominance)" (Nevicka et al., 2018). They can be charming, humorous, outgoing, confident, decisive, even charismatic. They are especially successful emerging as leaders of new groups that have not had enough opportunity

SECOND LOOK
Pattern of Leader Emergence

GENERAL PATTERN (PROCESS OF ELIMINATION)

Phase One

The "thou shalt nots" eliminate members from consideration

Task incompetent members are eliminated

Phase Two

Member who provides solution in time of crisis considered

Member who exhibits effective listening skills considered

Member who exhibits emotional intelligence considered

Member who acquires an advocate considered

If more than one member acquires an advocate—possible stalemate or shared leadership

Implicit Theories of Leader Emergence

Gender bias tends to diminish women's chances of selection as leaders.

Ethnic bias tends to diminish minority members' chances of selection as leaders.

Psychopaths considered because they can seem charming and self-confident.

Narcissists considered because they can seem decisive, confident, and charismatic.

beyond first impressions to observe and experience the narcissist's dark side displayed by a sense of entitlement, egocentrism, antagonism, lack of empathy, and a willingness to exploit others for personal gain. Such negative characteristics can be especially damaging to followers with low self-esteem (Nevicka et al., 2018). The narcissist's grandiose self-assessments "are not aligned with reality. Narcissistic leaders in fact hinder the processes for reaching high-quality decisions, and therefore diminish group performance" (Nevicka et al., 2011).

The troubling emergence of psychopathic and narcissistic leaders in groups underlines an essential point: Those who emerge as small group leaders do not necessarily prove to be effective leaders. Although as a student your exposure to either a psychopathic or narcissistic leader is likely to be remote, once you pursue your career in earnest if you haven't already, the likelihood that a boss will be either or both kinds of toxic leader is not so unlikely. Chapters 11 and 12 provide in-depth analysis and advice that is relevant to the obvious question on your mind, namely, "How do I deal with a toxic boss?" The answer is not some simple one-sentence formula.

Perspectives on Competent Leadership

Scholarly perspectives on leadership effectiveness have changed greatly over the almost century since the first serious research was conducted. In this section, the primary perspectives that have generated considerable interest are discussed. These perspectives unfold in a kind of historical progression, a story of how initial views on leadership effectiveness have evolved and improved. Leadership effectiveness not only serves as a powerful force for group achievement, but it is a ticket to retaining leadership. Groups don't typically dump leaders who are serving the group needs effectively.

Traits Perspective: The Born Leader View

This is the "leaders are born, not made" perspective. This perspective views leadership as a person, not a process. Thus, we hunt for the "heroic" and exceptionally talented individuals to idolize as model specimens of leadership. This journey has taken us to strange places. You can buy books on the leadership secrets of Pope Francis, Colin Powell, Meg Whitman, Barack Obama, Eleanor Roosevelt, Margaret Thatcher, Donald Trump, Steve Jobs, Attila the Hun, Genghis Khan, Osama bin Laden, and Santa Claus (not kidding).

One survey of CEOs in 60 countries asked which leaders respondents most admired. The top 10 list included Winston Churchill, Mahatma Gandhi, and

Napoleon Bonaparte—strikingly dissimilar choices. Among the same respondents, 96% of the male CEOs failed to mention a single female leader, and 83% of the female CEOs did likewise ("Leaders CEOs Most Admire," 2014). Similarly, a thousand Americans were asked to name a famous female leader in business technology. Respondents to this survey at the time could have named Susan Wojcicke (CEO of YouTube), Kimberly Bryant (founder and CEO of Black Girls Code and winner of multiple prestigious awards), Ginni Rometty (CEO of IBM), Safra Catz (CEO of Oracle), Meg Whitman (former CEO of Hewlett Packard), or Sheryl Sandberg (longtime COO of Facebook and bestselling author of *Lean In*). Nevertheless, 92% of respondents couldn't name a single female leader in tech, but "Siri" and "Alexa" were named by numerous respondents from the remaining 8%. Conversely, 57% of respondents could correctly name a male leader, with Steve Jobs, Bill Gates, Elon Musk, and Mark Zuckerberg heading the list. These results exhibit "Silicon Valley's ever-pervasive 'great man' culture, which too often mythologizes the work of male leaders without affording the same cultural cachet to their female counterparts" (Zara, 2018).

Finally, a Quinnipiac University poll found that 80% of American respondents viewed Russian President Vladimir Putin as dishonest and untrustworthy and 33% weren't sure about his mental stability, yet 57% saw him as possessing "strong leadership qualities" ("Obama Approval Inches Up," 2014). Clearly, such vastly disparate, male-dominated lists of perceived strong and admired leaders suggest a perspective with substantial limitations.

There remains the common belief that a universal set of traits conflates with leader effectiveness, sometimes with little consideration for ethical behavior. **Traits** are relatively enduring characteristics of an individual that highlight differences between people and that are displayed in most situations. There are physical traits such as height, weight, physique, beauty, and attractiveness. There are personality traits such as being outgoing, sociable, likable, or introverted and shy. There are traits associated with inherent capacities of an individual such as intelligence and quick-wittedness. There are also traits associated with consistent behaviors such as confidence, trustworthiness, and integrity.

A huge number of traits have been studied to discover the prototypical leader. We know, for instance, that being tall, physically fit, and attractive have a bearing on social influence (White et al., 2013). A Pew Research survey of 1,835 adults found that when asked which traits are "absolutely essential" for a leader to possess, honesty was at the top of the list (84%), followed by intelligence (80%) and decisiveness (80%) ("What Makes a Good Leader," 2015). A cross-cultural study of 62 countries found great variation among leadership traits chosen except for a single trait—charisma, universally viewed as an essential ingredient of leadership effectiveness (Javidan et al., 2006). "Despite the *insignificance* of charisma with regards to leadership effectiveness, you can ask anyone about

Per Grunditz/Shutterstock.com

Photo by Marla Aufmuth/Getty Images for Massachusetts Conference for Women 2019

Photo by Nathaniel S. Butler/NBAE via Getty Images

Michael Reynolds/Pool via AP

Identify traits that these four leaders—climate activist Greta Thunberg, youngest Nobel Prize winner Malala Yousafzai, L.A. Lakers team captain and James Family Foundation head LeBron James, and Facebook CEO Mark Zuckerberg—have in common. What traits clearly do not match? The trait perspective on leadership effectiveness is only minimally insightful, as the key differences among these four leaders attest.

the fundamental qualities of a leader and he or she will inevitably list charisma among the top traits" (Chamorro-Premuzic, 2019). Humble leaders, however, typically perform better (Peng et al., 2020). As one researcher concludes, "The research is clear: when we choose humble unassuming people as our leaders, the world around us becomes a better place. . . . Yet instead of following the lead of these unsung heroes, we appear hard-wired to search for superheroes: over-glorifying leaders who exude charisma" (Mayo, 2017).

Is there an ideal combination of traits that might make a leader effective? Fiedler and House (1988) claim that "effective leaders tend to have a high need to influence others, to achieve, and they tend to be bright, competent, and socially adept, rather than stupid, incompetent, and social disasters" (p. 87). In an extreme sense this is true. Stogdill (1948, 1974), however, twice reviewed hundreds of studies and concluded that no universal set of traits assures leader emergence or leader effectiveness.

How could it be otherwise? For example, traits such as intelligence, confidence, and attractiveness could be neutralized by unfriendliness, ethical indifference, laziness, arrogance, and/or insensitivity. One study of 3,700 business executives used 60 traits to assess leadership (Stamoulis & Mannion, 2014). Who could possibly possess all 60 traits, or even most? "To expect that a person would be born with all of the tools needed to lead just doesn't make sense based on what we know about the complexity of social groups and processes" (Riggio, 2009). A 25-year study by the Gallup Organization of 80,000 leaders found that the greatest leaders in the world don't share a common set of characteristics (Buckingham & Coffman, 1999).

Certain basic traits (intelligence, social and verbal skills, extroversion) may be the irreducible minimum qualifications to become a leader, but to retain the role of leader and ultimately to perform effectively requires much more. The principal problem with the trait approach is the assumption that effective leadership resides in the person, not in transactions between leaders and followers conducted within the group system (Northouse, 2019). No one set of leadership traits will fit every situation and group. Although the trait perspective is not entirely without merit, there's much more to leadership effectiveness. Effective leaders are not born; they are developed.

Styles Perspective: One Style Doesn't Fit All

Unsatisfied with the trait approach to leadership, Kurt Lewin and his associates developed a new approach based on three leadership styles: autocratic, democratic, and laissez-faire (Lewin et al., 1939). **Autocratic leadership style** exerts control over group members. The autocratic leader is highly directive. This leadership style does not encourage member participation. Autocratic leaders are not concerned about making friends or getting invited to parties. The autocratic style (usually referred

Thomas Barwick/Getty Images

Autocratic/directive leadership is effective in some instances but disastrous in others. Which do you think this is?

to more neutrally as the *directive style*) puts most of the emphasis on the task, with little concern for the social dimension of the group (high task, low social).

The **democratic leadership style** encourages participation and responsibility from group members. Democratic leaders work to improve the skills and abilities of group members. Followers have a say in what the group decides. The democratic style (usually referred to more neutrally as the *participative style*) puts a balanced emphasis on both the task and social dimensions of the group (high task, high social).

The **laissez-faire leadership style** is a do-nothing approach to leadership. It is "the avoidance or absence of leadership" in which individuals "avoid making decisions, hesitate in taking action, and are absent when needed" (Judge & Piccolo, 2004). Laissez-faire amounts to a sit-on-your-derriere style. This style doesn't try to influence anyone, so it is by definition nonleadership. "Without influence, leadership does not exist" (Northouse, 2019). Thus, it has been dropped from serious consideration in most of the research.

The extensive research comparing autocratic-directive and democratic-participative leadership styles shows both can be productive (Northouse, 2019). Participative leadership seems to work best when it springs naturally from the group itself. Not all small groups, however, want or expect their leaders to adopt the participative leadership style. Nevertheless, one survey of business leaders reported that 76% of 1,400 respondents viewed use of an inappropriate leadership style to be among the biggest failures of leaders ("Critical Leadership Skills," 2014). Typically, it is the autocratic/directive style that is overused and can backfire (Green, 2018).

What Is Your Leadership Style Preference?

Fill out the self-assessment on leadership styles. Note: The rating scale changes.

1. I like it when my supervisor at work admits openly that he/she made a mistake.
STRONGLY DISAGREE   STRONGLY AGREE
1   2   3   4   5

2. I want to be told what to do on the job, not have to figure it out for myself.
STRONGLY DISAGREE   STRONGLY AGREE
5   4   3   2   1

3. If my team were hiring a new applicant, I prefer that the entire team interview the candidate and make the final decision, not the team leader only.
STRONGLY DISAGREE   STRONGLY AGREE
1   2   3   4   5

4. I don't want my boss to be my friend; I prefer that my boss remain aloof from the group so he/she can be objective when decisions need to be made.
STRONGLY DISAGREE   STRONGLY AGREE
5   4   3   2   1

5. I do not think that my boss should reverse the decision of his/her team except in extraordinary circumstances (dangerous mistake).
STRONGLY DISAGREE   STRONGLY AGREE
1   2   3   4   5

6. I prefer to be told what decisions have been made and then informed what I should do to implement these decisions, not engage in time-consuming debate.
STRONGLY DISAGREE   STRONGLY AGREE
5   4   3   2   1

7. I prefer having many opportunities to provide input before my team leader makes a final decision.
STRONGLY DISAGREE   STRONGLY AGREE
1   2   3   4   5

8. I want my boss to make the important decisions, not get me and others on our team involved; that's why he/she gets paid the big bucks.
STRONGLY DISAGREE   STRONGLY AGREE
5   4   3   2   1

9. I want my boss to encourage robust debate and differences of opinion before any decisions are made.
STRONGLY DISAGREE   STRONGLY AGREE
1   2   3   4   5

10. I want my boss to be decisive, to make decisions confidently, and model a person who is totally in charge.
STRONGLY DISAGREE   STRONGLY AGREE
5   4   3   2   1

Tally your total score and divide by 10. The higher your average score, the more you prefer participative leadership from supervisors/bosses/team leaders. The lower your average score, the more you prefer the directive leadership style.

One weakness of the participative/directive leadership style duality is that these styles are viewed as extreme opposites. Individuals operate as either participative or directive leaders, but not both. Realistically, though, a combination of participative and directive leadership styles is required in small groups. Consider a "temp worker" who is new on a job. Should this person be consulted on how the job should be accomplished when he or she doesn't even have a good idea what the job entails? Should teachers consult their students before determining course content when the students know little or nothing about the subject? Should military commanders seek the participation of their troops before launching an offensive? "All those in favor of attacking the heavily armed enemy signal by saying aye; those opposed, nay. Okay, the nays have it. We'll stay put and live another day." Group members can't always meaningfully participate in decision making.

No one style of leadership will be suitable for all situations any more than one set of leadership traits will mesh with every situation. This realization has led researchers to explore yet another approach to leadership—the situational perspective.

Situational Perspective: Matching Styles with Circumstances

This is the "it depends" approach to leadership. Those leaders whose style fits well with their situation exhibit strong confidence and perform at a high level (Chemers, 2000). One caveat, however, should be noted: Leadership effectiveness may be influenced by situational forces beyond the control of any leader (Vroom & Jago, 2007). Military officers, coaches of sports teams, orchestra conductors, and others receive adulation for successes and blame for failures (recall the romance of leadership), but group effectiveness is systemic. Even the most capable leaders can be victimized by the harsh situational realities of inadequate resources, weak systemic support, and other external factors. For example, the San Francisco 49ers lost 27 players from injuries, some short-term but several key players for the entire year, by the 2020 midseason, most in the NFL. Three consecutive losses resulted at midpoint, and rumblings about firing head coach Kyle Shanahan, who guided his team to the Super Bowl in 2019, emerged. Unsurprisingly, the team finished with a 6–10 win–loss record. Nevertheless, despite unforeseen challenges, leaders who can adapt flexibly to systemic situations have the best chance of success.

Hersey and Blanchard have developed a popular situational leadership model that expands on the styles perspective (see Hersey et al., 2001). There are four leadership styles in this model. The **telling style** (high task, low relationship emphasis) is directive. A leader provides specific instructions on a task and closely supervises the performance of followers, but places minimal focus on developing social relationships with followers. The **selling style** (high task, high relationship) is also directive. A leader explains and clarifies decisions, but also tries to convince followers to accept directives. The **participating style** (low task, high relationship) is nondirective. A leader encourages shared decision making with special emphasis on developing relationships in the group. The **delegating style** (low task, low relationship) is also nondirective. A leader allows the group to be self-directed.

The primary situational variable that the leader must consider is the readiness level of followers. **Readiness** is "the extent to which a follower demonstrates the ability and willingness to accomplish a specific task" (Hersey et al., 2001). According to the model, as readiness levels increase, effective leadership requires reduced guidance and direction from the leader. When an individual is new to a team, leadership requires a directive style to educate the new member about group procedures, practices, and expectations. Then the selling style encourages the more informed member to feel a social identity, a connection to the group. This is followed by encouraging informed participation from the more "ready" member, and finally the delegating style exhibits trust by providing autonomy for decision making.

Despite its intuitive appeal, research on situational leadership is skimpy and contradictory (Northouse, 2019; Vecchio et al., 2006; Yukl, 2006), so much so that DuBrin (2019) in his extensive review of leadership research has completely dropped treatment of the Hersey and Blanchard model and its permutations (e.g., Situational Leadership II; Leadership Grid). These models also are leader-centric, downplaying the influence followers have on leadership effectiveness. Nevertheless, the situational leadership model, despite its overly formulaic and poorly supported approach, underlines the importance of flexible use of styles to fit differing situations. Leaders need to adapt to changing systemic circumstances and exhibit sensitivity to the fluctuations in the task and social requirements of groups.

One way of analyzing changing situations in a less detailed, prescriptive manner is simply to consider both the speed and quality of decision making. For example, in a crisis situation in which swift action is imperative, the autocratic/directive style is most appropriate. Crisis teams (e.g., first responders) are trained to take swift action and to follow the directions of those in command. There is not time to deliberate options while a building is on fire and people need to be rescued. Nevertheless, when an actual emergency is not occurring, a democratic/participative leadership style could encourage fruitful, creative problem solving among team members to improve response times and decision making. As situations change, leadership styles typically need to change.

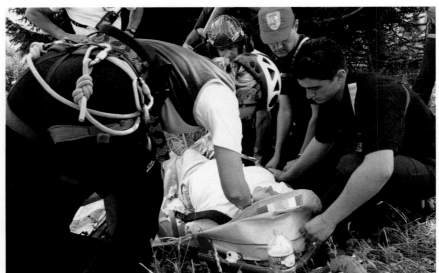

Rescue teams typically follow an autocratic/directive style of leadership because quick action is required to save lives. Democratic/participative leadership style, however, can be appropriate for later discussions concerning tactical improvement and better teamwork. One leadership style does not apply to every situation.

Photo by John van Hasselt/Corbis via Getty Images

Distributive Leadership: Sharing Functions

The **distributive, or shared, leadership perspective** recognizes that "we're all in this together." This perspective truly embraces the view that leadership is more a process than a person (Thomas et al., 2013). Distributive leadership tacitly recognizes the importance of the group's situation to leadership effectiveness but views changing situations from a functional angle (Morrison-Smith & Ruiz, 2020). There are certain functions, or responsibilities, that must be performed for the group to be successful. Typically, these functions fall into two categories: task requirements and social needs. Finding the right balance between these two is viewed as essential, and that balance varies with changing situations.

The list of task and maintenance roles previously identified in Chapter 6 indicates functions essential to a group's success (e.g., giving information, coordinating, facilitating, gatekeeping, relieving tension). Leadership as a shared responsibility is demonstrated when any member steps in and assumes whatever role in the group is required at a particular moment that has not been filled by any other member. What does the specific situation call for from alert members? When a group member dominates discussion, for example, this situation calls for any other member to act as a gatekeeper to quell the disruptive gabster ("I'd like to hear from some other members, and can we agree to keep our comments short, perhaps no longer than two minutes so everyone has an opportunity to contribute?"). When the group seems inclined to make a specific decision, but no mention has been forthcoming about possible disadvantages or potential pitfalls of such a decision, this situation calls for anyone to play devil's advocate ("Are we exhibiting confirmation bias? Have we sufficiently explored what might go wrong if we implement this plan?").

The distributive, shared leadership perspective takes the groups-as-systems view. Leadership is viewed as a system of interconnected networks of shared responsibility for group success, and research supports the effectiveness of shared leadership in groups (Wu et al., 2020). The more diverse the group membership is, however, the more challenging shared leadership becomes (Xu et al., 2019).

Team training is essential. One aspect of intensive training experienced by members of Navy SEAL teams, for example, is this shared leadership perspective. Trainees are divided into teams of six, the capacity of their landing rafts. "During boat exercises, trainees constantly trade positions and leadership roles" (Coyle, 2018). All members should be prepared to assume necessary roles that respond to new challenges and advance the progress of the group. Performing a necessary task or maintenance role can have a positive ripple effect throughout the group system. Research supports the effectiveness of shared leadership in both standard and virtual groups in concert with cooperative communication environments (Hoch & Dulebohn, 2017).

Servant Leadership Perspective: Ethical Necessity

Ethical leadership fundamentally involves how leaders treat followers. In Chapter 1, ethical criteria—honesty, respect, fairness, choice, and responsibility—were identified. One study of 195 global leaders ranked "high ethical and moral standards" as most important among 74 "leadership competencies" (Giles, 2016). Unfortunately, too often pragmatic concerns push ethical concerns about leader behavior into the background or make them virtually invisible (Knights, 2017). Servant leadership is well suited to both millennials and Gen Z individuals who typically highly value honesty, integrity, fairness, and serving others (Gomez et al., 2019; Parker & Igielnik, 2020).

A key principle of ethical leadership recently gaining popularity is the dictum to "serve others." Ethical leaders are **servant leaders** who "place the good of followers over their own self-interests and emphasize follower development . . . They demonstrate strong moral behavior toward followers" (Northouse, 2019). Initially offered by Robert Greenleaf (1977), the concept of servant leadership has been studied and developed more recently (Eva et al., 2019). Heavy emphasis is placed on caring for others, not advancing one's own self-interest. A leader must "operate beyond the ego, to put others first" (Knights, 2017).

Servant leadership embraces the five elements of communication ethics. A servant leader is scrupulously honest, respectful, and fair toward followers; provides choices for followers when possible; and is responsible for helping the group achieve goals in ethically acceptable ways. "A servant leader is therefore a moral leader" (DuBrin, 2019).

Servant leadership is also manifested by mentoring followers to become leaders in groups. When asked "How would you like to learn to lead," more than 60% of millennials responded, "I'd like a mentor." A remarkable 95% of those receiving mentoring from leaders received promotions at work within 18 months (Wartham, 2016). Helping others achieve their goals helps groups as well. Servant leadership is about building relationships with group members and creating an atmosphere of empowerment. "Servant leaders develop cultures in which followers become servant leaders" (Brown & Bryant, 2015). Research shows that ethically congruent servant leadership benefits group members by reducing stress and producing team effectiveness (Sajjadi et al., 2014).

The Cleveland Clinic, one of the world's premier healthcare providers, implemented a program of servant leadership in 2008 to improve team performance. The results were impressive. Patient satisfaction was greatly improved following extensive training of staff in servant leadership (Patrnchak, 2015). Note that it was entire staffs that were trained, not just those with authority and titles, underlining again that effective leadership is a shared, collaborative communication process permeating all levels of groups and organizations.

The servant leadership perspective is not just a "nice idea." Criticisms that servant leaders are subservient, weak leaders takes the incorrect view that leadership requires dominance and an autocratic style (Schwantes, 2016). The criticisms reflect the anachronistic stereotype of strong leaders being commanding and goal oriented, thus typically favoring men. Research shows that the movement toward servant leadership favors women, who seem to perform more effectively as groups increasingly value a communal emphasis and relationship development (Lemoine & Blum. 2019). Jim Olson, chief communications officer at Steward Health Care, notes the "seismic shift occurring in leadership from command-and-control leaders to servant leaders" (quoted by Henricks, 2018).

Culture and Leadership: Are There Universal Theories?

"Almost all of the prevailing theories of leadership, and about 98% of the empirical evidence at hand, are rather distinctly American in character" (House & Aditya, 1997). This hasn't changed appreciably in recent years. Can we apply the leadership effectiveness theories discussed in this chapter universally across cultures? At this point we simply don't know.

Nevertheless, research does suggest that some differences across cultures regarding leadership do exist. Even though in the United States the importance of leadership is widely taken for granted, other cultures do not necessarily share this view (Plaister-Ten, 2017). A huge research project called GLOBE, conducted by a collaborative group of 170 scholars worldwide, studied 62 cultures and 17,300 individuals in 951 organizations. It revealed that status and influence accorded leaders vary widely among cultures (House, 2004). Americans, Arabs, Asians, the British, Eastern Europeans, the French, Germans, Latin Americans, and Russians tend to idealize strong leaders, erecting statues and naming streets and buildings after those thought to be extraordinary. German-speaking parts of Switzerland, the Netherlands, and Scandinavia, however, are generally skeptical of strong leaders and fear their abuse of power. In these countries, public commemoration of leaders is sparse. Leadership characterized as elitist, self-centered, and egotistical is perceived to be slightly effective in Albania, Taiwan, Egypt, Iran, and Kuwait. All other countries in the GLOBE study, however, especially northern European countries, had a very negative opinion of such leadership. The participative leadership style, typically accepted or even preferred in Western cultures, is questionably effective in Eastern cultures (Dorfman, 2004). Directive leadership is strongly favored more in Middle Eastern cultures (Scandura et al., 1999).

There do seem to be some universals in the cross-cultural research on leadership. The GLOBE study revealed strong endorsement by all cultures examined of such leadership attributes as having foresight and planning ahead; being positive, encouraging, dynamic, motivating, communicative, and informed; and being a team builder. Also, research "has shown highly consistent results supporting the efficacy of servant leadership across national cultures" (Liden & Zhong, 2017). Conversely, "the portrait of an ineffective leader is someone who is asocial, malevolent, and self-focused. Clearly, people from all cultures find these characteristics to hinder effective leadership" (Northouse, 2019). Less clearly, being individualistic, status conscious, and a risk taker was viewed as enhancing outstanding leadership in some cultures but impeding outstanding leadership in other cultures (Dorfman et al., 2004). Also, an in-depth study of 1,500 corporate executives and public-sector leaders in 60 countries and 33 industries found that among the North American CEOs, 65% viewed integrity as a top trait for tomorrow's leaders, but only 29% to 48% of CEOs from other countries shared this view (Carr, 2010).

Again, even if agreement on a certain set of leadership traits existed across cultures, this would be very different from demonstrating effective leadership in actual practice. In any case, we still have much to learn about effective leadership across cultures.

Communication Competence Perspective: The Overarching View

"Extraordinary leadership is the product of extraordinary communication" (Hackman & Johnson, 2019). Communication competence is at the heart of leadership effectiveness. The evolving story of leadership perspectives discussed in this chapter offers useful insights, but ultimately all of these perspectives depend on competent communication for effective implementation. A survey of 1,400 leaders, managers, and executives found that the "most critical leadership skill" by far was the ability to communicate effectively and "the biggest mistake leaders make" is "inappropriate use of communication" ("Critical Leadership Skills," 2014). A Harris poll asked 1,000 workers to identify the "communication issues that prevent effective leadership." Respondents listed the following: not recognizing employee achievements (63%), not giving clear directions (57%), not having time to meet with employees (52%), refusing to talk to subordinates (51%), taking credit for others' ideas (47%), and not offering constructive feedback (39%) (cited by Solomon, 2015). A similar list added poor listening, micromanaging, and refusing to consider different opinions and ideas from one's own (Haden, 2013).

Effective leaders create a supportive, positive climate, encourage open communication, stimulate cooperation and a collaborative spirit, show empathy, and express optimism. The leader sets the emotional tone for the group. Leaders who fail typically do so because they exhibit indifference toward group members, are brutally critical, and are too demanding. In other words, inept leaders do not respect their followers. They don't care what they think or how they feel.

Showing respect for followers is a critical communication imperative for leaders and a key element of ethical communication (see Chapter 1). A survey of 20,000 employees worldwide by Georgetown University professor Christine Porath found that feeling respected by their superiors at work topped the list as the most important leadership behavior (cited by Rogers, 2018). Leaders exhibit respect by recognizing and appreciating the importance and worth of others. You praise good work, and when mistakes occur you engage in constructive dialogue to correct the error instead of criticizing and deflating the individual. You ask group members how you might help them improve. This can create a **virtuous cycle**—the more respect shown to those with less power in the group the more these lower power members typically become engaged and motivated to improve and provide creative solutions to problems (Cable, 2018). You act politely toward group members. In short, you exercise supportive, positive communication, not defensive, negative communication patterns (see Chapter 5). Because of the interconnectedness of leaders and followers, the more followers "feel respected by their leaders, the more they will 'return the favor' by being open to their leader's influence" (van Quaquebeke & Eckloff, 2010).

Unfortunately, respect from leaders is highly desired by followers but too rarely experienced (Porath, 2016). Consider the president of an organization whose open contempt and disrespect for his employees was reflected in his oft-stated motto: "Bring 'em in and burn 'em out." He seemed to enjoy disrespecting his workers. A junior staff member, for instance, announced that it was her birthday and offered pieces of cake to fellow workers, including the president. The president's response was to complain loudly to a nearby manager, "Can't you get your staff to work?" Then, to the junior staffer, he looked at her derisively and said, "And you sure don't need the calories in that cake" (quoted by Goleman et al., 2002, p. 194).

Virtual Group Leadership

Virtual groups pose unique leadership challenges. A study of 15,000 executives ranked leading virtual teams as by far their weakest skill ("The Ultimate Guide," 2021). As already noted, leadership is primarily a process more than a person, and distributed (shared) leadership is especially relevant. Exercising leadership with a dispersed group connected primarily or exclusively by electronic technology is difficult. It almost guarantees that "leadership focus shifts from individuals to networks of relationships because the Internet facilitates connecting so many people" (DuBrin, 2019). As also noted, there are cultural differences in attitudes toward hierarchy and authority. Multicultural groups may experience confusion and tension when there is no consensus regarding how leadership should be displayed.

Much of what has already been suggested in this and previous chapters about effective leadership requires added emphasis above and beyond what should occur for in-person groups. Research shows that distributive, shared leadership "provides many benefits to virtual teams such as emotional stability, agreeableness, mediating effects on the relationship between personality composition and team performance" and building trust and strong personal relationships among members (Morrison-Smith & Ruiz, 2020). Recognizing leadership of virtual groups as a shared responsibility, here are suggestions for enhancing effectiveness (DuBrin, 2019):

1. *Relationship building is essential*. There are "degrees of virtuality" (Hacker et al., 2019). Occasional face-to-face meetings of virtual group members can help build social relationships, enhance cohesiveness, and strengthen group collaboration to solve problems (Trees, 2017). As principal facilitator, scheduling an in-person meeting is especially important as an initial meet and greet. Provide praise and recognition as warranted. Admittedly, this can feel more awkward in a virtual environment that can seem impersonal, but it is important. Staying connected electronically with all group members is vital. Send congratulatory emails when a task is completed well, especially if it is a team effort. Holding virtual reward ceremonies, virtual

Cabeca de Marmore/Shutterstock

It is important when members of a virtual group meet for the first time that they share information about themselves and engage in casual conversation to begin the bonding process.

parties, and even mini lectures on shared interests all help create member connections. Again, any of these options can be a shared effort, not strictly the role of the designated group leader. Such shared leadership efforts create "commitment, trust, and cohesion among team members" (Morrison-Smith & Ruiz, 2020).

If some face-to-face contact is impossible, videoconferencing (Zoom meetings) must suffice as an alternative. Initially, sharing information about yourself with team members helps to build bonds. Engage in video conversations. Send pictures to the group. Share books and movies that you prefer. Engage in informal conversation to break down primary tension as you get to know each other. Connect with each other by texting, emailing, and social media options.

2. *Follow the detailed blueprint for conducting virtual meetings* offered in Chapter 3. Do not cut corners by ignoring some of the advice. Spending a couple of minutes before each virtual meeting interacting by sharing weather reports if members are geographically dispersed, recent activities, family outings, and the like as a warmup can be fruitful.

3. Facilitators *should set agendas, draft timelines and deadlines for projects, and schedule regular electronic communication* among group members.

4. *Establish ground rules* immediately for scrupulously avoiding defensive communication, and encouraging and monitoring abundant supportive communication. This should be a shared responsibility among all members but a group leader's prime directive. One rigidly enforced rule should be

that no group member should share negative information about individual group members or team conflicts with anyone outside of the virtual group. Confronting rumors and gossip can be particularly exasperating and complicated to address electronically.

5. *Set up chat rooms* that solicit a variety of opinions before the group makes decisions. You want to create a safe space for an exchange of differing points of view. Do not permit incivility during these exchanges. These chat rooms should never mimic blogging sites in which contributors engage in trashing anyone who disagrees. Chat rooms are not troll farms, spreading misinformation, inflaming emotions, and stoking conflict. Make sure that group members are active listeners, not active antagonists. Add this to the ground rules.

6. Institute suggestions discussed in Chapter 3 for *motivating member participation* and avoiding social loafing that is more prevalent in virtual groups.

Additional leadership strategies for addressing virtual group challenges are provided in the next chapter on teams. For now, take solace in the fact that what once was a rare experience has become a prevalent practice and will become increasingly easier as we all navigate our virtual environment.

So, in summary, considering all perspectives and viewpoints presented, what do we really know about leadership in small groups? Leadership is a leader–follower social influence process, directed toward positive change that reflects mutual purposes of group members and is largely accomplished through competent communication. Leaders emerge by a process of elimination. Our implicit theories of leadership initially and disproportionally lionize narcissists and psychopaths until we realize our egregious mistake. Women and ethnic minorities are disadvantaged in the emergence process. Leaders function within a system (leadership is a process, not just a person), and change is unavoidable in any system. That change may mean that leadership is distributed across many or even all group members depending on changing situations. The key to effective leadership is the ability to adapt to changing situations and to exhibit communication competence in the process. The "one leadership style fits all" approach is doomed to fail much of the time. Leadership and communication competence are inextricably bound. No specific set of traits, particular style, situational readiness, or set of functions or services will produce effective leadership without the knowledge, skills, sensitivity, commitment, and ethics of all group members participating in the leadership process together. Leadership is fundamentally a systemic, communication competence process in which adapting effectively to inevitable change is imperative, especially as virtual groups become ever more common.

QUESTIONS FOR CRITICAL THINKERS

1. If you worked in a culture that has difficulty accepting women as leaders, how should you address this issue?

2. Are there any instances in which being a servant leader might prove to be ineffective, even counterproductive for the group? Explain.

3. Why do you think that decisiveness seems to be highly valued as a leadership trait when corresponding emphasis on the quality of choices made decisively are so often absent?

TED TALKS AND YOUTUBE VIDEOS

"Great Leadership Comes Down to Only Two Rules" | Peter Anderton/ TEDxDerby

"It's Not You, It's Your Workplace" | Michelle P. King

"The Rarest Commodity Is Leadership Without Ego" | Bob Davids at TEDxESCP

"Servant Leadership: How to Lead with the Heart" | Liz Theophille

"What Working with Psychopaths Taught Me about Leadership" | Nashater Deu Solheim

"Why Do So Many Incompetent Men Become Leaders?" | Tomas Chamorro-Premuzic

"What Makes the Highest Performing Teams in the World" | Simon Sinek

VIDEO CASE STUDIES

Black Panther (2018). *Action/Adventure; PG-13*

Apply leadership perspectives to the main characters, especially concentrating on T'Challa, heir to the kingdom of Wakanda in this superhero film based on a Marvel character.

Bonus: See article partly about director Ryan Coogler and his leadership perspective as the film's director, at: *https://sites.psu.edu/leadership/2018/06/22/ servant-leaders-among-us/.*

Darkest Hour (2017). *Historical drama; PG-13*

Winston Churchill's rise to power as British prime minister during the early days of World War II is dramatized. Analyze the role implicit theories of leadership played in Churchill's rise to power, his leadership style, his influence on his country's citizens during a time of crisis, and his overall effectiveness.

Horrible Bosses (2011). *Dark comedy; R*

Three friends decide to murder their horrible bosses. This is a very funny movie in a very dark way. Beware the vulgarity. Examine the depiction of horrible bosses from the perspective of psychopathic and narcissistic leaders.

Jobs (2013). *Biography/Drama; PG-13*

A fairly bland, but still interesting, retelling of Steve Jobs's ascension from being a college dropout to one of the most influential and recognizable entrepreneurs of the twentieth century. Analyze Jobs's leadership style. Consider all perspectives (traits, style, etc.). Examine how he gains and especially tries to retain leadership.

McFarland, USA (2015). *Sports drama; PG*

Coach Jim White (Kevin Costner) faces a daunting task providing effective leadership for his cross-country high school team. Examine leadership styles, servant leadership, and the importance of adapting leadership styles to specific situations.

Star Trek: Into the Darkness (2013). *Action/Adventure/Sci-Fi; PG-13*

This is a terrific sequel to the initial reboot of the *Star Trek* motion picture series. Analyze Captain Kirk's (Chris Pine) leadership style. Does he adapt to the situation by changing his style to meet changing circumstances? Contrast Kirk's leadership style with Spock's style. Apply the distributive and the servant leadership perspectives to both individuals.

The Wolf of Wall Street (2013). *Biography/Comedy; R*

This is a depiction of a true story—the rise and fall of stockbroker Jordan Belfort (Leonardo DiCaprio). This movie is not for the faint of heart. There is very graphic sexual content and vulgarity. Is Belfort a psychopathic or narcissistic leader? Compare his positive traits with his negative qualities and analyze his leadership effectiveness. Any ethical issues?

Developing Effective Teams

8

It began as a ragtag group of street performers led by Guy Laliberte. It grew into something wild and wonderful. In 1984, Laliberte contacted the government in Quebec, Canada, to sponsor a show he called Cirque du Soleil (Circus of the Sun). With a small grant from the government to perform as part of Quebec's 450th anniversary celebration of Jacques Cartier's discovery of Canada, Laliberte's vision came to fruition. He wanted to create a circus of a much different sort, one that would mix street entertainment with traditional circus acts. The success of Cirque du Soleil is unparalleled. From its modest beginning, it has grown into a billion-dollar business as the largest theatrical production in the world (Kingsford-Smith, 2017). Almost 200 million people in 450 cities on every continent except Antarctica have attended its "mix of circus acts, street performance, unparalleled acrobatic feats and the avant-garde" (Rinne, 2019). It is also a grand exercise in teamwork. Lyn Heward, the creative director at Cirque du Soleil, explains that what's necessary for success is "in having a passionate strong team of people" (quoted by "Cirque du Soleil," 2011). The business became so successful that it offered team building and training modules for companies such as Google, Adobe, and Life Time Fitness, among many others (Xue, 2016). Their modules parallel much of what is discussed in this and previous chapters, especially those that address power balancing, communication climate, listening, conflict management, and competent leadership. Unfortunately, the massive success of Cirque du Soleil was seriously disrupted by the Covid-19-mandated shutdown of arena performances in 2020 and most of 2021.

In a starkly different direction, a disturbing study revealed the alarming statistic that more than 200,000 patients die each year from medical errors in hospitals (Kavanagh Oet al., 2017). Although the reasons for this stunning situation are complex, poor teamwork in our medical workplaces is emerging as a major cause (Mayo & Woolley, 2016). One study found that "more than 70% of medical errors are attributable to dysfunctional team dynamics" (Mitchell et al., 2014). "Patients receiving care with poor teamwork are almost five times as likely to experience complications or deaths" compared to those receiving care from effective medical teams (M. A. Rosen et al., 2019). A comprehensive study conducted by Rice University in concert with four other organizations found that team training of healthcare employees can reduce patient mortality by 15% and medical errors by 19% (Hughes et al., 2016; see also Morley & Cashell, 2017). "When all clinical and nonclinical staff collaborate

objectives

The primary purpose of this chapter is to explore how to build and sustain a wide variety of effective teams. Toward this end, there are five chapter objectives:

1. To distinguish teams from standard groups.

2. To identify qualities that make good and bad team members.

3. To discuss key communication elements that build and sustain effective teams.

4. To identify what constitutes effective team leadership.

5. To offer additional suggestions for improving virtual teams.

199

effectively, health care can improve patient outcomes, prevent medical errors, improve efficiency and increase patient satisfaction" (Bhatt & Swick, 2017; see also Hambley, 2020). One review of studies of teamwork in the medical field concludes that "communication and collaboration are crucial to the team function of nearly all frontline providers in and across the health care spectrum" (Dinh et al., 2020). With the appearance of Covid-19, "teamwork has become both more important and more challenging" (Tannenbaum et al., 2020).

Although the chances that you will ever join Cirque du Soleil are unlikely at best, and you may never enter a career in the medical field, the lessons these opening examples teach and what makes teams work or fail across myriad environments will sooner or later become critically important to you. The wisdom of teams is sometimes a tough sell in an individualistic culture such as the United States, where individual performance is extolled and personal ego is celebrated. Nevertheless, the wisdom of teams has become increasingly embraced in the workplace for practical reasons (Middleton, 2019). As Dom Price, head of Research and Development at Atlassian explains, "90 percent of organizations claim to be tackling issues so complex they need teams to solve them" (quoted by Welker, 2017). "Teams are at the core of how work is accomplished in business, medicine, science, the military, and sports—in virtually all human pursuits" (Kozlowski, 2018). This chapter explores team effectiveness.

Teamwork is the essence of Cirque du Soleil.

ADRIAN DENNIS/AFP via Getty Images

Standard Groups versus Teams

Despite some commonalities, standard groups, be they face-to-face or virtual, are distinct from teams. In this section, those distinctions are identified, and a specific definition of a team is provided and explained.

Distinctions: The Foremost Four

All teams are groups, but not all groups are teams. Teams are a special type of group. There are four principal characteristics that identify differences between standard groups and teams.

Level of Cooperation: The Working Together Imperative Teams typically manifest a higher level of cooperation than standard groups. Members of standard groups may be adversaries, not teammates working toward a common goal. Senate and House committees regularly battle over issues of taxes and spending, the size of government, and the like. Committee members act as adversaries, not team members. Student and faculty college senates operate the same way.

Collaborative interdependence is the essence of all teams (Benishek & Lazzara, 2019). Team members generally must work together to achieve their goals. One workplace survey reported that 86% of respondents blamed lack of collaboration and poor communication for team failures ("How to Improve Collaboration," 2015). When members work mostly for themselves, attempting to advance individual agendas (e.g., scoring more points than other teammates), that collaborative interdependence is missing.

For example, the 2004 U.S. men's Olympic basketball team was a huge disappointment (some would say an embarrassment compared to "dream teams" of previous Olympics). Composed entirely of star NBA players, these professionals displayed individual prowess at times but little actual teamwork (Killion, 2004). Dismantled 92–73 in a preliminary round by Puerto Rico, a team with just one NBA player, the United States went on to lose three games (equal to the total number of losses in all previous Olympics). Coach Larry Brown remarked after the loss to Puerto Rico, "We have to become a team in a short period of time. Throw your egos out the window" (quoted by Killion, 2004, p. 3D). With improved teamwork, the United States won the bronze medal, much better than another group of star NBA players who couldn't do better than sixth place for the United States in the 2002 World Games.

In contrast, the 2008 U.S. Olympic basketball team concentrated on teamwork, forgoing individual stardom. In its eight games, all victories, the U.S. team had more assists than its opponents in every game, emphasizing the players' willingness to pass and engage in team play. In the final against Spain, all five starters scored in double figures, exhibiting a willingness to spread the scoring around, not seek personal glory (Thamel, 2008). This "redeem team" won the gold medal with teamwork. Emphasizing similar teamwork, the United States repeated its gold medal performance in 2012, and again in 2016. The 2020 games were postponed because of Covid-19.

Diversity of Skills: Look for Complementarity In standard small groups, membership is usually a potluck. You may have lots of desserts but few main dishes. A kitchen staff in a fancy restaurant would perform badly if every chef were a master of desserts but none were able to cook more than the most basic entrees ("You want a burger—great! You want duck a l'orange—tough luck!"). Project groups in my classes often were stymied because no member had sufficient technical skills to permit the group to choose some of the project options. New members of the student senate are not typically chosen for how well they might blend with and complement other senate members. Often, they are chosen because no one else wants the job.

A team requires complementary, not identical, skills. At the IDEO design firm previously discussed, diverse teams are essential to success. Sometimes *unicorns*—"people who don't necessarily fit in a prescribed role, but have a unique perspective and combination of quirky skills"—are hired to avoid creating homogeneous teams that can stifle growth and creativity because of members' sameness

Collaborative interdependence is the core of teamwork. Each member of the Blue Angels must operate with exact precision as a unit or disaster would strike.

Photo by Joe McNally/Getty Images

(Pham, 2019). When ABC's *Nightline* challenged IDEO to redesign the common grocery store shopping cart, a diverse team composed of both men and women was assembled for the five-day challenge captured on camera. Engineers and industrial designers collaborated and brainstormed with team members whose backgrounds included psychology, architecture, business administration, linguistics, and biology. Similarly, scouts looking for talented individuals to join the Cirque du Soleil teams don't seek just dancers, gymnasts, or athletes. The list of team members includes contortionists, pickpockets, skateboarders, clowns, "giants," whistlers, fire jugglers, martial artists, and even a septuagenarian husband-and-wife acrobatic couple (Baghai & Quigley, 2011).

Group Identity: Operating as a Unit Teams typically have a stronger group identity than standard groups. In a standard small group, there are only superficial indicators of identity. When I served on my campus bookstore committee, no one would recognize from mere appearances what group was meeting. Members certainly didn't wear uniforms, brandish a team tattoo, sing a fight song, participate in team cheers ("Go e-books?"), or exhibit anything that might identify the group to the casual observer. Members would have to identify the group and its primary purpose to outsiders. A small group may not even have a specific name. Teams, however, are usually easily identified. Team names are important and sometimes the subject of intense disagreement. Consider the national kerfuffle regarding whether the name of the Washington Redskins NFL football team was racist. On July 13, 2020, it was officially announced that the offending nickname, after protracted national debate, would be replaced. Team members have a sense of cohesiveness and oneness that exceeds the typical, standard small group.

Time and Resources: Commitment to the Team Most small groups that we join require a limited time commitment and few resources to function. A hiring committee normally requires a few meetings. Once the decision has been made, the committee disbands (called an *ad hoc group*). Little or no money is necessary to sustain the panel. Teams, however, often require substantial resources and long-term time commitments. Sports teams play for a season and return the next year. Some members may change, but the team remains intact. Team members may devote huge time allotments to perfecting skills. There often is an emotional connection to the team. It is doubtful that you have an emotional connection with a study group composed of classmates chosen at random (e.g., "Count off 1, 2, 3, and 4 and join individuals with the same number"). You may come to like your group members but that is the luck of the draw and not necessarily bonding.

Definition of a Team: A Special Kind of Group

With the four characteristics that distinguish teams from standard groups in mind, a **team** is defined as a constellation of members with complementary knowledge and skills who act as an interdependent unit, are equally committed to a common mission, subscribe to a cooperative approach to accomplish that mission, and hold themselves accountable for team performance. Given this definition, obviously not all small groups can become teams. Boards of directors, student and faculty senates, class discussion groups, task forces, and standing committees are standard groups, but they are not usually teams. Members may simply represent diverse factions at odds with each other. Such groups often lack cohesiveness and cooperation, and group members are usually chosen for reasons other than their complementary knowledge and skills. Members are expected to attend periodic meetings in which discussion occurs and an occasional vote is taken, but they do not have to work together to accomplish the group's primary goals.

For example, a college board of directors is a standard group. Choosing a new college president may be its specific goal. Board members, however, often do not have complementary knowledge and skills and may become aggressive and hypercompetitive when advocating for a particular candidate, and adversarial debate may ultimately produce a split-vote decision. The goal is achieved (a president is chosen), but the process wasn't collaborative. Similarly, not every group dubbed a team truly qualifies. Those small groups that only half-heartedly exhibit the several criteria included in the preceding definition are more **pseudo-teams**—teams in name only (Benishek & Lazzara, 2019).

Boards of directors and boards of trustees do not operate as teams. Members often represent opposing constituencies. Although desirable, diverse membership is typically not required, as illustrated in this image. Collaboration is also not required, and members can become adversarial when representing constituent groups.

Amit.pansuriya/Shutterstock.com

Teams embody a central theme of this text—that cooperation in groups has distinct benefits that should be pursued. Research has found that the best performing teams exhibit high levels of cooperation. This is manifested by investing "extensive time and energy in coaching, teaching, and consulting" with team members. Every member shares knowledge, information, and insight across the entire team to improve every member's performance (DuBrin, 2019).

Although most material presented in other chapters applies to teams, the analysis and advice is sometimes too general to be practical enough to make teams successful. This chapter offers more specific detail to respond to the unique differences between teams and small groups, beginning with the importance of team composition.

Team Members

Group members are the raw materials of any successful team. Assembling the optimum combination of individuals is the starting point for team building (Mayo & Woolley, 2016). "The best way to build a great team is not to select individuals for their smarts or accomplishments, but to learn how they communicate and to shape and guide the team so that it follows successful communication patterns" (Pentland, 2015). Let's begin by identifying what you don't want in a team member before identifying what is best.

focus questions
1. Why is the attitude of team members at least as important as their aptitude?
2. What is the ideal team member?

Team Slayers: Members' Bad Attitudes and Bad Behavior

For teams to be effective, attitude is at least as important as aptitude. "Good attitudes . . . do not guarantee a team's success, but bad attitudes guarantee its failure" (Maxwell, 2001). Corresponding bad behavior that easily flows from bad attitudes diminishes team performance.

Egocentrism: Me-Deep in Omnipotence   Those who communicate egocentrically reveal the "Me-first" attitude that promotes team friction and weakens team cohesiveness. Egocentrics may even ridicule the fundamental underpinnings of teamwork, namely, cooperation. As one T-shirt trumpeted, "My idea of a team is a whole lot of people doing what I tell them to do." Egocentrism can be a significant problem. One study of data from 750,000 employees about 69,000 managers found that egocentric supervisors with superiority complexes (arrogance) typically have "fatal flaws" and weaknesses that negatively impact teams. On the other hand, supervisors who exhibit humility and a motivation to improve (mindfulness) are more likely to have "profound strength" and virtually no fatal flaws (Zenger & Folkman, 2015).

Members with a We-orientation have a very different effect on a team than egocentric members. We-oriented team members communicate with everyone equally; exhibit an infectious, energetic interest in others; listen at least as much as they talk; and socialize with all teammates (Pentland, 2012).

Cynicism: Communicating a Can't-Do Attitude Teams are systems, so even a single member can demoralize an entire team (the ripple effect). The attitude that most destroys teamwork and team effectiveness is cynicism (McKee, 2015). **Cynics** communicate negativity by being sneeringly distrustful, pessimistic, and blatantly contemptuous. They predict failure and look for someone or something to criticize, sapping the energy from the team with their negativity and spreading the cynicism disease among group members (Makela et al., 2021). "Cynicism is like cancer to the human soul" (Hyatt, 2016). Acclaimed journalist Sydney Harris characterized a cynic as someone "who is prematurely disappointed in the future." The term *cynic* is actually derived from the ancient Greek word for dog—*kynos*. The Greek philosophers who called themselves Cynics wanted to live like dogs, eschewing money, power, and even shelter. Diogenes, a prototypical Cynic, took to living in a ceramic jar on the streets of Athens (that's a story for another time). Present-day cynics are uninterested in living like canines on any street, but are distrustful of others and exhibit a scornful, jaded negative attitude. A review of numerous studies shows that cynics are less likely to exhibit competence than those who display a rosier disposition and attitude (Livni, 2018).

Experience and talent are not contagious, but attitude is (Weir, 2018). What you want in a team member is the communication of an optimistic, can-do attitude, not a cynical can't-do attitude. An optimistic attitude nourishes a team's spirit, braces it for coming challenges, and encourages aspirations to rise and motivation to increase. For example, on April 29, 2007, an overturned gas tanker-truck burst into a fireball and literally melted 165 feet of elevated freeway on the Interstate 80/I-580 connector ramp in the San Francisco Bay area. Initially predicted to take many months, even a year or more, and destined to create a gridlock traffic nightmare, the repair of this collapsed section of roadway was completed in only *18 days*. Clinton C. Meyers, the contractor on the job, explained how his crew managed to complete the monumental repair in so short a time: "I've got a tremendous organization behind me of dedicated can-do people. . . . This shows what you can accomplish when everyone works together as a team" (quoted in May, 2007).

Communicating Abuse: Incompetent Behavior Kills Teams Abuse is a prevalent problem in the workplace, and research shows that supervisor abusive communication produces significant problems for teams. Abuse that is perceived to be intentional is particularly destructive (Schyns et al., 2018). As serious as workplace abuse is, harmful behavior in intercollegiate sports is even worse. A study by the NCAA quoted Dr. Ben Tepper at Ohio State's Fisher College of Business whose specialty is abusive leadership in the workplace. He concluded based on substantial data: "Abusive leadership is two to three times as prevalent in college sports as in the orthodox workplace" (quoted by Hanson, 2020).

Coaches are key figures who dole out the abuse. For example, abusive coaches at various universities have been guilty of "persistent verbal abuse, fat-shaming, excessive practice times, and disregard for injuries" that targeted players on softball teams (Williams, 2019). Emotional abuse, such as "belittling, humiliating, shouting, scapegoating, rejecting, isolating, threatening, or ignoring" victimizes as much as 75% of young athletes, becoming more prevalent as the age of athletes increases. Such behaviors are clearly harmful on the individual victims (Singer, 2020), but they can destroy team morale and solidarity (Magnano, 2019).

No team should permit such bad behavior, but clear power differences make dealing with abusive coaches or any supervisor at work challenging, even risky. Abuse by those in authority in a variety of arenas is addressed extensively in Chapter 11. There is no simple solution, and any brief list of suggestions here would not do the issue justice or be academically credible.

Team Builders: Choosing and Developing Team Members

Unlike standard groups, teams aren't usually stuck with potluck when member composition is the focus. There are usually choices to be made. Who should become a team member depends on what each potential member has to offer the team. You want a diverse, complementary skill set.

Experience and Problem-Solving Abilities: Core Competencies "Experience and problem-solving ability are the core competencies that move a team toward its objective" (LaFasto & Larson, 2001). Look for experienced members when forming teams. No one wants to fly with an inexperienced pilot handling the plane. You don't want to mountain climb with a bunch of inexperienced team members. In each case, you may forfeit your life. Experience counts because it provides knowledge, and from knowledge comes problem-solving ability. Without appropriate teamwork knowledge and skill development, members of action teams (surgical teams, military units, expedition teams, rescue teams, and the like) "can be unprepared to work as an interdependent unit" (Ellis et al., 2005).

Communication Training: Developing Members' Competence Competent communication is critical to team effectiveness, and high-performing team members typically exhibit superior communication skills. According to Professor Cathy Davidson, Google conducted two studies using "every bit and byte of hiring, firing, and promotion data accumulated since the company's incorporation in 1998" to determine what promotes team success (quoted by Strauss, 2017). The first study, Project Oxygen, found that among the eight most important qualities of Google's top performing employees, STEM (science, technology, engineering, and math) expertise was dead last. "Soft skills" such as communicating and listening, empathy, supportiveness of team members, critical thinking, and problem solving were more important, all comprehensively addressed in this text. The second study, Project Aristotle, previously referenced, showed that "the best teams at Google exhibit a range of soft skills: equality, generosity, curiosity toward the ideas of your teammates [listening], empathy, and emotional intelligence" (quoted by Strauss, 2017).

Communication training must be an integral part of the team equation for success (McEwan et al., 2017). Completing a college small group communication class provides such critical training. Pursuing a communication studies major or even minor can provide even more comprehensive training. Workplace training, however, is often of dubious quality and efficacy. Dr. Eduardo Salas of Rice University notes, "If you send a group of executives into the wilderness for two days, they might have fun and learn something about one another—but it doesn't mean they'll magically develop teamwork skills" (quoted by Weir, 2018). Frequently, team training programs consist of little more than a weekend "dog and pony show" by an outside consultant, followed by "happy sheets" that indicate participants' degree of liking for the training. Liking, however, does not equal learning, and popularity ratings favor slick, cleverly packaged training programs that provide fun and entertainment but are as worthwhile as a sugar donut to a diabetic. You get pumped before reality hits.

Instead of these slick, superficial training sessions, you want ongoing, evidence-based, systemic training programs, not a one-time event followed months later by a booster shot from another consultant with a different slick show. Training should teach team members specific communication knowledge and skills relevant to the team's task (e.g., design teams solving problems).

Context-specific team training is effective in enhancing teamwork and team effectiveness (Salas et al., 2012). One study of operating room staff found that those groups trained in effective teamwork had significantly reduced deaths from surgical errors than those groups that did not receive such training (Neily et al., 2010). A training program at Maine General Hospital essentially taught the difference between defensive and supportive communication skills to its medical teams. The results were nothing short of astounding: Team members were 167% more likely to address directly anyone demonstrating poor teamwork behavior, and the same percentage were more likely to speak up when a doctor or nurse exhibited disrespectful behavior (Grenny, 2009). Communication training builds teams! If you set your sights on a high-risk, high-stress career such as firefighting or emergency service work, context-specific training is critical, and there is a plethora of college programs that provide such relevant training.

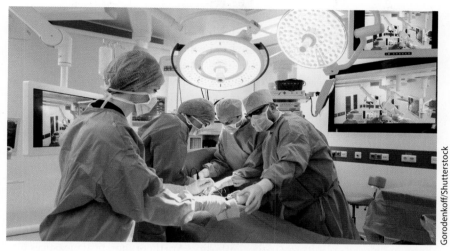

Gorodenkoff/Shutterstock

Team training is a vital part of team success. There is no magic to merely assembling individuals into a group, waving a wand, and declaring them a team. Surgical teams must undergo intense training, and communicating collaboratively is an important aspect of that training. The less they perform as a well-coordinated team that communicates competently, the greater the likelihood of medical errors and lethal consequences. Choosing surgical group members on the basis of availability in the absence of training in teamwork doesn't make such a group a team.

Developing Teamwork

Assembling members with appropriate communication training, attitude, experience, and humility is a necessary first step toward building competent teams, but much more needs to be done. Developing teamwork is a complicated process that unfolds over time. In this section, key aspects of building teamwork are discussed.

focus questions

1. What kinds of goals work best to build a team?
2. How is a team identity developed?
3. Should team roles be chosen by team members?

Developing Team Goals: The Four Cs

Setting specific goals is an important step in the team-building process (Klein et al., 2009). There are four criteria for setting effective team goals.

Clear Goals: Everyone on the Same Page For teams to become effective, clearly stated and understood goals are essential (Van der Hoek et al., 2016). Ambiguous goals, such as "do our best" or "make improvements," offer no clear direction for teams. "Complete the study of parking problems on campus by the end of the term," "raise $350,000 in donations within two years for a campus child care center," or "institute a textbook loan program on campus by the start of spring term" are clear, specific goals.

Terms such as "parking problems," "campus child care center," and "textbook loan program" should also be defined clearly at the very start of a team's effort. Definitional discussions should identify what is and is not included in the team's charge. The **charge** is the task of the team, such as to gather information, to analyze a problem and make recommendations, to make decisions and implement them, or to tackle a specific project from inception to completion. A clearly articulated goal is apparent when all members can identify how they will know when the charge has been accomplished. For example, is an oral or written report required? Does the team report its results to a higher authority? Are there statistical measures that indicate completion (e.g., $350,000 is raised for a child care center)?

In some cases, the goals will be specified by the organization within which teams operate. In other instances, the team will decide through discussion what goals they wish to pursue. In either case, the number of goals should be limited to what can reasonably be accomplished within the specified time period. A few clear goals that each team member can recite from memory are preferable to goals that are too numerous for members to recall.

Cooperative Goals: Interdependent Challenges Cooperative goals require interdependent effort from all team members. It is in every member's self-interest to promote the team goal and help each other achieve team success. Members share information freely, offer advice, share rewards, and apply their abilities to make every team member optimally effective (Mayo & Woolley, 2016). Research clearly shows that cooperative goals enhance team performance, while pursuing individual goals within a team structure diminishes team performance (Tjosvold & Yu, 2004; Van Mierlo & Kleingeld, 2010).

A **superordinate goal**, a specific kind of cooperative goal that overrides differences that members may have because it supersedes less important competitive goals, is particularly effective for developing teamwork (Sherif et al., 1988). When a group faces a common predicament that jeopardizes its very existence, for example, survival becomes the superordinate goal that can galvanize members to pull together in common cause.

Challenging Goals: Denting the Universe Accomplishing the mundane motivates no one. Teams need challenging goals to spark members' best efforts. Members need to feel that they are embarking on a shared mission, with a common

Bule Sky Studio/Shutterstock

A challenging goal can cement team cohesiveness and build teamwork.

vision of how to translate the dream into a team achievement. The team that built the first Macintosh computer had this elevated sense of purpose. Steve Jobs, the team leader, promised team members that they were going to develop a computer that would "put a dent in the universe." Amanda Steinberg, founder of DailyWorth, made her mission "to cultivate the self-worth and net-worth [sic] of women around the world" (quoted by Vozza 2014).

Changing the world, of course, doesn't have to be the team's dream. More down-to-earth visions can easily motivate team members. "Lowering the cost of textbooks by 25%," "doubling effective tutoring programs on campus," or "making the campus safer by replacing old lighting systems with brighter, energy-efficient systems" can be challenging team goals. Your team may not put a dent in the universe, but it may chip away at a serious local problem.

Commitment to Goals: A Passion to Succeed In a massive study for the Gallup organization of 1.4 million workers in 66 countries, one key finding was that coworkers who share a commitment to quality is a key to great team performance (Buckingham & Coffman, 2002a). Commitment is a key element of communication competence. It is also essential to team success.

One key way to create commitment is to have team members share in setting goals for the team (Pentland, 2016). Although not always possible, whenever participatory goal setting can be instituted, it is advisable to do so. Team members typically respond better to goals that they have had a hand in creating than to those that are foisted upon them by others.

Photo by Dennis Grombkowski/Getty Images

Which of the necessary qualities of team goals—clear, cooperative, challenging, and committed—are likely at this level of international soccer competition?

Developing a Team Identity: Unifying Members

A group becomes a team when it establishes its own identity, both to team members and to outsiders. **Team identity** is the sense members feel that they are a part of a group, that they belong. There are many benefits that derive from team identity. Research supports that team identity "is associated with higher levels of altruism, collective behaviors, cohesion and ultimately team performance while at the same time it is associated with lower levels of conflict, social loafing, and tardiness" (Robert & You, 2018). Strategies that develop team identity include developing fantasy themes, creating solidarity symbols, and using team talk.

Symbolic Convergence: Communicating Fantasy Themes Ernest Bormann (1986) developed what he termed **symbolic convergence theory**. Moving beyond an analysis of the individual, Bormann focused on how people communicating with each other develop and share stories that create a "convergence," a group identity that is larger and more coherent than the isolated experiences of individual group members. These stories, or fantasies, create a shared meaning for group members. As Daniel Coyle (2018) explains, "Stories are not just stories; they are the best invention ever created for delivering mental models that drive behavior."

Bormann defines fantasies without the negative connotation of "delusions" or "flights from reality." **Fantasies**, he says, are the dramatic stories that provide a shared interpretation of events that bind group members and offer them a shared identity. These fantasies will have heroes and villains, a plot, conflict—anything a well-told story would have (Kafle, 2014).

The fantasy theme serves as a motivation to team members to strive for goals and a vision that are extraordinary, not merely ordinary. Most start-up businesses small and large begin with a fantasy theme. Team members share a common vision and experience, and fantasies provide a shared interpretation of events. Each member can relate additional stories that play on the fantasy theme, creating **fantasy chains**—a string of connected stories that dramatize and amplify the theme. In this way, a team creates its own identity.

In my own communication studies department, a common **fantasy theme**—a consistent thread that runs through the stories told by departmental members—was the challenge to survive and thrive among many much larger departments with far greater clout. I periodically told the story of my early days at Cabrillo College when some members of the administration underappreciated our discipline. I related the drama over the battle for full-time replacements of two retiring instructors, how part-time faculty had their hopes for full-time positions dashed, how this battle got me kicked out of the president's office, and how I went before the college board, the faculty senate, and the faculty union to make our case successfully. The two positions were replaced. Each new member of the department got to hear a retelling of this story, embellished somewhat over the years.

After this initial success, the fantasy theme became "empire building." Initially seen as a dubious undertaking, the theme eventually gained adherents, and after years of coordinated rhetorical effort by both full-time and adjunct instructors, the department became one of the largest at the college. Additional stories played on the fantasy theme of a thriving and powerful department, creating a fantasy chain. New courses were imagined and creative teaching techniques were shared with elaboration from team members in a persistent effort to nurture a strong team identity campus-wide.

Solidarity Symbols: Unifying Nonverbally Another way to develop team identity is by creating "solidarity symbols" (Kelley & Littman, 2001). A team name, logo, uniform, or style of dress can all serve as solidarity symbols. Military uniforms or the jeans and T-shirt attire often found at IDEO are examples (Chion, 2013). In fact, T-shirts with individualized inscriptions or sayings—humorous, profound, or just plain whimsical (e.g., "It Might Look Like I'm Doing Nothing—But in My Head I'm Quite Busy")—help establish the loose team climate characteristic of design teams. During the Covid-19 pandemic, some businesses allowed, even encouraged, employees to wear masks with amusing messages to create a sense of camaraderie ("I Got a Mask; I Need a Cape"; "My Cussing Muffler"). In other instances, an entire team may wear T-shirts with the same inscription, such as a computer-programming team that wore T-shirts with the inscription "No Coffee, No Code" or a math club whose T-shirts were emblazoned with "Thank God It's Pi-Day."

Which solidarity symbols useful for creating team identity are apparent?

Hafiz Johari/Shutterstock.com

Team Talk: The Language of We Team talk is another strategy for creating a team identity and cohesiveness. Cirque du Soleil refers to auditions as "treasure hunting," intense training sessions as "boot camp," and describes teams as "family" (Baghai & Quigley, 2011). Teams establish an identity, a oneness, when they speak in terms of "we" and "our" and "us," not "he/her/they" (Carr, 2017). This language of shared identity is especially important for team leaders to use. For example, it is better for a team leader to say "*We* have to get this done by Friday" than "*You* have to . . ." Team talk emphasizes interdependence and avoids terminology that emphasizes individuality. Use terms such as *teammates* and *team members* instead of coworkers or employees (DuBrin, 2019). IDEO has "design community leaders" not "project managers." Groups at Pixar animation studio provide "notes" on initial versions of films and they "plus" them with suggestions for changes. As Coyle (2018) explains, "These might seem like small semantic differences, but they matter because they continually highlight the cooperative, interconnected nature of the work and reinforce the group's shared identity." Even failure is spoken of as "our" failure. The language of individual blame and criticism is avoided.

Designating Roles: Room for One Quarterback

Unlike most informal small groups in which roles emerge from the transactions of members, teams usually require a formal designation of roles. You don't want **role ambiguity** that produces confusion and duplication when team members are unsure of the parts they are expected to play (Klein et al., 2009). A football team can't function effectively if individual team members decide which roles they plan to play. You might end up with 15 quarterbacks or wide receivers but no cornerbacks or kickers. Remember that formal roles identify a position (goalie, defensive end, project leader, chief surgeon), and a description of the expected behavior is explicitly spelled out (orally or in writing by a coach, supervisor, or team leader).

A team must have every group function covered by a qualified member playing a specific role so there is little or no duplication of effort. If only some roles are played but others are ignored, several important team functions will be sacrificed, sometimes with disastrous results.

In a huge Gallup study of 80,000 managers and 1 million employees (Buckingham & Coffman, 1999), one manager, named Michael, who ran a highly successful restaurant in the Pacific Northwest was asked to tell about his best restaurant team ever. He told of his waitstaff of four individuals: Brad, Gary, Emma, and Susan. According to Michael's description, Brad was a professional waiter who aspired to be the best waiter in town. He could anticipate what customers wanted. Gary always smiled and was cheerful. Everyone liked him, especially the customers. He had an optimistic attitude. Emma was the unspoken team builder. She regularly assembled the team and alerted the crew members to potential problems. Finally, there was Susan, the greeter. She was lively, energetic, and pleasant. She kept track of customers at lunch who typically needed quick service to return to work. She was attentive.

Michael noted that each team member had his or her clearly defined role. "Brad is a great waiter, but he would be a terrible manager. . . . He respects the customers. He is less respectful of some of the new employees" (Buckingham &

Alvov/Shutterstock

Teams usually require a formal designation of roles, unlike informal small groups such as a college study group. Imagine this sailing team functioning efficiently with every member vying for captain of the boat. Someone has to steer and navigate the course during a race, other crew members handle the mainsail, others the jib or genoa, and still others raise the spinnaker during a reach.

Coffman, 1999). Qualities that made Susan a great greeter wouldn't necessarily translate into being an efficient waitperson. Emma worked well with her team members, but she had a quiet personality not particularly suitable for a greeter. Gary would have been a weak team builder. His joking around went too far. Finding the appropriate team member for each vital role permits full utilization of the team's resources.

The original reason that a person is asked to join a team may make role designation automatic. It is not unusual, however, to find that the roles originally contemplated for team members don't work well and must be changed to make the team more effective. One of the responsibilities of a team leader is to make determinations regarding role designations.

Team Empowerment: Enhancing Members' Capabilities

"Highly empowered teams are more effective than less empowered teams" (Jordan et al., 2002). This is true for both face-to-face and virtual teams (Kirkman et al., 2004). A key element of team building is structuring team empowerment.

Definition of Empowerment: Four Dimensions The concept of empowerment is the process of enhancing the capabilities and influence of individuals and groups. Research by IDEO of more than 500 organizations found that "teams that are empowered enough to challenge the status quo, have autonomy, and clear processes have 69 percent higher success rates" (Aycan et al., 2020).

There are four dimensions of empowerment: potency, meaningfulness, autonomy, and impact (Kirkman & Rosen, 1999). **Group potency** is "a team's generalized confidence in its ability to perform across a variety of situations" (Woodley et al., 2019). It's a can-do group attitude. There is a strong relationship between group potency and team performance. Those teams whose members are confident that their team can perform effectively, not just on a single task but across many different tasks, typically perform effectively, whereas teams with low group potency do not perform as well (Woodley et al., 2019). Feeling empowered to perform effectively as a team can contribute significantly to team success.

Meaningfulness is a team's perception that its tasks are important, valuable, and worthwhile. Meaningfulness is enormously important to team success (Carton, 2017b). When team members view a task as very meaningful, social loafing disappears, and they work harder collectively than they would individually (Karau & Elsaid, 2009).

Autonomy is "the degree to which team members experience substantial freedom, independence, and discretion in their work" (Kirkman & Rosen, 1999). Steve Jobs once said, "It doesn't make sense to hire smart people and tell them what to do; we hire smart people so they can tell us what to do." Choice empowers

Working to help animals can be extremely meaningful and can produce the positive group emotional contagion effect discussed in Chapter 2 that spreads excitement throughout the team and nourishes empowerment (Carton, 2017a).

team members. Team autonomy means that important decision making is a shared undertaking. Because of interconnectedness, no single team member entirely runs the show. Nevertheless, **autonomy doesn't mean that teams have no supervision or guidance.** "Leaders can foster autonomy by assuming the role of mentor or coach instead of micro-managing teams" (Aycan et al., 2020). Teams with a great deal of member autonomy and with limited supervision (facilitation, coordination) are far more effective than teams with virtually unlimited autonomy (DuBrin, 2019). IDEO has substantial member autonomy but some coaching by team leaders.

Impact is the degree of significance given by those outside of the team, typically the team's organization, to the work produced by the team (Kirkman & Rosen, 1999). Impact is often manifested by change outside of the team. If a team makes proposals for change in an organization but those proposals are mostly ignored and little change occurs, the message communicated is that the organization is indifferent to the team's suggestions.

Hierarchical Organizations: The Enemy of Team Empowerment Traditionally, organizations have been hierarchical, meaning that members of the organization are rank ordered in a kind of pyramid of power: CEOs, presidents, and vice presidents are at the top of the pyramid, upper management is next, followed by middle and lower management, and finally the common workers are spread out at the base (see Figure 8.1). Top-down decision making is the rule, with those at

Hierarchy of Traditional Organizations
(College)

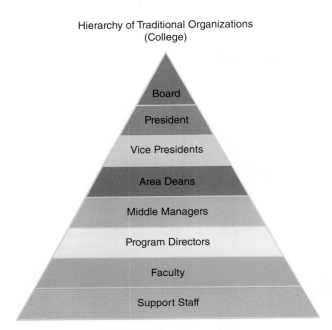

Figure 8.1 Hierarchy is the enemy of empowerment.

the top of the power pyramid issuing edicts to managers, who in turn tell the worker bees what to do. Employees at the bottom of the pyramid mostly check their brains at the door because they won't be asked to participate in decision making and problem solving. Their role is merely the "heavy lifting."

Hierarchy in traditional organizations is the enemy of empowerment and negatively impacts team effectiveness (Greer et al., 2018). Although some degree of hierarchy provides necessary structure for organizations, flattening traditional, rigid hierarchy somewhat is desirable. Empowerment flattens the organizational hierarchy by sharing power. The organizational system becomes more open with information and communication flowing in all directions, with few gatekeepers overly restricting the flow, and with decision making across the organizational spectrum encouraged. Groups can flatten hierarchies and encourage more egalitarian communication by monitoring the speaking times of participants. Reducing the speaking times of more dominant, loquacious participants can make room for those members who are less inclined to fight for the floor to be heard by the group (Khademi et al., 2020).

Self-Managing Work Teams: The IDEO Model Self-regulating teams that complete an entire task are called **self-managing work teams.** Most Fortune 1000 companies use self-managing teams within their organizational system (MacDonald, 2019). Self-managing work teams embrace empowerment. After sufficient training and education, team members share responsibility for planning, organizing, setting goals, making decisions, and solving problems. They have a great deal of autonomy, and since they control much of their own decision making and problem solving, team results seem meaningful to members and have impact on organizations. As self-managing teams manifest success, group potency increases, further reinforcing members' desire to continue with the team.

IDEO, a model for self-managing work teams, has a flattened hierarchy (Aroian, 2015). A team of designers, not "the boss," chooses new team members.

At IDEO, employees are treated as equals who set their own schedules (typically 50- to 60-hour workweeks) while meeting demanding standards and strict deadlines. Designers can pick project teams and even occasionally specific projects to tackle.

Impediments to Team Empowerment: No Buy-In   There are four primary impediments to team empowerment (Hollander & Offerman, 1990). First, organizations can sabotage their own teams. Teams functioning within organizations are subsystems operating within a larger system. Their interconnectedness requires that every part of the organizational structure embrace empowerment or team success suffers (Kennedy et al., 2009).

Second, not everyone embraces empowered teams. Those accustomed to receiving and following directives from supervisors may not adapt well to new responsibilities and autonomy. Some individuals' attitudes may be antagonistic to empowered teams. If so, they are unlikely to become effective, self-managing team members. This can be true of individuals assigned to teams to act as project leaders. If team leaders are held responsible for team failure when team decisions may contradict the leader's preference, it is not difficult to understand the reluctance of the leader to embrace self-managing teams.

Third, when participation in decision making is a sham, empowerment is thwarted. Collaborative effort will disintegrate if group members feel that their

SECOND LOOK

Typical Characteristics of Empowered Teams

1. Teams set their own goals and rules.
2. Team members often set their own work schedules.
3. Teams usually design their own workspace.
4. Workspace is divided relatively equally among members.
5. Members devise and embrace rules for appropriate member behavior.
6. Teams as a whole are accountable for team performance.
7. Teams determine their membership and remove members who are deemed ineffective or disruptive.
8. Team members are trained to communicate collaboratively and supportively.
9. Decision making is typically democratic, and leadership is participative.
10. Team members don't ask for permission from the team leader to take risks or make changes but negotiate with the team and strive for consensus.

participation merely rubber-stamps decisions already made by others with more power. If the team is not trusted to make careful, deliberative decisions, and if the team's choices are not respected, then participative decision making will be perceived as a deceptive illusion of choice.

Meaningful participation in decision making increases worker productivity and job satisfaction (Carton, 2017b). When participation is minimal, only some individuals are allowed to participate, the decisions teams are allowed to make are relatively inconsequential, or the team's choices are essentially ignored by upper management, then team productivity will fall.

Finally, when rewards are distributed based on individual effort or ability, not team success, empowerment is impeded. Individual merit reward systems "can often inhibit team members' willingness to work together and help one another, even when the success of the team depends on it" (Kozlowski & Ilgen, 2007). Research supports rewarding teams, not individuals, for maximum performance (Ladley et al., 2015).

Establishing Individual Accountability: Providing Feedback

Team accountability diffuses the blame for failure and spreads the praise for success. Team building, however, also requires **individual accountability**, which establishes a minimum standard of effort and performance for each team member to share the fruits of team success. Team effort is not truly cooperative if some members are slackers who let others do all the work. You must have a mechanism for individual accountability to discourage social loafing (Kozlowski & Ilgen, 2007). A team needs to catch errors, lapses in judgment, and slip-ups.

Individual accountability standards should not be set so high that they assure failure. Opportunities for social loafers to redeem themselves should be available. The focus should be on raising all team members above the minimum standards—way above if possible—not on looking for ways to designate failures (Druskat & Wolff, 1999). Minimum standards agreed to in advance by the group might include the following: no more than two missed meetings, no more than two incidents of tardiness or early exits from meetings, work turned in to the group on time, and work of satisfactory quality as determined by peer appraisal.

Individual accountability is different from ranking group members' performances or distributing rewards based on merit. Individual accountability merely provides feedback that establishes a floor below which no one should drop, not a ceiling that only a very few can reach. A plan to deal with social loafing was discussed in Chapter 4. Implement it.

Competent Team Leadership

Team leadership is a core component of teamwork (DuBrin, 2019). Teams require leadership even if they are self-managing. In fact, a survey by the Association of MBAs consisting of current MBA students and graduates found that 58% listed "poor leadership" as a top-three reason why their teams failed (Allen, 2018). In this section, communication strategies that produce competent team leadership are explored.

focus questions

1. Which style of leadership is usually most effective with teams? In all situations?
2. How does fear diminish teamwork and team effectiveness?
3. What are supportive rules and how should they be established in a team?

Nurturing Empowerment: A Shared Responsibility

A team may have a designated leader (coach, manager, project director), but leadership in teams is a shared responsibility. Linda Hill, professor of business administration at Harvard Business School, puts it succinctly when she notes that effective team leaders "understand that their job is to set the stage, not to perform on it" (quoted by Cook, 2015, p. 57). Team leaders don't act like bosses if they hope to be effective. As noted in Chapter 7, the days of "command and control" team leadership are quickly ending; increasingly being replaced with more "inspire and empower" leadership (Safian, 2017).

The most effective team leaders are teachers and facilitators—skill builders (Handrick, 2017). They are open to input from team members. One person cannot be expected to know everything, so effective team leadership encourages the sharing of knowledge and wisdom. Encouraging skill building, delegating meaningful responsibility, and sharing decision making and problem solving empowers members. Maximum utilization of team resources requires all members, not just the leader, to think for themselves. That's how group potency is fostered. As athletic coaches learn quickly, they can't think for the players when they're out on the field playing the game.

As explained in Chapter 7, a situation (such as a military combat unit in action) may require directive leadership, but the general leadership pattern for most teams should be a participative, shared approach (Collar, 2013; Pearce & Sims, 2002). A cardiac surgery team typically operates under directive leadership during the operation when swift, coordinated action by the entire team is essential, but participative leadership is appropriate when the surgical team considers new operating procedures, ways to improve coordination, and strategies to improve the team's communication. You want to involve team members in decision making and problem solving.

Requiring a Psychologically Safe Environment: Killing Fear and Ego

Autocratic/directive leadership typically operates from fear—fear of making a mistake, of looking foolish, and of being criticized. A team leader wants to drive away fear. Those who fear failure can be paralyzed into a play-it-safe stasis. Project Aristotle, previously referenced, found that the number one thing separating high-performing teams from others is **psychological safety**—where team members were free to make mistakes, ask questions, and take risks (O'Donovan et al., 2020). Effective team leaders create a climate in which making a mistake is an expected part of learning. At IDEO, there is a saying, "Fail often to succeed sooner." When mistakes are made, members are encouraged to learn from the errors. They are not ridiculed or made to feel stupid.

Effective team leaders also suppress their egos and model behavior typical of a cooperative climate (Hougaard & Carter, 2018). In 1984, former president Jimmy Carter expressed an interest in working with Habitat for Humanity. Millard Fuller, Habitat's founder, drew up a list of 15 possible roles the former president could play. Fuller expected Carter to agree to one or two roles, and almost everything on the list was a high-profile, prestige activity (speaking to the media, raising money, making a video). Carter agreed to all 15 roles, including working on a building crew. Rather than merely working on a crew for a one-day photo-op, as Fuller envisioned, Carter put together his own work crew, traveled by bus to Brooklyn, New York, worked vigorously every day for a week on building a Habitat house, and slept in a local church with the rest of his crew. Carter has assembled a building crew and served in similar fashion every year since, including during his bout with brain and liver cancer (Updegrove, 2018).

Imagine the result if Carter had demanded special treatment, played prima donna and swung a hammer on a building site only when cameras were rolling, and slept in luxury hotels while crew members slept uncomfortably in a church. Imagine the grumbling and disenchantment such egocentrism would have engendered. Who would have wanted to work with him, follow his lead, and be inspired by his example? Instead, Carter didn't expect special treatment, even though he was once the most powerful leader in the world. He completely suppressed any ego needs and became just one of the crew. When an aide summoned Carter to address the media at one home site, he responded, "You can't have me. We're not done yet." It wasn't about him; it was about the work to help the less fortunate (quoted by Emmons, 2013, p. A14).

AP Photo/Mark Humphrey

Former U.S. president, Jimmy Carter, works with a volunteer crew on a Habitat home. Even after a fall that left him with a large bruise and stitches over his left eye, at 94 years old the former president went to work at a Habitat site the day after his injury. Carter, along with his wife Rosalynn, "worked with over 103,000 volunteers and helped build and repair 4,331 homes across 14 countries" by the end of 2019 (Folley, 2019). The Jimmy and Rosalynn Carter Habitat for Humanity Work Project had to be suspended in 2020 and 2021 because of the Covid-19 pandemic.

Finally, effective team leaders work with team members to develop supportive rules. Please note: This does not mean that the leader concocts a set of rules and then imposes the rules on the team. It also does not mean that organizational policy rules ("always wear a suit to work" or "file an absence report immediately upon your return to work following an illness") should be followed without question. Supportive rules refer to communication behaviors that empower teams, not to policy rules in organizations. "Be open and honest" and "avoid gossiping" are two appropriate supportive rules.

Supportive rules should emerge from team discussion during the initial meeting of the team. All rules should help create a supportive environment and avoid a defensive climate. Some possible rules that the team could embrace might be "no personal attacks," "listen fully and patiently to team members before responding," "treat every member equally," "never bad-mouth a team member behind his or her back," and "always show up on time for meetings." Team members should agree to the rules, they should be posted, and there should be between 5 and 15 rules. Fewer than five rules likely means something has been left out; more than 15 makes it too difficult for team members to remember the rules.

Virtual Teams

Although distinctions between virtual groups and virtual teams are rarely offered by researchers and theorists, there are differences. They have electronic technologies and remote communication in common, but they differ in the same ways that conventional face-to-face groups and standard teams differ: degree of cooperation, diversity of skills, level of group identity, and commitment of members. For example, online class discussion groups are virtual groups but not virtual teams. Class members join online discussions to fulfill class requirements and share opinions. Little cooperation is required, class members are not chosen because of skill diversity, no real group identity is necessary or developed, and commitment to the online discussion may be lackluster and sporadic.

Choosing team members with diverse knowledge and skills is important to any team, but it is especially critical to virtual teams. As Keith Ferrazzi (2014), a consultant on virtual team development, explains, "We've found that successful virtual team players all have a few things in common: good communication skills, high emotional intelligence, an ability to work independently, and the resilience to recover from snafus that inevitably arise." You don't just plug in random individuals and expect them to flourish magically in a virtual environment. Individuals who can provide supportive communication, avoid defensive communication, exhibit shared leadership by playing key informal roles when certain functions need attending to, and can stringently avoid egocentrism, cynicism, and, of course, abuse of other team members are all essential to virtual team success. **Exhibiting empathy** that recognizes the inevitability of technological glitches, "challenges that people of historically underrepresented genders, races, ethnicities, language abilities, and other marginalized groups face in their organizations," and a host of problems that can arise in a virtual environment is especially critical (Meluso et al., 2020). Be understanding and kind.

Keeping virtual teams small, fewer than 10 members and preferably even smaller at 4–5 members, is also important for virtual team success. The larger the virtual team and the more spread out members' locations are (i.e., time zone differences), the more complicated and potentially frustrating and secondary tension producing this can be. Advice offered on conducting and participating in virtual group meetings (Chapter 3) is particularly essential as teams grow in size. When keeping virtual teams small is not possible because the task is especially complex, shared leadership becomes even more critical to success. Trying to navigate in a large virtual team is too complicated for a single leader to exercise effective control, nor is it desirable (Meluso et al., 2020).

Everything discussed so far that builds team success has to be magnified for virtual team success. In addition, advice offered in the next two chapters on group defective and effective decision making and problem solving should be added to the list of steps necessary to breed virtual team success.

In summary, teams have a higher level of cooperation, team members have more diverse skills, there is a stronger group identity in teams, and teams usually require greater allocation of time and resources than what is found in most standard small groups. Developing effective teams begins with assembling effective team members. The best team members eschew egocentrism, cynicism, and abusive communication practices, and they are experienced and have strong problem-solving abilities, are optimistic, and have received communication training. You build teamwork by developing team goals and team identity, designating clear and appropriate roles for each member, structuring empowerment into the fabric of the team, and having competent leadership. Competent team leadership is a shared process. Team leaders should foster participative leadership and insist on a cooperative team climate that they themselves also model. The next two chapters discuss defective and effective decision making and problem solving and vital considerations for teams as well as small groups in general.

QUESTIONS FOR CRITICAL THINKERS

1. Can you think of any teams that don't require clear, challenging goals, a team identity, and designated roles?

2. Can a team identity be established that doesn't conform to the team leader's preference?

3. How much say do you think a team member should have when roles are designated? Should this be the exclusive choice of the team leader?

TED TALKS AND YOUTUBE VIDEOS

"Abusive Leadership and College Coaches"
"5 Brilliant TED Talks on Team Building"

VIDEO CASE STUDIES

Glory Road (2006). *Drama; PG*

Above-average depiction of a true story. Coach Don Haskins molded a winning basketball team at Texas Western University in the early 1960s, eventually fielding an all-black starting five against an all-white Kentucky team in the NCAA final when racial tensions were heightened nationally. Examine the major elements of team building and teamwork, especially empowerment and identity.

Guardians of the Galaxy (2014). *Sci-Fi adventure; PG-13*

A motley group of intergalactic criminals must work as a team to stop a fanatical warrior from destroying the universe. Check out this teamwork analysis of the movie at https://www.careeraddict.com/what-guardians-of-the-galaxy-can-teach-us-about-teamwork. Do you agree with all of the analysis?

Invictus (2009). *Drama; PG-13*

Inspiring account of Nelson Mandela's quest to unify South Africa following the dismantling of apartheid by winning the 1995 World Rugby Cup. Examine the elements of team building and teamwork depicted in the film.

Pitch Perfect (2012). *Comedy/Musical; PG-13*

An all-female singing group, the Bellas, compete for campus fame and glory. Analyze elements of team composition, team identity, leadership, and team effectiveness.

The Finest Hours (2016). *Action/Drama; PG-13*

A crew of four perform a daring, true-life, sea rescue off the coast of Cape Cod after a pair of oil tankers are destroyed during a blizzard in 1952. Does the crew perform well as a team? Is leadership designated or emergent? Is leadership distributed across all crew members? Are roles designated?

Defective Decision Making and Problem Solving

9

On April 9, 2017, Dr. David Dao, a passenger on United Airlines Flight 3411, was forcibly removed from the plane by Chicago Department of Aviation officers. Dao had purchased a ticket for the flight and was not causing any disruption. A computer randomly picked him to disembark because the flight was overbooked, and not enough passengers accepted an offer of $800 and a hotel stay to leave the flight. Dao insisted that he could not "volunteer" to leave the overbooked flight because he had patients to see the next morning. The next available flight was in the afternoon the next day. Dao refused the offer. Three aviation officers and one aviation security sergeant were called, and the group boarded to demand that Dao deplane. When he again refused, they dragged him from his seat, inflicting numerous injuries, including a concussion, broken nose, and the loss of two front teeth. The security officers "mishandled a nonthreatening situation," according to a subsequent report by Chicago's inspector general (Salam, 2017).

Cellphone video by another passenger of this astonishing event went viral. The response from the Twitterverse was swift. One person tweeted, "United: You may be asked to vacate or be taken off the plane by force, but for $49.99 you can upgrade to trial by combat." Another tweeted, "In the unlikely event of an overbooking, please assume the crash position whilst we hunt down volunteers." Yet another individual offered this sardonic take on the event, "United: Putting the hospital in hospitality."

United CEO Oscar Munoz's initial response to this event was viewed as tone deaf by almost every news commentator, public figure, and contributor on social media. He initially blamed Dao for being "belligerent" and apologized for "having to re-accommodate" passengers because of overbooking the flight, making no direct mention that a human being had been brutally dragged by his arms and legs off a plane. As Dao noted in his first interview in 2019 about the incident, the onboard airline employees could have explained "nicely" and "reasonably" their justification for wanting to remove him from the flight. Passengers who observed this event close-up reported that Dao was "very polite" when asked to leave. Aviation officers were called to remove Dao from the plane with little attempt to

objectives

The principal purpose of this chapter is to explore sources of defective small group decision making and problem solving. There are five chapter objectives.

1. To analyze the adverse effects of excessive or insufficient information quantity.

2. To explain the role of mindsets in defective decision making/problem solving.

3. To explore collective inferential error.

4. To discuss group polarization.

5. To describe and analyze groupthink as an ineffective group decision-making process.

find an alternative. Initially, the officers tried to convince Dao to deplane, but suddenly treated Dao as you would a criminal, demanding he leave and then inflicting injurious force (Jacobs & Harrison, 2019).

Why did the flight crew stand by, seemingly impotent to offer an alternative means of dealing with this situation besides calling security (e.g., offering a more generous compensation)? Why did the security officers, acting as an enforcement group, mishandle the situation so dramatically?

Put succinctly, this chapter explores ways in which small groups manifest defective critical thinking, a major cause of bad decision making and problem solving. **Critical thinking** requires group members to analyze and evaluate ideas and information to reach sound judgments and conclusions based on high-quality reasoning and credible evidence. One note of caution is warranted. Russian author Fyodor Dostoyevsky once remarked that "everything seems stupid when it fails." Bad outcomes may result just from bad luck or external forces beyond a group's control, not from lack of critical thinking.

The terms *decision making* and *problem solving* are sometimes used synonymously. They are interconnected but not identical. A decision requires a choice between two or more alternatives. Groups make decisions during the problem-solving process. Not all decision making, however, involves a problem to be solved. A family, for example, may decide to vacation at a national park, not to solve a problem but just to have fun.

◥ Information Overload

Information is the raw material of group decision making and problem solving, but information overload has become a major problem. **Information overload** occurs when the rate of information flow into a system and/or the complexity of that information exceeds the system's processing capacity. This section will examine the scope and consequences of information overload, and effective coping strategies.

focus questions

1. What problems are created by information overload?
2. What ways do groups have of coping with information overload?

Scope of the Problem: The Information Avalanche

The research firm IDC (International Data Corporation) calculated that total digital data "created, captured, copied, and consumed" globally in 2020 was more than **64.2 zettabytes**. To provide some perspective, 1 zettabyte can store 250 billion DVDs ("The Zettabyte World," 2020). IDC also forecast that "the amount of digital data created over the next five years will be greater than twice the amount of data created since the advent of digital storage" ("Data Creation," 2021). Information that cannot be absorbed or understood because it overwhelms our processing capacity interferes with effective group decision making and problem solving. Electronic technology has created the age of information overload.

Information overload is largely a problem of too much openness in a system. The Internet provides ready access to an overwhelming abundance of information. Technology entrepreneur Mitchell Kapor once noted, "Getting information off the Internet is like taking a drink from a fire hydrant." The pervasive use of cellphones further exacerbates the problem. "Our smartphones have become Swiss army-knife-like appliances . . . They're more powerful and do more things than the most advanced computer at IBM corporate headquarters 30 years ago" (Levitin, 2015). One study found that the average "knowledge worker" checks emails and instant messaging every six minutes

Jon Feingersh Photography Inc/Getty Images

Information is so readily available and seems to inundate us from everywhere that information overload has become an impediment to effective group decision making and problem solving.

(MacKay, 2018). "Along with email, people chat through tweets, Gchat, Yik Yak, Snapchat, Facebook, Instagram, Viber, Skype, HipChat, Firechat, Cryptochat, and—perhaps most popular of all—text messaging" (LaFrance, 2016). Changes and new options have since emerged. One survey of Gen Z respondents ages 19–25 in 2020 ranked social media platforms in this order of usage: Instagram, TikTok, Snapchat, Facebook, and YouTube ("Gen Z," 2020). Popularity of media platforms are not static. Preferences are sure to change as we all just try to keep up with the never-ending, frenetic world of technological innovation.

The word *staggering* doesn't seem quite sufficient to capture the size of the challenge of information overload. Both useless and useful information is expanding at breakneck speed, making the task of separating the two for group decision making and problem solving ever more formidable.

Consequences: The Downside of Information Overload

Information overload is highly consequential. Aside from group members feeling overwhelmed by the avalanche of information, there are four main consequences of information overload relevant to group decision making and problem solving.

Critical Thinking Impairment: Separating Wheat from Chaff Jonathon Spira (2011), director of the Information Overload Research Group, states, "Information overload causes people to lose their ability to manage thoughts and ideas, contemplate, and even reason and think." One study found that constant emailing and text messaging decreases mental capacity by an average of 10 IQ points, like missing a night's sleep (Rock, 2009). Gathering vast quantities of information can increase a group's confidence in its decisions, but it may decrease the accuracy of those decisions (Hall et al., 2007). That's because much of that information may be useless, distracting noise. Consider a riddle that illustrates this point:

> Suppose you are a bus driver. On the first stop you pick up six men and two women. At the second stop two men leave and one woman boards the bus. At the third stop one man leaves and two women enter the bus. At the fourth stop three men get on and three women get off. At the fifth stop two men get off, three men get on, one woman gets off, and two women get on. What is the bus driver's name? (Halpern, 1984)

Don't reread the riddle! Have you figured it out? The answer, of course, is your name, since the riddle begins, "Suppose *you* are a bus driver." All the information about the passengers is irrelevant and merely diverts your attention from the obvious and correct answer.

Students working on group projects recognize the problem of information overload. Simply sorting through the gigaheaps of information on a subject easily accessed on the Internet with a few keystrokes leaves little time for group members to examine the information critically.

Indecisiveness: Conclusion Irresolution Our technological advances make "faster" possible, even necessary. Faster has become our expectation. We perceive a "need for speed" even when it isn't relevant. As psychologist Philip Zimbardo explains, "Technology makes us impatient for anything that takes more than seconds to achieve. You press a button and you expect instant access" (quoted by Gregoire, 2013). We become overly concerned that some new, instantly available fact or statistic that would invalidate a group decision will be overlooked, making the group appear foolish. Thus, groups, fearing such invalidation, can become indecisive, hesitant to finalize a decision.

Inattention: Difficulty Concentrating The mega-mountains of information competing for group members' attention make focusing on any one idea, concept, or problem extremely difficult. Despite the advantages of our new and

GaudiLab/Shutterstock

Technology makes "faster" the new norm. Information is almost instantly available, but decision making can be slow, even chaotic at times by comparison, potentially leading to impatience and indecision.

expanding electronic marvels, the use of these communication technologies can plague us with unexpected interruptions, massive increases in workload, and daily unpredictability making concentration on important tasks difficult (Ter Hoeven et al., 2016). For example, when cellphones go off repeatedly during group meetings, classes, and the like, everyone is distracted, and attention is diverted from decision making and problem solving. It can take a group as much as five minutes to refocus its attention after just a 30-second interruption (Spira, 2011). Employees at all levels of an organization spend more than 90 minutes a day, on average, recovering from email interruptions and returning to their normal tasks (Rosen et al., 2019).

Diminished Creativity: Preoccupation with the Mundane   When our minds are preoccupied with an abundance of mundane information, there is little opportunity for creative thought (Baror & Bar, 2016). A "quieter mind yields more creative ideas" (Baer, 2016). Burdened with the distraction of too much useless information, when do group members have a chance to think creatively and discover original solutions to complex problems?

Coping with Information Overload: Wrestling the Beast

Coping with information overload can't be accomplished by stuffing the technological genie back in the bottle. Information technologies will only expand, not retract. We're not reverting to the typewriter, carbon paper, or the rotary phone. There are several ways to cope with information overload and make information a useful and powerful resource for decision making and problem solving (Franganillo, 2017; Shin, 2014; Silver, 2012).

Ruthlessly Filter Information: Scan for Spam   Use spam filters to screen unwanted and undesirable information. You want to be hyper-selective when sifting through information to find what deserves your attention and what should be ignored. Often this requires nothing more than a quick scan of the topic and author of electronic messages.

"Eat the Frog": Tackle the Unpleasant Tasks First   This was movie producer Jake Eberts's memorable way of saying that whatever you look forward to tackling the least, metaphorically eating a frog, should be addressed early in the day. This is when you are best prepared physically and mentally to sort through mounds of tedious information.

Shut Down Technology: Hitting the Off Switch   Don't check emails and text messages until group meetings have ended. Put yourself on a Facebook,

Instagram, or YouTube diet. Your "friends" can wait to receive your response to a cute kitten video. Some companies have established quiet times when workers stay away from computers altogether and half days in which communicating electronically is prohibited to give employees time to think and problem solve and to meet in groups and deliberate. One study found that shutting off email for five days changed the group dynamics markedly. Group members communicated more face to face, and members were more focused on tasks and less distracted by attempts to multitask (Burkus, 2016).

Become Selective: On a Need-to-Know Basis Since group members can't attend to all information bombarding them, they should choose selectively based on group priorities and goals (Tartakovsky, 2013). Setting group priorities helps members select which information requires their urgent attention and which can be delayed or ignored entirely. Setting priorities distinguishes what we need to know from what there is to know. You need to find the few gold nuggets among the slag heap of iron pyrite.

Limit the Search: When Enough Is Enough The search for information must stop at some point to allow time to reflect and evaluate information (Tartakovsky, 2013). Setting deadlines for group decisions is critical. Deadlines force a group to bring a search for information to a halt. This means, however, that the search for information should begin early, instead of being postponed until the last minute. Otherwise, with time constraints, the search for relevant information may be far too limited to be effective.

Discern Patterns: Recognizing Irrelevant Information Pattern recognition narrows your search (Madsbjerg & Rasmussen, 2017). Discerning patterns is a group's best defense against information overload. "Once a pattern is perceived, 90% of information becomes irrelevant" (Klapp, 1978). Football teams preparing for a game against an opponent could not possibly perform effectively without a specific game plan (pattern). It simplifies the team's approach to the game and establishes recognizable patterns for players.

Focus: Don't Multitask As noted previously, you cannot concentrate on two competing stimuli simultaneously (Sma et al., 2018). Multitasking allows information overload to split your focus, producing bad results. As comedian Doug Benson "explains": "Just the other day I was walking down the street, I was putting eyedrops in my eyes, I was talking on my cellphone, and I was getting hit by a car." Vast research documents that multitasking decreases performance (Poljac et al., 2018; Schmidt, 2020). Stay focused on one task at a time, undisturbed by social media cruising.

pathdoc/Shutterstock

Resist multitasking. Admittedly, this is not always easy advice to follow. Despite what you may think, research shows that you are no good at it (D'Angelo, 2019). Your communication with group members becomes fragmented, unfocused, and in many cases simply chaotic when you attempt to juggle too many tasks at once. Picture a time when you attempted to communicate an important message to a peer group member, coworker, or boss while that person was texting on his or her cellphone. Did you feel that you were actively listened to, even though that person may have muttered "uh-huh" and "really" as you talked?

Information Underload

Although information overload is a far more prevalent and significant problem, information underload can also present problems for groups. **Information underload** refers to an insufficient amount of information (inadequate input) available to a group for decision-making purposes. This information underload often occurs in groups because an individual member sits on critical information and doesn't share it with the group, or time pressure impedes information sharing (Scholl et al., 2019).

Unshared information in groups leads to poor-quality decision making (Bowman & Wittenbaum, 2012). The problem of unshared information may even lead to disaster. One study revealed that flight crews all too commonly fail to provide necessary information to air traffic controllers (Howard, 2008). Fewer errors related to mishandling of the engines, hydraulic systems, fuel systems, misreading instruments, and failing to use ice protection were found when sufficient information was communicated to all crew members, in the cockpit, on the ground, and in the control tower.

Information underload is usually a problem of too much closedness in a system characterized by rigid boundaries limiting access to information (Lifshitz-Assaf, 2017). The principal solution to this problem is greater openness in the lines of communication and establishing a clear group goal that requires a genuine team effort to achieve (Scholl et al. 2019). A group climate that encourages sharing information without fear of negative consequences or role status impediments is essential. Address the problem of unshared information when groups initially form. Members from collectivist cultures may be hesitant to share information for a variety of reasons. Make it a group norm, an expectation, that information be shared without fear of criticism.

Mindsets: Critical Thinking Frozen Solid

A perceptual **mindset** is a psychological and cognitive predisposition to see the world in a particular way (Kitayama, 2013). It is rigid thinking. Cognitively, we are conditioned to view the world narrowly. Mindsets interfere with effective group decision making and problem solving. Patrick Smith, a pilot for a major airline, noted that the flight crew and agents involved in the United Airlines chapter opening case study fiasco were undoubtedly conditioned to follow strict company procedures without variance so that "summoning the police simply became the easiest way to pass the buck" (quoted by Strutner, 2017).

The ease with which we fall victim to mindsets can be demonstrated by this simple activity. Have your unsuspecting group members spell the word *shop* aloud. Now ask them to respond immediately to the rapid-fire question, "What do you do when you come to a green light?" Typically, they will unthinkingly reply "stop." Why? Because spelling the word *shop* predisposes us to answer with a word that rhymes relevant to a traffic signal even though the correct answer does not rhyme. Our minds are set to view the world in a particular way, even if this is inappropriate. Try asking a different group, "What do you do when you come to a green light?" without the "spell shop" prelude. Did everyone answer "go" or "continue driving?" Groups often are not even conscious of significant mindsets operating during decision making and problem solving. Consequently, two predominant mindsets are discussed in this section: confirmation bias and false dichotomies.

focus questions

1. Why does confirmation bias lead to defective decision making/problem solving?
2. Why is dichotomous (either–or) thinking usually false?

Try this on your study group in another class– Say to them: "Spell the word *joke* out loud together. Now, what do you call the white of an egg?" In almost all cases, group members will immediately say *yolk*. This is an illustration of perceptual mindset. Spelling *joke* primes your group members to think in terms of rhyme, so they say *yolk* instead of the correct answer, which is, of course, egg *white* or *albumen*.

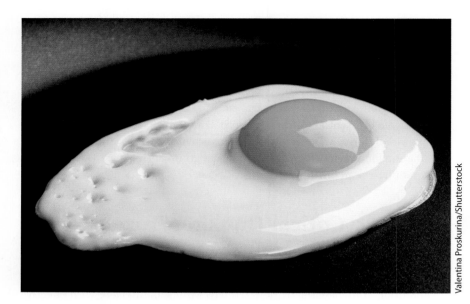

Valentina Proskurina/Shutterstock

Confirmation Bias: One-Sided Information Searches

Confirmation bias is our strong tendency to seek and attend to information that confirms our beliefs and attitudes and to ignore information that contradicts our currently held beliefs and attitudes. This is a particularly prevalent mindset problem in groups (Tschan et al., 2009).

The Problem: Poor Decisions and Solutions Looking for potential weaknesses and disconfirming evidence is an important element of effective group decision making and problem solving (Stanovich et al., 2013). Assessing positive qualities or consequences is not nearly as important. Thus, groups that resist confirmation bias and actively search for possible flaws in decisions and solutions usually make better choices than groups that don't.

The consequences of confirmation bias to group decision making and problem solving are serious (Madsbjerg & Rasmussen, 2017). For example, confirmation bias can lead to high rates of misdiagnoses by medical teams (Bhatti, 2018). "Diagnosticians tend to alter the information gained during a consultation to fit their preconceived diagnosis, rather than the converse" (O'Sullivan & Schofield, 2019).

A prominent historical example of confirmation bias and bad group decision making occurred in February 2003. The Department of Homeland

Security encouraged Americans to choose a "safe room" (an inner closet or the like) in their homes to seek protective shelter in case of a bioterrorist attack. The safe room was to be sealed with plastic sheeting and duct tape. This protection against a bioterrorist attack seemed to ignore the obvious downside of this recommendation: oxygen deprivation leading to death. "I mean, duct tape and plastic?" remarked Harold Schaitberger, president of the International Association of Fire Fighters. "Where's the good air coming from? How's it going to be recirculated? Beyond the fact that we already know, for nerve gas and other elements, the plastic is totally ineffective" (James, 2003). The negative consequences of such advice should have been obvious, but the recommendation fostered a false sense of security among Americans who emptied store shelves of duct tape and plastic sheeting. Why did the Homeland Security group that came up with this recommendation not recognize that the negative consequences nullified any perceived benefit? Think confirmation bias. Decision makers apparently didn't seriously consider the downside of their advice.

At work, confirmation bias can emerge in numerous ways. One simple example would be your supervisor who, let's say, believes that millennials and Gen Z employees are lazy and lack responsibility. When that supervisor sees such employees taking work breaks or chatting with colleagues, he or she sees this as confirmation of the stereotype. What that supervisor may not see is disconfirming information such as these same individuals arriving early to work, staying late to complete tasks, and chatting with team members, not as time wasters but as opportunities to gather relevant information on impending group decisions.

So, what happens when disconfirming information is unavoidable and seems indisputable? Groups may still engage in **rationalization of disconfirmation**—the invention of superficial, even glib alternative explanations for information that contradicts a belief. In the case of the stereotyping supervisor, perhaps younger employees do exhibit initiative and hard work that is unmistakable. The supervisor can still rationalize the disconfirming information as "the exception that proves the rule." This is not typical behavior but merely an atypical effort to impress the supervisor with a showy exhibition of faux hard work and dedication to task accomplishment when the supervisor is looking, but when the supervisor is out of sight lackluster effort and goofing off probably abound.

The perpetuation of unwarranted beliefs is the result of confirmation bias and its ally, rationalization of disconfirmation. False beliefs that pollute the decision-making and problem-solving group process won't be corrected when members aren't open to information that questions their beliefs and presuppositions (Sude et al., 2021).

Combating Confirmation Bias: A Plan There are several steps you can take to combat confirmation bias. They are:

1. *Seek disconfirming information and evidence.* Consider it your personal responsibility to find any disconfirming information and share it with the group. If, after a concerted effort, you find little disconfirming evidence of note, then your decision or solution has an excellent chance of turning out well.
2. *Vigorously present disconfirming evidence to the group.* Be persistent. Members will usually ignore information that disconfirms a strongly held belief unless you assert yourself.
3. *Play devil's advocate.* If a group establishes a norm of devil's advocacy, the responsibility won't fall only on a single member. Clearly indicate the intention to play this role to avoid any misunderstanding ("Let me play devil's advocate here").

False Dichotomies: Either–Or Thinking

A **false dichotomy** is the tendency to view the world in terms of only two opposing possibilities when other possibilities are available, and to describe this dichotomy in the language of extremes. Describing objects, events, and people in such extreme polarities as moral–immoral, good–bad, rich–poor, corrupt–honest, intelligent–stupid locks us into a mindset of narrow vision. Most of us don't qualify as either tall or short, fat or skinny, rich or poor; we're someplace in between these dichotomies. Most objects, events, and people are more accurately described in shades of gray, not black or white (pregnancy being a rare exception since it is difficult to be "sort of pregnant"). For instance, when does group success turn into failure? When does a small group become a large group? Dichotomous descriptions of events and objects are usually false because most of reality consists of more-to-less, not either–or.

False dichotomies contribute to defective group decision making and problem solving (Frenk & Gomez-Dantes, 2016). When group members' mindsets predispose them to see problems and solutions only in extremes, the vast middle ground goes largely unexplored. City councils, faced with reduced revenues during a recession, see only layoffs and reductions in public services when they think dichotomously (i.e., tax revenues up—fund services and jobs; tax revenues down—cut services and jobs). They may fail to explore other avenues for raising revenues besides taxes. Also, groups locked into the false dichotomy mindset may never consider a third alternative besides voting for or against some proposal. Postponing the decision until adequate study of the problem can take place and potential solutions can emerge may be a more viable option.

The competent communicator combats the problem of false dichotomies as follows:

1. *Be suspicious of absolutes.* When group members argue only two extreme possibilities (e.g., a solution is either all good or all bad), look for a third or even fourth possibility.
2. *Employ the language of provisionalism.* When engaged in group discussion, use provisional language—terms that express to what extent a claim is true. You'll be using terms such as *sometimes, rarely, occasionally, mostly, usually, unlikely,* and *moderately.* Avoid terms such as *always, never,* or *impossible.*

Collective Inferential Error: Uncritical Thinking

Two American women—a matronly grandmother and her attractive granddaughter—are seated in a railroad compartment with a Romanian officer and a Nazi officer during World War II. As the train passes through a dark tunnel, the sound of a loud kiss and an audible slap shatters the silence. As the train emerges from the tunnel, no words are spoken but a noticeable welt forming on the face of the Nazi officer is observed by all. The grandmother muses to herself, "What a fine granddaughter I have raised. I have no need to worry. She can take care of herself." The granddaughter thinks to herself, "Grandmother packs a powerful wallop for a woman of her years. She sure has spunk." The Nazi officer, none too pleased by the course of events, ruminates to himself, "This Romanian is clever. He steals a kiss and gets me slapped in the process." The Romanian officer chuckles to himself, "Not a bad ploy. I kissed my hand and slapped a Nazi."

This story illustrates the problem of inferential error. **Inferences** are conclusions about the unknown based on what is known. They are guesses varying by degrees from educated to uneducated (depending on the *quantity* and *quality* of information on which the inferences are based). We draw inferences from previous experiences, factual data, and predispositions. The limited facts of the story are that the sounds of a kiss followed by a slap are heard by all four individuals. Based on what is known, the three individuals who do not know for sure what happened all draw distinctly different and erroneous inferences.

Making inferences is not a problem in itself. The human thinking process is inferential. We could not function without making inferences. You can't know for certain that your project group will convene as scheduled, but you infer it will because it always has in the past weeks. This is a relatively safe inference, but an inference nonetheless because the unusual (e.g., the flu hits most members) may occur.

Inferences that rely on a quality information base in plentiful supply are educated guesses—not always correct, but probable. Inferences that are drawn from a limited and faulty information base, however, are uneducated guesses—likely to produce inferential errors.

AS photostudio/Shutterstock

Is this a college seminar class, a business meeting, or a luncheon get-together? Any guess that you make is inferential. For example, it is probably not a college seminar because a professor is not visibly apparent. It could be a business meeting because everyone is dressed in typical business attire and meeting around a boardroom-type table. It likely is not a luncheon meeting because only coffee cups are visible and no food is apparent. In each case, you make your conclusion about the unknown (what type of group) based on the known (apparent details that are observable). So, are these friends, business colleagues, or strangers meeting for the first time? Discuss!

focus questions

1. What are the primary, general sources of collective, inferential errors?

2. Why are most correlations noncausal?

Prevalence of the Problem: It's a Group Thing

The centrality of inferences to decision making and problem solving in groups is apparent (Khalvati et al., 2018). Gouran (1982) long ago explained:

> In virtually every phase of discussion, inferences come into play. Whether you are assessing facts, testing opinions, examining the merits of competing arguments, or exploring which of several alternatives best satisfies a set of decisional criteria, you will have occasion to draw inferences suggested by the information you are examining. How well you reason, therefore, can have as much to do with the effectiveness of a decision-making discussion as any other factor that enters the process.

Individuals are inclined to make inferential errors. The problem can be magnified in groups. Gouran called this **collective inferential error**. As many as half of a group's discussion statements may be inferences. Groups often accept these inferences uncritically. Why is this significant? Because ineffective groups that arrive at faulty decisions display more inferential errors in their discussions than effective groups (Hirokawa & Pace, 1983).

Sources of Inferential Errors: Distortions and Correlations

There are several specific sources of inferential errors. Two that are most significant are unrepresentativeness and correlation inferred as causation.

Unrepresentativeness: Distorting the Facts   Is a specific example representative of a general category? If the answer is yes, then the inference drawn from the representative example is on solid footing. If the example is unrepresentative, however, inferences drawn from it are likely to be erroneous. Focus groups, for example, usually composed of 6 to 10 members, are often used to conduct qualitative research in a variety of circumstances. You cannot reasonably infer much of anything about a larger population from a focus group, however, because the group is not a representative sample (Mack, 2017).

If an unrepresentative example is vivid, then the potential for inferential error is magnified. The grim, grisly, graphic, dramatic event draws our attention and becomes standard fare served up by the mass media hungry to draw viewers. As producer Gary David Goldberg once pointedly observed, "Left to their own devices, the networks would televise live executions. Except Fox—they'd televise live naked executions" ("TV or Not TV," 1993). The dramatic event, however, can distort our perception (Sunstein & Zeckhauser, 2009). A single airline disaster, for example, can make millions fear boarding a jetliner and induce them to choose driving their automobile instead. Yet the odds of dying in a plane crash are 1 in *11 million*, whereas the odds of dying in a car crash are 1 in *5,000* (Ropeik, 2008). The potential of a single dramatic example sticking in our minds, prompting us to overvalue such an event and undervalue statistical probabilities of such an event occurring, is called the **vividness effect** (Blonde & Girandola, 2018). Stanovich (2013) concluded that it "threatens to undermine the usefulness of any knowledge generated by any of the behavioral sciences."

Correlation Inferred as Causation: Covariation   Humans are predisposed to look for causes of events that remain unexplained. In the process, there is a strong inclination to draw causation (X causes Y) from mere correlation (X and Y occur together). A **correlation** is a consistent relationship between two or more variables.

The vividness effect is illustrated by the crash of Asiana Flight 214 at San Francisco International Airport. Judging from the look of the aftermath of this accident, it is surprising that almost all of the 307 passengers survived (3 died). Nevertheless, a single airplane accident can distort perception of the relative risks of air travel.

Photo by Ezra Shaw/Getty Images

There are two kinds of correlations: positive and negative. A positive correlation occurs when X increases and Y also increases (e.g., as you grow older, your ears grow larger—nature's practical joke on the elderly). A negative correlation occurs when X increases and Y decreases (e.g., as adults increase in age, their capacity to run long distances decreases).

The absurdity of inferring causation from mere correlation can be seen from a classic study conducted by a large research team in Taiwan. The team wanted to determine which variables best predicted use of birth control (Li, 1975). The study found that birth control usage increased as the number of electric appliances found in the home increased. So, does it make sense to you that a free microwave oven or electric blender for every teenager in high school would decrease teen pregnancy rates? I'm confident that you can see the absurdity of such a suggestion.

The birth control–electric appliances correlation is an obvious case where a correlation, even though a very strong one, is not a causation. The number of electric appliances more than likely reflects socioeconomic status and education levels, which undoubtedly have more to do with the rates of birth control usage than do the number of electric irons and toasters found in the home. To accentuate the absurdity of assuming correlations are causations, Tyler Vigen (2015), in his amusing book *Spurious Correlations*, cites numerous goofy correlations that no one would

The Uncritical Inference Test

Read the following story. For each statement about the story, circle "T" if it can be determined without a doubt from the information provided in the story that the statement is completely true, "F" if the statement directly contradicts information in the story, and "?" if you cannot determine from the information provided in the story whether the statement is either true or false. Read the story once only before answering.

The Story

Dr. Chris Cross, who works at St. Luke's Hospital, hurried into room #314 where Yoshi Yamamoto was lying in bed. Pat Sinclair, a registered nurse, was busy fluffing bed pillows when Dr. Cross entered. Dr. Cross said to the nurse in charge, "This bed should have been straightened out long ago." A look of anger came across Nurse Sinclair's face. Dr. Cross promptly turned around and hurried out the door.

1. Chris Cross is a medical doctor who works at St. Luke's Hospital.   **T   F   ?**

2. Dr. Cross is a man in a hurry.   **T   F   ?**

3. Yoshi Yamamoto, who is Japanese, was lying in bed.   **T   F   ?**

4. Pat Sinclair was in room #314 when Dr. Cross entered and found her fluffing bed pillows.   **T   F   ?**

5. Dr. Cross was irritated with Nurse Sinclair because the bed was not straightened out.   **T   F   ?**

6. Yoshi Yamamoto is a patient at St. Luke's Hospital.   **T   F   ?**

7. Nurse Sinclair's face reddened because Dr. Cross was stern with her.   **T   F   ?**

8. When Dr. Cross entered, he became the third person in room #314.   **T   F   ?**

9. This story takes place at St. Luke's Hospital.   **T   F   ?**

10. This story concerns a series of events in which only three persons are referred to: Dr. Cross, Nurse Sinclair, and Yoshi Yamamoto.   **T   F   ?**

Note: *Answers to all 10 questions are question marks. Can you figure out why?*

---

suggest are meaningful causal relations. For example, there is a strong correlation between per capita consumption of cheese and the number of people who died by becoming tangled in their bedsheets. The divorce rate correlates with the per capita consumption of margarine. The marriage rate in Kentucky correlates strongly with the number of people who drowned after falling out of a fishing boat.

I have witnessed the correlation-as-causation inferential error in my own classes. Consider the following discussion that took place in a small group in one of my classes:

> **Jamie:** I think we should choose capital punishment for our topic. I just did a paper on it. Fear of being executed should deter almost anyone from committing murder.
>
> **Alexis:** Yeah, in a lot of states that have it, murder rates have decreased. It's a strong deterrent.
>
> **Blaise:** Well, I heard that when they execute a guy, the murder rate goes up right after. I don't think capital punishment is a very effective deterrent to murder.

In this brief conversation, group members alleged the truth of an asserted causation based only on a correlation, affirmed the validity of the inferential error with a little common-sense reasoning about fear, and refuted the effectiveness of capital punishment by introducing yet another correlation assumed to be a causation. Murder rates go up and down for all kinds of reasons (e.g., socioeconomic conditions; police presence in communities). Correlations are not causations.

Error Correction: Practicing Critical Thinking

For the error-correction function of group discussion to kick in, competent communicators must recognize the sources of inferential errors just discussed. Assertively focusing the group's attention on sources of inferential error can help prevent faulty decision making from occurring. Group discussion promotes higher quality decision making when the following conditions occur:

1. The validity of inferences is carefully examined.
2. Inferences are grounded in credible and plentiful information.
3. At least one member of the group exerts influence to guide the group toward higher quality decisions, especially by acting as a devil's advocate.

Notice the last point. A single individual can prevent or minimize inferential error in group decision making because one person can affect the entire system. This creates a positive ripple effect.

Group Polarization: Extremely Uncritical Thinking

Researchers of small group decision making used to believe that group members inevitably influence each other to take greater collective risks than members' initial preferences. This was called the *risky shift phenomenon*, often seen when teenagers goad each other to engage in goofy and dangerous group actions (Tefft et al., 2012). We show off for our peers by taking risks.

After hundreds of studies, however, there is ample evidence that groups sometimes have a conservative shift rather than a risky shift (Dean, 2009a). Thus, group decisions tend to polarize.

focus questions
1. What are the negative consequences from group polarization?
2. What produces group polarization?

Polarization: From Gambling to Guarded

Group polarization is the group tendency to make a decision after discussion that is more extreme, either riskier or more cautious, than the initial preferences of group members. (Group polarization does not mean that disagreement among group members becomes more pronounced.) Groups tend to polarize decision making if there is a clear majority leaning one way (risk) or the other (caution). For example, in one study, 60 participants were assembled into 10 groups, each consisting of 5 to 7 members. Half the groups were from "liberal" Boulder, Colorado, and half were from "conservative" Colorado Springs, Colorado. All groups were instructed to deliberate on three controversial issues: affirmative action, civil unions for gays, and global warming. Groups that initially tended toward liberal positions on these issues took more extreme liberal positions after deliberations; conservative groups became more conservative. Discussion made civil unions, affirmative action, and a global warming treaty more appealing for liberal group members and less appealing for conservative group members (Hastie et al., 2006). This group polarization effect has been shown in hundreds of studies across many cultures (Hastie & Sunstein, 2015).

RAFA RIVAS/AFP via Getty Images

The running of the bulls at Pamplona, Spain, reminds us that groups can encourage risk-taking, sometimes to the point of dangerous excess. It used to be called the risky shift phenomenon, but group polarization shows extremes in either direction (risk-taking or playing it safe) depending on which direction the group initially leans.

If most members of a group lean slightly toward risk-taking initially, the group will become more prone to take even greater risks than any individual member might have initially preferred. If most members of a group lean slightly toward playing it safe, the group will likely become even more cautious than it was initially. **Groups composed entirely of like-minded members are the most prone to polarize** (Hastie & Sunstein, 2015). It is unlikely that a group will polarize when group members are about evenly split between risk-taking and playing it safe. This is where compromise, or *depolarization*, may result, or the group may be at an impasse.

Group polarization won't always produce erroneous decision making, but moving to the extreme can be problematic. Terrorism has been linked to the group polarization phenomenon of like-minded individuals stoking increasingly extremist behavior including suicide bombings (Sunstein, 2019). That's the crazy extreme, but in more common situations group polarization can be troublesome, even deadly. For example, fraternities and sororities at many campuses ignored warnings and threats of penalties and risked Covid-19 super-spreader parties (Goss, 2021; Reilly, 2020). The predictable results were large outbreaks of the virus in fraternity and sorority houses spreading to other students as well (Higgins-Dunn, 2020). Voices of caution can be drowned out when the group majority wants to party despite the serious risks.

Why Groups Polarize: Comparison and Persuasion

There are several explanations for group polarization (Sunstein, 2019). **The first is social comparison (normative influence).** The assumption here is that an individual uses the group norm regarding risk-taking or caution as a point of reference. The individual is inclined to shift after group discussion, to conform more closely to the perceived expectations of the group. If most group members initially tend toward riskiness, cautious members are inclined to move in the direction of the majority. If most members initially favor caution, all members feel pushed to be cautious.

A second primary explanation for the group polarization effect is **persuasive argumentation (informational influence)** (Kahneman et al., 2021). Individuals in a group will move toward either greater risk or caution when exposed to arguments and information that were not available to members when they made their initial decision. In general, the greater the number of arguments advanced during discussion that support the initial majority group opinion, the more cogent, reasonable, and persuasive they seem to be. Also, the more original or nonredundant the arguments are, the greater will be the group polarization (Van Swol, 2009). As these arguments get repeated during discussions, they validate the risk-taking or caution predominant in the group. Then group members become more confident in the correctness of their position, which has a further polarizing effect (Hastie & Sunstein, 2015).

A third explanation for group polarization is group identity. The more members like each other and feel a sense of belonging, of experiencing an emotional connection with the group, the greater is the likelihood of polarization. This is particularly germane to fraternities and sororities.

Research also reveals several lesser conditions that can influence risk-taking or caution in groups. The direction of the group polarization appears strongly influenced by the preference of the group's informal leader (Pescosolido, 2001). Culture also plays a role. For instance, individualist cultures are more likely to polarize in the direction of risk, whereas collectivist cultures are more likely to polarize in the direction of caution (Kim & Park, 2010). Risk could produce disharmony.

Combating Group Polarization: Necessary Steps

There are a number of steps that can be taken to address the problem of group polarization (Hastie & Sunstein, 2015). They are:

1. *Encourage a wide range of views on issues to be discussed in the group.* Group polarization thrives on uniformity of opinion and the squashing of dissent. Encourage differences of opinion.
2. *Act as a devil's advocate.* This may be the responsibility of a committee chair or designated leader, but any group member can provide opposing views to guard against group polarization. This can be difficult, however, if the group environment is not conducive to expressing dissenting views.
3. *Discuss issues openly before taking a firm position.* Juries, for example, are often counseled by judges to avoid taking an initial poll on guilt or innocence of a defendant before discussing evidence thoroughly. Once a position is publicly declared, it is difficult to switch. When a strong majority expresses a clear point of view initially, polarization can occur.

Groupthink: Critical Thinking in Suspended Animation

Sociologist Irving Janis (1982), who extensively analyzed decision-making debacles, argued that Pearl Harbor, the Bay of Pigs fiasco, Watergate, the escalation of the Vietnam War, and other blunders from U.S. history sprang from a defective decision-making process he calls groupthink. Janis defines **groupthink** as "a mode of thinking that people engage in when they are deeply involved in a cohesive in-group, when the members' strivings for unanimity override their motivation to realistically appraise alternative courses of action." The causes and effects of groupthink and its solutions are discussed in this section.

focus questions

1. What causes groupthink?

2. Do groups have to display all the symptoms of groupthink to exhibit poor-quality decisions like those that accompany full-blown groupthink?

Conditions: Excessive Cohesiveness and Concurrence Seeking

Cohesiveness and its companion, concurrence seeking, are the two general conditions necessary for groupthink to occur. Janis does not argue that all groups that are cohesive and seek agreement among their members exhibit groupthink. As discussed in Chapter 4, cohesiveness in a group can be a very positive factor. Groupthink, however, is rooted in excessive cohesiveness and a resulting pressure to present a united front to those outside of the group (Rovio et al., 2009).

Groupthink can be a primary source of poor decision making in groups (Jaeger, 2020; Lee, 2020). Sports psychologist and consultant Mitch Abrams argues that groups such as college athletic teams can have "a group dynamic that suppresses the individual point of view." He continues, "You might have a bunch of guys who have a great [individual] moral code, but inside a culture where there's groupthink that supports exploitation of women, mass consumption of alcohol that will impair judgment, and a feeling that they're above the law—there will be members who engage in bad behavior" (quoted by Lallanilla, 2006). This is not an indictment of all athletic teams, of course, but a recognition that some athletic teams can slide into groupthink. Lawrence Cohen and Anthony DeBenedet (2012) argue that the Penn State University cover-up of child sexual abuse by assistant football coach Jerry Sandusky that led to his conviction on 45 criminal counts was a prime example of groupthink. Without such an explanation, it is inconceivable that high-ranking members of a revered university would choose to cover up such egregious criminality. Groupthink also appears to have occurred in pack journalism, or copycat reporting (Matusitz & Breen, 2012). More recently, one study links groupthink to groups that opposed Covid-19 health mandates (Forsyth, 2020).

Identification of Groupthink: Main Symptoms

Janis lists eight specific symptoms of group-think, which he then divides into three types. The eight symptoms are discussed in this section within the context of the three types.

Overestimation of the Group's Power and Morality: Arrogance The *illusion of invulnerability* is a common precursor to major accidents. The Fukushima nuclear reactor was designed to withstand an earthquake as powerful as 8.6 in magnitude, in part because some seismologists thought that it was impossible that any earthquake larger than this could occur at this location (Silver, 2012). The plant was also built on the expectation that no tsunami wave from a major earthquake could rise higher than 5.7 meters. On March 11, 2011, however, Japan suffered a

The Deepwater Horizon oil spill and explosion in the Gulf of Mexico in 2010 is a case of the illusion of invulnerability that led to the disaster. Eleven men were killed and more than 200 million gallons of oil leaked into the sea. Almost 1,300 miles of coastline were contaminated. Years later "scientists are still figuring out exactly how the oil impacted the biology of the Gulf" (Borunda, 2020).

Photo by U.S. Coast Guard via Getty Images

9.0 magnitude earthquake that produced a 15-meter-high tsunami wave that engulfed the reactor and caused a meltdown and a radiation leak that killed almost 20,000 people (Aldhous, 2012).

In addition to a sense of invulnerability, groups sometimes overestimate their morality. The U.S. sense of higher moral purpose, according to Janis, contributed to the Bay of Pigs invasion during the Kennedy administration. The purpose, after all, was to upend a communist dictator (Castro) and free the Cubans. This *unquestioned belief in the inherent morality of the group* is symptomatic of groupthink.

Closed-Mindedness: Clinging to Assumptions Closed-mindedness is manifested by *rationalizations* that discount warnings or negative information that might cause the group to rethink its basic assumptions. The space shuttle *Columbia* disintegrated on its return to Earth because a chunk of foam knocked a hole in the shuttle's wing on takeoff. NASA knew that previous shuttle flights had been hit by foam debris, but shuttle engineers' weak efforts to sound a warning about possible catastrophic consequences from the debris went unheeded by NASA officials (Oberg, 2003; Wald & Schwartz, 2003). The operating assumption was that foam debris did not pose a serious problem to the safety of the shuttle mission.

Another aspect of closed-mindedness leading to groupthink is *negative stereotyped views of the enemy* as weak, stupid, puny, or evil. This characterization helps justify the recklessness of the group. This has become all too familiar in recent American politics (Drutman, 2020).

Pressures toward Uniformity: Presenting a United Front   The last type of symptom of groupthink is the pressure to maintain uniformity of opinion and behavior among group members. This pressure can be exhibited by *self-censorship*—squelching one's own viewpoint because of fear that the group opposes that view. A Pew Research study found that people generally engage in a "spiral of silence" when they perceive opposition to their points of view (Hampton et al., 2014). Social media only magnifies the problem (Gearhart & Zhang, 2015). It "has the effect of tamping down diversity of opinion and stifling debate about public affairs" (Miller, 2014). The group climate, however, is probably the strongest influence on whether dissent is permitted even encouraged or whether it is discouraged producing a spiral of silence among group members (Matthes et al., 2018).

Silence is considered assent. Other group members may have their doubts, but everyone assumes agreement exists and no one wants to rock the boat, so no one questions or raises an objection. Thus, an *illusion of unanimity* is fostered. If even a hint of dissent emerges, *direct pressure on deviants* is applied to squash it. Nonconformity is about as welcome as a thunderstorm at an outdoor wedding. *Self-appointed mindguards* protect the group from adverse information that might contradict shared illusions.

A group does not have to display all the symptoms to experience the poor-quality decisions that accompany full-blown groupthink. As Janis (1982) explains, "Even when some symptoms are absent, the others may be so pronounced that we can expect all the unfortunate consequences of groupthink" (p. 175). He argues that "the more frequently a group displays the symptoms, the worse will be the quality of its decisions, on the average" (p. 175).

Preventing Groupthink: Promoting Vigilance

To prevent groupthink, groups must become vigilant decision makers (Tasa & Whyte, 2005). Vigilant decision making requires that several steps be taken:

1. *Members must recognize the problem of groupthink as it begins to manifest itself.* The problem can be avoided if even a single member warns the group.
2. *The group must minimize status differences.* In one study, crews were subjected to flight simulations under conditions of severe weather and poor visibility.

Unknown to the crew members, the captains feigned incapacitation, then made serious errors that would lead to certain disaster. Airline officials were stunned that 25% of the flights would have crashed because no crew member took corrective action to override the captain's faulty judgment (Driskell & Salas, 1992). Asiana Airlines Flight 214 crashed short of the San Francisco airport runway on July 6, 2013, killing 3 people and injuring 181 others. The flight recorder revealed that the copilot was afraid to warn the captain about the low-speed landing (Wheeler, 2014).

The group leader, as high-status member, has the primary responsibility to minimize the influence of status differences. The leader could withhold his or her point of view from the group until everyone has had an opportunity to express an opinion. The high-status group member could also indicate ambivalence on an issue, thereby encouraging the open expression of a variety of viewpoints. Finally, a group leader could exhibit vulnerability, a recognition that everyone makes mistakes (Coyle, 2018). ("You think you messed up big time, I can top that story.")

3. *Members must develop a group norm that legitimizes disagreement.* Minority dissent stimulates divergent thought in groups and acts to prevent groupthink and improve decision making (Schultz-Hardt et al., 2006). Research clearly shows that group diversity—gender, ethnic, and cultural—is important to prevent uniformity of viewpoints that can contribute to groupthink (Hunt et al., 2018). A Pew Research study found that 89% of respondents viewed creating "a safe, respectful workplace" in which disagreement can flourish is "essential" and that female group leaders are far better at creating such an environment than male leaders (Parker, 2018).

This disagreement norm, bolstered by creating a positive, safe group climate (see Chapter 5), should be structured into the group process. Assign one or two group members to play devil's advocate (are you getting the impression that this role is critical for group success?). The primary group presents its proposals and arguments, and the devil's advocates critique it. This process can proceed through several rounds until the group is satisfied that the best decision has been made. Group leaders also should regularly invite input from all group members, welcoming civil disagreement and debate.

Finally, institute a dialectical inquiry (Sims, 1992). This procedure is very similar to devil's advocacy, except that in dialectical inquiry a subgroup develops a counterproposal and a debate takes place on two differing proposals. One or the other may be chosen by the group, both may be rejected in favor of further exploration and inquiry, or a compromise between the two proposals may be hammered out.

SECOND LOOK

Groupthink

Overestimation of Group's Power and Morality

Illusion of invulnerability

Unquestioned belief in the inherent morality of the group

Closed-Mindedness

Rationalization

Negative stereotyped views of the enemy

Pressures toward Uniformity

Self-censorship of contradictory opinion

Illusion of unanimity

Direct pressure applied to deviants

Self-appointed mindguards

Preventing Groupthink

Recognize groupthink when it first begins

Minimize status differences

Develop norm that legitimizes disagreement; create safe, respectful group climate

In summary, group members must exercise their critical-thinking abilities. The quality of decision making and problem solving in groups is significantly affected by problems of information quantity, mindsets, inferential errors, group polarization, and groupthink. If groups learn to cope with information overload and underload, recognize and counteract confirmation bias and false dichotomies, avoid or correct collective inferential errors, recognize and respond to group polarization, and avoid groupthink, then decision making and problem solving will be of higher quality.

QUESTIONS FOR CRITICAL THINKERS

1. Why is information overload such a problem when we have labor-saving technologies such as personal computers to process huge quantities of data?
2. Why are collective inferential errors more likely when issues are emotionally charged?
3. If cohesiveness is a positive small group attribute, why can it lead to groupthink?

TED TALKS AND YOUTUBE VIDEOS

"**Work Together Anywhere**" | **Lisette Sutherland**

"**Dare to Disagree**" | **Margaret Heffernan**

"**What to Trust in a 'Post Truth' World**" | **Alex Edmans**

VIDEO CASE STUDIES

Deepwater Horizon (2016). *Drama; PG-13*

This is a fairly gripping dramatization of the 2010 Deepwater Horizon oil rig catastrophic explosion and oil spill in the Gulf of Mexico. Examine elements of groupthink. Any other causes of poor decision making?

No End in Sight (2007). *Documentary; NR*

This is a documentary on the U.S. entry into the Iraq war and its ensuing difficulties. Examine this film's depiction of the war for illustrations of confirmation bias, inferential error, and groupthink.

Thirteen Days (2000). *Drama; PG-13*

Semi-accurate depiction of the harrowing 13 days of the Cuban Missile Crisis. The Kennedy administration avoided the groupthink mistakes that it made during the Bay of Pigs fiasco. Examine what prevented groupthink during the Cuban Missile Crisis. Identify any uncritical inferences made by various characters. Any mindsets? Information underload issues?

12 Angry Men (1957, 1997). *Drama; PG-13*

Either version of this taut drama that depicts a jury locked in animated argument because one juror votes "not guilty" in a capital murder case is wonderful entertainment. There are uncritical inferences aplenty. See if you can find them all. Any confirmation bias? False dichotomies?

Effective Decision Making and Problem Solving

10

Let's assume that you and your teammates have implemented all or at least most of the advice provided in previous chapters to overcome or avoid main causes of defective group decision making and problem solving. You and your fellow group members effectively addressed the specter of information overload, saw to it that information that is critical to effective decision making and problem solving is consistently shared with all members, recognized confirmation bias and groupthink and created a safe group climate for dissent to emerge, and vigilantly watched for collective inferential errors to rear their ugly heads and took immediate action to correct the problem. Your task is finished and group success is guaranteed, correct? Although corrective action to blunt or counter main causes of defective decision making and problem solving is a great start and a necessary one, there is still more work to be done.

▶ Group Discussion Functions and Procedures

In this section, functions and procedures for conducting effective group decision making and problem solving are presented. The importance of using a systematic approach is highlighted.

Phases and Functions: General Considerations

All decision-making and problem-solving groups exhibit recognizable phases. Identifying these phases helps guide understanding of what procedures work best to produce effective decisions and solutions to complex problems. The most widely accepted phasic model of group decision making is Poole's (1983) multiple sequence model of decision emergence.

objectives

The primary purpose of this chapter is to explore the importance of implementing processes for effective group decision making and problem solving beyond what has already been extensively detailed in previous chapters. Toward this end, there are four chapter objectives:

1. To explore structured procedures for effective decision making and problem solving.

2. To discuss ways to evaluate information to improve decision making and problem solving.

3. To explain several techniques for stimulating creative group problem solving.

4. To explore the unique decision-making and problem-solving challenges posed by small groups operating in the virtual arena.

focus questions

1. How are the Standard Agenda and the functional perspective related?

2. What constitutes a true consensus?

3. What are the advantages and disadvantages of various decision-making rules?

Multiple Sequence Model: Phases of Decision Making The multiple sequence model pictures groups moving along three activity tracks: *task*, *relational*, and *topic*. Some groups may devote a significant amount of time to the relational (social) activities of groups before proceeding to a task discussion; other groups may start right in on the task. Groups may also be sidetracked during discussions on task by relational conflicts that need to be addressed.

Groups take three principal paths in reaching decisions (Poole & Roth, 1989). The first path is called the *unitary sequence*. Groups on this path proceed in a rigid, step-by-step fashion toward a decision. The second path is called *complex cyclic*. This path repeats cycles of focusing on the problem, then the solution, and back again to the problem, and so forth. Finally, the third principal path is *solution oriented*. Here the group launches prematurely into discussion of solutions before adequate focus on the problem. One study of 106 top executives who represented 91 private and public-sector companies in 17 countries, found that 85% viewed their organizations as bad problem solvers. "Spurred by a penchant for action, managers tend to switch quickly into solution mode without checking whether they really understand the problem" (Wedell-Wedellsborg, 2017).

The multiple sequence model mostly *describes* the principal paths that groups often take. The functional perspective, however, *prescribes* procedures for effective decision making and problem solving.

Functional Perspective: Being Systematic Discussions that follow some systematic procedure tend to be more productive and result in better decisions than relatively unstructured discussions (Bohn, 2017; Honey-Roses et al., 2020). The drawbacks to unstructured, free-floating group discussions are aimless deliberations that are time-consuming and inefficient, premature focus on solutions (solution-oriented path), inclination to accept the first plausible solution that may not be the best option, discussion tangents and topic-hopping, talkaholics' windbaggery, and failure to address group conflict (Sunwolf & Frey, 2005).

There is no single, systematic discussion procedure that guarantees effective decision making and problem solving. Rigidly following a set of prescribed steps, such as the unitary sequence path, can stifle discussion and seem robotic. Steps in any systematic discussion procedure should be looked at as guidelines, not commandments. The more complex the task being discussed, the more likely the complex-cyclic path will emerge. Flashes of insight don't necessarily follow a preordained sequence of discussion steps. The group may need to backtrack occasionally.

Whatever path groups choose, the quality of decisions depends on the ability of members to use systematic procedures competently to accomplish five critical functions: problem analysis, establishment of evaluation criteria, generation of alternative solutions, evaluation of positive consequences of solutions, and evaluation of negative consequences of solutions (Orlitzky & Hirokawa, 2001). This functional perspective is reflected in the Standard Agenda. Arriving at an effective solution to a complex problem may take many meetings, so don't forget the necessary steps detailed in Chapter 3 for conducting effective meetings.

The Standard Agenda: Structuring Group Discussion

John Dewey (1910) described a process of rational decision making and problem solving that he called **reflective thinking**—a set of logical steps that incorporate the scientific method of defining, analyzing, and solving problems. The **Standard Agenda** is a direct outgrowth of Dewey's reflective thinking process. The Standard Agenda is exactly that, a precise agenda that guides what could be a series of meetings if the problem being addressed is especially complex and volatile. It is composed of six steps and focuses on a full analysis of the problem before considering solutions, thus eschewing the solution-oriented path that jumps to conclusions too quickly.

This section explains these steps by discussing the historical evolution of the smoking policy on the Cabrillo College campus. Although in actual fact campus meetings were not conducted precisely as advised in Chapter 3, resulting in some considerable turbulence and difficulties, for the sake of illustration let's pretend that they were. The purpose/impact statement guiding a series of extensive meetings on campus for this illustration therefore would have been: to determine whether the Cabrillo College smoking policy should be revised given the potential health risks and campus complaints regarding the permissive current policy.

Problem Identification: What's the Question?   The problem should be formulated into an open-ended question phrased as fact, value, or policy. The choice will identify the nature of the problem. A **question of fact** asks whether something is true and to what extent. Objective evidence can be used to determine an answer to the question "Are there serious dangers to nonsmokers from secondhand smoke?" A **question of value** focuses on the desirability of an object, idea, event, or person. For example, "Does permitting smoking on campus raise any quality-of-life concerns?" Quality of life is a subjective value judgment, and it can't be determined scientifically or statistically. Smokers might find the smell of smoke innocuous, whereas nonsmokers may find it grossly unpleasant.

A **question of policy** asks whether a specific course of action should be undertaken to solve a problem, such as "Should the campus smoking policy be changed?"

Once the problem is phrased as a question of fact, value, or policy, any ambiguous terms should be defined. "Quality of life," for example, would require some further description (e.g., no strong odors, freedom from pollutants that might trigger respiratory difficulties).

Problem Analysis: Causes and Effects The group researches and gathers information on the problem defined, tries to determine how serious the problem is, what harm or effect the problem produces, and what causes the problem. Smoking on campus was a contentious issue at Cabrillo College for many years. The conclusion of the student senate, after much research and debate, was that the smoking policy was too permissive, causing numerous hazards and significant unpleasantness for students. One note of caution: Although analyzing the problem is important and should be undertaken before exploring potential solutions, **analysis paralysis**, or bogging down by overly analyzing the problem, can prevent a group from ever making a decision.

Solution Criteria: Setting Standards This is a critical yet often ignored step in decision-making and problem solving. **Criteria** are standards used to evaluate decisions and solutions to problems. For example, the American Film Institute twice ranked *Citizen Kane* as the top all-time American film, in 1997 and again in 2007 ("*Citizen Kane*," 2007). For most college students of today, this must seem a perplexing choice. *Citizen Kane*, released in 1941, is a black-and-white film, it has no real body count, the action is plodding by today's frenetic standards, and the special effects probably seem laughable compared to recent blockbuster movies. Knowing that historical significance (especially cinematic innovations), critical recognition and awards, and popularity were primary criteria ("The Top Ten," 2017), however, helps you understand better why *Citizen Kane* received the top ranking twice.

Different criteria, however, can produce wildly different results. For example, University of Oregon, my alma mater, was ranked #103 on the list of top colleges in the United States by *U.S. News & World Report*, #225 by *Niche*, but #327 by *Money* magazine ("2021 Best National University Rankings"; "2021 College Rankings"; "Best Colleges," 2020). The criteria used by these sources explain the huge differences in rankings. *U.S. News* uses student retention and graduation rates, faculty resources, and what top academics at peer institutions think of each college. *Niche* uses academic grades, student loan amounts and alumni salaries, student-to-faculty ratios and faculty awards, diversity, and the quality of campus accommodations and facilities (Berkman, 2020). *Money* uses median SAT/ACT scores, affordability, and potential career earnings.

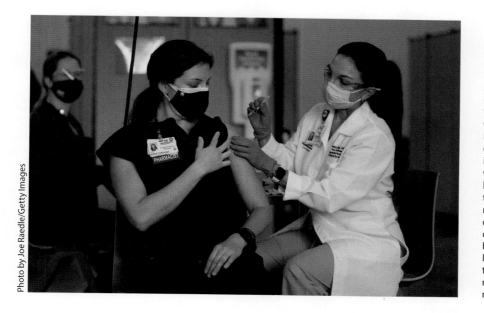

Photo by Joe Raedle/Getty Images

Prioritization for who received the Covid-19 vaccine first, second, and so forth was based on criteria offered by the Centers for Disease Control and Prevention. Healthcare workers and elderly individuals living in assisted living facilities were given top priority based on the rationale that groups at highest risk of acquiring the disease and potentially dying from it should be at the head of the line (J. Cohen, 2020). In this situation, decision-making criteria were a matter of life and death.

Groups should establish criteria for evaluating solutions before solutions are suggested. In some cases, the criteria are already dictated (e.g., the legal criterion of "beyond a reasonable doubt" in a murder case). Not all criteria, however, are created equal. The group must consider the relevance and appropriateness of each criterion. For example, ranking films based on criteria such as "buckets of blood spilled" or "number of sex scenes" would be dubious at best except perhaps for those with extremely narrow (some would say questionable) interests.

Some relevant and appropriate criteria on the smoking question devised by an ad hoc campus committee included: protect the health of nonsmokers, be simple to understand and enforce, avoid alienating either group (smokers or nonsmokers), cost less than $5,000, and maintain a comfortable environment. The criteria should be ranked in order of priority. The committee prioritized the criteria on the smoking policy in the order just listed.

Solution Suggestions: Generating Alternatives The group brainstorms possible solutions (see later in this chapter for proper brainstorming technique). Some possibilities on the smoking issue that emerged from the committee deliberations included mandating a total ban on smoking across the campus, designating certain locations outside for smoking, building outside shelters in designated locations around the campus to protect smokers from weather, permitting smoking only in automobiles, and allowing smoking only in parking lots, both in cars and outside.

Solution Evaluation and Selection: Deciding by Criteria   The story of a military briefing officer asked to devise a method for raising enemy submarines off the ocean floor illustrates the importance of this step. The briefing officer's solution? Heat the ocean to the boiling point. When bewildered Pentagon officials asked him how this could be done, he replied, "I don't know. I decided on the solution; you work out the details." The devil is in the details. Explore both the merits and demerits (avoid confirmation bias) of suggested solutions. Devil's advocacy and dialectical inquiry (see Chapter 9) are useful techniques for accomplishing this.

Consider each solution in terms of the criteria established earlier. For instance, protecting the health of faculty, staff, and students was a prime concern of those addressing the smoking policy. A *total ban* on smoking met this criterion best. Devil's advocates on the committee, however, raised the concern that a total ban might alienate student smokers to such an extent that significant enrollment declines would result, costing a great loss of money to the college. Smoking in *designated areas* seemed to be a promising solution and was tried on a temporary basis. Smokers, however, had difficulty determining where the designated smoking areas were on campus despite posted maps, smokers were exposed to some nasty weather (violating the "maintain a comfortable environment" criterion), and *building shelters* to address this complaint exceeded the $5,000 limit on expenses criterion. *Relegating smokers to their cars* also would ban smoking for those who chose mass transit or bicycled to campus.

Finally, the suggestion that smoking be *restricted to parking lots* protected the health of nonsmokers; was a simple, easily understood policy; cost less than $5,000 for signs and ashtrays; and mostly avoided alienating smokers because smoking was still permitted. Only the maintaining a comfortable environment criterion was not met completely because smokers were still not totally sheltered from the elements. They could, however, smoke in their cars or smoke in the two massive parking structures on campus that provide some shelter, especially from rain.

Permitting smoking only in parking lots was adopted by the board of trustees with support from the faculty and student senates. It made Cabrillo College one of the very first colleges in the nation to restrict smoking to this extent. The policy was later revisited, however, and in 2014, after extensive discussion by various groups, Cabrillo College joined a growing list of colleges that instituted a complete ban on smoking ("Smokefree and Tobacco-Free," 2020).

Solution Implementation: Follow-Through   A common failing of decision-making groups is that once they arrive at a decision, implementation faces two challenges. First, **Murphy's law**—which states that anything that can go wrong likely will go wrong, somewhere, sometime—is often not considered. Failing to make a backup copy of a final written report for a group project is flirting with Murphy's malevolence. NASA specializes in redundant systems in its spacecrafts because it expects the unexpected to occur.

Groups should consider what might go wrong before making a final decision. Once a bad decision is implemented, it is too late.

A second problem is that once a decision has been made, groups don't plan its implementation. One study found that only 30% of strategic initiatives in businesses are successfully implemented (Davis et al., 2010). **Force field analysis**, suggested by the work of Kurt Lewin (1947), is one method for planning implementation of a group solution or decision. Groups brainstorm a list of *driving forces* (those that encourage change) and *restraining forces* (those that resist change). Driving forces that encouraged implementation of the new smoking policy at Cabrillo College included multiple complaints from students, stated concerns about the health risks to nonsmokers, and a fear that many nonsmokers would stop enrolling at the college. Restraining forces working against implementation mostly involved concerns about enrollment and a more general resistance to change itself.

Systems resist change. One survey found that the number one barrier to change in business is "resistance to change," noted by 82% of respondents ("Survey of CEOs," 2007).

There are five conditions that reduce resistance to change:

1. *Group members have a part in the planning and decision making.* This gives them part ownership of the change. Imposing change produces psychological reactance (see Chapter 5).
2. *Change does not threaten group members.* The larger concern on the smoking issue was whether students would drop out of Cabrillo College because the policy was too restrictive.
3. *The need for change affects individuals directly.* The great majority of students at Cabrillo College are nonsmokers directly affected by a permissive smoking policy.
4. *Change is open to revision and modification.* The smoking policy change was presented as a temporary fix, subject to revision, which did occur.

5. *The three factors—degree, rate, and desirability of change—are considered.* The smoking policy at Cabrillo College addressed substantial degree of change by initially not banning smoking entirely, considered too rapid a rate of change by phasing in the policy (designated areas were tried first), and addressed desirability by conducting open hearings.

A helpful decision-making method that stipulates systematically how to implement small group decisions once resistance to change has been addressed is called *PERT (Program Evaluation Review Technique).* The steps in the PERT method are as follows:

1. *Determine what the final step should look like* (e.g., restrict smoking to parking lots).
2. *Specify any events that must occur before the final goal is realized* (e.g., obtain endorsement from the board of trustees).
3. *Put the events in chronological order* (e.g., the committee must secure the support of the student and faculty senates, then the college president, before going for board endorsement).
4. *Generate a list of activities, resources, and materials* that are required between events (e.g., hold a strategy session before making presentations).
5. *Develop a timeline for implementation.* Estimate how long each step will take.
6. *Match the total time estimate for implementation of the solution* with any deadlines (e.g., end of school year approaching). Modify your plan of action as needed.
7. *Specify which group members will have which responsibilities.* This prevents confusion.

Decision-Making Rules: Majority, Minority, and Unanimity

There are three primary group decision-making rules: majority, minority, and unanimity. There are pros and cons for each.

Majority Rule: Tyrannical or Practical Although majority rule is a popular method of group decision making, the quality of the group's decision is a particularly troublesome problem. Majorities can sometimes take ludicrous, even dangerous positions. Racism, sexism, and other bigotry in the United States have been the products of majority rule. Studies comparing unanimous and majority rule found several deficiencies in majority rule (Bor et al., 2020). First, deliberations are significantly shorter and less conscientious. Deliberations typically end once a requisite majority is reached (Hoe, 2017). Consequently, less

SECOND LOOK

Effective Problem-Solving Process

STANDARD AGENDA	TECHNIQUES
Problem identification	Form questions of fact, value, or policy
	Define ambiguous terms
Problem analysis	Explore causes of problem (gather information)
	Explore effects (significance) of the problem
	Avoid analysis paralysis
	Use framing/reframing
Solution criteria	Establish criteria
	Prioritize criteria
Solution suggestions	Brainstorm solutions
	Clarify ambiguous or confusing ideas
	Consolidate overlapping ideas
Solution evaluation/selection	Explore merits/demerits of solutions
	Use devil's advocacy
	Use dialectical inquiry
	Consider solutions in terms of criteria
	Use majority or minority rule, or consensus
Solution implementation	Use force field analysis
	Use PERT

error correction takes place, sometimes resulting in faulty decisions (Lee & Paradowski, 2007). Second, minority factions participate less frequently and are less influential, thereby underutilizing the group's resources. Third, members' overall satisfaction with the group is lower. Minorities feel the "tyranny of the majority" when their point of view is ignored and deliberations become combative and bullying.

Despite the disadvantages of majority rule, there are some advantages (Hastie & Kameda, 2005; Taylor et al., 2013). When issues are not very important, when decisions must be made relatively quickly, when groups become large, and when commitment of all members to the final decision is unimportant, majority rule can be useful. Majority rule is efficient and provides quick closure.

Minority Rule: Several Types Minority rule as a group decision-making method occurs in several forms. First, the group designates one of its members as an expert to make the decision. This method relieves group members from devoting time and energy to solving problems. Decision by designated expert, however, is mostly ineffective because determining who is the expert in the group is often difficult and contentious. Lack of group input also fails to capitalize on synergy.

Second, a designated authority (usually from outside the immediate group) makes the decision for the group, either after hearing discussion from group members or without their consultation. If group advice is treated as a mere formality, or the designated authority is a poor listener, then none of the benefits of group deliberations will accrue. Group members are also likely to vie competitively for attention, seek to impress the authority, and offer what the authority wants to hear, not what should be said.

Third, in some instances, executive committees must be delegated responsibility for making certain decisions because the workload for the larger group is overwhelming or the time constraints are prohibitive. The challenge here is to persuade the larger group to get behind the decision.

Finally, minority rule can take the form of a forceful faction deciding for the group by dominating less forceful members. On rare occasions this may be advisable when the minority faction consists of the most informed, committed members. Too often, however, dominant group members focus on personal gain more than on what's good for the group (Maner, 2017).

Unanimity Rule: Consensus Group consensus is based on the unanimity rule. **Consensus** is "a state of mutual agreement among members of a group where all legitimate concerns of individuals have been addressed to the satisfaction of the group" (Saint & Lawson, 1997). Consensus usually requires some give and take. If all members can agree on an acceptable choice, even if this alternative is not each member's preference, then you have come close to achieving a true consensus. A **true consensus**, however, requires not just agreement, but commitment and satisfaction (DeStephen & Hirokawa, 1988). Members show commitment by defending the unanimous decision to outsiders, not undermining it by agreeing in the group but disagreeing outside of the group. Group members feel satisfaction with the decision-making process when a cooperative group climate and reasonable opportunities for all members to participate meaningfully in the decision making occur (Gastil et al., 2007).

Groups that use a consensus approach tend to produce better decisions than groups using other decision rules. This occurs because full discussion of issues is required, every group member must embrace the decision, and minority members are heard (Lee & Paradowski, 2007). Women, who often are reticent to participate during group discussions when badly outnumbered by men, are more vocal when the unanimity rule is used (Karpowitz et al., 2012).

Nevertheless, there are three principal limitations to consensus decision making. First, achieving unanimous agreement from group members is very difficult. Some groups seem unable to agree even that gravity exists. Members who resist siding with the majority lengthen the deliberations and increase secondary tension (Taylor et al., 2013). Second, consensus is increasingly unlikely as groups grow larger. Groups of 15 or more rarely achieve a consensus. (Try getting 15 family members and friends to agree on a movie.) Seeking a consensus, however, even if never quite achieved, can still be beneficial. Third, consensus, because it takes substantial time, is usually inappropriate when quick action is required.

Several guidelines can help a group achieve a consensus (Saint & Lawson, 1997):

1. *Follow the Standard Agenda.* Structured group discussion, not aimless conversation, improves the chances of achieving consensus.
2. *Establish a cooperative group climate.* Supportive patterns of communication encourage consensus; defensive patterns discourage it.
3. *Identify the pluses and minuses of potential decisions under consideration.* This discourages confirmation bias.
4. *Discuss all concerns of group members and attempt to resolve them.* Try to find alternatives that will satisfy members' concerns. This avoids groupthink.
5. *Avoid adversarial, win–lose arguments.* Don't stubbornly argue for a position to achieve a personal victory. Avoid the "enemy–friend" competitive false dichotomy.
6. *Request a "stand aside."* A stand aside means a team member has reservations about the group decision but does not wish to block the group choice. This avoids the blocker role.

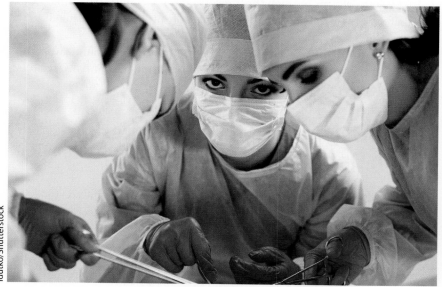

Idutko/Shutterstock

Both consensus and majority vote would be inappropriate for a surgical team performing an operation. "All those in favor of cutting here raise your hand" does not work! Split-second decisions must be made, so minority rule—the chief surgeon making the decisions—applies.

SECOND LOOK
Decision-Making Rules

Rules	Pros	Cons
Majority rule	Quick, efficient	Minorities vulnerable to tyranny of majority
	Expedient in large groups	Quality of decision questionable
		Usually alienates minority
		Underutilization of resources
Minority rule		
Designated expert	Saves time	Expertise hard to determine
		No group input
Designated authority	Clear, efficient	Members vie for attention
Executive committee	Divides labor	Weak commitment to decision
Forceful faction	Committed faction	Likely Me-, not We-oriented
Unanimity rule	Quality decisions	Time-consuming
	Commitment	Difficult
	Satisfaction	Tension-producing

Note: Although the consensus technique is used most directly during the solution criteria and solution evaluation/selection steps of the Standard Agenda, consensus rules may operate throughout the problem-solving process. Majority or minority rule may also be inserted at various steps if appropriate conditions exist.

7. *Avoid conflict-suppressing techniques such as coin flipping and swapping* ("I'll support your position this time if you support mine next time"). Conflict-suppressing techniques will not usually produce commitment to the group decision.

8. *If consensus is impossible, seek a supermajority* (a minimum two-thirds vote). It captures the spirit of consensus by requiring substantial, if not total, agreement.

▶ Evaluating Information: Countering "Truth Decay"

Group members must exercise their critical thinking abilities at every stage of the Standard Agenda to maximize the probabilities of effective decisions. Consequently, how you go about gathering and evaluating information should be primary concerns. Critical thinking has never been more important or challenging given the eruption of fake news, fabricated studies, "alternative facts," and fruit-loopy conspiracies disseminated on social media (Chan et al., 2017; Datz, 2020;

Debies-Carl, 2017). A Rand Report dubs this deterioration of critical thinking practices as "truth decay" (Kavanagh & Rich, 2018). Covid-19 unleashed what the World Health Organization dubbed a "massive infodemic" in which the desire to learn about this novel virus exploded, but so did the dissemination of misinformation and looney tunes nonsense. Holding your breath for 10 seconds as a test for Covid, Vladimir Putin releasing 500 lions to the streets of Moscow to keep residents indoors to fight the spread of the virus, and eating sea lettuce to prevent anyone from getting infected with Covid are just a few examples of the crazy misinformation spread on social media sites at the outset of the pandemic (Fleming, 2020).

Jonathan Swift long ago noted, "Falsehood flies, and the truth comes limping after it." Researchers at the Massachusetts Institute of Technology confirmed this by conducting a study on lies and false information spread on Twitter. Their results are troubling: Fake news is 70% more likely to be retweeted than real, substantiated news, and it takes the truth six times as long as misinformation to reach 1,500 people. Truthful information rarely spreads to more than 1,000 people, but the top 1% of false news routinely spreads to between 1,000 and 100,000 people on Twitter. They found that "bots" were not the culprits in spreading nonsense, but instead it is people who are more drawn to the novel, surprising, and emotional nature of most false information, rumor, and conspiracy theories (Vosoughi et al., 2018). As Dr. David L. Katz, founder of True Health Initiative, which counters fake health claims, observes, "Cyberspace is the ultimate, ecumenical echo chamber" (quoted by Krieger, 2018).

Clearly, knowing how to evaluate information and claims is a critical group function. There are five criteria for making such evaluations: credibility, currency, relevance, representativeness, and sufficiency.

Credibility: Is It Believable?

Consider several guidelines to determine **credibility**—trustworthiness of information. First, consider the source or lack thereof. For example, if an article on the Internet cites no author, be dubious. A slick-looking website can seem authoritative, but be a front for some questionable, even despicable viewpoints. A source's expertise should be apparent. An author's name without citation of his or her expertise lacks credibility. Wikipedia, the popular online encyclopedia, ironically cautions against using Wikipedia as a primary source because "anyone in the world can edit an article, deleting accurate information or adding false information" ("Wikipedia," 2017).

Even credible sources can provide misinformation, and that is doubly troubling. Research shows that corrections of misinformation are ineffective when the misinformation has been repeated multiple times and was originally provided by a credible source. When corrections are provided by a credible source, however, corrective messages tend to be more successful in changing peoples' minds (Walter & Tukachinsky, 2020).

Second, **check for bias** (gains something by taking certain positions). Research shows that ideologically leaning Internet news sources (e.g., Daily Kos; Drudge Report) have a strong biasing effect that produces "a distorted understanding of evidence, potentially promoting inaccurate beliefs" (Garrett et al., 2016). A Stanford University study showed that more than half of the college students participating thought the American College of Pediatricians (APC) was a reliable source after accessing the group's website and being given the opportunity to do a wider search online to check on this group. The Southern Poverty Law Center identifies the APC as a hate group because of its "history of propagating damaging falsehoods about LGBT people, including linking homosexuality to pedophilia, and claiming that LGBT people are more promiscuous than heterosexuals, and . . . a danger to children" ("Meet the Anti-LGBT Hate Group," 2015). A quick Google search easily reveals these details. Also, almost two-thirds of the same college student participants failed to recognize the political bias of a tweet about the National Rifle Association by the liberal group MoveOn.org (Wineburg et al., 2016).

Stanford researchers followed this study with another one that is just as discouraging. They gave 263 college students two tasks. One task had students evaluate the trustworthiness of a "news story" whose source was actually a satirical website. A second task asked students to evaluate a website claiming to sponsor "nonpartisan research" but was actually created by a Washington, D.C., public relations firm headed by a corporate lobbyist. Students were permitted to "use any online resources" to help with their evaluation. More than two-thirds of these students did not recognize the bogus "news story" as satirical. A whopping 95% never identified the PR firm as actually partisan, not nonpartisan (Wineburg et al., 2020). Students rarely explored additional websites to investigate the veracity of the "news story" and the "nonpartisan research" site.

Before considering a site as credible, especially if it is unfamiliar, type the site's organizational name into the Google search window and look for authoritative links that offer critiques of the organization, or flag it as bogus, highly partisan, or the work of troll farms. Such links are usually quite easy to locate. When researching on the Internet, search for websites that have no profit motive or ideological bent. If a site name ends in .gov or .edu, it is sponsored and maintained by a governmental or educational institution with a reputation to protect. Site names ending in .com or .org in their address are commercial ventures whose credibility varies. One study found that even subtle reminders about accuracy of information can decrease people's willingness to share false information (Pennycook et al., 2020).

Third, watch for authorities quoted outside of their field of expertise. Iben Browning predicted a "major" earthquake for December 3 and 4, 1990, along the New Madrid Fault located in the Midwest. Schools in several states were dismissed during these two days because of his prediction. Browning had some scientific expertise, but not on earthquakes. In fact, earthquake experts, with geotechnical engineering degrees and experience in seismology, denounced Browning's predictions because earthquakes cannot be predicted ("Can Earthquakes Be Predicted?" 2018). There wasn't a sizable earthquake on the New Madrid Fault until April 17, 2008, and it was considered "moderate" by quake experts and caused minimal damage.

Fourth, beware implausible statistics. For example, consider the statistic that *81% of white victims of homicide are "killed by blacks,"* attributed to the Crime Statistics Bureau in San Francisco and circulated on the Internet during the 2016 presidential campaign. First, there is no Crime Statistics Bureau in San Francisco. Second, according to the FBI, the actual statistic is *14%* of white victims are killed by African Americans (Fang, 2016). The original source for the wholly implausible 81% statistic was a neo-Nazi Twitter account (Sarlin, 2016).

The Internet can be a terrific repository of useful information, but it can also be a source of massive misinformation. Consult snopes.com to correct urban myths and implausible statistics, such as the spider and sex statistics that are silly manufactured stats.

Currency: Is It Up to Date?

Information should be as current as possible, especially when a phenomenon is volatile (e.g., weather, stock market performance, tech product prices) or all the facts are not known yet. What used to be taken as fact may be called into question with new information. For example, Covid-19 statistics on number of cases, deaths, positive test rates, vaccination distribution numbers, and vaccination completions were a constant reminder during the pandemic of the importance of accurate, credible, up-to-date statistics and information. Policies on school reopenings, return to in-person workplaces, and business reopenings and degree of safety measures required depended on the most current information. Also, Internet articles often post no date, so accuracy can be an issue. Check dates on any footnotes to guess the approximate date of authorship if none is provided.

Relevance: Looking for Logical Connections

Information should logically support claims made. Claiming that the public education system in the United States is the world's best because America spends more money in total than any other nation is irrelevant. Total spending doesn't necessarily equate with educational excellence, especially if the money is largely wasted or spent on the wrong priorities. The **ad populum fallacy**—basing a claim on popular opinion alone—lacks logical relevance. For example, a 2016 Chapman University survey found that almost a quarter of respondents do not believe astronauts landed on the moon, almost half believe in haunted houses, and more than half believe the U.S. government isn't telling the truth about the 9/11 terrorist attack (Poppy, 2017). More than 40% of Americans do not know that Earth orbits the Sun in a year-long cycle (Otto, 2016). A startling 52% of Americans do not know that dinosaurs and humans did not roam Earth at the same time—they were 65 million years apart (Sidky, 2018). Considering these results, basing a claim on mass opinion is logically irrelevant.

Representativeness: Reflecting the Facts

A single example, study, or statistic may or may not accurately reflect what is true in a particular instance. A single scientific study proves very little until thoroughly replicated by different experts. There are two principal guidelines for determining whether statistics are representative. First, the sample size (in polls, surveys, and studies) must be adequate. This can be determined most easily by the **margin of error**, which is the degree of sampling error accounted for by imperfections in selecting a sample. As the margin of error increases, the representativeness of the statistic decreases. If the margin of error reaches more than plus or minus 3%, the representativeness of the statistic becomes questionable. A margin of error of, say, plus or minus 7% means that a survey reporting that a majority of college students (51%) smoke marijuana could vary from a high of 58% (+7%) to a low of 44% (–7%). So, within that range, either a substantial minority or a sizable majority of college students smoke marijuana.

A second guideline for assuring statistics are representative is that the sample must be randomly selected, not self-selected. A **random sample** is a part of the population chosen in such a manner that every member of the entire population has an equal chance of being selected. A **self-selected sample** is one in which the most committed, passionate, or otherwise atypical parts of the population studied are more likely to participate. For example, the California Public Interest Research Group contacted almost 80,000 students 18 to 24 years old to complete an online survey on voter participation. A mere 1,057 students responded. When asked "Do you plan to vote in the June primaries?" a surprising 75% said yes. Historically, a primary in a nonpresidential election year has low voter turnout. Not surprisingly, only 25.2% of 18- to 24-year-olds ultimately voted (Manjikian & Rusch, 2014). Good intentions explain part of the discrepant statistics, but the self-selected sample represented mostly motivated young voters.

Sufficiency: When Enough Really Is Enough

When do you have enough information to support your claims? There is no magic formula. Nevertheless, remember that correlations alone are insufficient to assert causal relations (see Chapter 9). Also, inferences based on examples, anecdotes, or one or two easily accessed articles on Google are insufficient support for claims. Finally, extraordinary claims require extraordinary proof (Shermer, 2013). Despite the "moon landing was a hoax" crowd, astronauts landed on the moon six times, collected rocks, and returned to tell the story. Denying it is an extraordinary claim based mostly on raising mundane questions (Millis, 2017), and it ignores the fact that the moon landing is one of history's most thoroughly documented events. (See Appendix B for additional relevant material on critically examining information and claims.)

▶ Creative Problem Solving

Years ago, a prisoner escaped from a penitentiary in the western United States. He was recaptured after a few weeks. On his return, prison officials grilled him. "How did you cut through the bars?" they demanded. Finally, he confessed. He said he had taken bits of twine from the machine shop, dipped them in glue, then in emery. He smuggled these makeshift "hacksaws" back to his cell. For three months he laboriously sawed through the inch-thick steel bars. Prison officials accepted his story, locked him up, and kept him far away from the machine shop. Is that the end of the story? Not quite. Three and a half years later, he escaped again by cutting through the cell bars. He was never recaptured, but how he escaped became a legend in the underworld. It seems that his original story was a phony. He hadn't fashioned a hacksaw from any materials in the machine shop. Instead, he had used woolen strings from his socks, moistened them with spit, and rubbed them in abrasive dirt from the floor of his cell, then painstakingly sawed through the cell bars (Rossman, 1931). The prisoner had fashioned a creative solution, albeit for a nefarious reason, to a challenging problem. Creative problem solving is the focus of this section.

focus questions

1. How do imagination and knowledge relate to creative problem solving?

2. Is brainstorming a more effective creative process than nominal group technique?

3. What is reframing, and how does it work to produce creative ideas?

General Overview: The Creative Process

The story of the prisoner's resourceful escape highlights several important points about creativity and problem solving. First, to borrow Thomas Edison's comment on genius, creativity is more perspiration than inspiration. Finding **creative solutions to problems requires hard work.** This means devoting time and energy to the task, not hoping for imaginative ideas to fall from the sky and clunk us on the head.

Second, **creativity is spurred by challenges.** As the old adage says, "Necessity is the mother of invention." We are creative in response to some problem that requires a solution. The bigger the challenge, the more complex the problem, the greater is the need for creativity.

Third, **creativity flourishes in cooperative, not competitive environments.** In a competitive atmosphere, thinking "may be used to plan, strategize, and coerce rather than to problem solve and collaborate" (Carnevale & Probst, 1998).

Fourth, **creativity requires sound ideas, not just imaginative ones.** As Vincent Ruggiero (1988) puts it, creative ideas must be more than uncommon; they "must be uncommonly good" (p. 77). Creative solutions are original, but they also must work. I once heard a radio commentator read recipes submitted by children for preparing a Thanksgiving turkey. One child wrote: "Put 10 pounds of butter on the turkey and 5 pounds of salt. Cook it for 20 minutes." M-m-m-m-m good! Creative problem solving and decision making require both imagination and knowledge. Children create foolish things because they don't know any better. Competent communicators create solutions that are workable and effective.

Fifth, **creativity requires many ideas.** Although sheer quantity doesn't guarantee great solutions, the fewer the ideas, the less probable is the discovery of at least one good idea. IDEO generated more than 4,000 ideas for new toys. Of these, 230 were explored and only 12 were eventually produced by clients (Puccio et al., 2007).

Finally, *creativity requires breaking mindsets and thinking "outside the box."* Unless you try adopting different ways of approaching problems, you'll remain stuck in place (McCaffrey & Pearson, 2017).

Creative Techniques: Systematic Procedures

Haphazard, unfocused efforts to induce creativity are often not as productive as more focused efforts. Systematic procedures can spur creativity.

Idea Generation: Several Techniques Alex Osborn introduced the brainstorming technique in 1939. **Brainstorming** is a creative problem-solving technique that promotes plentiful, even zany, ideas in an atmosphere free from criticism and with enthusiastic participation from all group members. **Preparing for a brainstorming session can be important.** Studies show that the simple task of having group members each tell an embarrassing story about themselves in a 10-minute prep-session significantly increases both quantity and quality of brainstorming ideas generated afterward (Thompson, 2017). Such self-deprecation primes participants to loosen up and become less self-conscious about how others might judge them.

There are several guidelines for using the brainstorming technique ("Brainstorm Rules," 2018; Nussbaum, 2004):

1. *Encourage wild ideas.* At IDEO, this is a motto that appears in large print on the walls of each brainstorming room. Worry about the practical stuff after ideas have been generated in rapid-fire brainstorming sessions.
2. *Don't evaluate ideas while brainstorming.* Idea slayers, such as "That will never work" and "It's completely impractical," should be squelched by members. Even a positive evaluation, such as "great idea," is out of order because group members will quickly interpret absence of positive evaluation as a negative assessment of their ideas.
3. *Don't clarify or seek clarification of an idea.* This will slow down the process. Clarification can come later after a list of ideas has been generated.
4. *Do not engage in task-irrelevant discussion.* Idea generation is significantly diminished when conversation is permitted during brainstorming sessions. A brainstorming facilitator should invoke this rule.
5. *Stay focused on the topic.* You want all suggestions to be related to the topic. Wild ideas that are not on topic are not helpful.

6. *Expand on the ideas of other group members.* Look for opportunities to piggyback on the ideas of others, generating additional creative ideas. Such piggybacking can actually increase group cohesiveness and enhance idea generation (Henningsen & Henningsen, 2018).

7. *Evaluate ideas generated once the brainstorming phase is completed* (Sawyer, 2017). The group needs to decide what ideas generated are best to implement.

Brainstorming normally is instituted during the solutions suggestion step of the Standard Agenda. Determining the quality of the ideas generated from brainstorming comes during the solution evaluation and selection step. Ideas are evaluated based on solution criteria established earlier in the Standard Agenda process.

A second creative problem-solving method is **nominal group technique** (Delbecq et al., 1975). Individuals work by themselves generating lists of ideas on a problem, then convene in a group where they merely post their ideas (on a chart, whiteboard, or computer screen). Interaction occurs only to clarify ideas, not to discuss their merits and demerits. Individuals then select their five favorite ideas, write them on a card, and rank them from most to least favorite. The rankings are averaged and the ideas with the highest averages are the ones selected by the group. Voting is anonymous, so reticent members participate more readily, and consensus occurs. Dominant members are neutralized. Cross-fertilization of ideas that comes from group discussion is constrained, however, by the highly structured procedures, although procedures can be loosened.

When brainstorming, expand on the ideas of other group members.

REDPIXEL.PL/Shutterstock

Some research has shown nominal group technique generates more and better ideas than brainstorming (Paulus et al., 1993). Results, however, have been derived mostly from student groups that have no history together and no future as a group, have no training and experience brainstorming, are provided no opportunity to research the task prior to brainstorming, are given little time to think about the task, and are provided tasks often unrelated to students' interests, and brainstormers never evaluate ideas. Also, highly complex tasks, such as the design challenges faced by IDEO, have not been given to brainstormers to compare their results with nominal groups (Sutton, 2012).

Brainstorming, if done properly, can be highly effective (Cho, 2013; Goldenberg et al., 2013). Osborn suggested that the proper brainstorming format should involve first an individual, then a group, followed by an individual brainstorming session (Isaksen & Gaulin, 2005). Members should be provided with a well-defined problem a few days in advance so members can research it and think of ideas. Then members meet as a group to brainstorm. After this, individuals are given a few days to contemplate further ideas. There is experimental support for the Osborn approach as the "most effective brainstorming process" (Korde & Paulus, 2017).

"Never, ever, think outside the box."

Thinking outside the box is often a welcome method for engendering creative decision making, but it has its limits. Some "outside the box" ideas are just plain messy and ineffective. Thus, ideas generated by brainstorming require evaluation after brainstorming by the group to determine which are the best to implement.

Also, as a variation, there is the *6-3-5 method* of brainstorming. Here six group members sit around a table and write down three ideas on the subject. Then they pass these ideas to the person sitting immediately to their right, who then builds on those ideas. This is done five times until all members have had an opportunity to build on the ideas of others (Markman, 2017). The final list of ideas can be shared on a whiteboard or listed and sent as an email to all group members who can reassemble at a later time and conduct further open, standard brainstorming idea generation.

Brainstorming can also be improved in additional ways. Members should belong to a long-standing, not a zero-history, group of strangers. Deep diversity also enhances brainstorming creativity (Salazar et al., 2017). "Group genius can happen only if the brains in the team don't contain all the same stuff" (Sawyer, 2017). Brainstorming software, such as Ayoa (see *https://www.ayoa.com/brainstorming/*) can be quite useful as an aid to brainstorming by offering a process for **mind mapping** that takes ideas generated and forms them into a visual spiderweb of connections as brainstorming progresses (Pewsey, 2020). Training and experience in how to use the brainstorming technique is vital because this vastly improves idea generation (Baruah & Paulus, 2008). Having a trained facilitator improves idea generation significantly beyond nominal groups (Isaksen & Gaulin, 2005). Brainstorming is also superior to nominal groups in the final evaluation of ideas (Rietzschel et al., 2006). One final note: Research shows that brainstorming has the additional advantage of improving group cohesiveness and teamwork (Henningsen & Henningsen, 2018).

The brainstorming process somewhat parallels another creativity process called brainswarming, developed by cognitive psychologist Tom McCaffrey. Brainswarming is a complicated process best delineated by viewing videos that illustrate the technique (see video links at end of chapter for a detailed explanation).

Framing/Reframing: It's All in the Wording When MBA students and managers were informed that a corporate strategy had a 70% chance of success, most favored it. When it was framed as a 30% chance of failure, however, the majority opposed the strategy (Wolkomir & Wolkomir, 1990). When people were presented with two options for treating lung cancer, 84% chose the surgery option when it was framed in terms of living, while 56% chose the surgery option when it was presented in terms of dying (McNeil et al., 1982). A more recent study found that when participants were presented brief passages that either described crime as a "beast preying" on a city or as a "virus infecting" a city, those presented with the "beast" framing were likely to choose punishment as the solution but those presented with the "virus" framing were likely to choose reform measures (Thibodeau & Boroditsky, 2011). The reason for the difference lies in the **framing**—how language shapes our perception of choices.

Our frame of reference can lock us into a mindset, making solutions to problems difficult if not impossible to discover (Rathje, 2017). Consider the Covid-19 pandemic. "We find that exposure to framed messages regarding the origins of Covid-19 can have a powerful effect on people's beliefs about the cause of this global pandemic" (Bolsen et al., 2020). As the saying goes, "to the person with a hammer, every problem looks like a nail." This mental gridlock can block the free flow of creative ideas. Postman (1976) provides an example. You have the number VI. By the addition of a single line, make it into a seven. The answer is simple: VII. Now consider this problem: You have the number IX. By the addition of a single line, make it into a six. The answer is not so obvious because of your frame of reference, which identifies the number as a Roman numeral and all lines as straight. Not until you break away from this frame of reference by reframing the problem are you likely to solve it. Have you found the answer? How about **SIX**?

Frames determine whether people notice problems, how they understand and remember problems, and how they evaluate and act on them (Bilandzic et al., 2017; Fairhurst, 2010). **Reframing** is the creative process of breaking a mindset by describing the problem from a different frame of reference. For example, a service station proprietor put an out-of-order sign on a soda machine. Customers paid no attention to the sign, lost their money, then complained to the station owner. Frustrated and annoyed, the owner changed the sign to read "$5.00" for a soda. No one made the mistake of putting money in the faulty soda pop dispenser. The problem was reframed. Instead of wondering how to get customers to realize that the machine was on the fritz, the owner changed the frame of reference to one that would make customers not want to put money in the dispenser. Learning to reframe problems can significantly influence our perceptions (Tanner, 2020).

When groups become stumped by narrow or rigid frames of reference, interjecting certain open-ended questions can help reframe the problem and the search for solutions. In fact, Stanford professor Tina Seelig (2015) calls this **framestorming**—changing the framework for brainstorming before actually engaging in a brainstorming session by asking different questions. The group asks, "What if we don't accept this cutback in resources as inevitable?" instead of "How will we manage these cutbacks?" Brainstorming takes on a completely different direction depending on the framing of the question to be explored. "What if we tried working together instead of against each other?" instead of "How can

Meeting After Project Failure

Initial Frame

Reframed

Reframing can be a powerful creative problem-solving tool. If "disaster" is the frame, group members become defensive and fearful. If instead you reframe the project failure as an opportunity to "learn," you encourage creative ideas.

we beat this group?" is another example. Also, "How might we improve the proposal?" instead of "What happens if we reject the proposal?"

Clearly, what has been discussed so far demonstrates that small group decision making and problem solving are complicated processes. Virtual groups, not surprisingly, complicate the decision-making and problem-solving process even further, as this final section elaborates.

Virtual Groups and Decision Making

Extensive meta-analysis of hundreds of experimental studies on virtual groups compared to face-to-face groups concludes that virtual groups perform worse than face-to-face groups (Purvanova, 2014). Other research shows similar results (O'Neill et al., 2016). These studies, however, are aggregates of different types of virtual groups that contribute to the general results. When separated, field studies of virtual groups composed of skilled, trained professionals working in long-term (one- to two-year on average) teams on complex projects of shared concern (e.g., developing software, diagnosing and treating patients) are effective. "The virtual teams in the sample of case and field studies were largely successful at achieving their objectives, earning revenues for their companies, saving production costs and time, pleasing customers and managers alike, and engaging in collaborative decision making." Studies of student groups working on hypothetical case studies (e.g., "Lost at Sea," brainstorming uses of an extra thumb) for typically an hour, however, show that student virtual groups were not successful (Purvanova, 2014). This strongly suggests that extensive training, skill development, and long-term experience working virtually are necessary to improve the success of virtual group decision making and problem solving. Slapping student groups together in a virtual format without proper preparation in such an environment practically guarantees poor decision making and performance because copious advice provided already on how to make virtual groups successful has no time to develop (Garcia & Weiss, 2020).

Unquestionably, decision making and problem solving in virtual groups can be uniquely difficult. The more complex the group task, the worse team functioning is likely to be, requiring special emphasis on skillful communication among group members (Handke et al., 2020). Previous advice concerning how to conduct effective virtual meetings (Chapter 3), build group cohesiveness and discourage social loafing in virtual groups (Chapter 4), construct a positive, supportive virtual group climate (Chapter 5), and provide effective leadership in the virtual environment (Chapter 7) are all relevant to improving decision making and problem solving in virtual groups. Information overload, mindsets, collective inferential errors, and groupthink are as likely to produce defective group decision

metamorworks/Shutterstock

Virtual groups can engage in effective decision making, but when compared to face-to-face groups, it is more challenging in a virtual environment.

making and problem solving in virtual groups as in standard in-person groups, if not more so. Advice offered to combat these impediments to group effectiveness in Chapter 9 and this chapter may require amplification and greater vigilance when working virtually.

Pace of Decision Making: Synchronous and Asynchronous Media

The pace of decision making in virtual groups, however, is one troublesome issue not yet specifically addressed. A hefty 79% of respondents in the Solomon (2016) study reported that this was a significant concern. Text-only electronic technology, for example, may slow decision making if delays occur because group members haven't checked their email or bulletin board or don't respond immediately, for whatever reason. Students working in teams for online class projects may experience significant frustration with such delays or non-responsiveness from members. Unread email chains can also create disorganization and lost focus for team members (Gupta, 2015). Student groups can further be impeded by delayed feedback from instructors regarding ongoing term projects. Even scheduling videoconferences may not entirely solve the problem with delayed decision making. All members, or the instructor, may not be available for the meetings.

Sometimes this means using synchronous media and other times asynchronous media to address the unique challenges of virtual group work (Gillis & Krull, 2020). **Synchronous media** are those that permit simultaneous, same-time interactions among group members, modeled after face-to-face meetings.

Audioconferences, videoconferences, and instant messaging are examples of synchronous media. **Asynchronous media** are those that permit anytime/any-place communication among group members without interruption. Messages are posted and read at the convenience of other group members. Standard email, bulletin boards, blogs, Facebook postings, and text messaging are examples (Carr, 2017). If quick decisions are important, then synchronous media should be chosen whenever possible. If time is not a central concern but careful attention to detail and comprehensive research is desirable, then asynchronous media choices may serve the virtual group's purposes well.

Asynchronous media, however, can markedly magnify the challenge of information overload (Gunaratne et al., 2020). Emails, text messages, Twitter tweets, and other messages from social media options can quickly pile up, making it difficult, even impossible to attend to so many messages seemingly demanding responses from group members. At some point, the overload becomes too much and delayed responses can become complete non-responsiveness. Decisions delayed become decisions denied when group members become overwhelmed by too much information demanding attention.

Choosing either synchronous or asynchronous media for virtual group decision making, however, shouldn't be a dichotomous choice. Blending both synchronous and asynchronous media may provide the best choice for effective decision making and problem solving in virtual groups. Over time, virtual groups can adapt to the challenges of the virtual environment by varying group members' use of different media depending on circumstances (Handke et al. 2019). Video-conferencing or audioconferencing frequently enough to limit the asynchronous message barrage is one way to control the information flow and prevent virtual group impotence. Also, as a virtual group member, be cognizant of the importance of terse communication that makes your point directly, avoiding verbosity. Long-winded messages are likely to be scanned or ignored. Important follow-up details from a brief, direct message can be provided synchronously if necessary.

Virtual Creativity: Finding Your Comfort Zone

One final virtual group decision-making and problem-solving challenge concerns creativity. Does working in virtual groups help or hinder the creative process? Working remotely can make creative, innovative problem solving very difficult. Software engineer and entrepreneur Joyce Park explains it this way: "Fast feedback is what we're all about in this town [Silicon Valley]. That's what's gone away" (quoted by Baron, 2020). Also, motivation to be creative and innovative when working remotely is especially difficult in virtual groups (McGregor & Doshi, 2020). Casual conversations in hallways and in-person offices that can trigger brainstorms and original ideas to be pursued can't be replicated easily in virtual groups.

Others, however, believe that the emergence of virtual groups, especially resulting from Covid-19 restrictions, may actually spur greater creativity once groups adjust to the virtual environment (Thompson, 2021). Northwestern University management professor Leigh Thompson (2021) concludes, "Based on research I and others have conducted . . . I believe that the shift to remote work actually has the potential to improve group creativity and ideation, despite diminished in-person communication."

Creative problem solving may be more challenging, but conducting effective virtual meetings (Chapter 3), establishing trust that encourages creativity (Chapter 5), encouraging group members to be agile in assuming a variety of informal roles (Chapter 6), and having competent communication from leadership (Chapter 7) can produce creativity at least as impressive as in-person groups. Also, research shows that "secret virtual conversations" available from private chat options encourages majority group members to engage minority group members more often. In addition, "secret conversation opportunities may be a critical piece shaping the open communication norms that lead to cutting-edge innovation" (Swaab et al., 2016).

Then there is **electronic brainstorming** that can assist virtual group creativity. It occurs when group members sit at computer terminals and brainstorm ideas using a computer-based file-sharing procedure. This offers an additional method for improving idea generation and creativity. Group members type their contributions, then send the file to a shared pool. Ideas are added and shared with group members. This can be done anonymously if group members fear a critique. Electronic brainstorming has outperformed nominal groups in idea generation (Baruah & Paulus, 2016).

Virtual brainstorming, of course, can be conducted either synchronously or asynchronously. One company, Zapier, uses both. "For synchronous brainstorming, the company uses video calls and online whiteboards such as Miro, Stormboard, IPEVO Annotator, Limnu, and MURAL, but also urges employees to use asynchronous means of problem-solving through Slack channel threads" (Choudhury, 2020). A simpler alternative, especially for student groups, is to conduct a Zoom meeting of brainstormers without a computer file-sharing technology. A problem can be defined specifically in advance and shared with all group members who can generate preliminary ideas. During the Zoom meeting those ideas can be shared and new ideas can be triggered. A designated group member can record all ideas as they are presented. Recordings of Zoom brainstorming sessions can serve as "vaults and boneyards" that permit revisiting previously overlooked ideas (Thompson, 2021). If crosstalk becomes a problem, which is a common distraction in a virtual environment, the chat option can be used to add ideas while others are verbalizing their contributions. As groups become more comfortable in virtual groups, creativity does not have to be hindered.

In summary, there is no dichotomy between rational and creative decision making and problem solving. The two can be complementary paths to effective decisions in groups. The discussion process, however, should be systematic, not haphazard. Information gathering and evaluation should also be systematic. Consideration of the problem should come before deliberations on solutions. Standard Agenda is the most common and useful set of procedures for rational decision making. Consensus, when applicable, is an effective process for guiding members toward rational decisions. Brainstorming, nominal group technique, and reframing all provide systematic techniques for the discovery of creative solutions to problems. Virtual groups present additional challenges but as group members become more comfortable and experienced operating in a virtual environment, group effectiveness should improve.

QUESTIONS FOR CRITICAL THINKERS

1. Why is majority rule so popular when consensus decision making, by comparison, is often more advantageous?

2. Since a true consensus requires agreement, commitment, and satisfaction of group members, do you think groups are likely to achieve a true consensus?

3. What are some drawbacks to the Standard Agenda approach to decision making?

TED TALKS AND YOUTUBE VIDEOS

"Brainswarming"

(*Caveat: Despite the inaccurate claim by psychologist Tom McCaffrey that "brainstorming doesn't work," this short video on brainswarming provides an interesting illustration of this unique technique to generate ideas.*)

"Brainswarming"

(*Somewhat tedious, but illustrative video of the brainswarming technique.*)

"Fighting Truth Decay to Preserve the Value of Facts"

"How Can Groups Make Good Decisions?" | Mariano Sigman and Dan Ariely

"IDEO Brainstorming Video from IDEO U"

"Scientific Studies" | John Oliver (Warning: Raw Language)

"The Four Most Dangerous Words? A New Study Shows" | Laura Arnold

"Truth Decay: A Primer"

"Truth Decay and the Technology Threat" (Harris, Foroohar) | DLD Munich 20

"Why Do We Believe Things that Aren't True?" | Philip Fernbach

VIDEO CASE STUDIES

Apollo 13 (1995). *Drama; PG*

This dramatization of the nearly disastrous Apollo 13 space mission to the moon illustrates creative problem solving. What creative problem-solving techniques are exhibited?

Flight of the Phoenix (2004, 1966). *Drama; PG-13*

The original 1966 version of this taut drama, about a plane crash and efforts of survivors to literally rebuild their damaged plane into a smaller flying machine to escape their plight in the desert, is probably superior to the remake. In either case, examine the creative group problem solving required. What methods were used to create the final product?

The Martian (2015). *Adventure/Drama; PG-13*

Matt Damon plays the central character, an astronaut stranded on Mars and later rescued, to perfection. Identify the multitude of examples of creative problem solving depicted. What creative process does the technical group on the ground use to help solve the many problems?

Power in Groups

11

Access to bathrooms on the job rarely poses a problem for white-collar workers. Lawyers, business executives, and college professors don't need to ask for permission to relieve themselves, nor do they have their bathroom activities monitored. Because of their positions, they have the power to relieve themselves at will. This observation may strike you as too obvious to bother mentioning, but less powerful members of construction crews and groups of workers in factories, telephone-calling centers, and food-processing plants can be refused permission when they request a bathroom break. Individuals also can be timed while they are in the restroom, can be disciplined for frequent restroom visits, and can even be hunted like quarry by supervisors if they remain in the stalls too long. One manufacturing company polices potty practices of workers, and disciplines employees who exceed a six-minutes-per-day bathroom break (Clawson, 2014).

The courts have ruled that these common practices by supervisors are not necessarily illegal ("What Are the OSHA Restroom Break Laws?" 2021). Consequently, workers have in some instances taken to wearing adult diapers while toiling on assembly lines because bathroom breaks are not permitted often enough (Galimberti, 2018).

This seemingly mundane example illustrates that power is inescapable in human transactions. As social psychologist Dacher Keltner (2017) explains, "Power defines the waking life of every human being . . . emerges instantaneously when humans interact" and "shapes our every interaction, from those between parent and children to those between work colleagues." Power is a central underlying element in negotiating conflict, developing teamwork, engaging in group decision making and problem solving, creating normative behavior, designating formal roles, conducting effective meetings, creating a positive communication climate, and exercising leadership, just to name some of the relevant topics. To ignore or give only cursory treatment of power would be strikingly inadequate when exploring communication competence in groups and teams.

Covid-19 and the prospect of some future pandemic has spotlighted power as an inescapable, central group dynamic. In workplaces, for example, should masks be required to protect groups of employees, and who gets to create, communicate, and enforce the rules? Must social distancing be mandated and maintained, and

objectives

The primary purpose of this chapter is to explain how you can use power productively and constructively within small groups. There are five chapter objectives:

1. To define power, distinguishing its three types.

2. To identify various indicators of power and power resources.

3. To explore serious consequences that emanate from power imbalance.

4. To provide an explanation of the power-distance dimension of cultural communication and its implications.

5. To offer positive communication strategies that address power imbalances and their consequences.

are there small groups that should be exempt from this rule? Should vaccinations be mandatory for all employees in certain groups (healthcare teams, first responder teams, etc.)? What about student groups such as fraternities and sororities? Should mandatory vaccinating be a requirement to remain in such group housing? If you share an apartment with four roommates and one or more refuse to be vaccinated but you want everyone to get the vaccination, then what? How about college athletic teams? Who legitimately gets to make such meaningful decisions about vaccinations?

Battles regarding the bathroom break fiasco and Covid-19 contribute to a general negative perception of power. Lord Acton reputedly observed, "Power tends to corrupt, and absolute power corrupts absolutely." This is a popular perspective unless, of course, we are the ones with the power. Then, as former Secretary of the Navy John Lehman once quipped, "Power corrupts. Absolute power is kind of neat." It is commonplace to think of power as coercive, illegitimate, or even evil. References to "power plays," "power struggles," or "power politics" do not engender warm, fuzzy feelings of pleasant transactions.

Research on the communication behavior of high-power individuals doesn't help diminish this negative viewpoint. As Dacher Keltner (2007) disturbingly concludes, there is a "wealth of evidence that having power makes people more likely to act like sociopaths." He notes that unless we are vigilant, power can cause a host of unethical behaviors that include humiliating less powerful group members and shouting, swearing, and lying as an abusive pattern of behavior (see Fancher, 2016). Research also reveals that high-power individuals, exuding a misplaced confidence in their own self-efficacy, are inclined to ignore advice from lower-power group members who may even be experts on relevant subjects of discussion. Power doesn't just corrupt; it can induce poor listening and ultimately result in flawed judgment and decision making in group situations (Tost et al., 2010).

Exercising power, however, can be either corrupting or altruistic. Some may use power to bulldoze, bully, and badger others for personal gain at the expense of group goal attainment. Others may use power to achieve group goals, resolve group conflicts, and sustain important member relationships. There is no virtue in exercising little power (Aubin et al. 2016). Perceptions of powerlessness can induce indifference toward group tasks, diminish task performance, foster member passivity and withdrawal, destroy group cohesiveness, strain members' relationships, trigger stress, erode group members' self-esteem, and ignite destructive group conflict (Keltner, 2017; Laslo-Roth & Schmidt-Barad, 2020). No group can achieve its goals without exercising some power (Canary & Lakey, 2013). Your choice is not between using or not using power. "We only have options about whether to use power destructively or productively for ourselves and relationships" (Wilmot & Hocker, 2018).

Just to be clear, although intergroup power dynamics such as racist versus antiracist group confrontations is an interesting subject, one that has been explored in numerous books and articles, this is a small group communication text, not a primer on how to achieve large group power in the political arena. Thus, power dynamics within small groups, sometimes influenced by external forces within organizations, is the principal focus.

andresr/Getty Images

An Oxfam America report titled "No Relief" (2016), based on extensive research of the four largest poultry companies that control 60% of the market, found widespread abuse of workers' bathroom rights. "What would be shocking in most workplaces happens far too often in poultry plants: workers relieving themselves [wearing diapers] while standing at their work station." Power dynamics in small groups can play out in unusual, even disturbing ways.

The Nature of Power

Power is the ability to influence the attainment of goals sought by you or others. "Power is never the property of an individual; it belongs to a group and remains in existence only so long as the group keeps together" (Keltner, 2017). For example, individuals can be perceived as powerful leaders at work revered by all members of their teams, but viewed as bumbling messes at home with their families, branded as irredeemably ineffectual, especially by teenage children. So, are they powerful or powerless?

"Powerful or powerless" is a false dichotomy. The interconnectedness of components in a system means that all group members have some degree of influence, even if it is to defy or resist the group. Ever see a child pitch a fit in a grocery store, demanding some desired sweet from exasperated parents, and observe the parents cave to the demand just to stop the obnoxious din? Who's running the show in this little group, the parents or the child? If each person in a group has some degree of power, the appropriate question is not "Is person A powerful or powerless?" The apt question is "How much power does person A have compared to person B?" It is not an all-or-nothing proposition but a matter of relative influence.

focus questions

1. What does it mean to say that power is relational?
2. How do the primary forms of power differ from each other?

Forms of Power: Dominance, Prevention, and Empowerment

A captain spots a light in the distance, directly in the path of his ship. He orders the following message be sent: "Turn 10 degrees south." A response is transmitted: "*You* need to turn 10 degrees north." Irritated, the captain orders a second message transmitted: "I am this ship's captain, and I order you to turn 10 degrees south." An immediate reply ensues: "I am a seaman second class, and I am telling you to turn 10 degrees north." Outraged that his authority is being ignored by a lowly seaman second class, the captain responds: "This is a battleship coming right at you; turn 10 degrees south." This prompts a quick reply: "This is a lighthouse; turn 10 degrees north."

The captain and the seaman are engaged in a communication power struggle. The captain expects to be obeyed because of role status associated with rank and hierarchical rules. The role of seaman doesn't usually permit ordering captains to change course, but the seaman in this case is insistent to avoid calamity. Fighting over who has the legitimate power in a transaction could end up with a battleship on top of a lighthouse.

Such power struggles are the way we typically think of power playing out in the world, but there are three forms of power (see Figures 11.1 and 11.2), and they are considerably different from each other (Hollander & Offerman, 1990). **Dominance** is the active exercise of *power over* others. Bosses can interrupt an employee project team without asking permission to bloviate about the wonders of the video replay rule in football, but team members may feel obligated to endure the irrelevant rant in somnolent silence or ingratiating agreement.

Prevention is the reactive exercise of power used to thwart, take *power from* those with greater influence. It is the flipside of dominance. When someone tries to dominate us, psychological reactance rears its head. We wish to prevent the dominance. The willingness to say "no" can be formidable in the face of dominating attempts, but defiance comes with consequences, as detailed later.

Empowerment, as previously defined, is a *proactive* form of power derived from enhancing the capabilities, choices, and influence of individuals and groups. It is *power to* accomplish group goals through processes of group potency, meaningfulness, autonomy, and impact (see Chapter 8). Empowerment promotes power sharing, not power struggles. The group profits from all members gaining

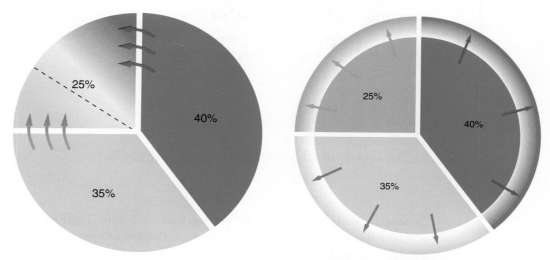

Depicted in these pie graphs, dominance-prevention power struggles (on the left) are based on seeing the power pie as a fixed, zero-sum contest. The more powerful try to poach power from the less powerful, and the less powerful try to prevent the poaching. Empowerment (on the right), conversely, sees the power pie as expandable. Every person may have the same proportion of power relative to others, but when the power pie grows larger everyone gains more pie.

the ability to succeed together. For example, group members who improve their speaking skills for a class presentation benefit the entire group.

Those who harbor a negative concept of power are usually responding to dominance and its companion form—prevention, and for good reason. "Dominance works as a tool to gain power, if not respect, but generally douses a group's well-being" ("Dominant Leaders," 2018).

Although likely to remain prevalent in our competitive society, the dominance-prevention power struggle is a poor model for small groups. "Social science reveals that one's ability to get or maintain power, even in small group situations, depends on one's ability to understand and advance the goals of other group members" (Keltner, 2007). Dominance-prevention cycles will not end, but empowerment can gain a wider audience and become more broadly applied.

SECOND LOOK
Forms of Power

Type	Definition	Description
Dominance	Power over	Active
Prevention	Power from	Reactive
Empowerment	Power to	Proactive

Communication Indicators of Power

Power indicators are the ways in which relative degrees of power are communicated in groups. You can understand the centrality of power in group transactions by understanding types of power indicators.

focus questions

1. "Those who define others exercise control." What does this mean?
2. What are the effects of "powerless" verbal and nonverbal communication patterns?
3. What are status cues in virtual groups?

General Indicators: Defining, Following, and Inhibiting There are several general indicators of power. First, those who can define others exercise power. Teachers define students (e.g., smart, slow learner), physicians define patients (hypochondriac, unhealthy), parents define children (sweet, incorrigible), and bosses define employees (good worker, loafer).

A second general indicator of power is whose decisions are followed. The individual with the position of authority in a group (e.g., designated leader) may not be exercising the most power. A more respected group member may be calling the shots, as indicated by whom the group follows.

Finally, communication inhibition is a general indicator of power (Cho & Keltner, 2020). The less powerful are more passive and withdrawn and more likely to be quiet and not express ideas, especially if those ideas might be unpopular or challenge more powerful individuals (Matthes et al., 2018). The more powerful are usually more vocal in groups, more expressive of opinions and ideas, and more assertive or aggressive in pushing those ideas and opinions.

Verbal Indicators: Language Choices The way we speak and how listeners evaluate these speech patterns indicate degrees of power. The speech of a less powerful person is often flooded with self-doubt, approval seeking, overqualification, hesitancy, personal diminishment, and deference to authority. "Powerless" language advertises a person's subordinate status. Examples of speech patterns commonly viewed as relatively powerless in U.S. culture include the following (see Dhawan, 2021; Leaper & Robnett, 2011):

> **Hedges** : "*Perhaps* a better way to decide is . . ." "I'm a *little* worried this *might* not work."
> **Hesitations** : "Well, *um*, the central point is . . ." "Gosh, *uh*, shouldn't we, *um*, act now?"

Tag Question : "This section of the report seems irrelevant, *doesn't it?*"

Disclaimers : "You *may disagree* with me, but . . ." "This idea is *probably silly*, but . . ."

Excessive Politeness : "I'm *extremely sorry* to interrupt, but . . ."

What usually is perceived as powerless forms of speech, however, may not be so in some circumstances. For example, a tag question doesn't necessarily communicate weakness. If your boss says, "You'll see that this is done, won't you?" this is authoritative, not weak. Also, members of a team may view a fellow member who uses "powerless" language as more collaborative and exuding greater warmth than those using "powerful" language (Fragale, 2006).

Unlike "powerless" language, powerful forms of language include being direct, fluent, declarative, commanding, and prone to interrupting or overlapping the speech of others. Group members who use more powerful language are perceived to be more credible, attractive, and persuasive than those using less powerful language (Palomares, 2008).

Powerful forms of speech, however, are not always appropriate. Incivility, or verbal abuse, can seem powerful, but it is inappropriate victimization of the less powerful by those with greater power (MacLennan, 2015). Sometimes deferential

Exaggerating to make the point, would you even bother listening to the ensuing message after hearing these disclaimers, hesitations, and the excessive politeness that scream "I'm not worthy"? Such powerless language communicates lack of self-confidence.

language is a sign of respect and politeness (Marsh, 2019). This is particularly true when cultural differences emerge. When negotiating teams from Japan and the United States meet, for example, misunderstandings triggered by different perceptions of what constitutes powerful or relatively powerless speech easily arise. Japanese negotiators use expressions such as "I think," "perhaps," and "probably" with great frequency because they strive to preserve harmony and cause no offense that would result in loss of face. This indirect language, however, is viewed as powerless by American negotiators more accustomed to the direct, explicit, "powerful" language of a low-context communication style (Kameda, 2007; Samovar et al., 2021).

Besides cultural differences, verbal indicators of power also show several gender differences. Men in general are more verbally aggressive, direct, opinionated, hostile, and judgmental. Sexist slurs mostly by males that reinforce feminine stereotypes are prevalent on social media. One study of Twitter tweets found 2.9 million tweets in one week that contained highly offensive terms for women, averaging 419,000 sexist slurs per day (Felmlee et al., 2019). Such slurs derogate and diminish women with their open hostility. Conversely, women typically use warmer, compassionate, and polite language (Brownlow, 2003; Park et al., 2016).

In conference meetings, men typically speak 75% of the time; women speak only 25% of the time. Interestingly, when using consensus instead of majority rule to make group decisions, this gender difference disappears. Giving women greater opportunities to speak also improved decision making (Wrenn, 2012). Then there is the case of referring to grown, adult, capable women as "girls" that can be demeaning and diminishing, especially when spoken by males in more powerful positions (Becker & Swim, 2011). "Hey boy" is also demeaning and diminishing, especially from an historical perspective of racism, when a white person refers to an African American adult male in such power sucking, abusive terminology.

Nonverbal Indicators: Silent Exercise of Power There are numerous nonverbal indicators of power (Moore et al., 2014). *Clothing*, for example, is a strong indicator of power. As Mark Twain once remarked, "Naked people have little or no influence on society." Most people typically associate uniforms with power and authority and suits with status involving financial success and position within an organization. Overly casual dress communicates lack of formality, even indifference or superficiality, especially in the workplace. Complicating the relationship between clothing and power in the workplace, however, is that "we live in a time in which our moguls dress in hoodies and t-shirts, and in which more and more workers are telecommuting—working not just from home, but from PJs" (Garber, 2016). This was amplified by the Covid-19 pandemic. "Shelter in place" and "work from home" became a first line of defense against the disease resulting in much greater acceptance of casual dress when Zooming meetings. We tend not to groom for the Zoom with the same attention to formality as when interacting in person.

Touch is another important nonverbal power indicator. The more powerful person can usually touch the less powerful person more frequently, and with fewer restrictions, than vice versa (Moore et al., 2014). Sexual harassment laws recognize this difference and try to protect subordinates from tactile abuse.

Eye contact also indicates a power difference. Staring is done more freely by the more powerful person (Moore et al., 2014). **Less powerful individuals must monitor their eye contact more carefully.** A boss can show lack of interest by looking away from subordinates, even ignoring them by reading a report, but a subordinate doing the same to a boss may invite a reprimand.

Space is the prerogative of the powerful. Parents get the master bedroom, while children get stacked vertically in bunk beds in a smaller bedroom. Imagine how odd the reverse would be. College faculty members typically have their own restricted parking lots, while students get to park in the next time zone. The higher up in the corporate hierarchy that you travel, the bigger is your office space. The reverse is true for those with lower status. Dorothy Parker once remarked, "He and I had an office so tiny that an inch smaller and it would have been adultery." White-collar workers are familiar with open-plan offices, dubbed "warehousing," in which large numbers of employees are clustered at desks separated only by insubstantial partitions that provide merely the illusion of privacy, and certainly little protection from infectious diseases as glaringly obvious with the recent pandemic. Some organizations practice "hot desking," which allocates space on a first-come, first-served basis, and rotates daily so no worker ever has dependable space of one's own. As such, employees cannot "clutter" their work space with personal items. Supervisors, in this arrangement of space, can subtly monitor subordinates' work habits, even rearrange office environments (Haslam & Knight, 2010). The powerful may violate the space of the less powerful, but not vice versa. You must be granted access to the chambers of the privileged. Research clearly shows, however, that workers highly value **autonomy**—the ability to control their own work space by decorating as they please without being monitored by supervisors—and such autonomy increases workers' productivity ("Workplace Effectiveness," 2020).

Much more could be added here, but the point seems clear. You can ascertain the relative distribution of power between individuals by observing general communication patterns and specific verbal and nonverbal communication behaviors.

Status Cues: Virtual Groups Power differences may be less obvious in virtual groups. Rank is less apparent when emailing group members than it is when

Monkey Business Images/Shutterstock

Executives typically do not work shoulder-to-shoulder with colleagues but have private offices. The less powerful are usually not accorded much private space, if any at all. Social distancing during the pandemic made such arrangements extremely risky, leading to work-at-home requirements, but some executives could continue to work and shelter in place in their semi-protected private offices.

Images Products/Shutterstock

communicating face to face. Even videoconferencing can minimize status differences. As professor of psychology Comila Shahani-Denning explains, "When we communicate via Zoom, participants are often presented side by side on the computer screen, with it being difficult to tell status and power, as all images are equal size except for the person speaking at the moment" (quoted by Lashbrook, 2020). When everyone is working from home, the formality of one's workspace often becomes more informal. Even the most powerful individuals on the planet appear less formidable when conducting a Zoom team meeting with a backdrop of a mere bookshelf or a wall with family pictures. Also, "Seeing your boss interact with children and pets, or seeing their own (possibly messy) office space humanizes them, which can erode hierarchical differences between employer and employee" (Lashbrook, 2020). Similarly, status cues such as the size of a person's office space are typically hidden. Conducting a videoconference in a large room can just create an echo effect and make the speaker appear diminutive, swallowed up by the extraneous space. In addition, micromanaging by supervisors can be diminished. You can't "manage by walking around" and engaging in surreptitious surveillance to monitor employees' focus on tasks.

This **status equalization effect**, however, is probably more prominent in text-only group discussion (Carr, 2017). **There are two types of status characteristics that are hidden from text-only communication:** (1) physical characteristics such as ethnicity, gender, and age, and (2) communication cues such as rapid speaking rate, fluency of speech (few pauses or disfluencies such as "ums" and "ahs"), emphatic tone of voice, strong eye contact when speaking, and head of the table seating location (Driskell et al., 2003). Email-only communication among group members screens these status markers that are immediately available in face-to-face communication.

Audioconferencing screens out some of these status markers, although age, gender, ethnicity, and even physical attributes can often be discerned from voice-only communication (Krauss et al., 2002). Even videoconferencing is not a perfect parallel to in-person group discussion in which nonverbal status cues are plentiful. For example, during Zoom meetings eye contact is unfocused as members stare at computer screens. "We lose the ability to observe others observing us, since we often don't know where their gaze is directed" (Keating, 2020). Are we taken seriously when we can't determine whether anyone is observing us? When team members stare at their computer screens, are they focusing on you as you speak or are they peering at other members?

Note, however, that this status equalization effect might be only temporary—experienced during the initial development of a virtual group. **More mature groups typically develop status markers even when restricted to text-only communication,** such as waiting a long time to respond to messages from less powerful group members, answering questions with curt responses, and using "powerful" language (Boughton, 2011; Rocheleau, 2002).

Conversely, grammatical errors and misspellings, especially if they occur often and in numerous messages, may taint a group member as poorly educated, careless, and unconcerned about credibility with other group members (all status-diminishing). Proofread text messages for appropriateness (following rules) before sending them to those expecting more professional-looking communication.

Power Resources: The Raw Materials of Influence

Thus far, power has been defined, types of power have been described, and indicators of power have been explained to sensitize you to the pervasive, unavoidable role that power plays in groups of all sizes. But how does power influence our transactions in groups in an ongoing basis? To begin this discussion, understanding what power resources are available and how they might be used for good or ill is important.

A **power resource** is anything that enables individuals or groups to achieve their goals, assists others to achieve their goals, or interferes with the goal attainment of others (Folger et al., 1993). This section lays out the primary resources from which power is derived, both classic views (Raven, 1993) and more recent modifications that I and others offer (Peyton et al, 2018).

Information: Good and Plenty Unquestionably, information is power (Spikes & Moyers, 2017). "Group members can turn information into power by providing it to others who need it, by keeping it from others, by organizing it, increasing it, or even falsifying it" (Forsyth, 2019). For example, a young woman in my small group communication class told her project group that she could get a highly technical, information-rich report on the subject chosen for the class project. The information from this report, so she claimed, was unavailable anywhere else, but she could get the report from her father, who had access to it because of his high position in a company. Her group members were thrilled. Her prestige and influence in the group immediately soared. Unfortunately, she never produced the report, and two weeks after she offered to obtain the report, she dropped the class. Scarce or restricted information has power potential, but only if you can actually produce it for the group's benefit.

Our society, our world runs increasingly on information, but as Chapter 9 previously explored, information overload is an enormous challenge. Information loses its power potential when it is overly abundant and unmanageable. Suggestions for addressing information overload were provided.

Expertise: Information Plus Know-How Information and expertise are closely related, but not identical (Canary & Lakey, 2013). An **expert** understands the information and knows how to use it wisely and skillfully. A person can have critical information without being an expert. You might possess a valuable technical report without being able to decipher any of the information. A team of corporate lawyers presumably know the law, but they may not practice it skillfully in the courtroom. Expertise "maximizes collective intelligence" when group members feel free to share their knowledge in a safe, supportive group environment (Mayo & Woolley, 2016). Interculturally, however, recognizing who are actual experts within a group can be confusing. One study discovered that communication indicators of expertise can produce misattributions in which nonexperts can be mistaken for actual experts and vice versa. For example, "conversational control" exhibited by behaviors such as "speaks frequently," "tends to come on strong," and "likes to determine the directions of our group conversation" showed "a huge variation in expertise evaluation of a given person" when comparing Chinese and non-Asian group participants. In addition, the communication of confidence "is a culturally shared cue for expertise judgment" even though such confidence may be undeserved (Yuan et al., 2019).

Expertise has also become devalued as a power resource, according to Tom Nichols (2017), in his thoughtful book with the somewhat overstated title, *The Death of Expertise*. He argues persuasively that "a Google-fueled, Wikipedia-based, blog-sodden collapse of any division between professionals and laypeople, students and teachers, knowers and wonderers—in other words, between those of any achievement in an area and those with none at all" underlines the need to recognize the difference between mere access to information and understanding and ability to offer intelligent advice on subjects of critical importance. The quality of group decision making is diminished when expertise is undervalued.

Legitimate Authority: You Will Obey In a series of famous studies by social psychologist Stanley Milgram (1974), participants were told to deliver increasingly painful electric shocks to an innocent victim for every wrong answer on a word-association test. Two-thirds of the participants in some of the studies obeyed the experimenter and delivered the maximum shock to the victim, who in some cases screamed in agony. No shocks, however, were delivered. The experiments were made to seem real, though, and none of the participants suspected trickery. In all, 19 variations of these obedience-to-authority studies were conducted. Others have replicated and updated results of obedience studies with similar findings. One replication required participants to shock a cute, fluffy puppy. The shocks in this case were real, not faked, but surreptitiously reduced some in intensity. Three-fourths of the participants, all college students, were obedient to the end, shocking the helpless puppy whose pain they could witness (Sheridan & King, 1972). More recent studies suggest that nothing much has changed since Milgram conducted his experiments (Bocchiaro & Zimbardo, 2017; Burger, 2009).

Ivanova N/Shutterstock

Would you administer 450-volt shocks to this cute puppy? In one experiment, 100% of college women and 54% of college men did just that to a puppy, or so they thought, obeying a perceived legitimate authority.

Participants in the Milgram studies followed orders, not because they were evil or sadistic, but because they couldn't resist legitimate authority (Milgram, 1974). A **legitimate authority** is someone perceived to have a right to direct others' behavior because of his or her position, title, role, experience, or knowledge. The experimenter was the legitimate authority because of his role, appearance, and position as the person in charge of the study. To have power potential, authority must be viewed as legitimate. Authority that springs from the group (e.g., being voted by membership to represent the group in bargaining talks or earning it by demonstrating competence) has a solid base of legitimacy.

Group members, however, do not have to be the pawns of legitimate authority. One of the Milgram studies found that in groups of three participants, when two confederates defied the experimenter (authority) and refused to administer shocks beyond 210 volts, 90% of the naïve subjects who didn't know the setup also refused to comply with the experimenter's commands. Yet in a comparison study where the naïve subject faced the experimenter alone, only 35% refused to comply with the experimenter's command, and refusal never occurred before 300 volts (Milgram, 1974). Conformity to group norms can sometimes prove to be a more powerful tendency than obeying authority. The defectors created a group norm that opposed shocking victims against their will. This punctuates the power of groups to withstand the unethical or wrongheaded directives of a powerful group leader or member.

Although results from obedience studies are disturbing, defiance of all authority is as empty-headed as ceaseless compliance. What kind of society would you live in if few people obeyed police, teachers, parents, judges, bosses, or physicians? What grade point average might you expect if you and your class project groups consistently ignored your instructors' assignment directions because you didn't want to be "told what to do"? The answer to the excessive influence of legitimate authority rests with your ability to discriminate between appropriate and inappropriate use of authority, not the exercise of indiscriminate rebellion against all authority. Ethical criteria—respect, honesty, fairness, choice, and responsibility—are guidelines for choosing when to defy and when to comply, not always an easy choice.

Rewards and Punishments: Pleasure and Pain   Distributing rewards and punishments can be an important source of power. Salaries, bonuses, work schedules, perks, hirings, and firings are typical job-related rewards and punishments.

The power potential of punishment depends on the degree of certainty that the punishment will be administered. Idle threats have little influence on behavior. Punishment is a source of power if it can, and likely will, be exercised. Verbal threats without follow-through become impotent bluster. It also needs to be proportional to the offense.

Punishment can be used positively to change behavior from antisocial to prosocial, but it also is coercive and reinforces dominance. Consequently, it easily triggers backlash. A sign found in some workplaces—"The beatings will continue until morale improves"—expresses ironically the challenge of using punishment to produce positive outcomes. Individuals on the receiving end of punishment typically rebel. We don't normally like our tormenters.

A reward can be an effective power resource, but there is a difference between *intrinsic* and *extrinsic rewards*. An **intrinsic reward** is enjoying what one does for its own sake and because it gives you pleasure, such as acting in a play just because it is fun. An **extrinsic reward** is an external inducement, such as money, grades, recognition, awards, or prestige. "Work sucks, but I need the bucks" captures the essence of an extrinsic reward. One study of more than 500 organizations and 200,000 employees found that money was way down the list of what motivates employees to excel at their jobs. An "intrinsic desire to do a good job" came in second just behind "peer camaraderie" ("The 7 Trends," 2020). Offering group members the power of choice (autonomy), providing meaningful challenges (a mission), creating a supportive team climate (connection), praising effort even if success does not occur immediately, and encouraging persistence in the face of difficulties as small progress on challenging tasks proceeds are some ways group leaders can stimulate intrinsic rewards to motivate excellence (Ben-Hur & Kinley, 2016).

Personal Qualities: A Powerful Persona Some individuals exhibit personal qualities that appeal to groups. Being charismatic, for example, can be powerful and is strongly associated with likability (Tousley, 2017). Likable people receive more job offers and promotions and are perceived as more credible (Vozza, 2015). Also, good looks, an attractive personality, dynamism, persuasive skills, warmth, and charm are some of the personal qualities that make an individual charismatic. There is no precise formula for determining charisma, however. What is attractive to you may be unattractive to others. Charisma, however, as noted earlier, does not necessarily translate into group leadership effectiveness despite its power potential. Prevailing research shows that leaders who exhibit personal qualities of humility and persistence, and nurture the talent of other group members were more likely to produce high-performing teams than charismatic leaders (Chamorro-Premuzic, 2019).

Before leaving this section on power resources, one final point should be emphasized. A person does not possess power; a person is granted power by others. Charisma means little in a job interview if a hiring committee prefers diligence, expertise, and efficiency. In this case, charisma might look like flash without follow-through (Rast et al., 2016). A reward that nobody in your group wants will influence no one. Information that is irrelevant to the needs of groups has no power potential. Expertise on a subject of no consequence or interest to the group engaged in problem solving lacks potency.

Consequences of Power Imbalances

Power can be seductive and tempt anyone to use it unethically and harmfully. As Dacher Keltner notes based on voluminous research, "The skills most important to obtaining power and leading effectively are the very skills that deteriorate once we have power" (quoted by Schaarschmidt, 2017). In this section, some significant consequences of power imbalances in groups, especially in the workplace where you either are currently engaged or will be in the future, are explored.

Bias Against Women and Ethnic Minorities: Leadership Gap

Although women hold more than half of all professional and management positions in the United States, they held only slightly more than 7% of Fortune 500 CEO positions in 2020, and that was a record (Connley, 2020). The percentage of female S&P 500 CEOs actually fell slightly in 2020 to 5.4% (Schwartz, 2020). As previously cited, women also held only 23% of board directorships at the 3,000 largest U.S. companies. Although 10% of new board directors are women of color, a mere 7.4% of board chairs are women ("Women on Corporate Boards," 2020). At the current pace, America will have established a fully functioning human colony on Mars before gender equity in corporate power positions is a reality.

Women, and especially women of color, still have a difficult time emerging to top executive leadership roles. This *Fortune* magazine–sponsored annual Most Powerful Women conference highlights those women who have bucked the system and emerged as powerful leaders. From left to right, Bari Williams, Tracey Patterson, Jamie-Clare Flaherty, and Ellen McGirt are pictured.

Photo by Joe Scarnici/Getty Images for Fortune

So, do these statistics prove gender bias exists? Perhaps not as many women are qualified for high-level positions. Not true. Women earn the majority of college degrees at every level, and this has been consistent since 1981 (Tanzi, 2018). There are more women than men in the U.S. workforce who have a college degree (Fry, 2019). Consistently, studies show that women outscore men on leadership capabilities tested, suggesting that they make "better leaders for the 21st century" (Andersen, 2018; Young, 2016).

Why do numerous well-qualified women not rise to the top of corporate America? First, the prevalence of sexual harassment primarily against women certainly has a dampening effect on women remaining in the corporate workplace long enough to advance to group leadership positions (Peck, 2017). More than half of women in the workplace have experienced sexual harassment (Zetlin, 2018). Almost half of the women who have been victims of sexual harassment leave their jobs or switch careers (Beras, 2018). That diminishes their chain of experience to compete for top-level positions.

Second, equally qualified women with children are perceived to be less reliable and committed to their jobs than men with children, a myth that persists but is refuted by substantial research. This stereotype emanates from a typical view that women are the primary caregivers to their children. Male applicants experience no such parental penalty (Padavic et al.,2020).

Third, even when women tough it out in the sometimes-corporate Hunger Games, quite often gender stereotyping thwarts female job advancement. Men occupy most of the positions of power that determine job advancement, and they typically perceive women as better "caretakers" ("Catalyst Study," 2017). Thus, according to a comprehensive study, viewing women in this way means they are "more likely to be shunted into support roles rather than landing the core positions that lead to executive jobs" (Silverman, 2015). They're expected to play more maintenance roles (supporter-encourager; harmonizer-tension reliever) than powerful task roles (facilitator; devil's advocate).

Fourth, studies of biased performance reviews of female employees, most often conducted by male supervisors, showed that, compared to male employees, women received 2.5 times as many complaints about "aggressive communication styles" and half as many references to their technical expertise and vision for the company. Women were far more frequently described as having a speaking style that is "off-putting" or "shrill" (Silverman, 2015). As Kathy Caprino (2017) at *Forbes* explains, women "are perceived far more negatively than men for communicating in the same forceful way and manner as men do."

You don't have to be a high-level female manager striving for promotion to feel the frustration of gender bias. *New York Times* columnist Susan Chira (2017) observes, "Academic studies and countless anecdotes make it clear that being interrupted, talked over, shut down or penalized for speaking out is nearly a universal experience for women when they are outnumbered by men."

In 2017, a term was coined for this propensity of men to dismiss or derogate women's contributions in meetings but then later to repeat the exact same ideas as their own brilliant contribution. It was termed *hepeating*.

Finally, according to one report, women get **less access to leaders** in organizations. They ask for feedback from managers as often as men but receive far less. When they negotiate for promotion or higher compensation **they are 30% more likely than men to receive negative feedback** that they are "bossy," "too aggressive," or "intimidating" ("Women in the Workplace," 2016).

So what steps need to be taken to help end gender bias? Men especially who are in positions of power, until greater gender equity is achieved, need to assist women (discussed later as alliances). Creating collaborative, supportive group climates also produces greater female leadership emergence in leaderless groups (Lindzon, 2016; Roebuck et al., 2019). A Pew Research study, however, found that 23% of female respondents reported that they "were treated as if they were not competent," compared to only 6% of male respondents making the same claim. Also, 16% of the female respondents "experienced repeated, small slights at work, compared to only 5% of male respondents" (Bailey, 2017). These **microaggressions** can create a negative group climate and marginalize women in the workplace.

Thirty years of research involving more than 12,000 executive leaders conducted by Suzanne Peterson and her colleagues (2020) suggests that women use a "blended style of leadership" to overcome bias. "Women must walk a narrow tightrope: they must have the courage to interrupt, use fewer nonfluencies, and use more intense words while blending in more relational and empathetic responses." These researchers "wish this weren't the case" that bias and discrimination limiting women's rise to positions of power didn't exist, but the blended style of leadership can be a benefit as an interim step until gender equality is eventually realized. A blended style, however, does not mean avoiding assertiveness. Women must persist in their desire to gain powerful leadership positions by remaining assertive (discussed later in this chapter) and challenging "hepeating." Finally, women who have cracked the glass ceiling also should act as mentors to less powerful women to assist them in rising to more powerful leadership positions.

The dismal statistics on gender inequity in general are bad enough, but **for both women and men of color the picture is even worse** (Somvichian-Clausen, 2020). The number of African American CEOs, *both male and female*, at Fortune 500 companies hit its zenith at 7 in 2007, and, for Hispanic/Latinos, it peaked at 13 in 2008. African American women held *zero* positions as CEOs of Fortune 500 companies, and only *five* African American men held such positions at the end of 2020 (Wahba, 2020). According to the Hispanic Association on Corporate Responsibility, fewer than 2% of Fortune 500 CEOs were Hispanic at the end of 2020 ("Only 9 Hispanic CEOs," 2020).

Potential solutions to this problem mirror steps to help women crack the glass ceiling just outlined. In addition, include "voluntary diversity training as opposed to forced sessions, getting managers on board through college recruitment programs targeted to women and people of color, and formal mentoring for underrepresented groups" (Clouse, 2018). Finally, in general, "individuals are more likely to pursue leadership when they receive feedback suggesting that they might be good at it" (Bear et al., 2017). Thus, encouragement can go a long way toward nurturing leadership emergence among women and ethnic minorities.

Bullying: Verbal and Nonverbal Aggression

Workplace bullying is "persistent verbal and nonverbal aggression" that "includes public humiliation, constant criticism, ridicule, gossip, insults, and social ostracism—communication that makes work tasks difficult or impossible, and socially isolates, stigmatizes, and discredits those targeted" (Lutgen-Sandvik, 2006). It is unethical behavior, egregiously disrespectful, and irresponsible action against others.

Workplace bullying is common. In a survey by the Workplace Bullying Institute and Zogby International, 19% of U.S. employees reported having suffered abusive conduct in the workplace, and an additional 19% witnessed bullying ("Work Shouldn't Hurt," 2021). That's almost 61 million workers affected by bullying. Workplace bullying is especially problematic for LGBTQ workers, with 56% reporting being repeatedly bullied at their job (Nauen, 2017). Online bullying, dubbed **cyberbullying**, is also a widespread problem in the workplace (Kowalski et al., 2018). Women are disproportionately targets of such online abuse (Felmlee et al., 2019). Damage from workplace bullying is significant: increases in depression, anxiety, absenteeism, sick days, and turnover rates, as well as decreases in productivity, not only from the targets, but also from witnesses to the bullying (Rock, 2017).

Workplace bullying is fundamentally a dominance–prevention power struggle (Young, 2016). Bullying persists primarily because most transgressors are in more powerful positions than victims. Research on workplace bullying, for example, reveals a stunningly common problem of disrespecting team members and employees throughout groups and organizations. Descriptions offered in one study of workplace victims reveal a bubbling cauldron of vitriol by toxic bosses waiting to be spewed daily on long-suffering group members. As one victim described such an event: "[She] was intimidating—right in your face— less than an inch away from your face, where her spit would hit you in the face. She would scream at us, her face getting all red and her eyes watering. It was almost like she wanted to reach out and choke you" (quoted in Lutgen-Sandvik, 2006). Another victim described it this way: "He'd scream and yell every day. Veins would pop out of his head; he'd spit, he'd point, he'd threaten daily, all day long to anyone in his way, every day that I was there. Every single day . . . He'd swear profusely." Rage (and apparently flying spit) appear to be common manifestations of workplace bullying by those in positions of power. Ironically, for all the bluff and bluster, these toxic bosses not only create significant group and organizational harm (Kim et al., 2020), but "the primary intent of toxic leaders is to conceal lack of relevant competence and maintain a position of control" (Milosevic et al., 2020). Their rage and abuse are typically a cover for their own inadequacies as leaders.

Bullying, however, is not relegated only to the workplace. A significant amount of bullying among college students occurs. Although peer-to-peer bullying is problematic, a surprising amount of bullying is instigated by university personnel (teaching, research, and administrative personnel) who "hold roles of authority and power within the higher education setting" (Porhola et al.,2020).

How victims should address bullies is a complicated challenge (Tye-Williams et al., 2020). The steps offered in Chapter 2 regarding how to deal with difficult group members may seem appropriate, and this is true to an extent, but bullying that emanates from an imbalance of power within the group presents additional challenges. Confrontation, for example, one of the suggested steps, may get you fired or more abuse may be heaped on you until you quit either your job or drop out of college. Some victims try avoidance, by keeping as much distance as possible between themselves and the bully. You can't become invisible, however, and sometimes you end up on groups and teams with a bully as the leader, and avoiding college personnel is not always possible since they make decisions that affect your educational advancement. Workers quit their jobs, but in tough economic times, this may not be a feasible option. Finally, victims of bullying may file formal grievances with external groups (e.g., unions, courts, governmental agencies, administrative personnel). This usually takes years, however, and it doesn't guarantee a satisfactory outcome for victims.

Ultimately, prevention is far more effective than any of the preceding strategies (Nielsen & Einarsen, 2018). A zero-tolerance policy in organizations and educational institutions for any acts of bullying is the place to start. Addressing directly the first signs of bullying behavior and providing training for bullies to change their ways is important. Mediation from a neutral person trained in conflict resolution can be effective, but it usually needs to be instituted early when bullying first occurs (Lempp et al., 2020).

Enlightened leadership can create a group culture that discourages social dominance that encourages bullying behavior (Khan et al., 2016). If and when you are in such a position of leadership, it becomes your responsibility to snuff out the first signs of bullying group members. When clear policies exist, and are enforced to discourage bullying, such victimization can dissipate. If the bullying persists, this should be followed by firing the offender or ousting the perpetrator from the group. Developing a positive communication climate is also essential.

Power Distance: Cultural Variation

Cultures vary widely in their attitudes concerning the appropriateness of power imbalances. These variations in the *acceptability of unequal distribution of power* in relationships, institutions, and organizations are called the **power distance (PD) dimension** (Hofstede & Hofstede, 2010). The extent to which members of a culture, both relatively powerful and powerless, *endorse* the society's overall level of inequality determines its place on the PD dimension (Hofstede, 2012).

General Description: Horizontal and Vertical Cultures

All cultures are **stratified**—divided into various levels of power that put distance between the haves and the have-nots. The difference on the PD dimension lies in whether the culture tends to accept or reject stratification, even though it is a fact of life. For example, the AFL-CIO study of executive pay in the United States found that the average CEO for a major U.S. corporation was paid 299 times the average annual compensation of workers ("8 Facts from the Executive Paywatch," 2021). So, how do Americans in general view such pay disparity? A study by the Rock Center for Corporate Governance at Stanford University, in a national survey, found that 74% of respondents believe CEOs are vastly overpaid. Only 16% disagree (Larcker et al., 2016).

The United States is a low PD culture (see Figure 11.3). A **low PD culture**, or what Triandis (2012) calls a horizontal culture, values relatively equal power sharing and discourages attention to status differences and ranking in society. Challenging authority, flattening organizational hierarchies to reduce status differences between management and employees, and using power legitimately are encouraged in a low PD culture. Low PD cultures do not expect power disparities to be eliminated. Nevertheless, in low PD cultures such as the United States, Great Britain, Sweden, Denmark, Austria, Israel, and New Zealand, norms that minimize power distinctions act as guides for appropriate behavior (Samovar et al., 2021).

High PD cultures, or what Triandis (2012) calls vertical cultures, have a relatively strong emphasis on maintaining power differences. The norms of cultures such as Malaysia, Guatemala, the Philippines, Mexico, India, Singapore, and Hong Kong encourage power distinctions. Authorities are rarely challenged, the most powerful are thought to have a legitimate right to exercise their power, and organizational and social hierarchies are nurtured.

Comparing piggy banks as a metaphor. Vast pay disparities in the low-PD United States is common, but it can create a huge power imbalance and can be a source of worker dissatisfaction and conflict.

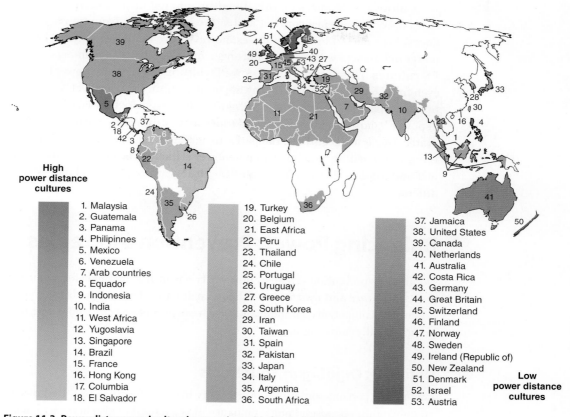

Figure 11.3 Power distance and cultural comparisons (Hofstede & Hofstede, 2010)

High
power distance
cultures

1. Malaysia
2. Guatemala
3. Panama
4. Philipinnes
5. Mexico
6. Venezuela
7. Arab countries
8. Equador
9. Indonesia
10. India
11. West Africa
12. Yugoslavia
13. Singapore
14. Brazil
15. France
16. Hong Kong
17. Columbia
18. El Salvador

19. Turkey
20. Belgium
21. East Africa
22. Peru
23. Thailand
24. Chile
25. Portugal
26. Uruguay
27. Greece
28. South Korea
29. Iran
30. Taiwan
31. Spain
32. Pakistan
33. Japan
34. Italy
35. Argentina
36. South Africa

37. Jamaica
38. United States
39. Canada
40. Netherlands
41. Australia
42. Costa Rica
43. Germany
44. Great Britain
45. Switzerland
46. Finland
47. Norway
48. Sweden
49. Ireland (Republic of)
50. New Zealand
51. Denmark
52. Israel
53. Austria

Low
power distance
cultures

Communication Differences: With Whom May You Communicate?

Communication in low PD cultures reflects the minimization of power disparities. Workers may disagree with their supervisors; in fact, some bosses may encourage disagreement. Socializing outside the work environment and communication on a first-name basis between team members and bosses, and teachers and students, are not unusual.

Communication in high PD cultures reflects the desire to maintain power disparities. Workers typically avoid disagreeing with their bosses. Friendship between a worker and a boss would appear inappropriate (Hofstede & Hofstede, 2010). A small group of workers grabbing a brew at the local pub with their boss would not even occur to employees as an option. Students typically avoid socializing with their teachers.

Cultural differences on this dimension do not mean that high PD cultures never experience conflict and aggression arising from power imbalances. Members of low PD cultures, however, are more likely to respond to power imbalances with frustration, anger, and hostility than members of high PD cultures. This occurs because low PD cultures subscribe to power balance even though the reality of everyday life in such cultures may reflect significant power disparities. Many groups recognize this disparity between the "ideal" of power balance and the reality of socioeconomic disadvantage in the United States. In a low PD culture, the battle to achieve the ideal of balanced power is more compelling, and the denial of power is likely to be viewed as more unjust and intolerable than in a high PD culture, where power balance is seen differently.

Balancing Power: Prevention Strategies

Dominance-prevention struggles produce two principal methods for balancing power: *defiance* and *resistance*. Although neither of these methods inherently produces incompetent communication, each can produce negative outcomes that groups usually cannot ignore.

Defiance: Digging in Your Heels

Low-power persons sometimes overtly defy higher power persons. **Defiance** is unambiguous, purposeful noncompliance. It is a refusal to give in to those with greater power. Defiance is the prevention form of power where one stands against those who attempt to dominate.

Defiance can be contagious. A single worker who defiantly walks off the job may encourage a wildcat strike. Those in authority are anxious to halt defiance before it spreads, especially with the ready availability of social media to raise awareness of such acts. The very nature of defiance is disagreeable to those who want compliance, and they normally are the most powerful. Usually, defiance should be considered an option of last resort because the potential negative consequences can be significant, especially to the less powerful. You can be socially ostracized and branded a social leper, or you can be severely punished. Supervisors may simply brand your defiance as "insubordination," using this as justification for demotion or termination of your employment.

Nevertheless, defiance may be the ethical choice in some workplace situations (recall the Milgram obedience studies). As psychologists Piero Bocchiaro and Philip Zimbardo (2017) note, "We should encourage obedience to just authority, while promoting defiant disobedience against all forms of unjust authority." They further claim that "any organization can benefit from 'intelligent disobedience,' a behavior typical of individuals who have the courage to speak up when they realize that certain positions are wrong or that obedience would produce harm." When is intelligent disobedience most likely to occur? When the workplace environment established by group leaders encourages candor, and when those who defy unjust authority are listened to by those with power who are not the actual perpetrators of unethical conduct, intelligent disobedience will occur in appropriate situations.

Resistance: Dragging Your Feet

While defiance is overt, unambiguous noncompliance, **resistance** is covert, ambiguous noncompliance. It is often duplicitous and manipulative. Resisters are subtle saboteurs. Truly successful resistance leaves people wondering if it even occurred. Although defiance is chosen in some instances and it may be a moral imperative in certain circumstances, resistance is far more often the choice of the less powerful to prevent dominance from others. One study found that the autocratic leadership style provokes passive aggression (Johnson & Klee, 2007). Resistance is also a far more complex strategy for low-power group members than defiance.

Resistance has an advantage over defiance. When faced with a more powerful person or group, it is often safer to use indirect means of noncompliance than direct confrontation. Those who are defiant dig in their heels, but those who resist merely drag their feet.

Resistance strategies are sometimes referred to as **passive aggression** (Wilmot & Hocker, 2018). The passive part is a seeming willingness to comply with an authority's dictates. The aggressive part is the undermining of those with more power to require compliance. Several common passive-aggressive resistance strategies are discussed next. Most of these strategies are magnified in virtual groups.

Sluggish Effort: How Slow Can You Go? When a group member is unmotivated to perform a portion of a group task, he or she may exhibit frustratingly sluggish "progress" to either communicate dissatisfaction with working on the designated task or undermine the authority of an autocratic group leader, or both, without having to be blatantly defiant. This resistance strategy is especially prevalent in virtual groups. Invented excuses for slack behavior are plentiful in virtual groups: technical difficulties, scheduling problems, unavailability of Internet connectivity, and so forth.

Strategic Stupidity: Smart People Acting Dumb This is the "playing stupid" strategy. Strategic stupidity works exceedingly well when the low-power person claims "not to know how," is forced to attempt the task anyway, and then performs it ineptly. The poor performance becomes "proof" that the stupidity was real. The strategic stupidity in the workplace is particularly prevalent in the technological realm. Technology changes so rapidly and can be enormously complex. It can seem quite reasonable, at least initially, for team members to exhibit difficulty mastering computer systems, when they just don't want to be forced to assume certain tasks that they perceive are not in their job description. Online instruction necessitated by the Covid-19 pandemic created a steep learning curve, but it also provided opportunities for some to employ passive-aggressive excuses for poor academic performance.

Loss of Motor Function: Conscious Carelessness This resistance strategy is an effective companion to strategic stupidity. The resister doesn't act stupid, just incredibly clumsy, often resulting in costly damage. Being required to perform "menial tasks" can be frustrating, even humiliating. "Inadvertently" breaking the copy machine, printer, or some other expensive piece of equipment makes assigning such tasks to that person risky, so they may just avoid such tasks while more compliant group members get to do the jobs. There is a mixed message here of resistance on the one hand but apparent effort on the other.

The Misunderstanding Mirage: Confusion Illusion This is the "I thought you meant" or the "I could have sworn you said" strategy. The resistance is expressed with great sincerity. A deadline is "misunderstood" as a mere "target to shoot for," not a critical time table to complete a project. As project requirements become more complex, especially with the widespread emergence of virtual groups, this strategy can be employed more easily. The implicit message is that since this is a simple misunderstanding, a penalty would be unfair.

Selective Amnesia: Fake Forgetfulness Have you ever noticed that some people are particularly forgetful about those things that they clearly do not want to do? This temporary amnesia is highly selective when used as a resistance strategy because selective amnesiacs rarely forget what is most important to them. No outward signs of resistance are manifested. Resisters agree to perform the task—but conveniently let it slip their minds. "Forgetting" important documents for a critical meeting is one way of striking back at perceived disrespect or indifference shown by managers.

Tactical Tardiness: Late by Design When you really don't want to attend a meeting, you can show contempt by arriving late. Tactical tardiness irritates and frustrates those who value the event. It can hold an entire group hostage while everyone waits for the late person to arrive. With the pervasiveness of virtual work groups, tactical tardiness has become easier to employ. Assembling group members virtually can be a daunting task. Being late or missing a virtual meeting entirely can easily be excused by arguing scheduling issues across time zones.

Purposeful Procrastination: Deliberate Delays Most people put off doing what they dislike, but there is nothing "purposeful" about this. Purposeful procrastinators, however, pretend that they will pursue a task "soon." While promising imminent results, they deliberately refuse to commit to a specific time or date for task completion. They delay the completion of tasks on purpose. Trying to pin down a purposeful procrastinator is like trying to nail Jell-O to a wall—it won't stick. Really clever resisters can provide an almost endless stream of plausible excuses for not meeting deadlines. If those waiting for the task to be completed express exasperation, they can appear to be excessively compulsive about time constraints.

Dependence on electronic speed-of-light technology ironically can be excruciatingly slow even without users intending to be passive-aggressive procrastinators. Emails to group members with attachments that need to be reviewed are unlikely to receive quick attention in the best of circumstances. If virtual group members are in different countries, time zones interfere with prompt responses because some group members will be asleep when the email or text message arrives. Think how easy it is, however, to feign attempts to reply "as soon as possible" but "a computer glitch occurred" or cellphones lost their charge. The procrastination may be on purpose, but it can be challenging to prove it.

Ethically, resistance strategies are questionable. In most cases, they are not examples of competent communication. Too often, being passive-aggressive is a strategic way of being a social loafer. In extreme cases, however, these strategies may be the only feasible option available to fight against ill treatment and a toxic group atmosphere fostered by more powerful group members.

From the standpoint of competent communication, however, emphasis must be on how to deal effectively with resistance since the resistance is only rarely noble. There are three principal ways to combat them.

1. First, *confront the strategy directly.* Identify your belief that passive-aggressive strategies are being employed by a worker. Describe in detail what behaviors you have observed that lead you to make such a conclusion. Discuss why the strategy has been used and work cooperatively with the resister to find an equitable solution so that resistance strategies are not used.

Passive aggression is one way to combat power imbalances, which should generally be recognized as a sign of a toxic group environment. Constructing a positive, supportive group environment (see Chapter 5) and confronting passive-aggressive strategies constructively, rather than encouraging their use, however, should be the focus.

2. Second, *be very clear*. Instructions must be precise and easy to understand. If there are several steps necessary to complete tasks, make sure that the steps are clearly outlined and explained. The misunderstanding mirage can operate effectively as a resistance strategy only if task instructions are murky.

3. Third, *produce consequences for resistance*. We become enablers when we allow ourselves to be ensnared in the resister's net of duplicity. When we continue to wait for the tactically tardy, we encourage the behavior. If, when frustrated by purposeful procrastination, you perform the tasks or assign them to more pliable and responsible group members because it's just easier than cage fighting with a passive-aggressor, you reward the resistance and guarantee that such strategies will persist.

Addressing passive aggression is important, but allow for human failing. Sometimes a person just makes a mistake. Look for a pattern of behavior before assessing that it is passive aggression. Despite the negative aspects of resistance

SECOND LOOK

Resistance Strategies

Sluggish Effort—not a thyroid problem; purposely slowing down

Strategic Stupidity—smart people playing dumb; feigned stupidity

Loss of Motor Function—sudden attack of the clumsies

The Misunderstanding Mirage—illusory mistakes

Selective Amnesia—no fear of Alzheimer's; forgetting only the distasteful

Tactical Tardiness—late for reasons within your control

Purposeful Procrastination—promising to do that which you have no intention of doing

strategies, reducing power imbalances and fostering a constructive communication environment, discussed in Chapter 5, can markedly diminish any desire to resist.

Balancing Power Positively: Enhancing Empowerment

Individuals become empowered by learning to communicate competently. Acquiring communication knowledge and developing a broad range of communication skills can give you the confidence to adapt your communication appropriately in groups of all types. Empowerment has previously been discussed at length regarding the development of teamwork. In this section, several ways to empower less powerful members for the benefit of the group are explored.

Developing Assertiveness: Exhibiting Confidence and Skill

The terms assertive and aggressive are often confused. **Assertiveness** is "the ability to communicate the full range of your thoughts and emotions with confidence and skill" (Adler, 1977). Those who confuse assertiveness with aggressiveness tend to ignore the last part of this definition. Assertiveness isn't merely imposing your thoughts and emotions on others. Too often abrasive behavior is excused as "simply being assertive." Assertiveness requires competent communication of thoughts and feelings, not some infantile, cathartic rant dressed up in a scary clown suit and modeled under the pretense of assertiveness.

Assertiveness falls between the extremes of aggressiveness and passivity, and it is distinctly different from both. Aggressiveness puts one's own needs first; you

Communicating confidence and skill is the essence of **assertiveness:** a willingness to stand your ground when challenged. Assertiveness, however, is not "constructive aggression" as some have "asserted." **Aggression** is defined as "behavior that is intended to harm another person" (Allen & Anderson, 2017). That is not "constructive." You can be determined, yet respectful toward others. You can be firm without being rude.

El Nariz/Shutterstock

wipe your shoes on other people. Passivity underemphasizes one's needs; you're a doormat in a world of muddy shoes. **Assertiveness considers both your needs and the needs of others.**

Although assertiveness can be used to defy others, it is primarily an empowering skill. Assertive individuals try to enhance their significance in the eyes of others, not alienate anyone. "People gain power . . . by speaking up first, offering a possible answer to a problem, being first to assert an opinion, freeing up everyone's thinking by throwing out a wild suggestion, question, or humorous observation that gets the creative juices flowing" (Keltner, 2017). When passive, reticent individuals learn assertiveness, they become better contributors. When aggressive group members learn assertiveness, they can change the group climate from negative to positive.

Assertiveness requires practice, and it involves five key communication steps (Bower & Bower, 1976):

1. *Describe your needs, rights, and desires* or the basis of your conflict with others. "I need us to work more energetically on this presentation."
2. *Express how you feel.* "I feel anxious when our team appears to be falling behind schedule to complete this project." Understand, however, that there is no magic in beginning a statement with "I feel." For example, "I feel that you are an imperious, pathetic jerk" or "I feel that you are a terrible boss" is not being assertive. It is an aggressive attack.

3. *Specify the behavior or objective you are seeking.* "I suggest that we commit to meeting from noon to 3:00 twice a week on Mondays and Wednesdays for the next three weeks, if that works for everyone's schedule."

4. *Identify consequences.* The emphasis should be on positive, not negative, consequences. "Finishing this project on time after concerted effort will make us all proud of our accomplishment." This is a better statement than "If we don't finish on time and make a concerted effort to produce a quality proposal, then we'll all have hell to pay."

5. *Remain respectful.* You can remain firm and direct and still be unwaveringly polite and respectful. Tone of voice is especially important. A weak, quavering voice communicates passivity, and a loud voice can seem aggressive. Find the balance in between the two. (See Box 11.1.)

Being assertive is particularly challenging when participating in virtual groups. Emailing or texting written messages without companion nonverbal cues (e.g., facial expressions, tone of voice, gestures, and eye contact) can easily be perceived as aggressive. "I need this document to be changed immediately" can seem pushy and demanding when intended to be merely direct and firm. Soften the tone: "Please make the required changes to this document by tomorrow. Thank you." This version is polite but firm, and it avoids the undertone of a demand. Using **emojis** can sometimes convey a softer tone as well, but as noted earlier some may be misinterpreted (Glikson et al., 2017). Also, crosstalk and overlapping stop-start conversations—so typical of Zoom meetings in which participants appear to be interrupting, then apologizing, then clearly interrupting and appearing aggressive in seizing the group's attention—complicate perceptions of assertiveness versus aggressiveness in virtual small groups. Online etiquette rules that may require exaggerated politeness that during in-person conversations would appear to be using "powerless" language, in some instances may be necessary to avoid the appearance of overly aggressive behavior. A strong meeting facilitator following the specific steps delineated in Chapter 3 can make certain that all group members have ample opportunities to contribute to discussions without having to fight for attention.

The appropriateness of assertiveness, aggressiveness, or passivity is situational. Assertiveness, although generally a desirable skill, is not always appropriate, especially if harm may come to you or others (e.g., your boss will fire you). Also, as noted previously, collectivist cultures are accustomed to high-context communication, and individuals from such cultures typically do not respond well to assertiveness. Conversely, aggressiveness, although generally an undesirable communication pattern, is sometimes appropriate and effective (e.g., with sexual harassers who won't back off). Occasionally, passivity is the appropriate choice if it avoids threatening consequences.

BOX 11.1

"STAND UP, SIT DOWN": AN EXERCISE IN ASSERTIVENESS

Studies reveal that most individuals do not accurately perceive how they come across to others in the workplace: too passive, aggressive, or appropriately assertive (Ames & Wazlawek, 2014). I have used an instructive exercise in dozens of classroom and boardroom presentations to demonstrate this very point. Try it with a group of friends, a study group, or a group of coworkers and see what happens. It requires the following steps:

1. The group is divided into pairs and these dyads indicate by simple agreement who will be person A and who will be person B.

2. Person A is instructed to say "Stand up" to person B, *using absolutely no other words*.

3. Person B is told to physically stand up only if he/she feels that person A has said it assertively. If it seems like an order (aggressive) or a plea (passive), then person B remains seated but provides feedback (e.g., "Too aggressive"; "Too passive"). Once successful, person A says "Sit down" with the same instructions. Partners switch roles after several successful attempts and following the same steps.

4. Participants then break into groups of six to nine members. Each member, in turn, makes the statement "Stand up" to the group. Each group member is told to make an independent judgment about whether the statement is said assertively, aggressively, or passively. Group members obey only when the statement is deemed assertive. Sometimes all group members obey simultaneously, and sometimes compliance is sporadic. Each member must get every group member to stand up before making the statement "Sit down." Individuals remain standing until every group member has risen.

When every group member rises or sits in unison, this occurs when all nonverbal cues seem to communicate assertiveness. The more typical mixed reactions, however, occur because nonverbal cues are mixed. This underlines a key point that assertiveness is mostly nonverbal in nature. The statements "Stand up" and "Sit down" seem to be inherently commands and therefore aggressive. Yet this exercise clearly demonstrates that the verbal "command" can be communicated in an exceedingly passive way through hesitant or questioning tone of voice, lack of eye contact, soft-spokenness, nervous twitches, frozen facial expressions, and so forth. Thus, what you say is often not as important as how you say it when you are trying to be assertive. Depending on which nonverbal cues each group member focuses on, reactions can be split. If you are sitting beside the person issuing the statement, for example, you cannot use eye contact or facial expressions as nonverbal cues for determining assertiveness, aggressiveness, or passivity. Tone of voice thus becomes more salient.

This is a surprisingly difficult exercise for most people. I have witnessed CEOs of organizations large and small appear baffled and increasingly frustrated that other people perceive aggressiveness when they are convinced that they have toned down the statements to be assertive, even passive. In some cases, the opposite occurs. Individuals up and down the status hierarchy of an organization come off as passive when they think they are being obviously aggressive.

Alliances: Forming Coalitions

Sometimes we just need help in balancing power in the groups. Forming **alliances**—associations in the form of subgroups entered into for mutual benefit or achievement of a common objective—can be quite powerful. Bullying and abuse at work or in student groups can be decreased if others object to such behavior, even if they are not the target, but merely witnesses (Shavin, 2014). They become allies of the abused. To address gender bias, it can be especially helpful to gain male coworkers as allies who support gender equity in the workplace. Men in more powerful positions can provide requested feedback that especially highlights women's strengths. They need to increase women's access to managers and resist the tendency to view women negatively who negotiate for promotions and compensation in the same ways that men do. As Greg Young (2016) observes, "Clearly, men play a big part in women getting the real power in companies." In addition, a report by the Rockefeller Foundation found that two-thirds of women believe it is critical to have female mentors in leadership positions. Powerful female leaders can help other women change sexist policies, encourage a diverse workplace by affecting hiring practices and promotional decisions, and fight the wage gap that favors men ("Women in Leadership," 2016). The same holds true for ethnic minorities. There is strength in numbers. Gaining allies can be extremely helpful in balancing power in all types of small groups that operate in organizations.

fizkes/Shutterstock

Acquiring a mentor at work can be a great aid, especially for women just starting in a new job.

Gaining a **mentor**—someone knowledgeable and experienced who can help you learn to function effectively in a group—is a key way to enhance your power especially for women faced with barriers already discussed. Briefly addressed generally in Chapter 6 in regard to newcomers joining small groups, choosing a mentor and proactively developing an ally for your personal advancement that makes you an improved team member involves several steps (D'Angelo, 2020).

1. Decide what gaps in your knowledge exist and what you most hope to learn from a mentor.
2. Do not look to a mentor for an intense friendship. The mentor-mentee relationship can be professional, but casual.
3. Seek a mentor who is well informed, not necessarily a manager or higher-status person. You might choose a knowledgeable peer in a student group or a coworker who knows the ropes much better than you, especially if you are just embarking on your career or job. Sometimes someone from outside of the group can provide important perspective and wisdom.
4. Build an interpersonal relationship with your potential mentor. Meet for coffee or lunch, in person or virtually, and converse casually about work or outside activities. Once you feel comfortable with this person, you can ease into asking him or her to mentor you.
5. Plan to meet occasionally with your mentor, but you do not have to schedule formal meetings. In some instances, social media contacts in which you seek specific advice on a project or proposal, exchange relevant articles or research, or simply check in with your mentor works well.

Mentors are your allies. Becoming empowered requires assistance from others.

Increasing Personal Power Resources: Benefiting the Group

I previously identified power resources that can be exploited to enhance power within groups: information, expertise, rewards and punishments, legitimate authority, and personal qualities. Developing expertise that can be communicated to those with greater power can be enormously empowering. One study found expert power to be the most influential among power resources (Meng et al., 2014). Another study found that "the most convincing way to display expert power is by solving important problems, making good decisions, providing sound advice, and successfully completing challenging but high visibility projects" (Meng et al., 2014).

You do not have to be the designated leader of a group to be an expert. If your student project group is working on climate change as a subject, for example, and you have majored in oceanography and ecological science, your academic expertise makes you potentially a highly influential group member capable of helping your group achieve success.

In addition, receiving education or training to expand your capabilities makes you a more influential group member. As Maureen Habel (2015) observes about nurse–physician power relationships, "Encouraging nurses to obtain more nursing education and specialty certification is an important way to support nurses in becoming intellectual peers with physicians." Beyond this, "nurses can continue to expand their clinical expertise through participation in continuing education programs." As Habel puts it, nurses then have "separate but equal" complementary knowledge and skills with physicians as they work together as a team.

Enhancing personal qualities also can prove to be a valuable source of empowerment. Earlier, humility and persistence were noted as more important personal qualities than charisma when reviewing research on leadership and group effectiveness. Keltner (2017) adds to this the importance of exhibiting kindness. Referring to "natural state experiments," he concludes that "it was the individuals who were kind and focused on others who enjoyed enduring power in schools, workplaces, and military units." He further concludes that "groups give power to individuals who advance the greater good, and they diminish the standing of those who stray from this principle." Recall the power of servant leadership discussed at length in Chapter 7.

In summary, power is a central dynamic in all groups. Power is the ability to influence the attainment of goals sought by yourself and others. Power is not a property of any individual. It is the product of transactions between group members. Information, expertise, rewards and punishments, personal qualities, and legitimate authority are primary resources of power. Groups must endorse these resources before they have power potential. You can approximate the distribution of power in groups by observing certain general patterns of communication, plus verbal and nonverbal indicators and status cues in virtual groups. An imbalance of power in groups promotes abuses and conflict. Defiance and resistance are typically the product of toxic group climates and power imbalances, and although they may be used to balance power in groups, they are for the most part negative ways to achieve such balance. More productive ways involve building empowerment among group members. This can be accomplished by exhibiting assertiveness, forming alliances, and expanding personal power resources.

QUESTIONS FOR CRITICAL THINKERS

1. Information is power. Can misinformation also serve as a power resource?
2. If punishment has significant drawbacks, why is it used more frequently than reward?
3. Have you ever used resistance strategies? Did they work?
4. Can you think of instances in your own experience in which assertiveness was inappropriate?

TED TALKS AND YOUTUBE VIDEOS

"The Power Paradox: How We Gain and Lose Influence" | Dacher Keltner, Ph.D.

"Why Ordinary People Need to Understand Power" | Eric Liu

"Why Cultivating Power Is the Secret to Success" | Jeffrey Pfeffer

"We Have to Stop Calling Women Girls" | Mayim Bialik

VIDEO CASE STUDIES

Miss Sloane (2016). *Drama; R*

Jessica Chastain plays a political power broker in Washington, D.C. Examine what power resources emerge and what type of power is predominant.

Morning Glory (2010). *Comedy/Drama; PG-13*

Workaholic Becky Fuller, played by Rachel McAdams, is the executive producer of a failing early morning network TV show. Desperate to raise the ratings, she hires egomaniacal news reporter Mike Pomeroy (Harrison Ford) to cohost the show. Identify and analyze resistance strategies used by Pomeroy. What are the power resources used?

The Assistant (2019). *Drama; R*

Jane, played by Julia Garner, is a recent college graduate who begins her "dream job" as a junior assistant to a powerful entertainment mogul. She begins to suspect that her boss is abusing his powerful position, but she gets no help from the HR director when she raises concerns about possible sexual harassment and other abuses of power. Examine these abuses subtly indicated as the movie progresses.

The Great Debaters (2007). *Drama; PG-13*

African American poet Mel Tolson (Denzel Washington) forms a debate team at historically black Wiley College in the 1930s. Based on a true story, the Wiley College debate team achieves such distinction that it earns an opportunity to debate powerhouse Harvard University in 1935. Analyze the power dynamics of the debate team with Tolson as its coach. What power resources are used by each character? Are there any defiance or resistance strategies used?

Three Billboards Outside Ebbing, Missouri (2017). *Drama; R*

Award-winning film about a mother who challenges local authorities to solve her daughter's brutal murder. Does the main character, played by Frances McDormand, use defiance or resistance strategies, or both? How do authorities respond? What power resources are evidently displayed?

Conflict Management and Negotiation

12

Open warfare raged for almost a year at public radio station K-I-L-L (slogan: "Live radio that'll knock you dead"). The station operated from facilities on the campus of Bayview Community College in Tsunami, California. KILL radio had 1,000 watts of power, enough to reach into the local Tsunami community (population 42,000).

The program director quit after a feud with the general manager (GM). The GM resigned soon after. His reasons included: the volunteer staff (community members who were not students) inappropriately slanted and presented blatantly false information while reading news on the air and presented only one side on controversial issues, both violations of Federal Communications Commission (FCC) regulations for public radio stations. The FCC notes that "rigging or slanting the news is a most heinous act against the public interest" and "the FCC will investigate a station for news distortion if it receives documented evidence of rigging or slanting" ("The Public and Broadcasting," 2019). In addition, the volunteers were "insubordinate" when they refused to obey his directives concerning substitution of other programs for previously scheduled regular shows; and the volunteers threatened him with bodily injury when he ordered them either to implement his directives or terminate their association with the station.

The volunteer staff countered these allegations with the following: The GM showed them little respect and treated them abusively; they were overworked and underappreciated; and the GM never sought their input on programming and scheduling concerns. The volunteers issued the following demands: Programming should be determined by a consensus of the staff; program substitution should be made only when prior notice (at least two weeks in advance) has been given so staff members will not prepare material destined to be preempted at the last minute; and volunteers should run the station since they do the lion's share of the work and are the only ones with the necessary technical expertise. The volunteer staff threatened to quit en masse unless their demands were met.

The college supported the station with $85,000 annually but seriously considered a drastic cut in the station's budget due to the persistent conflict and because students were not actively involved in the station. The administration wanted the station to be a learning laboratory for students interested in pursuing careers in broadcasting. The school's board of trustees got twitchy because of

objectives

The principal purpose of this chapter is to show constructive ways to manage group conflict beyond what has already been presented in previous chapters. There are six chapter objectives:

1. To define conflict, distinguishing its constructive and destructive form.

2. To explain the pros and cons of five communication styles of conflict management.

3. To discuss how to negotiate conflict effectively in small groups.

4. To explore ways to manage your anger and the anger of others.

5. To recognize cultural influences on conflict management in groups.

6. To address the added challenge of conflict in virtual groups.

all the commotion. The local community highly valued the station and was upset. The college administration, in desperation, named the chair of the mass communication department as the new general manager and temporary program director of the station, a position he relished as much as poking a wasp's nest with a stick. Based on real events, what should have been done to manage this complicated conflict, and in most instances did occur, is discussed throughout this chapter.

Group conflict is pervasive. Roommate and housemate conflicts are a typical instance. A national survey of 31,500 first-year college students reported that 50.1% of women and 44.1% of men experienced "frequent" or "occasional" conflict with roommates or housemates (Liu et al., 2008), and living situations with multiple roommates can increase the complexity of such conflicts. You may simply not like your roommates, and this produces tension and disagreements.

The most extensive and often cited study of conflict in the workplace was conducted by CPP, Inc. The study surveyed 5,000 full-time employees in nine countries from the United States and Europe and found that 85% of respondents address workplace conflict at various times, and 29% (36% in the United States) do so "always" or "frequently." Only 11% have never experienced a disagreement that escalated into personal attacks and project failures (Hayes, 2008). The prevalence of conflict in the workplace finds further support from a more recent study of nurses, teachers, and social workers. This study found that 93% of the 1,299 subjects experienced conflict in their work settings (Tafvelin et al., 2019). Although conflict is a common occurrence in groups, managing conflict competently is not so commonplace (Hastings, 2012).

Workplace conflict is a common event. Effectively addressing workplace conflict is not so common.

fizkes/Shutterstock

In previous chapters, several sources of conflict were discussed at length. Briefly, these included: ethical challenges within groups; an oversized ripple effect on an entire group system from even a single difficult group member; boundary control issues; cultural value differences; negative group climates; listening problems posed by competitive interrupting, ambushing, and shift responses; social loafers; group members who display disruptive roles; role conflict; psychopathic and narcissistic group leaders; the impediments from hierarchy to team building; challenges posed by "truth decay"; and especially imbalances of power—"a fundamental element of every conflict interaction" (Canary & Lakey, 2013). Corresponding antidotes to each of these sources of group conflict were provided in detail. As a result, this chapter on conflict management appears last because so much of this necessary groundwork needed to be laid before addressing final objectives in this chapter.

Nature of Conflict

The KILL radio case study provides a means of explaining the general definition of conflict. In this section, destructive and constructive conflict are also differentiated.

Definition: Incompatible, Interconnected Struggle

In general, **conflict** is the expressed struggle of interconnected parties who perceive incompatible goals and interference from each other in attaining those goals (Wilmot & Hocker, 2018). You can see all elements of this definition in the KILL radio battle.

First, **conflict is an expressed struggle between parties**. If the participants in the radio station conflict had merely silently stewed over perceived outrages, then no conflict would have existed because parties involved wouldn't have known there was a problem. Often the expression of a struggle is verbally manifested as in threatening bodily injury, such as occurred between the parties at the radio station. Occasionally, the expression is nonverbal, as in ignoring specific directions from the GM.

Second, **conflict occurs between interconnected parties**. For a conflict to exist, the behavior of one or more parties must produce consequences for the other party or parties. Clearly, consequences to opposing parties in the radio station conflict were evident. Both the GM and the program director quit, leaving the station in chaos.

Third, conflict involves perceived incompatible goals (Canary & Lakey, 2013). The staff demand that it run the station was incompatible with the role of the GM. The program director and the staff were engaged in a power struggle regarding programming decisions.

Finally, conflict involves interference from each other in attaining desired goals. Unless one party attempts to block the attainment of another party's goal, there is no conflict. Clearly, both sides in the KILL radio dispute interfered with attainment of respective goals.

Benefits of Conflict: Dissent Can Be Productive

Conflict is not an event that most people welcome. Most conflict probably seems destructive given how poorly conflict is typically managed in groups (Kerwin et al., 2011), and frequent conflict can be counterproductive for groups because it can interfere with task accomplishment (Hanif et al., 2016). Moderate amounts of conflict, however, can be a constructive force in groups if the conflict is managed competently. Conflict can disturb the group system and instigate positive changes that foster individual and group growth; it can promote creative problem solving, encourage power balancing, enhance group cohesiveness, and prevent groupthink (Dovidio et al., 2009; Omisore & Abiodun, 2014). "The benefits of conflict are much more likely to arise when conflicts are discussed openly, and when discussion skillfully promotes new ideas and generates creative insights and agreements" (Elgoibar et al., 2017). Authentic dissent, genuine disagreement, can provoke constructive conflict and make group decision making and problem solving more effective. Encouraging dissenting voices is very useful. How this genuine dissent is communicated, of course, often a big challenge for social and political action groups, determines whether the conflict will be constructive or destructive.

Destructive and Constructive Conflict: Differences

Destructive conflict is characterized by dominating, escalating, retaliating, competing, and acting defensively and inflexibly (Wilmot & Hocker, 2018). When conflicts spiral out of control, a system's dynamic equilibrium and its ability to manage an acceptable range between stability and change is disrupted. Participants lose sight of their initial goals and focus on hurting their adversary, threatening the very existence of the group. The KILL radio fracas was essentially a destructive conflict. Escalation, threats, shouting, inflexibility on both sides, and expressions of contempt and ridicule occurred. Neither side seemed able to work together to find a mutually satisfactory solution to the conflict.

Recognizing destructive conflict while it is occurring may not always be easy. When it becomes obvious to you that "Gee, I'm getting stupid," you're engaged in destructive conflict (Donohue & Kolt, 1992), but this requires a certain amount of self-awareness and mindfulness ("Conflict Is Destructive," 2018). When you see yourself engaging in petty, even infantile, tactics to win an argument, you're getting stupid. Gossiping, backstabbing, and spreading malicious rumors are additional, obvious examples of stoking destructive conflict. Becoming physically and verbally aggressive also moves the conflict into destructive territory. This doesn't mean that you can never raise your voice, express frustration, or disagree with other group members. **Conflict can remain constructive even when discussion becomes somewhat contentious because it remains within the bounds of dynamic equilibrium.** When conflict becomes more emotional than reasonable, and when you can't think straight because you are too consumed by anger, then conflict has become destructive (Fisher & Shapiro, 2005; Wilmot and Hocker, 2018). The interconnectedness of parts in group systems, however, emphasizes the likelihood of the ripple effect or what some researchers have dubbed **conflict contagion**—when one or more group members can spread nasty conflict among an entire team (Shah et al., 2020).

Constructive conflict is characterized by We-oriented, de-escalating, cooperative, supportive, and flexible communication patterns (Wilmot & Hocker, 2018). **The principal focus is on trying to achieve a solution between struggling parties that is mutually satisfactory to everyone.** Even if no mutually satisfactory solution is achieved or even possible (e.g., you disagree with the company dress code but it is set by "corporate" and cannot be changed locally), the communication process that characterizes constructive conflict allows conflicting parties to maintain cordial relationships while agreeing to disagree.

Prostock-studio/Shutterstock

When coworkers escalate a conflict to the point of "getting stupid" they exhibit destructive conflict.

▶ Communication Styles of Conflict Management

Communication is central to conflict in groups. Our communication can signal that conflict exists, it can create conflict, and it can be the means for managing conflict constructively or destructively (Wilmot & Hocker, 2018). Consequently, communication styles have been the center of much research and discussion. A **communication style of conflict management** is an orientation toward conflict. Styles exhibit tendencies regarding the way conflict is managed in groups. Individual group members may exhibit a specific style, or an entire group may adopt a normative preference for a certain style of conflict management. There are five communication styles of conflict management: collaborating, accommodating, compromising, avoiding, and competing (Howell, 2014; Kilmann & Thomas, 1977).

Before delving into a discussion of these styles, one clarification is warranted. The term conflict *management*, not *resolution*, has been chosen because it is more appropriate for a systems perspective. "Resolution" suggests settling conflict by ending it (Elgoibar et al., 2017), as if that is always desirable. Since conflict can be an essential catalyst for growth in a system, increasing conflict may be required to evoke change (Johnson & Johnson, 2000). Women who file sexual harassment lawsuits provoke conflict to end an evil. "Managing conflict" implies no end to the struggle. Although some conflict episodes end, and are therefore resolved, conflict overall in a system is a continuous phenomenon that waxes and wanes.

focus questions

1. How do communication styles of conflict management differ on task and social dimensions of small groups?
2. Should group members always use the collaborating style and avoid the competing (power-forcing) style?

Collaborating: Problem Solving

The most complex and potentially productive communication style of conflict management is collaborating, or what some refer to as problem solving. The **collaborating style** is a win–win, cooperative approach to conflict that attempts to satisfy all parties. The emphasis is on what Daniel Shapiro (2017), founder and director of the Harvard International Negotiation Program, calls the "relentless We." Conflict is viewed as "a shared challenge," not an us-against-them degeneration into tribal clashes. Someone employing this style balances a high concern for both task and social relationships in groups. A collaborating style has three key components: confrontation, integration, and smoothing.

Confrontation: Directly Addressing the Problem The overt recognition that conflict exists in a group and the direct effort to manage it effectively is called **confrontation.** Confrontation as a conflict-management technique incorporates all the elements already discussed at length regarding assertiveness (describe, express, specify, and identify consequences, and remain respectful) and supportive communication patterns (description, problem orientation, etc.). The purpose of confrontation is to manage conflict in a productive way for all parties (DuBrin, 2019).

The KILL radio case cried out for collaboration. The new GM should, and did, immediately meet with the volunteers individually, and actively listened to their perspective. He let them tell their story without offering correction or rebuttal. Staff members felt unappreciated and undervalued. Supportive, confirming statements concerning the essential role volunteers played in the functioning of the station were made to all involved.

Not all issues are worth confronting (De Dreu & Van Vianen, 2001). As Dorothy Parker once said, "I don't have to attend every argument I'm invited to." Members who confront even trivial differences of opinion or can't let a momentary flash of pique go unaddressed can be like annoying online pop-up ads. Groups must decide which issues and concerns are priorities and which are tangential. You can overuse confrontation.

Min C. Chiu/Shutterstock

Although the news media are fond of using the term *confrontation* in a negative sense, as in a nose-to-nose face-off, a contest of wills such as "There was a violent confrontation between protesters and police," this is not the meaning relevant to this discussion.

Integration: Seeking Joint Gains Decision making often involves conflicts of interest. **Integration** is a creative approach that addresses conflicts of interest; it searches for solutions that benefit everyone. There are two key forms: expanding the pie and bridging. **Expanding the pie** refers to increasing the resources as a solution to a problem ("Integrative Bargaining Examples," 2017). When faced with scarce resources, groups often become competitive and experience serious strife, warring over who gets the biggest or best piece of the limited resource pie. Groups, however, sometimes accept the inevitability of scarce resources—called the **"bias of the fixed pie"**—without fully exploring options that might expand the resources ("Creating Value," 2020). For example, projects can sometimes be crowdfunded to raise money outside of traditional budgetary sources ("Crowdfunding," 2017).

Integrating the KILL radio station into the college curriculum was actually a fairly simple process. Involving students in the actual operation of the station as supervised interns earning class credit satisfied a primary concern of the administration and board. This also expanded the resources of the station by training additional individuals to help staff members who already felt overworked.

Bridging is the second type of integrative solution to conflicts. **Bridging** looks for overarching (sometimes referred to as superordinate) goals that find common ground to move beyond conflicts of interest toward mutual interest ("Four Conflict Negotiating Strategies," 2018). In the KILL radio station conflict, the overarching goal of all parties was to keep the station running. Violating FCC regulations could have resulted in the loss of the station's license, resulting in the shutdown of the station ("The Public and Broadcasting," 2019). No one wanted that to occur. Impetus to resolve the dispute was galvanized once the new GM made it clear that all parties must pull together in mutual interest (maintaining the viability of the station).

Try the following steps to promote integrative solutions to conflicts:

1. *Parties in conflict must determine whether a real conflict of interest exists.* Family members argue over whether to get a dog or not. The two teens say they want a dog; the parents say they do not. On the surface, this looks like a standard conflict of interest. Yet when the issue is discussed, what becomes clear is that the mother doesn't want to take care of the dog, and the father dislikes barking. When asked whether a cat would serve as an adequate substitute, the teenagers agree since they just want a pet. No conflict exists since the parents like cats, which are low maintenance and mostly quiet, except around mealtime.

2. *The parties in disagreement should stick to their goals but remain flexible regarding the means of attaining them.* Both expanding the pie and bridging allow conflicting parties to find flexible, creative means of attaining goals without compromising them.

3. *If stalemated, concede on low-priority issues or discard low-priority interests.* You give on minor issues that are relatively unimportant to you but are important to the other party.

Smoothing: Calming Troubled Waters   The act of calming the agitated feelings of group members during a conflict episode is called **smoothing**. When tempers ignite and anger morphs into screaming and shedding of tears, no collaboration is possible. A simple "I'm sorry" is a useful smoothing response. "Let's all calm down. Attacking each other won't help us find a solution" is another example of smoothing. Calming the emotional storm opens the way to confronting conflict and brainstorming integrative solutions. In the KILL radio case, smoothing hurt feelings was essential for the new GM to address. Smoothing statements (e.g., "We're starting fresh. I want us to work together") were delivered to the staff to calm troubled waters.

Since collaborating is such an effective communication style for solving conflicts of interest, why isn't it always used in these situations? There are several reasons. First, collaborating usually requires a significant investment of time and effort along with greater-than-ordinary communication skills. Even if you want to collaborate, it requires mutually agreeable parties. Second, collaboration is built on trust. If parties are suspicious of each other and worry that one will betray the other by not honoring agreements, then even an integrative solution may be rejected. Third, parties in a conflict sometimes do not share the same emotional investment in finding a mutually agreeable solution. Hypercompetitive group members want a clear "victory," not a solution that benefits all parties.

Accommodating: Yielding

The **accommodating** style yields to the concerns and desires of others. Someone using this style shows a high concern for social relationships but low concern for task accomplishment. This style may camouflage deep divisions among group members to maintain the appearance of harmony. If the task can be accomplished without social disruption, fine. If accomplishing the task threatens to jeopardize the harmonious relationships within the group, however, a person using this style will opt for giving members what they want, even though this may sacrifice productivity. Generally, group members with less power are expected to accommodate more often and to a greater degree than more powerful members.

Although we tend to view accommodating in a negative light, as appeasement with all its negative connotations, this style can be positive. A group that has experienced protracted strife may rejoice when one side accommodates, even on an issue of only minor importance (Shonk, 2018b).

Compromising: Halving the Loaf

When **compromising**, we give up something to get something. Some have referred to this as a lose–lose style of conflict management because neither party is ever fully satisfied with the solution. Compromising is choosing a middle ground. Someone using this style shows a moderate concern for both task and social relationships in groups (Zarankin, 2008). The emphasis is on workable but not necessarily optimal solutions.

In the KILL radio case, a couple of experimental programs were tried as a compromise when community preferences did not match staff preferences in programming. Some compromise on program substitution (a one-week prior notice, not two weeks as demanded) was also instituted with agreeable success.

Compromise evokes ambivalence—both negative and positive reactions (Jaffe, 2012). We speak disparagingly of those who would "compromise their integrity." On some issues, usually moral or ethical conflicts, compromise is thought to be intolerable. Yet despite this negative view, members of task forces, ad hoc groups, and committees of many shapes and sizes often seek a compromise as an admirable goal. Half a loaf is better than starvation—not in all circumstances, but certainly in some. When an integrative solution cannot be achieved, when a temporary settlement is the only feasible alternative, or when the issues involved are not considered critical to the group, compromise can be useful.

Avoiding: Withdrawing

Avoiding is a communicating style of withdrawing from potentially contentious and unpleasant struggles. *Flights from fights* may seem constructive at the time because they circumvent unpleasantness. Facing problems, however, proves to be more effective than running from them. Someone using the avoiding conflict style shows little concern for both task and social relationships in groups. Avoiders shrink from conflict, even fear it. By avoiding conflict, they hope it will disappear. It may instead increase relationship conflict and blow up like a geyser later (Impett et al., 2005).

Avoiding, nevertheless, is sometimes appropriate (Elgoibar et al., 2017). If you are a low-power person in a group and the consequences of confrontation are potentially hazardous to you, avoiding might be a reasonable strategy until other alternatives present themselves. Standing up to a bully may work out well in movies, but confronting antisocial types who look like they eat raw meat for breakfast and might eat you for lunch may not be a very bright choice. Staying out of a bully's way, although perhaps ego-deflating, may be the best *temporary option* in a bad situation.

If the advantages of confrontation do not outweigh the disadvantages, avoiding the conflict might be a desirable course of action. In some cases, tempers need to cool. Avoiding contentious issues for a time may prove to be constructive. ("Let's deal with this later when we've had a chance to simmer down a bit,

As Keith Ferrazzi and his colleagues (2021) suggest: "When it feels like there's an elephant in the room, leaders of high-performing teams create what we call 'candor breaks' to encourage team members to share their thoughts and feelings." Avoiding the obvious difficult controversies even when they are small can lead to much greater and more troublesome conflict later.

okay?") We often make foolish, irrational choices when we are highly stressed. In addition, if differences among group members are intractable (e.g., personality clashes), avoiding the differences and focusing on task accomplishment may be a desirable approach (De Dreu & Van Vianen, 2001). Again, in the KILL radio case, the demand that the volunteers run the station was pointless. There was no way that the college board would accommodate this demand and approve funds to support a public radio station run by unsupervised volunteers. More than likely, however, this demand was made without any expectation that it would be accepted. The GM wisely avoided the issue, no staff member raised it again, and it disappeared into the ether.

In most cases, however, avoiding rather than confronting is highly counterproductive (Elgoibar et al., 2017). Failure to address conflict promptly can lead to destructive conflict later, while addressing conflict without delay usually prevents escalation into destructive conflict (Behfar et al., 2008; Greer et al., 2008).

Competing: Power-Forcing

When we approach conflict as a win–lose contest, we are using the **competing style**. This style is communicated in a variety of ways that are likely to produce destructive conflict: threats, criticism, contempt, hostile remarks and jokes, sarcasm, ridicule, intimidation, fault-finding and blaming, and denials of responsibility (Wilmot & Hocker, 2018). The competing style is aggressive, not assertive. It is not confrontation as previously defined; it is an attack. It flows from the dominance perspective on power. Someone using a competing or forcing style shows high concern for task but low concern for relationships. If accomplishing the group task requires a few wounded egos, that is thought to be the unavoidable price of productivity.

The power-forcing style is a tug-of-war between competing parties in a win–lose effort.

PHOTOCREO Michal Bednarek/Shutterstock

In the KILL radio case, power-forcing would have been required if staff violations of FCC regulations continued. The staff's desire to editorialize on the air at will was irrelevant. The law could not be violated. Handling other issues effectively, however, reduced this issue to virtual irrelevance.

All five styles of conflict management show different emphases on task and social dimensions of groups. Nevertheless, someone using the competing style, for example, may in some circumstances manifest genuine concern for social climate. Low concern doesn't mean no concern. **All of these styles represent tendencies, not unalterably fixed ways of managing conflict in every situation.**

Comparing Styles: Likelihood of Success

Research clearly favors some conflict styles over others, even though more than one style may need to be used, as was required in the KILL radio case. Overall, the collaborating style produces the best decisions and greatest satisfaction from parties in conflict (DuBrin, 2019), avoiding typically produces poor results ("The Right Way," 2016), and the competing/forcing style is least effective (Prieto-Remon et al., 2015). This is true for both face-to-face and virtual groups (Paul et al., 2005). Collaborating encourages constructive conflict; competing tends to promote destructive conflict. You have a choice. As author Max Lucado observes, "Conflict is inevitable, but combat is optional."

Despite the clear benefits of collaborating, poor results of avoiding, the disadvantages of competing, and mixed results for accommodating and compromising, we seem to use the least effective styles most often to manage conflict in groups. Studies of doctor–nurse abuse, for example, found that avoidance was a chief style used by nurses and fewer than 7% of nurses confronted abusive doctors (Johnson, 2009; Maxfield et al., 2005). In the nursing profession overall, conflict styles are typically used in this order of frequency: compromising, competing, avoiding, accommodating, and finally collaborating (Iglesias & Vallejo, 2012). In a review of more than two dozen workplace studies, the power-forcing style was the most common approach used by managers, both male and female, with employee groups (Dildar & Amjad, 2017). Among employees engaged in conflict with their peers at work, "male employees consistently use more competing strategy (dominating) than female employees" (Rahim & Katz, 2019).

SECOND LOOK

Communication Styles of Conflict Management

Style	Task–Social Dimension
Collaborating (problem solving)	High task, high social
Accommodating (yielding)	Low task, high social
Compromising (halving the loaf)	Moderate task, moderate social
Avoiding (withdrawing)	Low task, low social
Competing (power-forcing)	High task, low social

Even if the style with the greatest likelihood of success is chosen, when and how it is used must also be figured into the equation. Confrontation used as a collaborative tactic can be highly effective, but it won't be if used in a hit-and-run fashion. Confronting contentious issues five minutes before the group is due to adjourn or just before you leave to attend class provides no time for another person to respond constructively. Hit-and-run confrontations look like guerrilla tactics, not attempts to communicate competently and work out disputes. Likewise, when to use power-forcing is an important concern. Competing/power-forcing should be a style of last resort, except in times of emergencies in which quick, decisive action must be taken and discussion has no place (Elgoibar et al., 2017). Power-forcing typically produces psychological reactance (see Chapter 5). If you try to force before using other styles and are met with defiance, then you attempt to collaborate or accommodate, you may find that this sequence of styles will fail. Trying to collaborate after unsuccessfully forcing will be seen as the disingenuous act of a person whose bluff and bluster were challenged. On the other hand, temporarily withdrawing after a protracted feud has stalemated might allow heads to clear and passions to cool. Sometimes we just need a "time out," a chance to think calmly.

SECOND LOOK

Conditions for Communication Styles

	Appropriate	Inappropriate
Collaborating	Complex issues	Trivial issues
	First approach	Last resort
	Ample time	
Accommodating	Trivial issues	Complex issues
	Issues significant only to one side	Issues significant to all parties
	Maintaining relationships	Social relationships temporary
	Large power imbalance	Relatively equal power
Compromising	No integrative solution	
	Temporary solution better than no agreement	Giving up too soon on critical issues
Avoiding	Issues are trivial	Issues are significant
	Hazardous to confront	Ignoring disagreements may damage relationships
	Need temporary break	May increase anger by ignoring issues
Competing	Timely decision required	Time not constrained
	Last resort	First option
	Disruptive member unresponsive to other approaches	Concern for positive social relations critical (especially collectivist cultures)

Situational Factors

Although some conflict styles have a higher probability of effectiveness than others, the choice of styles always operates within a context. To understand how to transact conflict effectively in a small group context, certain situational factors should be considered, such as the type of conflict and cultural views of conflict-management communication styles.

focus questions

1. How do group members short-circuit conflict spirals?
2. Why is principled negotiation superior to other negotiating strategies?

Task Conflict: Routine and Nonroutine

Whether conflicts regarding group tasks are beneficial or detrimental depends largely on the type of task, routine or nonroutine, performed by the group (Jehn, 1995; Yousaf et al., 2020). A **routine task** is one in which the group performs processes and procedures that have little variability and little likelihood of change. Ad hoc groups organizing protests must acquire proper permits to march within city limits. Arguing about "the senseless bureaucracy" of this routine task is unproductive. It's a requirement and can't be changed before protesters take to the streets. A **nonroutine task** is one that requires problem solving, has few set procedures, and has a high level of uncertainty (e.g., student group deciding who to invite to make the college commencement address). Conflicts regarding routine tasks easily deteriorate into gripe sessions with little opportunity for resolution. Conflicts about nonroutine tasks, however, can promote team accomplishment in both face-to-face and virtual groups (Tafvelin et al., 2019). These positive results, of course, are predicated on group members choosing a collaborative instead of a competing style.

Relationship Conflict: It's Personal

Conflicts are not always about task accomplishment; some are about group relationships. In fact, relationship conflict is far more likely to impact group cohesion and productivity negatively than task conflict (Tafvelin et al., 2019). Some of the most frustrating and volatile conflicts are provoked by personality clashes and outright dislike between group members (Varela et al., 2008).

We make style choices depending on our relationships with group members. Confronting roommates about their narcissistic personality, for example, is usually a fool's errand. People don't change their personality easily even after concentrated effort and training (Vitelli, 2015). You may choose avoidance when personality clashes occur. You may even redesign your space to avoid volatile conflicts until a more favorable living arrangement emerges. The reality of power imbalances clearly influences conflict management style choices. In a review of 28 workplace studies, both men and women chose predominately the competing style when acting in management positions but the accommodating style when in a subordinate position with others (Dildar & Amjad, 2017). Lower power group members may want to collaborate. Dominating, high-power group members may see little need to collaborate since they can impose their will on less powerful group members ("Do it because I say so"). Accommodation may be necessary to avoid negative consequences of defiance.

A conflict initially about task accomplishment can easily become a relationship conflict (Kerwin et al., 2011) that can have a toxic impact on teams, especially startup entrepreneurial groups (Kozusznik et al., 2020). When working on a group project for class, some group members may exhibit social loafing. Such lackluster effort from some members can trigger relationship conflict. Those members who wish to achieve a high grade may lash out at loafers. Anger can erupt, and relationship conflict can escalate into destructive conflict and poor overall group performance (Curseu & Schruijer, 2010). As previously discussed, conflict is sometimes constructive, but not when it deteriorates into nasty relationship conflict, as it did in the KILL radio kerfuffle.

Establishing trust among group members is a key component necessary to prevent task conflict from mutating into relationship conflict (Curseu & Schruijer 2010). In relationships poisoned by mistrust, as occurred in the KILL radio case, a collaborative attempt by one party may be seen as a ploy to gain some unforeseen advantage. Accommodating by one party, even as a gesture to change the negative dynamics of the parties in conflict, may be viewed as weakness and a sign that capitulation is likely to occur after a period of waiting. Also, research shows that perceived team performance impacts the rise or fall of relationship conflict in groups. Low performing teams experience increased relationship conflict; high performing teams experience the opposite (Guenter et al., 2016).

Values Conflict: Deeply Felt Struggles

The most difficult disputes to manage are often values conflicts ("Four Conflict Negotiation Strategies," 2018). **Values** are the most deeply felt views of what is deemed good, worthwhile, or ethically right. We may clash over beliefs and still walk away as friends, especially if the ideas do not touch much on values. **Beliefs** are what we think is true or probable. "Smartphones are an indispensable means of communicating" or "Texting is more efficient than using email" are beliefs that don't ordinarily degenerate into fistfights or verbal assaults. How odd would that be if they did? When disputes about beliefs spill over into value clashes, however, especially when the values are held passionately, then you have a conflict of a different ilk. Battles over immigration, hate speech, and the like are fundamentally about values such as morality, freedom, and equality. Such conflicts do not lend themselves much to compromise (would you compromise your values?). When dichotomous battle lines are drawn—friends versus enemies—power-forcing is often the style required for conflict management. The courts have had to settle these issues by declaring what is permissible and what is prohibited.

Culture and Conflict: Communication Differences

Cultures can vary widely in their preferences for communication styles of conflict management (Gunkel et al., 2016). Individualist and collectivist values significantly affect the communication styles of conflict management chosen when conflict occurs (Samovar et al., 2021). Individualist, low-context cultures tend to favor direct competitive/forcing or compromising styles of conflict management. Communication during conflict is explicit and direct. Americans as individualists "can become frustrated if conflicts are not managed openly and directly" (Canary & Lakey, 2013). Collectivist, high-context cultures favor avoiding or accommodating styles of conflict management (Kim, 2016). Assertive confrontation is considered rude and offensive. It is too direct, explicit, and unsettling. It can be perceived as face-threatening (Sadri, 2018). For example, avoidance of confrontation is "a core element of Thai culture. Expressions of emotion and excitement are seen as impolite, improper, and threatening" (Knutson & Posirisuk, 2006). A Thai avoids conflict and exhibits respect, tactfulness, politeness, modesty, and emotional control (Knutson et al., 2003).

Consider a comparison between typical Chinese and American approaches to conflict. Harmony is the essential foundation of Chinese communication (Chen, 2011). This philosophy translates into avoiding conflicts that might stir up trouble and disharmony. Conflicts handled ineptly might bring shame on the individual and the entire group. Thus, while Americans tend to focus immediately on task conflicts, Chinese tend to focus on relationship conflicts (i.e., saving or losing face) and avoid task conflicts until the relationships among all disputing parties have had time to build (Merkin, 2015). To Americans, this may look like stalling to gain advantage.

Conflicts with individuals and groups from other cultures (out-groups), however, are often handled differently in collectivist cultures than are conflicts within the culture (in-group). Although not the initial choice, competing (power-forcing) is not an uncommon way to approach conflict with outsiders, especially if the interests of the opposing parties are highly incompatible. Vicious quarrels, even physical fights, are not uncommon in such circumstances (Chen & Starosta, 1998).

Managing intercultural conflicts is challenging where expectations differ on the appropriateness of different communication styles. Remaining flexible by employing a style that is well suited to cultural expectations is a key to effective conflict management in such situations (Knutson et al., 2003). One study found that the more sensitive and accepting individuals are of cultural differences, the more likely they are to choose integration and compromising conflict styles and the less likely they are to choose avoiding and power/forcing styles (Yu & Chen, 2008). Competing/power-forcing is ineffective and inappropriate in most intercultural conflicts (Sadri, 2018).

Always remember, however, that cultural generalizations are just that—generalizations. Remaining flexible when managing cross-cultural conflicts means more than adapting conflict styles to typical cultural expectations of appropriateness. It also means adapting to individuals who may not embrace predominant cultural values (Shonk, 2020c)! Be careful not to stereotype an entire culture. Remain open to individual differences.

Negotiation Strategies

Negotiation is "a process by which a joint decision is made by two or more parties" (Pruitt, 1981, p. 1). Negotiating strategies are the ways we transact these joint decisions when conflicts arise. In this section, commonly used strategies for negotiating conflict are discussed.

Positional Bargaining: Hard and Soft Negotiating

In positional bargaining, parties take positions on contested issues, then they haggle back and forth until concessions are made and an agreement is reached. There are two styles of positional bargaining: hard and soft. **Hard bargainers** (sometimes called *tough bargainers*) see negotiation as a contest of wills. Hard bargaining is the "negotiate from strength" approach to conflicts of interest. The focus is on conveying strength and resilience so the other party or parties will yield. Volunteers who made "demands" during the KILL radio conflict engaged in hard bargaining tactics.

Hard bargaining is a competing/forcing strategy. Hard bargainers can be abusive or sarcastic to gain an advantage over the other party. When both sides adopt a hard-bargaining style, the battle is joined. Both sides attempt to cut the best deal for themselves (Me-Not-We orientation), instead of finding the most equitable and constructive solution to the conflicts of interest. Opening positions typically are extreme and unreasonable ("Ten Hard-Bargaining Tactics," 2020). The more hard bargainers publicly defend these positions, the more hardened the positions tend to become. Egos become identified with positions. Task conflict transforms into relationship conflict as well. Concessions easily take on the appearance of "selling out." Making threats, lying, belittling alternatives, flinging personal insults at perceived adversaries, making "nonnegotiable take-it-or-leave-it" demands, walking out on the negotiations in a huff, exhibiting negative emotions through facial expressions (e.g., anger, contempt), and dominating space are commonplace verbal and nonverbal tactics in hard positional bargaining (Semnani-Azad & Adair, 2011; "Ten Hard-Bargaining Tactics," 2020). "Getting stupid" is a common hard-bargaining tactic.

Consider this example of hard positional bargaining among housemates:

A: I want to have a party here at the house on Saturday.

B: Hey, that's a great idea.

C: Sorry, you can't. I have to study for my law exam, and I sure can't do that with your belching, retching friends cranking the music to a decibel level equivalent to a jet airplane taking off. I'd have to lug a truckload of stuff to the library or anywhere else I might choose to study.

A: Who appointed you king? This is our house too. Since when do you dictate what can and can't happen around here?

C: Since I pay a third of the rent and am not about to sacrifice my standing in law school so you can get drunk with your brain-dead friends and act like imbeciles. I'm vetoing your little beer bash.

B: I don't even know why we're bothering to ask for your permission to hold this party. There's no way you can stop us anyway. I say we just go ahead and do it. If you don't like it, sue us.

A: Yeah! Get used to the idea because we're going to have this party and there isn't anything you can do about it.

C: On the contrary, there is a great deal I can do about it. Suing you is actually an option that appeals to me. I could sue you for damages, especially if I do poorly on the exam. I could also argue in small claims court that you violated a verbal contract not to have parties without the consent of all housemates—I have witnesses affirming that you both agreed to such an arrangement. So, don't start issuing ultimatums unless you want this party to cost a lot more than the price of beer.

And on and on the silliness escalates—a ludicrous contest of wills.

Hard bargaining doesn't have to mean ruthless bargaining and obstinacy. A person can achieve positive results by acting tough (Shapiro, 2017). Eventually, though, there must be some give and take for a stalemate to be avoided if all parties assume a hard-bargaining strategy. Even a token concession "can be a powerful way of prompting reciprocation from counterparts" engaged in negotiations (Shonk, 2018b). **The key to making hard bargaining a constructive conflict strategy is to appear tough but fair.** The main difficulty with this strategy is determining how tough you should be without seeming pigheaded. **As with any competitive strategy, when hard bargainers face off against each other, their transactional moves and countermoves can easily produce an impasse** ("Ten Hard-Bargaining Tactics," 2020).

Conversely, **soft bargainers**, recognizing the high costs of hard bargaining on relationships with people they may have to interact with once the negotiations are concluded, yield to pressure. To soft bargainers, making an agreement and

Hard bargaining negotiation strategies build walls that often prevent effective conflict management.

remaining friends is more important than winning a victory. The major drawback to soft bargaining is that the accommodator may give away too much to maintain harmonious relationships during negotiations. Hard bargainers looking to enhance self-interest, not group interests, often exploit those who desire cooperation if a soft bargaining approach is taken (Schei & Rognes, 2005).

Principled Negotiation: Interest-Based Bargaining

Fisher and his associates (2011) offer a third choice besides hard and soft positional bargaining—**principled negotiation**, or interest-based bargaining. Principled negotiation embodies the essential elements of competent communication. Active listening is an overarching competent communication imperative for successful principled negotiation. "If there is a common denominator in virtually all successful negotiations, it is to be an *active listener*" ("The New Conflict Management," 2012). Bobby Covic (2003), author of *Everything's Negotiable*, notes: "There's a saying among negotiators that whoever talks the most during negotiation loses." Active listening is essential to building trust that enhances interest-based bargaining (Goodman, 2016). This means avoiding competitive interrupting and shift responses that divert attention from concerns of other parties negotiating, and eschewing ambushing (preparing rebuttals while half-listening). Instead, paraphrase and probe for understanding before offering your own issues and viewpoint (review Chapter 5).

The Four Principles: Appropriate Rules There are four basic elements to principled negotiation, with corresponding principles for each element. They are:

People:	Separate the people from the problem.
Interests:	Focus on interests, not positions.
Options:	Generate a variety of possibilities before deciding what to do.
Criteria:	Insist that the result be based on some objective standards.
	(Fisher et al., 2011)

Separating the people from the problem reaffirms the importance of supportive climates (e.g., description, problem orientation, empathy, equality, or provisionalism) and the inappropriateness of defensive communication patterns (e.g., evaluation, control, superiority, or certainty) during negotiations. Principled negotiation also focuses on task conflicts and strives to diminish relationship conflicts during negotiations. Set the table to ensure that there is no "power seat," no dominant position at the negotiating table that could devolve into relationship strife (Crampton, 2013). Empower all parties to feel "on equal footing," safe to express their viewpoints by employing a rule that requires everyone treat each other with respect throughout the negotiations.

When Frank Lorenzo became president of Eastern Airlines, relations between management and labor immediately became tense and personal, and after a year of fruitless negotiations, Eastern's machinists and pilots went on strike. The machinist union targeted Lorenzo as the issue in negotiations, painting him as an unscrupulous takeover artist. The Airline Pilots Association characterized Lorenzo as a Machiavellian sleazeball whose middle name was Greed. Lorenzo fired back, calling the pilots' role in the strike "suicidal" and akin to the Jonestown cult mass suicide tragedy. Eastern filed for bankruptcy, and thousands lost their jobs because the parties in conflict could not separate the people from the problem. It became personal, not productive.

Negotiating interests first, not arguing positions, is critical (Patton, 2018). **Positions** are the concrete things one party wants. **Interests** are the intangible motivations—needs, desires, concerns, fears, aspirations—that lead a party in the conflict to take a position (Ury, 1993). For instance, a group in my class working on a symposium presentation got into a dispute over topic choice (positions). Two members wanted the group to choose "climate change." Two other members pushed for "capital punishment." The three remaining group members advocated "animal rights." Bickering broke out as each faction chose a hard-bargaining approach. Nobody was willing to budge. Put-downs, snide comments, and abusive remarks were flung back and forth (relationship conflict).

When instructed to explore their interests, not their positions, both the capital punishment and climate change factions revealed that their primary interest was time management. They wanted to "double dip" by using research for two classes instead of just one. The animal rights faction simply wanted to do a presentation that dealt with an issue of values, not some "dry, scientific report." Once the interests of each faction were identified and discussed, everyone realized that the capital punishment faction had already done most of the necessary research for the entire group presentation. The animal rights group agreed that capital punishment was an issue of values, so the group settled on capital punishment as the group topic.

Generating a variety of options is another aspect of principled negotiation. This involves brainstorming, as already explained in Chapter 10. Integration by expanding the pie or bridging may be discovered in a brainstorming session. The nominal group technique may also prove to be useful here.

Finally, principled negotiation rests on establishing objective standards (criteria) for weighing the merits and demerits of any proposal (see Chapter 10). In the conflict over topic choice just discussed, one primary objective standard that was agreed to was "the least number of hours doing research."

Remaining Unconditionally Constructive: Sound Judgment What do you do if the other parties insist on hard bargaining, not principled negotiations? Remain unconditionally constructive. In real situations, however, we tend to employ a **tit-for-tat strategy**—we're inclined to adopt those conflict strategies that are used by other parties during a conflict ("Ten Hard Bargaining Tactics," 2020). If you begin with a cooperative opening move, tit-for-tat could prove constructive if the cooperative gesture is reciprocated (McCarthy, 2017). The tit-for-tat strategy, however, runs the risk of provoking **conflict spirals**—the escalating cycle of negative communication that produces destructive conflict. The KILL radio case was a clear instance of conflict spiraling out of control.

If someone tries to cheat, blackmail, or exploit you in a dispute, should you reciprocate in kind? If another party has a snit fit, should you likewise throw a temper tantrum? If your antagonist demands outrageous concessions from you, should you mindlessly match the demands? Does any of this sound to you like competent communication? As Fisher and Brown (1988) explain, "If you are acting in ways that injure your own competence, there is no reason for me to do the same. Two heads are better than one, but one is better than none" (p. 202). Tit-for-tat predisposes us to stoop to whatever level the other party is willing to sink.

Being unconditionally constructive means you make choices and take only those actions that benefit both you and the other parties in the dispute, regardless of whether the other parties reciprocate. Remaining unconditionally constructive during negotiations short-circuits conflict spirals. If they become abusive, you remain civil. If they purposely misunderstand or confuse issues, you clarify. If they try to bully, you neither yield nor bully back. You try to persuade them on the merits of your proposal. If they try to deceive you, neither trust nor deceive them. You remain trustworthy throughout the negotiations. If they do not listen carefully, you nevertheless listen to them carefully and empathically. You remain unconditionally constructive because it serves your best interests to do so (Falcao, 2010).

If one of your interests is fairness, ask the other parties to explain how their position is fair. Don't assert that the other side offers an unfair proposal. Asking the hard bargainers to justify their position translates positions (e.g., no parties on weekends) into interests (e.g., peace and quiet to study). Personal attacks, threats, and bullying tactics can be handled by confronting them openly and immediately. For example, "Threats are not constructive. They won't work. I negotiate only on merit. Can we return to the substantive issues?" Research shows that labeling the hard-bargaining tactic as ineffective and refusing to reciprocate bad bargaining behavior effectively refocuses the negotiations on interest-based issues and prevents conflict spirals (Brett et al., 1998). If necessary, redirect the hard bargainers' game plan by forthrightly asking for the rules operating, a key aspect of setting system boundaries. For instance, "Before we go any further, I need to know what rules we are following during this bargaining. Does everyone here want to achieve a fair settlement in the quickest amount of time, or are we going to play the hard-bargaining game where blind stubbornness wins out?" Make them convince you that their intentions are honorable. In the process they may convince themselves that hard bargaining isn't appropriate. You want to bring hard bargainers to their senses, not to their knees (Ury, 1993).

The BATNA: Best Alternative to a Negotiated Agreement You also need to develop a BATNA as a standard against which any proposal can be measured ("BATNA Strategy," 2021). Your **BATNA** tells you what is the best that you can do if negotiations fail to produce an agreement. Most important, your BATNA can prevent a serious mistake (Fisher et al., 2011).

For instance, if you have ever visited towns on the Mexican side of the border with the United States, you have undoubtedly engaged in street negotiations with local merchants on items such as handcrafted rugs, sunglasses, and pottery. Not having a BATNA before negotiating with merchants can result in overpaying for merchandise. If you have no idea how much comparable items would cost in the United States, then you are likely to make a charitable contribution to the Mexican economy when negotiating with a savvy merchant on what you think is a hot deal. Your BATNA in this instance is a comparable item that sells at a slightly higher price in the United States, a similar item of better quality for more money, or a similar item of lesser quality for less money. You know when you've negotiated a real value if you have such a BATNA.

Anger Management

Conflict often produces anger. Anger was a key component of the KILL radio blowup. Anger can easily trigger a tit-for-tat response that disrupts constructive negotiations. As one study concluded, "Negotiators who felt angry engaged in more competitive and less cooperative behavior" (Liu, 2009). Common communication behaviors associated with workplace anger include: yelling, swearing, hurling insults, using sarcasm, criticizing, crying, giving dirty looks, making angry gestures, throwing things, and physical assault (Johnson, 2009). Thus, managing anger is an important aspect of constructive conflict management in groups.

Constructive and Destructive Anger: Intensity and Duration

Anger is sometimes justified (e.g., in cases of injustice). The difference between constructive and destructive anger depends on two conditions: the intensity and the duration of the anger expression (Adler et al., 2021). This pertains to a system's boundary control and remaining within a group's dynamic equilibrium range. The **intensity** of anger can vary from mild irritation to outright rage. The more intense the anger, the more likely it is that outcomes will be negative. Mild to moderate expressions of anger can signal problems that must be addressed in groups. Rage, however, is destructive. It is the antithesis of competent communication because the group member expressing the rage is out of control. Temper tantrums, ranting, and screaming fits make you look like a lunatic because you're "getting stupid." When used as a power-forcing strategy during conflict, it will likely provoke counter-rage that can even provoke physical aggression.

The **duration**, or how long the anger lasts, also determines whether anger is constructive or destructive. The length of an anger episode can vary from momentary to prolonged. Quick flashes of anger may hardly cause group members to notice. Even intense anger, if brief, can underline that you are very upset without causing irreparable damage. Prolonged expressions of anger, however, even if mild, can cause group members to tune out and ignore you. Highly intense anger that is long-lasting is a combustible combination. Venting anger, despite popular notions to the contrary, doesn't typically reduce it. On the contrary, it rehearses the anger and can increase it (Bushman, 2002; Fradera, 2017).

Antonio Guillem/Shutterstock

Anger that is intense and of long duration is destructive.

Learning to manage your own anger and the anger of other group members is a hallmark of *emotional intelligence* (Lopez-Zafra et al., 2008). When groups exhibit maximum emotional intelligence, group performance is enhanced (Hjerto & Paulsen, 2016).

Managing Your Own Anger: Taking Control

There are several steps you can take to diffuse your own anger when you sense that it is approaching the destructive stage of intensity and duration.

1. *Reframe self-talk.* Thoughts trigger anger. If you think a group member meant to hurt you intentionally, you feel righteously angry. If you believe that no harm was intended, then anger usually doesn't ignite. Try assuming group members did not intend to harm you unless there is clear evidence to the contrary. Reframing the way we think about events can deflate our anger before it escalates (Gottman & Gottman, 2006; "The Right Way," 2016).

2. *Listen nondefensively.* When group members criticize, blame, or ridicule you, refuse to be defensive. Reframe the criticism or blame as a challenge or problem, not an opportunity for retaliation. Counter defensive communication from others with supportive communication (Chapter 5).

3. *"Wag more, bark less."* Learn the lesson of one of my favorite bumper stickers. The more "barking" that you do, the more anger you express, the more you increase your anger.

4. *Deliberately calm yourself.* Exercise discipline and refuse to vent your anger. A cooling-off period often works well to calm your anger (Gottman & Gottman, 2006). Typically, it takes about 20 minutes to recover from a surge of adrenaline that accompanies anger (Goleman, 1995).

5. *Find distractions.* Ruminating, focusing your thoughts on what makes you angry, can bring them to a boiling point. Distract yourself when old wounds resurface (Bushman, 2002). Read a newspaper, watch television, play with the dog, or take a walk with someone and discuss subjects unrelated to the anger-inducing subject.

Don't attempt to employ all four of these steps at once. Pick one and work on making it an automatic response when your anger wells up, then try a second step, and so on.

Managing the Anger of Others: Communication Jujitsu

Managing conflict constructively means defusing and de-escalating the anger of group members so you can confront issues without eruptions of verbal or physical aggression. **Try these suggestions for defusing the anger of others** (Lickerman, 2013):

1. *Be asymmetrical.* When a group member is expressing anger, especially if it turns to rage, it is critical that you not strike back in kind. Be **asymmetrical**, which means do the opposite. Counter rage with absolute calm. Stay composed. Hostage negotiators are trained to defuse highly volatile individuals by remaining absolutely calm throughout the interaction. Imagine the outcome if hostage negotiators flew into a rage while talking to hostage takers. Use smoothing techniques to quiet the enraged group member.

2. *Validate the other person* (Fisher & Shapiro, 2005). You can validate another person in several ways. First, you can take responsibility for the other person's anger. "I deserve your anger; I was wrong" acknowledges your role in provoking anger. Second, you can apologize. "I'm sorry; I'll do better" can be a very powerful validation of the other person (Shapiro, 2017). Apologies, of course, should be offered only when truly warranted. Third, actively listening to the other person can also be validating. "I know it upsets you when I don't come to meetings on time" makes the other person feel heard, even if conflict remains.

3. *Probe.* Seek information from an angry group member so you can understand his or her anger (Gottman & Gottman, 2006). When you ask a question of an angry group member, it forces the person to shift from emotional outburst to rational response. Simply asking, "Can we sit down and discuss this calmly so I can understand your point of view?" can momentarily defuse a group member's anger.

4. *Distract.* Shifting the focus of attention when a person is out of control can sometimes short-circuit rage (Rusting & Nolen-Hoeksema, 1998). A humorous quip, an odd question, a request for help, or pointing to an unrelated event can break a rage cycle.

5. *Assume a problem orientation.* This is supportive communication. This step should occur once you have calmed the angry group member by using previous steps. Approach the anger display as a problem to be solved, not a reason to retaliate. The question "What would you like to see occur?" invites problem solving.

6. *Refuse to be abused.* Even if you are wrong, feel guilty, or deserve another person's anger, do not permit yourself to be verbally battered. Verbal aggression is unproductive no matter who is at fault in a conflict. "I can see you're upset, but verbally assaulting me won't lead to a solution" sets a ground rule on how anger can be expressed.

7. *Disengage.* This step is especially important if the person continues to be enraged and abusive despite your best efforts to calm the emotional storm. Firmly state, "This meeting is over. I'm leaving. We'll discuss this another time."

Keeping track of all seven steps to quell the anger of group members, particularly when faced with an enraged person, is too much to expect. Concentrate on one or two steps until they become almost a reflex reaction, a habit. Being asymmetrical is the crucial first step, with validation a close second. The remaining steps can gradually become part of your anger-defusing skill package.

Anger is a common companion of group conflict. The constructive management of conflict can occur only when anger is kept under control. This does not mean squelching anger. A group member can feel angry for good reasons. Anger acts as a signal that changes need to occur. Anger should not be used as a weapon, however, to abuse others. We want to learn ways to cope with and express anger constructively, not be devoured by it.

Virtual Groups and Conflict

As already discussed, not all conflict is counterproductive for groups. Conflict that is competently managed can promote important, positive changes. There are differences, however, between virtual and face-to-face groups in conflict management. Overall, virtual groups experience more task and relationship conflict than face-to-face groups (Petersen, 2014). The Solomon (2016) study found that 82% of respondents considered managing conflict to be more challenging in virtual teams than in face-to-face teams. When conflict arises, face-to-face groups engage in significantly more constructive conflict management than virtual groups.

Trust and cohesiveness are critical to engendering constructive conflict and minimizing or preventing destructive conflict (Tamir, 2020).

Virtual groups are more likely to move in the direction of destructive conflict than are face-to-face groups because of the disinhibition effect—the tendency to say online what you wouldn't normally say in person (Voggeser et al., 2018), and briefly referenced in Chapter 5. "Blowing off steam," especially online (Martin et al., 2013), awakens our anger. It doesn't put it to bed. The anger of a single virtual group member can trigger emotional contagion in a ripple effect across the group (Chesin et al., 2011). A prodigious 84% of respondents in one survey "admitted they become more easily exasperated and enraged at others online than they ever would in person" (Macrae, 2015). Young people were particularly prone to social media rage, with 26% of 18- to 24-year-olds admitting they "are always worked up when using social media," followed by 18% of 35- and 44-year-olds with the same proclivity (Macrae, 2015).

Communication filters that operate in face-to-face communication to short-circuit emotional incontinence are less apparent when communicating electronically. Nonverbal indicators of disapproval, such as a glance, a frown, or an eye roll, are missing from text-only and audio-only group interactions. What you wouldn't say to a member's face you might say in an email or text message. Misunderstandings can be a big problem for virtual teams because perceived slights, insults, or a negative tone in emails may not be quickly cleared up. Members may have to stew over a perceived insult for a day, even a week, if an email response is not accessed right away.

Although this disinhibition effect and emotional contagion are more likely in text-only or audio-only virtual group communication, even in videoconferences with greater access to nonverbal cues, this disinhibition effect can play out negatively to provoke destructive conflict. Skype or Zoom meetings do not create the same feeling of presence of fellow group members that in-person discussions produce. Social cues that can reinforce norms that support appropriate etiquette online are not as apparent (Voggeser et al., 2018). Gestures can be more restrained, and eye rolling or even muttering under one's breath can be muted or indiscernible. Intemperate comments can be added to chat options during videoconferences.

Differences that emerge from virtual group membership representing several diverse cultures can also lead to misunderstandings and perceived insults (Baba et al., 2004; Krawczyk-Brylka, 2017). Misunderstanding emerging from cultural and language differences was identified in one survey as the greatest challenge of working in virtual groups (Economist Intelligence Unit, 2009). Establishing group norms can be difficult in virtual groups when cultural differences create clashes about approaches to addressing conflicts, directness of communication, and respect for high-power group members. Cultural differences are often challenging to address in face-to-face groups, but they can be doubly so when text-only or sometimes even audio-only communication is available. The ambiguity of language discussed in Chapter 1 is not easily recognized or clarified when the communication media limit nonverbal contextual cues that help with understanding messages.

Text-only communication, however, may be appropriate when face-to-face communication among members has a history of being awkward or intimidating. Sometimes we can be more honest and assertive in an email than in person. A group member who is feeling angry may be able to choose words more carefully and edit messages for tone more judiciously when writing an email than when communicating face to face. How often have you replayed a hostile conversation in your mind and wished you hadn't made certain statements or had cushioned negative comments? In some instances, setting aside an angry email response to a perceived insult or slight by another group member and deciding, upon reflection, to delete it entirely is a wise choice. Email allows you to edit intemperate messages, but only by adopting a standard practice of never responding heatedly to an email until you have had time to reflect, simmer down, and edit offensive remarks.

Essentially, virtual group conflict management requires a higher dose of what has already been explained comprehensively throughout this text. In-person initial meetings are critical to establishing cohesiveness and trust among virtual group members (Kahlow et al., 2020). Emphasis must be placed on developing and maintaining a positive, supportive group climate as detailed in Chapter 5. Procedural and behavioral ground rules play an important part in preventing discussions from devolving into destructive conflict. Servant and shared leadership should be the preferred approach for guiding virtual groups toward success. Such leadership should encourage constructive dissent and devil's advocacy. The Standard Agenda provides a structured decision-making and problem-solving process that is highly relevant to virtual groups to prevent relationship conflict while focusing on task accomplishment. Bullying and abuse should be strictly prohibited, especially as a leadership function. Successful virtual groups and teams are less likely to experience conflict, especially destructive versions.

In summary, conflict is a reality of group life. Although most people would prefer that conflict didn't exist, there are both positive and negative aspects to conflict. Constructive management of conflict can turn a dispute into a positive experience for the group. The five primary communication styles of conflict management—collaborating, accommodating, compromising, avoiding, and competing—all have pros and cons, depending on the situation. Nevertheless, collaborating has a higher probability of producing constructive outcomes than does competing. Negotiation is a universal process used to manage conflicts of interests. Principled negotiation is the most productive means of resolving conflicts of interests.

This concludes my discussion of communication competence in small groups. One of the central points that I hope has come through loudly and clearly is that one person can make an enormous difference in the quality of the group experience. What you individually do or don't do may be the difference between a successful and a less-than-successful group. Competent communication begins with you. The We-orientation is the core of group effectiveness. Don't look to others to make groups work. Take the knowledge you've garnered from this textbook and the skills that you will develop as you put this knowledge into practice and focus them on improving the group experience.

QUESTIONS FOR CRITICAL THINKERS

1. If competition has so many disadvantages, why would the competing/forcing style ever be appropriate for a competent communicator?

2. If principled negotiating is so effective, why isn't it used more often?

TED TALKS AND YOUTUBE VIDEOS

"Why There's So Much Conflict at Work and What You Can Do to Fix It" | **Liz Kislik**

"3 Ways to Resolve a Conflict" | **Dorothy Walker**

"The Gift of Conflict" | **Amy E. Gallo**

VIDEO CASE STUDIES

The Insult (2017). *Drama; R*

A personal rift between a Lebanese Christian and a Palestinian refugee explodes into a bitter conflict. Analyze the different types of conflict and how one relates to another. What elements of destructive conflict are exhibited? This film was Oscar nominated for Best Foreign Language Film.

The Social Network (2010). *Biography/Drama; PG-13*

Facebook CEO Mark Zuckerberg's meteoric rise to social networking superstar is presented in this well-made movie. Analyze the communication styles of conflict management used by Zuckerberg and others. What negotiating strategies are used, especially in response to a lawsuit filed against Zuckerberg contesting who came up with the initial idea for Facebook?

The Upside of Anger (2005). *Drama; R*

Compelling story of a woman (Joan Allen) whose husband appears to have walked out on her and his four daughters and the residual anger that wells up inside of her and others as a result. Kevin Costner plays an ex-baseball player turned radio personality who insinuates himself into the family. Examine anger as destructive or constructive. How do characters handle their anger?

What's Cooking? (2000). *Comedy/Drama; PG-13*

This is a portrayal of four separate, yet interrelated families (African American, Vietnamese, Mexican American, and Jewish) trying to celebrate Thanksgiving. Identify the communication styles of conflict management used by the characters. Are conflicts mostly task, relationship, or values? How does culture affect conflict management? In what ways is anger managed? Are these ways effective?

Appendix A
Group Oral Presentations

▶ Groups sometimes have public-speaking responsibilities. In some cases, the group has been formed to present information orally before an audience of interested people. To assist those with little or no training or experience in public speaking, I am including this brief appendix, which covers some of the basics of oral presentation. I discuss types of group oral presentations, speech anxiety, attention strategies, organization, and use of visual aids.

Typical Types of Group Oral Presentations

There are three main types of oral group presentations. They are panel discussions, symposiums, and forums.

Panel Discussions: Free Exchange of Ideas

Panel discussions assemble a small group of participants, usually experts, to engage in a free exchange of information and ideas on a specific issue or problem before an audience. Purposes of a panel discussion include solving a difficult problem, informing an audience on an issue or topic of interest, or stimulating audience members to think about the pros and cons of a controversial issue.

Panel discussions require a moderator. The moderator usually organizes the group presentation by soliciting panel members who represent different points of view on the topic or issue. Panel members should be informed in advance of the topic to be discussed and major issues that should be addressed by panelists. The moderator should follow several steps to make the panel discussion successful.

1. Suitable physical arrangements for the panel discussion should be organized in advance. Usually, the number of panelists should be no fewer than three and no more than seven. Panelists should be seated at a long table in front of the audience, normally on a stage overlooking audience members. When group discussions involve more than four or five participants, seating panelists at two tables formed in a slight

V-shape to the audience helps panelists address each other during discussions without closing off the audience. Name cards placed on the table in front of each speaker will help the audience become familiar with each panelist. If the room where the panel discussion takes place is relatively large, a microphone at the table should be available for each speaker. If panelists request a DVD player and monitor, computer hookup, Smartboard, easel, whiteboard, or other means of presenting visual aids, provide these if possible and place them in a location where access to them is easy and will not block the audience's view.

2. The moderator usually begins by welcoming the audience, providing a brief background on the topic or issue to be discussed, and introducing each panel member, citing specific background and qualifications of each speaker.

3. Panelists should be encouraged to bring notes but discouraged from reading a prepared manuscript.

4. Begin the discussion with a question posed to the panel (e.g., "What is the extent of the problem of binge drinking on college campuses?"). The opening question can be posed to the entire panel, or a specific panelist can be asked to begin the discussion. The moderator identifies who has the floor during the discussion.

5. The moderator acts as a discussion guide. If a panelist has been left out of the discussion, the moderator may direct a question to him or her. If a panelist begins to dominate discussion, the moderator should step in and request participation from other panelists. Controversy should be encouraged, but polite conversation should be the norm. It is the responsibility of the moderator to keep the conversation civil. If it begins to turn ugly, the moderator should remind panelists to disagree without being disagreeable. Move the discussion along so that all major issues are discussed in the allotted time (usually about 45 minutes to an hour).

6. The moderator closes discussion by summarizing main points made by panelists and identifying new issues raised during the discussion to be further explored.

Symposiums: Structured Group Presentations

A **symposium** is a relatively structured group presentation to an audience. It is composed of several individuals who present uninterrupted speeches with contrasting points of view on a central topic. Unlike a panel discussion, speakers do not engage in a discussion with each other. Each speaker presents a relatively short speech (usually four to six minutes apiece) addressing a separate segment of the overall topic. The primary purpose of a symposium is to enlighten an audience on a controversial issue or to inform audience members on a subject of interest.

A symposium also benefits from having a moderator. The moderator should follow a few important steps to ensure a successful symposium.

1. Physical arrangements made for a panel discussion, just discussed, should also be used for a symposium.
2. To avoid redundancy, speakers should be chosen who represent different points of view.
3. The moderator should provide a brief background on the subject, introduce the speakers, and identify the speakers' order of presentation.

Forum Discussion: Audience Participation

A **forum discussion** allows members of an audience listening to a public speech, panel discussion, symposium, or debate to participate in a discussion of ideas presented. The primary purpose of a forum is to engage the audience in the discussion of issues raised. The moderator's role is critical to the success of a forum discussion. Some suggestions for the moderator who directs the forum include:

1. Announce to the audience that an open forum will occur after a panel discussion or symposium has concluded. Audience members can prepare questions or short remarks as they listen to speakers.
2. Rules for forum participation should be clearly articulated before any discussion occurs. Rules may include: raise your hand to be recognized or stand in a line where a microphone has been placed and wait your turn; keep remarks and questions very brief (about 15 to 30 seconds); each person should ask only one follow-up question.
3. Set a time limit for the forum (usually about 30 minutes). Indicate when there is time for only one or two more questions. Accept questions until the deadline has been reached, then conclude the forum by thanking the audience for its participation.
4. Encourage diverse points of view from the audience. A pro and con line might be established. The moderator could move back and forth, recognizing audience members on both sides so a balanced series of questions and comments will be presented.

5. If a question cannot be heard by all members of the audience, the moderator should repeat the question. If a question is confusing, the moderator may ask for a restatement or try to paraphrase the question so panelists or forum speakers can answer.

Speech Anxiety

Mark Twain once remarked, "There are two types of speakers: those who are nervous and those who are liars." Overstated perhaps, but fear of public speaking is widespread (Pull, 2012). A survey by Chapman University of 1,500 respondents puts the fear factor at 62% ("The Chapman University Study," 2015). This same study also showed fear of public speaking as greater than fear of heights (61%), drowning (47%), flying (39%), and, yes, zombies (18%). The fear of public speaking holds true for both face-to-face and web-based "online" speeches given to remote audiences (Campbell & Larson, 2012).

You can "cure" speech anxiety with heavy doses of tranquilizers, but, aside from the physiological dangers associated with them (they're potentially addictive), they will make you appear witless in front of an audience because they deaden mental acuity. So, if you're concerned about appearing lobotomized in front of groups, avoid using drugs as a cure for anxiety.

Speech anxiety, however, is not necessarily a demon to be exorcised. The degree of anxiety, not the anxiety itself, requires attention. A moderate amount of anxiety can enhance performance and energize a speaker. You can present a more dynamic, forceful presentation when energized than when you feel so comfortable that you become almost listless and unchallenged by the speaking experience.

When the intensity of your fear about speaking in front of people gets out of control, however, it becomes debilitative and detracts from your performance. Intense anxiety can be cause for real concern if ignored. It will congest your thought pathways, thereby clogging your free flow of ideas. In such a condition, every speaker's nightmare—going blank—will likely occur. Also, a terror-stricken speaker feels an urge to escape. Consequently, a seven-minute speech is compressed into three minutes by a staccato, hyper-drive delivery. The quicker the speech presentation, the quicker the escape.

The causes of speech anxiety are complex and varied. Space does not permit a thorough discussion of these causes. Generally speaking, the causes of speech anxiety are self-defeating thoughts and situational factors.

Self-defeating thoughts include negative thoughts that predict failure, desire for complete approval from an audience, and an awareness that audience members will evaluate your speaking performance. Negative thoughts about your speaking performance can wildly exaggerate potential problems and thus stoke the furnace of anxiety. Those harboring negative thoughts predict not just momentary lapses of memory, but a complete meltdown of mental functions ("I know I'll forget my entire speech, and I'll just stand there like an idiot"). Minor problems of organization are magnified into graphic episodes of total incoherence and nonstop babbling. Perfectionists also anguish over every flaw in their speech and overgeneralize the significance of even minor defects. A flawless public-speaking performance is a desirable goal, but why beat up on yourself when it doesn't happen? Perfectionists make self-defeating statements to themselves such as "I'm such a fool. I mispronounced the name of one of the experts I quoted" and "I must have said 'um' at least a dozen times. I sounded like a moron." Ironically, the imperfections so glaringly noticeable to perfectionists usually go unnoticed by most people in the audience. This overestimation of the extent to which audience members detect a speaker's nervousness is called the **illusion of transparency** (MacInnis et al., 2010). Even the most talented and experienced public speakers make occasional errors that go unnoticed in otherwise riveting performances.

Another self-defeating thought that triggers speech anxiety is the desire for complete approval from your audience, especially from those whose opinion we value. It is irrational thinking, however, to accept nothing less than complete approval from an audience. You cannot please everyone, especially if you take a stand on a controversial issue. When you set standards for success at unreachable heights, you are bound to take a tumble.

The fact that an audience evaluates you every time you give a speech, even if no one is formally grading your performance, will usually trigger some anxiety. Human beings are social creatures who dislike, even fear, disapproval from others. Even if you aren't seeking complete approval or adulation from your listeners, you would be a rare individual if you were completely immune to the judgments of others hearing you speak. Public speaking becomes doubly intense when formal grades are given for each speech performance.

There are many situational causes of speech anxiety. Two prominent ones are novel situations and conspicuousness. Novel situations—ones that are new to you—create uncertainty, and uncertainty can easily make you tense. For most students, public speaking is a novel situation. Few students have given many speeches in their lifetime, and some have never given a formal public address. Fortunately, as you gain experience speaking in front of audiences, the novelty wears off and your anxiety will diminish.

The conspicuousness of the public-speaking situation increases most people's anxiety. Most students tell me that speaking to one or two persons is usually not very difficult, but speaking in front of an entire class or an auditorium filled with a thousand people really makes them want to toss their lunch. Here the interaction of conspicuousness and approval can be easily seen. Standing alone before a few people and possibly failing is not nearly as big a deal as possibly failing in front of a huge crowd. In the former situation, your potential failure would likely remain an isolated event, but in the latter situation the entire school might be in on your humiliation—so goes the logic.

So how do you manage your speech anxiety, given the variety of causes that induce it? Numerous individuals have suggested to me that picturing your audience nude, or clothed only in underwear or in diapers, can be helpful (assuming you can stifle your laughter when the image pops into your mind). Breathing deeply is also a favorite tidbit of wisdom offered by many as a quick-fix coping strategy for stage fright. These remedies have some merit, especially if they work for you. None of them, however, offers a reliable solution to speech anxiety. There are many more effective methods.

First, there is no substitute for adequate preparation. Conducting proper research on your speech topic, organizing your speech clearly and carefully, and practicing it several times are all essential if you hope to manage your anxiety effectively. Adequate preparation also must include physiological preparation, such as ensuring proper nutrition just prior to the speech event. Ignoring your physiological preparation for a speech may cancel out the benefits of other methods used to manage your speech anxiety. Consequently, do not deliver a speech on an empty stomach, but also do not fill your stomach with empty calories. You need high-quality fuel such as complex carbohydrates to sustain you while you're speaking. Simple sugars (doughnuts, Twinkies), caffeine (coffee, colas, chocolate), and nicotine (cigarettes) should be avoided or ingested in very small quantities. Adequate preparation will reduce uncertainty and the fear of failure.

Second, gain perspective on your speech situation. Consider the difference between rational and irrational speech anxiety. A colleague of mine, Darrell Beck, worked out a simple formula for determining the difference between the two. The severity of the feared occurrence times the probability of the feared occurrence provides a rough approximation of how much anxiety is rational and when you have crossed the line into irrational anxiety. Severity is approximated by imagining what would happen to you if your worst fears came true—you bombed the speech. Would you leave the state? Would you drop out of school? Probably not, since even dreadful speaking performances do not warrant such drastic steps. You might consider dropping the class, but even this is unlikely since fellow students are very understanding when a classmate delivers a poor speech. So even a poor speech does not rationally warrant joining the monastic life or making any significant life changes. The probability that your worst nightmare will come true and you will give a horrible speech, however, is extremely unlikely if you have adequately prepared. Thus, working yourself into a lather over an impending speech lacks proper perspective if you follow the advice given here.

Third, refocus your attention on your message and your audience and away from yourself (Motley, 1995). You cannot concentrate on two things at the same time. If you dwell on your nervousness, you will be distracted from presenting your message effectively. Focus on presenting your message clearly and enthusiastically. View the speaking experience as a challenge to keep your audience interested, maybe even an opportunity to change their minds on an issue.

Fourth, make coping statements to yourself as you give your speech, especially when you momentarily stumble. When inexperienced speakers make mistakes during a speech, they tend to make negative statements to themselves. You forget a point, momentarily lose your train of thought, or stammer. Immediately, the tendency is for you to say to yourself "I knew I would mess up this speech" or "I told everybody I couldn't give a decent speech." Instead, try making coping statements while you're delivering the speech. When problems arise say "I can do better" or "I'm getting to the good part of my speech." Talk to yourself during your speech in positive ways to counteract self-talk that defeats you. When parts of your speech go well, compliment yourself on a job well done (to yourself, of course, not out loud). This sustains and energizes you as you proceed through the speech.

Gaining and Maintaining Attention

Audience interest doesn't just happen magically. Interest is garnered by carefully planning and utilizing strategies of attention. Although gaining and maintaining attention throughout your speech is an important goal for any speaker, attention strategies should enhance a speech, not detract from it. A disorganized speech gains attention but in a negative way. Frequent verbal and vocal fillers such as "you know," "um," and "ah" draw attention to inarticulateness.

Some attributes of stimuli, by their very nature, attract attention. Consider just a few of these attributes and how they can become attention strategies.

First, intensity is a concentrated stimulus that draws attention. Intensity is an extreme degree of emotion, thought, or activity. Relating a story of a woman fleeing for her life from a stalker can be intense, especially for those who fear such an occurrence. Don't be too graphic when describing emotionally charged events, however, or you may offend and alienate your audience.

There are several basic stylistic techniques that promote intensity and rivet an audience's attention. Direct, penetrating eye contact is a useful technique. How does a daydreamer continue to ignore you when you are zeroing in on the daydreamer? The lack of eye contact so typical of manuscript speeches, in which every word of your speech is written on the paper in front of you, underlines the importance of not reading a speech to an audience because you break connection with your listeners. Direct eye contact is an attention builder, but lack of eye contact is an attention destroyer.

Variation in vocal volume is a second technique for provoking intensity. A raised voice can be quite intense. It punctuates portions of your speech much as an exclamation point punctuates a written sentence. The use of a raised voice, however, can be a rather shattering experience for an audience. Incessant, unrelenting, bombastic delivery of a message irritates and alienates an audience. Punctuate with a raised voice only those points that are especially significant and deserve closer attention lest your speech sounds like a rant.

Silence can also be intense. A pregnant pause—silence held a bit longer than usual if you were merely taking a breath—interjects drama into your speech and spotlights significant points.

A second stimulus attribute that induces attention is being startling. You try to stun, surprise, and shake up your audience. A startling statement, fact, or statistic can do this quite effectively. Startling statements such as "Climate change clearly has the potential to decimate the human population," "Calories can kill you," and "You may be living next door to a terrorist" can make an audience sit up and take notice. That it costs more to feed and house a criminal in prison than it does to send him or her to the most expensive university in the country is a startling fact. Of course, you do not want to startle your audience if you can't support your claims with evidence.

Every startling stimulus does not produce constructive attention from an audience. Speakers can startle and offend at the same time. A few examples from my own experience and those of my colleagues make this point. One student (during a speech on food poisoning) gained attention by vomiting scrambled eggs into his handkerchief, raising serious doubts about the speaker's good taste. Another student punched himself so hard in the face that he was momentarily staggered (the speech was on violence in America). These examples have one thing in common: The speakers startled their audience but lost credibility in the process. Tasteless jokes, ethnic slurs, and offensive language will also startle an audience and gain attention, but at a substantial cost to the speaker. The general rule applies—attention strategies should be appropriate and enhance the effectiveness of your speech, not detract from it.

Making a problem or issue appear **vital** to an audience is a third attention strategy. There are two principal ways to do this. First, the problem must be made vital not in some abstract or general sense, but in a specific, immediate, and meaningful sense. An audience's primary question when told that a problem exists is "How does it affect me?" The problem becomes vital and therefore meaningful when listeners can see how the consequences of inaction directly affect their interests and well-being. "One out of every ten women in this audience will contract breast cancer, and a similar number of men listening to me will contract prostate cancer. Those of you who escape the disease will likely know one or more friends or relatives who will die from these forms of cancer" is an example of how to personalize a problem and make it seem vital to an audience. Be careful, however, not to overstate your case by depicting relatively trivial concerns as vital. For an issue to be accepted as vital, it must have the ring of truth. Credible evidence must substantiate your claim that the problem is vital.

Using **novelty** is a fourth attention strategy. Audiences are naturally drawn to the new and different. Unusual examples, clever quotations, and uncommon stories attract attention because they are new and different. Beginning your speech with a novel introduction is especially important. Do not begin by telling the audience what your topic is. That is very unoriginal and boring. Create interest in your topic with a novel opening—an unusual news event, story, or human interest example related to your subject. For instance, notice how the following introduction using a real "news of the weird" item grabs attention by using novelty:

> Acting as his own attorney, an Oklahoma City robbery suspect became agitated when a witness identified him in court as the guilty party. "I should have blown your head off," he screamed, adding on quick reflection, "if I'd been the one that was there." The verdict? Guilty. Lesson to be learned? Acting as your own attorney is a foolish idea.

Novelty can be a very effective attention strategy, especially for the introduction to your speech, but also throughout your presentation.

Finally, using **humor** is a superior attention strategy if used adroitly. You should be able to incorporate humorous anecdotes, quotations, and personal stories throughout your speech. There are several important guidelines, however, for using humor effectively as an attention strategy. First, don't force humor. If you aren't a particularly funny person and have never told a joke without omitting crucial details or flubbing the punch line, then don't try to be a comedian in front of your audience. Humorous quotations, funny stories, and amusing occurrences can be used without setting them up as jokes. Simply offer them as illustrations of key points, and, if the audience members are amused, they will laugh.

Second, use only relevant humor. Unrelated stories and jokes may be suitable for a comic whose principal purpose is to make an audience laugh, but a formal speech requires you to make important points. Your use of humor needs to make a relevant contribution to the advancement of the speech's purpose.

Third, use good taste. Coarse vulgarities, obscenities, and sick jokes invite anger and hostility. Humor that rests on stereotypes and put-downs may alienate vast sections of your audience. Sexist, racist, and homophobic jokes that denigrate groups exhibit bad taste and poor judgment.

Fourth, don't overuse humor. Don't become enamored with your own wittiness. Telling joke after joke or telling one amusing story after another will likely produce laughter, but the audience will also be dissatisfied if you substitute humor for substance.

Humor can be risky but very satisfying when it works. Using humor is probably the most effective attention strategy when used appropriately and skillfully.

Organizing and Outlining

Presenting a well-organized speech is critical to your success as a speaker. This section, by necessity, will be a cursory treatment of organization and outlining.

Perhaps the easiest way of developing the organization of your speech is to think of your speech as an inverted pyramid. The base of your upside-down pyramid represents the most general part of your speech, namely, the topic. Moving down toward the tip of the pyramid, you fill in the purpose statement, then the main points that flow from the purpose statement, then elaborate on each main point with subpoints and sub-subpoints, and so forth. You begin with the abstract and work toward the concrete and specific.

Let's say that your group has chosen for its symposium topic the problem of violence in America. First, your group must divide this general topic into manageable subtopics so each group member will have about a four- to six-minute speech. Subtopics might include violence on television, violence in the movies, guns and violence, gang violence, social and economic causes of violence, and potential solutions to violence (which could be divided even further into specific proposals such as "three strikes and you're out," outlawing handguns, prison reform, and social programs). Each group member would then be given his or her subtopic.

Once you have your subtopic for the symposium, each group member must construct a specific purpose statement. A **purpose statement** is a concise, precise, declarative statement phrased in simple, clear language that provides both the general purpose (to inform or to persuade) and the specific purpose (exactly what you want the audience to understand, believe, feel, or do). A purpose statement ordinarily considers the interests and knowledge level of a particular audience. Your group presentation should always be mindful of audience interest, depth of understanding, and experience of audience members.

> TOPIC: Guns and violence
> PURPOSE STATEMENT: To inform you that handgun violence is a serious problem in America.

Your purpose statement becomes the blueprint for your entire speech. You determine your main points from your purpose statement.

> MAIN POINT I: Death from handguns is a serious problem.
> MAIN POINT II: Serious injury from handguns also poses a serious problem for America.

Each main point is then divided into subpoints, sub-subpoints, and so on.

> MAIN POINT I: Death from handguns is a serious problem.
> SUBPOINT A: There are more than 16,000 murders from handguns every year in America; Japan has fewer than 100.
> SUBPOINT B: More than 1,400 American youths between the ages of 10 and 19 commit suicide or attempt suicide with resulting injuries with a handgun each year.

Each subpoint is then broken down further with more detail, examples, and supporting evidence.

> SUBPOINT A: There are more than 16,000 murders from handguns every year in America; Japan has fewer than 100.

SUB-SUBPOINT 1: Teenage homicide from handguns has almost doubled in the last decade to more than 5,000 annually.

SUB-SUBPOINT 2: The teenage handgun death rate now exceeds the mortality rate for young people from all natural causes combined.

SUB-SUBPOINT 3: Three times more American young men are killed by handguns every 100 hours than were killed during the 100-hour Persian Gulf War.

SUB-SUBPOINT 4: Provide examples of teenagers gunned down in street violence.

SUBPOINT B: More than 1,400 American youths between the ages of 10 and 19 commit suicide or attempt suicide with resulting injuries with a handgun each year.

SUB-SUBPOINT 1: Nearly two-thirds of suicides are from handguns.

SUB-SUBPOINT 2: Handguns put at risk large numbers of young people who consider suicide.

SUB-SUB-SUBPOINT a: More than one in four high school students seriously contemplate suicide.

SUB-SUB-SUBPOINT b: Sixteen percent of high-schoolers make a specific plan to commit suicide, and half of these actually try to kill themselves.

SUB-SUB-SUBPOINT c: Ready availability of handguns makes teen suicide more likely.

SUB-SUB-SUBPOINT d: Tell the story of 14-year-old Paul Hoffman.

The resulting outline for your first main point would look as follows:

PURPOSE STATEMENT: To inform you that handgun violence is a serious problem in America.

I. Death from handguns is a serious problem.

   A. There are more than 16,000 murders from handguns every year in America; Japan has fewer than 100.

      1. Teenage homicide from handguns has almost doubled in the last decade to more than 5,000 annually.

      2. The teenage handgun death rate now exceeds the mortality rate for young people from all natural causes combined.

   3. Three times more American young men are killed by hand-guns in 100 hours than were killed during the 100-hour Persian Gulf War.
   4. Provide examples of specific teenagers gunned down in street violence.
B. More than 1,400 American youths between the ages of 10 and 19 commit suicide or attempt suicide with resulting injuries with a handgun each year.
   1. Nearly two-thirds of suicides are from handguns.
   2. Handguns put at risk large numbers of young people who consider suicide.
      a. More than one in four high school students seriously contemplate suicide.
      b. Sixteen percent of high-schoolers make a specific plan to commit suicide, and half of these actually try to kill themselves.
      c. Ready availability of handguns makes teen suicide more likely.
      d. Tell the story of 14-year-old Paul Hoffman.

You follow the same procedure for outlining your second main point. Note that every subpoint must relate specifically to the main point and likewise every sub-subpoint must relate specifically to the subpoint above it.

The form used in the sample outline follows a standard set of symbols composed of Roman numerals, capital letters, and Arabic numbers. Indent all subdivisions of a more general point. This will help you follow the development of your points as you speak. Every point that is subdivided has at least two subpoints.

Preparing the body of your speech is your most difficult and primary organizational task. The introduction, however, creates the all-important first impression with an audience. Your introduction should satisfy the following objectives, usually in this order:

1. Gain the attention of the audience.
2. Provide your purpose statement.
3. Relate the topic and purpose statement to the needs and interests of the audience (answering the question "Why should the audience care about your topic and purpose?").
4. Preview the main points of your speech (state them exactly as they appear in your outline).

The conclusion of your speech should strive to accomplish two objectives:

1. Wrap up the speech with a brief summary of your main points.
2. End the speech with an effective attention strategy that brings closure to the speech.

Once you have prepared your speech outline composed of your introduction, body, and conclusion, practice your speech several times. Speaking from an outline instead of a written manuscript is called the **extemporaneous style of speaking** (**extemp**, for short). When you have prepared your full-sentence outline as already explained, you may want to condense full sentences into terse words or phrases for your actual speaking outline. Under pressure of performing before an audience, it is usually easier to speak extemporaneously when you do not have to read whole sentences. Glancing at a few words or a phrase to remind you of a point allows you to maintain strong eye contact with your listeners without losing your train of thought.

Finally, as you present your speech, signpost your primary points. **Signposts** indicate exactly where you are in your speech so the audience can follow along easily. Restating your main points as you get to each one is an example of signposting. If you had "three causes of gun violence in America," you would signpost each one as you addressed them in turn, such as "the first cause of gun violence is poverty," "the second cause of gun violence is the ready availability of guns," and "the third cause of gun violence is the breakdown of the criminal justice system." In this way, signposting underscores your important points as you present your speech.

Using Visual Aids

Visual aids can add interest, clarify complex material, make points memorable, and enhance the credibility of the speaker. There are many types of visual aids, and with the advent of computer graphics and technologies still being developed, the possibilities are almost limitless. For inexperienced speakers, however, it is best to keep visual aids simple. Photographs, diagrams, charts, graphs, physical models, video clips, and PowerPoint slides are the standard types of visual aids.

Poorly designed and clumsily used visual aids will detract from your speech. The following guidelines will assist you in preparing and displaying visual aids effectively:

1. *Keep visual aids simple.* Visual aids that work well in books, magazines, or newspapers rarely work well in a speech. In printed material a visual aid can be studied carefully. A complicated visual aid used in a speech will distract audience members from listening to the speaker while they try to figure out the complex graph, chart, or diagram.

2. *Visual aids should be large enough to be seen easily.* The general rule of thumb here is that a person in the back of the room should be able to see the visual aid easily.

3. *Visual aids should be neat and attractive.* Sloppy, hastily constructed visual aids are worse than no visual aids at all. Long lists of bulleted points on PowerPoint slides are boring. Remember, PowerPoint slides are supposed to be *visual* aids. Make slides visually attractive and attention getting.

4. *Display the visual aid where all members of the audience can see it easily.* Audience members should not have to stand up or elongate their necks to see the visual aid. A PowerPoint presentation shown on a small computer screen instead of projected on a large screen is inadequate in almost all group presentations.

5. *Practice with the visual aids.* Remember Murphy's law—whatever can go wrong likely will go wrong. Make certain that any equipment used is in proper working order. Do not attempt to use electronic technology without practicing with it first.

6. *Talk to the audience, not the visual aid.* Don't turn your back on your audience while explaining your visual aid (a common practice even by professional speakers when referring to projected PowerPoint images). Stand facing your audience, point the toes of your feet straight ahead, and imagine that your feet have been nailed to the floor. Stand beside the visual aid when referring to it and use your finger or a laser pointer to guide the audience.

7. *Keep the visual aid out of sight when it is not in use.* Audience members may be distracted by the visual aid when you are talking about an unrelated point. I once had a symposium group, whose topic was surfing, play a surfing movie during all members' speeches. Not surprisingly, the audience was far more attentive to the wave riders than the speakers. When showing a series of PowerPoint slides, insert blank slides in places where you won't be referring to a slide for some time.

8. *Do not circulate a visual aid among the audience members.* Passing around pictures or other visual aids while you're still speaking will distract listeners.

Appendix B
Critical Thinking Revisited: Arguments and Fallacies

▶ Chapters 9 and 10 have already delved substantially into the process of critical thinking in small group decision making and problem solving. Group members must be able to recognize and deal effectively with problems of information overload and underload, confirmation bias, false dichotomies, collective inferential error, group polarization, and groupthink. In addition, critical thinking is involved in every step of the Standard Agenda, especially when information is gathered and evaluated, criteria for decision making are developed and applied, and final decisions are made by the group.

This bonus appendix is included because in classrooms in some parts of the country, heavier emphasis is placed on reasoning and use of evidence in the small group context than is true of other parts of the country. This appendix is divided into two segments: the structure of arguments and types of fallacies.

The Structure of Arguments

An argument or "train of reasoning" is composed of several constituent parts (Toulmin et al., 1979). These parts are: the **claim**—that which is asserted and remains to be proven; **data**—the grounds (support/evidence) for the claim, such as statistical evidence, expert testimony, documents, objects, exhibits, conclusions from test results, verifiable facts, and conclusions previously established; **warrant**—the reasoning used to link the data to the claim, usually assumed (implied), not stated directly; **backing**—additional evidence and reasoning used to support the inference made in the warrant; **rebuttal**—exceptions or refutation that diminish the force of the claim; and **qualifier**—degree of truth of the claim (e.g., highly probable, plausible, possible).

Consider the following example of all six parts of an argument:

Claim:	Jim Davis should be given antibiotics.
Data:	Davis suffered severe cuts and injuries on his arms and legs in an auto accident.
Warrant:	There is a risk of infection in such injuries.
Backing:	Hospital reports and numerous studies indicate that risk of infection is serious and that antibiotics can prevent infection from occurring.

Rebuttal:	Overuse of antibiotics can produce superbugs. Antibiotics should be used only when absolutely necessary, or they will eventually be useless to fight disease.
Qualifier:	"Probable." This is a strong claim based on solid evidence and reasoning.

Fallacies

Understanding fallacies will help you determine the validity of your claim, the strength of your data, and the solidity of your warrant and backing. **Fallacies** are errors in the use of supporting materials, the process of reasoning, or resting claims on emotional appeals instead of logic and evidence. The following list of fallacies is not exhaustive. I have chosen only those specific fallacies that seem to occur frequently and that students are likely to encounter almost daily. I am dividing this list of fallacies into three types: **material fallacies**—errors in the process of using supporting materials as proof; **logical fallacies**—errors in the process of reasoning; and **psychological fallacies**—claims that rest on emotional appeal rather than logic and evidence.

Material Fallacies: Misuse of Statistics

There are two primary material fallacies: misuse of statistics and misuse of authority. Misuse of statistics fallacies are numerous. I cover five common ones.

Manufactured or Questionable Statistics: Making Them Up This fallacy consists of statistics that have been fabricated, or statistics whose validity is highly questionable because there is no reasonable method for compiling such statistics, or that which is quantified is too trivial to warrant the time, effort, and resources necessary to compile accurate statistics. Every year the claim is made during the Academy Awards that the presentation of Oscars is viewed by 1 billion people worldwide. Considering that only 23.6 million viewers in the United States watched it in 2020, according to Nielsen ratings surveys, and that the Academy Awards is of greater interest to Americans than to other countries because most movies nominated for Oscars are American made, and further considering that the program is aired in English, which is not the language of most other countries, the 1 billion viewers claim is almost certainly a preposterously inflated statistic of pure fabrication. *The Hollywood Reporter*, which compiles data and estimates for key market viewership, puts the likely worldwide total at 65 million (Szalai & Roxborough, 2016). The Oscars popularity has fallen since this estimate.

Irrelevant Statistic: Does Not Apply These are statistics that do not directly prove the implied or stated claim, yet they are offered as evidence supporting the claim. For example, "The United States spends a trillion dollars a year on health care, more than any other nation. Clearly, our health care system is the world's best." The amount of money spent doesn't prove money was spent wisely, efficiently, or effectively.

Sample Size Inadequate or Unspecified: Not Nearly Enough This fallacy occurs when the sample size is very small, resulting in a margin of error in excess of plus or minus 3%, or when you are left guessing what the sample size might have been. For example, "80% of those surveyed support the cable TV legislation." How many were surveyed? Ten people, eight of whom favored the legislation?

Self-Selected Sample: Not Exactly Random Call-in polls by local television stations, and surveys or questionnaires printed in magazines asking readers to respond, are examples. Those who are angry or have a vested interest in the outcome are most likely to participate. The "Drudge Report," a conservative blog, conducted an online reader poll in 2014. Results showed that 209,381 (73%) of the self-selected respondents wanted President Obama impeached (Jackson, 2014). A CNN poll of randomly selected subjects, however, showed that only 35% favored impeachment, almost the identical amount in past surveys that favored impeachment of George W. Bush and Bill Clinton (Blumer, 2014).

Dated Statistics: Lack of Currency Statistics should be as up to date as possible, especially if the event, phenomenon, or situation is volatile and likely to change quickly (e.g., number of unemployed, long-term interest rates on mortgages, murder rates in various cities, international monetary exchange rates). Some phenomena change very slowly, if at all, over time (e.g., percentage of U.S. population who call themselves Catholics, Protestants, and other denominations). They require less attention to the recency of statistics. "According to the Department of Housing and Urban Development in a 2015 report to Congress, the median price of a new home in the United States is $120,000" is a statistic that hardly qualifies as current in today's volatile housing market.

Material Fallacies: Misuse of Authority

Testimony of experts and authorities is useful as supporting material for claims because experts draw on a larger data and knowledge base than do nonexperts. Experts are not always correct, but they are more reliable than someone who is uninformed or only marginally knowledgeable, especially about a highly technical subject (Nichols, 2017).

Incomplete Citation: Reference Is Neither Specific Nor Complete Minimum requirements for a complete citation include the qualifications of the authority (if not obvious), place of publication, and date of reference. For example, "The President's Commission on Mental Health, in its January report of this year entitled 'Mental Health, Mental Illness,' concludes, 'The biggest stigma in America is the mental illness label.'" "Research indicates" (unless offered by an expert interpreting the latest results in his or her field), "studies show," "some people say," and the like are incomplete or nonexistent citations.

Biased Source: Ax Grinders Special-interest groups or individuals who stand to gain money, prestige, power, or influence simply by taking a certain position on an issue, or crusaders for a cause, are all biased even though they may have expertise. An example is quoting R. J. Reynolds Tobacco Company on the safety of cigarette smoking or vaping. Pharmaceutical companies regularly, and tediously, advertise the efficacy of their latest drugs.

Authority Quoted Out of His or Her Field: Expertise Is Not Generic Quote experts in their area of specialization. "Professor of Biology, Dr. Ernhard Bousterhaus, claims that electric cars are impractical and will remain so for at least the next 50 years" is quoting an expert in one field that has little to do with the claim regarding electric cars.

Logical Fallacies: Reasoning Gone Awry

Reasoning is the basis of warrants for arguments. Sometimes our logic is faulty.

Hasty Generalization: Overgeneralizing Drawing conclusions (generalizations) from too few or atypical examples is called a hasty generalization. Testimonials exalting cancer cures, faith healings, and so on are generalizations based on too few and probably atypical experiences of individuals. Audience members at a talk show generalizing from their individual experiences is another example.

False Analogy: Bogus Comparison A false analogy occurs when two items, events, or phenomena with superficial similarities are viewed as identical, even when a significant point or points of difference exist between the two things compared. "In Turkey, farmers grow poppies (source of heroin) as a cash crop. In the United States, farmers grow corn and soybeans for cash crops. Why outlaw poppies when we don't outlaw corn and soybeans?" This is a false analogy because the poppy crop is not a critical food source capable of feeding the hungry of the world, but corn and soybeans are. Also, poppies are grown as a source of drugs. Although corn can be made into alcohol, that is not its primary purpose.

Correlation Mistaken for Causation: Covariation Fallacy When two phenomena vary at the same time, a causal linkage is often incorrectly asserted. "I ate a lot of chocolate this week, and now my face has acne. I guess I'll have to stop eating chocolate so I can get rid of these blasted pimples." This is an example of correlation incorrectly asserted as causation.

Single Cause: Complexity Oversimplified Attributing only one cause to a complex phenomenon with many causes is a single-cause fallacy. "Poor communication is the reason for the alarming increase in the divorce rate" is an example. Poor communication is probably a cause of some divorces, but not necessarily the most important or the only cause.

Psychological Fallacies: Emotion Disguised as Logic

Pretending that an emotional attack is logical steps into fallacious territory. Consider two primary examples: ad hominem and ad populum.

Ad Hominem: Personal Attack Attacking the messenger to divert attention away from the message is an ad hominem fallacy. Not all attacks on a person's credibility, character, and qualifications, however, are fallacious. If character or credibility is the real issue, then it is relevant argumentation.

"Why are you always on my back for not studying? Last semester your GPA fell nearly a full point" is an ad hominem fallacy.

Ad Populum: Popular Opinion A claim based on popular opinion rather than reasoning and evidence is an ad populum fallacy. "Go ahead and smoke marijuana. More than a third of all college students do" is an example.

Glossary

▶ A glossary of terms does not substitute for clear understanding of the concepts represented. You can memorize a definition without knowing what it means. Clear understanding requires a context for the terms. By reading the following terms in the context of this book, you will see the interconnections between and among the terms. All terms included in the glossary appear in **boldfaced** type in the body of the text (see the index for location).

Accommodating style of conflict management Yields to the concerns and desires of others.

Activities groups Groups that engage in specific activities such as chess teams and sports teams.

Adaptability to change The adjustment of group boundaries in response to changing environmental conditions.

Ad populum fallacy Basing a claim on popular opinion alone.

Aggregation A collection of individuals who do not interact with each other or influence each other to achieve common goals.

Aggression Any physical or verbal behavior intended to hurt or destroy a person.

Allen Curve Decreasing the distance between workers in offices to 6 meters massively increases communication among workers and also increases a sense of belonging to the group.

Alliances Associations in the form of subgroups entered into for mutual benefit or achievement of a common objective.

Ambushing Biased listening in which the listener focuses on attacking a speaker's points instead of striving to comprehend them.

Analysis paralysis Bogging down decision making by analyzing a problem too extensively.

Appropriateness Complying with contextual rules and their accompanying expectations.

Artistic groups Groups that form to perform artistic endeavors such as choirs, bands, and quilting.

Assertiveness "The ability to communicate the full range of your thoughts and emotions with confidence and skill."

Asymmetry Behaving opposite to how others behave, especially when others are angry or enraged.

Asynchronous media Those forms of communicating that permit anytime/anyplace interaction among group members without interruption.

Autocratic leadership style A style of leadership that exerts control over group members; highly directive.

Autonomy (and empowerment) The degree to which team members experience substantial freedom, independence, and discretion in their work.

Avoiding style of conflict management Group member withdraws from potentially contentious and unpleasant struggles.

Babble effect Result of group members who seem to believe that aimless and endless discussion improves decision making when it actually impedes success.

Backing Additional evidence and reasoning used to support the inference made in the warrant.

Bad apples Disruptive members who poison the group.

BATNA (Best Alternative to a Negotiated Agreement) A fallback position that identifies the best alternative available if a negotiated settlement fails to occur.

Behavioral ground rules Specified rules that assist in managing contributions and communication during group meetings.

Behavioral output control theory Social loafing can be addressed effectively by comparing group members' performance with predetermined behavioral expectations and holding members accountable to meeting those expectations.

Beliefs What we think is true or probable.

Bias of the fixed pie Acceptance of the inevitability of scarce resources without fully exploring options that might expand the resources.

Boundary control Regulation that determines the amount of access to input and consequent exposure to change in a system.

Brainstorming A creative problem-solving technique that promotes plentiful, even zany, ideas in an atmosphere free from criticism and encourages enthusiastic participation from all group members.

Bridging An integrative problem-solving technique that offers a new option devised to satisfy all parties on important conflicting issues by appealing to common ground or superordinate goals.

Charge The task of a team, such as to gather information, to analyze a problem and make recommendations, to make decisions and implement them, or to tackle a specific project from inception to completion.

Charisma A constellation of personal attributes that people find highly attractive in an individual and strongly influential.

Charismatic leaders All leaders are transformational to some degree, but charismatic leaders are thought to be *highly* transformational.

Civility Treating people with respect both verbally and nonverbally.

Claim That which is asserted and remains to be proven.

Co-culture Any group that is part of a dominant culture yet often has a common history and shares some differences in values, beliefs, and practices from the dominant culture.

Coercion Forced choice.

Cohesiveness The degree to which members feel a part of a group, wish to stay in the group, and are committed to each other and to the group's work.

Collaborating style of conflict management Recognizes the interconnection between the task and social components of groups and deals directly with both requirements; win–win cooperative approach to conflict management that attempts to satisfy all parties.

Collective effort model (CEM) It suggests that group members are strongly motivated to perform well in a group if they are convinced that their individual effort will likely help in attaining valued results.

Collective inferential error Mistakes made by groups when drawing conclusions based on limited and faulty information base.

Commitment Persistent effort to achieve goals and produce excellence.

Communication A transactional process of sharing meaning with others.

Communication competence Engaging in communication behavior with others that is both effective and appropriate in a given context.

Communication skill The ability to perform a communication behavior effectively and repeatedly.

Communication style of conflict management An orientation toward conflict; predisposition or tendency regarding the way conflict is managed in groups.

Competing (power/forcing) style of conflict management Attempts to force one's will on another group member or the group as a whole by use of threats, criticism, contempt, hostile remarks and jokes, sarcasm, ridicule, intimidation, fault-finding and blaming, and denials of responsibility.

Competition A mutually exclusive goal attainment process.

Compromising Style of conflict management that gives up something to get something.

Conference call An audioconference or teleconference that is devoid of video access.

Confirmation bias A strong tendency to seek information that confirms our beliefs and attitudes and to ignore information that contradicts our currently held beliefs and attitudes.

Conflict The expressed struggle of interconnected parties who perceive incompatible goals and interference from each other in attaining those goals.

Conflict contagion When one or more group members can spread nasty conflicts among an entire team.

Conflict spirals The escalating cycle of negative communication that produces destructive conflict.

Conformity The adherence to group norms by group members.

Confrontation A collaborative component of conflict management characterized by the overt recognition that conflict exists in a group and the direct effort to manage it effectively.

Consensus A state of mutual agreement among members of a group in which all legitimate concerns of individuals have been addressed to the satisfaction of the group.

Constructive competition Occurs when rivalry produces positive, enjoyable experiences and generates increased effort to achieve without jeopardizing positive interpersonal relationships and personal well-being.

Constructive conflict Conflict that is characterized by communication that is We-oriented, cooperative, de-escalating, supportive, and flexible.

Content dimension (of messages) The information transmitted.

Context An environment in which meaning emerges, consisting of who communicates to whom, why the communicator does it, and where, when, and how it is done.

Cooperation A mutually inclusive goal attainment process.

Correlation A consistent relationship between two or more variables.

Credibility A composite of competence (knowledge, skills), trustworthiness (honesty, consistency, character), and dynamism (confidence, assertiveness).

Criteria Standards by which decisions and solutions to problems can be evaluated.

Critical thinking Analyzing and evaluating ideas and information to reach sound judgments and conclusions based on high-quality reasoning and credible evidence.

Criticism sandwich Offering praise, then criticism, then praise.

Culture A learned set of enduring values, beliefs, and practices that are shared by an identifiable, large group of people with a common history.

Cyberbullying Online bullying.

Cyberostracism A form of remote ostracism or isolation from a group that occurs in virtual groups.

Cynics They focus on the negative, predicting failure and looking for someone or something to criticize, sapping the energy from a team with their negativity.

Data The grounds (support/evidence) for the claim, such as statistical evidence, expert testimony, documents, objects, exhibits, conclusions from test results, verifiable facts, and conclusions previously established as credible.

Deep diversity Substantial variation among members in task-relevant skills, knowledge, abilities, beliefs, values, perspectives, and problem-solving strategies.

Defensive communication Patterns of communication characterized by evaluation, control, indifference, manipulation, superiority, and certainty.

Defensiveness A reaction to a perceived attack on our self-concept and self-esteem.

Defiance An overt form of communicating noncompliance; unambiguous noncompliance.

Delegating style (of situational leadership) Nondirective leadership that has low task, low relationship emphasis; lets other group members shoulder the burdens once the leader deems them ready.

Democratic leadership style A style of leadership that encourages participation and responsibility from group members.

Designated leaders Appointed leaders by a higher authority or elected by the group membership.

Destructive conflict Conflict that is characterized by domination, escalation, retaliation, competition, defensiveness, and inflexible communication patterns.

Digital divide Inequitable distribution of access to technology that tends to benefit wealthier individuals, especially students experiencing online learning, and disadvantages poorer individuals.

Disinhibition effect Tendency to say online what you wouldn't normally say in person.

Disruptive roles Informal group roles that serve individual needs or goals while impeding attainment of group goals.

Distributive leadership Shared leadership among group members.

Dominance A form of power in which individuals actively attempt to gain power over others.

Duration One of two key indicators that distinguish constructive and destructive anger; a measure of how long anger lasts.

Dyad Academic term for a two-person transaction.

Dynamic equilibrium A range in which systems can manage change effectively to promote growth and success without destroying the system with too much instability.

Effectiveness How well we have progressed toward the achievement of goals.

Electronic brainstorming Occurs when group members sit at computer terminals and brainstorm ideas using a computer-based, file-sharing procedure, or engage in brainstorming via Zoom-type meeting.

Emergent leader A group member who becomes leader by earning the admiration of members and influencing them even though he or she has no formal authority.

Emojis Typed icons or digital images meant to express an idea or emotional tone; a substitute for nonverbal communication in written text messages.

Emotional intelligence The ability to perceive, glean information from, and manage one's own and others' emotions.

Empathic listening Intent listening that requires that we try to see from the perspective of the other person, perceiving the needs, desires, and feelings of a group member because that is what we would want others to do for us.

Empathy Capacity to experience what someone else is thinking or feeling.

Empowerment A proactive form of power derived from enhancing the capabilities, choices, and influence of individuals and groups.

Entropy A measure of a system's movement toward disorganization and eventual termination.

Environment The context within which a system operates, such as a team within an organization or a student project group within a college class.

Equifinality Accomplishment of similar or identical goals in highly diverse ways by different groups.

Extemporaneous style of speaking Speaking from an outline instead of a written manuscript.

Ethics A system for judging the moral correctness of human behavior by weighing that behavior against an agreed-upon set of standards regarding what constitutes right and wrong.

Ethnocentrism Exalting one's own culture while disparaging other cultures.

Expanding the pie An integrative problem-solving technique in which creative means of increasing resources as a solution to a conflict are generated.

Expert A person who not only has valuable and useful information for a group but also understands the information and knows how to use it to help the group.

Explicit norms Rules in groups that expressly identify acceptable and unacceptable behavior.

Extrinsic reward An external inducement such as money, grades, praise, recognition, or prestige that motivates us to behave or perform.

Fallacies Errors in the use of supporting materials, the process of reasoning, or resting claims on emotional appeal instead of logic and evidence.

False dichotomy The tendency to view the world in terms of only two opposing possibilities when other possibilities are available, and to describe this dichotomy in the language of extremes.

Fantasies Prime element of symbolic convergence theory; dramatic stories that provide a shared interpretation of events that bind group members and offer them a shared identity.

Fantasy chain A string of connected stories that dramatize and amplify a fantasy theme.

Fantasy theme A consistent thread that runs through the stories that create a shared group identity.

Force field analysis A process for group implementation of decisions by anticipating the driving forces (those that encourage change) and restraining forces (those that resist change).

Formal role A *position* assigned by an organization or specifically designated by the group leader or the result of a formal election.

Forum discussion Permits members of an audience listening to a public speech, panel discussion, symposium, or debate to participate in a discussion of ideas presented.

Framing The way in which language shapes our perception of choices.

Framestorming Changing the framework for brainstorming before actually engaging in a brainstorming session by asking different questions.

Group A human communication system composed of three or more individuals interacting for the achievement of some common goal(s), who influence and are influenced by each other.

Group climate The emotional atmosphere, the enveloping tone that is created by the way we communicate in groups.

Group emotional contagion "The transfer of moods among people in a group and its influence on work group dynamics."

Grouphate The hostility people harbor from having to work in groups.

Group polarization The group tendency to make a decision after discussion that is more extreme, either riskier or more cautious, than the initial preferences of group members.

Group potency (and empowerment) The shared belief among team members that they can be effective as a team across a variety of situations.

Group socialization The communication process in which new and established group members adjust to one another.

Groupthink A mode of thinking that people engage in when they are deeply involved in a cohesive in-group, and members' strivings for unanimity override their motivation to realistically appraise alternative courses of action.

Hard bargaining Negotiating from strength approach to conflicts of interest; a contest of wills.

Hazing Any humiliating or dangerous activity that degrades, abuses, or endangers them expected of individuals to join a group, regardless of their willingness to participate in the activity.

Hidden agendas Personal goals of group members that are not revealed openly and that can interfere with group accomplishment.

High-context communication style Cultural tendency to emphasize the cultural context of a message when determining meaning. It is indirect, imprecise, and implicit.

High PD cultures Vertical cultures that have a relatively strong emphasis on maintaining power differences.

Hindsight bias The tendency to overestimate our prior knowledge once we have been told the correct answers.

Hypercompetitiveness An excessive emphasis on defeating others to achieve one's goals.

Illusion of transparency Overestimation of the extent to which audience members detect a speaker's nervousness.

Impact (and empowerment) The degree of significance that is given by those outside of the team, typically the team's organization, to the work produced by the team.

Implicit norms Rules in groups that are indirectly indicated by uniformities in the behavior and expressed attitudes of members.

Implicit theories of leadership Individuals' expectations, beliefs, and assumptions about what traits and abilities constitute an effective leader.

Incivility Commonplace acts of rudeness and disrespect.

Individual accountability An established minimum standard of effort and performance for each team member to share the fruits of team success.

Individual achievement The attainment of a personal goal without having to defeat another person.

Individualism–collectivism dimension (of cultures) The degree to which cultural values emphasize either the individual or the group as paramount.

Inferences Conclusions about the unknown based on what is known.

Informal role A role that emerges in a group from the group transactions; it emphasizes *functions*, not positions.

Information overload The rate of information flow into a system or the complexity of that information exceeds the system's processing capacity; excessive input.

Information underload The amount of information available to a group for decision-making purposes is insufficient (input is inadequate).

Input Resources that come from outside a system, such as energy (sunlight, electricity), information (Internet, books), and people (a new group member).

Integration Creative approach to conflicts of interest that searches for solutions that benefit everyone.

Intensity One of two key variables that distinguish constructive from destructive anger; an indicator of the magnitude of feelings of anger.

Interests The intangible motivations such as needs, desires, concerns, fears, and aspirations that lead a party in a conflict to take a position.

Interpersonal communication Communication that is between two people (dyads).

Intrinsic reward Enjoying what one does for its own sake; an inner motivation to continue doing what brings us pleasure.

Laissez-faire leadership style A do-nothing style of leadership; therefore, no leadership.

Language A structured system of symbols for sharing meaning.

Leadership A leader–follower influence process, directed toward positive change that reflects mutual purposes of group members and is largely achieved through competent communication.

Learning groups Groups that enhance members' knowledge, such as college seminar groups and class study groups.

Legitimate authority Someone perceived to have a right to direct others' behavior because of his or her position, title, role, experience, or knowledge.

Logical fallacies Errors in the process of reasoning.

Low-context communication style Cultural tendency to emphasize the explicit content of a message when determining meaning. It is verbally precise, direct, literal, and explicit.

Low PD culture A horizontal culture that values relatively equal power sharing and discourages attention to status differences and ranking.

Maintenance roles Informal group roles that focus on social relationships among group members.

Margin of error A degree of sampling error in polls, surveys, and studies accounted for by imperfections in selecting a sample.

Material fallacies Errors in the process of using supporting materials as proof.

Meaningfulness (and empowerment) A team's perception that its tasks are important, valuable, and worthwhile.

Mentors Knowledgeable individuals who have achieved some success in their profession or jobs and who assist individuals trying to get started in a line of work.

Microaggressions Small slights targeted toward some group members, often women and minorities, that accumulate to create a negative group climate.

Mindfulness Contemplating our communication with others and making changes to become more effective.

Mindlessness Paying little attention to our communication with others and putting little or no effort into improving it.

Mind mapping A creative problem-solving process that takes ideas generated and forms them into a visual spiderweb of connections as brainstorming progresses.

Mindsets Psychological and cognitive predispositions to see the world in a particular way, such as biases, preconceptions, and assumptions.

Mixed message Positive verbal and negative non-verbal communication, or vice versa; contradictory verbal and nonverbal communication.

Murphy's law Anything that can go wrong likely will go wrong, somewhere, sometime.

Music groups Groups that provide a creative outlet for members who participate in choirs, bands, and the like.

Myths Beliefs contradicted by fact.

Narcissist Someone who exhibits "a grandiose sense of self-importance; arrogant behavior or attitudes; a lack of empathy for others; a preoccupation with fantasies of unlimited success or power; and a desire for excessive admiration from others."

Negative climate Group members do not feel valued, supported, and respected; trust is minimal; and members perceive that they are not treated well.

Negative synergy Group members working together produce a worse result than expected based on perceived individual skills and abilities of members.

Negativity bias Our strong tendency to be influenced more heavily by negative than positive information.

Negotiation A process by which a joint decision is made by two or more parties.

Neighborhood groups Groups that provide a sense of community, such as homeowners associations and PTAs.

Network A structured pattern of information flow and personal contact.

Nominal group technique A creative problem-solving method in which individuals work by themselves generating lists of ideas on a problem, then convene in a group where they merely record the ideas generated and interaction occurs only to clarify ideas. Rankings of each member's five favorite ideas are averaged with the highest average ideas selected by the group.

Nonconformity Violation of a group norm.

Nonroutine task Work to be accomplished that requires problem solving, has few set procedures, and has a high level of uncertainty.

Nonverbal communication Sharing meaning with others without using words.

Norms Rules that establish standards of appropriate behavior in groups.

Openness Degree of continuous interchange with the environment outside of a system.

Output The continual results of the group's throughput (the transformation of input), such as decisions made, solutions created, and projects completed.

Overclaiming of responsibility Group members who may have contributed little or nothing to the group's output claim undeserved equal contributions.

Panel discussions Small groups of participants who engage in an exchange of information and ideas on a specific issue or problem before an audience.

Paraphrasing A concise response to a speaker that states the essence of the speaker's content in the listener's own words.

Parking lot A visual (e.g., whiteboard, flip chart) location for questions and topics that are worthy of discussion but are not on the meeting agenda.

Parliamentary procedure A set of hundreds of rules for conducting especially large, formal group meetings.

Participant-observer A self-monitoring process whereby you assume a detached view of yourself communicating in groups.

Participative style (of leadership) Leadership behavior that puts emphasis on social dimensions of the group.

Passive aggression Resistance strategies to thwart efforts to gain compliance initiated by more powerful group members.

Perception checking A process involving three steps: (1) neutral description of an observable fact, (2) two possible interpretations of an aforementioned fact, and (3) a request for clarification.

PERT (Program Evaluation Review Technique) A systematic process for group implementation of decisions.

Platinum rule Treat others as they want to be treated.

Positions Concrete things that one party wants in a negotiation.

Positive climate Group members perceive that they are valued, supported, and treated well.

Power The ability to influence the attainment of goals sought by you or others.

Power distance (PD) dimension (of cultures) Degree to which different cultures vary in their attitudes concerning the acceptability of unequal distribution of power in relationships, institutions, and organizations.

Power indicators Ways in which relative degrees of power are communicated in groups.

Power resource Anything that enables individuals or groups to achieve their goals, assists others to achieve their goals, or interferes with the goal attainment of others.

Pre-reads Essential materials assigned for review by group members before a meeting commences.

Prevention A form of power in which group members reactively resist or defy attempts to be dominated by other group members.

Primary groups Groups that provide a sense of belonging and affection such as family and friends.

Primary tension The initial jitters and uneasiness felt by individuals when they first join a group.

Principled negotiation Interest-based bargaining process that uses a collaborative approach to negotiating conflicts of interest, focusing on merits of arguments, not on hard-bargaining strategies.

Probing Seeking additional information from a speaker by asking questions.

Procedural ground rules Specified rules that help a meeting process.

Productivity The result of the efficient and effective accomplishment of a group task.

Project groups Groups that work on specific tasks such as self-managing work teams and task forces.

Provisionalism Qualifying statements and avoiding absolute claims.

Pseudo-teams Small groups that only half-heartedly exhibit the several criteria that constitute a true team. They give the appearance of being teams and of engaging in teamwork without exhibiting the substance of teams.

Psychological fallacies Claims that rest on emotional appeal rather than logic and evidence.

Psychological reactance The more someone tries to control us by telling us what to do, the more we are inclined to resist such efforts or even to do the opposite.

Psychological safety Team members feel free to make mistakes, ask questions, and take risks.

Psychopath Someone who has no conscience and feels no remorse or empathy.

Public speaking Communication in a formal setting between a clearly identified speaker and an audience of listeners.

Purpose/impact (P/I) statement The guiding statement for group meetings that specifies a clear goal and an expected outcome from the meeting.

Purpose statement A concise, precise, declarative statement phrased in simple, clear language that provides both the general purpose (to inform or persuade) and the specific purpose (exactly what you want the audience to understand, believe, feel, or do).

Qualifier Degree of truth of the claim (e.g., highly probable, plausible, possible).

Question of fact Asks whether something is true and to what extent.

Question of policy Asks whether a specific course of action should be undertaken to solve a problem.

Question of value Asks for an evaluation of the desirability of an object, idea, event, or person.

Random sample A part of the population for a poll, survey, or study chosen in such a way that every member of the population has an equal chance of being selected.

Rationalization of disconfirmation Inventing superficial, glib alternative explanations for information that contradicts beliefs.

Readiness How ready a person is to perform a particular task; determined by ability and willingness of the person.

Rebuttal Exceptions or refutations that diminish the force of the claim.

Reciprocal pattern A tit-for-tat interaction between rivals during a conflict negotiation or a cycle of defensive communication patterns.

Reflective thinking A set of logical steps that incorporate the scientific method of defining, analyzing, and solving problems.

Reframing A creative process of breaking a mindset by placing the problem in a different frame of reference.

Relationship dimension (of messages) How messages define or redefine the relationship between group members.

Resistance A covert, ambiguous form of communicating noncompliance; often duplicitous and manipulative.

Ripple effect A chain reaction that begins in one part of a system and spreads across an entire system.

Role A pattern of expected behavior associated with parts that members play in groups.

Role ambiguity Confusion and duplication when team members are unsure of the parts they are expected to play.

Role conflict When group members play roles in different groups that contradict each other.

Role fixation The acting out of a specific role, and only that role, no matter what the situation might require.

Role flexibility The capacity to recognize the current requirements of the group and then enact the role-specific behaviors most appropriate in the given context.

Role reversal Stepping into a role distinctly different from or opposite of a role one usually plays.

Role specialization When an individual group member settles into his or her primary role.

Role status The relative importance, prestige, or power accorded each group role.

Romance of leadership The tendency to give too much credit to leaders for group outcomes, both good and bad, that makes it appear one can lead successfully without willing and capable followers.

Routine task Work to be accomplished in which the group performs processes and procedures that have little variability and little likelihood of change.

Rule Prescription that indicates what you should or shouldn't do in specific contexts.

Rule of seven Each member added to a group of seven reduces decision-making effectiveness by about 10%.

Secondary tension The stress and strain that occurs within a group when disagreements and conflicts emerge, and decisions must be made.

Self-centered, disruptive roles Roles that serve individual needs or goals (Me-oriented) while impeding attainment of group goals.

Self-justification Providing excuses that absolve us of blame.

Self-managing work teams Teams that complete an entire task under self-regulation.

Self-selected sample The most committed, passionate, or otherwise atypical parts of the population studied are more likely to participate in a study, poll, or survey.

Selling style (of situational leadership) Directive leadership that is high task, high relationship in emphasis.

Sensitivity Receptive accuracy whereby you can detect, decode, and comprehend signals sent in groups.

Servant leadership A perspective on leadership that places the emphasis on the needs of followers and helps them to become more knowledgeable, freer, more autonomous; "a moral leader."

Service groups Groups that provide social service to others, such as fraternities and sororities and Rotary and Lions clubs.

Shift response An attention-getting initiative by listeners in which the listeners attempt to shift the focus of attention from others to themselves by changing the topic of discussion.

Signposts A speech organizational technique that indicates exactly where you are in your speech so the audience can follow along easily.

Smoothing Collaborative component of conflict management characterized by acting to calm agitated feelings during a conflict episode.

Social compensation A group member's increased motivation to work harder on a group task to counterbalance the lackluster performance of other members.

Social dimension (of groups) The relationships that form among members in a group and their impact on the group as a whole.

Social groups Groups that provide social connections and whose goal is to help others.

Social identity theory Explains that groups provide us with a meaningful identity.

Social loafing The tendency of a group member to exert less effort on a task when working in a group than when working individually.

Social media networks Groups that communicate via Facebook, Twitter, and other social networking sites.

Soft bargaining Negotiating strategy that typically yields to pressure from hard bargainers.

Standard Agenda A six-step process for structuring group discussion and decision making that begins with a focus on the problem and ends with consideration of solutions and their implementation.

Status equalization effect A leveling of role status among group members especially in text-only messaging.

Stratification Divisions of a culture into various levels of power that put distance between the haves and the have-nots.

Structuration theory Explains that systems, such as groups, establish structures for discussion and problem solving by creating rules, roles, norms, and power distribution to permit the system to function effectively and sustain itself.

Structure The systematic interrelation of all parts to the whole, providing form and shape.

Superordinate goal A specific kind of cooperative goal that overrides differences that members may have because the goal supersedes less important competitive goals.

Support groups Groups that provide social support to address life problems.

Supportive communication Patterns of communication characterized by description, problem orientation, empathy, assertiveness, equality, and provisionalism.

Support response An attention-giving, cooperative process in which listeners focus their attention on another group member, not on themselves, during discussion.

Symbolic convergence theory Focuses on how group members communicating with each other develop and share stories (fantasies) to create a convergence or group identity that is larger and more coherent than the isolated experiences of individual group members.

Symbols Representations of referents (whatever the symbol refers to).

Symposium A relatively structured group presentation to an audience composed of several individuals who present uninterrupted speeches with contrasting points of view on a central topic.

Synchronous media Those forms of communicating that permit simultaneous interactions among group members modeled after face-to-face meetings.

Synergy Occurs when group performance from joint action of members exceeds expectations based on perceived abilities and skills of individual group members.

System A set of interconnected parts working together to form a whole in the context of a changing environment.

Task dimension (of groups) The work to be performed by a group.

Task roles Informal group roles that move the group toward attainment of its goals.

Team A constellation of group members with complementary skills who act as an interdependent unit, are equally committed to a common mission, subscribe to a cooperative approach to accomplish that mission, and hold themselves accountable for team performance.

Team identity The sense members feel that they are a part of a group, that they belong.

Telling style (of situational leadership) Directive leadership that is high task, low relationship in emphasis.

Throughput The *process* of transforming input into output to keep a system functioning.

Tit-for-tat strategy Negotiating strategy in which one either cooperates or competes with rivals, depending on what the other party does; you give back what you receive.

Tokenism Giving the appearance of diversity inclusion in a group by adding a single minority, woman, or person of a markedly different age or gender identification without exhibiting real diversity in actual practice. It's all for show.

Traits Relatively enduring characteristics of an individual that highlight differences between people and that are displayed in most situations.

Transactional communication A process in which each person communicating is both a sender and a receiver simultaneously, not merely a sender or receiver, and all parties influence each other.

Transactional leadership Leadership often associated with management that typically strives to maintain the status quo efficiently.

Transformational leadership Leadership often associated with changing the status quo; frequently linked to charisma.

True consensus Requires not just unanimous agreement, but commitment to and satisfaction with a group decision.

Uncertainty reduction theory Posits that when strangers first meet, the principal goal is to reduce uncertainty and increase predictability.

Values The most deeply felt views of what is deemed good, worthwhile, or ethically right.

Videoconference Virtual group process that incorporates nonverbal cues such as facial expressions, gestures, posture, and eye contact; Zoom meetings.

Virtual group A small group whose members rarely, if ever, interact in person and who mostly communicate by means of electronic technologies.

Virtuous cycle The more respect shown to those with power in the group the more the more lower power members typically become engaged and motivated to improve and provide creative solutions to problems.

Vividness effect A graphic, outrageous, shocking, controversial, dramatic event that draws our attention and sticks in our minds, prompting us to overvalue such events and undervalue statistical probabilities of such an event occurring.

WAIT "Why Am I Talking?" acronym; helps determine whether a group member's comment will add or subtract from the conversation.

Warrant The reasoning used to link the data to the claim; usually assumed, not stated directly.

Work-from-anywhere Group members can connect from home, at their office, or virtually anyplace for group meetings.

Workplace bullying Persistent verbal and nonverbal aggression at work that includes public humiliation, constant criticism, ridicule, gossip, insults, and social ostracism; form of badgering, abuse, and "hammering away" at targets who have less power than their bullies.

References

About IDEO. (2021). *IDEO.* https://www.ideo.com/about

Abrams, D., Weick, M., Thomas, D., Colbe, H., & Franklin, K. M. (2010). On-line ostracism affects children differently from adolescents and adults. *British Journal of Developmental Psychology, 29,* 110–123. https://doi.org/10.1348/026151010x494089

Adesina, T. (2017, March 2). The 80/20 rule of diversity & inclusion in the workplace: The long and short of it. *LinkedIn.* https://www.linkedin.com/pulse/8020-rule-diversity-inclusion-workplace-long-short-tayo-adesina

Adler, R. B. (1977). *Confidence in communication: A guide to assertive and social skills.* Holt, Rinehart & Winston.

Adler, R. B., Elmhorst, J. M., & Lucas, K. (2013). *Communicating at work: Principles and practices for business and the professions.* McGraw-Hill.

Adler, R. B., Rosenfeld, L. B., & Proctor, R. F. (2021). *Interplay: The process of interpersonal communication.* Oxford University Press.

Afifi, T. D., Shahnazi, A. F., Coveleski, S., et al. (2017). Testing the ideology outcomes: The comparative effects of talking, writing, and avoiding a stressor on rumination and health. *Human Communication Research, 43,* 76–101. https://doi.org/10.1111/hcre.12096

Agerholm, H. (2016, September 15). 1 in 5 CEOs are psychopaths according to a new study: Here's why. *Business Insider.* https://www.businessinsider.com/1-in-5-ceos-are-psychopaths-according-to-a-new-study-2016-9

Aldhous, P. (2012, March 9). Fukushima's fate inspires nuclear safety rethink. *New Scientist.* https://www.newscientist.com/article/dn21556-fukushimas-fate-inspires-nuclear-safety-rethink

Alessandra, T. (2020). The platinum rule: What it is and how does it apply to you? *C-Suite.* https://c-suitenetwork.com/news/the-platinum-rule-what-is-it-and-how-does-it-apply-to-you-2/

Allan, E. J., & Madden, M. (2008, March 11). Hazing in view: College students at risk: Initial findings from the National Study of Student Hazing. *University of Maine.* Retrieved from http://www.umaine.edu/hazingstudy/hazinginview1.htm

Allen, J. A., Lehmann-Willenbrock, N., Rogelberg, S. G. (2018). Let's get this meeting started: Meeting lateness and actual meeting outcomes. *Journal of Organizational Behavior, 39,* 1008–1021. https://doi.org/10.1002/job.2276

Allen, J. J., & Anderson, C. A. (2017, September 8). Aggression and violence: Definitions and distinctions. *The Wiley handbook of violence and aggression.* https://onlinelibrary.wiley.com/doi/abs/10.1002/9781119057574.whbva001

Allen, N. (2018, May 22). Why teams fail, according to MBAs. *Poets & Quants.* https://poetsandquants.com/2018/05/22/why-teams-fail-according-to-mbas/?pq-category=business-school-news/

Ames, D. R., & Wazlawek, A. S. (2014). Pushing in the dark: Causes and consequences of limited self-awareness for interpersonal assertiveness. *Personality and Social Psychology.* https://doi.org/10.1177%2F0146167214525474

Anderson, C. M., Riddle, B. L., & Martin, M. M. (1999). Socialization processes in groups. In L. R. Frey (Ed.), *Handbook of group communication theory & research.* SAGE.

Andersen, M. K. (2018, May 7). Why are women better leaders than men? *Linkedin.* https://www.linkedin.com/pulse/why-women-better-leaders-than-men-mortenkamp-andersen

Anderson, R., & Ross, V. (2002). *Questions of communication: A practical introduction to theory.* St. Martin's Press.

Anthony, J. (2020). 46 virtual team statistics you can't ignore: 2020 data analysis, benefits & challenges. *Finances Online.* https://financesonline.com/virtual-team-statistics/

Antoci, A., Boneli, L., Paglieri, F., Reggiani, T. G., & Sabatini, F. (2018). Civility and trust in social media. *IZA Institute of Labor Economics.* http://ftp.iza.org/dp11290.pdf

Anwar, K. (2016). Working with group-tasks and group cohesiveness. *International Education Studies, 9,* 105–111. https://files.eric.ed.gov/fulltext/EJ1110205.pdf

Apgar, T. T. (2020, September 20). Hazing in the virtual world. *Hazing Prevention.org.* https://

hazingprevention.org/wp-content/uploads/2020-NHPW-Resource-Guide-Final.pdf

Are six heads as good as twelve? (2004, May 28). *American Psychological Association*. http://www.apa.org/research/action/jury.aspx

Aritz, J., & Walker, R. C. (2014). Leadership styles in multicultural groups: Americans and East Asians working together. *Journal of Business Communication, 51*, 72–92. https://citeseerx.ist.psu.edu/viewdoc/download?doi=10.1.1.902.811&rep=rep1&type=pdf

Aroian, K. (2015). Designing teamwork: An interview with Dana Cho of IDEO. *Wavelength*. https://wavelength.asana.com/ideo-design-project-management/

Aronson, E., & Aronson, J. (2018). *The social animal*. Worth.

Aronson, E., Wilson, T. D., & Akert, R. M. (2016). *Social psychology*. Pearson.

Artinger, S., & Vulkan, N. (2016). Does group size matter for behavior in online trust dilemmas? *PLoSOne*. http://journals.plos.org/plosone/article?id=10.1371/journal.pone.0166279

Artz, B., Goodall, A., & Oswald, A. J. (2018, June 25). Research: Women ask for raises as often as men, but are less likely to get them. *Harvard Business Review*. https://hbr.org/2018/06/research-women-ask-for-raises-as-often-as-men-but-are-less-likely-to-get-them

Asch, S. E. (1955). Opinions and social pressure. *Scientific American, 19*, 31–35.

Aube, C., Rousseau, V., & Tremblay, S. (2011). Team size and quality of group experience: The more the merrier? *Group Dynamics: Theory, Research, and Practice, 15*, 357–375. https://psycnet.apa.org/doi/10.1037/a0025400

Aubin, R. M., Amiot, C. E., & Fontaine-Boyte, C. (2016). The impact of group power and its perceived stability on hope and collective action: Applying the concept of hopelessness at the collective level of analysis. *Group Dynamics: Theory, Research, and Practice, 20*(2), 105–119. https://psycnet.apa.org/doi/10.1037/gdn0000045

Axtell, P. (1998). *Gestures: The DO's and TABOOs of body language around the world*. John Wiley & Sons, Inc.

Axtell, P. (2015, July 14). 5 Ways to improve employee engagement in meetings . . . and why it matters. *Lucid Meetings*. https://blog.lucidmeetings.com/blog/5-ways-to-improve-employee-engagement-in-meetings-and-why-it-matters

Aycan, D., Duffy, M. W., & Hale, A. (2020, April 30). Building empowered teams is good for business. *IDEO Creative Difference*. https://medium.com/@ideoCD/building-empowered-teams-is-good-for-business-4e578c010d77

Baba, M. L., Gluesing, J., Ratner, H., & Wagner, K. H. (2004). The contexts of knowing: Natural history of a globally distributed team. *Journal of Organizational Behavior, 25*, 547–587. https://psycnet.apa.org/doi/10.1002/job.259

Babiak, P., & Hare, R. D. (2006). *Snakes in suits: When psychopaths go to work*. HarperCollins.

Baer, D. (2016, June 20). Unloaded minds are the most creative. *The Cut*. https://www.thecut.com/2016/06/unloaded-minds-are-the-most-creative.html

Bagchi, R., Koukova, N. T., Gurnani, H., Nagarajan, M., & Oza, S. S. (2016). Walking in my shoes: How expectations of role reversal in future negotiations affect present behaviors. *Journal of Marketing Research, 3*, 381–395. https://www.researchgate.net/deref/http%3A%2F%2Fdx.doi.org%2F10.1509%2Fjmr.13.0426

Baghai, M., & Quigley, J. (2011). *As one: Individual action, collective power*. Portfolio.

Bailey, R. (2017, December 20). Pew survey: US women and gender discrimination at work. *African Seer*. https://www.africanseer.com/news/world/559724-pew-survey-us-women-and-gender-discrimination-at-work.html

Baker, G. (2015, July 31). Five top causes of "business communication problems." *AdvanceConsulting*. https://www.advanceconsulting.com/blog/five-top-causes-of-business-communication-problems/

Baron, E. (2020, December 13). Does remote work hurt Valley's tech innovation? *The Mercury News*, pp. A1, A8.

Baror, S., & Bar, M. (2016). Associative activation and its relation to exploration and exploitation in the brain. *Psychological Science, 27*, 776–789. https://doi.org/10.1177%2F0956797616634487

Barsade, S. G. (2002). The ripple effect: Emotional contagion and its influence on group behavior. *Administrative Science Quarterly, 47*, 644–675. https://doi.org/10.2307%2F3094912

Barsade, S. G. (2020, March 26). The contagion we can control. *Harvard Business Review*. https://hbr.org/2020/03/the-contagion-we-can-control

Barsade, S. G., Coutifaris, C. G. V., & Pillemer, J. (2018). Emotional contagion in organizational life. *Research in Organizational Behavior, 38*, 137–151. https://doi.org/10.1016/j.riob.2018.11.005

Baruah, J., & Paulus, P. B. (2008). Effects of training on idea generation in groups. *Small Group Research*, *39*, 523–541. https://doi.org/10.1177%2F1046496408320049

Baruah, J., & Paulus, P. B. (2016). The role of time and category relatedness in electronic brainstorming. *Small Group Research*, *47*, 333–342. https://doi.org/10.1177%2F1046496416642296

Bass, B. M., & Bass, R. (2008). *The Bass handbook of leadership: Theory, research, and managerial applications.* Free Press.

BATNA Strategy: Should you reveal your BATNA? (2021, January 12). *Program on Negotiation/Harvard Law School.* https://www.pon.harvard.edu/daily/batna/negotiation-research-you-can-use-should-you-brandish-your-batna-nb/?utm

Bauer-Wolf, J. (2018, February 23). Overconfident students, dubious employers. *Inside Higher Ed.* https://www.insidehighered.com/news/2018/02/23/study-students-believe-they-are-prepared-workplace-employers-disagree

Bauer-Wolf, J. (2019, January 17). Survey: Employers want "soft skills" from graduates. *Inside Higher Education.* https://www.insidehighered.com/quicktakes/2019/01/17/survey-employers-want-soft-skills-graduates

Bean-Mellinger, B. (2019, March 1). Most important employee skills in the workplace. *Chron.* https://smallbusiness.chron.com/important-employee-skills-workplace-24708.html

Bear, J. B., Cushenberry, L., London, M., & Sherman, G. D. (2017). Performance feedback, power retention, and the gender gap in leadership. *The Leadership Quarterly.* http://dx.doi.org/10.1016/j.leaqua.2017.02.003

Becker, J. C., & Swim, J. K. (2011). Seeing the unseen: Attention to daily encounters with sexism as way to reduce sexist beliefs. *Psychology of Women Quarterly*, *35*, 227–242. https://journals.sagepub.com/doi/10.1177/0361684310397509

Behfar, K., Peterson, R., Mannix, E. A., & Trochim, W. (2008). The critical role of conflict resolution in teams: A close look at the links between conflict type, conflict management strategies, and team outcomes. *Journal of Applied Psychology*, *93*, 170–180. https://psycnet.apa.org/doi/10.1037/0021-9010.93.1.170

Belbin, R. (1996). *Team roles at work.* Butterworth-Heinemann.

Benenson, J. F., Gordon, A. J., & Roy, R. (2000). Children's evaluative appraisals of competition in tetrads versus dyads. *Small Group Research*, *31*, 635–652. https://citeseerx.ist.psu.edu/viewdoc/download?doi=10.1.1.853.5509&rep=rep1&type=pdf

Ben-Hur, S., & Kinley, N. (2016, May). Intrinsic motivation: the missing piece in changing employee behavior. *IMD.* https://www.imd.org/research-knowledge/articles/intrinsic-motivation-the-missing-piece-in-changing-employee-behavior/

Benishek, L. E., & Lazzara, E. H. (2019, May 9). Teams in a new era: Some considerations and implications. *Frontiers in Psychology.* https://doi.org/10.3389/fpsyg.2019.01006

Benne, K., & Sheats, P. (1948). Functional roles of group members. *Journal of Social Issues*, *4*, 41–49.

Bennis, W. (2007). The challenges of leadership in the modern world. *American Psychologist*, *62*, 2–5.

Benson, K. (2017, October 4). The magic relationship ratio, according to science. *The Gottman Institute.* https://www.gottman.com/blog/the-magic-relationship-ratio-according-science/

Beqiri, G. (2017, September 8). Essential business skills for success in the workplace. *Virtual Speech.* https://virtualspeech.com/blog/business-skills-for-success-in-the-workplace

Beras, E. (2018, March 9). Poll: Nearly half of the women who experienced sexual harassment leave their jobs or switch careers. *Marketplace.* https://www.marketplace.org/2018/03/09/new-numbers-reflect-lasting-effects-workplace-harassment-women/

Berger, P. (2016, November 4). Juror: Debate among Bridgegate jury was so heated they were sent home early. *App: USA Today Network.* https://www.app.com/story/news/politics/new-jersey/chris-christie/2016/11/04/juror-debate-among-bridgegate-jury-so-heated-they-were-sent-home-early/93315484

Berkman, J. (2020, October 4). All the college ranking lists you should read. *PrepScholar.* https://blog.prepscholar.com/all-the-college-ranking-lists-you-should-read

Bernieri, F. J. (2001). Toward a taxonomy of interpersonal sensitivity. In J. A. Hall & F. J. Bernieri (Eds.), *Interpersonal sensitivity: Theory and measurement.* Erlbaum.

Bernstein, E. (2014, October). The transparency trap. *Harvard Business Review.* https://hbr.org/2014/10/the-transparency-trap

Best colleges in America, ranked by value. (2020, August 25). *Money.* https://money.com/best-colleges/

Beugelsdijk, S., Maseland, R., & van Hoorn, A. (2015). Are scores on Hofstede's dimensions of national culture stable over time? A cohort analysis. *Global Strategy Journal, 5.* https://onlinelibrary.wiley.com/doi/full/10.1002/gsj.1098

Beugelsdijk, S., & Wetzel, C. (2018). Dimensions and dynamics of national culture: Synthesizing Hofstede with Inglehart. *Journal of Cross-Cultural Psychology, 49,* 1469–1505. https://doi.org/10.1177%2F0022022118798505

Bhatti, A. (2018). Cognitive bias in clinical practice—nurturing healthy skepticism among medical students. *Advances in Medical Education and Practice, 9,* 235–237. https://doi.org/10.2147/amep.s149558

Bhatt, J., & Swick, M. (2017). Focusing on teamwork and communication to improve patient safety. *American Hospital Association.* https://www.aha.org/news/blog/2017-03-15-focusing-teamwork-and-communication-improve-patient-safety

Bilandzic, H., Kalch, A., & Soentgen, J. (2017). Effects of goal framing and emotions on perceived threat and willingness to sacrifice for climate change. *Science Communication, 39,* 466–491. https://doi.org/10.1177%2F1075547017718553

Binge drinking statistics. (2013). *The Century Council.* http://www.centurycouncil.org/binge-drinking/statistics

Blenko, M. W., Mankins, M. C., & Rogers, P. (2010). *Decide & deliver: 5 steps to breakthrough performance in your organization.* Harvard Business Review Press.

Blom, M. (2015). Less followership, less leadership? An inquiry into the basic but seemingly forgotten downsides of leadership. *Management, 18,* 266–282. https://www.cairn.info/revue-management-2015-3-page-266.htm

Blonde, J., & Girandola, F. (2018). Are vivid (vs. pallid) threats persuasive? Examining the effects of threat vividness in health communications. *Basic and Applied Social Psychology, 40*(1), 36–48. https://doi.org/10.1080/01973533.2017.1412969

Blumer, T. (2014, July 28). At CNN, poll results on impeachment released Friday morning, but Romney whipping Obama held until Sunday. *MRC News Busters.* http://www.newsbusters.org/blogs/tom-blumer/2014/07/28/cnn-poll-results-impeachment-released-friday-morning-romney-whipping-oba

Bocchiaro, P., & Zimbardo, P. (2017). On the dynamics of disobedience: Experimental investigations of defying unjust authority. *Psychology Research and Behavioral Management, 10,* 219–229. https://dx.doi.org/10.2147%2FPRBM.S135094

Bohn, R. (2017, Fall). Stop fighting fires. *Harvard Business Review OnPoint, pp.* 93–101.

Bolden-Barrett, V. (2019, August 16). Most people have cried at work at least once, survey says. *HR Dive.* https://www.hrdive.com/news/most-people-have-cried-at-work-at-least-once-survey-says/560940/

Bolsen, T., Palm, R., & Kingsland, J. T. (2020). Framing the origins of COVID-19. *Science Communication, 42,* 562–585. https://doi.org/10.1177%2F1075547020953603

Bolton, R. (1979). *People skills: How to assert yourself, listen to others and resolve conflicts.* Simon & Schuster.

Bonebright, D. A. (2010). 40 years of storming: A historical review of Tuckman's model of small group development. *Human Resource Development International, 13,* 111–120. https://doi.org/10.1080/13678861003589099

Boorstin, J. (2021, March 5). At the current rate, corporate boards won't hit gender parity until 2032, new report warns. *CNBC.* https://www.cnbc.com/2021/03/05/corporate-boards-wont-hit-gender-parity-until-2032-new-report-warns.html

Bor, A., Mazepus, H., Bokemper, S. E., & DeScioli, P. (2020). When should the majority rule? Experimental evidence for Madisonian judgment in five cultures. *Journal of Experimental Political Science, 8,* 41–50. https://doi.org/10.1017/XPS.2020.8

Bormann, E. G. (1986). Symbolic convergence theory and group decision making. In R. Y. Hirokawa & M. S. Poole (Eds.), *Communication and group decision making.* SAGE.

Bormann, E. G. (1990). *Small group communication: Theory and practice.* Harper & Row.

Borunda, A. (2020, April 20). We still don't know the full impacts of the BP oil spill, 10 years later. *National Geographic.* https://www.nationalgeographic.com/science/2020/04/bp-oil-spill-still-dont-know-effects-decade-later/

Bostrom, R. (1970). Patterns of communicative interaction in small groups. *Speech Monographs, 37,* 257–263.

Boudreau, J. (2007, August 12). Beijing brushes up on its English skills. *San Jose Mercury News,* p. 17A.

Boughton, M. (2011). *Power, influence tactics, and influence processes in virtual teams.* Unpublished doctoral dissertation, University of North Carolina.

http://libres.uncg.edu/ir/uncc/f/Boughton_uncc_0694D_10213.pdf

Bower, S., & Bower, G. (1976). *Asserting yourself.* Addison-Wesley.

Bowman, J. M., & Wittenbaum, G. M. (2012). Time pressure affects process and performance in hidden-profile groups. *Small Group Research, 43,* 295–314.

Bradberry, T. (2020). How successful people handle toxic people. *Two Paths.* http://tpiwellness.com/successful-people-handle-toxic-people-travis-bradberry

Brainstorm rules. (2018). *IDEO.* http://www.designkit.org/methods/28

Brannigan, M. (1997, May 30). Why Delta Air Lines decided it was time for CEO to take off. *Wall Street Journal,* pp. A1, A8.

Braun, M. T., Kozlowski, T. A., Brown, R., et al. (2020). Exploring the dynamic team cohesion-performance and coordination-performance relationships of newly formed teams. *Small Group Research, 51,* 551–580. https://doi.org/10.1177%2F1046496420907157

Brehm, J. (1972). *Responses to loss of freedom: A theory of psychological resistance.* General Learning Press.

Brett, J. M., Shapiro, D. L., & Lytle, A. L. (1998). Breaking the bonds of reciprocity in negotiations. *Academy of Management Journal, 41,* 410–425.

Breuer, C., Huffmeier, J., & Hertel, G. (2016). Does trust matter more in virtual teams? A meta-analysis of trust and team effectiveness considering virtuality and documentation as moderators. *Journal of Applied Psychology, 101,* 1151–1177. https://psycnet.apa.org/doi/10.1037/apl0000113

Brewer, C. S., Kovner, C. T., Obeidat, R. F., & Budin, W. C. (2013). Positive work environments of early-career registered nurses and the correlation with physician verbal abuse. *Nursing Outlook, 61,* 408–416.

Brittle, Z. (2015, April 1). Turn towards instead of away. *The Gottman Institute.* https://www.gottman.com/blog/turn-toward-instead-of-away/

Brown, D. (2013, December 29). Living in a digital minefield. *San Jose Mercury News,* pp. A1, A16.

Brown, D. J. (2013). *The boys in the boat: Nine Americans and their epic quest for gold at the 1936 Berlin Olympics.* Penguin.

Brown, S., & Bryant, P. (2015). Getting to know the elephant: A call to advance servant leadership through construct consensus, empirical evidence, and multi-level theoretical development. *Servant Leadership: Theory and Practice, 2,* 10–35.

Brownlow, S. (2003). Gender-linked linguistic behavior in television interviews. *Sex Roles, 49,* 121–132.

Bryant, M., & Higgins, V. (2010). Self-confessed troublemakers: An interactionist view of deviance during organizational change. *Human Relations, 63,* 249–277. https://doi.org/10.1177%2F0018726709338637

Buckingham, M., & Coffman, C. (1999). *First, break all the rules: What the world's greatest managers do differently.* Simon & Schuster.

Buckingham, M., & Coffman, C. W. (2002a, Spring). Item 9: Doing quality work. *Gallup Management Journal.* http://news.gallup.com/businessjournal/508/item-doing-quality-work.aspx

Buckingham, M., & Coffman, C. W. (2002b, Spring). Recognition or praise. *Gallup Management Journal.* http://www.gallupjournal.com/q12Center/articles/19990412.asp

Budds, D. (2016, February 2). IDEO, Silicon Valley's most influential design firm, sells a minority stake. *Fastcodesign.* https://www.fastcodesign.com/3056415/ideo-silicon-valleys-most-influential-design-firm-sells-a-minority-stake

Burger, J. M. (2009). Replicating Milgram: Would people still obey today? *American Psychologist, 64,* 1–11. https://www.apa.org/pubs/journals/releases/amp-64-1-1.pdf

Burke, M., Kraut, R., & Joyce, E. (2010). Membership claims and requests: Conversation level newcomer socialization strategies in online groups. *Small Group Research, 41,* 4–40. https://doi.org/10.1177%2F1046496409351936

Burkus, D. (2016, May 16). Why your inbox is your enemy. *Inc.* https://www.inc.com/david-burkus/youre-kidding-yourself-email-is-actually-killing-your-productivity.html

Burn, S. M. (2019, May 17). What to do when your group's norms make you uneasy. *Psychology Today.* https://www.psychologytoday.com/us/blog/presence-mind/201905/what-do-when-your-groups-norms-make-you-uneasy

Burnett, A., & Badzinski, D. M (2005). Judge nonverbal communication on trial: Do mock trial jurors notice? *Journal of Communication, 55,* 209–224. https://doi.org/10.1111/j.1460-2466.2005.tb02668.x

Bushman, B. J. (2002). Does venting anger feed or extinguish the flame? Catharsis, rumination, distraction, anger, and aggressive responding. *Personality and Social Psychology Bulletin, 28,* 724–731. https://doi.org/10.1177%2F0146167202289002

Cable, D. (2018, April 23). How humble leadership really works. *Harvard Business Review*. https://hbr.org/2018/04/how-humble-leadership-really-works?utm_medium=email&utm_source=tgr_subengagement_digital&utm_campaign=insider-welcome_newpriorday&deliveryName=DM111410

Campbell, S., & Larson, J. (2012). Public speaking anxiety: Comparing face-to-face and web-based speeches. *Journal of Instructional Pedagogies*. http://www.aabri.com/manuscripts/121343.pdf

Can earthquakes be predicted? (2018). *American Geosciences Institute*. https://www.americangeosciences.org/critical-issues/faq/can-earthquakes-be-predicted

Canary, D. J., & Lakey, S. (2013). *Strategic conflict*. Routledge.

Caprino, K. (2017, June 15). Gender bias at work—why men call forceful women "hysterical" and try to silence them. *Forbes*. https://www.forbes.com/sites/kathycaprino/2017/06/15/gender-bias-at-work-why-men-call-forceful-women-hysterical-and-try-to-silence-them/#5a6775f3ea2a

Carey, H. R., & Laughlin, P. R. (2012). Groups perform better than the best individuals on letters-to-numbers problems: Effects of induced strategies. *Group Processes and Intergroup Relations, 15*, 231–242. https://doi.apa.org/doi/10.1037/0022-3514.90.4.644

Carnevale, P., & Probst, T. (1998). Social values and social conflict in creative problem solving. *Journal of Personality and Social Psychology, 74*, 1300–1309.

Carino, M. M. (2019, October 21). Ellipses and emoji: How age affects communication at work. *Marketplace*. https://www.marketplace.org/2019/10/21/ellipses-and-emoji-how-age-affects-communication-at-work/

Carr, A. (2010, May 18). The most important leadership quality for CEOs? Creativity. *Fast Company*. http://www.fastcompany.com/1648943/most-important-leadership-quality-ceos-creativity

Carr, C. (2017). Social media and intergroup communication. *Oxford Research Encyclopedia*. http://communication.oxfordre.com/view/10.1093/acrefore/9780190228613.001.0001/acrefore-9780190228613-e-460

Carter, S., & West, M. (1998). Reflexivity, effectiveness, and mental health in BBC-TV production teams. *Small Group Research, 29*, 583–601. https://doi.org/10.1177%2F1046496498295003

Carton, A. (2017a, March 16). Meaningful work: What leaders can learn from NASA and the space race. *Knowledge@Wharton*. http://knowledge.wharton.upenn.edu/article/what-leaders-can-learn-from-nasa

Carton, A. (2017b). "I'm not mopping floors, I'm putting a man on the moon": How NASA leaders enhanced the meaningfulness of work by changing the meaning of work. *Administrative Science Quarterly, 63*, 323–369. https://doi.org/10.1177%2F0001839217713748

Castles, A. (2017, October 5). Why Atlassian is using a rubber chicken named Helmut to run more effective meetings. *Smart Company*. https://www.smartcompany.com.au/startupsmart/advice/atlassian-using-rubber-chicken-called-helmut-run-effective-meetings/

Catalyst study exposes how gender-based stereotyping sabotages women in the workplace. (2017). *Catalyst*. Retrieved from http://www.catalyst.org/media/catalyst-study-exposes-how-gender-based-stereotyping-sabotages-women-workplace

Caulderwood, K. (2013, October 8). Delta Airlines (DAL) CEO Richard Anderson charts independent course: Buying a refinery, half of a rival, and avoiding gas guzzlers. *International Business Times*. http://www.ibtimes.com/delta-air-lines-dal-ceo-richard-anderson-charts-independent-course-buying-refinery-half-rival

Celik, K. (2013). The effect of role ambiguity and role conflict on performance of vice principals: The mediating role of burnout. *Egitim Arastirmalari/Eurasian Journal of Educational Research, 51*, 195–214.

Chamorro-Premuzic, T. (2019). *Why do so many incompetent men become leaders?* Harvard Business Review Press.

Chan, M. S., Jones, C. R., & Jamieson, K. H. (2017). Debunking: A meta-analysis of the psychological efficacy of messages countering misinformation. *Psychological Science, 28*, 1531–1546. https://doi.org/10.1177%2F0956797617714579

Chang, A., Duck, J., & Bordia, P. (2006). Understanding the multidimensionality of group development. *Small Group Research, 37*, 327–350. https://doi.org/10.1177%2F1046496406290564

The Chapman University survey on American fears. (2015, May 17). *Chapman University*. https://www.chapman.edu/wilkinson/research-centers/babbie-center/fear-survey-faqs.aspx

Chemers, M. M. (2000). Leadership research and theory: A functional integration. *Group Dynamics: Theory, Research, and Practice, 4*, 27–43.

Chen, G-M. (2011). An introduction to key concepts in understanding the Chinese: Harmony as the foundation of Chinese communication. *China Media Research*, *7*, 1–12. https://core.ac.uk/download/pdf/56694323.pdf

Chen, G., & Starosta, W. (1998). *Foundations of intercultural communication*. Allyn & Bacon.

Cherry, K. (2020, May 6). How hindsight bias affects how we view the past. *VeryWellMind*. https://www.verywellmind.com/what-is-a-hindsight-bias-2795236

Chesin, A., Rafaeli, A., & Bos, N. (2011). Anger and happiness in virtual teams: Emotional influences of text and behavior on others' affect in the absence of non-verbal cues. *Organizational Behavior and Human Decision Processes*, *116*, 2–16. https://www.mgt.unm.edu/behavioral-lab/assets/documents/research-articles/cheshin.pdf

Chidambaram, L., & Tung, L. L. (2005). Is out of sight, out of mind? An empirical study of social loafing in technology-supported groups. *Information Systems Research*, *16*, 149–160.

Chion, J. (2013, October 24). What it's like to work at IDEO. *Leadership Journal*. https://medium.com/leadership-journal/6ca2c961aae4

Chira, S. (2017, June 14). The universal phenomenon of men interrupting women. *New York Times*. https://www.nytimes.com/2017/06/14/business/women-sexism-work-huffington-kamala-harris.html

Cho, M. (2013, October 14). A better way to group brainstorm. *Lifehacker.com*. https://lifehacker.com/a-better-way-to-group-brainstorm-1445054503

Cho, M., & Keltner, D. (2020). Power, approach, and inhibition: Empirical advances of a theory. *Current Opinion in Psychology*, *33*, 196–200. https://doi.org/10.1016/j.copsyc.2019.08.013

Choudhury, P. (2020, November–December). Our work-from-anywhere future. *Harvard Business Review*. https://hbr.org/2020/11/our-work-from-anywhere-future

Cirque du Soleil on teamwork and creativity. (2011, June 28). *Business Banter*. http://businessbanter.wordpress.com/2011/06/28/cirque-du-soleil-on-teamwork-and-creativity

Citizen Kane holds its spot as AFI's top American film. (2007, June 21). *San Jose Mercury News*, p. 2A.

Clawson, L. (2014, July 11). Company tracks worker bathroom visits so it can punish people who need to pee too much. *Daily Kos*. https://www.dailykos.com/stories/2014/7/11/1313307/-Company-tracks-worker-bathroom-visits-so-it-can-punish-people-who-need-to-pee-too-much

Clouse, C. J. (2018, January 10). It's lonely at the top for people of color in corporate America—and CEOs know it. *Huffington Post*. https://www.huffingtonpost.com/entry/corporate-america-is-lonely-at-the-top-for-people-of-color_us_5a552b29e4b003133ecd51c8

Cohen, A. (2020, September 9). The surprising traits of good remote leaders. *BBC Worklife*. https://www.bbc.com/worklife/article/20200827-why-in-person-leaders-may-not-be-the-best-virtual-ones

Cohen, L. J., & DeBenedet, A. T. (2012, July 17). Penn State cover-up: Groupthink in action. *Time*. http://ideas.time.com/2012/07/17/penn-state-cover-up-group-think-in-action

Cohen, N. A., & Yoon, J. (2021). Who makes whom charismatic? Leadership identity negotiation in work teams. *Journal of Leadership & Organizational Studies*. https://www.amirza.org/media/991344CRS809677.pdf

Cohen, S. (2014, January 11). Tweets and threats: Gang activity grows on Net, police watching—and making arrests. *Fox News*. http://www.foxnews.com/us/2014/01/11/tweets-and-threats-gang-activity-grows-on-net-police-watching-and-making.html

Cole, M. (2016, March 21). What makes a good manager: The case for listening and assessing skills. *Association for Talent Development*. https://www.td.org/Publications/Blogs/Management-Blog/2016/03/Makes-a-Good-Manager-the-Case-for-Listening-and-Assessing-Skills

Cole, S. (2015, February 26). New research shows we're all bad listeners who think we work too much. *Fast Company*. https://www.fastcompany.com/3042863/new-research-shows-were-all-bad-listeners-who-think-we-work-too-much

Collar, M. (2013, March 29). Collective leadership. *Society for Human Resource Management*. https://www.shrm.org/hr-today/news/hr-news/Pages/spring-2013-collective-leadership.aspx

College drinking. (2020, February). *National Institute on Alcohol Abuse and Alcoholism*. https://www.niaaa.nih.gov/publications/brochures-and-fact-sheets/college-drinking

Conflict is destructive in the workplace, but it can be addressed. (2018, April 9). *Harvard Business Review*. https://www.physicianleaders.org/news/conflict-is-destructive-in-the-workplace-but-it-can-be-addressed

Connley, C. (2020, May 19). The number of women running Fortune 500 companies hits a new high. *CNBC*.

https://www.cnbc.com/2020/05/19/the-number-of-women-running-fortune-500-companies-hits-a-new-high.html

Cook, G. (2015, March–April). All together now. *Scientific American Mind*, pp. 54–57.

Cote, S., Lopes, P. N., Salovey, P., & Miners, C. T. H. (2010). Emotional intelligence and leadership emergence in small groups. *Leadership Quarterly, 21*, 684–685.

Cotton, G. (2013, August 13). Gestures to avoid in cross-cultural business: In other words, "Keep your fingers to yourself." *Huffington Post*. https://www.huffpost.com/entry/cross-cultural-gestures_b_3437653

Courville, R. (2017, August 1). Survey results: What's the problem with online meetings? *Eventbuilder*. http://www.eventbuilder.rocks/survey-results-whats-problem-online-meetings

Covic, B. (2003). *Everything's negotiable: How to bargain better to get what you want*. Pendulum.

COVID-19 coronavirus pandemic. (2021, August 1). *Worldometer*. https://www.worldometers.info/coronavirus/

Coyle, D. (2018). *The culture code: The secrets of highly successful groups*. Bantam Books.

Crampton, A. (2013). Elder mediation in theory and practice: Study results from a national caregiver mediation demonstration project. *Journal of Gerontological Social Work, 56*, 423–437. https://doi.org/10.1080/01634372.2013.777684

Creating value in integrative negotiations: Myth of the fixed-pie of resources. (2020, September 24). *Program on Negotiation/Harvard Law School*. https://www.pon.harvard.edu/daily/negotiation-skills-daily/when-the-pie-seems-too-small/?utm_source=WhatCountsEmail&utm_medium=daily&utm_date=2020-09-24-13-30-00&mqsc=E4120720

Critical leadership skills. (2014, March). *The Ken Blanchard Companies*. http://www.everestla.org/images/pdfs/4_3%20Critical%20Leadership%20Skills%20-%20Ken%20Blanchard.pdf

Croucher, S. M., Sommier, M., & Rahmani, D. (2015). Intercultural communication: Where we've been, where we're going, issues we face. *Communication Research and Practice, 1*, 71–87. https://doi.org/10.1080/22041451.2015.1042422

Crowdfunding: How to fund your business idea. (2017, May 22). Business.gov.au. https://www.business.gov.au/info/run/finance-and-accounting/finance/crowdfunding-how-to-fund-your-business-idea

Crowley, T. (2016, September 7). The platinum rule for creating a culture of diversity and inclusion. *LinkedIn*. https://www.linkedin.com/pulse/platinum-rule-creating-culture-diversity-inclusion-tim-crowley

Crown, D. F. (2007). The use of group and group-centric individual goals for culturally heterogeneous and homogeneous task groups: An assessment of European work teams. *Small Group Research, 38*, 489–508. https://doi.org/10.1177%2F1046496407300486

Cumberland, D. M., & Alagaraja, M. (2016). No place like the frontline: A qualitative study on what participant CEOs learned from Undercover Boss. *Human Resource Development Quarterly, 27*, 271–296. https://doi.org/10.1002/hrdq.21252

Curseu, P. L., & Schruijer, S. G. L. (2010). Does conflict shatter trust or does trust obliterate conflict? Revisiting the relationships between team diversity, conflict, and trust. *Group Dynamics: Theory, Research, and Practice, 14*, 66–79.

Dahlstrom, M. F. (2014). Using narratives and storytelling to communicate science with nonexpert audiences. *Proceedings of the National Academy of Sciences of the United States of America, 111*(Suppl. 4), 13614–13620. http://www.pnas.org/content/111/Supplement_4/13614

Daimler, M. (2016, May 25). Listening is an overlooked leadership tool. *Harvard Business Review*. https://hbr.org/2016/05/listening-is-an-overlooked-leadership-tool

D'Angelo, M. (2020, December 23). How to find a mentor. *Business News Daily*. https://www.businessnewsdaily.com/6248-how-to-find-mentor.html

Data creation and replication will grow at a faster rate than installed storage capacity, according to the IDC GlobalDatasphere and StorageSphere forecasts. (2021, March 24). IDC. https://www.idc.com/getdoc.jsp?containerId=prUS47560321&utm_medium=rss_feed&utm_source=alert&utm_campaign=rss_syndication

Datz, L. (2020, October 17). America is experiencing "truth decay" at an alarming rate, experts warn. *Syracuse University News*. https://news.syr.edu/blog/2020/10/17/america-is-experiencing-truth-decay-at-an-alarming-rate-experts-warn/

Davis, J., Frechette, H. M., & Boswell, E. H. (2010). *Strategic speed: Mobilize people, accelerate execution*. Harvard Business Press.

Dean, J. (2009a, September). Group polarization: The trend to extreme decisions. *PsyBlog*. http://www.spring.org.uk/2009/09/group-polarization-the-trend-to-extreme-decisions.php

Dean, J. (2009b). How newcomers can influence established groups. *Psyblog*. http://www.spring.org.uk/2009/07/how-newcomers-can-influence-established-groups.php

Debies-Carl, J. S. (2017, November /December). Pizzagate and beyond: Using social research to understand conspiracy legends. *Skeptical Inquirer*, pp. 34–37.

De Dreu, C. K. W., & Van Vianen, A. E. M. (2001). Managing relationship conflict and the effectiveness of organizational teams. *Journal of Organizational Behavior, 22*, 309–328. https://doi.org/10.1002/job.71

Delbecq, A., Van de Ven, A. H., & Gustafson, D. H. (1975). *Group techniques for program planning*. Scott, Foresman.

The Deloitte Global Millennial Survey. (2020). *Deloitte*. https://www2.deloitte.com/content/dam/Deloitte/global/Documents/About-Deloitte/deloitte-2020-millennial-survey.pdf

Delton, A. W., & Cimino, A. (2010). Exploring the evolved concept of newcomer: Experimental tests of a cognitive model. *Evolutionary Psychology, 8*, 317–335. https://doi.org/10.1177%2F147470491000800214

de Marcellis-Warin, N., Munoz, J. M., & Warin, T. (2020, July 31). Coronavirus and the widening educational digital divide: The perfect storm for inequalities. *California Management Review*. https://cmr.berkeley.edu/2020/07/covid-education/

Denworth, L. (2017, December). I feel your pain. *Scientific American*, pp. 58–63.

Derber, C. (1979). *The pursuit of attention: Power and individualism in everyday life*. New Oxford University Press.

DeRuy, E. (2018). The old college try. *Mercury News*, pp. 1A, 6A.

DeStephen, R., & Hirokawa, R. (1988). Small group consensus: Stability of group support of the decision, task process, and group relationships. *Small Group Behavior, 19*, 227–239.

De Waele, A. Schoofs, L., & Claeys, A-S. (2020). The power of empathy: The dual impacts of an emotional voice in organizational crisis communication. *Journal of Applied Communication Research, 48*, 350–371. https://doi.org/10.1080/00909882.2020.1750669

Dewey, J. (1910). *How we think*. D. C. Heath.

Dhawan, E. (2021). *Digital body language: How to build trust & connection, no matter the distance*. St. Martin's Press.

Dildar, S., & Amjad, N. (2017). Gender differences in conflict resolution styles (CRS) in different roles: A systematic review. *Pakistan Journal of Social and Clinical Psychology, 15*, 37–41. https://gcu.edu.pk/wp-content/uploads/2020/04/pjscp20172-6.pdf

Dinh, J. V., Traylor, A. M., Kilcullen, M. P., et al. (2020). Cross-disciplinary care: A systematic review on teamwork processes in health care. *Small Group Research, 51*, 125–166. https://doi.org/10.1177%2F1046496419872002

Dombeck, M. (2010, August). Psychological self-help tools: Assertiveness training. *CenterSite.net*. https://www.centersite.net/poc/view_doc.php?type=doc&id=9779&cn=353

Dominant leaders are bad for groups. Why do they succeed? (2018, January 8). *Association for Psychological Science*. https://www.psychologicalscience.org/news/minds-business/dominant-leaders-are-bad-for-groups.html

Donohue, W., & Kolt, R. (1992). *Managing interpersonal conflict*. SAGE.

Doodle. (2019). The state of meetings report. https://meeting-report.com/

Dorfman, P. W. (2004). International and cross-cultural leadership research. In B. J. Punnett & O. Shenkar (Eds.), *Handbook for international management research*. University of Michigan Press.

Dorfman, P. W., Hanges, P. J., & Brodbeck, F. C. (2004). Leadership and cultural variation: The identification of culturally endorsed leadership profiles. In R. J. House, P. J. Hanges, M. Javidan, P. W. Dorfman, & V. Gupta (Eds.), *Culture, leadership, and organizations: The GLOBE study of 62 societies*. SAGE.

Dotan-Eliaz, O., Sommer, K. L., & Rubin, Y. S. (2009). Multilingual groups: Effects of linguistic ostracism on felt rejection and anger, coworker attraction, perceived team potency, and creative performance. *Basic and Applied Social Psychology, 31*, 363–375.

Dovidio, J. F., Saguy, T., & Shnabel, N. (2009). Cooperation and conflict within groups: Bridging intragroup and intergroup processes. *Journal of Social Issues, 65*, 429–449. https://doi.org/10.1111/j.1540-4560.2009.01607.x

Dowell, N. M. M., Nixon, T. M., & Graesser, A. (2017). Group communication analysis: A computational linguistics approach for detecting sociocognitive roles in multi-party interactions. *Arxiv.org.* https://arxiv.org/ftp/arxiv/papers/1801/1801.03563.pdf

Drake, N., & Turner, B. (2021, January 18). Best video conferencing software in 2021. *Techradar.* https://www.techradar.com/best/best-video-conferencing-software

Drinking and drug abuse in Greek life. (2018, March 22). *Addiction Center.* https://www.addictioncenter.com/college/drinking-drug-abuse-greek-life

Driskell, J., Radtke, P., & Salas, E. (2003). Virtual teams: Effects of technological mediation on team performance. *Group Dynamics: Theory, Research, and Practice, 7,* 297–323. https://doi.apa.org/doi/10.1037/1089-2699.7.4.297

Driskell, J., & Salas, E. (1992, June). Collective behavior and team performance. *Human Factors, 34,* 277–288.

Druskat, V. U., & Wolff, S. B. (1999). Effects and timing of developmental peer appraisals in self-managing work groups. *Journal of Applied Psychology, 84,* 58–74.

Drutman, L. (2020, October 5). How hatred came to dominate American politics. *FiveThirtyEight.* https://fivethirtyeight.com/features/how-hatred-negative-partisanship-came-to-dominate-american-politics/

DuBrin, A. J. (2019). *Leadership: Research findings, practice, and skills.* Cengage.

Duhigg, C. (2016, February 25). What Google learned from its quest to build the perfect team. *New York Times.* https://www.nytimes.com/2016/02/28/magazine/what-google-learned-from-its-quest-to-build-the-perfect-team.html

Dunning, K. (2003). Why people fail to recognize their own incompetence. *Current Directions in Psychological Science, 22,* 77–87.

Dutton, K. (2016, September–October). Would you vote for a psychopath? *Scientific American Mind,* pp. 48–55.

Early, C. (1989). Social loafing and collectivism: A comparison of the United States and the People's Republic of China. *Administrative Science Quarterly, 34,* 555–581.

Ebert, R. J., & Griffin, R. W. (2011). *Leadership and decision making.* Pearson.

Ebrahim, N. A., Ahmed, S., & Taha, Z. (2009). Virtual teams: A literature review. *Australian Journal of Basic and Applied Sciences, 3,* 2653–2669.

Economist Intelligence Unit. (2009). Managing virtual teams. *The Economist.* http://graphics.eiu.com/upload/eb/NEC_Managing_virtual_teams_WEB.pdf

Edinger, S., Gallo, A., Schwarz, R., & Saunders, E. (2018, September 7). Stop Scheduling Conference Calls and Finally Commit to Videoconferencing. *Harvard Business Review.* https://hbr.org/2018/06/stop-scheduling-conference-calls-and-finally-commit-to-videoconferencing

8 facts from the 2021 Executive Paywatch report you need to know. (2021, July 14). AFL-CIO. https://aflcio.org/2021/7/14/8-facts-2021-executive-paywatch-report-you-need-know

Elgoibar, P., Euwema, M., & Munduate, L. (2017). Conflict management. *Oxford Research Encyclopedia.* http://psychology.oxfordre.com/view/10.1093/acrefore/9780190236557.001.0001/acrefore-9780190236557-e-5

Ellis, A. P. J., Bell, B. S., Ployhart, R. E., Hollenbeck, J. R., & Ilgen, D. R. (2005). An evaluation of generic teamwork skill training with action teams: Effects on cognitive and skill-based outcomes. *Personnel Psychology, 58,* 641–672.

Ellison, S. (2009). *Taking the war out of our words.* Wyatt-MacKenzie.

Emmons, M. (2013, October 9). *Ex-president helps build East San Jose home. San Jose Mercury News,* p. A14.

Eswaran, V. (2019, April 29). The business case for diversity in the workplace is now overwhelming. *World Economic Forum.* https://www.weforum.org/agenda/2019/04/business-case-for-diversity-in-the-workplace/

Eva, N., Robin, M., Sendjaya, S., et al. (2019). Servant leadership: A systematic review and call for future research. *The Leadership Quarterly, 30,* 111–132. https://doi.org/10.1016/j.leaqua.2018.07.004

Evans, C. R., & Dion, K. L. (2012). Group cohesion and performance: A meta-analysis. *Small Group Research, 43,* 690–701. https://doi.org/10.1177%2F1046496412468074

Executive paywatch. (2020, July 29). *AFL-CIO.* https://aflcio.org/paywatch

Eys, M., & Kim, J. (2017). Team building and group cohesion in the context of sport and performance psychology. *Sport Psychology.* http://psychology.oxfordre.com/view/10.1093/acrefore/9780190236557.001.0001/acrefore-9780190236557-e-186

Fadiman, C. (Ed.). (1985). *The Little, Brown book of anecdotes.* Little, Brown.

Fairhurst, G. (2010). *The power of framing: Creating the language of leadership.* Jossey-Bass.

Falcao, H. (2010). *Value negotiation: How to finally get the win-win right.* Prentice-Hall.

Fancher, L. (2016, June 17). Dacher Keltner's "The Paradox of Power" dishes the details on its uses and abuses. *Mercury News.* https://www.mercurynews.com/2016/06/17/dacher-keltners-the-power-paradox-dishes-the-details-on-its-uses-and-abuses

Fang, M. (2016, February 27). GOP presidential field scrambles to attack Donald Trump, deepening the party's split. *Huffington Post.* Retrieved from http://www.huffingtonpost.com/entry/donald-trump-republican-party_us_56d21fe8e4b0871f60eba9ab

Felmlee, D., Rodis, P. I., & Zhang, A. (2019). Sexist slurs: Reinforcing feminine stereotypes. *Sex Roles, 83,* 16–28. https://doi.org/10.1007/s11199-019-01095-z

Felps, W., Mitchell, T. R., & Byington, E. (2006). How, when, and why bad apples spoil the barrel: Negative group members and dysfunctional groups. *Research in Organizational Behavior, 27,* 175–222. https://doi.org/10.1016/S0191-3085(06)27005-9

Fernandes, C. R., & Polzer, J. T. (2015). Diversity in groups. In R. A. Scott & S. Kosslyn (Eds.), *Emerging trends in the social and behavioral sciences.* Wiley.

Ferrara, S., Mohammadi, N., Taylor, J., & Javernick-Will, A. (2016, June 28). Toward a more nuanced understanding of the generational digital divide in virtual teams. *Engineering Project Organization Conference.* http://www.epossociety.org/EPOC2016/papers/Ferrara%20et%20al_EPOC_2016.pdf

Ferrazzi, K. (2014, December). Getting virtual teams right. *Harvard Business Review.* https://hbr.org/2014/12/getting-virtual-teams-right

Ferrazzi, K. (2017, September 27). How to run a great virtual meeting. *Harvard Business Review.* https://hbr.org/2015/03/how-to-run-a-great-virtual-meeting

Ferrazzi, K., Race, M-C., & Vincent, A. (2021, January 21). 7 strategies to build a more resilient team. *Harvard Business Review.* https://hbr.org/2021/01/7-strategies-to-build-a-more-resilient-team

Fiedler, F., & House, R. (1988). Leadership theory and research: A report of progress. In C. Cooper & I. Robertson (Eds.), *International review of industrial and organizational psychology.* Wiley.

Fisher, R., & Brown, S. (1988). *Getting together: Building a relationship that gets to yes.* Houghton Mifflin.

Fisher, R., & Shapiro, D. (2005). *Beyond reason: Using emotions as you negotiate.* Penguin.

Fisher, R., Ury, W. L., & Patton, B. (2011). *Getting to yes: Negotiating agreement without giving in.* Penguin.

Fitzpatrick, B., Martinez, J., Polidan, E., & Angelis, E. (2015). The big impact of small groups on college drinking. *Journal of Artificial Societies and Social Stimulation.* http://jasss.soc.surrey.ac.uk/18/3/4.html

Fleming, N. (2020, June 17). Coronavirus misinformation, and how scientists can help to fight it. *Nature.* https://www.nature.com/articles/d41586-020-01834-3

Folger, J., Poole, M., & Stutman, R. (1993). *Working through conflict: A communication perspective.* Scott, Foresman.

Folley, A. (2019, October 7). Jimmy Carter back to building homes for Habitat for Humanity one day after fall. *The Hill.* https://thehill.com/blogs/in-the-know/in-the-know/464705-jimmy-carter-back-to-building-homes-for-habitat-for-humanity

Forbes Insights Team. (2017, October 30). Optimizing team performance: How and why video conferencing trumps audio. *Forbes.* https://www.forbes.com/sites/insights-zoom/2017/10/30/optimizing-team-performance-how-and-why-video-conferencing-trumps-audio/?sh=1788c49f720a

Ford, H. (2003). *My life and work.* Kessinger.

Forsyth, D. (2013, February 23). The costs of hazing. *Group Dynamics.* http://donforsythgroups.wordpress.com/2013/02/23/the-costs-of-hazing

Forsyth, D. (2019). *Group dynamics.* Wadsworth, Cengage Learning.

Forsyth, D. (2020). Group-level resistance to health mandates during COVID-19 pandemic: A groupthink approach. *Group Dynamics: Theory, Research, and Practice, 24,* 139–152. https://doi.apa.org/fulltext/2020-59628-001.html

Four conflict negotiation strategies for resolving value-based disputes. (2018, January 18). *Program on Negotiation/Harvard Law School.* https://www.pon.harvard.edu/daily/dispute-resolution/four-negotiation-strategies-for-resolving-values-based-disputes

Foust, D. (2009, May 14). How Delta climbed out of bankruptcy. *Bloomberg Businessweek.* http://www.businessweek.com/print/magazine/content/09_21_b4132036798289.htm

Fradera, A. (2017, March 23). Workplace venting makes it harder to bounce back from bad experiences. *The British Psychological Society Research Digest.* https://digest.bps.org.uk/2017/03/23/workplace-venting-makes-it-harder-to-bounce-back-from-bad-experiences/

Fragale, A. R. (2006). The power of powerless speech: The effects of speech style and task interdependence on status control. *Organizational Behavior and Human Decision Processes, 101,* 243–261. https://

alisonfragale.com/wp-content/uploads/2020/09/AlisonFragale_PowerofPowerlessSpeach.pdf

Franganillo, J. (2017, May). Information overload, why it matters and how to combat it. *Interaction Design Foundation*. https://www.interaction-design.org/literature/article/information-overload-why-it-matters-and-how-to-combat-it

Fredrickson, B. L. (2009). *Positivity: Top-notch research reveals the 3-to-1 ratio that will change your life*. Three Rivers.

Freeman, V. (2019, October 21). College hazing: What it is and how to stop it. *Best Colleges*. https://www.bestcolleges.com/blog/college-hazing

Frenk, J., & Gomez-Dantes, O. (2016). False dichotomies in global health: The need for integrative thinking. *The Lancet, 389*, 667–670. https://doi.org/10.1016/s0140-6736(16)30181-7

Frisch, B., & Greene, C. (2017, September 27). The right way to cut people off in meetings. *Harvard Business Review*. https://hbr.org/2016/04/the-right-way-to-cut-people-off-in-meetings

Fry, R. (2019, June 20). U.S. women near milestone in the college-educated labor force. *Pew Research*. https://www.pewresearch.org/fact-tank/2019/06/20/u-s-women-near-milestone-in-the-college-educated-labor-force/?

Fulop, M., & Orosz, G. (2015). State of the art in competition research. In R. Scott & S. Kosslyn (Eds.), *Emerging trends in the social and behavioral sciences*. Wiley.

Fulwiler, M. (2018). Managing conflict: Solvable vs. perpetual problems. *The Gottman Institute*. https://www.gottman.com/blog/managing-conflict-solvable-vs-perpetual-problems

Galimberti, A. (2018, January 30). Lives on the line: The human cost of cheap chicken. *Oxfam America*. https://www.iatp.org/sites/default/files/2018-02/Oxfam%20Poultry%20Webinar%20with%20IATP.pdf

Garber, M. (2016, May 25). Casual Friday and the "end of the office dress code." *The Atlantic*. https://www.theatlantic.com/entertainment/archive/2016/05/casual-friday-and-the-end-of-the-office-dress-code/484334/

Garcia, E., & Weiss, E. (2020, September 10). COVID-19 and student performance, equity, and U.S. education policy. *Economic Policy Institute*. https://www.epi.org/publication/the-consequences-of-the-covid-19-pandemic-for-education-performance-and-equity-in-the-united-states-what-can-we-learn-from-pre-pandemic-research-to-inform-relief-recovery-and-rebuilding/

Garrett, R. K., Weeks, B. E., & Neo, R. L. (2016). Driving a wedge between evidence and beliefs: How online ideological news exposure promotes political misperceptions. *Journal of Computer-Mediated Communication, 21*, 331–348. https://doi.org/10.1111/jcc4.12164

Gastil, J., Burkhalter, S., & Black, L. W. (2007). Do juries deliberate? A study of deliberation, individual difference, and group member satisfaction at a municipal courthouse. *Small Group Research, 38*, 337–359. https://doi.org/10.1177%2F1046496407301967

Gauche, C., de Beer, L. T., & Brink, L. (2017). Exploring demands from the perspective of employees identified as being at risk of burnout. *International Journal of Qualitative Studies on Health and Well-Being, 12(1)*. https://psycnet.apa.org/doi/10.1080/17482631.2017.1361783

Gearhart, S., & Zhang, W. (2015, April 16). "Was it something I said?" "No, it was something you posted!" A study of the spiral of silence theory in social media contexts. *Cyberpsychology, Behavior, and Social Networking*. https://www.liebertpub.com/doi/abs/10.1089/cyber.2014.0443?journalCode=cyber

Generation gap in American politics. (2018, March 1). *Pew Research Center*. https://www.pewresearch.org/politics/2018/03/01/the-generation-gap-in-american-politics/

Gentry, W. A., Weber, T. J., & Sadri, G. (2016). Empathy in the workplace: A tool for effective leadership. *Center for Creative Leadership*. http://www.ccl.org/wp-content/uploads/2015/04/EmpathyInTheWorkplace.pdf

Gen Z & Millennials' 5 favorite social media platforms now (2020, May 6). *YPulse*. https://www.ypulse.com/article/2020/05/06/gen-z-millennials-5-favorite-social-media-platforms-now/

Gerrig, R. J. (2013). *Psychology and life*. Pearson.

Gibb, J. (1961). Defensive communication. *Journal of Communication, 11*, 141–148.

Gilani, P., Bolat, E., Nordberg, D., et al. (2019). Mirror, mirror on the wall: Shifting leader-follower power dynamics in a social media context. *Leadership, 16*, 343–363. https://doi.org/10.1177%2F1742715019889817

Gilbert, P., Mcewan, K., Bellew, R., et al. (2008). The dark side of competition: How competitive behavior and striving to avoid inferiority are linked to depression, anxiety, stress, and self-harm. *Psychology and Psychotherapy Theory Research and Practice, 82*, 123–136. https://www.researchgate.net/deref/http%3A%2F%2Fdx.doi.org%2F10.1348%2F147608308X379806

Giles, S. (2016, March 15). The most important leadership competencies, according to leaders around the world. *Harvard Business Review*. https://hbr.org/2016/03/the-most-important-leadership-competencies-according-to-leaders-around-the-world

Gillis, A., & Krull, L. M. (2020, September 22). COVID-19 remote learning transition in spring 2020: Class structures, student perceptions, and inequality in college courses. *Teaching Sociology*. https://journals.sagepub.com/doi/full/10.1177/0092055X20954263

Gilmour, C. (2016, June 8). The Stanford Prison Experiment: "Put people in bad barrels and they'll become bad apples." *Independent*. http://www.independent.co.uk/arts-entertainment/music/features/the-stanford-prison-experiment-put-people-in-bad-barrels-and-they-ll-become-bad-apples-a7070596.html

Glikson, E., Cheshin, A., & van Kleef, G. A. (2017). The dark side of a smiley: Effects of smiling emoticons on virtual first impressions. *Social Psychological and Personality Science, 9*, 614–625. https://doi.org/10.1177%2F1948550617720269

Goff-Dupont, S. (2019, February 27). Types of meetings: 6 to keep, and 2 to cancel. *Atlassian*. https://www.atlassian.com/blog/teamwork/types-of-meetings

Goldenberg, O., Larson, J. R., & Wiley, J. (2013). Goal instructions, response formats, and idea generation in groups. *Small Group Research, 44*, 227–256.

Goldhaber, G. (1990). *Organizational communication*. Brown.

Goleman, D. (1995). *Emotional intelligence: Why it can matter more than I.Q.* Bantam.

Goleman, D. (2013). *Focus: The hidden driver of excellence*. HarperCollins.

Goleman, D., Boyatzis, R., & McKee, A. (2002). *Primal leadership: Realizing the power of emotional intelligence*. Harvard Business School Press.

Gomez, K., Mawhinney, T., & Betts, K. (2019). Welcome to Generation Z. *Deloitte*. https://www2.deloitte.com/content/dam/Deloitte/us/Documents/consumer-business/welcome-to-gen-z.pdf

Goodman, B. (2016, June 9). The art of negotiation. *Psychology Today*. https://www.psychologytoday.com/articles/200701/the-art-negotiation

Goss, E. (2021, February 1). Santa Clara University fraternity faces consequences for super-spreader event. *Fox KTVU*. https://www.ktvu.com/news/santa-clara-university-fraternity-faces-consequences-for-super-spreader-event

Gottman, J. M., & Gottman, J. S. (2006). *10 lessons to transform your marriage*. Crown.

Goudreau, J. (2012, November 16). The 10 worst communication mistakes for your career. *Forbes*. https://www.forbes.com/sites/jennagoudreau/2012/11/16/the-10-worst-communication-mistakes-for-your-career/#23877fd37562

Gould, T. (2016, May 18). New grads don't have skills needed for today's work world, report says. *HR Mornings*. https://www.hrmorning.com/articles/new-grads-dont-have-skills-needed-for-todays-work-world-report-says/

Gouran, D. (1982). *Making decisions in groups: Choices and consequences*. Scott, Foresman.

Grace, D. M., & Platow, M. J. (2015). Showing leadership by not showing your face: An anonymous leadership effect. *SAGE Open, 5*. https://journals.sagepub.com/doi/pdf/10.1177/2158244014567476

Grasz, J. (2017, January 12). CareerBuilder releases annual list of strangest interview and body language mistakes. *CareerBuilder*. https://www.careerbuilder.com/share/aboutus/pressreleasesdetail.aspx?sd=1%2F12%2F2017&id=pr984&ed=12%2F31%2F2017

Green, A. (2018, February 1). A university negotiates accusations of autocratic leadership. *Program on Negotiation/Harvard Law School*. https://www.pon.harvard.edu/daily/leadership-skills-daily/a-university-negotiates-accusations-of-autocratic-leadership/?utm_source=WhatCountsEmail&utm_medium=daily&utm_date=2018-02-01-13-55-00&mqsc=E3933802

Greengross, G., & Miller, G. F. (2008). Dissing oneself versus dissing rivals: Effects of status, personality, and sex on the short-term and long-term attractiveness of self-deprecating and other-deprecating humor. *Evolutionary Psychology Journal, 6*, 393–408. https://doi.org/10.1177%2F147470490800600303

Greenleaf, R. K. (1977). *Servant leadership: A journey into the nature of legitimate power and greatness*. Paulist.

Greer, L. L., De Jong, B., Schouten, M., & Dannals, J. (2018). Why and when hierarchy impacts team effectiveness: A meta-analytic examination. *Journal of Applied Psychology, 103,* 591–613. https://doi.apa.org/doi/10.1037/apl0000291

Greer, L. L., Jehn, K. A., & Manniz, E. A. (2008). Conflict transformation: A longitudinal investigation of the relationship between different types of intragroup conflict and the moderating role of conflict resolution. *Small Group Research, 39,* 278–302. https://doi.org/10.1177%2F1046496408317793

Gregoire, C. (2013, December 6). How technology speeds up time (and how to slow it down again). *Huffington Post.* http://www.huffingtonpost.com/2013/12/06/technology-time-perception_n_4378010.html

Grenny, J. (2009). Crucial conversations: The most potent force for eliminating disruptive behavior. *Physician Executive Journal, 35,* 30–33. https://doi.org/10.1097/01.cnq.0000343136.57813.f6

Grenny, J. (2017, April 20). What to do about mediocrity on your team. *Harvard Business Review.* https://hbr.org/2017/04/what-to-do-about-mediocrity-on-your-team

Grenny, J. (2019, June 17). How to be resilient in the face of harsh criticism. *Harvard Business Review.* https://hbr.org/2019/06/how-to-be-resilient-in-the-face-of-harsh-criticism

Griffin, E. (2006). *A first look at communication theory.* McGraw-Hill.

Group cohesiveness. (2017). *Management Study HQ.* http://www.managementstudyhq.com/group-cohesiveness.html

Grove, L. (2014, January 24). John Boehner live and unhinged with Jay Leno. *The Daily Beast.* https://www.thedailybeast.com/john-boehner-live-and-unhinged-with-jay-leno

Guastello, S. J., Correro, A. N., & Marra, D. E. (2018). Do emergent leaders experience greater workload? The swallowtail catastrophe model and changes in leadership in an emergency response simulation. *Group Dynamics: Theory, Research, and Practice, 22*(4), 200–222. https://psycnet.apa.org/doi/10.1037/gdn0000091

Guenter, H., van Emmerik, H., & Schreurs, B., Kuypers, T., van Iterson, A., & Notelaers, G. (2016). When task conflict becomes personal: The impact on perceived team performance. *Small Group Research, 47,* 569–604. https://doi.org/10.1177/1046496416667816

Gully, S., Devine, D., & Whitney, D. (2012). A meta-analysis of cohesion and performance: Effects of level of analysis and task interdependence. *Small Group Research, 43,* 702–725. https://doi.org/10.1177%2F1046496412468069

Gunaratne, C., Baral, N. Rand, W., et al. (2020). The effects of information overload on online conversation dynamics. *Computational and Mathematical Organizational Theory, 26,* 255–276. https://doi.org/10.1007/s10588-020-09314-9

Gundemir, S., Homan, A. C., de Dreu, C. K. W., & van Vugt, M. (2014). Think leader, think white? Capturing and weakening an implicit pro-white leadership bias. *PLOS One.* https://journals.plos.org/plosone/article?id=10.1371/journal.pone.0083915

Gunkel, M., Schlaegel, C., & Taras, V. (2016). Cultural values, emotional intelligence, and conflict handling styles: A global study. *Journal of World Business, 51,* 568–585. https://doi.org/10.1016/j.jwb.2016.02.001

Gupta, H. (2015). *Social media usage and its effect on virtual team dynamics: A transactive memory system approach.* Unpublished doctoral dissertation, University of Canterbury.

Guynn, J., & Schrotenboer, B. (2021, February 4). Why are there still so few Black executives in America? *USA Today.* https://www.usatoday.com/in-depth/money/business/2020/08/20/racism-black-america-corporate-america-facebook-apple-netflix-nike-diversity/5557003002/

Haass, R. N., & Knell, G. E. (2016, September). What college-aged students know about the world: A survey on global literacy. *Council on Foreign Relations & National Geographic Society.* https://www.cfr.org/content/newsletter/files/CFR_NatGeo_ASurveyon GlobalLiteracy.pdf

Habel, M. (2015, July 1). Building collegial nurse-physician relationships. *OR Today.* http://ortoday.com/building-collegial-nurse-physician-relationships

Habitat's history. (2020). *Habitat for Humanity.* https://www.habitat.org/about/history

Hacker, J. V., Johnson, M., Saunders, C., & Thayer, A. L. (2019). Trust in virtual teams: A multidisciplinary review and integration. *Australasian Journal of Information Systems.* DOI: 10.3127/ajis.v23i0.1757

Hackman, M., & Johnson, C. (2019). *Leadership: A communication perspective.* Waveland Press.

Haden, J. (2013, March 14). 8 most common complaints about the boss. *Inc.* https://www.inc.com/jeff-haden/8-most-common-complaints-employees-have-about-their-boss.html

Hall, C. C., Ariss, L., & Todorov, A. (2007). The illusion of knowledge: When more information reduces accuracy and increases confidence. *Organizational Behavior and Human Decision Processes, 103*, 277–290. https://psycnet.apa.org/doi/10.1016/j.obhdp.2007.01.003

Hall, E., & Hall, M. (1987). *Understanding cultural difference*. Intercultural Press.

Hall, J. A., & Bernieri, F. J. (Eds.). (2001). *Interpersonal sensitivity: Theory and measurement*. Erlbaum.

Halpern, D. (1984). *Thought and knowledge: An introduction to critical thinking*. Erlbaum.

Hambley, C. (2020, February 28). Five ways to build a better medical team. *Medical Economics*. https://www.medicaleconomics.com/view/5-ways-build-better-medical-team

Hampton, K., Rainie, L., Dwyer, M., Shin, I., & Purcell, K. (2014, August 26). Social media and the "spiral of silence." *Pew Research Center*. http://www.pewinternet.org/2014/08/26/social-media-and-the-spiral-of-silence

Handke, L., Klonek, F. E., Parker, S. K., et al. (2019). Interactive effects of team virtuality and work design on team functioning. *Small Group Research, 51*, 3–47. https://journals.sagepub.com/doi/full/10.1177/1046496419863490

Handke, L., Schulte, E-M., Schneider, K., et al. (2020). Teams, time, and technology: Variations of media use over project phases. *Small Group Research, 50*, 266–305. https://doi.org/10.1177%2F1046496418824151

Handrick, L. (2017, November 1). Self-management: 5 steps to a self-managed workplace. *FitSmallBusiness*. https://fitsmallbusiness.com/self-management

Hanif, F., Khan, M., Adeel, M., & Shah, S. M. (2016). Impact of intra-group conflict on group performance-moderating role of cultural diversity. *Universal Journal of Management, 4*, 72–78. http://www.hrpub.org/download/20160130/UJM4-12105635.pdf

Hannah, R. (2019, March 20). Dynamic Signal's annual state of employee communication and engagement study—the 2019 findings are in! *Dynamic Signal*. https://dynamicsignal.com/2019/03/20/2019-employee-communication-and-engagement-study/

Hanson, B. (2020). Research on abuse in sport and athlete welfare. *Athlete Assessments.com*. https://www.athleteassessments.com/research-on-athlete-welfare-and-abusive-coaching/

Hanson, M., & Turner, B. (2020, October 2). Best conference phones of 2020: Audio conferencing for online meetings. *Techradar.pro*. https://www.techradar.com/best/best-conference-phones

Hanson, R. (2016, October 26). Confronting the negativity bias. *RickHanson.net*. http://www.rickhanson.net/how-your-brain-makes-you-easily-intimidated

Hare, A. P. (2013). Roles, relationships, and groups in organizations: Some conclusions and recommendations. *Small Group Research, 34*, 123–154. https://doi.org/10.1177%2F1046496402250430

Harrison, D. A., Price, K. H., Gavin, J. H., & Florey, A. T. (2002). Time, teams, and task performance: Changing attitudes of surface and deep-level diversity on group functioning. *Academy of Management Journal, 445*, 1029–1045.

Haslam, S. A., & Knight, C. (2010, September/October). Cubicle, sweet cubicle. *Scientific American Mind*, pp. 31–35.

Haslam, S. A., Reicher, S. D., & Platow, M. J. (2011). *The new psychology of leadership: Identity, influence and power*. Psychology Press.

Hastie, R., & Kameda, T. (2005). The robust beauty of majority rules in group decision. *Psychological Review, 112*, 494–508. https://psycnet.apa.org/doi/10.1037/0033-295X.112.2.494

Hastie, R., & Sunstein, C. R. (2015, July 21). Polarization: One reason groups fail. *Chicago Booth Review*. http://review.chicagobooth.edu/magazine/spring-2015/one-reason-groups-fail-polarization

Hastie, R., Schkade, D., & Sunstein, C. R. (2006). *What really happened on deliberation day?* Unpublished manuscript, University of Chicago Law School.

Hastings, R. R. (2012, August 17). Bosses seen as ineffective conflict managers. *SHRM*. https://www.shrm.org/resourcesandtools/hr-topics/employee-relations/pages/bosses-seen-as-ineffective-conflict-managers.aspx

Hayes, J. (2008, July). Workplace conflict and how business can harness it to thrive. *CPP Global Human Capital Report*. https://shop.cpp.com/Pdfs/CPP_Global_Human_Capital_Report_Workplace_Conflict.pdf

Hayes, L. N. (2018, February 22). The most unusual interview mistakes and biggest body language mishaps, according to annual CareerBuilder survey. *CareerBuilder*. http://press.careerbuilder.com/2018-02-22-The-Most-Unusual-Interview-Mistakes-and-Biggest-Body-Language-Mishaps-According-to-Annual-CareerBuilder-Survey

Haynie, D. (2016, May 10). Millennial leaders around the world. *U.S. News & World Report*. https://www.usnews.com/news/best-countries/slideshows/10-millennial-leaders-around-the-globe

He, H., Baruch, Y., & Lin, C-P. (2014). Modeling team knowledge sharing and team flexibility: The role of within-team competition. *Human Relations, 67,* 947–978. https://doi.org/10.1177%2F0018726713508797

Heaney, K. (2013, June 11). Everyone is using their smartphones on the toilet. *BuzzFeed.* http://www.buzzfeed.com/katieheaney/everyone-is-using-their-smartphones-on-the-toilet

Hennigan, K., & Spanovic, M. (2012). Gang dynamics through the lens of social identity theory. In F. A. Esbensen & C. Maxson (Eds.), *Gangs in international perspective.* Springer.

Henningsen, D. D., & Henningsen, M. L. M. (2018). Does brainstorming promote cohesiveness? How the rules of brainstorming mirror symbolic convergence. *Communication Reports, 31,* 103–114. https://doi.org/10.1080/08934215.2017.1394476

Henricks, M. (2018, October 30). The mantle of leadership isn't held only by one pay grade. *The Homes Report.* https://www.holmesreport.com/latest/article/the-mantle-of-leadership-isn-t-held-only-by-one-pay-grade

Herley, T. (2015). Perceptions of role conflict and workplace stress among women working in two traditionally male professions. *Walden University Scholars Work.* http://scholarworks.waldenu.edu/cgi/viewcontent.cgi?article=1263&context=dissertations

Hersey, P., Blanchard, K. H., & Johnson, D. E. (2001). *Management of organizational behavior: Leading human resources.* Prentice Hall.

Higginbottom, K. (2018, May 31). Why empathy matters in the workplace. *Forbes.* https://www.forbes.com/sites/karenhigginbottom/2018/05/31/why-empathy-matters-in-the-workplace/#3f5d6e071130

Higgins-Dunn, N. (2020, September 11). Fraternities blamed for campus coronavirus outbreaks as universities struggle to keep students in class. *CNBC.* https://www.cnbc.com/2020/09/09/coronavirus-universities-blame-greek-life-for-campus-reopening-headaches-were-having-a-significant-issue.html

Hirokawa, R., & Pace, R. (1983). A descriptive investigation of the possible communication-based reasons for effective and ineffective group decision-making. *Communication Monographs, 50,* 363–379.

Hitlan, R. T., Kelly, K. M., Schepman, S., Schneider, K. T., & Zarate, M. A. (2006). Language exclusion and the consequences of perceived ostracism in the workplace. *Group Dynamics: Theory, Research, and Practice, 10,* 56–70. https://psycnet.apa.org/doi/10.1037/1089-2699.10.1.56

Hjerto, K. B., & Paulsen, J. M. (2016). Beyond collective beliefs: Predicting team academic performance from collective emotional intelligence. *Small Group Research, 47,* 510–541. https://doi.org/10.1177%2F1046496416661236

Hoch, J. E., & Dulebohn, J. H. (2017). Team personality composition, emergent leadership and shared leadership in virtual teams: A theoretical framework. *Human Resource Management Review, 27,* 678–693. https://psycnet.apa.org/doi/10.1016/j.hrmr.2016.12.012

Hoch, M. (2021, January 29). The insider: Leadership isn't about a to-do list. *Harvard Business Review.* https://mail.google.com/mail/u/0/#inbox/FMfcgxwLsJvLLhhpcTpnbHjtRsqjCgKn

Hoe, R. (2017, June 6). Pros and cons of majority-rule explained in 5 minutes. *Consensus.* https://consensusg.com/2017/06/06/pros-and-cons-of-majority-rule-explained-in-5-minutes

Hoffer, T., Reppeto, L., White, L., Greeley, A., & Kirpalani, A. (2013, April). *Jurors' body language: Why we look, what to notice and what to ignore.* Paper presented at the ABA Section of Litigation: Section Annual Conference, Chicago. https://www.americanbar.org

Hoffman, R. (2020, June 22). Social loafing: Definition, examples and theory. *Simply Psychology.* https://www.simplypsychology.org/social-loafing.html

Hofstede, G. (2012). Dimensionalizing cultures: The Hostede model in context. In S. A. Samovar, R. E. Porter, & E. R. McDaniel (Eds.), *Intercultural communication: A reader.* Wadsworth/Cengage.

Hofstede, G., & Hofstede, G. J. (2010). *Cultures and organizations: Software of the mind.* McGraw-Hill.

Hogg, M. A. (2018). Social identity theory. In P. J. Burke (Ed.), *Contemporary social psychological theories.* Stanford University Press.

Hoigaard, R., & Ommundsen, Y. (2007). Perceived social loafing and anticipated effort reduction among young football (soccer) players: An achievement goal perspective. *Psychological Reports, 100,* 857–875.

Hollander, E., & Offerman, L. (1990, February). Power and leadership in organizations. *American Psychologist, 45,* 179–189.

Homan, A. C., Greer, L. L., Jehn, K. A., & Koning, L. (2010). Believing shapes seeing: The impact of diversity beliefs on the construal of group composition. *Group Processes & Intergroup Relations, 13,* 477–493.

Honey-Roses, J., Canessa, M., Daitch, S., et al. (2020). Comparing structured and unstructured facilitation approaches in consultation workshops: A field experiment. *Group Decision and Negotiation, 29*, 949–967. https://doi.org/10.1007/s10726-020-09688-w

Hong, Y-Y., & Cheon, B. K. (2017). How does culture matter in the face of globalization? *Perspectives on Psychological Science, 12*, 810–823. https://doi.org/10.1177%2F1745691617700496

Hoption, C., Barling, J., & Turner, N. (2013). "It's not you, it's me": Transformational leadership and self-deprecating humor. *Leadership & Organizational Development Journal, 34*, 4–19. https://psycnet.apa.org/doi/10.1108/01437731311289947

Horila, T., & Siitonen, M. (2020). A time to lead: Changes in relational leadership processes over time. *Management Communication Quarterly, 34*, 558– 584. https://journals.sagepub.com/doi/full/10.1177/0893318920949700

Hornsey, M. J., Grice, T., Jetten, J., Paulsen, N., & Callan, V. (2007). Group-directed criticisms and recommendations for change: Why newcomers arouse more defensiveness than old-timers. *Personality and Social Psychology Bulletin, 33*, 1036–1048. https://psycnet.apa.org/doi/10.1177/0146167207301029

Hosman, L. A., & Siltanen, S. A. (2006). Powerful and powerless language forms: Their consequences for impression formation, attributions of control of self and control of others, cognitive responses, and message memory. *Journal of Language and Social Psychology, 25*, 33–46. https://doi.org/10.1177%2F0261927X05284477

Hougaard, R., & Carter, J. (2018, November 6). Ego is the enemy of good leadership. *Harvard Business Review.* https://hbr.org/2018/11/ego-is-the-enemy-of-good-leadership

House, R. J. (2004). Illustrative examples of GLOBE findings. In R. J. House, P. J. Hanges, M. Javidan, P. W. Dorfman, & V. Gupta (Eds.), *Culture, leadership, and organizations: The GLOBE study of 62 societies.* SAGE.

House, R. J., & Aditya, R. N. (1997). The social scientific study of leadership: Quo vadis? *Journal of Management, 23*, 409–473.

Housman, M., & Minor, D. (2015). Toxic workers [Working Paper 16-047]. *Harvard Business School.*

Howell, E., & Hickok, K. (2020, March 31). Apollo 13: The moon-mission that dodged disaster. *Space.com.* https://www.space.com/17250-apollo-13-facts.html

Howell, S. E. (2014). Conflict management: A literature review and study. *Radiology Management.* http://www.ahra.org/AM/Downloads/OI/qc/RM365_p14-23_Features.pdf

How to improve collaboration and teamwork skills with whole brain thinking. (2015). *Hermann Solutions.* https://www.herrmannsolutions.com/how-to-improve-collaboration-and-teamwork-skills-with-whole-brain-thinking

Howard, J. W. (2008). "Tower, am I cleared to land?": Problematic communication in aviation discourse. *Human Communication Research, 34*, 370–391. https://doi.org/10.1111/j.1468-2958.2008.00325.x

Hsieh, C-J., Fific, M., & Yang, C-T. (2020, September 17). A new measure of group decision-making efficiency. *Cognitive Research: Principles and Implications, 5*, 45. https://doi.org/10.1186/s41235-020-00244-3

Hughes, A, M., Gregory, M. E., Joseph, D. L., et al. (2016). Saving lives: A meta-analysis of team training in healthcare. *Journal of Applied Psychology, 101*(9), 1266–1304. https://doi.org/10.1037/apl0000120

Hunt, V., Yea, L., Prince, S., & Dixon-Fyle, S. (2018, January). Delivering through diversity. *McKinsey & Company.* https://www.mckinsey.com/~/media/mckinsey/business%20functions/organization/our%20insights/delivering%20through%20diversity/delivering-through-diversity_full-report.ashx

Hyatt, M. (2016). How to treat the scourge of cynicism. *MichaelHyatt.com.* https://michaelhyatt.com/the-scourge-of-cynicism

Iglesias, M. E. L., & Vallejo, R. B. (2012). Conflict resolution styles in nursing profession. *Contemporary Nurse, 43*, 73–80.

Impett, E. A., Gable, S. L., & Peplau, L. A. (2005). Giving up and giving in: The costs and benefits of daily sacrifice in intimate relationships. *Journal of Personality and Social Psychology, 89*, 327–344. https://psycnet.apa.org/doi/10.1037/0022-3514.89.3.327

Integrative bargaining examples: Expanding the pie—Integrative versus distributive bargaining negotiation strategies. (2017, November 28). *Program on Negotiation/Harvard Law School.* https://www.pon.harvard.edu/daily/negotiation-skills-daily/negotiation-skills-expanding-the-pie-integrative-bargaining-versus-distributive-bargaining

Internet world users by language. (2021). *Internet World Stats.* https://www.internetworldstats.com/stats7.htm

Is your team too big? Too small? What's the right number? (2006). *Wharton Business School, University of Pennsylvania*. http://knowledge.wharton.upenn.edu/article/is-your-team-too-big-too-small-whats-the-right-number-2

Isaac, M. L. (2012). "I hate group work!" Social loafers, indignant peers, and the drama of the classroom. *The English Journal, 101*, 83–89. https://www.jstor.org/stable/41415478

Isaksen, S. G., & Gaulin, J. P. (2005). A reexamination of brainstorming research: Implications for research and practice. *Gifted Child Quarterly, 49*, 315–329. https://doi.org/10.1177%2F001698620504900405

Jackson, G. P. (2014, July 9). Shock poll: 73% support the impeachment of President Obama. *Word Press*. https://thespeechatimeforchoosing.wordpress.com/2014/07/09/shock-poll-73-support-the-impeachment-of-president-obama

Jacobs, J., & Harrison, C. (2019, April 9). Doctor dragged off United Airlines flight after watching viral video of himself: "I just cried." *ABC News*. https://abcnews.go.com/US/doctor-dragged-off-united-airlines-flight-watching-viral/story?id=62250271

Jaeger, E. L. (2020). Not the desired outcome: Groupthink undermines the work of a literacy council. *Small Group Research, 51*, 517–541. https://doi.org/10.1177%2F1046496419890684

Jaffe, E. (2012). Give and take: Empirical strategies for compromise. *Observer, 25*, 9–11.

Jaksa, J., & Pritchard, M. (1994). *Communication ethics: Methods of analysis*. Wadsworth.

James, D., & Clarke, S. (1993). Women, men, and interruptions: A critical review. In D. Tannen (Ed.), *Gender and conversational interaction*. Oxford University Press.

James, F. (2003, February 13). Critics unglued by government's advice on duct tape. *Chicago Tribune*. http://www.chicagotribune.com/sns-terror-ducttape-ct-story.html

Janis, I. (1982). *Groupthink: Psychological studies of policy decisions and fiascoes*. Houghton Mifflin.

Janusik, L., & Rouillard, J. (2020, July). Research findings on listening. *Global Listening Centre*. https://www.globallisteningcentre.org/wp-content/uploads/2020/07/research-findings-on-listening-laura-janusik.pdf

Jarc, R. (2012, October 31). The ethics of American youth: 2012. *Josephson Institute Center for Youth Ethics*. http://charactercounts.org/programs/reportcard/2012/installment_report-card_bullying-youth-violence.html

Javidan, M., House, R. J., Dorfman, P. W., et al. (2006). Conceptualizing and measuring cultures and their consequences: A comparative review of GLOBE's and Hostede's approaches. *Journal of International Business Studies, 37*, 897–914. https://doi.org/10.1057/palgrave.jibs.8400234

Jaworski, M. (2021). The negativity bias: Why the bad stuff sticks. *Psycom*. https://www.psycom.net/negativity-bias

Jehn, K. A. (1995). A multimethod examination of the benefits and detriments of intragroup conflict. *Administrative Science Quarterly, 40*, 256–282.

Jenkins, S., & Delbridge, R. (2016). Trusted to deceive: A case study of "strategic deception" and the normalization of lying at work. *Organizational Studies, 38*, 53–76. https://doi.org/10.1177%2F0170840616655481

Jennings, C. A. (2020, November 1). How to relax Robert's Rules. *Dummies*. https://www.dummies.com/careers/business-skills/how-to-relax-roberts-rules/

Jerabek, I., & Muoio, D. (2017). Lone wolf, lone sheep: Why some of the best-and-worst-employees hate teamwork. *Human Resources*. https://www.researchgate.net/publication/320456667_Lone_Wolf_Lone_Sheep_Why_Some_Of_The_Best-And-Worst-Employees_Hate_Teamwork

Jiang, J., Chen, C., Dai, B., Shi, G., Ding, G., Liu, L., & Lu, C. (2015). Leader emergence through interpersonal neural synchronization. *Proceedings of the National Academy of Sciences of the United States of America, 112*, 4274–4279.

Jiang, M. (2020, April 22). The reason Zoom calls drain your energy. *BBC*. https://www.bbc.com/worklife/article/20200421-why-zoom-video-chats-are-so-exhausting

Jobidon, M-E., Turcotte, I., & Aube, C. (2016). Role variability in self-organizing teams working in crisis management. *Small Group Research, 48*, 62–92. https://doi.org/10.1177%2F1046496416676892

Johannessen, H. A., Tynes, T., & Sterud, R. (2013). Effects of occupational role conflict and emotional demands on subsequent psychological distress. *Journal of Occupational and Environmental Medicine, 55*, 605–613. https://doi.org/10.1097/jom.0b013e3182917899

Johnson, C. (2009). Bad blood: Doctor–nurse behavior problems impact patient care. *Physician Executive Journal, 35*, 6–10. https://www.svhs.org.au/

ArticleDocuments/3393/doctornursebehavior%20
2009.pdf.aspx?embed=y

Johnson, D. T. (2016). Juries in the Japanese legal system: The continuing struggle for citizen participation and democracy. *Social Science Japan Journal, 19,* 116–119.

Johnson, D. W. (2003). Social interdependence: Interrelationships among theory, research, and practice. *American Psychologist, 58,* 934–945. https://doi.apa.org/doi/10.1037/0003-066X.58.11.934

Johnson, D. W., & Johnson, R. T. (2000, June). *Teaching students to be peacemakers; Results of twelve years of research.* Paper presented at the Society for the Psychological Study of Social Issues Convention, Long Beach, California.

Johnson, D. W., & Johnson, R. T. (2009). An educational psychology success story: Social interdependence theory and cooperative learning. *Educational Researcher, 38,* 365–379. https://doi.org/10.3102%2F0013189X09339057

Johnson, D. W., & Johnson, R. T. (2015). Cooperation and competition. *International Encyclopedia of the Social & Behavioral Sciences (2nd ed.).* https://www.sciencedirect.com/science/article/pii/B9780080970868240518?via%3Dihub

Johnson, D. W., Johnson, R. T., & Smith, K. A. (2014). Cooperative learning: Improving university instruction by basing practice on validated theory. *Journal of Excellence in College Teaching, 25,* 85–118.

Johnson, N., & Klee, T. (2007). Passive-aggressive behavior and leadership styles in organizations. *Journal of Leadership & Organizational Studies, 14,* 130–142. https://doi.org/10.1177%2F1071791907308044

Johnson, S. K., Bettenhausen, K., & Gibbons, E. (2009). Realities of working in virtual teams: Affective and attitudinal outcomes of using computer-mediated communication. *Small Group Research, 40,* 623–649. https://doi.org/10.1177%2F1046496409346448

Jones, E. E., & Kelly, J. R. (2007). Contributions to a group discussion and perceptions of leadership: Does quantity always count more than quality? *Group Dynamics: Theory, Research, and Practice, 11,* 15–30. https://psycnet.apa.org/doi/10.1037/1089-2699.11.1.15

Jordan, M. H., Field, H. S., & Armenakis, A. A. (2002). The relationships of group process variables and team performance. *Small Group Research, 33,* 121–150.

Josephson, M. (2002). *Making ethical decisions.* Josephson Institute of Ethics.

Judge, T. A., & Piccolo, R. F. (2004). Transformational and transactional leadership: A meta-analytic test of their relative validity. *Journal of Applied Psychology, 89,* 755–768. https://psycnet.apa.org/doi/10.1037/0021-9010.89.5.755

Juergens, J., & Hampton, D. (2020, December 1). Drinking and drug abuse in Greek life. *Addiction Center.* https://www.addictioncenter.com/college/drinking-drug-abuse-greek-life/

Jurors' body language: Why we look, what to notice—and what to ignore. (2017, February 23). *DecisionQuest.* https://www.decisionquest.com/jurors-body-language-why-we-look-what-to-notice-and-what-to-ignore/

Kafle, H. R. (2014). Symbolic convergence theory: Revisiting its relevance to team communication. *International Journal of Communication, 24,* 16–29.

Kahlow, J., Klecka, H., & Ruppel, E. (2020). What the differences in conflict between online and face-to-face work groups mean for hybrid groups: A state-of-the-art review. *Review of Communication Research, 8,* 50–77. https://www.rcommunicationr.org/index.php/rcr/article/view/53/61

Kahneman, D., Sibony, O., & Sunstein, C. R. (2021). *Noise: A flaw in human judgment.* Little, Brown Spark.

Kameda, N. (2007). Communicative challenges for Japanese companies: Strategies in the global marketplace. In *Proceedings of the Association for Business Communication 7th Asia-Pacific Conference.* Association for Business Communication.

Kameda, N. (2014). Japanese business discourse of oneness: A personal perspective. *International Journal of Business Communication, 51,* 93–113. https://doi.org/10.1177%2F2329488413516210

Kao, A. B., & Couzin, I. D. (2014). Decision accuracy in complex environments is often maximized by small group sizes. *Proceedings of the Royal Society B, 281*(178). https://doi.org/10.1098/rspb.2013.3305

Karau, S. J., & Elsaid, A. M. M. K. (2009). Individual differences in beliefs about groups. *Group Dynamics: Theory, Research, and Practice, 13,* 1–13.

Karpowitz, C. F., Mendelberg, T., & Shaker, L. (2012). Gender inequality in deliberative participation. *American Political Science Review, 106,* 533–547.

Katz, D., & Kahn, R. (1978). *The social psychology of organizations.* Wiley.

Kavanagh, J., & Rich, M. D. (2018). *Truth decay: An initial exploration of the diminishing role of facts and analysis in American public life.* Rand.

Kavanagh, K. T., Saman, D., Bartel, R., & Westerman, K. (2017). Estimating hospital-related deaths due to medical error: A perspective from patient advocates. *Journal of Patient Safety, 13,* 1–5.

Keating, E. (2020, October 20). Why do virtual meetings feel so weird? *Sapiens.* https://www.sapiens.org/language/nonverbal-communication-online/

Keck, S., & Tang, W. (2020). Enhancing the wisdom of the crowd with cognitive-process diversity: The benefits of aggregating intuitive and analytical judgments. *Psychological Science, 31,* 1272–1282. https://doi.org/10.1177%2F0956797620941840

Kelemen, T. K., Matthews, S. H., et al. (2020). When does gender diversity enhance team performance? The dual need for visionary leadership and team tenure. *Journal of Applied Social Psychology, 9,* 501–511. https://doi.org/10.1111/jasp.12690

Kelley, T., & Littman, J. (2001). *The art of innovation.* Doubleday.

Keltner, D. (2007, December 1). The power paradox. *Greater Good Magazine.* https://greatergood.berkeley.edu/article/item/power_paradox

Keltner, D. (2017). *The power paradox: How we gain and lose influence.* Penguin Books.

Kennedy, F. A., Loughry, M. L., Klammer, T. P., & Beyerlein, M. M. (2009). Effects of organizational support on potency in work teams. *Small Group Research, 40,* 72–93.

Kenski, K., Coe, K., & Rains, S. A. (2020). Perceptions of uncivil discourse online: An examination of types and predictors. *Communication Research, 47,* 795–814. https://doi.org/10.1177%2F0093650217699933

Kerwin, S., Doherty, A., & Harman, A. (2011). "It's not conflict, it's differences of opinion": An in-depth examination of conflict in nonprofit boards. *Small Group Research, 42,* 562–594.

Keyton, J., & Beck, S. J. (2010). Examining laughter functionality in jury deliberations. *Small Group Research, 41,* 386–407.

Khademi, M., Schmidt-Mast, M., & Frauendorfer, D. (2020). From hierarchical to egalitarian: Hierarchy steepness depends on speaking time feedback and task interdependence. *Group Dynamics: Theory, Research, and Practice, 24*(4), 261–275. https://psycnet.apa.org/doi/10.1037/gdn0000114

Khalvati, K., Park, S. A., Philippe, R., et al. (2018, September 17). Bayesian inference of other minds explains human decisions in a group decision making task. *BioTxiv.*

https://www.biorxiv.org/content/10.1101/419515v1.full

Khan, A. K., Moss, S., Quratulain, S., & Hameed, I. (2016). When and how subordinate performance leads to abusive supervision: A social dominance perspective. *Journal of Management, 44,* 2801–2826. https://doi.org/10.1177%2F0149206316653930

Kidder, R. M, Mirk, P., & Loges, W. E. (2002). Maricopa values & ethics survey. *The Institute for Global Ethics.* https://www.maricopa.edu/gvbd/vei/Values%20&%20Ethics%20Survey.pdf

Killion, A. (2004, August 16). Yet another "wake-up call" won't rouse this U.S. team. *San Jose Mercury News,* pp. 1D, 3D.

Kilmann, R., & Thomas, K. (1977). Developing a force-choice measure of conflict-handling behavior: The MODE instrument. *Educational and Psychological Measurement, 37,* 309–325.

Kim, D-Y., & Park, J. (2010). Cultural differences in risk: the group facilitation effect. *Judgment and Decision Making, 5,* 380–390.

Kim, M-S. (2016, October). Intercultural conflict. *Oxford Research Encyclopedia.* http://communication.oxfordre.com/view/10.1093/acrefore/9780190228613.001.0001/acrefore-9780190228613-e-24

Kim, S. L., Lee, S., & Yun, S. (2020). The trickle-down effect of abusive supervision: The moderating effects of supervisors' task performance and employee promotion focus. *Journal of Leadership & Organizational Studies, 27,* 241–255. https://doi.org/10.1177%2F1548051820933321

King, E. B., Hebl, M. R., & Beal, D. J. (2009). Conflict and cooperation in diverse workgroups. *Journal of Social Issues, 65,* 261–285.

King, M. (2020, March 24). One invisible barrier holding back women at work: the conformity bind. *Ideas. TED.com.* https://ideas.ted.com/one-invisible-barrier-holding-back-women-at-work-the-conformity-bind/

Kingsford-Smith, A. (2017, July 12). Cirque du Soleil: The circus that took over the world. *The Culture Trip.* https://theculturetrip.com/north-america/canada/quebec/articles/cirque-du-soleil-the-circus-that-took-over-the-world

Kirkman, B., & Rosen, B. (1999). Beyond self-management: Antecedents and consequences of team empowerment. *Academy of Management Journal, 42,* 58–74.

Kirkman, B. L., Rosen, B., Tesluk, P. E., & Gibson, C. B. (2004). Team empowerment on virtual team performance: The moderating role of face-to-face interaction. *Academy of Management Journal, 47*, 175–192.

Kitayama, S. (2013). Mapping mindsets: The world of cultural neuroscience. *Observer, 26*, 21–23.

Klapp, O. (1978). *Opening and closing: Strategies of information adaptation in society*. Cambridge University Press.

Klein, C., DiazGranados, D., Salas, E., Le, H., Burke, C. S., & Goodwin, G. F. (2009). Does teambuilding work? *Small Group Research, 40*, 181–222.

Kluger, J. (2009, March 2). Why bosses tend to be blowhards. *Time*, p. 48.

Knapp, M. L., Hall, J. A., & Horgan, T. G. (2014). *Nonverbal communication in human interaction*. Wadsworth, Cengage.

Knights, J. (2017). How to develop ethical leaders. *Routledge*. https://www.routledge.com/rsc/downloads/Transpersonal_Leadership_WP1.pdf

Knowles, M. (2018, June 27). 1 in 3 nurses have reported sexual harassment by physicians; no action taken 74% of the time. *Becker's Hospital Review*. https://www.beckershospitalreview.com/workforce/1-in-3-nurses-have-reported-sexual-harassment-by-physicians-no-action-taken-74-of-the-time.html

Knutson, T. J., Komolsevin, R., Chatiketu, P., & Smith, V. R. (2003). A cross-cultural comparison of Thai and U.S. American rhetorical sensitivity: Implications for intercultural communication effectiveness. *International Journal of Relations, 27*, 63–78.

Knutson, T. J., & Posirisuk, S. (2006). Thai relational development and rhetorical sensitivity as potential contributors to intercultural communication effectiveness: Jai Yen Yen. *Journal of Intercultural Communication Research, 35*, 205–217.

Ko, V. (2013, April 14). Can you cope with criticism at work? *CNN*. https://www.cnn.com/2013/04/14/business/criticism-praise-feedback-work-life/index.html

Koenig, A. M., Eagly, A. H., Mitchell, A. A., & Ristikari, T. (2011). Are leader stereotypes masculine? A meta-analysis of three research paradigms. *Psychological Bulletin, 137*, 616–642.

Kohn, A. (1992). *No contest: The case against competition*. Houghton Mifflin.

Konstantinova, M., & Astakhova, K. (2018, November 16). Experts say . . . Is communication really only 7% verbal? Truth vs. marketing. *Medium Marketing*. https://medium.com/@neurodatalab/experts-say-is-communication-really-only-7-verbal-truth-vs-marketing-9a8e7428fd0f

Korde, R. M., & Paulus, P. (2017). Alternating individual and group idea generation: Finding the elusive synergy. *Journal of Experimental Social Psychology, 70*, 177–190. https://doi.org/10.1016/j.jesp.2016.11.002

Kowalski, R. M., Toth, A., & Morgan, M. (2018). Bullying and cyberbullying in adulthood and the workplace. *The Journal of Social Psychology, 158*, 64–81. https://doi.org/10.1080/00224545.2017.1302402

Kozlowski, S. W. J. (2018). Enhancing the effectiveness of work groups and teams: A reflection. *Perspectives on Psychological Science, 13*, 205–212.

Kozlowski, S. W. J., & Ilgen, D. R. (2007, June/July). The science of team success. *Scientific American Mind*, pp. 54–61.

Kozusznik, M. W., Aaldering, H., & Euwema, M. C. (2020). Star(tup) wars: Decoupling task from relationship conflict. *International Journal of Conflict Management, 31*, 393–415. https://doi.org/10.1108/IJCMA-09-2019-0167

Krause, S., James, R., Faria, J. J., Ruxton, G. D., & Krause, J. (2011). Swarm intelligence in humans: Diversity can trump ability. *Animal Behavior, 81*, 941–948.

Krauss, R. M., Freyberg, R., & Morsella, E. (2002). Inferring speakers' physical attributes from their voices. *Journal of Experimental Social Psychology, 38*, 618–625.

Krawczyk-Brylka, B. (2017). Intercultural challenges in virtual teams. *Journal of Intercultural Management, 8*(3), 69–85. https://content.sciendo.com/configurable/contentpage/journals$002fjoim$002f8$002f3$002farticle-p69.xml

Krieger, L. M. (2018, March 9). In Twittersphere, false information travels fast. *Mercury News*, p. 1A, 6A.

Krieger, L. M. (2021, January 24). A grim tally. *The Mercury News*, pp. A1, A8.

Kristinsson, K., Jonsdottir, I. J., & Snorrason, S. K. (2019). Employees' perceptions of supervisors' listening skills and their work-related quality of life. *Communication Reports*. https://doi.org/10.1080/08934215.2019.1634748

Kruger, J., Epley, N., Parker, J., & Ng, Z-W. (2005). Egocentrism over E-mail: Can we communicate as well as we think? *Journal of Personality and Social Psychology, 89*, 925-936.

Kuhel, J. (2020). Giving back, while moving forward. *Shaker Life*. https://shaker.life/schools/mac-scholars/

Ladkin, D. (2020). Donald Trump's response to COVID-19 teaches us: It's time for our romance with leaders to end. *Leadership, 16*, 273–278. https://doi.org/10.1177 %2F1742715020929134

Ladley, D., Wilkinson, I., & Young, L. (2015). The impact of individual versus group rewards on work group performance and cooperation: A computational social science approach. *Journal of Business Research, 68*, 2412–2425.

LaFasto, F., & Larson, C. (2001). *When teams work best: 6,000 team members and leaders tell what it takes to succeed*. SAGE.

LaFrance, A. (2016, January 6). The triumph of email. *The Atlantic*. https://www.theatlantic.com/technology/archive/2016/01/what-comes-after-email/422625

Lallanilla, M. (2006, April 20). Team psychology can contribute to assaults. *ABC News*. https://abcnews.go.com/Sports/story?id=1867104

Lamb, L. (2015, August 10). Inside the creative office cultures of Facebook. IDEO, and Virgin Air. *Fast Company*. https://www.fastcompany.com/3049282/inside-the-creative-office-culture-at-facebook-ideo-and-virgin-airlines

Landers, A. (1995, February 25). Low income families need fire protection too. *Santa Cruz Sentinel*, p. D5.

Lange, C., Costley, J., & Han, S. L. (2016). Informal cooperative learning in small groups: The effect of scaffolding on participation. *Issues in Educational Research, 26*, 260–279. https://www.iier.org.au/iier26/lange.pdf

Lapakko, D. (2007). Communication is 93% nonverbal: An urban legend proliferates. *Communication and Theater Association of Minnesota Journal, 34*, 7–19.S.

Larcker, D. F., Donatiello, N. E., & Tayan, B. (2016, February). Americans and CEO pay: 2016 public perception survey on CEO compensation. *Stanford Business*. https://www.gsb.stanford.edu/faculty-research/publications/americans-ceo-pay-2016-public-perception-survey-ceo-compensation

Larson, J. R. (2007). Deep diversity and strong synergy: Modeling the impact of variability in members' problem-solving strategies on group problem-solving performance. *Small Group Research, 38*, 413–436.

Lashbrook, A. (2020, July 21). Remote work can actually flip the power dynamic with your boss. *OneZero*. https://onezero.medium.com/remote-work-can-actually-flip-the-power-dynamic-with-your-boss-c6d232fbcbf

Laslo-Roth, R., & Schmidt-Barad, T. (2020). Personal sense of power, emotion and compliance in the workplace: A moderated mediation approach. *International Journal of Conflict Management, 32*, 39–61. https://doi.org/10.1108/IJCMA-07-2019-0113

Lauby, S. (2017, April 29). The only 3 reasons to hold a business meeting. SHRM. https://www.hrbartender.com/2015/training/the-only-3-reasons-to-hold-a-business-meeting/

Laughlin, P. R., Hatch, E. C., Silver, J. S., & Boh, L. (2006). Groups perform better than the best individuals on letter-to-numbers problems: Effects of group size. *Journal of Personality and Social Psychology, 90*, 644–650.

Leaders CEOs most admire. (2014). *PWC*. http://www.pwc.com/gx/en/ceo-survey/2013/key-findings/admired-leaders-leadership-attributes.jhtml

Leaper, C., & Robnett, R. D. (2011). Women are more likely than men to use tentative language, aren't they? A meta-analysis testing gender differences and moderators. *Psychology of Women Quarterly, 35*, 129–142.

Leavitt, H. (1964). *Managerial psychology*. University of Chicago Press.

Lee, M. D., & Paradowski, M. J. (2007). Group decision-making on an optimal stopping problem. *Journal of Problem Solving, 1*, 53–73.

Lee, T. C. (2020). Groupthink, qualitative comparative analysis, and the 1989 Tiananmen Square disaster. *Small Group Research, 51*, 435–463. https://doi.org/10.1177 %2F1046496419879759

Lemoine, G. J., & Blum, T. C. (2019, November 27). Servant leadership, leader gender, and team gender role: Testing a female advantage in a cascading model of performance. *Personnel Psychology, 74*, 3–28. https://doi.org/10.1111/peps.12379

Lempp, F., Blackwood, K., & Gordon, M. (2020). Exploring the efficacy of mediation in cases of workplace bullying. *International Journal of Conflict Management, 31*, 665–685. https://doi.org/10.1108/IJCMA-09-2019-0145

Lenaghan, J. A., & Sengupta, K. (2007). Role conflict, role balance and affect: A model of well-being of the working student. *Institute of Behavioral and Applied Management, 9*, 88–109. https://psycnet.apa.org/record/2008-17316-005

Levin, M. (2010, July 13). It's hard out here for a snitch. *Mother Jones*. http://motherjones.com/politics/2010/07/osha-whistleblowers-protection-retaliation

Levitan, L. C., & Verhulst, B. (2016). Conformity in groups: The effects of others' views on expressed attitudes and attitude change. *Political Behavior, 38*, 277–315.

Levitin, D. J. (2015, January 18). Why the modern world is bad for your brain. *The Guardian.* https://www.theguardian.com/science/2015/jan/18/modern-world-bad-for-brain-daniel-j-levitin-organized-mind-information-overload

Levitt, J. (2013). Seven symptoms of bad meetings and what you can do about them. *LCE.* https://www.lce.com/Seven-Symptoms-of-Bad-Meetings-and-What-You-Can-Do-About-Them-1408.html

Lewin, K. (1947). Frontiers in group dynamics. *Human Relations, 1,* 5–42.

Lewin, K., Lippitt, R., & White, R. (1939). Patterns of aggressive behavior in experimentally created social climates. *Journal of Social Psychology, 10,* 271–299.

Li, C. (1975). *Path analysis: A primer.* Boxwood.

Lickerman, A. (2013, November 10). Dealing with anger. *Psychology Today.* https://www.psychologytoday.com/blog/happiness-in-world/201311/dealing-anger

Liden, R. C., & Zhong, M. (2017, January). Highlights of scientific research on servant leadership. *To Serve First: The Servant Leadership Journey.* https://www.toservefirst.com/research-highlights.html

Lieberman, M. D. (2013). *Social: Why our brains are wired to connect.* Broadway Books.

Lifshitz-Assaf, H. (2017). Dismantling knowledge boundaries at NASA: The critical role of professional identity in open innovation. *Administrative Science Quarterly, 63,* 746–782. https://doi.org/10.1177%2F0001839217747876

Lindzon, J. (2016, September 12). How women leaders emerge from leaderless groups. *Fast Company.* https://www.fastcompany.com/3063599/research-suggests-that-women-are-more-likely-to-emerge-as-leaders-in-lead

Lipman, V. (2013, June 13). New employee study shows recognition matters more than money. *Psychology Today.* http://www.psychologytoday.com/blog/mind-the-manager/201306/new-employee-study-shows-recognition-matters-more-money

Lipman-Blumen, J., & Leavitt, H. J. (1999). *Hot groups.* Oxford University Press.

Littlejohn, S. W., Foss, K. A., & Oetzel, J. G. (2021). *Theories of human communication.* Waveland.

Liu, A., Sharkness, J., & Pryor, J. H. (2008). *Findings from the 2007 administration of your first college year (YFCY): National aggregates.* Higher Education Research, University of California, Los Angeles.

Liu, M. (2009). The intrapersonal and interpersonal effects of anger on negotiation strategies: A cross-cultural investigation. *Human Communication Research, 35,* 148–169.

Livni, E. (2018, July 18). Cynicism isn't as smart as we think it is. *Quartz.* https://qz.com/1329802/cynicism-isnt-as-smart-as-we-think-it-is/

Lodewijkx, H. F., van Zomeren, M., & Syroit, J. E. M. M. (2005). The anticipation of a severe initiation: Gender differences in effects on affiliation tendency and group attraction. *Small Group Research, 36,* 237–262.

Lopez, C., & Ward, M. (2020, June 5). 13 things you should never say to your LGBTQ coworkers. *Business Insider.* https://www.businessinsider.com/lgbtq-workers-discrimination-things-not-to-say-2019-9

Lopez-Zafra, E., Garcia-Retamero, R., & Landa, J. M. A. (2008). The role of transformational leadership, emotional intelligence, and group cohesiveness on leadership emergence. *Journal of Leadership Studies, 2,* 37–49.

Lovett, M. (2016, August 14). Exploring the Mehrabian myth. *Storytelling with Impact.* https://www.storytellingwithimpact.com/exploring-the-mehrabian-myth/

Lublin, J. S. (2017, December 13). Talkaholics sink partnerships, presentations—and careers. *Wall Street Journal.* https://www.wsj.com/articles/talkaholics-sink-partnerships-presentationsand-careers-1513173600

Lutgen-Sandvik, P. (2006). Take this job and . . . Quitting and other forms of resistance to workplace bullying. *Communication Monographs, 73,* 406–433.

Lybormirsky, S., King, L., & Diener, E. (2005). The benefits of frequent positive affect: Does happiness lead to success? *Psychological Bulletin, 131,* 803–855.

Lykken, D. T. (1997). The American crime factory. *Psychological Inquiry, 8,* 261–270.

MacDonald, L. (2019, March 7). What is a self-managed team? *Chron.* https://smallbusiness.chron.com/selfmanaged-team-18236.html

MacKay, J. (2018, July 11). Communication overload: Our research shows most workers can't go 6 minutes without checking email or IM. *RescueTime.* https://blog.rescuetime.com/communication-multitasking-switches/

MacInnis, C. C., MacKinnon, S. P., & MacIntyre, P. D. (2010). The illusion of transparency and normative beliefs about anxiety during public speaking. *Current Research in Social Psychology, 15*(4), 42–52.

Mack, S. (2017). Disadvantage of a focus group interview. *Chron.* http://smallbusiness.chron.com/disadvantage-focus-group-interview-22097.html

MacLennan, H. L. (2015). Incivility by degree: The influence of educational attainment on workplace civility. *Journal of Conflict Management, 3*, 35–51.

Macrae, F. (2015, March 11). Twitter anger "is road rage": Psychologist says distance from victim and having vast platform to vent irritation encourages users to be more aggressive. *Daily Mail.* http://www.dailymail.co.uk/sciencetech/article-2989040/Twitter-anger-like-road-rage-Psychologist-says-distance-victim-having-vast-platform-vent-irritation-encourages-users-aggressive.html

Madsbjerg, C., & Rasmussen, M. B. (2017, Fall). An anthropologist walks into a bar . . . *Harvard Business Review OnPoint*, pp. 64–72.

Magnano, M. (2019, January 31). Under-acknowledged, yet common: Preventing emotional abuse in sport. *Michigan State University College of Education.* https://education.msu.edu/sport-coaching-leadership/how-to/under-acknowledged-yet-common-preventing-emotional-abuse-in-sport/

Makela, L., Tanskanen, J., & De Cieri, H. (2021). Do relationships matter? Investigating the link between supervisor and subordinate dedication and cynicism via the quality of leader-member exchange. *Journal of Leadership & Organizational Studies, 28*, 76–90. https://doi.org/10.1177%2F1548051820967010

Malhotra, N., Zietsma, C., & Morris, T. (2020). Handling resistance to change when societal and workplace logics conflict. *Administrative Science Quarterly, 1*, 1–46. https://doi.org/10.1177%2F0001839220962760

Managing age diversity in the workplace. (2020, April 28). *NatWest.* https://natwestbusinesshub.com/articles/managing-age-diversity-in-the-workplace

Maner, J. K. (2017). Dominance and prestige: A tale of two hierarchies. *Current Directions in Psychological Science, 26*, 526–531. https://doi.org/10.1177%2F0963721417714323

Manjikian, G., & Rusch, E. (2014, September). The voting intentions and opinions of students. *CALPIRG Education Fund.* https://calpirgstudents.org/sites/student/files/reports/Results%20of%20CALPIRG%20Student%20Survey.pdf

Mannix, E., & Neale, M. A. (2005). What differences make a difference: The promise and reality of diverse teams in organizations. *Psychological Science in the Public Interest, 6*, 31–55.

Manolaki, A. (2016, August 30). Translating body language signs in different cultures. *Terminology Coordination: European Parliament.* https://termcoord.eu/2016/08/translating-body-language-signs-in-different-cultures/

Markman, A. (2017, May 18). Your team is brainstorming all wrong. *Harvard Business Review.* https://hbr.org/2017/05/your-team-is-brainstorming-all-wrong

Marmarosh, C. L., Forsyth, D. R., Strauss, B., & Burlingame, G. M (2020). The psychology of the COVID-19 pandemic: A group-level perspective. *Group Dynamics: Theory, Research, and Practice, 24*(3), 122–138. http://dx.doi.org/10.1037/gdn0000142

Marsh, J. (2019). Why say it that way? Evasive answers and politeness theory. *Journal of Politeness Research, Language, Behaviour, Culture, 15*, 55–75.

Martin, R. C., Coyier, K. R., VanSistine, L. M., & Schroeder, K. L. (2013). Anger on the Internet: The perceived value of rant-sites. *Cyberpsychology, Behavior, and Social Networking, 16*, 119–122.

Martin, S. (2014, February 3). Status update: 10 years in, Facebook still a force. *USA Today.* http://www.usatoday.com/story/tech/2014/02/03/facebook-juggernaut/4849409

Marzulli, J. (2014, November 1). Exclusive: Jurors come to blows during trial of reputed Brooklyn drug dealers charged with torturing and murdering victims. *New York Daily News.* https://www.nydailynews.com/new-york/nyc-crime/exclusive-jurors-blows-alleged-drug-dealers-trial-article-1.2028368

Matthes, J., Knoll, J., & von Sikorski, C. (2018). The "spiral of silence" revisited: A meta-analysis on the relationship between perceptions of opinion support and political opinion expression. *Communication Research, 45*, 3–33. https://doi.org/10.1177%2F0093650217745429

Matusitz, J., & Breen, G. (2012). An examination of pack journalism as a form of groupthink: A theoretical and qualitative analysis. *Journal of Human Behavior in the Social Environment, 22*, 896–915.

Maxfield, D., Grenny, J., McMillan, R., Patterson, K., & Switzler, A. (2005). Silence kills: The seven crucial conversations in healthcare. *VitalSmarts.* http://www.silencekills.com/UPDL/SilenceKillsExecSummary.pdf

Maxwell, J. C. (2001). *The 17 indisputable laws of teamwork: Embrace them and empower your team.* Thomas Nelson.

Mayo, M. (2017, April 7). If humble people make the best leaders, why do we fall for charismatic narcissists?

Harvard Business Review. https://hbr.org/2017/04/if-humble-people-make-the-best-leaders-why-do-we-fall-for-charismatic-narcissists

May, P. (2007, May 26). Governor salutes rapid repair of Maze. *San Jose Mercury News*, pp. 1B, 6B.

Mayo, A. T., & Woolley, A. W. (2016). Teamwork in health care: Maximizing collective intelligence via inclusive collaboration and open communication. *AMA Journal of Ethics, 18*(9), 933–940. http://journalofethics.ama-assn.org/2016/09/stas2-1609.html

McCaffrey, T., & Pearson, J. (2017, Fall). Find innovation where you least expect it. *Harvard Business Review OnPoint*, pp. 103–109.

McCarthy, K. (2017, July 5). How to approach negotiations: Game theory and generous tit for tat. *McCarthy Garber Law.* https://mccarthygarberlaw.com/approach-negotiations-game-theory-generous-tit-tat

McClean, E., Martin, S. R., Emich, K., & Woodruff, T. (2017). The social consequences of voice: An examination of voice type and gender on status and subsequent leader emergence. *Academy of Management Journal, 61.* http://amj.aom.org/content/early/2017/09/14/amj.2016.0148.abstract

McCoy, B. R. (2016, January). Digital distractions in the classroom phase II: Student classroom use of digital devices for non-class relation purposes. *Journal of Media Education, 7*, 5–32. https://en.calameo.com/read/00009178915b8f5b352ba

McCoy, B. R. (2020, April). Gen Z and digital distractions in the classroom: Student classroom use of digital devices for non-class related purposes. *Journal of Media Education, 11*, 5–23. https://en.calameo.com/read/0000917898a07ac2096e4

McCracken, H. (2017, October). Microsoft rewrites the code. *Fast Company*, pp. 50–58.

McEwan, B. (2016). Communication of communities: Linguistic signals of online groups. *Information, Communication & Society, 19*, 1233–1249.

McEwan, D., Ruissen, G. R., Eys, M. A., Zumbo, B. D., & Beauchamp, M. R. (2017). The effectiveness of teamwork training on teamwork behaviors and team performance: A systematic review and meta-analysis of controlled interventions. *PLoSOne.* http://journals.plos.org/plosone/article?id=10.1371/journal.pone.0169604

McGregor, L., & Doshi, N. (2020, April 9). How to keep your team motivated, remotely. *Harvard Business Review.* https://hbr.org/2020/04/how-to-keep-your-team-motivated-remotely

McKee, A. (2015, July 16). The emotional impulses that poison healthy teams. *Harvard Business Review.* https://hbr.org/2015/07/the-emotional-impulses-that-poison-healthy-teams

McLachlan, S. (2021, January 20). 27 Facebook demographics to inform your strategy in 2021. *Hootsuite.* https://blog.hootsuite.com/facebook-demographics/

McLaughlin, M., & Brame, D. (2020, May 28). The best video conferencing software. *PC Magazine.* https://www.pcmag.com/picks/the-best-video-conferencing-software?test_uuid=01jrZgWNXhmA3ocG7ZHXevj&test_variant=a

McNeil, B. J., Pauker, S. G., Sox, H. C., & Tversky, A. (1982). On the elicitation of preferences for alternative therapies. *New England Journal of Medicine, 306*, 1259–1262.

McNutt, P. (1997, October /November). When strategic decisions are ignored. *Fast Company*, pp. 17–22.

McQuaid, M. (2015, March 6). The strengths revolution transforming our workplaces. *Psychology Today.* https://www.huffingtonpost.com/michelle-mcquaid/the-strengths-revolution-transforming-our-workplace_b_6810192.html

McQueen, N. (2018, June 26). Workplace culture trends: The key to hiring (and keeping) top talent in 2018. *Linkedin.* https://blog.linkedin.com/2018/april/19/the-u-s-is-facing-a-critical-skills-shortage-reskilling-can-be-part-of-the-solution

Meet the anti-LGBT hate group that filed an amicus brief with the Alabama Supreme Court. (2015, November 13). *Southern Poverty Law Center.* https://www.splcenter.org/hatewatch/2015/11/13/meet-anti-lgbt-hate-group-filed-amicus-brief-alabama-supreme-court

Meetings: The good, the bad, and the ugly. (2015, September 16). *Wharton.* http://knowledge.wharton.upenn.edu/article/meetings-the-good-the-bad-and-the-ugly

Mehrabian, A. (1971). *Silent messages.* Wadsworth.

Meluso, J., Johnson, S., & Bagrow, J. (2020). Making virtual teams work: Redesigning collaboration for the future. *SocArXiv Papers.* https://osf.io/preprints/socarxiv/wehsk/

Mendoza, N. F. (2020, April 15). How too many virtual meetings can cause employee productivity to plummet. *TechRepublic.* https://www.techrepublic.com/article/how-too-many-virtual-meetings-cause-employee-productivity-to-plummet/

Meng, Y, He, J., & Luo, C. (2014). Science research group leader's power and members' compliance and satisfaction with supervision. *Research Management Review, 20,* 1–15. https://files.eric.ed.gov/fulltext/EJ1022035.pdf

Merkin, R. (2015). The relationship between individualism/collectivism: Consultation and harmony needs. *Journal of Intercultural Communication.* http://immi.se/intercultural/nr39/merkin.html

Middleton, T. (2019, May 15). The importance of teamwork (as proven by science). *Work Life.* https://www.atlassian.com/blog/teamwork/the-importance-of-teamwork

Milgram, S. (1974). *Obedience to authority.* Harper & Row.

Miller, C. C. (2014, August 24). How social media silences debate. *New York Times.* https://www.nytimes.com/2014/08/27/upshot/how-social-media-silences-debate.html?abt=0002&abg=1&_r=1

Miller, D. (2018, November 29). Developing Generation Z leaders. *Workforce Institute.* https://workforceinstitute.org/developing-generation-z-leaders/

Millis, J. P. (2017, July 11). Yes, men really landed on the moon. *ThoughtCo.* https://www.thoughtco.com/did-men-really-land-on-moon-3072611

Milosevic, I., Maric, S., & Loncar, D. (2020). Defeating the toxic boss: the nature of toxic leadership and the role of followers. *Journal of Leadership & Organizational Studies, 27,* 117–137. https://doi.org/10.1177%2F1548051819833374

Mitchell, R., Giles, P. V., & Boyle, B. (2014). The ABC of health care team dynamics: Understanding complex affective, behavioral, and cognitive dynamics in interprofessional teams. *Health Care Management Review, 39,* 1–9. https://doi.org/10.1097/hcm.0b013e3182766504

Mokhtari, R. B., Homayouni, T. S., Baluch, N., et al. (2017, March 30). Combination therapy in combating cancer. *Oncotarget: An Open Access Impact Journal.* https://www.ncbi.nlm.nih.gov/pmc/articles/PMC5514969/

Molavi, C. (2015, October 8). What's the optimal team size for workplace productivity? *Flow.* https://www.getflow.com/blog/optimal-team-size-workplace-productivity

Moore, S. (2019). Reactance theory & employee performance. *Chron.* https://smallbusiness.chron.com/reactance-theory-employee-performance-34456.html

Moore, N-J., Hickson, M., & Stacks, D. W. (2014). *Nonverbal communication: Studies and applications.* Oxford University Press.

Moreland, R. L. (2010). Are dyads really groups? *Small Group Research, 41,* 251–267.

Moreland, R., & Levine, J. (1987). Group dynamics over time: Development and socialization in small groups. In J. McGrath (Ed.), *The social psychology of time.* SAGE.

Morieux, Y. (2017, Fall). Smart rules: Six ways to get people to solve problems without you. *Harvard Business Review,* pp. 74–81.

Moring, C. (2017). *Newcomer information seeking: The role of information seeking in newcomer socialization and learning in the workplace.* Proceedings of ISIC, the Information Behaviour Conference, Zadar, Croatia. http://www.informationr.net/ir/22-1/isic/isic1616.html

Morley, L., & Cashell, A. (2017). Collaboration in health care. *Journal of Medical Imaging and Radiation Sciences.* https://www.researchgate.net/publication/317297419_Collaboration_in_Health_Care

Morrison-Smith, S., & Ruiz, J. (2020, May 20). Challenges and barriers in virtual teams: A literature review. *SN Applied Sciences.* https://link.springer.com/article/10.1007/s42452-020-2801-5

Motley, M. (1995). *Overcoming your fear of public speaking: A proven method.* McGraw-Hill.

Mouawad, J. (2016, February 3). Richard Anderson, Delta chief who led airline's rebound, will retire. *New York Times.* https://www.nytimes.com/2016/02/04/business/delta-chief-who-led-airlines-rebound-will-retire.html

Muceldili, B., & Erdil, O. (2015). *Cultivating group cohesiveness: The role of collective energy.* Paper presented at 11th International Strategic Management Conference 2015. https://core.ac.uk/download/pdf/82157095.pdf

Muddiman, A., Pond-Cobb, J., & Matson, J. E. (2020). Negativity bias or backlash: Interaction with civil and uncivil online political news content. *Communication Research, 47,* 815–837. https://doi.org/10.1177%2F0093650216685625

Mudrack, P. E., Bloodgood, J. M., & Turnley, W. H. (2012). Some ethical implications of individual competitiveness. *Journal of Business Ethics, 108,* 347–359. https://www.researchgate.net/publication/254426814_Some_Ethical_Implications_of_Individual_Competitiveness

Mudrack, P., & Farrell, G. (1995). An examination of functional role behavior and its consequences for individuals in group settings. *Small Group Research, 26,* 542–571.

Muir, T. (2019). *The collaborative classroom: Teaching students how to work together now and for the rest of their lives.* Dave Burgess Consulting, Inc.

Murphy, H. (2018, March 16). Picture a leader: Is she a woman? *New York Times.* https://www.nytimes.com/2018/03/16/health/women-leadership-workplace.html?&moduleDetail=section-news-2&action=click&contentCollection=Health&region=Footer&module=MoreInSection&version=WhatsNext&contentID=WhatsNext&pgtype=Blogs

Murphy, M. (2020, January 21). If you want to have great listening skills, stop saying these three phrases. *Forbes.* https://www.forbes.com/sites/markmurphy/2020/01/21/if-you-want-to-have-great-listening-skills-stop-saying-these-three-phrases/?sh=41548c625bf7

Myers, C. (2017, April 28). How to become a more decisive leader. *Forbes.* https://www.forbes.com/sites/chrismyers/2017/04/28/how-to-become-a-more-decisive-leader/#62d5fd974336

Myers, D. G. (2002). *Intuition: Its power and perils.* Yale University Press.

Nass, C. (2010). *The man who lied to his laptop: What machines teach us about human relationships.* Portfolio Penguin.

National Geographic–Roper Public Affairs Geographic Literacy Study (2006, May). *Final Report.* http://www.nationalgeographic.com/foundation/pdf/NGS-Roper2006Report.pdf

Nauen, R. (2017, October 19). Two in five LGBT workers feel bullied at work. *CareerBuilder.* http://press.careerbuilder.com/2017-10-19-Two-in-Five-LGBT-Workers-Feel-Bullied-at-Work-According-to-Recent-CareerBuilder-Survey?_ga=2.201454993.1655842223.1609542300-435713707.1609542300

Neily, J., Mills, P. D., Young-Xu, Y., Carney B. T., West, P., Berger, D. H., . . . Bagian, J. P. (2010). Association between implementation of a medical team training program and surgical mortality, *Journal of the American Medical Association, 304,* 1693–1700.

Neuliep, J. W. (2014). *Intercultural communication: A contextual approach.* SAGE.

Nevicka, B., De Hoogh, A. H. B., Hartog, D. N. D., et al. (2018). Narcissistic leaders and their victims: Followers low on self-esteem and low on core self-evaluations suffer most. *Frontiers in Psychology, 9,* 422. https://www.frontiersin.org/articles/10.3389/fpsyg.2018.00422/full#B40

Nevicka, B., Ten Velden, F. S., De Hoogh, A. H. B., & Van Vianen, A. E. M. (2011). Reality at odds with perceptions: Narcissistic leaders and group performance. *Psychological Science, 22,* 1259–1264.

The new conflict management: Effective conflict resolution strategies to avoid litigation. (2012). *Program on Negotiation/Harvard Law School.* https://www.pon.harvard.edu/freemium/new-conflict-management-effective-conflict-resolution-strategies-to-avoid-litigation

Nezlek, J. B., Wesselmann, E. D., Wheeler, L., & Williams, K. D. (2012). Ostracism in everyday life. *Group Dynamics: Theory, Research, and Practice, 16,* 91–104.

Nichols, T. (2017). *The death of expertise: The campaign against established knowledge and why it matters.* Oxford University Press.

Nicola, M., Alsafi, Z., Sohrabi, et al. (2020, June). The socio-economic implications of the coronavirus pandemic (COVID-19): A review. *International Journal of Surgery, 78,* 185–193. https://www.ncbi.nlm.nih.gov/pmc/articles/PMC7162753/

Nielsen, M. B., & Einarsen, S. V. (2018). What we know, what we do not know, and what we should and could have known about workplace bullying: An overview of the literature and agenda for future research. *Aggression and Violent Behavior, 42,* 71–83. https://doi.org/10.1016/j.avb.2018.06.007

Noe-Bustamante, L., Mora, L., & Lopez, M. H. (2020, August 11). *About one-in-four U.S. Hispanics have heard of Latinx, but just 3% use it. Pew Research Center.* https://www.pewresearch.org/hispanic/2020/08/11/about-one-in-four-u-s-hispanics-have-heard-of-latinx-but-just-3-use-it/

Northouse, P. (2019). *Leadership: Theory and practice.* SAGE.

Nussbaum, B. (2004, May 17). The power of design. *Business Week,* pp. 86–94.

Obama approval inches up, tied with Putin as leader, Quinnipiac University national poll finds. (2014, April 2). *Quinnipiac University.* http://www.quinnipiac.edu/news-and-events/quinnipiac-university-poll/national/release-detail?ReleaseID=2027

Oberg, A. (2003, August 26). From Challenger to Columbia. *San Jose Mercury News,* p. 7B.

O'Brien, T. (1995, November 5). No jerks allowed. *West,* pp. 8–26.

Odine, M. (2015). Communication problems in management. *Journal of Emerging Issues in Economics, Finance and Banking, 4,* 1615–1630.

O'Donovan, R., Van Dun, D., & McAuliffe, E. (2020). Measuring psychological safety in healthcare teams: Developing observational measure to complement survey methods. *BMC Medical Research Methodology, 20*, 203. https://doi.org/10.1186/s12874-020-01066-z

Oglensky, B. D. (2008). The ambivalent dynamics of loyalty in mentorship. *Human Relations, 61*, 419–448.

O'Malley, M. (2019, December 12). What the "best companies to work for" do differently. *Harvard Business Review*. https://hbr.org/2019/12/what-the-best-companies-to-work-for-do-differently

Omisore, B. O., & Abiodun, A. R. (2014). Organizational conflicts: Causes, effects and remedies. *International Journal of Academic Research in Economics and Management Sciences, 3*, 118–137. https://pdfs.semanticscholar.org/dc47/343acf285d3c6e7af9d5bb935981ac251c02.pdf

101+ social media sites you need to know in 2021. (2021, January 27). *Influencer Marketing Hub*. https://influencermarketinghub.com/social-media-sites/

O'Neill, T. A., Hancock, S. E., Zivkov, K., et al. (2016). Team decision making in virtual and face-to-face environments. *Group Decision and Negotiation, 25*, 995–1020. https://doi.org/10.1007/s10726-015-9465-3

Only 9 Hispanic CEOs at top 500 companies. (2020, September 10). *Mexican American Professional Archives*. https://mexican-american-proarchive.com/2020/09/only-9-hispanic-ceos-at-top-500-companies/

Organizational dynamics survey: Most businesses have a teamwork problem. (2016, December 8). *5 Dynamics*. https://www.simpli5.com/organizational-dynamics-survey-most-businesses-have-a-teamwork-problem/

Orlitzky, M., & Hirokawa, R. Y. (2001). To err is human, to correct for it divine: A meta-analysis of research testing the functional theory of group decision-making effectiveness. *Small Group Research, 32*, 313–341.

O'Sullivan, E. D., & Schofield, S. J. (2019, January 8). A cognitive forcing tool to mitigate cognitive bias—a randomised control trial. *BMC Medical Education, 9*, 1444–1445. https://doi.org/10.1186/s12909-018-1444-3

Otto, S. (2016). *The war on science: Who's waging it, why it matters, what can be done about it*. Milkweed.

Oxfam America. (2016). *No relief: Denial of bathroom breaks in the poultry industry*. https://www.oxfamamerica.org/static/media/files/No_Relief_Embargo.pdf

Padavic, I., Ely, R. J., & Reid, E. M. (2020). Explaining the persistence of gender inequality: The work-family narrative as a social defense against the 24/7 work culture. *Administrative Science Quarterly, 65*, 61–111. https://doi.org/10.1177%2F0001839219832310

Palomares, N. A. (2008). Explaining gender-based language use: Effects of gender identity salience on references to emotion and tentative language in intra-and inter-group contexts. *Human Communication Research, 34*, 263–286.

Park, G., Yaden, D. B., Schwartz, H. A., Kern, M. L., Eichstaedt, J. C., Kosinski, M., . . . Seligman, M. E. P. (2016, May 25). Women are warmer but no less assertive than men: Gender and language on Facebook. *PLoSOne Journal*. http://journals.plos.org/plosone/article?id=10.1371%2Fjournal.pone.0155885#sec009

Parker, K. (2018, September 25). *Many Americans say women are better than men at creating safe, respectful workplaces*. Pew Research. https://www.pewresearch.org/fact-tank/2018/09/25/many-americans-say-women-are-better-than-men-at-creating-safe-respectful-workplaces/

Parker, K., & Igielnik, R. (2020, May 14). *On the cusp of adulthood and facing an uncertain future: What we know about Gen Z so far*. Pew Research Center. https://www.pewsocialtrends.org/essay/on-the-cusp-of-adulthood-and-facing-an-uncertain-future-what-we-know-about-gen-z-so-far/

Patnaik, S. (2020, April 2). Zoom's daily participants jumped from 10 million to over 200 million in 3 months (updated). *Venture Beat*. https://venturebeat.com/2020/04/02/zooms-daily-active-users-jumped-from-10-million-to-over-200-million-in-3-months/

Patrnchak, J. M. (2015). Implementing servant leadership at Cleveland Clinic: A case study in organizational change. *Servant Leadership: Theory and Practice, 2*, 36–48.

Patton, B. (2018, January 28). The Sunday minute. *Program on Negotiation/Harvard Law School*. https://correo.cabrillo.edu/Session/4824-Tibpue6uGJqAZ67ViwJT/Message.wssp?Mailbox=INBOX&MSG=101399

Patton, D. (2017, May 4). The haunting soil media trail left by a teen gang member. *Vice*. https://www.vice.com/en_us/article/43nwqm/the-square-is-a-brilliant-takedown-of-the-art-world

Paul, S., Seetharaman, P., Samarah, I., & Mykytyn, P. (2005). Understanding conflict in virtual teams: An experimental investigation using content analysis. In R. H. Sprague (Ed.), *Proceedings of the 38th Hawaii International Conference on Systems Sciences*. IEEE Computer Society.

Paulus, P., Dzindolet, M., Poletes, G., & Camacho, M. L. (1993). Perceptions of performance in group brainstorming: The illusion of group productivity. *Personality and Social Psychology Bulletin, 19,* 78–89.

Pearce, C. L., & Sims, H. P. (2002). Vertical versus shared leadership as predictors of the effectiveness of change management teams: An examination of aversive, directive, transactional, transformational, and empowering leader behaviors. *Group Dynamics: Theory, Research, and Practice, 6,* 172–197.

Peck, E. (2017, December 3). Sheryl Sandberg warns of ≠MeToo backlash against women. *Huffington Post.* https://www.huffingtonpost.com/entry/sheryl-sandberg-sexual-harassment-backlash_us_5a22c2a5e4b03350e0b710eb

Peng, A. C., Wang, B., Schaubroeck, J. M., et al. (2020). Can humble leaders get results? The indirect and contextual influences of skip-level leaders. *Journal of Leadership & Organizational Studies, 27,* 329–339. https://doi.org/10.1177%2F1548051820952402

Pennycook, G., McPhetres, J., Zhang, Y., et al. (2020). Fighting COVID-19 misinformation on social media: Experimental evidence for a scalable accuracy-nudge intervention. *Psychological Science, 31,* 770–780. https://doi.org/10.1177%2F0956797620939054

Pentland, A. S. (2012, April). The new science of building great teams. *Harvard Business Review.* https://hbr.org/2012/04/the-new-science-of-building-great-teams

Pentland, A. S. (2015, March 27). Alex "Sandy" Pentland (Harvard Business Review): The new science of building great teams. *Emergent Cognition Project.* https://emergentcognition.com/2015/03/27/alex-sandy-pentland-harvard-business-review-the-new-science-of-building-great-teams

Pentland, A. S. (2016, September /October). Betting on people power. *Scientific American Mind,* pp. 32–37.

People hate being managed—what organizations (and managers) need to do instead. (2018, March 29). *Betterworks.* https://blog.betterworks.com/people-hate-being-managed-what-organizations-and-managers-need-to-do-instead/

Perlow, L. A., Hadley, C. N., & Eun, E. (2017, August). Stop the meeting madness. *Harvard Business Review.* https://hbr.org/2017/07/stop-the-meeting-madness

Perman, C. (2011, September 2). Think your boss is a psychopath? That may be true. *CNBC.* http://www.cnbc.com/id/44376401

Perretti, F., & Negro, G. (2007). Mixing genres and matching people: A study in innovation and team composition in Hollywood. *Journal of Organizational Behavior, 28,* 563–586. https://doi.org/10.1002/job.464

Pescosolido, A. T. (2001). Informal leaders and the development of group efficacy. *Small Group Research, 32,* 74–93. https://doi.org/10.1177%2F104649640103200104

Petersen, D. (2014, November 7). Lindred Greer: Why virtual teams have more conflict. *Stanford Business.* https://www.gsb.stanford.edu/insights/lindred-greer-why-virtual-teams-have-more-conflict

Peterson, S. J., Abramson, R., & Stutman, R. K. (2020, November–December). How to develop your leadership style. *Harvard Business Review.* https://hbr.org/2020/11/how-to-develop-your-leadership-style

Pewsey, R. (2020, January 24). 7 mind mapping uses for students. *AYOA.* https://www.ayoa.com/ourblog/7-mind-mapping-uses-for-students/

Peyton, T., Zigarmi, D., & Fowler, S. N. (2018). Examining the relationship between leaders' power use, followers' motivational outlooks, and followers' work intentions. *Frontiers of Psychology, 9,* 2620. https://www.ncbi.nlm.nih.gov/pmc/articles/PMC6367254/

Pfeffer, J. (2015). *Leadership BS: Fixing workplaces and careers one truth at a time.* HarperCollins.

Pham, H. (2019, April 2). "How we culture" with Michelle Lee and Jenny Gottstein of IDEO. *Culture Summit.* https://www.culturesummit.co/articles/how-we-culture-michelle-jenny-ideo/

Phillips, K. W. (2014, October 1). Diversity makes us smarter. *Scientific American.* https://www.scientificamerican.com/article/how-diversity-makes-us-smarter

Phillips, K. W., Liljenquist, K. A., & Neale, M. A. (2009). Is the pain worth the gain? The advantages and liabilities of agreeing with socially distinct newcomers. *Personality and Social Psychology Bulletin, 35,* 336–350. https://doi.org/10.1177%2F0146167208328062

Plaister-Ten, J. (2017). *Leading across cultures: Developing leaders for global organizations.* Routledge. https://www.crcpress.com/go/white_paper_leading_across_cultures_developing_leaders_for_global_organisat

PlaneBusiness Ron Allen airline management award. (2008, February). *PlaneBusiness.* https://www.planebusiness.com/ronallen.shtml

Platow, M. J., Haslam, S. A., Reicher, S. D., & Steffens, N. K. (2015). There is no leadership if no-one follows: Why leadership is necessarily a group process. *International Coaching Psychology Review, 10*, 20–37.

Poljac, E., Kiesel, A., Koch, I., & Muller, H. (2018). New perspectives on human multitasking. *Psychological Research, 82*, 1–3. https://doi.org/10.1007/s00426-018-0970-2

Poole, M. S. (1983). Decision development in small groups III: A multiple sequence model of group decision making. *Communication Monographs, 50*, 321–341.

Poole, M. S., & Roth, J. (1989). Decision development in small groups IV: A typology of group decision paths. *Human Communication Research, 15*, 323–356.

Poole, M. S., Seibold, D. R., & McPhee, R. D. (1996). The structuration of group decisions. In R. Hirokawa & M. S. Poole (Eds.), *Communication and group decision making*. SAGE.

Poppy, C. (2017, January /February). Survey shows Americans fear ghosts, the government, and each other. *Skeptical Inquirer*, pp. 16–18.

Porath, C. (2016). *Mastering civility: A manifesto for the workplace*. Grand Central.

Porhola, M., Cvancara, K., Kaal, E. K., et al. (2019). Bullying in university between peers and by personnel: Cultural variation in prevalence, forms, and gender differences in four countries. *Social Psychology of Education, 23*, 143–169. https://doi.org/10.1007/s11218-019-09523-4

Postman, N. (1976). *Crazy talk, stupid talk*. Dell.

Poston, D., & Saenz, R. (2019, May 25). *Demographic trends spell the end of the white majority in 2044. Associated Press*. https://apnews.com/article/4a60c86e938045fa80dad97f67ce9120

The power of praise and recognition. (2014, February 18). *Training Journal*. https://www.trainingjournal.com/articles/feature/power-praise-and-recognition

Prieto-Remon, T. C., Cobo-Benita, J. R., Ortiz-Marcos, I., Uruburu, A. (2015). Conflict resolution to project performance. *ResearchGate*. https://www.researchgate.net/publication/282556551_Conflict_Resolution_to_Project_Performance

Protecting teachers under attack by students. (2020, January 21). *CaseGuard*. https://caseguard.com/articles/protecting-teachers-under-attack-by-students/?p=5479

Prudenti, A. G. (2020, January 14). Juror misconduct is a threat to criminal justice system. *Long Island Business News*. https://libn.com/2020/01/14/prudenti-juror-misconduct-is-a-threat-to-criminal-justice-system/

Pruitt, D. (1981). *Negotiation behavior*. Academic Press.

The public and broadcasting. (2019, August 2). *Federal Communications Commission*. https://www.fcc.gov/media/radio/public-and-broadcasting#CRITICISM

Puccio, G. J., Murdock, M. C., & Mance, M. (2007). *Creative leadership: Skills that drive change*. SAGE.

Pull, C. B. (2012). Current status of knowledge on public speaking anxiety. *Current Opinion in Psychiatry, 25*, 32–38.

Purvanova, R. K. (2014). Face-to-face versus virtual teams: What have we really learned? *Psychologist-Manager Journal, 17*, 2–29. https://psycnet.apa.org/doi/10.1037/mgr0000009

Purvanova, R. K., Charlier, S. D., Reeves, C. J., et al. (2020). Who emerges into virtual team leadership roles? The role of achievement and ascription antecedents for leadership emergence across the virtuality spectrum. *Journal of Business and Psychology, 1*, 1–21. https://doi.org/10.1007/s10869-020-09698-0

Rabi, M., Pattermann, J., Schlogl, S., & Canham, N. (2019, May 28). The use of digital devices in the university classroom: Exploring and comparing students' perceptions and practices. *International Workshop on Learning Technology for Education in Cloud*. https://link.springer.com/chapter/10.1007/978-3-030-20798-4_10

Rahim, M. A., & Katz, J. P. (2019). Forty years of conflict: The effects of gender and generation on conflict-management strategies. *International Journal of Conflict Management, 31*, 1–16. https://doi.org/10.1108/IJCMA-03-2019-0045

Rahmani, D. (2017). Apprehension and anxiety in communication. *Oxford Research Encyclopedias*. http://communication.oxfordre.com/view/10.1093/acrefore/9780190228613.001.0001/acrefore-9780190228613-e-414

Ramos-Villagrasa, P. J., Marques-Quinteiro, P., Navarro, J., et al. (2018). Teams as complex adaptive systems: Reviewing 17 years of research. *Small Group Research, 49*, 135–176. https://doi.org/10.1177%2F1046496417713849

Rast, D. E., Hogg, M. A., & Giessner, S. R. (2016). Who trusts charismatic leaders who champion change? The role of group identification, membership centrality, and self-uncertainty. *Group Dynamics: Theory,*

Research, and Practice, 20(4), 259–275. https://psycnet.apa.org/doi/10.1037/gdn0000053

Rathje, S. (2017, July 20). The power of framing: It's not what you say, it's how you say it. *The Guardian.* https://www.theguardian.com/science/head-quarters/2017/jul/20/the-power-of-framing-its-not-what-you-say-its-how-you-say-it

Raven, B. H. (1993). The basis of power, origins and recent developments. *Journal of Social Issues, 49,* 227–251. https://doi.org/10.1111/j.1540-4560.1993.tb01191.x

Reilly, K. (2020, July 13). Coronavirus outbreaks linked to fraternity houses are a warning for college campuses. *Time.* https://time.com/5865251/coronavirus-fraternities-colleges/

Reinsel, D., Gantz, J., & Rydning, J. (2018, November). The digitization of the world: From edge to core. *IDC.* http://cloudcode.me/media/1014/idc.pdf

Reitzig, M., & Maciejovsky, B. (2015). Corporate hierarchy and vertical information flow inside the firm—a behavioral view. *Strategic Management Journal, 36,* 1979–1999. https://doi.org/10.1002/smj.2334

Reynolds, A., & Lewis, D. (2017, March 30). Teams solve problems faster when they're more cognitively diverse. *Harvard Business Review.* https://hbr.org/2017/03/teams-solve-problems-faster-when-theyre-more-cognitively-diverse

Reyes, D. L., & Salas, E. (2019). What makes a team of experts and expert team? In R. F. Subotnik, P. Olszewski-Kubilius, & F. C. Worrell (Eds.), *The psychology of high performance: Developing human potential into domain-specific talent* (pp. 141–159). *American Psychological Association.* https://psycnet.apa.org/record/2018-59444-007

Rietzschel, E. F., Nijstad, B. A., & Strobe, W. (2006). Productivity is not enough: A comparison of interactive and nominal brainstorming groups on idea generation and selection. *Journal of Experimental Social Psychology, 42,* 244–251.

Riggio, R. E., Riggio, H. R., Salinas, C., & Cole, E. J. (2003). The role of social and emotional communication skills in leader emergence and effectiveness. *Group Dynamics: Theory, Research, and Practice, 7,* 83–103.

Riggio, R. E. (2009, March 18). Leaders: Born or made? *Psychology Today.* http://www.psychologytoday.com/blog/cutting-edge-leadership/200903/leaders-born-or-made

The right way to regulate emotion in negotiation. (2016, December 15). *Program on Negotiation/Harvard Law School.* https://www.pon.harvard.edu/daily/dispute-resolution/dealing-with-difficult-people-the-right-way-to-regulate-emotion

Rinne, J. D. (2019, April 25). 16 jaw-dropping facts about Cirque du Soleil. *Mental Floss.* https://mentalfloss.com/article/540342/cirque-du-soleil-facts

Riordan, M. A., & Trichtinger, L. A. (2017). Overconfidence at the keyboard: confidence and accuracy in interpreting affect in e-mail exchanges. *Human Communication Research, 43,* 1–24. https://doi.org/10.1111/hcre.12093

Robbins, A. (2015, April 29). Doctors throwing fits. *Slate.* http://www.slate.com/articles/health_and_science/medical_examiner/2015/04/doctors_bully_nurses_hospital_mistreatment_is_a_danger_to_patient_health.html

Robert, L. P. (2020). Behavior-output control theory, trust, and social loafing in virtual teams. *Multimodal Technologies and Interaction.* https://deepblue.lib.umich.edu/bitstream/handle/2027.42/156029/Robert%202020.pdf?sequence=1&isAllowed=y

Robert, L. P., & You, S. (2018, January 7). Disaggregating the impacts of virtuality on team identification. *Proceedings of the ACM International Conference on Supporting Group Work.* https://deepblue.lib.umich.edu/bitstream/handle/2027.42/138817/Old%20Version?sequence=1&isAllowed=y

Rocheleau, B. (2002). E-mail: Does it need to be managed? Can it be managed? *Public Administration & Management: An Interactive Journal, 7,* 83–116.

Rock, D. (2009). *Your brain at work.* HarperCollins.

Rock, J. (2017, March 2). Workplace bullying may be linked to long-term health issues. *Association for Psychological Science.* https://www.psychologicalscience.org/news/minds-business/workplace-bullying-may-be-linked-to-long-term-health-issues.html

Roebuck, A., Thomas, A., & Biermeier-Hanson, B. (2019). Organizational culture mitigates lower ratings of female supervisors. *Journal of Leadership & Organizational Studies, 26,* 454–464. https://journals.sagepub.com/doi/full/10.1177/1548051818781815

Rogelberg, S. G., Scott, C. W., Agypt, B., Williams, J., Kello, J. E., McCausland, T., & Olien, J. L. (2013). Lateness to meetings: Examination of an unexplored temporal phenomenon. *European Journal of Work and Organizational Psychology, 23,* 323–341. https://doi.org/10.1080/1359432X.2012.745988

Rogelberg, S. G., Shanock, L. R., & Scott, C. W. (2012). Wasted time and money in meetings: Increasing return on investment. *Small Group Research, 43,* 236–245. https://doi.org/10.1177%2F1046496411429170

Rogers, K. (2018, July–August). Do your employees feel respected? *Harvard Business Review.* https://hbr.org/2018/07/do-your-employees-feel-respected

Rohlin, M. (2018, February 21). Getting the message. *Mercury News,* pp. C1, C3.

Romero, E., & Pescosolido, A. (2008). Humor and group effectiveness. *Human Relations, 61,* 395–418. https://doi.org/10.1177%2F0018726708088999

Ropeik, D. (2008, April 13). How risky is flying? *NOVA.* http://www.pbs.org/wgbh/nova/planecrash/risky.html

Rosen, C. C., Simon, L. S., Gajendran, R. S., et al. (2019). Boxed in by your inbox: Implications of daily e-mail demands for managers' leadership behaviors. *Journal of Applied Psychology, 104,* 19–33. https://doi.org/10.1037/apl0000343

Rosen, M. A., DiazGranados, D., Dietz, A. S., et al. (2019). Teamwork in healthcare: Key discoveries enabling safer, high-quality care. *American Psychologist, 73*(4), 433–450. https://dx.doi.org/10.1037%2Famp0000298

Ross, M. (2017, April 9). Civility suits the workplace. *San Jose Mercury News,* pp. D1, D8.

Rossman, J. (1931). *The psychology of the inventor.* Inventors' Publishing.

Rost, J. C. (1991). *Leadership for the twenty-first century.* Praeger.

Rovio, E., Eskola, J., Kozub, S. A., Duda, J. L., & Lintunen, T. (2009). Can high group cohesion be harmful? A case study of a junior ice-hockey team. *Small Group Research, 40,* 421–435. https://psycnet.apa.org/doi/10.1177/1046496409334359

Ruback, B. R., & Jweng, D. (2006). Territorial defense in parking lots: Retaliation against waiting drivers. *Journal of Applied Social Psychology, 27,* 821–834. https://doi.org/10.1111/j.1559-1816.1997.tb00661.x

Ruggiero, V. R. (1988). *The art of thinking: A guide to critical and creative thought.* Harper & Row.

Rusting, C. L., & Nolen-Hoeksema (1998). Regulating responses to anger: Effects of rumination and distraction on angry mood. *Journal of Personality and Social Psychology, 74,* 790–803. https://doi.org/10.1037//0022-3514.74.3.790

Ryall, J. (2019, May 22). Why are Japanese citizens refusing to show up for jury duty? *South China Morning Post.* https://www.scmp.com/week-asia/society/article/3011303/japanese-citizens-are-refusing-show-jury-duty-claiming-it-takes

Ryan, N. (2020, February 19). The four horsemen: Signs your relationship is in trouble. *Sacwellness.* https://sacwellness.com/the-four-horsemen-signs-your-relationship-is-in-trouble/

Sadri, G. (2018). *Choosing conflict resolution by culture. Institute of Industrial & Systems Engineers.* http://www.iise.org/Details.aspx?id=35396

Safian, R. (2017, October). How to lead with empathy. *Fast Company,* p. 12.

Saint, S., & Lawson, J. (1997). *Rules for reaching consensus.* Pfeiffer.

Sajjadi, A., Karimkhani, M., & Mehrpour, M. (2014). New emerging leadership theories and styles. *Technical Journal of Engineering and Applied Sciences, 3,* 180–188.

Salam, M. (2017, October 17). Security officers fired for United Airlines dragging episode. *New York Times.* https://www.nytimes.com/2017/10/17/us/united-airlines-david-dao.html

Salas, E., Tannenbaum, S. I., Kraiger, K., & Smith-Jentsch, K. A. (2012). The science of training and development in organizations: What matters in practice. *Psychological Science in the Public Interest, 13,* 74–101.

Salazar, A. (1995). Understanding the synergistic effects of communication in small groups. *Small Group Research, 26,* 169–199. https://doi.org/10.1177%2F1046496495262002

Salazar, M. R., Feitosa, J., & Salas, E. (2017). Diversity and team creativity: Exploring underlying mechanisms. *Group Dynamics: Theory, Research, and Practice.* https://psycnet.apa.org/record/2017-53952-001

Samovar, L. A., Porter, R. E., McDaniel, E. R., & Roy, C. S. (2021). *Communication between cultures.* Cengage.

Sanders, G. I. (2020). Employee productivity statistics: Everything you need to know. *Dynamic Signal.* https://dynamicsignal.com/2020/03/06/employee-productivity-statistics-2020/

Santos, H. C., Varnum, M. E. W, & Grossmann, I. (2017). Global increases in individualism. *Psychological Science, 28,* 1228–1239. https://doi.org/10.1177%2F0956797617700622

Sarlin, B. (2016, January 22). *Donald Trump tweets apparent neo-Nazi supporter. MSNBC.*

http://www.msnbc.com/msnbc/donald-trump-tweets-apparent-neo-nazi-supporter

Satell, G. (2015, February 6). Why communication is today's most important skill. *Forbes.* https://www.forbes.com/sites/gregsatell/2015/02/06/why-communication-is-todays-most-important-skill/#5f5775841100

Sawyer, K. (2017). *Group genius: The creative power of collaboration.* Basic Books.

Scandura, R. A., Von Glinow, M. A., & Lowe, K. B. (1999). When East meets West: Leadership "best practices" in the United States and the Middle East. In W. Mobley, M. J. Gessner, & V. Arnold (Eds.), *Advances in global leadership.* JAI.

Schaarschmidt, T. (2017, May/June). Power moves. *Scientific American Mind,* pp. 51–55.

Schei, V., & Rognes, J. K. (2005). Small group negotiation: When members differ in motivational orientation. *Small Group Research, 36,* 289–320. https://doi.org/10.1177%2F1046496404273145

Schmidt, S. J. (2020). Distracted learning: Big problem and golden opportunity. *Journal of Food Science Education, 19,* 278–291. https://onlinelibrary.wiley.com/doi/pdf/10.1111/1541-4329.12206

Scholl, A., Landkammer, F., & Sassenberg, K. (2019, March 11). When those who know do share: Group goals facilitate information sharing, but social power does not undermine it. *PLOS ONE.* https://journals.plos.org/plosone/article?id=10.1371/journal.pone.0213795

Schrodt, P., Witt, P. L., Myers, S. A., Turman, P. D., Barton, M. H., & Jernberg, K. A. (2008). Learner empowerment and teacher evaluations as functions of teacher power use in the college classroom. *Communication Education, 57,* 180–200.

Schroeder, J., Caruso, E. M., & Epley, N. (2016). Many hands make overlooked work: Over-claiming of responsibility increases with group size. *Journal of Experimental Psychology: Applied, 22,* 238–246. https://doi.org/10.1037/xap0000080

Schroth, H. (2019). Are you ready for Gen Z in the workplace? *California Management Review.* https://cmr.berkeley.edu/assets/documents/sample-articles/61-3-schroth.pdf

Schultz-Hardt, S., Brodbeck, F. C., Mojzisch, A., Kerschreiter, R., & Frey, D. (2006). Group decision making in hidden profile situations: Dissent as a facilitator for decision quality. *Journal of Personality & Social Psychology, 80,* 918–930. https://psycnet.apa.org/doi/10.1037/0022-3514.91.6.1080

Schur, K. (2019, September 20). The toxicity of a hyper-competitive work environment. *ApplicantOne.* https://www.applicantonesource.com/blog/toxic-competition-workplace

Schwantes, M. (2016, September 1). 10 compelling reasons servant leadership may be best, says science. *Inc.* https://www.inc.com/marcel-schwantes/10-convincing-reasons-to-consider-servant-leadership-according-to-research.html

Schwartz, E. (2020, February 11). The mystery of the disappearing female CEO. *Econlife.* https://econlife.com/2020/02/fewer-female-ceos-2/

Schwarz, R. (2017, December 6). How to design an agenda for an effective meeting. *Harvard Business Review.* https://hbr.org/2015/03/how-to-design-an-agenda-for-an-effective-meeting

Schyns, B., Felfe, J., & Schilling, J. (2018). Is it me or you? How reactions to abusive supervision are shaped by leader behavior and follower reactions. *Frontiers in Psychology.* https://dx.doi.org/10.3389%2Ffpsyg.2018.01309

Sciacovelli, P. (2017, April 25). Teams going virtual: Why focusing on trust matters. *Science for Work.* https://scienceforwork.com/blog/virtual-teams-trust

Seelig, T. (2015). Insight Out: Get ideas out of your head and into the world. *HarperOne.*

Semnani-Azad, Z., & Adair, W. L. (2011). The display of "dominant" nonverbal cues in negotiation: The role of culture and gender. *International Negotiations, 16,* 451–479.

The 7 trends impacting today's workplace. (2020). *Tinypulse.* https://www.tinypulse.com/2014-employee-engagement-organizational-culture-report

Sexual harassment at work. (2019). *Equal Rights Advocates.* https://www.equalrights.org/legal-help/know-your-rights/sexual-harassment-at-work/

Shaffner, G. (1999). *The arithmetic of life and death.* Ballantine.

Shah, P. P., Peterson, R., Jones, S. L., & Ferguson, A. (2020). Things are not always what they seem: the origins and evolution of intragroup conflict. *Administrative Science Quarterly.* DOI: 10.1177/0001839220965186

Shakers. (2020, September 16). *Wikipedia.* https://en.wikipedia.org/wiki/Shakers

Shandwick, W., & Tate, P. (2017). *Civility in America VII: The state of civility. Weber Shandwick. KRC Research.* http://www.webershandwick.com/uploads/news/files/Civility_in_America_the_State_of_Civility.pdf

Shapiro, D. (2017). *Negotiating the nonnegotiable: How to resolve your most emotionally charged conflicts.* Penguin.

Shavin, N. (2014, June 25). What workplace bullying looks like in 2014—and how to intervene. *Forbes.* https://www.forbes.com/sites/naomishavin/2014/06/25/what-work-place-bullying-looks-like-in-2014-and-how-to-intervene/2/#3dbabfa0293b

Sheridan, C., & King, R. (1972). Obedience to authority with an authentic victim. *Proceedings of the 80th Annual Convention, American Psychological Association, 7,* 165–166.

Sheridan, S., & Williams, P. (2011). Developing individual goals, shared goals, and the goals of others: Dimensions of constructive competition in learning contexts. *Scandinavian Journal of Educational Research, 55,* 145–164. https://doi.org/10.1080/00313831.2011.554694

Sherif, M., Harvey, O. J., White, B. J., Hood, W. R., & Sherif, C. W. (1988). *The Robbers Cave Experiment.* Wesleyan University Press.

Shermer, M. (2013, February 1). What is skepticism, anyway? *Huffington Post.* http://www.huffingtonpost.com/michael-shermer/what-is-skepticism-anyway_b_2581917.html

Sherrer, K. (2018, February 26). *What is tokenism, and why does it matter in the workplace? Vanderbilt University.* https://business.vanderbilt.edu/news/2018/02/26/tokenism-in-the-workplace/

Shimanoff, S. B. (2009). *Rules theory.* In S. W. Littlejohn & K. A. Foss (Eds.), *Encyclopedia of communication theory.* SAGE.

Shin, L. (2014, November 14). 10 steps to conquering information overload. *Forbes.* https://www.forbes.com/sites/laurashin/2014/11/14/10-steps-to-conquering-information-overload/#509cf4bb7b08

Shollen, S. L. (2010, December). The value of collaborative leadership: Leadership approach and leader emergence in virtual work groups. Paper presented at the 12th Annual ILA Global Conference, Boston.

Shonk, K. (2018, January 29). A token concession: In negotiation, the gift that keeps on giving. *Program on Negotiation/Harvard Law School.* https://www.pon.harvard.edu/daily/negotiation-skills-daily/token-concession-negotiation-gift-keeps-giving/?utm_source=WhatCountsEmail&utm_medium=daily&utm_date=2018-01-29-13-55-00&mqsc=E3933168

Shonk, K. (2020a, October 19). Managing difficult employees, and those who just seem difficult. *Program on Negotiation/Harvard Law School.* https://www.pon.harvard.edu/daily/dealing-with-difficult-people-daily/managing-difficult-employees-just-seem-difficult/

Shonk, K. (2020b, October 1). How to resolve cultural conflict: Overcoming cultural barriers at the negotiation table. *Program on Negotiation/Harvard Law School.* https://www.pon.harvard.edu/daily/conflict-resolution/a-cross-cultural-negotiation-example-how-to-overcome-cultural-barriers/

Sidky, H. (2018, March /April). The war on science, anti-intellectualism, and "alternative ways of knowing" in 21st-century America. *Skeptical Inquirer,* pp. 38–43.

Silver, N. (2012). *The signal and the noise: Why so many predictions fail—but some don't.* Penguin.

Silverman, R. W. (2015, September 30). Gender bias at work turns up in feedback. *Wall Street Journal.* https://www.wsj.com/articles/gender-bias-at-work-turns-up-in-feedback-1443600759

Silverman, S. B., Johnson, R. E., McConnell, N., & Carr, A. (2012). Arrogance: A formula for leadership failure. *The Industrial-Organizational Psychologist, 50,* 21–28.

Sims, R. (1992). Linking groupthink to unethical behavior in organizations. *Journal of Business Ethics, 11,* 651–662. https://doi.org/10.1007/BF01686345

Singer, J. (2020). The long-term effects of abusive coaching practices. *Psychologically Speaking.* https://drjacksinger.com/the-long-term-effects-of-abusive-coaching-practices/

Singh, A. (2019, July 16). How a team-based model can help build the organization of the future. *Ceridian.* https://www.ceridian.com/blog/how-a-team-based-model-can-help-build-the-organization-of-the-future

Sittenthaler, S., Traut-Mattausch, E., & Jonas, E. (2015, October 8). Observing the restriction of another person: Vicarious reactance and the role of self-construal and culture. *Frontiers in Psychology.* https://www.frontiersin.org/articles/10.3389/fpsyg.2015.01052/full

Sleek, S. (2016). The science of sameness: The neural mechanics of conformity. *Observer, 29,* 18–20.

Sma, S., Schrift, R. Y., & Zauberman, G. (2018). The illusion of multitasking and its positive effect on performance. *Psychological Science, 29,* 1942-1955.

Smith, R., Morgan, J., & Monks, C. (2017). Students' perceptions of the effect of social media ostracism on wellbeing. *Computers in Human Behavior, 68,* 276–285. https://psycnet.apa.org/doi/10.1016/j. chb.2016.11.041

Smokefree and tobacco-free U.S. and tribal colleges and universities. (2020). *American Nonsmokers Rights Foundation.* http://no-smoke.org/wp-content/ uploads/pdf/smokefreecollegesuniversities.pdf

Snyder, K. (2014, August 26). The abrasiveness trap: High-achieving men and women are described differently in reviews. *Fortune.* https://fortune. com/2014/08/26/performance-review-gender-bias/

Solomon, C. (2016). Trends in global virtual teams. *CultureWizard.* http://cdn.culturewizard.com/PDF/ Trends_in_VT_Report_4-17-2016.pdf

Solomon, L. (2015, June 24). The top complaints from employees about their leaders. *Harvard Business Review.* https://hbr.org/2015/06/the-top-complaints-from-employees-about-their-leaders

Sommers, S. R. (2006). On racial diversity and group decision making: Identifying multiple effects of racial composition on jury deliberations. *Journal of Personality and Social Psychology, 90,* 597–612. https://www.apa.org/pubs/journals/releases/psp-904597.pdf

Somvichian-Clausen, A. (2020, May 19). Female CEOs in the Fortune 500 hit an all-time record high. *The Hill.* https://thehill.com/changing-america/respect/equality/498582-female-ceos-in-the-fortune-500-hit-an-all-time-record-high

Sorensen, S. (1981, May). *Grouphate.* Paper presented at the International Communication Association, Minneapolis, MN.

Spikes, M., & Moyers, B. (2017, March 12). Making sense of the news: The power of information. *Salon.* https:// www.salon.com/2017/03/12/making-sense-of-the-news-the-power-of-information_partner

Spira, J. B. (2011). *Overload: How too much information is hazardous to your organization.* Wiley.

Spitzberg, B. H. (2015). Intercultural communication competence. In L. A. Samovar, R. E. Porter, E. R. McDaniel, & C. S. Roy (Eds.), *Intercultural communication: A reader.* Cengage.

Stamoulis, D., & Mannion, E. (2014). Making it to the top: Nine attributes that differentiate CEOs. *Russell Reynolds Associates.* http://www.russellreynolds.com/content/ making-it-top-nine-attributes-differentiate-ceos

Stanovich, K. (2013). *How to think straight about psychology.* HarperCollins.

Stanovich, K. E., West, R. F., & Toplak, M. E. (2013). Myside bias, rational thinking, and intelligence. *Current Directions in Psychological Science, 22,* 259–264. https://doi.org/10.1177%2F0963721413480174

Stark, P. B. (2017). Arrogance is leadership kryptonite. *PeterBarronStark Companies.* https://peterstark. com/arrogance-leadership-kryptonite/

Stephens, K. K., Houser, M. L., & Cowan, R. L. (2009). R U able to meat me: The impact of students' overly casual email messages to instructors. *Communication Education, 58,* 303–326. https://doi. org/10.1080/03634520802582598

Stewart, M. (2009). *The management myth: Debunking modern business philosophy.* Norton.

Stogdill, R. M. (1948). Personal factors associated with leadership: A survey of the literature. *Journal of Psychology, 25,* 35–71.

Stogdill, R. M. (1974). *Handbook of leadership.* New York: Free Press.

Stosny, S. (2014, April 18). What's wrong with criticism. *Psychology Today.* https://www.psychologytoday. com/blog/anger-in-the-age-entitlement/201404/ whats-wrong-criticism

Strauss, V. (2017, December 20). The surprising thing Google learned about its employees—and what it means for today's students. *Washington Post.* https://www. washingtonpost.com/amphtml/news/answer-sheet/ wp/2017/12/20/the-surprising-thing-google-learned-about-its-employees-and-what-it-means-for-todays-students

Strutner, S. (2017, April 12). Pilots sound off on United's massive mistake. *Huffington Post.* https:// www.huffingtonpost.com/entry/pilots-united_us_ 58ecfb45e4b0ca64d9198e1b

Student activities. (2021, January). *Ohio State University.* https://activities.osu.edu/involvement/ student_organizations/find_a_student_org/

Student-led clubs & organizations. (2021, January). *UC Santa Cruz.* https://admissions.ucsc.edu/why-ucsc/ organizations.html

Sude, D. J., Pearson, G. D. H., & Knobloch-Westerwick, S. (2021). Self-expression just a click away: Source interactivity impacts on confirmation bias and political attitudes. *Computers in Human Behavior.* https:// www.sciencedirect.com/science/article/abs/pii/ S0747563220303198

Sulek, J. P. (2004, November 8). A nod means "I agree"... or does it? *San Jose Mercury News*, pp. 1A, 9A.

Sunstein, C. R. (2019, May 17). Conformity and the dangers of group polarization. *Quillette*. https://quillette.com/2019/05/17/conformity-and-the-dangers-of-group-polarization/

Sunstein, C., & Zeckhauser, R. (2009). Overreaction to fearsome risks. In E. Michel-Kerjan and P. Slovic (Eds.), *The irrational economist: Future directions in behavioral economics and risk management*. Public Affairs.

Sunwolf, D. R., & Frey, L. R. (2005). Facilitating group communication. In S. A. Wheelan (Ed.), *The handbook of group research and practice*. SAGE.

Superhuman heroes. (1998, June 6). *Economist*, pp. 10–12.

Supiano, B. (2020, April 23). Why is Zoom so exhausting? *The Chronicle of Higher Education*. https://www.chronicle.com/article/why-is-zoom-so-exhausting/

The surprising truth about virtual vs. in-person conferences. (2020, May 1). *Promoleaf*. https://promoleaf.com/blog/the-surprising-truth-about-virtual-vs-in-person-conferences

Survey of CEOs regarding business transformation: Barriers to success. (2007). *EquaTerra*. http://www.cisco.com/en/US/services/ps2961/ps2664/ent_social_software_whitepaper_services.pdf

Sutton, B. (2012, January). Why the New Yorker's claim that brainstorming "doesn't work" is an overstatement and possibly wrong. *Bob Sutton Work Matters*. https://bobsutton.typepad.com/my_weblog/2012/01/why-the-new-yorkers-claim-that-brainstorming-doesnt-work-is-an-overstatement-and-possibly-wrong.html

Sutton, R. (2011, October 24). A few troublesome employees can outweigh the good. *Wall Street Journal*. http://online.wsj.com/news/articles/SB10001424052970203499704576622550325233260

Sverdrup, T. E., Schei, V., & Tjolsen, O. A. (2017). Expecting the unexpected: Using team charters to handle disruptions and facilitate team performance. *Group Dynamics: Theory, Research, and Practice*, *21*, 53–59. https://psycnet.apa.org/doiLanding?doi=10.1037%2Fgdn0000059

Swaab, R. I., Phillips, K. W., & Schaerer, M. (2016). Secret conversation opportunities facilitate minority influence in virtual groups: the influence on majority power, information processing, and decision quality. *Organizational Behavior and Human Decision Processes*, *133*, 17–32. https://psycnet.apa.org/doi/10.1016/j.obhdp.2015.07.003

Synnott, C. K. (2016). Guides to reducing social loafing in group projects: Faculty development. *Journal of Higher Education Management*, *31*, 211–221.

Szalai, G., & Roxborough, S. (2016, February 23). Oscars: How many people watch the ceremony worldwide? *Hollywood Reporter*. http://www.hollywoodreporter.com/news/oscars-worldwide-tv-audience-867554

Tabuchi, H., & McDonald, M. (2009, August 7). In first return to Japan court, jurors convict and sentence. *New York Times*. http://www.nytimes.com/2009/08/07/world/asia/07japan.html?_r=1&pagewanted=print

Tafvelin, S., Keisu, B-I., & Kvist, E. (2019). The prevalence and consequences of intragroup conflicts for employee well-being in women-dominated work. *Human Service Organizations: Management, Leadership & Governance*. https://www.tandfonline.com/doi/full/10.1080/23303131.2019.1661321

Tamir, S. (2020, December 3). The characteristics of virtual teams, when to use them and determinants of their success. *CQ Net*. https://www.ckju.net/en/dossier/characteristics-virtual-teams-when-use-them-and-determinants-their-success

Tannenbaum, S. I., Traylor, A. M., Thomas, E. J., & Salas, E. (2020). Managing teamwork in the face of pandemic: Evidence-based tips. *BMJ Quality & Safety*. https://qualitysafety.bmj.com/content/30/1/59

Tanner, R. (2020, November 20). Reframing for innovative and creative problem solving. *Management Is a Journey*. https://managementisajourney.com/reframing-for-innovative-and-creative-problem-solving/

Tanzi, A. (2018, August 6). U.S. women outpacing men in higher education: Demographic trends. *Bloomberg*. https://www.bloomberg.com/news/articles/2018-08-06/u-s-women-outpacing-men-in-higher-education-demographic-trends

Tartakovsky, M. (2013). Overcoming information overload. *Psych Central*. http://psychcentral.com/blog/archives/2013/01/21/overcoming-information-overload

Tasa, K., & Whyte, G. (2005). Collective efficacy and vigilant problem solving in group decision making: A non-linear model. *Organizational Behavior and Human Decision Processes*, *96*, 119–129. https://psycnet.apa.org/doi/10.1016/j.obhdp.2005.01.002

Tavris, C., & Aronson, E. (2016). *Mistakes were made (but not by me)*. Mariner.

Taylor, E., Hewitt, K., Reeves, R.A., & Lawless, W. F. (2013). Group decision-making: Consensus rule versus majority rule. *Science Direct*. https://www.researchgate.net/publication/274037111_Group_Decision-making_Consensus_Rule_Versus_Majority_Rule

Teams work better when employees care about each other. (2020, March 23). *Business News Daily*. https://www.businessnewsdaily.com/8585-teams-care-about-others.html

Tefft, B. C., Williams, A. F., & Grabowski, J. G. (2012, May). Teen driver risk in relation to age and number of passengers. *AAA Foundation for Traffic Safety*. https://www.aaafoundation.org/sites/default/files/research_reports/2012TeenDriverRiskAgePassengers.pdf

Temme, L. (2019, August 27). Social media use by juries: Is there any way to stop it? *FindLaw*. https://blogs.findlaw.com/technologist/2019/08/social-media-use-by-juries-is-there-any-way-to-stop-it.html

Ten hard-bargaining tactics to watch out for in a negotiation. (2020, September 28). *Program on Negotiation/Harvard Law School*. https://www.pon.harvard.edu/daily/batna/10-hardball-tactics-in-negotiation/

Tenzer, H., Terjesen, S., & Harzing, A-W. (2017). Language in international business: A review and agenda for future research. *Management International Review*. https://www.researchgate.net/publication/317253086_Language_in_International_Business_A_Review_and_Agenda_for_Future_Research

Ter Hoeven, C. L., van Zoonen, W., & Fonner, K. L. (2016). The practical paradox of technology: the influence of communication technology use on employee burnout and engagement. *Communication Monographs*, *83*, 239–263. https://www.tandfonline.com/doi/full/10.1080/03637751.2015.1133920?src=recsys

Thamel, P. (2008, August 24). US basketball returns to the top. *New York Times*. https://www.nytimes.com/2008/08/25/sports/olympics/25bball.html

Thanawala, S. (2016, April 24). California jurors misusing the Internet could face fines up to $1,500. *Associated Press*. https://apnews.com/47a337400517448fbe58b4aba4ce1d41/california-jurors-misusing-internet-could-face-fines

Thibodeau, P. H., & Boroditsky, L. (2011). Metaphors we think with: The role of metaphor in reasoning. *PLoSOne*. http://journals.plos.org/plosone/article?id=10.1371/journal.pone.0016782

Thomas, G., Martin, R., & Riggio, R. E. (2013). Leading groups: Leadership as a group process. *Group Processes & Intergroup Relations*, *16*, 3–16. https://psycnet.apa.org/doi/10.1177/1368430212462497

Thomas, L. (2018, January 16). Communication methods do not work equally across diverse teams. *PhysOrg*. https://phys.org/news/2018-01-methods-equally-diverse-teams.html

Thompson, L. (2017, October 2). Research: For better brainstorming, tell an embarrassing story. *Harvard Business Review*. https://hbr.org/2017/10/research-for-better-brainstorming-tell-an-embarrassing-story

Thompson, L. (2021, Winter). Virtual collaboration won't be the death of creativity. *MIT Sloan Management Review*. https://sloanreview.mit.edu/article/virtual-collaboration-wont-be-the-death-of-creativity/

Tian, X., Solomon, D. H., & Brisini, K. S. C. (2020). How the comforting process fails: Psychological reactance to support messages. *Journal of Communication*, *70*, 13–34. https://academic.oup.com/joc/article-abstract/70/1/13/5739595?redirectedFrom=fulltext

Tierney, J., & Baumeister, R. F. (2020). *The power of bad: How the negativity effect rules us and how we can rule it*. Penguin Press.

Ting-Toomey, S., & Chung, L. C. (2012). *Understanding intercultural communication*. Oxford University Press.

Ting-Toomey, S., & Dorjee, T. (2018). *Communicating across cultures*. Guilford Press.

Tipping. (2020, January 19). *Wikitravel*. http://wikitravel.org/en/Tipping

Tjosvold, D., Johnson, D. W., Johnson, R. T., & Sun, H. (2003). Can interpersonal competition be constructive within organizations? *Journal of Psychology*, *137*, 63–84. https://doi.org/10.1080/00223980309600600

Tjosvold, D., Johnson, D. W., Johnson, R. T., & Sun, H. (2006). Competitive motives and strategies: Understanding constructive competition. *Group Dynamics: Theory, Research, and Practice*, *10*, 87–99. https://psycnet.apa.org/doi/10.1037/1089-2699.10.2.87

Tjosvold, D., & Yu, Z. (2004). Goal interdependence and applying abilities for team in-role and extra-role performance in China. *Group Dynamics: Theory, Research, and Practice*, *8*, 98–111.

Toegel, G., & Barsoux, J-L. (2016, June 8). 3 situations where cross-cultural communication breaks down. *Harvard Business Review*. https://hbr.org/2016/06/3-situations-where-cross-cultural-communication-breaks-down

The top ten: American Film Institute's greatest movies of all time. (2017, February 28). *Infoplease*. https://www.infoplease.com/culture-entertainment/film/top-ten-american-film-institutes-greatest-movies-all-time

Tost, L. P., Gino, F., & Larrick, R. P. (2010). Power, competitiveness, and advice taking: Why the powerful don't listen. *Organizational Behavior and Human Decision Processes*. https://www.academia.edu/15431294/Power_competitiveness_and_advice_taking_Why_the_powerful_don_t_listen?email_work_card=view-paper

Toulmin, S., Rieker, R., & Janik, A. (1979). *An introduction to reasoning*. Macmillan.

Tousley, S. (2017, January 25). How to be charismatic: The 9 habits of insanely likable people. *HubSpot*. https://blog.hubspot.com/sales/habits-of-likable-people

Tran, K. T., Nguyen, P. V., Dang, T. T. U., & Ton, T. N. B. (2018). The impacts of the high-quality workplace relationships on job performance: A perspective on staff nurses in Vietnam. *Behavioral Sciences*, *8*, 109–121. https://www.ncbi.nlm.nih.gov/pmc/articles/PMC6316783/

Trees, L. (2017, May 26). Why employees hate virtual collaboration and what to do about it. *SmartBrief*. http://www.smartbrief.com/original/2017/05/why-employees-hate-virtual-collaboration-and-what-do-about-it

Triandis, H. C. (1995). *Individualism and collectivism*. Westview Press.

Triandis, H. C. (2009). Ecological determinants of cultural variations. In R. S. Wyer, C. Chiu, Y. Hong, & D. Cohen (Eds.), *Understanding culture: Theory, research and applications*. Psychology Press.

Triandis, H. C. (2012). Culture and conflict. In S. A. Samovar, R. E. Porter, & E. R. McDaniel (Eds.), *Intercultural communication: A reader*. Wadsworth/Cengage.

Troster, C., Mehra, A., & van Knippenberg, D. (2014). Structuring for team success: The interactive effects of network structure and cultural diversity on team potency and performance. *Organizational Behavior and Human Decision Processes*, *124*, 245–255. https://doi.org/10.1016/j.obhdp.2014.04.003

The trouble with meetings. (2017, August 23). *MyHubIntranet*. https://www.myhubintranet.com/trouble-with-meetings

Tsao, T. (2017, February 22). Why you need to be rotating meeting roles. *Meeteor*. https://www.meeteor.com/post/rotating-meeting-roles

Tschan, F., Semmer, N. K., Gurtner, A., Bizzari, L., Spychiger, M., Breuer, M., & Marsch, S. U. (2009). Explicit reasoning, confirmation bias, and illusory transactive memory: A simulation study of group medical decision making. *Small Group Research*, *40*, 271–300. https://doi.org/10.1177%2F1046496409332928

Tuckman, B. (1965). Developmental sequences in small groups. *Psychological Bulletin*, *63*, 384–399.

Turgeon, J. (2017, January/February). Permitting jurors to ask questions during trials. *Pennsylvania Lawyer*. http://www.ncsc-jurystudies.org/~/media/Microsites/Files/CJS/Other/JF%2017%20Lawyer%20JurorQuestionssm%20(002).ashx

TV or not TV. (1993, April 19). *San Jose Mercury News*, p. 5E.

12 UK phrases and sayings. (2017, December 21). *Veem*. https://www.veem.com/library/12-uk-business-phrases-and-sayings/

Twenge, J. M., VanLandingham, H., & Campbell, W. K. (2017). The seven words you can never say on television: Increases in the use of swear words in American books, 1950–2008. *SAGE Journals*. https://journals.sagepub.com/doi/10.1177/2158244017723689

2021 best national university rankings. (2021). *U.S. News & World Report*. https://www.usnews.com/best-colleges/rankings/national-universities

2021 college rankings. (2021). *Niche*. https://www.niche.com/colleges/rankings/

Tye-Williams, S., Carbo, J., D'Cruz, P., & Hollis, L. P. (2020). Exploring workplace bullying from diverse perspectives: A *Journal of Applied Communication Research* Forum. *Journal of Applied Communication Research*, *48*, 637–653. https://www.tandfonline.com/doi/full/10.1080/00909882.2020.1830148

The ultimate guide to virtual leadership. (2021). *DDI*. https://lp.ddiworld.com/eg/the-ultimate-guide-to-virtual-leadership?utm_source=google&utm_medium=cpc&utm_campaign=VC&utm_content=300X600&gclid=CjwKCAiAudD_BRBXEiwAudakX2lxbT2MpiNFFCLeDAghkCTzW_Uh8QyyPO12JZ-VRjmyeegc1I_VQxoCHsMQAvD_BwE

University of Phoenix survey reveals nearly seven-in-ten workers have been part of dysfunctional teams. (2013, January 16). *University of Phoenix*. https://markets.financialcontent.com/stocks/news/read?GUID=23212959

Updegrove, M. K. (2018, February 18). Building a better world. *Parade*, pp. 8, 9, 20–22.

Ury, W. (1993). *Getting past no: Negotiating your way from confrontation to cooperation*. Bantam.

Valcea, S., Hamden, M., & Bradley, B. (2019). Weakest link goal orientation and team expertise: Implications for team performance. *Small Group Research*, *50*, 315–347. https://journals.sagepub.com/doi/full/10.1177/1046496418825302

Van der Hoek, M., Groeneveld, S., & Kuipers, B. (2016). Goal setting in teams: Goal clarity and team performance in the public sector. *Review of Public Personnel Administration.* https://journals.sagepub.com/doi/full/10.1177/0734371X16682815

Vangelisti, A., Knapp, M., & Daly, J. (1990). Conversational narcissism. *Communication Monographs, 57,* 251–274. https://doi.org/10.1080/03637759009376202

Van Mierlo, H., & Kleingeld, A. (2010). Goals, strategies, and group performance: Some limits of goal setting in groups. *Small Group Research, 41,* 524–555. https://doi.org/10.1177%2F1046496410373628

Vanoverbeke, D. (2015). *Juries in the Japanese legal system.* Routledge.

Van Quaquebeke, N., & Eckloff, T. (2010). Defining respectful leadership: What it is, how it can be measured, and another glimpse at what it is related to. *Journal of Business Ethics, 91,* 343–358. https://psycnet.apa.org/doi/10.1007/s10551-009-0087-z

Van Swol, L. M. (2009). Extreme members and group polarization. *Social Influence, 4,* 185–199.

Van Swol, L. M., & Kane, A. A. (2019). Language and group processes: An integrative, interdisciplinary review. *Small Group Research, 50,* 3–38. https://journals.sagepub.com/doi/full/10.1177/1046496418785019

Varela, O. E., Burke, M. J., & Landis, R. S. (2008). A model of emergence and dysfunctional effects of emotional conflict in groups. *Group Dynamics: Theory, Research, and Practice, 12,* 112–126. https://psycnet.apa.org/doi/10.1037/1089-2699.12.2.112

Vecchio, R. P., Bullis, R. C., & Brazil, D. M. (2006). The utility of situational leadership theory. *Small Group Research, 37,* 407–424. https://psycnet.apa.org/doi/10.1177/1046496406291560

Victor, D. A. (2007, March 27–31). *What is the language of business? Affecting business outcome before you say a word.* Proceedings of the Association for Business Communication, 7th Asia-Pacific Conference, City University of Hong Kong.

Vigen, T. (2015). *Spurious correlations.* Hachette.

Vitelli, R. (2015, September 7). Can you change your personality? *Psychology Today.* https://www.psychologytoday.com/blog/media-spotlight/201509/can-you-change-your-personality

Voggeser, B. J., Singh, R. K., & Goritz, A. S. (2018). Self-control in online discussions: Disinhibited online behavior as a failure to recognize social cues.
Frontiers in Psychology. https://dx.doi.org/10.3389%2Ffpsyg.2017.02372

Vosoughi, S., Roy, D., & Aral, S. (2018). The spread of true and false news online. *Science, 359,* 1146–1151.

Vozza, S. (2014, February 25). Personal mission statements of 5 famous CEOs (and why you should write one too). *Fast Company.* https://www.fastcompany.com/3026791/personal-mission-statements-of-5-famous-ceos-and-why-you-should-write-one-too

Vozza, S. (2015, May 15). Seven habits of likable people. *Fast Company.* https://www.fastcompany.com/3046228/seven-habits-of-likable-people

Vroom, V. H., & Jago, A. G. (2007). The role of the situation in leadership. *American Psychologist, 62,* 17–24. https://psycnet.apa.org/doi/10.1037/0003-066X.62.1.17

Wahba, P. (2020, June 1). The number of black CEOs in the Fortune 500 remains very low. *Fortune.* https://fortune.com/2020/06/01/black-ceos-fortune-500-2020-african-american-business-leaders/

Waheed, A., & Malik, S. (2013). Impact of role conflict, role balance on general well-being with students who work. *Journal of Humanities and Social Science, 6,* 26–30. https://citeseerx.ist.psu.edu/viewdoc/download?doi=10.1.1.1063.1649&rep=rep1&type=pdf

Wakefield, N., Abbatiello, A., Agarwal, D., et al. (2016). Leadership awakened: Generations, teams science. *Deloitte University.* file:///C:/Users/darot/Downloads/Global%20Human%20Capital%20Trends%202016_%20The%20new%20organization8719.pdf

Wald, M. L., & Schwartz, J. (2003, July 12). Shuttle probe blames managers, foam equally. *San Jose Mercury News,* p. 8A.

Walker, B. (2017). How to create change in your organization. *IDEO.* https://www.ideou.com/blogs/inspiration/how-to-create-change-in-your-organization

Walter, N., & Tukachinsky, R. (2020). A meta-analytic examination of the continued influence of misinformation in the face of correction: How powerful is it, why does it happen, and how to stop it? *Communication Research, 47,* 155–177. https://journals.sagepub.com/doi/full/10.1177/0093650219854600

Ward, A. F., Duke, K., Gneezy, A., & Bos, M. W. (2017, April 3). Brain drain: The mere presence of one's own smartphone reduces available cognitive capacity. *The University of Chicago Press Journals, 2,* 140–154. https://www.journals.uchicago.edu/doi/10.1086/691462?mobileUi=0&

Wartham, A. (2016, October 14). Four key trends driving the corporate learning and development. *The Evolllution.* https://evolllution.com/revenue-streams/corporate_partnerships/four-key-trends-driving-the-corporate-learning-and-development-market

Watanabe, A. (2012, June 3). Japan's "lay judge" system to be revised. *Asian Correspondent.* http://asiancorrespondent.com/83631/japans-lay-judge-system-to-be-revised

Watzlawick, P., Beavin, J. H., & Jackson, D. D. (1967). *Pragmatics of human communication.* Norton.

Wax, A., DeChurch, L. A., & Contractor, N. S. (2017). Self-organizing into winning teams: Understanding the mechanisms that drive successful collaborations. *Small Group Research, 48,* 665–718. https://doi.org/10.1177%2F1046496417724209

Wedell-Wedellsborg, T. (2017, January-February). Are you solving the right problems? *Harvard Business Review.* https://hbr.org/2017/01/are-you-solving-the-right-problems

Weedmark, D. (2019, June 1). Importance of English in business communication. *Bizfluent.* https://bizfluent.com/list-6631343-major-trends-international-business.html

Weingart, L. R., & Todorova, G. (2010). Jury tensions: Applying communication theories and methods to study group dynamics. *Small Group Research, 41,* 495–502. https://doi.org/10.1177%2F1046496410369564

Weir, K. (2018). What makes teams work? *Monitor.* https://www.apa.org/monitor/2018/09/cover-teams

Weiss, T. (2011). The blurring border between the police and the military: A debate without foundation. *Cooperation and Conflict, 46,* 396–405.

Weisser, D. (2013, March). 2013 trends report: The state of employee engagement. *Quantum Workplace.* http://www.quantumworkplace.com/wp-content/uploads/2013/03/Resources-Whitepapers-2013-Employee-Engagement-Trends-Report.pdf

Welker, M. (2017, July 27). The future of productivity: AI and machine learning. *Entrepreneur.* https://www.entrepreneur.com/article/295264

West, R., & Turner, L. H. (2020). *Introducing communication theory: Analysis and application.* McGraw-Hill.

What are OSHA restroom break laws? (2021). *360 Training.* https://www.360training.com/blog/osha-restroom-break-laws

What did the writers' strike cost? (2008, February 12). *Newsweek.* http://www.newsweek.com/id/110892

What makes a good leader, and does gender matter? (2015, January 14). *Pew Research Center.* http://www.pewsocialtrends.org/2015/01/14/chapter-2-what-makes-a-good-leader-and-does-gender-matter

Wheelan, S. A. (2009). Group size, group development, and group productivity. *Small Group Research, 40,* 247–262. https://doi.org/10.1177%2F1046496408328703

Wheelan, S. A., Davidson, B., & Tilin, F. (2003). Group development across time: Reality or illusion? *Small Group Research, 34,* 223–245. https://doi.org/10.1177%2F1046496403251608

Wheeler, M. (2014, February 17). Asiana Airlines: "Sorry captain. You're wrong." *LinkedIn.* https://www.linkedin.com/pulse/20140217220032-266437464-asiana-airlines-sorry-captain-you-re-wrong

White, A. E., Kenrick, D. T., & Neuberg, S. L. (2013). Beauty at the ballot box. *Psychological Science, 24,* 2429–2436. https://doi.org/10.1177%2F0956797613493642

Why do hospital nurses leave their jobs? (2018, August 6). *CentraState Blog.* https://www.centrastatejobs.com/why-do-hospital-nurses-leave-their-jobs/

Wikipedia: Citing Wikipedia. (2017). *Wikipedia.org.* https://en.wikipedia.org/wiki/Wikipedia:Citing_Wikipedia

Wilding, M. (2018, June 11). The surprising truth about crying at work. *Forbes.* https://www.forbes.com/sites/melodywilding/2018/06/11/the-surprising-truth-about-crying-at-work/?sh=75538fa44e79

Williams, C. (2019, October 8). College athletes beginning to rebel against abusive coaches. *Global Sport Matters.* https://globalsportmatters.com/health/2019/10/08/college-athletes-beginning-to-rebel-against-abusive-coaches/

Williams, K. D. (2007). Ostracism: The kiss of social death. *Social and Personality Psychology Compass, 1,* 236–247. https://psycnet.apa.org/doi/10.1111/j.1751-9004.2007.00004.x

Wilmot, W., & Hocker, J. (2018). *Interpersonal conflict.* McGraw-Hill.

Wilson, D. (2016, October 20). Failure to communicate. *Flight Safety Foundation.* https://flightsafety.org/asw-article/failure-to-communicate/

Wimmer, J., Backmann, J., & Hoegl, M. (2019). In or out? Exploring the inconsistency and permeability of team boundaries. *Small Group Research, 50,* 699–727. https://journals.sagepub.com/doi/full/10.1177/1046496419851842

Wineburg, S., Breakstone, J., Ziv, N., & Smith, M. (2020). Educating for misunderstanding: How approaches to teaching digital literacy make students susceptible to scammers, rogues, bad actors, and hate mongers.

Stanford Digital Repository. https://purl.stanford.edu/mf412bt5333

Wineburg, S., McGrew, S., Breakstone, J., & Ortega, T. (2016). Evaluating information: The cornerstone of civic online reasoning. *Stanford Digital Repository.* https://cor.stanford.edu/research/evaluating-information-the-cornerstone-of-cor/

Wise, S. (2014). Can a team have too much cohesion? The dark side of network density. *European Management Journal, 32,* 703–711. https://doi.org/10.1016/j.emj.2013.12.005

Wolf, M., Krause, J., Carney, P. A., Bogart, A., & Kurvers, R. H. J. M. (2015). Collective intelligence meets medical decision-making: The collective outperforms the best radiologist. *PLOS ONE.* https://www.ncbi.nlm.nih.gov/pmc/articles/PMC4534443/

Wolkomir, R., & Wolkomir, J. (1990, February). How to make smart choices. *Reader's Digest,* pp. 27–32.

Women in leadership: Why it matters. (2016, May 12). *Rockefeller Foundation.* https://www.rockefellerfoundation.org/report/women-in-leadership-why-it-matters/

Women in the workplace 2016. (2016). *LeanIn.org.* https://leanin.org/news-inspiration/wiw-2016

Women on corporate boards: Quick take. (2020, March 13). *Catalyst.* https://www.catalyst.org/research/women-on-corporate-boards/

Wood, J. T. (2019). *Gendered lives: Communication, gender, and culture.* Cengage Learning.

Woodley, H. J. R., McLarnon, M. J. W., & O'Neill, T. A. (2019, May 3). The emergence of group potency and its implications for team effectiveness. *Frontiers of Psychology.* https://doi.org/10.3389/fpsyg.2019.00992

Woolley, A. W., Chabris, C. F., Pentland, A., Hashmi, N., & Malone, T. W. (2010). Evidence for a collective intelligence factor in the performance of human groups. *Science, 330,* 686–688.

Workplace effectiveness has declined. (2020). *Gensler: US. Workplace Survey 2020.* https://www.gensler.com/uploads/document/677/file/Gensler_US_WPS_Report_2020.pdf

Work shouldn't hurt. (2021, February 6). *Workplace Bullying Institute.* https://workplacebullying.org/

Worley, T. R., & Shelton, M. R. (2020). Work-family conflict, relational turbulence mechanisms, conflict tactics and marital satisfaction. *Journal of Applied Communication Research, 48,* 248–269. https://www.tandfonline.com/doi/full/10.1080/00909882.2020.1735647

Wrenn, E. (2012, September 19). The great gender debate: Men will dominate 75% of the conversation during conference meetings, study suggests. *Daily Mail.* http://www.dailymail.co.uk/sciencetech/article-2205502/The-great-gender-debate-Men-dominate-75-conversation-conference-meetings-study-suggests.html

Wright, L. (2018, April 19). New survey explores the changing landscape of teamwork. *Microsoft.* https://www.microsoft.com/en-us/microsoft-365/blog/2018/04/19/new-survey-explores-the-changing-landscape-of-teamwork/

Wu, J. (2020, August 18). The pandemic is a perfect time to address the digital divide. *Forbes.* https://www.forbes.com/sites/junwu1/2020/08/18/the-pandemic-is-a-perfect-time-to-address-the-digital-divide/?sh=7720ed376129

Xie, B., Hurlstone, M. J., & Walker, I. (2018). Correct me if I'm wrong: Groups outperform individuals in the climate stabilization task. *Frontiers in Psychology.* https://doi.org/10.3389/fpsyg.2018.02274

Xu, N., Chiu, C-Y, Treadway, D. C. (2019). Tensions between diversity and shared leadership: The role of team political skill. *Small Group Research, 50,* 507–538. https://journals.sagepub.com/doi/full/10.1177/1046496419840432

Xue, J. (2016, September 20). Team building principles Google, Adobe and Life Time Fitness learned from Cirque du Soleil. *Business.com.* https://www.business.com/articles/the-team-building-principles-google-adobe-and-life-time-fitness-learned-from-cirque-du-soleil/

Yaakobi, E. (2017, September 6). Ostracism: Recent neurological, cognitive and personality research. *iMedPub Journals.* https://www.imedpub.com/articles/ostracism-recent-neurological-cognitiveand-personality-research.pdf

Yang, J. L. (2006, June 12). The power of number 4.6. *Fortune,* p. 122.

Yang, Z., Sun, J., Zhang, Y., & Wang, Y. (2018). Virtual collaboration with mobile social media in multiple-organization projects. *Proceedings of the 51st Hawaii International Conference on System Sciences.* IEEE. https://scholarspace.manoa.hawaii.edu/bitstream/10125/49956/1/paper0069.pdf

Yavuk, F., & Celik, O. (2017). The importance of listening in communication. *Global Journal of Psychology Research: New Trends and Issues, 7,* 8–11. https://pdfs.semanticscholar.org/422c/a8f532edfb735064e3fc52e16f173f3245ff.pdf

Yoerger, M., Allen, J. A., & Crowe, J. (2018). The impact of premeeting talk on group performance. *Small Group Research*, *49*, 226–258. https://journals.sagepub.com/doi/full/10.1177/1046496417744883

Young, G. (2016, August 12). Women, naturally better leaders for the 21st century. *LeaderShape*. https://www.routledge.com/rsc/downloads/WP-TL2-2016_Transpersonal_Leadership_WP2_FINAL.pdf

Yousaf, A., Shaukat, R., & Umrani, W. A. (2020). Linkages between group level task conflict and individual outcomes in non-routine technical jobs. *International Journal of Conflict Management*, *32*, 158–176. https://doi.org/10.1108/IJCMA-08-2019-0128

Youyou, W., Stillwell, D., Schwartz, H. A., et al. (2017). Birds of a feather do flock together: Behavior-based personality assessment method reveals personality similarity among couples and friends. *Psychological Science*, *28*, 276–284. https://journals.sagepub.com/doi/full/10.1177/0956797616678187

Yu, R., & Chen, G-M. (2008). Intercultural sensitivity and conflict management styles in cross-cultural situations. *Intercultural Communication Studies*, *47*, 149–161. https://web.uri.edu/iaics/files/12-Tong-Yu-GM-Chen.pdf

Yu, R., & Sun, S. (2013, May 17). To conform or not to conform: Spontaneous conformity diminishes the sensitivity to monetary outcomes. *PLoSOne*. http://journals.plos.org/plosone/article?id=10.1371/journal.pone.0064530

Yu, X. (1998). The Chinese "native" perspective on Mao-dun (conflict) and Mao-dun resolution strategies: A qualitative investigation. *Intercultural Communication Studies*, *7*, 63–82.

Yuan, Y. C., Liao, W., & Bazarova, N. N. (2019). Judging expertise through communication styles in intercultural collaboration. *Management Communication Quarterly*, *33*, 238–271. https://journals.sagepub.com/doi/full/10.1177/0893318918824674

Yukl, G. (2006). *Leadership in organizations*. Prentice Hall.

Yung, C. T., & Tsai, K. C. (2013). Followership: An important partner of leadership. *Business and Management Horizons*, *1*, 47–55.

Yurkiw, J. (2013, May 8). Benchbook for U.S. District Court judges adds a section on e-discovery and jury instructions for jurors' use of social media and electronic devices. *Technology Law Source*. http://www.technologylawsource.com/2013/05/articles/information-technology/benchbook-for-us-district-court-judges-adds-new-section-on-ediscovery-and-jury-instructions-for-jurors-use-of-social-media-and-electronic-devices

Zak, P. J. (2017, January/February). The neuroscience of trust. *Harvard Business Review*. https://hbr.org/2017/01/the-neuroscience-of-trust

Zander, A. (1982). The psychology of removing group members and recruiting new ones. *Human Relations*, *29*, 1–8.

Zara, C. (2018, March 20). People were asked to name women tech leaders: They said "Alexa" and "Siri." *Fast Company*. https://www.fastcompany.com/40547212/people-were-asked-to-name-women-tech-leaders-they-said-alexa-and-siri

Zarankin, T. G. (2008). A new look at conflict styles: Goal orientation and outcome preferences. *International Journal of Conflict Management*, *19*, 167–184. https://psycnet.apa.org/doi/10.1108/10444060810856094

Zenger, J., & Folkman, J. (2015, November 10). We like leaders who underrate themselves. *Harvard Business Review*. https://hbr.org/2015/11/we-like-leaders-who-underrate-themselves

Zetlin, M. (2018, April). 54 percent of women report workplace harassment. How is your company responding? *Inc. Magazine*. https://www.inc.com/magazine/201804/minda-zetlin/sexual-harassment-workplace-policy-metoo.html

Zimbardo, P. (2007). *The Lucifer effect: Understanding how good people turn evil*. Random House.

Index